SENTENCING and the PENAL SYSTEM:

TEXT and MATERIALS

Second Edition

by

Christopher Harding, B.A., LL.M.
Professor of Law,
University College of Wales, Aberystwyth

and

Laurence Koffman, B.A.
Reader in Law,
University of Sussex

LONDON
SWEET & MAXWELL
1995

Published in 1995 by
Sweet & Maxwell Limited of
South Quay Plaza, 183 Marsh Wall,
London, E14 9FT

Typeset by Selwood Systems,
Midsomer Norton
Printed in Great Britain by Butler & Tanner Limited,
Frome and London

No natural forests were destroyed to make this product:
only farmed timber was used and re-planted

ISBN 0 421 47140 9

**A catalogue record for this book is
available from the British Library**

ERRATUM

Following an oversight in the publishing process, references from the Tables in the first edition of this book have been duplicated in this second edition. The following references should therefore be ignored.

Campbell and Fell v. U.K. (1985)
Kiss v. U.K. (1976)
R. v. Barbery (1975)
R. v. Barnes (1984)
R. v. Burgess (1974)
R. v. Burke (1974)
R. v. Clarke (1982)
R. v. Cole (1983)
R. v. Collier (Geoffrey) (1987)
R. v. Dawson (1983)
R. v. Deputy Governor of Camp
    Hill Prison *ex p.* King (1984)
R. v. Doab (1983)
R. v. Downs (1976)
R. v. Drummond (1972)
R. v. Eastlake (1980)
R. v. Fairman (1983)
R. v. Fell (1975)
R. v. Fox (1980)
R. v. Freeman (1980)
R. v. Gardiner (1967)
R. v. Genese (1976)
R. v. George (1984)
R. v. Gilby (John Thomas) (1975)
R. v. Glossop (1981)
R. v. Godfrey (1973)
R. v. Gomez, Cooper and
    Bovington (1972)
R. v. Grieve (1975)
R. v. Hannah (1983)
R. v. Hercules (1980)
R. v. Hillyer (1968)
R. v. House (1974)
R. v. Ingham (1980)
R. v. Jones (1980)
R. v. Kelly (1986)

R. v. Knight (1980)
R. v. Leigh (David Roger) (1969)
R. v. McCann (1980)
R. v. McAleny and Griffiths (1975)
R. v. Marquis (1974)
R. v. Maynard (1983)
R. v. Miller (1976)
R. v. Newbury and Jones (1975)
R. v. Parr (1982)
R. v. Paton (1982)
R. v. Raphael (1972)
R. v. Reeves (Raymond) (1972)
R. v. Roberts and Roberts (1982)
R. v. Roe (1982)
R. v. Ross (1984)
R. v. Sapiano (Mary) (1968)
R. v. Satterthwaite and
    Satterthwaite (1981)
R. v. Sawyer (1985)
R. v. Secretary of State for the Home
    Department *ex p.* Tarrant and
    another (1984)
R. v. Sharkey (1976)
R. v. Skilton and Blackham (1982)
R. v. Smedley (1981)
R. v. Smith (1982)
R. v. Storey (1984)
R. v. Taylor (1983)
R. v. Turner (1966)
R. v. Upton (1980)
R. v. Whitton (1986)
R. v. Williams (1971)
R. v. Williams (1983)
Silver and Others v. U.K. (1983)
Williams v. Home Office (No. 2) (1981)
Mental Health Act 1959, s. 123

PREFACE TO THE SECOND EDITION

The passage of time since the appearance of the first edition of this work, witnessing a great deal of legislative activity, policy development and a number of significant events within the field of criminal justice and the penal system, has made the preparation of a second edition a matter of increasing urgency. Policy is always evolving in this area and in the early 1990s there have been significant recommendations and statements concerning a number of aspects of the British penal system, notably the 1990 Government White Paper, *Crime, Justice and Protecting the Public*; the Woolf Report in 1991 and the Report of the Royal Commission on Criminal Justice in 1993. The White Paper was the precursor of the significant 1991 Criminal Justice Act, but there had already been an earlier Criminal Justice Act in 1988. Further criminal justice legislation has followed in 1993 and 1994, while there had also been legislation concerning the procedure for dealing with mentally disordered offenders in 1991. While some of this new legislation has altered—or, rather, sought to clarify—the framework of sentencing, there have also been significant developments as regards the organisation and administration of the prison system. Some measures have disappeared, such as the care order in criminal proceedings and the partly suspended sentence, and there are some new concepts (in particular that of the community sentence), although not all of these may become operative (as in the case of the curfew order). The first edition stated matters as they stood in mid-1987; seven years later there is a great deal of new material and new developments to discuss.

We have retained the basic format of the first edition, but some of the chapters have been recast to take into account new trends and legal changes and we have generally introduced more comparative material. Discussion of the theoretical basis of the subject in Chapter One has been extended to deal with different kinds of criminality, the methodology of punishment and the issue of "net-widening". Chapter Two, although still concerned generally with the pre-sentence stage, now includes a substantial section on diversionary policy and practice so as to reflect the greater attention which needs to be given to this area of the subject and to the concept of "diversion" itself. The discussion of information for sentencers has been relocated in an expanded chapter on the sentencing process, and the chapters on both imprisonment and non-custodial measures have inevitably had to incorporate much new material. The structure of the more specific chapters relating to young offenders and mentally disordered offenders remains similar, but again there has been a good deal to update. Regrettably, as the subject changes and expands in this way, there are inevitable casualties in the process of keeping the book within manageable proportions. The topic of prisoners' rights has become very large in itself and is now dealt with more systematically and fully in other works. We therefore decided that a necessarily short and summary account in the chapter on imprisonment did little justice to the subject. We also felt that the final chapter in the first edition, dealing with the evaluation of sentences, had a rather different orientation compared to the remainder of the work and, although the topic has not been lost altogether, it was decided to remove the separate chapter and relocate its main points wherever appropriate elsewhere in the book.

In this edition we have brought the subject up-to-date as of November 1994. Both authors wish to thank the staff of the Hugh Owen Library in Aberystwyth for their considerable help. Laurence Koffman wishes to thank Christine Davies for her speedy and accurate typing. He would also like to express his deep gratitude to his wife, Valerie, and daughter, Angela, for their constant encouragement, support and patience.

Aberystwyth   Christopher Harding
November, 1994   Laurence Koffman

ACKNOWLEDGEMENTS

Grateful acknowledgement is made to the following authors and publishers for permission to reproduce part of their works:

ALLEN, R., "Out of Jail: The Reduction in the Use of Penal Custody for Male Juveniles, 1981–8" (1991) 30 *Howard Journal* 30

ASHWORTH, A., "Judicial Independence and Sentencing Reform," in *The Future of Sentencing* (Thomas, D.A. ed., 1982, University of Cambridge Occasional Papers, No. 8)

ASHWORTH, A., "Prosecution, Police and Public—A Guide to Good Gate-keeping?" (1984) 23 *Howard Journal* 65

ASHWORTH, A., "Reducing the Prison Population in the 1980s: The Need for Sentencing Reform" in *A Prison System for the 1980s and Beyond* (1982, NACRO)

ASHWORTH, A., *Sentencing and Criminal Justice* (1992, Weidenfeld and Nicolson)

ASHWORTH, A., "The Criminal Justice Act 1991" in *Sentencing Judicial Discretion and Training*, (Munro, C. and Wasik, M. eds., 1992, Sweet & Maxwell)

ASHWORTH, A. & GIBSON, B., "Altering the Sentencing Framework" [1994] Crim.L.R. 101

ASQUITH, A., "Justice, Retribution and Children" in *Providing Criminal Justice for Children* (Morris, A. L. and Giller, H. eds., 1983, Edward Arnold)

BALDWIN, J., "The Compulsory Training of the Magistracy" [1975] Crim.L.R. 634

BALDWIN, J., "Pre-Trial Settlement in Magistrates' Courts" (1985) 24 *Howard Journal* 108

BALL, C., "Young Offenders and the Youth Court", (1992) Crim.L.R. 277

BASIL BLACKWELL, Extracts from the *Howard Journal*

BOTTOMS, A. E., "The Efficacy of the Fine: The Case for Agnosticism" [1973] Crim.L.R. 543

BOTTOMS, A. E., "The Suspended Sentence in England 1967–78" (1981) 21 B.J.Crim. 1

BOTTOMS, A. *et al.*, *Intermediate Treatment and Juvenile Justice: Key Findings and Implications from a National Survey of Intermediate Treatment Policy and Practice*, (1990)

BRANTS, C. & FIELD, S., "Discretion and Accountability: A Comparative

Perspective on Keeping Crime out of Court" in *Criminal Justice in Europe* (Fennel, P. *et al.* eds., 1995, Clarendon Press)

BREDAR, J. K. *Justice Informed: The Pre-Sentence Report Pilot Trials in the Crown Court* Vol. 1 (1992, HMSO, London)

BUTLER COMMITTEE, *Mentally Abnormal Offenders*, Report on, Cmnd. 6244 (1975, HMSO, London)

BUTTERWORTH LAW PUBLISHERS LTD., *All England Law Reports* and extracts from various other publications.

CAVADINO, P., "The White Paper – Will it Achieve its Objectives?" (1990) 80 *Prison Services Journal* 5.

COMMITTEE FOR INQUIRY INTO THE UNITED KINGDOM PRISON SERVICES, Cmnd. 7673 (1979, HMSO, London)

CROW, I., "Black People and Criminal Justice in the U.K. (1987) 26 *Howard Journal* 303

DINGWALL, G., "Making Fines Work—or Learning from our Mistakes" (1994) 47 *Criminal Lawyer* 3

DITCHFIELD, J., "Controls in Prisons: Review of the Literature", (1990, H.O.R.S. No. 118)

DOHERTY, M. & EAST, R., "Bail Decisions in Magistrates' Courts" (1985) B.J.Crim. 251

DYER, C., "Making a Snap Decision", *The Guardian*, February 14, 1990

EUROPEAN HUMAN RIGHTS REPORTS, THE (Sweet & Maxwell) Extracts from various cases

FITZGERALD, G. & SIM, J., *British Prisons* (2nd ed., 1992, Blackwell)

FREEMAN, M. D. A., "The Rights of Children when they do Wrong" (1981) 21 B.J.Crim. 210

GELSTHORPE, L. & GILLER, H., "More Justice for Juveniles: Does More Mean Better?" [1990] Crim.L.R. 153

GELSTHORPE, L. & TUTT, N. "The Attendance Centre Order" [1986] Crim. L.R. 146

GLADSTONE COMMITTEE, *Prisons*, Report on, Cmnd. 7702 (1985, HMSO, London)

GLIDEWELL, Lord Justice, "The Judicial Studies Board" in *Sentencing, Judicial Discretion and Training* (Munro, C. & Wasik, M. eds., 1992, Sweet & Maxwell)

GOSTIN, L. & STAUNTON, M., "The Case for Prison Standards: Conditions of Confinement, Segregation and Medical Treatment" in *Accountability and Prisons* (Maguire, M., Vagg, J. & Morgan, R. eds., 1985)

GOWER PUBLISHING COMPANY LTD., Extracts from various publications

GUNN, J., "Psychiatry and the Prison Medical Service", in *Secure Provision* (Larry Gostin ed., 1985, Tavistock)

HARDING, C. & IRELAND, R., *Punishment: Rhetoric, Rule and Practice* (1989, Routledge)

HART, H. L. A., *Punishment and Responsibility* (1968, Oxford University Press)

HER MAJESTY'S STATIONERY OFFICE: Various extracts reprinted with permission of the Controller, HMSO

HOGGETT, B., *Mental Health Law* (3rd ed., 1990)

HOOD, R., "Criminology and Penal Change" in *Crime, Criminology and Public Policy*, (Hood ed., 1974, Heinemann)

HOOD, R., *Race and Sentencing: A Study in the Crown Court* (1992, Clarendon Press)

HOWARD LEAGUE FOR PENAL REFORM: Extracts from various articles published in the Howard Journal

INCORPORATED COUNCIL OF LAW REPORTING FOR ENGLAND AND WALES, THE: *Official Reports, Weekly Law Reports*

JUSTICE, *Negotiated Justice: A Closer Look at the Implications of Plea Bargains* (1993, JUSTICE)

KELK, C. & KOFFMAN, L., SILVIS, J., "Sentencing Practice, Policy and Discretion" in *Criminal Justice in Europe*, (P. Fennell *et al* eds., 1994, Clarendon Press)

KNAPP, M., ROBERTSON, E. and McIVOR, G., "The Comparative Costs of Community Service and Custody in Scotland" (1992) 31 *Howard Journal* 8

LAW COMMISSION, THE, Draft Criminal Code, Clause 38

LIEBLING, A., *Suicides in Prison*, (1992, Routledge)

McMAHON, M., *The Persistent Prison* (University of Toronto Press, 1992)

McWILLIAMS, W., "Probation, Pragmatism and Policy", (1987) 26 *Howard Journal* 97

MIERS, D. A., "The Responsibilities and Rights of Victims of Crime", (1992) 55 M.L.R. 483

MORRIS, A., "Legal Representation and Justice" in *Providing Criminal Justice for Children* (Morris, A. & Giller, H. eds., 1983, Edward Arnold)

MOXON, D., "The Use of Compensation Orders in Magistrates' Courts" (1993) H.O. Research Bulletin)

NACRO, *The Cost of Penal Measures* (1992, NACRO Briefing Paper, 23)

NACRO, *The Electronic Monitoring of Offenders* (1989, NACRO Briefing Paper)

NATIONAL STANDARDS FOR THE SUPERVISION OF OFFENDERS IN THE COMMUNITY (1992)

NELLIS, M., "The Electronic Monitoring of Offenders in England and Wales" (1991) 31 B.J.Crim. 165

OZTURK V. GERMANY, Judgment of the European Court of Human Rights (1984) 6 E.H.R.R. 409

PATERSON, A., *Paterson on Prisons* (S.K. Ruck ed., 1951, Muller)
PARSLOE, P., *Juvenile Justice in Britain and the United States* (1978, R.K.P.)
PATERSON, A. A. & BATES, T. ST. J. N., *The Legal System of Scotland* (3rd ed., 1993, W. Green/Sweet & Maxwell)
PEASE, K., *Community Service Orders—A First Decade of Promise* (1981, Howard League)
PEASE, K., "Cross-National Imprisonment Rates", (1994) 34 B.J.Crim. 117
PEAY, J., *Tribunals on Trial: A Study of Decision-Making Under the Mental Health Act 1983* (1989, Clarendon Press)
PLAYER, E. & JENKINS, M., *Prisons After Woolf* (1994, Routledge)
PRIESTLEY, P., *Victorian Prison Lives* (1985, Methuen)
PRINS, H., *Offenders, Deviants or Patients?* (1980, Tavistock)

RADZINOWICZ, L. & HOOD, R., *A History of the English Criminal Law, Vol. 5: The Emergence of Penal Policy* (1986, Stevens)
RADZINOWICZ, L. & KING, J., *The Growth of Crime* (Hamilton, 1987)
RICHARDSON, G., *Law, Process and Custody: Prisoners and Patients* (1993, Weidenfeld and Nicolson)
ROBENS COMMITTEE, *Safety and Health at Work*, Cmnd. 5034 (1972, HMSO, London)
ROSS, A., *On Guilt, Responsibility and Punishment* (1975, Stevens)
ROYAL COMMISSION ON CRIMINAL JUSTICE, Report, Cm. 2263 (1993, HMSO, London)
RUTHERFORD, A., *Prisons and the Process of Justice*, (1984, Heinemann)
RYAN, M. & WARD, T., *Privatisation and the Penal System* (1989, Open University Press)

SELECT COMMITTEE ON MURDER AND LIFE IMPRISONMENT, Report (1988–89, H.L. 78) (HMSO, London)
SIM, J., "Reforming the Penal Wasteland?" in *Prison After Woolf* (Player, E. & Jenkins, M. eds., 1994, Routledge)
SPENCER, J. N., "Current Thinking on the Imposition of a Fine as a Sentence—or the Re-introduction of the Unit Fine System by the Back Door?" (1994) 158 *Justice of the Peace* 115
SPENCER, J. R., "Do We Need a Prosecution Appeal Against Sentence?" [1987] Crim.L.R. 724
STERN, V., *Bricks of Shame* (2nd ed., 1993, Penguin)
STONE, N., "Pre-Sentence Reports, Culpability and the 1991 Act" [1992] Crim.L.R. 558
STONE, N., "The Suspended Sentence Since the Criminal Justice Act, 1991" [1994] Crim.L.R. 399
STUART-WHITE, C., (JUDGE), "The Exercise of Judicial discretion in Sentencing Decisions", (1989) 45 *The Magistrate* 194

SWEET & MAXWELL LTD., Extracts from the *Criminal Law Review* and various other publications

TAYLOR, M., AND PEASE, K., "Private Prisons and Penal Purpose" in *Privatising Criminal Justice*, (R. Matthews ed., Sage)
THOMAS, D., "Penalties Without a Plan", *The Times*, February 13, 1990
THOMAS, D., "Why the Sentence Fits the Crime", *The Guardian*, March 22, 1994
THOMAS, J. E., "Policy and Administration in Penal Establishments" in *Progress in Penal Reform* (Blom-Cooper, L. ed., Open University Press, 1974)
TEVERTON-JONES, G., *Imprisonment: The Legal Status and Rights of Prisoners*, (1989, Sweet & Maxwell)
TURNER, A. J., "Sentencing in the Magistrates' Court" in *Sentencing, Judicial Discretion and Training* (Munro, C. & Wasik, M. eds., 1992, Sweet & Maxwell)

VASS, A., *Alternatives to Prison*, (1990, Sage)

WALMSLEY, R., *Special Security Units*, Home Office Research Study No. 109 (1989, HMSO, London)
WASIK, M. & TURNER, A., "Sentencing Guidelines for the Magistrates' Courts", (1993) Crim.L.R. 345
WASIK, M. & VON HIRSCH, A., *Statutory Sentencing Principles: the 1990 White Paper* (1990) 53 M.L.R. 508
WASIK, M. & VON HIRSCH, A., "Section 29 Revised: Previous Convictions in Sentencing" [1994] Crim.L.R. 409
WASIK, M., "Arrangements for Early Release" [1992] Crim.L.R. 252
WHITE PAPER, *Crime, Justice and Protecting the Public*, Cm. 965 (1990, HMSO, London)
WILLIAMSON, D., *Questions of Punishment*, (1990) 80 *Prison Service Journal* 18
WILLIS, A., "Community Service as an Alternative to Imprisonment" (1977) 24 *Probation Journal* 120
WOOLF, LORD JUSTICE AND TUMIN, JUDGE, *Prison Disturbances, April 1990*, Report of Inquiry into, Cm. 1456 (1991, HMSO, London)

X v. UK (RE DETENTION OF A MENTAL PATIENT), Judgment of the European Court of Human Rights (1982) 4 E.H.R.R. 188

N.B. The extract from Hoggett, *Mental Health Law*, on pp. 423–424 is from the third edition of the book, published in 1990. Sweet & Maxwell expect to publish a fourth edition of this book in 1996.

ABBREVIATIONS

Am. J. Soc.	*American Journal of Sociology*
B.J.Crim.	*British Journal of Criminology*
Crim.L.R.	*Criminal Law Review*
H.O.	Home Office
H.O.R.S.	Home Office Research Study
Howard Journal	*Howard Journal of Penology and Crime Prevention* (until 1983)
	Howard Journal of Criminal Justice (from 1984)
J.C.L.	*Journal of Criminal law, Criminology and Police Science*
M.L.R.	*Modern Law Review*
NACRO	National Council for the Care and Resettlement of Offenders
NCCL	National Council for Civil Liberties
Oxford J.L.St.	*Oxford Journal of Legal Studies*
RAP	Radical Alternatives to Imprisonment

CONTENTS

CHAPTER FOUR: **IMPRISONMENT**

CHAPTER FIVE: **NON-CUSTODIAL SENTENCES**

CHAPTER SIX: **YOUNG OFFENDERS**

CHAPTER SEVEN: **MENTALLY DISORDERED OFFENDERS**

TABLE OF CASES

TABLE OF STATUTES

TABLE OF STATUTORY INSTRUMENTS

CHAPTER ONE

THE FUNCTIONS AND OBJECTIVES OF THE SENTENCING AND PENAL SYSTEMS

I. INTRODUCTION

The process of sentencing and the collection of procedures, measures, institutions and personnel which comprises what is often termed the penal system represents the state's response to the problem of how to deal with criminal law-breaking. The pre-eminent position of the state in this matter is a relatively modern phenomenon and most societies have progressed from procedures based upon self-help and private prosecution to the adoption of a system which assumes an overriding interest in infractions of the criminal code on the part of centrally organised state authorities. This tendency towards state involvement can be seen even in the last hundred years as the state has gradually taken over what were originally private welfare initiatives and incorporated these into a centralised structure. But although the main scope of the subject is therefore concerned with the state's sentencing and penal and corrective apparatus, it would be misleading to leave out of account altogether a number of private and non-state responses to the problem of crime. For that reason, the relation between state-based and other sanctions will be considered first of all in this chapter.

However, when focusing on the machinery of the state in this area, a variety of descriptions and categorisations is possible. It is naturally convenient to distinguish that stage at which measures for criminal wrongdoers are decided upon – the sentencing process – from the subsequent application of those measures. This later activity may be described as penal or corrective depending upon the nature and purpose of the measures adopted. Even so there may not always be a neat or clear distinction: the same measure may have both penal and corrective characteristics and may also serve other purposes such as public protection which may not be easily subsumed under either of these headings. Terminology and classification are naturally important for purposes of exposition and discussion but it is also necessary that such organisational language is as consistent and clear as possible so as to minimise any confusion in discussion of aims and policy. Particular attention should therefore be paid to setting up a useful and workable framework for the overall subject-matter of discussion.

Finally, it should be noted that the approach adopted here departs in some respects from the more traditional treatment, according to which theoretical aspects of the sentencing and penal systems have been viewed as a department of moral philosophy. Much of the literature in that vein concentrated upon the problem of justifying state action in its classical form of "punishment". Here, a wider view will be taken by emphasising the range of state interventions. To that extent, "penal system" may be something of a misleading title, but is retained as being the general description in common usage which most readily suggests the full complement of options available to the authorities in this area.

II. Criminal Law and Non-State Sanctions

H. L. A. Hart, *Punishment and Responsibility* (1968), pp. 4–5.

Here I shall simply draw upon the recent admirable work scattered through English philosophical journals and add to it only an admonition of my own against the abuse of definition in the philosophical discussion of punishment. So with Mr Benn and Professor Flew I shall define the standard or central case of "punishment" in terms of five elements:

   (i)   It must involve pain or other consequences normally considered unpleasant.
   (ii) It must be for an offence against legal rules
   (iii) It must be of an actual or supposed offender for his offence.
   (iv) It must be intentionally administered by human beings other than the offender.
   (v)   It must be imposed and administered by an authority constituted by a legal system against which the offence is committed.

In calling this the standard or central case of punishment I shall relegate to the position of sub-standard or secondary cases the following among many other possibilities:

   (a) Punishments for breaches of legal rules imposed or administered otherwise than by officials (decentralised sanctions).
   (b) Punishments for breaches of non-legal rules or orders (punishments in a family or school).
   (c) Vicarious or collective punishment of some member of a social group for actions done by others without the former's authorisation, encouragement, control or permission.
   (d) Punishment of persons (otherwise than under (c)) who neither are in fact nor supposed to be offenders.

Hart, in his definition of the central institution of punishment, identifies "standard" and "sub-standard" cases. His reasons for doing so are bound up with moral arguments as to when it is justifiable to impose punishment. In particular, he wishes to preclude a reliance on deterrence as a justification if this would define away objections to morally unacceptable extremes of deterrence, for example, by saying that extreme measures taken against innocent people for deterrent purposes do not qualify as punishment. Hart wishes to say that measures taken against innocent people, scapegoats or as a means of imposing vicarious responsibility – all of which may have a useful deterrent effect – cannot be conveniently dismissed, by means of a "definitional stop", as not amounting to punishment. According to his argument, they are a form of punishment but not what is usually referred to as such in debates about punishment. Hart's "central" or "standard" case is the measure imposed by a state agency in respect of an infringement of the state's system of criminal law.

Christopher Harding and Richard Ireland, *Punishment: Rhetoric, Rule and Practice* (1989), pp. 21–24.

The authors take issue with Hart's categorisation of punishment into "standard" and "substandard" cases and emphasise that in social terms the latter may play a dominant role.

Another danger that we are seeking to avoid – indeed, our eagerness to avoid it may attract considerable criticism from some quarters – is that of using stipulative definitions to close off the subject-matter for analysis. Philosophers of punishment have not always resisted this temptation, not through any sinister motive but simply because their sphere of investigation has been limited and they have accordingly adopted limited definitions. But, once these self-imposed terms of reference are challenged, the definitions produced by such theorising appear as manifestly arbitrary. So, for example, H. L. A. Hart, in his influential writing on the subject, has been concerned to avoid what he calls use of a "definitional stop", which simply rules out of court any discussion of matter not contained within the convenient definition. He does this, more precisely, by listing a number of "substandard" or "secondary" cases of punishment, which include "among many other possibilities":

(a) Punishments for breaches of legal rules imposed or administered otherwise than by officials (decentralised sanctions).
(b) Punishment for breaches of non-legal rules or orders (punishments in a family or school).
(c) Vicarious or collective punishment of some member of a social group for actions done by others without the former's authorisation, encouragement, control or permission.
(d) Punishment of persons (otherwise than under (c)) who neither are in fact nor supposed to be offenders.

That the contents of this list may perfectly properly be described as instances of punishment is clear from the fact that Hart himself uses that term. But what Hart has done is to move the definitional stop from the definition of "punishment" to that of the "standard" or "central" case of punishment. While it may be accepted that this definition provides the standard case for Hart, that is also to accept Hart's position as a legal philosopher; but there is no other reason, certainly none supplied by Hart himself, why *we* should adopt the same viewpoint, nor why, for example, a man who loses his job because he has taken home the company's stationery or a boy who has been slapped by his father for being insolent should be corrected when they say that they have been punished but reassured that their statements are true in a substandard or secondary sense.

Hart's own introduction to this question of definition itself raises the issue that he is content to marginalise by definition rather than by argument. He states:

There is, I think, an analogy worth considering between the concept of punishment and that of property. In both cases we have to do with a social institution of which the centrally important form is a structure of *legal* rules, even if it would be dogmatic to deny the names of punishment or property to the similar though more rudimentary rule-regulated practices within groups such as a family or a school, or in customary societies whose customs may lack some of the standard or salient features of law (e.g. legislation, organised sanctions, courts).

Leaving aside the question of whether the analogy is appropriate (i.e. whether punishment can be spoken of in the same way as property, as an institution), the reasons for designating one instance of punishment (the "legal") as "the most centrally important form" really ought to be stated. Certainly, the self-evidence of this presumed centrality is not warranted on grounds of popular contact with, or perhaps even popular perception of, punishment (though the latter is an untestable hypothesis). Many more readers of this book will have been punished at home or at school than will have encountered the penal process of the legal system.

Nor do the reasons of those writers who seek to articulate their reasons for such a standpoint necessarily impress any more than Hart's silence. The editors of a work entitled *Contemporary Punishment* show that they are sufficiently aware of the problems being discussed here to observe (with what justification we shall discuss later) in relation to Flew's classic definition of punishment: "If quarrels must be picked with such a masterly performance one might raise the question of punishment for the breach of rules outside the legal realm." But they proceed to explain their preferred focus on criminal law punishment: "It is here that the problems of social control by coercive means take on a crucial significance. Not only are the means frequently harsh, such as loss of liberty, but they always involve [the] latent quality of moral condemnation."[1]

This simply will not do. The first limb of the distinction differentiates criminal law punishment only on the ground of its severity, a weak enough distinction, even if true; but it is a difference that, in any case, would be disputed by the relatives of those punished for breaching the rules of criminal gangs such as the Mafia, who may have suffered a much more severe penalty than that imposed by many legal codes. Nor is the second limb of the distinction, that of moral condemnation, convincing. It is neither sufficient to include cases where a breach of the law does not provoke a moral censure but may be met with either moral indifference or even popular support, nor does it cater for other cases where rules are supported by moral censure (such as rules of morality themselves!), yet attract no legal sanction. The easy conflation of law and morality with no further investigation is simply inadequate as an argument.

The other line of enquiry into punishment, which has become significant recently once again, tends to concern itself with punishment as employed by the state – indeed, it is this relation it is most eager to explore. Although the editors of a recent "sociological" critique, arguing for a critical reappraisal of thoughts about punishment, are well aware that the practice is to be found in social contexts other than that of state intervention, their recognition of this fact is consigned to a footnote, so as to concentrate on their concept of "penality", which is one related to state activity.[2] Indeed, much recent critical investigation often sees its task as being an explanation of "the roots of the modern penal system". To be sure, this is a valuable enterprise, yet once more we would simply assert that much of this work, while purporting to examine the implement, is in fact fascinated by the user. State-centred theorists use the model of the western industrialised capitalist state (the existence of which is not, of course, a precondition for the use of punishment) and tell us how it uses its tools. The danger in such discussion is that the language and ideology entailed in a critique of the agent (the state) becomes too closely identified with the instrument of punishment itself. Moreover, such an argument does not consider some ideas which, in our view, should be seen as fundamental. It is not, we suggest, absurd to regard as crucial in the history of state punishment, the

---

[1] R. J. Gerber and P. D. McAnany, *Contemporary Punishment* (1972).
[2] *The Power to Punish: Contemporary Penality and Social Analysis* (David Garland and Peter Young eds., 1983).

question of when and how the state arrogated to itself the right and the power to punish, taking it away, in whole or in part, from other social groupings, such as the kindred or the local community. With few exceptions, the power of the state to punish has been received as a datum and what are investigated are rather the changes in the exercise of that power. Such transitions in the exercise and forms of punishment are important, but to accept the assumption of this power by the state, which is not a matter lost in the mists of ancient history (certainly not in the case of British penal practice), but is itself a subject of important enquiry.

There are thus important reasons for considering the "secondary" or "non-standard" cases of punishment which lie outside the traditional debates of moral philosophy. In practice it is clearly not only the state which reacts to instances of criminal law-breaking. Often, there are also adverse consequences of a broader social nature, in particular loss of respect, friendship, position or employment and dislocation of family life. These may be validly regarded as society's punishment of the offence and operate concurrently with the imposition of state measures. Moreover, a criminal offence may at the same time amount to a breach of non-legal rules or may attract sanctions from non-state institutions, for instance, censure by a professional body or expulsion from an organisation. Hart refers to these responses as "decentralised sanctions" and they may operate irrespective of whether any use has been made of the criminal law. Thus many breaches of the rules of educational, trade or professional institutions are never dealt with as criminal offences although technically qualifying as such. Yet the use of such sanctions is an important fact of social organisation and, in so far as they operate alongside the criminal law and its system of punishment, raise questions of a moral nature about the risk of "double jeopardy" (being dealt with more than once in respect of the same offence), although this concept has been customarily used in a legal rather than a socio-legal context, usually to guard against prosecution in more than one jurisdiction, or in respect of overlapping offences. See Article 13 of the Harvard Research Draft Convention on Jurisdiction with respect to Crime 1935, 29 A.J.I.L., Supp., 443.

It could be argued that in some circumstances the experience of conviction by itself would carry a sufficient punitive, deterrent or reformative impact to make the application of any further measures unnecessary, as for instance in the case of an offender for whom conviction would entail the loss of professional status, family or friends. What function would then be served by the imposition of "additional" penal measures by the state?

To the extent that sentencers do take into account the social consequences of conviction it is for purposes of mitigation, that is, to reduce the quantum of the sentence rather than eliminate it altogether. Such pleas in mitigation are principally relevant if a prison sentence is being considered by the court, since imprisonment is the measure likely to have the most severely dislocating social effects. (See, for instance, the case of Geoffrey Collier, who received a suspended prison sentence for illicit trading in shares; the judge pointed out that Collier would face "other penalties," *The Observer*, July 5, 1987.) But it may also be a worthwhile strategy in other contexts: for instance, in motoring cases, to minimise the impact of a measure such as disqualification. See also the discussion by Andrew Ashworth (1992), pp. 134–6.

A study by J. P. Martin and D. Webster (1971) revealed that the social circumstances of offenders are important, but in a way that does not always relate to the intentions underlying penal law. In particular, their suggestion that the type of person for whom criminal activities hold the most attraction is the least likely to be deterred by the risk of penalties is something which should be borne in mind by policy-makers when designing schemes of deterrence. But, conversely, experience of the penal system may eventually help to detach a professional criminal from his previous and habitual culture. John McVicar's account of this transition is informative (from Laurie Taylor (1985), pp. 187–8):

> "I could see it for what it was .... When you're young, you've got a few things going for you in crime. You"ve got more liberty ahead of you. But as the years go on, you get more convictions, you've got less time to play with. You've got less life. And you begin to edge a bit more .... Emotionally, it still plucked.... And that's what makes it hard to unshackle a criminal identity. You have to take all the emotional pressure to go back to your ways – you can't do it in one, it's not like giving up smoking or drinking where you can keep a check; you get caught up again in subtle things...."

The impact of social consequences is borne out by an earlier study by H. D. Wilcock and J. Stokes (1968). A sample of young men were asked to rank fear of assumed consequences of appearing in a criminal court. 49 per cent were most concerned abut family reaction, 22 per cent about loss of employment, 12 per cent about the associated publicity or shame but only 10 per cent were most concerned about the possible penalty. This was found to be broadly true even of those youths among the sample who had committed a wide variety of offences and might have been assumed to be less fearful of such social consequences.

III. The Sentencing Repertoire

It is misleading to think of the modern sentencing process as involving simply a decision as to an appropriate penal measure. There exist options for the sentencer which cannot properly be described as penal, such as probation or hospital orders, and even those which are commonly thought of as being measures of punishment may comprise elements which are corrective or preventive. "Penal system" is used here as a convenient shorthand term to describe the collection of different measures which may be employed by the state as a response to criminal law-breaking. Similarly, it would be unduly restrictive to term the discussion of the aims of and justification for such measures as the "theory of punishment." Although punishment remains an important response to the problem of crime, the present diversity of sanctions necessitates a broader base for discussion.

Some attempt at categorisation may, however, be useful for purposes of exposition. Although not satisfactory in all respects, the following heads may be suggested in order to discuss the range of measures in question: 1. penal measures; 2. corrective measures (including methods of "reform" or types of "treatment" or "training"); 3. preventive measures (including methods of public protection and disqualification).

These broad groupings are suggested since within each there is likely to be some identity of justification and aim. These concepts of justification and aim are used to answer questions about the appropriate use of different measures and whether such measures are morally acceptable. Given that the measures in question are likely to be coercive, entailing a restriction of individual rights, their use requires justification, and this is likely to differ according to whether the measure is penal, corrective or preventive in character. The purpose or aim of the measure may coincide with its justification, or may be different.

Alf Ross, *On Guilt, Responsibility and Punishment* (1975), pp. 61–63.

According to the prevailing view among legal writers "theories of punishment" have to do with the question of the *aim* of punishment, *i.e.* with the nature of the results that are (or ought to be) aimed at by means of the existence and enforcement of penal laws. And it is maintained that from far back in history there has been a fundamental opposition between those who say that this aim is retribution (the absolute theories, *quia peccatum est*), and those who say it is prevention, *i.e.* the combating of acts that are classified as crimes because they are socially harmful (the relative theories, *ne peccetur*).

This interpretation of the traditional problem is, as we have said, altogether mistaken. Theories of punishment have from old times been ethical theories concerning the State's (moral) right and/or duty to punish. Precisely because punishment is the deliberate infliction of pain or suffering, a system of ethics which assumes suffering to be a basic evil and the forbidding of the (unauthorised) harming of others a fundamental moral law, must find it a problem to justify and delimit the State's right to inflict suffering through punishment – suffering which often consists in the deprivation of the greatest human goods, for example freedom and even life itself.

It is this ethical question to which each of these two essentially quite different viewpoints offers an answer. According to the one view the State's right derives from an ethical principle – the principle of justice, which allows – perhaps even requires – that evil be repaid with evil. The State is accordingly entitled (even bound) to inflict punishment on someone who has broken the law in a way which makes it proper to hold him responsible. According to the second view the right to punish derives from the socially beneficial effects of imposing punishments: the law-breaker must suffer pain of punishment because it is necessary for the maintenance of certain ideals of social life. It is punishment's aim, one might say, that justifies it.

But in both cases the topic is not the aim of punishment but its moral justification. The aim only comes in indirectly in so far as, according to the relative theories, it provides the ground for the moral justification. Retributive theories, for their part, quite clearly have nothing at all to do with the aim of punishment.

The two theories, or types of theory, are thus divergent solutions to the same problem, the moral-philosophical problem of the ethical status of punishment as the State's right or duty....

... The absurdity is manifest. Retribution has never been understood by retributivists themselves as an aim – an intended effect – of punishment, but its legitimation and a principle for its measurement. This is quite clear in the case of modern authors like Hart, who settle for the requirement of guilt (*mens rea*) as a restrictive principle counter to considerations of purpose. But it is also true of classical theorists like Kant, Stahl, Hegel, Binding and any other one cares to mention. If it has ceased to be obvious, then, this is due in the first instance, simply to the fact that these authors are no longer read. People simply parrot one another's hearsay that the absolute theorist's claim retribution, and not prevention, to be the aim of punishment. No one stops to consider how unreasonable such an assumption is; how a thinker of Kant's calibre could have thought anything so foolish. And even people who take the trouble to read the original works often lack the required familiarity with natural law conceptions to grasp their meaning. Admittedly the going is often heavy. A special difficulty is the lack of analytical rigour with which the problem itself and the basic concepts are presented, and the fact that they are only intelligible on the basis of assumptions quite foreign to contemporary modes of thought. The universe of discourse in which the reader must move is aprioristic, and he must bear in mind that in that universe expressions like "law", "legal ground", "necessity", "consequence" – and even "aim" – have meanings quite different from those he would normally give them.

H. L. A. Hart, *Punishment and Responsibility* (1968), pp. 8–13.

I shall not here criticise the intelligibility or consistency or adequacy of those theories that are united in denying that the practice of a system of punishment is justified by its beneficial consequences and claim instead that the main justification of the practice lies in the fact that when breach of the law involves moral guilt the application to the offender of the pain of punishment is itself a thing of value. A great variety of claims of this character, designating "Retribution" or "Expiation" or "Reprobation" as the justifying aim, fall in spite of differences under this rough general description. Though in fact I agree with Mr Benn in thinking that these all either avoid the question of justification altogether or are in spite of their protestations disguised forms of Utilitarianism, I shall assume that Retribution, defined simply as the application of the pains of punishment to an offender who is morally guilty, may figure among the conceivable justifying aims of a system of punishment. Here I shall merely insist that it is one thing to use the word Retribution *at this point* in an account of the principle of punishment in order to designate the General Justifying Aim of the system, and quite another to use it to secure that to the question "To whom may punishment be applied?" (the question of Distribution), the answer given is "Only to an offender for an offence". Failure to distinguish Retribution as a General Justifying Aim from retribution as the simple insistence that only those who have broken the law – and voluntarily broken it – may be punished, may be traced in many writers: even perhaps in Mr J. D. Mabbott's otherwise most illuminating essay. We shall distinguish the latter from Retribution in General Aim as "retribution in Distribution". Much confusing shadow-fighting between utilitarians and their opponents may be avoided if it is recognised that it is perfectly consistent to assert *both* that the General Justifying Aim of the practice of punishment is its beneficial consequences *and* that the pursuit of this General Aim should be qualified or restricted out of deference to principles of Distribution which require that punishment should be only of an offender for an offence. Conversely it does not in the least follow from the admission of the latter principle of retribution in Distribution that the General Justifying Aim of punishment is Retribution though of course Retribution in General Aim entails retribution in Distribution.

We shall consider later the principles of justice lying at the root of retribution in Distribution. Meanwhile it is worth observing that both the old fashioned Retributionist (in General Aim) and the most modern sceptic often make the same (and, I think, wholly mistaken) assumption that sense can only be made of the restrictive principle that punishment be applied only to an offender for an offence if the General Justifying Aim of the practice of punishment is Retribution. The sceptic consequently imputes to all systems of punishment (when they are restricted by the principle of retribution in Distribution) all the irrationality he finds in the idea of Retribution as a General Justifying Aim; conversely the advocates of the latter think the admission of retribution in Distribution is a refutation of the utilitarian claim that the social consequences of punishment are its Justifying Aim.

The most general lesson to be learnt from this extends beyond the topic of punishment. It is, that in relation to any social institution, after stating what general aim or value its maintenance fosters we should enquire whether there are any and if so what principles limiting the unqualified pursuit of that aim or value. Just because the pursuit of any single social aim always has its restrictive qualifier, our main social institutions always possess a plurality of features which can only be understood as a compromise between partly discrepant principles. This is true even of relatively minor legal institutions like that of a contract. In general this is designed to enable individuals to give effect to their wishes to create structures of legal rights and duties, and so to change, in certain ways, their legal position. Yet at the same time there is need to protect those who, in good faith, understand a verbal offer made to them to mean what it would ordinarily mean, accept it, and then act on the footing that a valid contract has been concluded. As against them, it would be unfair to allow the other party to say that the words he used in his verbal offer or the interpretation put on them did not express his real wishes or intention. Hence principles of "estoppel" or doctrines of the "objective sense" of a contract are introduced to prevent this and to qualify the principle that the law enforces contracts in order to give effect to the joint wishes of the contracting parties.

Distribution

This as in the case of property has two aspects (i) Liability (Who may be punished?) and (ii) Amount. In this section I shall chiefly be concerned with the first of these.

From the foregoing discussions two things emerge. First, though we may be clear as to what value the practice of punishment is to promote, we have still to answer as a question of Distribution "Who may be punished?" Secondly, if in answer to this question we say "only an offender for an offence" this admission of retribution in Distribution is not a principle from which anything follows as to the severity or amount of punishment; in particular it neither licenses nor requires, as Retribution in General Aim does, more severe punishments than deterrence or other utilitarian criteria would require.

The root question to be considered is, however, why we attach the moral importance which we do to retribution in Distribution. Here I shall consider the efforts made to show that restriction of punishment to offenders is a simple consequence of whatever principles (Retributive or Utilitarian) constitute the Justifying Aim of punishment.

The standard example used by philosophers to bring out the importance of retribution in Distribution is that of a wholly innocent person who has not even unintentionally done anything which the law punishes if done intentionally. It is supposed that in order to avert some social catastrophe officials of the system fabricate evidence on which he is charged, tried, convicted and sent to prison or death. Or it is supposed that without resort to any fraud more persons may be deterred from crime if wives and children of offenders were punished vicariously for their crimes. In some forms this kind of thing may be ruled out by a consistent sufficiently comprehensive utilitarianism. Certainly expedients involving fraud or faked charges might be very difficult to justify on utilitarian grounds. We can of course imagine that a negro girl might be sent to prison or executed on a false charge of rape in order to avoid widespread lynching of many others; but a system which openly empowered authorities to do this kind of thing, even if it succeeded in averting specific evils like lynching, would awaken such apprehension and insecurity that any gain from the exercise of these powers would by any utilitarian calculation be offset by the misery caused by their existence. But official resort to this kind of fraud on a particular occasion in breach of the rules and the subsequent indemnification of the officials responsible might save many lives and so be thought to yield a clear surplus of value. Certainly vicarious punishment of an offender's family might do so and legal systems have occasionally though exceptionally resorted to this. An example of it is the Roman *Lex Quisquis* providing for the punishment of the children of those guilty of majestas. In extreme cases many might still think it right to resort to these expedients but we should do so with the sense of sacrificing an important principle. We should be conscious of choosing the lesser of two evils, and this would be inexplicable if the principle sacrificed to utility were itself only a requirement of utility.

Similarly the moral importance of the restriction of punishment to the offender cannot be explained as merely a consequence of the principle that the General Justifying Aim is Retribution for immorality involved in breaking the law. Retribution in the Distribution of punishment has a value quite independent of Retribution as Justifying Aim. This is shown by the fact that we attach importance to the restrictive principle that only offenders may be punished, even where breach of law might not be thought immoral. Indeed even where the laws themselves are hideously immoral as in Nazi Germany, *e.g.* forbidding activities (helping the sick or destitute of some racial group) which might be thought morally obligatory, the absence of the principle restricting punishment to the offender would be a further special iniquity; whereas admission of this principle would represent some residual respect for justice shown in the administration of morally bad laws.

Notes

For a critical overview of the literature and theorising on the justification for punishment see Nicola Lacey (1988), Chapter 2; A. Duff and D. Garland (1994), Chapter 1.

1.   Both Hart and Ross are concerned with one of the enduring problems of moral philosophy: the ethical basis for society's use of coercive measures against law-breaking individuals. Both refer to the opposition between those who justify such actions in terms of the requirements of a just social order (often described as "retributivists"), which entails the necessity of punishment to avoid unfairness, and those who prefer to support such measures by reference to their perceived beneficial consequences, broadly an overall reduction in crime, and labelled for that reason "utilitarians" or "consequentialists". Hart accepts that the moral basis of coercive measures may take either of these forms but argues that the application or "distribution" of sanctions should be conditioned upon retributive ideas of proportionality and responsibility. Ross, on the other hand, eschews Hart's open-minded "general justifying aim" and argues for a "pure" concept of justification which is kept distinct from future-looking aims and objectives. In this way, for Ross, the justification for the state's use of coercive measures

is always rooted in retributive argument, whatever the character of the aims being pursued in the application of these sanctions.

2.   Is it possible to divorce retributive and utilitarian concerns as neatly as in Ross' argument? It may be helpful to postulate questions about the origin of our feeling that it would be unjust not to take action against law-breakers. Does it simply spring from an ethical conviction? Or is it also and inextricably bound up with a (utilitarian) idea that not to take such action would inevitably undermine the authority of both the system of criminal law and the moral code upon which it is based? If so, the broad ethical basis for state action is a fusion of retributive and utilitarian concerns. The advantages of Hart's approach is that it sees no problems in this, but at the same time his insistence of "retribution in distribution" guards against the morally unacceptable application of sanctions, for example, to those who were not responsible for their actions or to a degree which does not broadly reflect the nature and impact of the law-breaking.

3.   The American writer, Herbert L. Packer, also insists upon the role of responsibility as a limiting principle (*Limits of the Criminal Sanction* (1969), pp. 65–66):

> "Law, including the criminal law, must in a free society be judged ultimately on the basis of its success in promoting human autonomy and the capacity for individual human growth and development. The prevention of crime is an essential aspect of the environmental pro-tection required if autonomy is to flourish. It is, however, a negative aspect and one which, pursued with single-minded zeal, may end up creating an environment in which all are safe but none is free. The limitations included in the concept of culpability are justified not by an appeal to the Kantian dogma of 'just deserts' but by their usefulness in keeping the state's powers of protection at a decent remove from the lives of its citizens."

Note that Packer rests the justification for state intervention on the "promotion of human autonomy and the capacity for individual human growth and development". Is this very different from more traditional retributive ideas based on a concept of justice? Packer's justification is taken a stage further by Nicola Lacey (1988) in her preference for a "community conception" of punishment, according to which a promotion of similar values is moulded by the wider community of individuals:

> "... the strongest possible arguments for punishment can be developed within a communitarian conception which envisages a society genuinely committed to pursuing with equal concern the welfare and autonomy of each of its citizens, and of creating an environment in which human beings may flourish and develop, whilst acknowledging the role of the community in constructing the values and human interests which it seeks to defend." (*State Punishment: Political Principles and Community Values* (1988), pp. 198–199).

Would Packer have disagreed with such an argument?

4.   However, Hart's analysis is valid in so far as what is at issue is the use of punishment. If the measure in question is adopted, not as a necessary response (on either ethical or policy grounds) to a criminal act, but as necessary treatment for a condition or disorder or as a means of public protection, then the question of both its justification and application will be dependent on considerations of personal or public well-being. Issues of justice enter the discussion only to the extent that such measures should not be more restrictive of individual freedom than is strictly required by the objectives of effective treatment and protection. In this context the fact of the offence loses much of its significance, being relegated from the essential reason for taking action to a form of evidence for the need to take action. For example, hospital and restriction orders under the Mental Health legislation are justified as coercive means because of an overriding need for treatment or public protection; their nature and extent may be limited by arguments of proportionality, but these are linked to considerations of treatment and protection, not to any criminal offence.

5.   In practice, nice theoretical distinctions between punishment and treatment may not be easy to draw. Incarceration may be used for purposes of punishment, treatment or public protection. But, in theoretical terms, it may be difficult to justify it for reasons of both punishment and treatment, since widely accepted ideas of responsibility render these two options mutually exclusive, although either could be validly coupled with the need for public protection. In this connection, note that, if a hospital order is made by a court under section 37 of the Mental Health Act 1983, section 37(8) prohibits the concurrent use of a sentence of imprisonment, fine, probation order or custodial measure for young offenders. For a discussion of the ability of the courts, in the first years when hospital orders were available, to distinguish between objectives of treatment and punishment, see: D. A. Thomas (1965) and Nigel Walker and Sarah McCabe (1973), pp. 99–104, especially at p. 101:

> "On the whole, however, Mr Thomas was probably right if he meant that in the ordinary case in which a hospital order is proposed courts tend to reason in a utilitarian way. If so, legislation on the disposal of disordered offenders seems to have reached a very interesting stage. This can be defined briefly by saying that in their case the offence itself seems to be in the process of relegation from the position of *justification* for the measures applied to the position of a mere *occasion* for them."

6.   Some thirty years ago Baroness Wootton (1963) argued for an abandonment of punitive and retributive principles and their replacement by a system of disposals which is designed to prevent any reoccurrence of the anti-social conduct in question. The outward act (*actus reus*) of such conduct would be sufficient to render a person liable to some form of appropriate "treatment" and any moral questions about responsibility for the action are neatly side-stepped. Wootton argues that "the prevention of accidental

deaths presents different problems from those involved in the prevention of wilful murders. The results of the actions of the careless, the mistaken, the wicked and the merely unfortunate may be indistinguishable from one another, but each case calls for a different treatment" (p. 48). Such an exclusive focus on questions of prevention, resulting in a neutral, blame-free system of disposals has attracted considerable doubt and criticism; see in particular Hart (1968), pp. 177–85; 193–209. *Cf.* more recent "abolitionist" argument, much of it inspired by "critical criminology": see H. Bianchi (1994).

IV. NON-CRIMINAL LAW SANCTIONS AND DECRIMINALISATION

Underlying much of this discussion is an inevitable tension between two features of any kind of anti- social conduct: the state of mind in which it is carried out, and its effects. Traditionally, criminal law has concentrated upon the first of these. Thus a deliberate theft of a small amount of money is a "serious" offence, punishable (in theory) with a maximum of ten years imprisonment, despite its small social impact. On the other hand, unintentionally causing the death of another person may not amount to a criminal offence at all but clearly has a devastating social effect. Theorists such as Baroness Wootton wish to stress social damage as a primary concern of the legal system and point to the inevitable difficulties involved in deciding questions of moral culpability. Many, however, would still accept that the proper and necessary function of the criminal law is to deal with anti-social acts which are morally blameworthy. That does not mean that the law should not seek to control other anti-social conduct, but there may be persuasive arguments that the latter should not be the subject of criminal law sanctions.

Report of the Committee on Safety and Health at Work **(Robens Committee), Cmnd. 5034 (1972), Chapter 9, paragraphs 260–262**

260. The picture which emerges is, in many ways, a curious one. From the discussions we had it was obvious to us that many doubts exist within the inspectorates as to the value and efficacy of prosecution as a means of promoting acceptable standards of safety and health at work. It is fair to say that inspectors value the *threat* of possible prosecution as a potent sanction, and that they attach importance to the deterrent effect of the adverse local publicity which prosecutions frequently attract. Nevertheless, the weight of the evidence points to the conclusion that the lengthy process of investigation, warning, institution of criminal proceedings, conviction and ultimate fine is not a very effective way of producing an early remedy for known unsatisfactory conditions. In sum, we do not believe that the traditional sanction commands any very widespread degree of respect or confidence in this field. Why is this?

261. The fact is – and we believe this to be widely recognised – that the traditional concepts of the criminal law are not readily applicable to the majority of infringements which arise under this type of legislation. Relatively few offences are clear-cut, few arise from reckless indifference to the possibility of causing injury,

few can be laid without qualification at the door of a particular individual. The typical infringement or combination of infringements arises rather through carelessness, oversight, lack of knowledge or means, inadequate supervision or sheer inefficiency. In such circumstances the process of prosecution and punishment by the criminal courts is largely an irrelevancy. The real need is for a constructive means of ensuring that practical improvements are made and preventive measures adopted. Whatever the value of the threat of prosecution, the actual process of prosecution makes little direct contribution towards this end. On the contrary, the laborious work of preparing prosecutions – and in the case of the Factory Inspectorate, of actually conducting them – consumes much valuable time which the inspectorates are naturally reluctant to devote to such little purpose. On the other side of the coin – and this is equally important – in those relatively rare cases where deterrent punishment is clearly called for, the penalties available fall far short of what might be expected to make any real impact, particularly on the larger firms.

262. Thus the traditional sanction of criminal proceedings falls between two stools. On the one hand the character of criminal proceedings is inappropriate to the majority of situations which arise, and the process involved make little positive contribution towards the real objective of improving future standards and performance. On the other hand, the penalties available are too light to have any real impact in the minority of cases where exemplary punishment is called for. What is needed is an approach which recognises that different types of situation call for different types of remedy. The sanctions available should provide scope for distinguishing between situations where the accent should be on punishment, and the more frequent situations where the accent should be on constructive remedial action...

Notes

1.   The extract from the Report of the Robens Committee presents clear and persuasive arguments in favour of the use of "administrative" sanctions in the area of health and safety at work, to be reinforced by criminal law sanctions only in cases of recalcitrance or blatant disregard of standards. The underlying idea is that, in the area of regulation of commercial and social activities beyond the scope of traditional criminality, the use of criminal law sanctions is excessive and also sometimes an unwieldy and blunt instrument of control. There may be a cost, both in economic terms and through a self-defeating process of stigmatisation, in using the criminal law in such cases. A number of continental European legal systems have adopted a system of administrative offences in the field of economic and social regulation, with different agencies and procedures of enforcement and sanctions of a formally distinct nature. Similarly in European Community law, the investigation of alleged infringements of the competition rules and the imposition of sanctions in that context comprises the use of "administrative procedures" and "administrative penalties" (see generally Christopher Harding (1992); also, House of Lords Select Committee on the European Communities, *Enforcement of Community Competition Rules,* H.L. Paper 7-I (1993)).

2.   An advantage of court proceedings is that they represent open justice whereby any discretionary decision-taking can be publicly scrutinised. Conversely, the risk inherent in the more flexible but less visible administrative procedures described above is that the individual is less easily provided with

legal safeguards. One method of legal protection in this respect is to provide for the possibility of appeal to a court if the subject of the procedure feels genuinely aggrieved about the way in which the administrative authority has handled the case. At the same time, there may be a disincentive to easy or spurious complaints if, by making the appeal, the individual in effect "criminalises" the proceedings, so raising the possibility of a criminal rather than administrative sanction. This approach has been adopted in the German Federal Republic, under a system of *Ordnungswidrigkeiten* (petty offences), which has involved the removal of a large number of "regulatory" offences from the ambit of the criminal law into a scheme of administrative prosecutions and penalties. See: John H. Langbein, "Controlling Prosecutorial Discretion in Germany" (1973–4) 41 *University of Chicago Law Review* 439.

Ozturk v. Germany, **Judgment of the European Court of Human Rights (1984) 6 *European Human Rights Reports* 409, paragraphs 51–53.**

51. Under German law, the facts alleged against Mr Öztürk – non-observance of Regulation 1(2) of the Road Traffic Regulations – amounted to a "regulatory offence". They did not fall within the ambit of the criminal law, but of section 17 of the *Ordnungswidrigkeitengesetz* and of section 24(2) of the Road Traffic Act. The 1968/1975 legislation marks an important step in the process of "decriminalisation" of petty offences in the Federal Republic of Germany. Although legal commentators in Germany do not seem unanimous in considering that the law on "regulatory offences" no longer belongs in reality to criminal law, the drafting history of the 1968/1975 Act nonetheless makes it clear that the offences in question have been removed from the criminal law sphere by that Act.

Whilst the Court thus accepts the Government's arguments on this point, it has nonetheless not lost sight of the fact that no absolute partition separates German criminal law from the law on "regulatory offences", in particular where there exists a close connection between a criminal offence and a "regulatory offence". Nor has the Court overlooked that the provisions of the ordinary law governing criminal procedure apply by analogy to "regulatory" proceedings, notably in relation to the judicial stage, if any, of such proceedings.

52. In any event, the indications furnished by the domestic law of the respondent State have only a relative value. The second criterion stated above – the very nature of the offence, considered also in relation to the nature of the corresponding penalty – represents a factor of appreciation of greater weight.

In the opinion of the Commission – with the exception of five of its members – and of Mr Öztürk, the offence committed by the latter was criminal in character.

For the Government in contrast, the offence in question was beyond doubt one of those contraventions of minor importance – numbering approximately five million each year in the Federal Republic of Germany – which came within a category of quite a different order from that of criminal offences. The Government's submissions can be summarised as follows. By means of criminal law, society endeavoured to safeguard its very foundations as well as the right and interests essential for the life of the community. The law on *Ordnungswidrigkeiten*, on the other hand, sought above all to maintain public order. As a general rule and in any event in the instant case, commission of a "regulatory offence" did not involve a degree of ethical unworthiness such as to merit for its perpetrator the moral value-judgment of reproach (*Unwerturteil*) that characterised penal punishment (*Strafe*). The difference between "regulatory offences" and criminal offences found expression both in procedural terms and in relation to the attendant penalties and other legal consequences.

In the first place, so the Government's argument continued, in removing "regulatory offences" from the criminal law the German legislature had introduced a simplified procedure of prosecution and punishment conducted before administrative authorities save in the event of subsequent appeal to a court. Although general laws on criminal procedure were in principle applicable by analogy, the procedure laid down under the 1968/1975 Act was distinguishable in many respects from criminal procedure. For example, prosecution of *Ordnungswidrigkeiten* fell within the discretionary power of the competent authorities and the 1968/1975 Act greatly limited the possibilities of restricting the personal liberty of the individual at the stage of the preliminary investigations.

In the second place, instead of a penal fine (*Geldstrafe*) and imprisonment the legislature had substituted a mere "regulatory" fine (*Geldbusse*). Imprisonment was not an alternative (*Ersatzfreiheitsstrafe*) to the latter type of fine as it was to the former and no coercive imprisonment (*Erzwingungshaft*) could be ordered unless the person concerned had failed to pay the sum due without having established his inability to pay. Furthermore, a "regulatory offence" was not entered in the judicial criminal records but solely, in certain circumstances, on the central traffic register.

The reforms accomplished in 1968/1975 thus, so the Government concluded, reflected a concern to "decriminalise" minor offences to the benefit not only of the individual, who would no longer be answerable in criminal terms for his act and who could even avoid all court proceedings, but also of the effective functioning of the courts, henceforth relieved in principle of the task of dealing with the great majority of such offences.

53. The Court does not underestimate the cogency of this argument. The Court recognises that the legislation in question marks an important stage in the history of the reform of German criminal law and that the innovations introduced in 1968/1975 represent more than a simple change of terminology.

Nonetheless, the Court would firstly note that, according to the ordinary meaning of the terms, there generally come within the ambit of the criminal law offences that make their perpetrator liable to penalties intended, *inter alia*, to be deterrent and usually consisting of fines and of measures depriving the person of his liberty.

In addition, misconduct of the kind committed by Mr Öztürk continues to be classified as part of the criminal law in the vast majority of the Contracting States, as it was in the Federal Republic of Germany until the entry into force of the 1968/1975 legislation; in those other States, such misconduct, being regarded as illegal and reprehensible, is punishable by criminal penalties.

Moreover, the changes resulting from the 1968/1975 legislation relate essentially to procedural matters and to the range of sanctions, henceforth limited to *Geldbussen*. Whilst the latter penalty appears less burdensome in some respects than *Geldstrafen*, it has nonetheless retained a punitive character, which is the customary distinguishing feature of criminal penalties. The rule of law infringed by the applicant has, for its part, undergone no change of content. It is a rule that is directed, not towards a given group possessing a special status – in the manner, for example, of disciplinary law –, but towards all citizens in their capacity as road-users; it prescribes conduct of a certain kind and makes the resultant requirement subject to a sanction that is punitive. Indeed, the sanction – and this the Government did not contest – seeks to punish as well as to deter. It matters little whether the legal provision contravened by Mr Öztürk is aimed at protecting the rights and interests of others or solely at meeting the demands of road traffic. These two ends are not mutually exclusive. Above all, the general character of the rule and the purpose of the penalty, being both deterrent and punitive, suffice to show that the offence in question was, in terms of Article 6 of the Convention, criminal in nature.

The fact that it was admittedly a minor offence hardly likely to harm the reputation of the offender does not take it outside the ambit of Article 6. There is in fact nothing to suggest that the criminal offence referred to in the Convention necessarily implies a certain degree of seriousness. In this connection, a number of Contracting States still draw a distinction, as did the Federal Republic at the time when the Convention was opened for the signature of the Governments, between the most serious offences (*crimes*), lesser offences (*délits*) and petty offences (*contraventions*), whilst qualifying them all as criminal offences. Furthermore, it would be contrary to the object and purpose of Article 6, which guarantees to "everyone charged with a criminal offence" the right to a court and to a fair trial, if the State were allowed to remove from the scope of this Article a whole category of offences merely on the ground of regarding them as petty. Nor does the Federal Republic deprive the presumed perpetrators of *Ordnungswidrigkeiten* of this right since it grants them the faculty – of which the applicant availed himself – of appealing to a court against the administrative decision.

Note

The question of legal protection for those subject to administrative procedures and sanctions, whether at the national or European Community level, has become increasingly a matter for debate, especially in relation to the applicability of Article 6 of the European Convention on Human Rights, as exemplified by the above extract from the judgment of the Court of Human Rights in the *Öztürk* case. The Court has made it clear that the national description of a procedure as "administrative" rather than "criminal" is not sufficient to divert the protection offered by the Convention; the function of the procedure and nature of the sanction are decisive in this respect (see also *Stenuit v. France*, (1993) 16 *European Human Rights Reports* 97). At the Community level, there is increasingly an acceptance of the need for a level of protection analogous to that provided by the European Convention on Human Rights and a recognition that the nature of competition investigations and their consequent sanctions is not far removed from the conventional idea of criminal proceedings (see, for instance, the remarks of Advocate-General Vesterdorf in Case T-7/89, *Re the Polypropylene Cartel, Hercules Chemicals v. Commission* [1992] 11 E.C.R. 1711; [1991] 4 C.M.L.R. 84, at p. 100: "In many instances the parties' submissions can only be understood with the help of the terminology and concepts in criminal law and procedure".)

V. DIFFERENT KINDS OF CRIMINALITY

The use of different kinds of sanction – criminal law or otherwise – begs questions about the nature of the conduct which it is sought to control. The discussion above has drawn a distinction between "traditional" criminality and infractions of economic and social codes of regulation, and this distinction is used to justify the separate treatment of some conduct by means of "administrative" or "regulatory" means of enforcement. Decisions as to the appropriate method of enforcement and type of sanction is thus inextricably bound up with perceptions of the offending conduct, and in particular the force of the moral condemnation of that conduct. It is a well-recognised fact, for instance, that in both social practice and moral argument breaches of trading regulations attract less censure than acts of physical violence. Categorisation of offending behaviour therefore determines the strategies of legal control, in terms of such matters as the allocation of resources, the responsibility of different agencies of enforcement, the kinds of procedure and sanction, and the extent to which control is left as a matter of private initiative (for instance, as a matter of civil rather than criminal liability). This kind of discussion impinges upon not only the question of non-criminal law sanctions (Section IV, above), but also upon strategies of diversion from formal criminal proceedings (discussed in Chapter Two, below).

But the delinquency or criminality inherent in certain conduct may also be analysed in terms of the character and background of the actors involved and this also can have some bearing on the kind of enforcement and sanction which is employed. Whether the offender's situation should have such an impact on questions of process may be a controversial matter, especially if factors of status and social class appear to be determinative. In particular, difficult questions have arisen in relation to the differential treatment of categories such as "white-collar" and "corporate" offenders.

This kind of discussion demonstrates the way in which perceptions of the character of the offender may affect a number of aspects of the criminal justice process: the determination of criminal liability, enforcement of criminal law, and trial and sentence. It is commonly accepted in criminological literature that "white collar" and "corporate" delinquency entail particular problems for purposes of enforcing criminal law. These are summarised by Croall (1992, Chapter 1) as: low visibility; complexity; diffusion of responsibility; diffusion of victimisation; problems of detection and prosecution; ambiguous law; and ambiguous criminal status. A further underlying problem has arisen from the concept of "white collar" crime and its definition. The pioneering definition by Edwin Sutherland (1949) – "a crime committed by a person of respectability and high social status in the course of his occupation" – has been subsequently subject to re-definition, broadly to suggest the idea of crime committed in the course of legitimate employment and involving the abuse of an occupational role (see the discussion in Croall, Chapter 1).

Levi's discussion of the infamous Guinness share-support trial in 1991 refers to some of the difficulties of enforcement but also argues that the case – a successful prosecution – resulted in a disproportionate amount of media attention (what Levi considered to be a "nauseating" spectacle of "popular justice" in full swing, (1991, p. 276)) and sentences which were unduly severe. Were the Guinness defendants victims of a sense of frustration within the legal system as regards the legal control of financial criminality? Subsequently, one of the leading defendants in the Guinness trial, Ernest Saunders, successfully appealed to the European Commission on Human Rights, arguing a violation of Article 6 of the Convention in that evidence obtained under compulsion as part of a Department of Trade and Industry investigation had been used against him in the criminal proceedings (Application No. 19187/91, *Saunders v. U.K.*, 1994). Interestingly, a further complaint that the trial had been prejudiced by excessive press coverage was ruled inadmissible by the Human Rights Commission since the applicant had not specified in what way he had been prejudiced by the press coverage: the mere existence of publicity concerning events which became the subject matter of a trial is not in itself sufficient to cast doubt on the fairness of the proceedings.

For a study of changing policy in relation to the prosecution of crime such as fraud in the financial sector, see Brants (1994). The level of prosecution of financial fraud increased dramatically in the Netherlands during the 1980s, leading to some major and "spectacular" fraud trials, in which most of the defendants were acquitted. Prosecution of this kind of conduct then tailed off at the beginning of the 1990s. Brants argues that what was exposed as the source of the problem was not the existence of "easily identifiable criminal stereotypes to whom traditionally an equally stereotype solution can be applied, but structural aspects of the legitimate economy" (1994, p. 124).

Field and Jorg (1991) discuss a different problem, and for the most part one comprising a different area of delinquency: dangerous activities, rather than fraud or financial manoeuverings. They present a critique of the traditional basis for corporate liability, which identifies the corporate person with the "controlling" human actors. But, as they point out, this approach not only enables an evasion of liability in many cases but also begs questions about the real nature of corporate decision-making and activity. There is a vigorous recent literature on the problem of corporate responsibility for criminal activity: see in particular, Stephen Box (1983), P. French (1984), Brent Fisse and John Braithwaite (1988), and Celia Wells (1993).

VI. LEVELS OF PUNISHMENT

Just as it is necessary, in order to gain a full picture, to consider sanctions and reactions which originate outside the legal system and also legal penalties and procedures which are not of a criminal law character, it is also important to bear in mind that *within the structure of the penal measure* there may be a sub-system of penalties. The application of such lesser penalties may give rise to questions and problems, the resolution of which may be a subject for legal argument or review. The most important context in which such a situation arises is the use of imprisonment, where the body of internal regulations and procedures includes the possible use of sanctions to back up requirements of control and discipline within the prison system. When a prisoner is punished for a breach of internal prison rules, is this to be viewed in the same way as an offence under the state's system of criminal law? If so, it would follow that the prisoner in such a situation should be accorded the same degree of legal protection as an accused person facing a criminal prosecution. Or should a distinction be drawn between the two types of procedure, by saying that the prison proceedings are internal or "disciplinary" in character and so do not raise the same issues of "public law" as normal criminal proceedings? Has the convicted prisoner, by reason of his status after conviction, forfeited his basic rights of legal protection in this context? A further question relates to the justification for imposing additional punishment within the prison regime, apart from matters of breach of discipline. In so far as imprisonment is a punishment, does the penal element reside only in the deprivation of liberty or can it extend to the character of the regime?

Alexander Paterson, "Why prisons?", Chapter 1 in *Paterson on Prisons* (S. K. Ruck ed., 1951), p. 23.

The first duty of a prison then, as an institution of the State, is to perform the function assigned to it by the law, and its administration must therefore ensure that a sentence of imprisonment is a form of punishment. It must, however, be clear from the outset to all concerned that it is the sentence of imprisonment, and not the treatment accorded in prison, that constitutes the punishment. Men come to prison as a punishment, not *for* punishment. It is doubtful whether any of the amenities granted in some modern prisons can in any way compensate for the punishment involved in the deprivation of liberty. It is the length of the sentence that measures the degree of punishment and not the conditions under which it is served. A man would rather spend a week in hell than a year in an almshouse. It is therefore possible to have considerable variety in prison treatment without disregarding the basic fact that a prison sentence is still used by the Courts as a form of punishment.

Philip Priestley, *Victorian Prison Lives* (1985), pp. 124–131.

Hard Labour

The Earl of Carnarvon and his 1863 Select Committee were predictably distressed to discover "the widest possible differences of opinions held as to what constitutes *hard labour*". During the drafting of the bill that followed their endeavours "great efforts were made ... to devise a general definition which should indicate what was intended by the above phrase, and a proposal which was made, though not adopted, that it should be defined as "work which visibly quickens the breath and opens the pores', sufficiently indicates the idea intended." The report itself concluded that, "of the various forms which are in force in the several prisons, the treadwheel, crank and shot-drill alone appear to the Committee properly to merit this designation of hard labour."

The treadwheel, the first of Carnarvon's candidates for "real" hard labour, appeared to opponents of the purely "penal" philosophy to be an infernal machine: "the absence of any human sound – the dull, soughing voice of the wheel, like the agony of drowning men – the dark shadows toiling and treading in a journey which knows no progress – force on the mind involuntary sensations of horror and disgust."

Its invention was claimed by Mr William Cubitt, a civil engineer from Lowestoft, during a visit to the gaol at Bury St Edmunds. In 1818, "the inmates", according to the narration Governor Chesterton received from Cubitt's own lips, "were seen lounging idly about, and the whole aspect indicated a demoralising waste of strength and time." "'I wish to God, Mr. Cubitt,' said the justice who escorted him, 'you could suggest to us some mode of employing these fellows! Could nothing like a wheel become available?' Mr. Cubitt ... whispered to himself, 'the wheel elongated!'" and thus was conceived the treadwheel. The most obvious use of such a wheel was to pump water, "as in the old days in some monasteries", says Basil Thomson, which suggests that Cubitt had merely extended an old principle. At Reading, the wheel supplied water to "various cisterns", and the one at Stafford was "employed in grinding wheat for the consumption of the prison, and of the two lunatic asylums in the neighbourhood". A more typical employment was for the wheel to "grind the wind", a fact which helped to fan the flames of the controversy between those who thought penal labour should be productive and those who thought it should not.

Mr Cubitt had clearly intended his device to be put to some practical use, perhaps in "a mill or manufactory, near the boundary wall of a prison, through which only a single shaft, or axle, would have to pass to communicate the power and motion". And Henry Mayhew was assured at Cold Bath Fields "that advertisements have often been inserted in the journals, offering to lease the tread-mill power, but without any result." But the "utility" party in this debate earned for itself the derision of Sir Edmund DuCane, who wrote in the *Nineteenth Century*:

> They think the moral disadvantage of mechanical labour, such as the tread-wheel, &c., may be surmounted by connecting it with machinery which does useful work, such as grinding corn for the prisoners' own consumption. It seems to me that this view is founded on an amiable delusion as to the imagination prisoners are likely to indulge in on these subjects, and further in an absolute failure to perceive the mode in which, or the reason why, industrial employment may have a good effect on a prisoner's mind.

That Sir Edmund himself harboured few delusions on the subject, and certainly none that could be called amiable, is sufficiently indicated by the title of his article, which was "The unavoidable uselessness of prison work"....

... Next on Carnarvon's list was the crank; sometimes known as "Appold's hard labour machine", and which, like the wheel, as often as not "ground nothing but the air". It was still in use for the military prisoners at Millbank when Mayor Arthur Griffiths went there as deputy governor in 1872; it comprised a "wheel set against cogs that exercised a resisting pressure, and turned by a handle weighted at will to fix the amount of effort required to make the revolution. Apart from the humiliating sensation of labouring hard to achieve no sort of result, the process was to be condemned as inflicting the most unequal toil, for these cranks were of very imperfect construction, continually out of order, so that the precise amount of work could never be exactly calculated."

Like the wheel, the cranks could also be put to productive use if required. At the Leicester County Gaol they were linked to the production of firewood. "The 'saw' was worked by thirty men, ten changing every quarter of an hour, thus twenty were constantly turning the 'crank handles' and ten resting. The 'saw' crank was fixed in a long building so that twenty men could stand in one long row, each in a small 'stall'". But at Cold Bath Fields, in a fiendish refinement beyond anything William Cubitt had thought of, the cranks had been set up as "counter-weights at each end of the axle of the tread-wheel ... so that whilst one group of prisoners is forcing the wheel round with their legs, others are using the strength of their arms to turn the cranks. And as the crank turns in the opposite direction to the wheel it follows that the motion of the one works against that of the other." "I know of nothing harder or more degrading than this work," says M. Moreau-Christophe, *"les dètenus que j'y ai vus appliquès m'ont paru le subir avec une vèritable humiliation".*

Notwithstanding all its advantages, and the enthusiastic endorsements of the Carnarvon Committee, local prisons did not take up the crank in large numbers.

One of the reasons for their reticence may have been a scandal investigated by Royal Commission in 1853. At the Leicester County Gaol, the crank had been the centre-piece of a penal regime that struck even the mid-Victorians as extreme. Men were worked so hard at the machine that they developed symptoms generally described in the surgeon's journal as "crank oedema". They were also deprived of their food if they failed to reach the number of revolutions prescribed as their "task". The Commission condemned this coupling of the crank to the supply of food, describing it as "altogether unwarranted by the law of England". But the practice was common enough for George Bidwell to quote a tariff: "before the occupant can have his breakfast he must turn the handle 1,875 revolutions. His dinner must be earned with 5,000 and his supper with 4,000 turns." ...

... The third kind of hard labour favoured by the Carnarvon Committee was shot drill, described by Arthur Griffiths (a former major in the 63rd West Suffolk regiment) as "the last survival of those barbarous personal punishments by which a century ago military discipline was maintained". The practice slowly fell into disuse, but One-who-has-tried-them "once watched the prisoners at Lewes engaged in this cheerful amusement". "It consists", he says, "of stooping down (without bending the knees) and picking up a thirty-two pounder round shot, bringing it slowly up until it is on a level with the chest, then taking two steps to the right and replacing it on the ground again." Griffiths recalls it as a 24-pound shot, carried six paces, which "went on for four hours, with only a halt of five minutes every half hour to rest the strained and tortured muscles." Another version had lines of men stationed between piles of shot, and the exercise then consisted "in passing the shot, composing the pyramids at one end of the line, down the entire length of the ranks, one after another, until they have all been handed along the file of men, and piled up into similar pyramids at the other end of the line; and when that is done, the operation is reversed and the cannon balls passed back again." Variations on the theme were limited only by geometry and the capacity of the human frame. Carnarvon recommended it with one proviso; that "if the shot be slightly raised from the ground, this punishment is free from all possible objection in a physical point of view." In the event, *i.e.* with hindsight, his recommendation assumes an almost wistful air, since prisons proved more likely to opt for the crank, and even more the wheel – two true creations of the machine age; and they virtually ignored the military athletics of the shot.

Notes

1.   The prison regime prior to 1895 was clearly designed to be punitive so that there were, so to speak, two layers of punishment. The end of this approach was signalled by the Report of the Gladstone Committee (1895), which condemned "useless" labour and advocated a system of "useful" prison work as a component of a reformative regime. Rule 1 of the Prison Rules now states: "the purpose of the training and treatment of convicted prisoners shall be to encourage and assist them to lead a good and useful life." Theoretically, therefore, what happens to the prisoner inside the prison should not involve any additional punishment, although the repressive nature of the institution will itself inevitably involve further restriction of the prisoner's liberty. Such restrictions in themselves, since they are not imposed as a response to any kind of offence, are best described as measures of control and may as such be distinguished from measures applied in connection with breaches of discipline or other prison rules.

2.   An example of litigation arising out of disciplinary proceedings is the

case of *Campbell and Fell v. U.K.*, June 28, 1984, (1985) 7 E.H.R.R. 165. The disciplinary proceedings were taken after an incident at Albany Prison in September 1976. Some prison officers had been injured when trying to bring to an end a protest by a group of prisoners. The applicants were charged with disciplinary offences under the Prison Rules; in subsequent proceedings before the prison Board of Visitors they were found guilty and, amongst other sanctions, lost a substantial period of remission of sentence then normally awarded for good conduct. One of the questions was whether the safeguards laid down in Article 6 of the European Convention on Human Rights were applicable to their proceedings; this required a decision as to whether the disciplinary charges were in substance "criminal" charges. The Court of Human Rights ruled:

> "Taking into account, therefore, both the 'especially grave' character of the offences with which Mr Campbell was charged and the nature and severity of the penalty that he risked incurring – and did in fact incur – the Court finds that Article 6 is applicable to the Board of Visitors" adjudication in his case."

3. A number of cases, both under the European Convention and in the British courts, discuss the distinction between the deprivation of rights and of privileges (see *R v. Hull Prison Board of Visitors, ex p. St Germain and others* [1979] 1 All E.R. 701, C.A.; and the *Engel* case, June 8, 1976, (1979–80) 1 E.H.R.R. 647. Is this a useful approach, at either a juridical or a practical level, to the question of whether a measure may be viewed as a punishment? Even if a measure is strictly speaking a loss of a privilege, this is still something experienced in a real sense as a disadvantage; and surely an important fact, as stated by the European Court, is the loss of an expectation. Granted, a prisoner could automatically expect to be given remission, but every fixed term prisoner started his sentence with the possibility of remission. And since loss of remission was incurred in respect of behaviour within the prison considered by the authorities there to be unacceptable, there seems to be no convincing reason why the measure should not be considered as punitive in character.

4. However, the distinction drawn under the European Convention is between "criminal" and "disciplinary" proceedings. It would seem that the latter are characterised by their internal relevance to the institution in question, but the Court has been willing to say that, even if the need for such proceedings springs from internal requirements of control and security, they may have an overlapping character with proceedings outside the prison if the offence is "grave" and the penalty "severe," in which case the protection of the Convention should be available. Although the Court's jurisdiction is limited by Article 6 of the Convention to questions arising out of "the determination of ... civil rights and obligations or of any criminal charge", this has been given a broad interpretation in order to invade the "closed" sphere of prison discipline. It is uncertain how far the Court is likely to proceed in this direction. For instance, would it decide

that the guarantees of Article 6 should be extended to proceedings relating to an offence not classified under Rule 47 of the Prison Rules as "especially grave" (for example, using abusive, insolent, threatening or other improper language, under Rule 47(14); or refusing to work when required to do so, under Rule 47(17))? If "justice cannot stop at the prison gates" (see paragraph 69 of the judgment), why should it stop short of such lesser breaches of discipline? Is the wording of the Convention fatal to any further extension of the scope of Article 6?

5. This discussion illustrates the distinction drawn by Hart and other writers between "central" and "secondary" cases of punishment. It would be wrong to say that disciplinary sanctions are not a form of punishment, but for procedural and other legal purposes, they have been held distinct from penal measures imposed by the courts. What justifies such a distinction? The fact that the sanctions are applied by different authorities? The fact that the prisoner is subject to a different legal regime under which he has forfeited his normal complement of legal rights and protections? Until the relatively recent development of the concept of prisoners' rights, this was a subject which had received little articulation.

Williams v. Home Office (No. 2) [1982] 2 All E.R. 564, C.A.

In this action, the plaintiff claims damages, including an award of exemplary damages, for the tort of false imprisonment. The action relates to a period of 180 days which the plaintiff spent between August 23, 1974 and February 18, 1975 in a part of Wakefield Prison known as the control unit whilst he was serving a sentence of 14 years' imprisonment. The plaintiff sues the Home Office alleging that the tort was committed against him by his detention in the unit....

... On February 17, 1971 the plaintiff, who is now aged 39, was convicted at Glamorgan Assizes on one of three counts in an indictment charging him with armed robbery of a bank in Cardiff. His sentence of 14 years was an extended sentence. The plaintiff served his sentence in various prisons. In August 1974 the governor of Hull Prison described the plaintiff as a "high notoriety category A prisoner" and as "a totally subversive and dedicated troublemaker". The control unit was established as a means of containing and controlling prisoners who were considered to be troublemakers in prisons and it was the assessment of the plaintiff as such which caused his transfer to the unit....

... for some time there had been considerable concern and anxiety among the administrators of prisons at the influence which troublemakers were exercising on prison life. In 1968 a subcommittee of the Advisory Council on the Penal System, under the chairmanship of Professor Radzinowicz, had recommended the setting up of segregation units at dispersal prisons for violent prisoners or for those who were able to disrupt prison life because of their ability to dominate and manipulate other prisoners....

... In 1972 there was widespread disruption and disorder in a large number of prisons....

... Against that background, a working party was set up to consider the question of control in the dispersal prisons.... Whilst the working party committee recommended the continuation of segregation units as a means of removing disruptive prisoners from ordinary prison life, it was of the opinion that segregation units had not been wholly effective for a number of reasons. Among the reasons was the fact that the segregation units were not sufficiently insulated or isolated from the main part of the prison. Thus the inmates were still able to influence the prisoners in the main prison. The committee therefore recommended that special control units should be set up in dispersal prisons, physically separate and insulated from the main prison, and that prisoners who were allocated to it should not come from the prison in which the unit was situated....

... The question I have to decide is whether the regime was punitive in character. Mr Allum agreed in cross- examination that the regime might appear punitive to a prisoner in the same way as a prison might appear punitive to a member of the public. Mr Emes agreed that one of the reasons for isolation was to make it sufficiently disagreeable so that it would be worthwhile for a man to work his passage. He said that it was known that the prisoner would find the regime disagreeable. The intention was to ensure that he did not continue to make a nuisance of himself in the prison system. He said that there were two elements in the regime: first, to teach the prisoner that it was not going to pay him to go on being a troublemaker and, secondly, to make him not want to go back. In this sense, according to Mr Emes, there was an element of deterrence, but he added that many things can be deterrent without being a punishment. For him punishment is the response to a proven act.

I do not think that the regime was devised to punish the prisoners; nor do I think that the plaintiff was in fact being punished when he was sent there. As I have already said, punishment is not within the ambit of r. 43. If this rule were used merely as a device to punish a particular prisoner, it would be highly improper and there would be a breach of the rule, although with what legal effect I have yet to consider. Junior counsel for the defendant pointed out that, objectively viewed, a punishment regime and a r. 43 regime can appear to be close together. If a prisoner is beaten up and the governor strongly suspects, but is unable to prove, that a particular prisoner is responsible, he would be fully entitled to place the suspect on r. 43, not to punish the prisoner, but to prevent a repetition of the incident in the interests of good order and discipline...

Notes

1. Various arguments were put forward in this case to establish the illegality of the control units (actually discontinued before the date of this judgment as a result of political pressure). It was contended, amongst other things, that, having their legal basis in Rule 43 of the Prison Rules, the units were *ultra vires* that provision since that allows for a prisoner's removal from association for the maintenance of good order and discipline or in his own interests, but does not authorise such segregation as a punishment. Tudor Evans J. rejected the view that the units were punitive in character. But while it would be true to say that the units were ultimately concerned with the maintenance of good order and discipline within the prison system, is this not also a long-term function of punishment in the criminal justice system? The function of the control units was not purely preventive: they were operated in such a way as to teach a prisoner a lesson and act as a deterrent – a disagreeable regime was used as a response to disruptive conduct. These arguments are another demonstration of the practical importance of achieving a consistent analysis of what is involved in the process of punishment.

2. Can a measure ever be a deterrent without at least incorporating a prospect of punishment? Is it meaningful to try to separate processes of deterrence and punishment?

VII. METHODS OF PUNISHMENT

Any discussion of the range of penal measures is in effect an evaluation and comparison of various penal methods and this in turn is the main substance of the field of enquiry often described as "Penology". A number of the subsequent chapters in this book comprise a description and evaluation of the penal measures used at the present time in the British criminal justice system. But at this point it would be useful to indicate some of the important transitions in penal methodology and to say something about the phenomenon of "net-widening", which is a reflection of how the choice of particular measures may have an impact on the scope of the penal system.

The most commonly identified process of transition in the use of penal methods over the last two hundred years or so in Western society, is that from corporal methods of punishment to incarceration, and then more recently from incarceration towards community-based measures. The first element in this transition, from corporal punishment to incarceration, seen as occurring around the end of the eighteenth century, was stressed in particular in the work of the French writer Michel Foucault (especially in *Discipline and Punish: The Birth of the Prison* (1975, 1977)), which has been very influential in the work of other theorists over the past 25 years. Foucault's perception of the increasingly incursive operation of the carceral method in the penal system (classically stated in the metaphor of the "carceral archipelago") has stimulated an interpretation of penal activity as involving a sinister "net-widening" effect. However, there has been some resistance to this interpretation; see, for instance and in particular, Anthony E. Bottoms, "Neglected Features of Contemporary Penal Systems", Chapter 8 in *The Power to Punish: Contemporary Penality and Social Analysis* (David Garland and Peter Young eds., 1983).

Maeve McMahon, *The Persistent Prison* (1992) pp. 31–35, 37–38.

This critical consensus about empirical trends in imprisonment and alternatives was clearly evident by the mid- 1980s. The core elements of the conventional wisdom are apparent, for example, in Cohen's (1985: 44) state-of-the-art summary of what is really going on "inside the system":

> Let us start with the (apparently) simple question of whether the decarceration strategy has worked in reducing the rates of juvenile and adult offenders sent to custodial institutions. The obvious index of success is not simply the proliferation of new programmes, but whether custodial institutions are being replaced, phased out or at least are beginning to receive fewer offenders overall. The statistical evidence here is by no means easy to decipher and there are complicated methodological problems in picking out even the crudest of changes. But all the evidence here indicates failure – that in Britain, Canada and the USA rates of incarceration are not at all declining and in some spheres are even increasing. Community control has supplemented rather than replaced traditional methods.

Similar messages about the limited effects of community corrections have repeatedly appeared in the critical literature. For example, Canadian authors Lowman, Menzies, and Palys (1987: 211) confidently state that, "designed originally to provide a community *alternative* to incarceration ... these programmes have become a *supplement* to them. Instead of *fewer* individuals going to prison, there are now more than ever. And instead of directing individuals out of the criminal justice system, the new programmes have directed more people *into* it .... The bottom line, therefore, is that more and more individuals are becoming subject to the scrutiny and surveillance of criminal justice personnel."

One notable characteristic of the critical literature on decarceration has been the tendency to express the empirical basis of arguments as much through metaphors and analogies as through specific statistical statements about identifiable penal populations. In the course of this analytical strategy, the language and theme of net-widening have become prominent in depicting the scenario whereby alternatives become add-ons to pre-existing prison populations. Probation, parole, and other community programs have been said to have reduced liberty, and to have introduced many new people into the "control net" (Matthews 1979: 115). As the process of "widening the net" is said to have been accompanied by that of "thinning the mesh," the predominant image is that of a system in perpetual expansion: deviants are continually subjected to new, more intense and pervasive forms of control that are woven into, and beyond, traditional institutional networks of penal control.

As the notions of "widening" and "thinning" suggest, the development of alternatives is seen by critics as not only yielding an expansion in the numbers of people subject to penal control, but also giving rise to an intensification of the substance of control. When these changes are depicted, the concept of "net-widening" is typically allied with – and often presented as incorporating – those of "stronger" and "different" nets. Again, Cohen (1985: 44) has provided an adroit specification of these key images. According to him, with the development of alternatives

(1) there is an increase in the total number of deviants getting into the system in the first place and many of these are new deviants who would not have been processed previously (wider nets);
(2) there is an increase in the overall intensity of intervention, with old and new deviants being subject to levels of intervention (including traditional institutionalisation) which they might not have previously received (denser nets);
(3) new agencies and services are supplementing rather than replacing the original set of control mechanisms (different nets).

In turn, the overarching concept of "net-widening" is linked to other evocative images. The prison, for example, is described as the "hard end" of the system, with the boundaries between it and other control institutions becoming increasingly "blurred". Community and private institutions – such as the family, school, neighbourhood, and workplace – are seen as subject to "penetration" and "absorption" by formal modes of social control. As the "hard end" gets harder, and as the "soft end" gets wider, "bifurcation" is said to be occurring. Meanwhile, the processing of deviants "accelerates." In light of these developments, the "holy trinity" of reform rhetoric about the virtues of alternatives in terms of costs, effectiveness, and humaneness, is revealed as mythical. The "dreams" of progressive reformers are said to be better understood as "nightmares".

Analysts of decarceration portray the net effect of these trends as involving a "dispersal of discipline": the prison retains its institutional strength, and is interwoven with, and dependent on, a "carceral continuum" that powerfully pervades social life in ever more subtle, complex, and effective ways ... These key empirical points of the conventional wisdom can be expressed more mundanely: prison populations are maintained and increased, while community alternatives proliferate. The predominant penal trend is that of an expansion of penal control.

Perceptions of the Maintenance and Increase of Imprisonment

While claims about net-widening are most clearly expressed in the literature on decarceration, wider debates about penal control also tend to reinforce perceptions about prison and penal expansion. For example, in an important article, "Neglected Features of Contemporary Penal Systems," Anthony Bottoms (1983) calls attention to developments that have been overlooked by analysts of decarceration, and points to the need for an empirically based research agenda. Yet, at the same time, he accepts that increasing numbers of people in different countries are being subjected to imprisonment.

Bottoms's analytical objective is a critique of the "extension of discipline" thesis, particularly as advanced by Cohen (1979) and Mathiesen (1983). In developing his points, Bottoms identifies the *proportionate* decline in the use of imprisonment for indictable offences in England and Wales when figures for 1938, 1959, and 1980 are compared. On the basis of sentencing data for these years, Bottoms goes on to make a convincing argument that the gap has been filled, not, as one might expect, by a proportionate increase in the use of probation or discharge, but rather by the imposition of fines: as the use of imprisonment proportionately decreased, that of fines increased.

Bottoms does not use these data to dispute the net-widening thesis. More at issue for him is the question of whether these trends accord with wider perceptions of the "dispersal of discipline". Decarceration analysts have emphasised the growth of "disciplinary" penalties, such as probation. But, according to Bottoms, the fine is a non-disciplinary penalty, the area in which the most dramatic increases have taken place. For Bottoms, therefore, analytical issues about the disciplinary or non-disciplinary nature of penal dispositions are very important.

Questions about whether specific penal practices should or should not be classified as "disciplinary" are interesting and difficult to answer. Related debates derive largely from the translation of Foucault's *Surveillir et punir* as *Discipline and Punish*. Had *surveillir* been translated as "supervision," "inspection," or "observation," rather than "discipline", issues of the "disciplinary society" would hardly have come to such prominence. The ambiguity of the notion of "discipline," as exacerbated by the idiosyncracies of Foucault's literary approach and its translation, has given rise to stimulating disputes about the character of contemporary penal control and preferred concepts in elucidating it . . . . At this point, however, I am more concerned with the empirical than with the theoretical aspects of the debate. Of particular interest is Bottoms's acceptance of observations about the maintenance and growth of imprisonment.

Pointing to Bottoms's agreement about the growth of imprisonment may initially appear puzzling in light of his emphasis on the proportionate decline in the imposition of imprisonment compared to other dispositions. But, stability or growth in imprisonment, coupled with a proportionate decline in its use in sentencing, is possible when there is a growth in the numbers of those convicted in the first place. Such a trend indeed occurred in England and Wales. Therefore, in conjunction with his observations about the proportionate decline in imprisonment, Bottoms makes the "very important" observation: "many more people are being sent to prison per annum now than before the Second World War." One example he cites is that the "number of adults given prison sentences in England and Wales rose from less than 13,000 in 1938 to 36,000 in 1980" (1983: 183–4). According to Bottoms, this represents the "same kind of result" as that represented by Hylton's (1981) data for the Canadian province of Saskatchewan, which demonstrate an increasing imprisonment rate both in absolute numbers and in rates per 100,000 population. He also points to Chan and Ericson's (1981) study of Canadian data as showing such an increase. Bottoms further notes that these studies demonstrate concurrent and rapid increases in community supervision, with those put on probation growing in rates per head of population as well as in absolute numbers.

Where Bottoms takes issue with Hylton, and Chan and Ericson, is with respect to their omission of broader sentencing data. This omission, he says, leads them to overlook the possibility of increasing numbers of people being convicted, and a declining proportion being sentenced to imprisonment. Such data could lead to different inferences about developments in the nature of power exercised by the state. By contrast – and despite Bottoms's focus on the methodologies of Hylton's and Chan and Ericson's studies – he does not take issue with what they include. Bottoms thereby accepts their propositions that both prison and probation populations are growing in Canada. In sum, whether or not one considers that the "features" Bottoms has identified fit with the "dispersal of discipline" thesis, they certainly do accord with the conventional wisdom of the decarceration literature: an international trend of growth in those subject to imprisonment – and to criminal-justice processing more generally – is clearly identified....

... Other critical analysts either downplay or ignore the potential importance of Bottoms's observations about the relevance of proportionate declines in the use of imprisonment in sentencing. Cohen (1985: 84, 295), for example, makes only passing reference to the phenomenon, and cites Bottoms in a note. In the main narrative, he goes on to say: "beyond all the complex empirical problems, historical comparisons and implied value judgements, there is the over-riding fact of proliferation, elaboration and diversification." Again, while the analytical significance of events may be disputable, the factuality of penal expansion is not. Meanwhile, Bottoms (1987) himself has pointed to the proportionate decrease in the use of fines that occurred in the 1980s, at least partly in favour of the use of imprisonment. These more recent trends may render it even more unlikely that Bottoms's historical observations will disturb conventional-wisdom analyses.

Adherence to the conventional wisdom has, on occasion, been associated with extremely deterministic views about penal reform. According to Roger Matthews (1979: 115), for example: "the introduction of parole, probation, indeterminate sentences, diversion programmes, and the whole array of recent control strategies have served, *invariably*, to ... increase lengths of incarceration, loss of liberty, or surveillance ... and to introduce many, particularly the young, into the control net for 'offences' that prior to the setting up of such programmes would have gone unnoticed or seem to be inconsequential" (emphasis added). While Matthews (1987, 1989) has now modified his view, many critical criminologists have continued to assume that the development of alternatives yields an expansion of the prison and penal system.

An article by Muncie and Coventry (1989) is a prototype of this kind of thinking. Muncie and Coventry's subject is the non-custodial sanction of the Youth Attendance Order (involving community work and activities), introduced in the Australian province of Victoria in 1988. While making customary reference to the possibility of different experiences in different places, and having acknowledged that no evaluative research on the new community program is available to them, the authors grant themselves "poetic licence" in using the findings of decarceration research elsewhere to make predictions about the consequences of the program.

Through this approach, and in the absence of data on the Youth Attendance Order in Victoria, Muncie and Coventry confidently state that, several years hence, it will have been seen that the community order program "acts as a funnel towards custody rather than a route out of it"; that the order "is not treated as a true alternative to custody"; that the order "is used as an *addition* rather than an *alternative* to existing sentencing options"; that it is "net-widening," and is but one in the series of reform innovations that have "established a system which appears to be forever expanding" (1989: 185–6; emphasis in original). For Muncie and Coventry, conventional-wisdom knowledge provides a basis for social-scientific premonition.

In sum, the critical literature on alternatives sees them as not simply different, but more intense, and more ominous, than earlier forms of control. The portrait is of an oppressive situation that appears to be becoming worse. In making this argument, statements about the persistence and growth of imprisonment are central: evidence for the worsening nature of the situation largely derives from the observation that alternatives are merely "add-ons" to imprisonment. If alternatives "really" were alternatives, and prison population was declining, arguments about the expansion of penal control would lose much of their analytical force.

Note

There is not so much argument about the general character of penal transitions during the modern period (corporal, to carceral, to community measures), as about the sinister interpretation of these developments, especially in terms of a "net-widening" outcome. The work of the main writers in this school of interpretation (*e.g.* Foucault (1975, 1977), Cohen (1979) and (1985) and Mathiesen (1983)) has been challenged and refined by the kind of argument contained in the extract above. Both Bottoms and McMahon point to the development and use of measures which are outside the "dispersal of discipline" identified by Foucault and Cohen; and McMahon is especially critical of the rigour and methodology of the net-widening arguments. Nelken (1989) points to some fuzziness in the debate: is it about developments in the criminal justice system or in the wider, more diffuse realm of social control? Nelken's discussion is specifically concerned with the use of contracts and working agreements in social work and he concludes that categorisation according to whether or not something is part of the criminal justice system may not be very helpful:

> "in seeking to understand marginal forms of crime control, such as the use of contracts by social workers, only limited insight is gained by arguing whether they count as extensions of the criminal justice system (Cohen (1979)) or whether they belong outside it (Bottoms 1983) ... instead their specific characteristics need to be identified for their own sake." (1989, p. 253)

VIII. REPARATION AND THE ROLE OF THE VICTIM OF CRIMINAL OFFENCES

The modern criminal justice system has been predominantly concerned with the relationship between the offender and those agencies responsible for the enforcement of criminal and penal law (*e.g.* police, prosecutors, lawyers, penal and corrective agents), often to the exclusion of the position of the victim of criminal offences. The victim's role has therefore become, for the most part, procedural and evidential: making initial complaints about offences and testifying to their commission. This is in marked contrast to earlier forms of criminal proceedings, in which the victim's role in prosecution and need for compensation were much more significant features of the process. More recently, however, there has been a revival of interest in the position of the victim, and it is possible to identify two main ways in which the latter's role within the criminal justice system may be enhanced. First, and perhaps most important, the system of criminal proceedings could entail greater consideration of the victim's need for support and compensation, involving possibly some development of the reparative character of certain penal measures. Secondly, it may be that the victim could make a greater and more positive contribution to decision-making at different points in the criminal justice process. The changing attitude towards the position of victims of crime can be seen in a number of official statements and legal instruments during the 1980s and 1990s: for instance, the U.N. Declaration on the *Basic Principles of Justice for Victims of Crime and Abuse of Power* (1985); the European Convention on the *Compensation of Victims of Violent Crime* (1983); and in Britain, the *Victim's Charter*, issued by the Home Office in 1990.

As regards the compensation of victims of crime, this had been for some time viewed as a function of the civil process, which, however, on account of such factors as cost and the probable lack of funds on the part of many offenders, offered little real prospect of success. A state-funded criminal injuries compensation scheme was set up in 1964 and put on a statutory basis in the Criminal Justice Act of 1988, and this has undoubtedly improved the position of those injured as a result of crimes of violence. Moreover, since 1972 criminal courts have been able to make compensation orders when exercising their sentencing powers and this measure has been given higher priority in both the 1982 and 1988 Criminal Justice Acts (for a discussion of these measures, see pp. 340 *et seq.* below). On the operation of the criminal injuries compensation scheme, see Atiyah (1987), Chapter 13; Shapland, Willmore and Duff (1985), Chapter 9; David Miers, *Compensation for Criminal Injuries* (1990).

The possibility of a more positive contribution by the victim to the criminal justice process generally was considered by J. Shapland, J. Willmore and P. Duff in *Victims in the Criminal Justice System* (1985, at p. 81):

"... victims see their role as continuing throughout this process of prosecution, paralleling that of the police. They wish to follow what is happening and to help where they can, being ready to intervene when they are needed. They expect the police to facilitate this by providing information and by consulting them. In contrast the police appear to wish to preserve the prosecution process to themselves, requiring victims to jump the hurdle of deciding to press charges as soon as possible and then seeing them as having little further role until the time comes to give evidence in court. The expectations of victims are not matched by those of the police. The result is that victims are not valued and perceive themselves not to be valued."

See, in particular, Chapter 5 of their book. What benefits may arise for the criminal justice system generally if there were a larger participation of victims of crime in criminal law proceedings? For further discussion of these questions, see Andrew Ashworth (1986); Joanna Shapland and David Cohen (1987); Mike Maguire and John Ponting eds., (1988); Paul Rock (1990); David Miers (1992); Lucia Zedner (1994).

The following extracts explore some of the theoretical and practical problems which may be involved in any policy of enhancing the victim's role in criminal proceedings and attempt to relate this question to the more general issue, considered so far, of what may be seen to be the functions and aims of the sentencing and penal system.

David Miers, "The Responsibilities and Rights of Victims of Crime", (1992) 55 *Modern Law Review* 483, pp. 495–498

Alternative Models of Criminal Justice

It has for some time been a matter of mundane note that the interests of victims of crime have traditionally been "subordinated to powerful and persisting objectives of the criminal justice system."[3] The response of the police to a victim's reported crime determines its status and the nature of any subsequent dealings with it. This response is informed by considerations which may have little to do with the victim's interests: clear-up criteria, offence priorities, the usefulness of the offender as a Crown witness, sentencing factors and so on. Bureaucratic and operational imperatives likewise inform the trial and sentencing processes.[4] There is a very substantial North American literature concerning this matter,[5] but it is only recently that any systematic research undertaken in this country has generated the same general conclusions and validated what has been anecdotally known for some time.[6] The bitter remarks of a legal practitioner who sustained serious personal injuries following an assault are now amply evidenced:

> I write as a lawyer aware of the rules of procedure, the rules of court and knowing best how to behave as a witness. But what of all the other victims who do not possess this knowledge and have no way of getting it? What of those traumatised already who are told in no uncertain terms that they must keep away from the prosecution (who are supposedly acting in their interests), who have no right to a lawyer – and certainly no legal aid – who are terrified

---

[3] Ziegenhagen, *Victims, Crime and Social Control* (1978) p. 75. T. Newburn and S. Merry, *Keeping in Touch* (London: HMSO. Home Office Research Study 116, 1990) note that, following the initial reporting of the incident, subsequent contact between the police and the victim was almost always for the purpose of satisfying police requirements (clarifying statements, etc.,).

[4] A Goldstein, "Defining the Role of the Victim in the Criminal Prosecution" (1982) 52 *Mississippi* L.J. 515–61.

[5] See, *e.g.* (1983–4) 11 *Pepperdine* L.R. 1 182 and Lamborn (1986).

[6] Newburn and Merry (1990). See also I. Burrows, *Burglary, Police Action and Victims' Views* (London: HMSO, Home Office RPU Paper 37, 1986) Ch. 7 and W. Skogan, *The Police and Public in England and Wales* (London: HMSO, Home Office Research Study 117, 1990) Ch. 2.

in court and must face, within close physical proximity, "the attacker"? What of the interminable waiting periods, the impersonal summons in the morning post, the total, but total silence from the people who are representing the victim's interests? In short, the victim is made to feel like a criminal.[7]

Since the secondary victimisation of victims is not a new phenomenon, the question arises, why has it only lately become a political issue? There are a number of strands to the answer. One is associated with the earlier dominance of a criminological paradigm in which the *offender* figured as the victim of a biased criminal justice system, or in stronger Marxist critiques, as the victim of the contradictions of capitalism.[8] A corollary of this paradigm was the virtual exclusion of the victim from any radical agenda, an ideological subordination reflected also in the criminal justice debate of the 1960s. This was conducted principally in terms of the conflicting goals idealised in the crime control and due process models.[9] In emphasising either the bureaucratic values of speed and productivity, or those of doing justice to defendants, both models were able to underpin a system structurally and operationally insensitive to the victim. Both models are thus equally susceptible to criticisms which take victims' rights as their basic premise. Those of an essentially conservative stance can maintain their objection to the due process model, since it neither does justice to victims nor reduces crime,[10] while those of the left can maintain their objection to the crime control model, since it conduces to secondary victimisation, in particular of such groups as blacks, homosexuals and women, who have traditionally been marginalised or ill-treated by criminal justice personnel, whether as offenders or as consumers of criminal justice services. The crucial point is that in the criminal justice debate, concern for the interests of victims of crime constitutes an almost unassailable moral position[11] and, whereas formerly the debate was between the right and the left, each can now pursue ideological objectives that do not, *prima facie*, conflict. The superficial similarity of the rhetoric of "victims' rights" disguises, however, the same fundamental differences of ideology. As espoused by the left, the victim movement is in the tradition of the radical politics of the 1960s; as espoused by the right, it advocates a return to an earlier set of values in which crime control is central,[12] and victims'' rights, to borrow Dworkin's metaphor, trump those of the defendant. Such advocacy, often couched in terms of redressing the balance between victim and offender, may well be prompted by a

---

[7] L. Spry-Leverton, *The Guardian* May 2, 1985. See also J. Shapland, "The Criminal Justice System and the Victim" (1985) 10 *Victimology* 585–99 and "Victims and the Criminal Justice System" in Fattah (1986) 210–7.

[8] A. Phipps, "Radical Criminology and Criminal Victimisation" in *Confronting Crime* (R. Matthews and J. Young eds., 1986). See also F. Heidensohn, *Crime and Society* (1989), 158–77.

[9] H. Packer, *The Limits of the Criminal Sanction* (Stanford: Stanford UP, 1969).

[10] A perennial complaint is that the state has "gone soft" on crime in the pursuit of non-retributivist penal policies: see e.g. *The Times* letters page, October 23, 1991.

[11] As L. Henderson, "The Wrongs of Victims' Rights" (1984–5) 37 *Stanford LR* 937–1021, 953 suggests, "victims' rights" is a symbol that overwhelms critical analysis in two ways: firstly, by playing on the seductive appeal of a concern for "the innocent victim", and secondly, by confusing the experience of victimisation with the fear of crime to justify crime control measures.

[12] See e.g. the explicit linking of proper support for victims of crime with the reform of the right to silence (Mr A. Eastwood, Chairman of the Police Federation, *The Times*, May 23, 1991). As Henderson (p. 953) remarks, "'victims' rights' has produced an emerging structure of criminal law and procedure that closely resembles the 'crime control' model so antithetical to liberal thought." Likewise, the emphasis on "just desserts" for offenders is deeply appealing to the radical right. While "victims'" rights" presents an attractive platform for politicians, many of those looking for easy votes have become embarrassed by the "rightist" sentiments of some of their advocates: B. Smith, "Trends in the Victims' Rights Movement and Implications for Future Research" (1985) 10 *Victimology* 34–43.

genuine concern to see improvements in the ways in which victims are treated by the criminal justice system: more information about the progress of the case, more sensitive responses by the police and other officials, and the easier availability of compensation. To others may be attributed less charitable motives. There are clearly some who use reported or predicted rates of personal victimisation to criticise the political decisions which they feel have contributed to the offending behaviour: courts are too lenient, the welfare state erodes personal responsibility, schools, parents and other moral guardians are not communicating appropriate moral standards, and so on. Such rhetoric is an integral part of the politics of victimisation.

Another strand lies in the failure of the police to control crime. As was noted earlier, one official response has been an explicit insistence upon the victim's share of the public responsibility which defines the police's role in preventing and clearing up crime; but, as the recorded crime rate apparently shows no sign of abating, the victims" movement can be seen as a response both to the perceived failure of the two dominant models of criminal justice policy to incorporate victims' interests in its decision criteria (a failure which can be used to serve ideological objectives), and to the anger generated by a policing policy that demands the curtailment of the *victim's* freedom of movement and of association as a technique for coping with the failure of the police to control that of the *offender*.

A further consideration is the inevitable reliance of the criminal justice system upon victims as its principal information source. The system depends upon the exchange of information and, frequently, this is uniquely known to the victim. The BCS confirm that it is victims who are the gatekeepers to the mobilisation of its personnel,[13] and so it must be in the interests of the system to encourage free and spontaneous reporting, as well as subsequent verification and authorisation for trial purposes. Since research suggests that when victims feel unsympathetic to the system's goals and values they will be less likely to supply or validate information, it follows that such a tendency could be countered by the system's adopting a more sensitive response to the victim's interests.[14] A practice that could go a substantial way towards meeting at least one of those interests is the routine and unsolicited communication to victims of the progress of the investigation and subsequent trial. Recent research unequivocally confirms the importance victims attach to being kept informed,[15] but it remains to be seen whether the inclusion in the *Victim's Charter* of such a requirement will be realised in practice.

Apart from the development of a variety of victim services, a second consequence of the concern to re-establish the victim's place in the criminal justice system[16] has been the introduction of schemes designed to divert offenders from the normal criminal justice pathways, typically coupled with some form of reparation for the victim.[17] During the 1980s, a number of experimental schemes were financed by the

---

[13] Hough and Mayhew (1985) p. 19.

[14] *e.g.* M. Wolfgang, "Making the Criminal Justice System Accountable" (1972) *Crime and Delinquency* 15–22. A useful cross national study is M. Joutsen, *The Role of the Victim of Crime in European Criminal Justice Systems* (Finland: Helsinki Institute for Crime Prevention and Control, 1987).

[15] Newburn and Merry (1990).

[16] It is often argued that there was a "golden age" in which the victims' interests were at least given the same value as those of the offender: whether this argument can, as a matter of historical interpretation, be sustained is debatable: see Miers (1990), 317–8.

[17] Such developments have been especially prominent in the United States in recent years; e.g. C. Abel and F. Marsh, *Punishment and Restitution* (1984) and B. Galaway, "Victim Participation in the Penal Corrective Process" (1985) 10 *Victimology* 617–30. In this country, see M. Wright, *Making Good* (1982), "The Impact of Victim/Offender Mediation upon the Victim" (1985) 10 *Victimology* 631–44, and *Justice for Victims and Offenders* (1991); J. Harding, *Victims and Offenders: Needs and Responsibilities* (1982) and *Alternatives to Custody* (J. Pointing ed., 1987).

Home Office.[18] Mediation is considered apt where there is an existing relationship between the offender and the victim which is likely to continue, the harm is not serious, and there is a dispute amenable to resolution. What is avoided is the all-or-nothing outcome of a trial, the stigma of conviction, and the expense of time and effort typically involved in such proceedings. What is gained are the positive virtues of a settlement negotiated by individuals who retain their dignity and who share active responsibility for the normative framework of their future relationship. These values will be instantly recognised as those that are sought, in civil law, by arbitration and small claims procedures; more broadly, mediation is but one analogue for the paradigmatic private settlement: contract.[19]

Attractive though this option may seem, it disguises some real difficulties both in terms of its objectives and its implementation. The preliminary study produced by the RPU identified ten objectives, not all of which were mutually compatible: victims regaining control over "their" dispute, promoting cathartic exchange between the parties, achieving restitution, giving victims a greater voice in criminal justice decisions, encouraging the offender to accept responsibility for his or her actions, reducing the likelihood of reoffending, to divert the offender from the criminal justice system, to encourage a smaller sentence, to develop the probation service, and to involve the community. Similarly, the report highlighted some difficulties in reconciling the public nature of criminal justice decision criteria with the essentially private nature of mediation, which may generate considerations inimical to the public aspect of offensive behaviour.[20]

There are yet stronger versions of this diversionary policy, associated in particular with Christie's argument that conflicts "belong" to their participants, who should be allowed to resolve them, with consequential benefits to them and to their community,[21] arguments which, as has just been noted, appear among the objectives of the mediation schemes now in place. Associated, and equally radical, is Barnett's thesis that restitution should be the prime objective of legal proceedings following an offence causing injury.[22] While these ideas too may appear attractive, Ashworth has cogently demonstrated their impracticability given existing social-structural and, more particularly, legal-systemic arrangements.[23]

These developments further underline the shift which has occurred in the recent past of responsibility for significant elements of the implementation of criminal justice policy, from the public to the private sector. Private policing has long been with us and, as noted, the tenor of official advice on crime prevention and on the provision of victim services is that they properly entail private sector activity. The Criminal Justice Act 1991 makes provision for the contracting out of prisons, while the development of mediation and reparation programmes emphasises the private, and binding, settlement of disputes. These developments were, until recently,

---

[18] Four experimental schemes were established during 1984 and 1985 in which offenders were encouraged to make compensation in kind (*e.g.* gardening, repairing damage) as part of a mediation programme; HC Deb vol. 58, col 515 (April 12, 1984). T. Marshall, "Reparation, Conciliation and Mediation" (London: HMSO, Home Office RPU Paper 27, 1984), T. Marshall and M. Walpole, "Bringing People Together" (London; HMSO, Home Office RPU Paper 33, 1985), C. Williams, "Reparation and Mediation in the Criminal Justice System" (1986) 136 *New L.J.* 1106–8, 1141–2, S. Walklate, "Reparation: A Merseyside View" (1986) 26 *B. J. Crim.* 287–98, and H. Blogg, "Reparation and Justice for Juveniles" (1985) 25 *B. J. Crim.* 267–79. See also *The Times*, September 21, 1991.

[19] R. Boldt, "Restitution, Criminal Law and the Ideology of Individuality" (1987) *J Crim. Law and Criminology* 962–1022.

[20] G. Davis *et al.*, "A Preliminary Study of Victim Offender Mediation and Reparation Schemes in England and Wales" (London: HMSO, Home Office RPU Paper 42, 1987).

[21] N. Christie, "Conflicts as Property" (1977) 27 *B. J. Crim.* 1–15.

[22] R. Barnett, "Restitution: A New Paradigm in Criminal Justice" (1976) 87 *Ethics* 279–301.

[23] A. Ashworth, "Punishment and Compensation: Victims, Offenders and the State" (1986) 6 *Oxford J Legal Studies* 86–122.

adventitious, but they now figure as key components in the Home Office's multi-agency approach to crime prevention; an approach that owes as much to the wisdom of a policy of preventative medicine as it does to an acceptance of the futility of post-offence treatment of offenders.[24] If this shift continues, we may expect correspondingly stronger claims that victims be given rights in the determination of criminal justice decisions.

Royal Commission on Criminal Justice, *Report*, Cm. 2263. (1993) pp. 79–80 (paragraphs 44–48); pp. 128–130 (paras 36–40, 42–47)

44. The evidence of victims and other witnesses is crucial to the criminal justice process because prosecutions will founder, and guilty people thus escape justice, if victims and other witnesses are not prepared to make statements to the police and thereafter to give evidence. It is important therefore that everything possible is done to support and, where necessary, protect witnesses in what is often an unenviable role. We received a great deal of evidence that for witnesses to give evidence in a criminal trial is a daunting (and sometimes even dangerous) task and one that many come to regret having undertaken. This is particularly so where women have been the victims of rape or other sexual crimes or of domestic violence. We have therefore taken very seriously the many suggestions put to us for improvement of the way in which victims and other witnesses are treated at the various stages of the criminal justice process. The police have the most involvement with prosecution witnesses, although the decisions that affect those witnesses are most frequently taken by the CPS. There is therefore a risk that communication between the CPS and prosecution witnesses may be inadequate, that the victim's views may be insufficiently taken into account, and that the victim may not be kept informed of crucial decisions. The following recommendations are designed to reduce this risk.

45. The Code for Crown Prosecutors, before setting out the public interest criteria that may lead to a decision not to prosecute, states that, although the public interest will be the paramount consideration, the interests of the victim are an important factor in determining the balance of the public interest and should be taken into account. We agree with this general approach. Important though the feelings of the victim are, they cannot override the public interest and no one has suggested to us that the victim should have the right to decide whether or not a prosecution goes ahead. Equally the CPS are accountable in general to Parliament and to the courts for the manner in which they exercise their discretion whether or not to prosecute; they are not accountable to the victims in individual cases. That said, we recommend that victims should so far as practicable be kept informed of the progress and outcome of cases, including decisions not to prosecute and, in some cases, the results of bail applications or successful appeals.

46. Since the views of victims may not always be apparent from the case papers, it seems to us that the CPS should in appropriate cases take steps to ascertain those views before decisions are taken. This will not be possible in all cases but should be the aim in at least those in which the potential consequences for the victim are serious. In particular, when the CPS are considering whether or not to oppose bail, they should be in possession of adequate information on the likely consequences for the victim of any decision to release on bail. If they do not have that information, they should ask for it. The CPS and the police should together agree the categories of case in which the police would be requested to provide the information routinely to the CPS where there is an objection to bail. Cases in which women have been the victims of crimes of violence or of rape or other sexual offences need particular care. In cases of domestic violence the woman may well be in danger of losing her home or of suffering further

---

[24] See Rock (1989) 254–69.

violence if bail is granted to the defendant. In other cases also distress, intimidation or physical harm to the victim may well occur. Close liaison with the police is needed and steps must be taken to minimise the risk of further violence if bail is granted. It is in our view essential that local authority social services departments are able to place vulnerable women in refuges if that is the only way of ensuring their safety.

47. Normally, communications between the CPS and witnesses take place through the police. As a general rule this is sensible because the police will be more likely to be aware of the witness's circumstances and so be in a better position to pass on the information, taking into account any untoward factors such as the victim's mental or emotional state. Nevertheless, there are times when it would be better for the CPS to pass on the information direct. This is particularly so when a decision has been made in advance of the day of trial not to prosecute or to prosecute on a less serious charge and the police are either not in a position to convey to the victim the full reasons for this decision or fail to convey the information convincingly because they themselves are not in sympathy with it.

48. Particular care, however, and the continued involvement of the police, will be necessary in cases where the victim fears for his or her personal safety because a defendant is to be released on bail. It is also important for victims to be warned if someone convicted of an offence against them has appealed against conviction, been released on bail pending appeal, or has been released because the appeal was successful. In such cases it is essential that the victim receives timely warning and, if appropriate, advice and assistance from the police. We so recommend....

36. The efficient management of a trial and the clear presentation of issues to the jury depend heavily on the willingness of victims and other witnesses to testify. It should be a key objective of the system that their cooperation is freely given, that everything possible is done to ensure that waiting and other facilities are adequate, that they are protected from intimidation and that in all other ways they are given the support and encouragement that many will need when undergoing the daunting and sometimes distressing experience of appearing in court.

37. Before the trial it is current best practice for the police to refer to the voluntary organisation, Victim Support, all cases of domestic burglary, assault, robbery, arson, criminal damage to private property and many cases of theft. If the victim (or, in cases of homicide, the relatives) consents, the police will also refer cases of homicide, sexual offences and domestic violence. We understand that Victim Support would like to extend its support to other witnesses who fear or are suffering from intimidation, and does so already in areas where it has sufficient resources.

38. Victim Support has embarked on a programme of support schemes which in time should cover all the main Crown Court centres. The aim of these schemes is to ensure that victims and other prosecution witnesses know what to expect and that, when they arrive at the court for the trial, they know where to turn to for advice and help should they need it. We were told by Victim Support that all inner city areas would have a scheme by the end of 1992 and that all Crown Court centres would be covered by 1995, provided that Government funding was available. We recommend that the necessary priority is given to establishing such schemes in all Crown Court centres.

39. An important feature of the witness support schemes that we have described is that they help to prevent a witness from feeling isolated in what may well be unfamiliar and intimidating surroundings. This may be particularly necessary when the victim goes into the witness box, especially if he or she has been the victim of a sexual offence or an offence of violence.[25] We judge that it is perfectly acceptable in

---

[25] It is not unknown, however, for victims in rape cases to be permitted to give their evidence from the main body of the court out of sight of the accused without going into the witness box. We would not wish to rule out such an arrangement.

such circumstances for the witness to be accompanied by a friend or supporter who sits in the body of the court, although he or she should not accompany the witness into the witness box nor sit close to the witness box while the witness is giving evidence. This is to avoid any suggestion that the witness is not giving his or her evidence unaided. We understand that it may still be the case in some Crown Court centres that a friend or supporter of the witness will be excluded from the court or placed in the public gallery. This seems to us to be wrong; the admission of the witness's friend or supporter to the body of the court though not to the witness box itself seems to us to be an acceptable compromise.

40. Before the trial begins, several agencies may be involved in providing victims and other witnesses with information about what they should expect. The police and CPS may well be in touch; the Home Office produce a leaflet, which is used by Victim Support among others. We have been told that this leaflet is being updated and improved, and that the possibility of different leaflets for the magistrates' courts and the Crown Court is being considered. The CPS intend to provide better information for witnesses by sending them detailed letters about court procedures, what is expected of them and how long they may be required. It seems to us that there may be a need for coordination between these agencies so as to ensure that there is no unnecessary duplication of effort or inconsistency in the information provided from the different sources. But we welcome the general intention behind these initiatives....

42. We recommend that, where the case is known to be a sensitive one and the victim may be in a distressed or vulnerable state, the case should wherever possible be given a fixed date for hearing.

43. In keeping with our wish to see judges take a more interventionist approach where necessary, we recommend that they should be particularly vigilant to check unfair and intimidatory cross-examination by counsel of witnesses who in the nature of the case are likely to be distressed or vulnerable. The needs of child witnesses have recently been considered by the Pigot Committee, some of whose recommendations were implemented in the Criminal Justice Act 1991. It seems to us that any further changes, including extension of the Act's provisions to vulnerable witnesses other than children, should await experience of how the Act works in practice. It has, however, been suggested to us that the use of screens or live video links may tend to prejudice the defendant in the minds of the jury and we recommend that, where this is not already being done, the judge should, in any opening introductory remarks at the trial, explain to the jury the reasons for using such links or screens.

44. Witnesses may find the publicity, or threat of it, surrounding their appearance in the witness box a powerful disincentive to giving evidence. We accept that a trial must in principle continue to be a public proceeding. Nevertheless, we think that certain steps can and should be taken to mitigate the fear of publicity. We believe that witnesses who do not wish to have their addresses read out in court should be allowed to hand them into court or be able to use accommodation addresses, with the leave of the judge. We also believe that greater use could be made of section 23 of the Criminal Justice Act 1988. This section allows the court to give leave for the statement of a witness to be read out where the witness is afraid to give oral evidence. Section 26 provides that the court should not give leave unless it is in the interests of justice to admit the statement. It is rare for section 23 to be used where the intimidated witness is the main witness, as the defendant would not be able to cross-examine. We would, however, like to see more use made of the section for other witnesses. One difficulty is that the CPS have no way of knowing in advance whether the statement will be admitted or not. We therefore suggest that this is one of the matters which ought to be resolved prior to trial in accordance with the procedures which we have proposed in chapter seven.

45. We further recommend that, in certain sensitive cases, there should be guidelines for judges to follow when deciding whether or not to exercise their discretion to allow a witness to remain anonymous. We received disquieting evidence of cases in which witnesses, for example victims of blackmail, had been led to expect anonymity only to discover that the judge was not prepared to allow it. It seems to us that witnesses should be told what to expect in such circumstances. Anonymity, however, raises difficult issues for a trial process which assumes that, whenever possible, justice must be seen to be done. We accept that it should only be permitted where the case for it is fully made out. We recommend, however, that, where it becomes an issue, it is resolved in the course of the pre-trial procedures that we recommend in chapter seven, with the judge being asked to rule as early as practicable at a preparatory hearing if the defence and prosecution do not reach agreement.

46. We also recommend that, at the conclusion of cases that involve sexual offences, victims' statements should be returned to the instructing solicitor. The defendant must have the right to read them before and during the trial but he or she should not have the right to retain them after it. We were disturbed by evidence that we received that victims' statements were being freely circulated for various dubious purposes quite unconnected with the trial.

47. Finally, it was put to us that, particularly if a plea of guilty has been entered, the victim may have slurs cast upon him or her during the defence speech in mitigation of the likely sentence. Such remarks are privileged and may be reported by the press with impunity and with no opportunity for the victim to obtain redress. This is a difficult problem since we have no wish to restrict the freedom of the press and the defendant's counsel is under a duty to carry out his or her client's instructions. Nevertheless, we believe that it should be possible to prevent wholly unfair attacks on the victim during speeches in mitigation. In appropriate cases, the prosecution should intervene and the CPS have told us that it is their policy to do so where the defence depart from the facts in a material aspect. Such a course, however, cannot be embarked upon lightly since there may have to be a separate hearing, following an adjournment, if the defence persist in their version of the facts. We believe that, if prosecuting counsel intervened more often, defendants would become less prone to launching unsupported attacks on the characters of victims and other witnesses (or even on occasion people who have not appeared at the trial at all), since such attacks would be likely to be counter-productive when it came to sentence. We recommend, however, that a power be vested in the judge to prohibit in the last resort the reporting of unsupported allegations made during a speech in mitigation. We envisage this as a discretionary power to be used in the extreme case of a defendant apparently using the opportunity of a speech in mitigation to do as much damage as possible to the reputation of the victim or a third party without any risk of retaliation.

Notes

1. The extract from the article by Miers seeks to locate responses to the position of the victim within the criminal justice process in a framework of changing ideology and so explain some of the developing official concern for the situation of victims of crime. The extract from the Report of the Royal Commission on Criminal Justice describes some of the victim-oriented measures and policies which have been implemented at different points in the criminal justice process, and the Royal Commission has recommended further action in some areas. All of this demonstrates how the subject of the victim has moved higher on the agenda of policy and practice over the

last ten to twenty years. However, as most writers on the subject acknow-ledge, this represents an intrusion into the "public interest" orientation of traditional criminal justice, while also affecting the balance of the calculation of gravity of offences (harm caused assumes greater importance) and perceptions of offending behaviour (as Zedner (1994) notes: "labelling, theory... will surely never assume the same status again" (1994, at p. 1240)). In future works on criminal justice, victims may have a whole chapter to themselves.

2.   The Criminal Injuries Compensation Board (CICB) was replaced by a new Criminal Injuries Compensation Authority in 1994. The CICB's annual report for 1992–3 had shown an increased total annual payout of over £152 million, six per cent more than the previous year's record payout. Of the £909 million paid out since the scheme started in 1964, £405 million had been paid out in the period 1990–1993.

CHAPTER TWO

PRE-SENTENCE DECISION-MAKING

I. INTRODUCTION

Although the sentencing and penal process is usually considered to begin after the end of the defendant's trial, it would be misleading to isolate sentencing dispositions wholly from decisions and events occurring before the trial takes place. There are a number of decisions taken earlier in the criminal justice process in connection with prosecution policy and matters such as bail and the defendant's plea which are both significant in themselves as elements of criminal procedure and may have, to a greater or lesser extent, a bearing on the outcome of the case as a "criminal case". In particular, there are a number of decisions taken during these earlier stages of "criminal procedure" which may "divert" an offender from the formal process of prosecution, trial and sentence. Such "diversion" in effect constitutes an important alternative method of dealing with certain types of offender and can take a number of forms which are often specific to certain categories of offender and offending. This whole package of diversionary action merits careful consideration alongside the conventional system of sentencing. Decisions as to bail have custodial implications and in practice the outcome of such decisions have important consequences for the operation and management of the prison system. Finally, as a prosecution case proceeds to trial, there are likely to be discussions (especially in relation to more serious cases at the Crown Court level) as to the plea to be entered by the defendant, which affect not only the outcome of the trial but also may determine to some extent the nature and severity of the sentence. It is therefore necessary to consider in a critical fashion the operation and consequences of these types of pre-sentence decision-making, bearing in mind two general features of such activity: its low level of public visibility (bail decisions excepted) as compared to formal sentencing decisions; and its tendency to undermine the autonomy of the conventional sentencing and penal decision-makers.

II. DIVERSION

The term "diversion" is often used in a loose sense to encompass more widely "diversion from crime" (crime prevention policies) and "diversion from custody" (alternatives to imprisonment). For present purposes the term will be used more narrowly to refer to policies and measures which result in diversion of alleged offenders from the formal process of prosecution, trial and sentence.

Andrew Ashworth, "Prosecution, Police and Public – A Guide to Good Gatekeeping?" (1984) 23 *Howard Journal* 65, pp 66–68

It would be possible to have a system of criminal procedure whereby the prosecutor is obliged to bring a prosecution in all cases in which there is sufficient evidence against a person. This, indeed, is the Austrian system, and in West Germany the same obligation rests upon prosecutors when dealing with offences which carry a maximum of more than one year's imprisonment. There are strong arguments of principle in favour of mandatory prosecution. Criminal justice is seen to be administered in an even-handed way: the sense of unfairness sometimes generated by selective prosecution policies is avoided, as is the scope for prejudice, bias and even corruption among those who prosecute. All persons against whom there is sufficient evidence are dealt with in open court. Secondly, it would seem unconstitutional for members of the Executive, such as police and prosecutors, to dilute the laws laid down by Parliament by prosecuting for some and not for others. Thirdly, mandatory prosecution might be expected to have denunciatory and general deterrent effects, and thereby to promote greater observance of the law. Fourthly, since it is well known that most offences which the police record are brought to their attention by members of the public, mandatory prosecution might be supported as implementing the wishes of the public in relation to prosecution policy.

In view of these apparently weighty arguments of principle, why is it that not only has the English approach always favoured discretion in prosecution policy, but also that even those countries which proclaim mandatory prosecution appear nevertheless to find ways of avoiding the prosecution of certain offences and offenders? First and foremost, the argument based on justice may be turned on its head. Whilst inconsistent prosecution policies do strike citizens as unjust, it is not expected that every single person against whom there is sufficient evidence will be prosecuted. Indeed there might be a loss of public respect for the law if it were thought to be administered harshly and unsympathetically, as by prosecuting the old, the infirm or the afflicted. This may be linked to a second argument: prosecution in court may have a great human cost, even for a defendant who is ultimately acquitted. When the possible psychological consequences to the defendant, together with social and economic consequences, are placed in the scales, they should only be outweighed when there is demonstrable need to prosecute rather than to take some other action. This leads to the third argument, which is that there is no compelling evidence for the view that prosecution, conviction and sentence constitute the most effective means of preventing further crimes. Other approaches might be no less effective. Fourthly, the constitutional argument is less strong than it appears at first sight. In some instances Parliament has framed offences widely so as to allow room for sensitive and selective prosecution policies: the offence of unlawful sexual intercourse with a girl aged under 16 is the clearest example. On other occasions, as when enacting a single offence of theft with a maximum sentence of ten years, it might be said that Parliament did not expect every little dishonest taking to be prosecuted in court.

The balance of these arguments is, I believe, in favour of allowing prosecutorial discretion. This brings a flexibility which is essential because the very experience of being prosecuted in court may either generate anxiety or stigma out of all proportion to the alleged offence, or be unnecessary for the purpose of preventing further crime. But discretion may also leave scope for the intrusion of bias, prejudice and irrelevant considerations into decisions on prosecution. This is a familiar objection, to which there is a familiar answer. Although one cannot eradicate all possibility of the intrusion of irrelevant considerations, it is possible to structure and to control the use of discretion. This approach was advocated by the Royal Commission on Criminal Procedure (1981), when it recommended that the police should retain the initial discretion on whether to prosecute an offender, administer a formal caution or take no further action, and that the Crown prosecutor should have the discretion to drop a case which the police had decided to prosecute (paras. 7.55, 7.59 and 8.10). The Royal Commission recommended that guidelines be drawn up for the guidance of police and prosecutors, and in February 1983 the Attorney-General issued a set of Guidelines. I believe that the method is an appropriate one, and that it is also appropriate for these Guidelines to be the subject of public discussion. After all, the police and prosecutors would surely claim to be acting in the interests of society or in the public interest when they take their decisions, and the Attorney-General's Guidelines deal extensively with the "public interest". We are members of the public. It is our right, if not our duty, to consider whether prosecution policy is taking a proper course.

Report of the Royal Commission on Criminal Justice, Cm. 2263, (1993) pp. 81–83

56. Many witnesses, including the police service and the CPS, recommended to us that more should be done to keep out of the courts cases which did not seem to call for prosecution and which could be dealt with in some other way. We have therefore considered the case for encouraging the police and prosecution services to keep from the courts more cases which do not need to be considered by the judicial process. As we have already said, failure to prosecute in cases that demand it can do great damage to public confidence in the criminal justice system. Also, as we noted in the same paragraph, the Code for Crown Prosecutors acknowledges that the interests of the victim should be taken into account in deciding where the balance of the public interest lies. We do not therefore advocate any system of automatically enabling offenders in particular types of case to evade the consequences of their actions. There may, however, be scope for dealing efficiently and less expensively with some offenders without the need for a court appearance.

57. The most common means of diverting first and petty offenders from the criminal justice process, particularly in the case of juveniles, is the caution. The number and range of cases in which people are cautioned by the police have increased steadily over the years, with 279,000 being cautioned in 1991, an increase of 4 per cent on the previous year. Of these, 170,000[1] related to indictable or either way offences, mainly shoplifting. This was 8 per cent up on the year before. We believe that there may be many more petty offenders who could be treated similarly. Cautioning practice, however, needs to be subject to national guidelines and applied more consistently across police force areas than appears to be the case at present. We recommend that police cautioning should be governed by statute, under which national guidelines, drawn up in consultation with the CPS and police service among others, should be laid down in regulations. These regulations should also govern the keeping of records of cautions so that information about whether a suspect has been cautioned previously can easily be transferred between police forces.

58. We do not recommend that proposals to caution should have to be referred for approval to the CPS. The police, however, should be free, as they are at present, to ask for CPS advice on whether or not a caution should be administered in cases where they consider that appropriate. Also where a case is sent to the CPS by the

[1] Aged 10–13:	21,000 males;	6,300 females
Aged 14–16:	41,000 males;	14,800 females
Aged 17–20:	28,000 males;	8,400 females
Aged 21 and over:	41,400 males;	19,000 females

police to consider whether a prosecution would be justified, we recommend that the CPS should be enabled to require the police in lieu of prosecution to administer a caution, provided always that the defendant admits the offence, as the present cautioning guidelines require. At present, if the police refuse to administer a caution at the request of the CPS, the CPS will usually discontinue proceedings so that no further action at all is taken. This may not always be a desirable outcome.

59. The decision whether or not to charge (or take other action) in a case is normally a matter for police discretion and often they will decide to take no further action. This may be for a variety of reasons, including the absence of sufficient evidence against the suspect. It has been suggested to us that the decision to take no further action should, as happens in some overseas jurisdictions, for example Germany, only be taken by the CPS. We see no compelling reason for this in principle and in practice it would place a severe and perhaps insupportable burden on the CPS. We therefore make no recommendation on the matter.

60. Several witnesses, including the CPS, pressed on us the desirability of combining the caution with a requirement on the offender to cooperate with social work agencies or the probation service or to agree to consult a doctor or attend a clinic. We were attracted by this idea, particularly where the offender may be suffering from mental disorder or social handicap and criminal proceedings seem inappropriate as a means of dealing with the case. We were told, however, that neither the police nor the CPS felt that it should take the lead in administering such schemes. We agree that they may in fact not be the most appropriate services to take the overall responsibility. The most suitable candidate would seem to be the probation service. We understand that in at least one police area an informal system has been jointly developed between the police and the local probation service. This may well provide a model for national development and we recommend that the topic be looked at further.

61. We learnt with interest that in Inner London and in Coventry, Oldham and Newcastle, schemes exist, run by the probation service, which aim to increase the quantity and quality of information available to the CPS to enable them to consider fully the case for discontinuance in less serious offences. These schemes, known as Public Interest Case Assessment (PICA) schemes, are based on magistrates' courts and collect information on offenders which is then sent to the CPS in order to inform its decisions whether or not to continue the prosecution. We were told that, in the Inner London scheme based on Horseferry Road, Marlborough Street and Marylebone Magistrates Courts, 31 per cent of the reports submitted to the CPS in the latest year of operation led to a decision to discontinue in the public interest. In 67 per cent of those cases, the PICA report provided information that was crucial to the decision to discontinue and in 86 per cent it led to the CPS having information to which they would not otherwise have had access. This leads us to think it likely that expansion of PICA across the country would lead to significant benefits. We recognise that there are resource implications but we would expect these to be offset at least to some extent by the savings in court time and otherwise resulting from the identification of cases which did not have to be prosecuted. We understand that an evaluation of the PICA schemes by the Home Office Research and Planning Unit is due in 1993. Subject to that we recommend that the scheme be put on a formal and systematic basis and extended as far as practicable across the country.

62. In some continental jurisdictions, the prosecution authorities are empowered to levy fines direct on offenders, with their agreement, as an alternative to taking formal proceedings against them in court. In England and Wales there exists the machinery for imposing fixed penalties for motoring offences. In recent years, a fixed penalty system for a wide variety of offences has been introduced in Scotland. Under section 56 of the Criminal Justice (Scotland) Act 1987, the procurator fiscal

has the power to make a "conditional offer" to an alleged offender as regards any offence triable in the district court (that is minor summary offences). The substance of the offer is that if the offender pays a fixed penalty (or the first instalment thereof) to the clerk of the relevant district court within a specified time, proceedings will not be brought. Acceptance of the offer through making the relevant payment does not count as a criminal conviction (although a record is kept locally by procurators fiscal of the imposition and payment of the fine). Such a penalty is known as a "fiscal fine". The fiscal fine is a fixed sum (currently £25) and is payable in instalments of £5 at fortnightly intervals. The fiscal fine emerged as a result of the deliberations of the Stewart Committee,[2] which was set up to study alternatives to prosecution in an effort to ease the pressure of work on both the court system and the prosecution service. The scheme is used in a significant number of cases: in 1991, there were 15,599 fiscal fines.

63. We believe that similar arrangements should be introduced in England and Wales. There would be a small cost to the magistrates' courts' fine collection machinery but this should be considerably outweighed by the savings in magistrates' court trials. We therefore recommend that prosecution fines on the Scottish model be introduced in England and Wales for use instead of prosecution in appropriate cases. We recommend, however, that instead of one level of fine as in Scotland there should be an appropriate range of fines. As in Scotland the imposition of such fines should only be possible with the agreement of the offender. In some areas there might be a requirement that the defendant pay compensation to the victim with or without a prosecution fine. In such cases it would be very relevant to take the views of victims into account before reaching a decision.

Notes

1. Both Ashworth, writing in the early 1980s, and the Royal Commission on Criminal Justice, reporting ten years later, acknowledge the existence and usefulness of prosecutorial discretion and diversionary policy. Underlying this approval of diversion are, on the one hand, a sense of proportionality coupled with a recognition of the self-defeating nature of formal prosecution and sentencing in some types of case, and on the other hand a belief in the penal and corrective efficacy of some alternative methods of dealing with offenders. Thus, arguments related to the stigma, trauma and economic cost inherent in the formal process of criminal justice (especially for defendants eventually acquitted) are linked to the need for a selective policy of prosecution which leaves aside minor and more condonable cases of offending. These arguments are further reinforced by a growing belief in the effectiveness of less formal methods, such as cautioning, informal fixed penalties and compounding, discussed further below.

2. But at the same time, the relative informality of diversionary methods is productive of some concern about potential arbitrariness and inconsistency in the way in which offenders are dealt with – problems which are less evident in the more visible and public context of formal criminal justice. Cautioning rates have been notoriously variable over geographical areas, provoking calls for a more structured and accountable system, based on

---

[2] *Keeping Offenders Out of Court: Further Alternatives to Prosecution*, Cmnd. 8958 (1983).

clearly agreed policy and centrally produced guidelines. Informal negotiated settlements, such as compounding, are inherently difficult to monitor and indeed part of what is agreed to be the effectiveness of this kind of approach resides in its flexibility and its responsiveness to individual circumstances. Most diversionary policies are therefore based upon an equation according to which the benefits of (a) a sensible and proportionate use of resources and of (b) penal and corrective effectiveness are balanced against (c) the risks of arbitrary and inconsistent application. More simply this equation may be expressed in the following terms:

$$\text{justification for diversion} \quad = \quad \frac{\text{best use of resources} \times \text{effectiveness}}{\text{due process}}$$

Due process considerations should embrace not only defendants but also victims of offending, some of whom may be aggrieved by the use of what may be perceived as "softer" diversionary measures, and whose interests therefore ought not to be left out of account in deciding upon the use of such measures (see the discussion of victims' interests in Chapter One, above).

3. It should be appreciated that the scope for diversion in the overall process of criminal justice is considerable: it can and does take place at a number of different stages and on the initiative of different parties. Right up to the point of sentence it is possible to identify the following opportunities for diversion, linked to the principal stages of process: investigation, prosecution, trial and sentence.

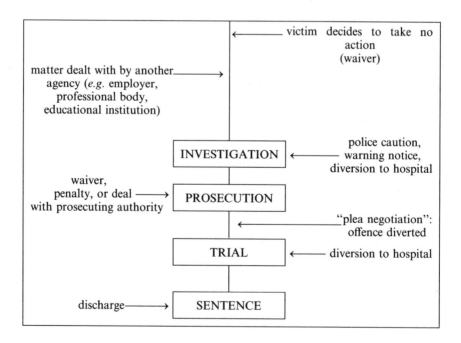

Some of these instances of diversion may be regarded as more "official" and "formal" than others. At one end of the scale, victim "waiver" and resolution within the workplace, family, college and other contexts of civil society are naturally obscure and difficult to measure and monitor. At the other extreme, committal to hospital (see Chapter Seven, below) and discharge in place of sentence (see Chapter Five), are regulated by legislation and carried out through public decision-making. In between the two extremes lie the official but informal processes such as cautioning, compounding and other types of negotiated settlement, and bargaining about pleas, all of which have been subject to increasing academic and official scrutiny and, in most cases, greater legal control, as discussed below.

4. On the question of proceedings and sanctions as carried out by non-State agencies, see Chapter One, Section 11, above. Professional and educational disciplinary proceedings constitute important processes of social control which may to some extent be subject to external legal scrutiny (for instance, via judicial review). But there is as yet little in the way of detailed and systematic knowledge about the operation of this kind of sanctioning process. See generally on the wider theoretical aspects of this topic, Harding and Ireland (1989), Chapter 8.

5. An interesting example of diversion to an "alternative" jurisdiction occurred in 1994 in Washington State (U.S.) when a sentencing judge handed over two Tlingit Indian offenders from Alaska to a tribal court to decide on an appropriate penalty after being convicted of robbery in Washington. The Council of Elders on Prince of Wales Island, Alaska sentenced the two offenders to banishment of between twelve and eighteen months on separate uninhabited islands off the south-east Alaskan coast. At the same time the tribe stated that it would compensate the victim of the robbery, who was seriously injured at the time of the offence. On the other hand, Washington prosecutors have objected to the decision, criticising a differential disposal on the basis of ethnic origin. (See, *The Independent*, August 28, 1994; September 4, 1994).

Andrew Ashworth, "*Prosecution, Police and Public – A Guide to Good Gatekeeping?*", pp. 82–84

Of the 7,000 or more criminal offences in this country, many are enforced rarely and some are not enforced at all. To some extent this is the choice of members of the public, for it is well known that they refrain from reporting certain offences or certain offenders to the police (Hough and Mayhew 1983). To some extent it is the choice of the police and the many other law enforcement agencies, in that they do not look for every conceivable offence which is being committed, and do not even record as an offence every criminal incident reported to them by members of the public or coming to their attention during the course of duty. The Royal Commission on Criminal Procedure (1981) took it for granted that we must retain the police officer's discretion to turn a blind eye to some offences or to deal with them by an informal warning, without making a formal crime report (para. 6.31). The Interdepartmental Working Party on Road Traffic Law (1981) stated that it is "obviously right" for the police to "have discretion to caution a driver in lieu of any other action" (p. 38), that is instead of imposing a fixed penalty for an offence (such as speeding) for which this would be possible. The result of leaving this large area of discretion is that it is not only types of offences but also types of offender who may benefit from the "blind eye". And whilst one can look to the new prosecution arrangements for a framework within which decisions to prosecute reported offenders can be structured, there seems much less scope for ensuring that the day-to-day working practices of many thousands of policemen can be shaped into a coherent and consistent policy for invoking the criminal law and recording an offence in the first place.

Yet it is the patterns of law enforcement which determine the kinds of offence and kinds of offender who go through to the next stage of being reported with a view to caution, prosecution or other alternative, and henceforward into the criminal process. There is a real sense in which the police and other agencies are the gatekeepers of the criminal process: their decisions determine who goes into the criminal process and who stays out, thus effectively fixing the bite of the criminal law. Decisions taken at a high level within the police affect patterns of law enforcement: "the Chief Constable's policies on the disposition of his officers in an area and the priorities of their investigative activity can critically affect what offences are prosecuted in that area" (R.C.C.P. 1981, para. 6.60). Decisions taken at the practical everyday level are dictated not by the abstract prescriptions of the criminal law but, as research amply demonstrates, by the perceived demands of the particular situation, of the general public, of senior officers and of colleagues, and to some extent by the feelings of the individual officer. Even without going into great detail, then, it can be accepted that what is important is not the law as it is stated in the books and in the Acts of Parliament but the law as it is enforced in practice, and the police have considerable room for pursuing particular policies within the broad avenues of legal prohibition.

The police might seek to defend the way in which they exercise this discretion by reference to the wishes of the public. Presumably they would claim to be acting in the public interest, since the police forces themselves cannot be said to have an independent right to choose which laws to enforce and to what extent. But how is the public interest to be determined? To what extent should the police be influenced by vocal groups of local people? Even if some local variation in policies is acceptable, what about problems which do not materially differ from one part of the country to another, such as shoplifting or football hooliganism? Answers to questions of this kind must be placed in the context of the enforcement of the law in general. It is well known that a considerable number of non-police agencies in law enforcement rarely invoke the criminal process, and in many cases this is for conduct which is no less serious than that for which the police bring prosecutions. My reason for introducing this consideration is that any conception of the public interest in this sphere must surely be based on a rounded view of lawbreaking in its multifarious forms. Fairness in the administration of the criminal law means comparing the seriousness of some of the offences which are only rarely prosecuted with the seriousness of some which are regularly prosecuted. The comparison between the moderate rate at which D.H.S.S. frauds are prosecuted and the rarity of a prosecution for tax evasion is a stark one (Lidstone et al. 1980; Uglow 1984), but it is merely a starting point. Thefts from an employer are rarely brought to the attention of the police, and are sometimes tolerated and almost accepted; by comparison, thefts from shops are reported with relative frequency. It is widely believed that the amount of dishonest obtaining of property or evasion of liability which takes place on the so-called "black economy" vastly outstrips the losses to shops through shoplifting and the losses to the Government through D.H.S.S. frauds. Yet patterns of law enforcement do not mirror patterns of offending: minor offences against the property of individuals and of shops receive far more attention than more substantial dishonesty in matters of business and personal taxation. To achieve a sense of proportion in prosecution policy we need to have a sense of proportion in law enforcement. That calls for more accurate information and beliefs about the totality of lawbreaking in society, and it should lead to a more realistic view of the social significance of minor thefts such as those for which a fixed penalty system has been proposed.

See further: Hough, M. and Mayhew, P., *British Crime Survey* (Home Office Research Study No. 76, 1983); Interdepartmental Working Party on Road Traffic Law, *Report*, 1981; Lidstone, K. W., Hogg, R. and Sutcliffe, F., *Prosecution by Private Individuals and Non-Police Agencies* (Royal Commission on Criminal Procedure Research Study, No. 10, 1980); Royal Commission on Criminal Procedure, *Report*, Cmnd. 8092, 1981; Uglow, S., "Defrauding the Public Purse", (1984) *Criminal Law Review 128*.

Notes

1. According to Hough and Mayhew in the first British Crime Survey (1983),

> "the reasons mentioned most frequently by respondents for not inform-ing the police [of offences committed against them] were that the incidents involved no loss or damage, or were regarded as trivial (particularly true, for example, for thefts from motor vehicles). A further important reason for not reporting was the belief (probably realistic) that the police would not have been able to do anything; this applied to many instances of vandalism for instance. More victims of violent offences were likely to feel that their incidents were inappropriate for the police, in some cases squaring the matter themselves. Other reasons (dislike of the police, fear of reprisals, inconvenience) which it is sometimes suggested that victims have for non-reporting were rarely mentioned." (p. 11)

This suggests that a good deal of "victim waiver" is based upon a mix of pragmatic writing-off of the matter and self-help. In a sense, victim waiver may be regarded as a form of private settlement.

2. There are thus two levels of "gate-keeping", to adopt Ashworth's terminology: first, victims of crime themselves; secondly, the police and other agents of enforcement. Ashworth emphasises the crucial role of the latter in determining the flow of people into the formal criminal justice process.

Chrisje Brants and Stewart Field, "Discretion and Accountability: A Comparative Perspective on Keeping Crime Out of Court", Chapter 7 in Fennell *et al*, *Criminal Justice in Europe* (1995), pp. 130–133

In the United Kingdom there are a limited number of ways that the ordinary offender may be diverted from prosecution. The most formal mechanism is the police caution. This is an official warning which, since 1985, may be cited in court as part of a criminal record and which will affect subsequent prosecution decisions.

Cautions also form part of the official criminal statistics. In recent years there has been a significant increase in the use of formal cautions. In 1985 the Home Office issued new cautioning guidelines which made much of the advantages of diversion, primarily as a way of dealing with juveniles. In 1990, the Home Office issued further guidelines designed to encourage police forces to use cautioning more often for adult offenders.[3] Indeed, cautioning rates have already increased appreciably in the late 1980s. In 1985, 7 per cent of both 17–21-year-old males and men of 21 or over were cautioned for indictable offences. By 1990, the rates were 21 per cent for the younger group and 15 per cent for the older. Rates for women 21 or over started from a higher base (19 per cent in 1985) but showed similar rates of increase (to 33 per cent in 1990). The police may also informally caution. The only consequence of this is that a record may be kept which may influence later prosecutions. Home Office Guidelines state that informal cautions should only be given where the criteria for a formal caution are met but a formal caution is considered inappropriate.[4] Figures on this are not kept, so the figures quoted above are for the formal caution only....

... Andrew Sanders has argued recently that the relatively slow and uncertain development of diversion by the police caution in the United Kingdom is the product of two obvious but contradictory impulses:

    (a) the desire to avoid the stigma and labelling of criminal proceedings (recognised by Home Office circulars on cautioning)
    (b) the view widely held by police officers and magistrates that warnings are not enough to prevent offending and can therefore be used only for a small minority of trivial offences.[5]

Sanders sees a way of reconciling these two viewpoints by moving toward more diverse conditional diversion mechanisms such as exist on the Continent.[6] He stresses that the effect of the system is to avoid the stigma of a court appearance while not "letting off" the offender in that conditions have to be fulfilled. He points to an experimental scheme in Cumbria as a possible model for expansion. The police selected juveniles who were then asked to offer to make reparation to the victim (apologies, compensation, or community work). If they agreed they were cautioned, not prosecuted. But the Home Office responded negatively to the scheme, in part because it feared that it made the police investigator prosecutor, judge, and sentencer.

Despite official rhetoric, a 1987–8 survey of police forces suggested that eighteen of forty-two were operating some form of "caution plus" system whereby cautions would be given with conditions attached to them, such as attending an intermediate treatment group and participating in reparation or mediation schemes. These schemes mainly exist on a localised basis: only three forces operate the system throughout the force area. Furthermore, they are almost exclusively applied to juveniles: only one force had a scheme for adults. The use of caution plus was squared with official rhetoric by some officers by insisting the decision to caution was made independently of the agreement to participate in treatment or reparation.

---

[3] Home Office Circular 59/1990, July 16, 1990, *The Cautioning of Offenders*.

[4] *ibid.* Annex C.

[5] A. Sanders, "Diverting Offenders from Prosecution – Can we learn from Other Countries?" (1986) *Justice of the Peace* 614. This attitude has been confirmed by recent interviews with officers, see R. Evans, "Police Cautioning and the Young Adult Offender" [1991] *Crim. L. R.* 598 at 601–2.

[6] A. Ashworth has also repeatedly argued for the adoption of various conditional diversion schemes. See "Prosecution, Police and Public" and "The Public Interest Element in Prosecutions" [1987] *Crim. L. R.* 595 at 604.

Others accepted that the caution decision was affected by such an agreement.[7]

In interviews officers showed a growing interest in giving cautions teeth by use of such conditions.[8] More recently, the idea of developing conditional forms of diversion has surfaced again in official debate. In April 1990, the House of Commons Home Affairs Select Committee made radical proposals for an extension of the range of diversionary options available within the criminal justice system.[9]

The Committee was very keen to extend the level of diversion from prosecution and suggested, very much as Sanders had done, that one way of doing this would be to extend the range of available disposals. It argued that more offenders might be cautioned if some form of penalty were attached to the caution. The CPS recommended to it that a system of "caution plus" should be introduced whereby an offender who consented could be dealt with by a caution and a form of penalty. Penalties envisaged were compensation for property broken or stolen from other forms of reparation.

As interesting as the proposal is the reaction to it. In evidence to the Committee, the National Association for the Care and Resettlement of Offenders, one of Britain's most prominent liberal penal pressure groups, welcomed the idea of increased diversion but expressed considerable concern at an "alternative criminal system" which did not have the safeguards of due process. They were also concerned about the "net-widening effect". The Select Committee was not impressed by these worries and recommended the introduction of such a system. It felt the fact that the consent of the offender was required was a sufficient safeguard. Furthermore, the Committee felt the power to administer the system should remain exclusively with the police, and that the CPS should continue to deal only with prosecutions.

The Government rejected this proposal curtly: "The police do not wish to become involved in sentencing, believing that this would be contrary to the basic principles of the criminal justice system ... and the Government endorses this position."[10] In July 1990, the Home Office issued cautioning guidelines to replace the 1985 version, which attempted to broaden the use of diversion by emphasising that cautioning was suitable for age-groups other than juveniles. However the Guidelines reflected the Government's rejection of the Select Committee's proposals, preferring to rely on encouraging the traditional police caution. The guidelines do stress that the effectiveness of cautions is likely to be enhanced if they are backed up by arrangements for referring offenders to welfare agencies for support and guidance. However, "[s]uch referrals should be on a voluntary basis but any agreement to be referred should not be made a condition of a caution." It appears that conditional diversion has been dismissed for the immediate future.

Notes

1.   The Royal Commission on Criminal Justice has reported in favour of a system of conditional diversion (pp. 82–83 of its Report), and suggested

---

[7] Circular 59/1990 specifically suggested when considering a caution that the police should consider the offender's "attitude to the offence, including practical expressions of regret" (Annex B, para. 3). The scope for covert conditional diversion linked to reparation is surely apparent: R. Evans and C. Wilkinson, "Variations in Police Cautioning Policy and Practice in England and Wales" in (1990) 29 *Howard Journal* 155 at 169.

[8] C. Wilkinson and R. Evans, "Police Cautioning of Juveniles" [1990] *Crim. L. R.* 165 at 171.

[9] Home Affairs Committee, Fourth Report, i. *The Crown Prosecution Service*, House of Commons Papers, Session 1989–90. Select Committees are non-executive cross-party committees of the legislature that "shadow" and comment on matters within the responsibility of particular departments.

[10] Crown Prosecution Service, The Government's Reply to the Fourth Report of the Home Affairs Committee (HMSO, 1990).

liaison with the probation service for this purpose. Note also the Royal Commission's recommendation that police cautioning should be governed by statute, under which a system of national guidelines should be issued.
2.   More recently, Home Office Circular 18/1994 has sought to "clarify" key aspects of Government guidance on cautioning policy and practice. It adopts a more restrictive approach compared to earlier Home Office circulars on cautioning and in particular seeks to discourage the use of cautioning in relation to offences triable only on indictment, and also the use of multiple cautioning (on the ground that it brings the practice into disrepute). It also attempts to promote greater consistency as between police force areas and better recording of cautions. Finally, police are encouraged to monitor the use of "caution plus" and to liase with local statutory and voluntary agencies as regards measures designed to prevent juvenile re-offending. The future of conditional cautions (or "caution plus") appears uncertain at the present time, therefore, despite the enthusiasm of the House of Commons Home Affairs Committee and the Royal Commission on Criminal Justice.

A. A. Paterson and T. St J. N. Bates, *The Legal System of Scotland*, (3rd ed., 1993), pp. 76–79.

One factor of increasing significance in relation to the decision as to whether to initiate a prosecution or not, is the range of options available to the fiscal other than prosecution in the courts. Over the last 15 years the number of recorded crimes has risen by over 70 per cent. Inevitably, there has been a similar rise in the number of police reports to the fiscal service. Some commentators have gone so far as to say that the criminal justice system in Scotland is in crisis. Just as ADR is increasingly being talked of as a possible solution to the problems of the civil justice system, so increasingly we find the prosecution service relying on non-court methods of disposal to tackle the growing caseload with which they are confronted. These include: no proceedings, warnings, conditional offers, fiscal fines and diversions. Thus in 1976, 93 per cent of police reports resulted in a prosecution in court – the comparable figure for 1991 was only 53 per cent.

Obviously, if the fiscal concludes that there is insufficient evidence to warrant a prosecution he or she may determine to mark the report as a "no pro" (no proceedings). But the decision to take no proceedings may also be taken if the case is a trivial one, one in which the fiscal considers that no useful purpose would be served by a prosecution or because of certain mitigating factors, *e.g.* the length of time which has passed since the offence was committed, age or other factors relating to the accused and the attitude of the victim.

In 1986, "no pro-ing" was the most commonly used non-court option. However, thereafter it has taken second place behind conditional offers of fixed financial penalties – a trend that was accelerated as "no pro-ing" became more contentious following the publication of a report by the National Audit Office in 1989, *Prosecution of Crime in Scotland*, which, *inter alia*, highlighted the considerable variations between areas in terms of "no pro" percentages. (Not the least curious feature was that it was not always the busiest courts which had the highest percentages and vice versa. Thus a table published in 1990 shows that whilst the "no pro" rate in Glasgow was 23 per cent the figures for Edinburgh and Aberdeen were 10 per cent and 6 per cent respectively. Equally while Stornoway had a rate of 2 per cent Rothesay's was 16 per cent. [See 1990 S.L.T. (News) 275].)

Alternatively, the fiscal may determine that the case requires some action short of prosecution or an administrative penalty and issue a formal warning to the accused either personally or by letter. Such warnings cannot be referred to in any subsequent court proceedings although it appears that lists of those who have been so warned are retained by fiscals. Warnings are most commonly used in shoplifting, speeding and breach of the peace cases. Easily the most commonly used alternative to court proceedings now are conditional offers of fixed financial penalties by fiscals to accused persons in a wide range of road traffic cases.

A majority of the Stewart Committee in their report, *Keeping Offenders Out of Court*, Cmnd. 8958 (1983) recommended that fiscals should be able to impose a fine of up to £50 on offenders, without reference to a court. However, there were powerful opponents to this proposal. Nevertheless, fiscal fines were introduced in 1988 under s. 56 of the Criminal Justice (Scotland) Act 1987 in relation to cases which could be prosecuted in the District Court (other than motoring offences). The fiscal offers the offender an opportunity of paying a fixed sum (currently £25) either as a lump sum or by instalment, to the court. If payment is made no prosecution is brought. Moreover payment is not a tacit admission of guilt and accepted fines are not recorded as convictions. [See K. Meechan, "Extrajudicial Punishment and Procurator Fiscal Fines," 1991 S.L.T. (News) 1.] It has now been suggested by the Scottish Office that the police should be able to offer "on the spot" fixed penalties to alleged road traffic offenders.

The Stewart Committee was united in its support for pre-trial diversion schemes in terms of which minor offenders in suitable cases are referred to agencies which can offer help to the offender. Social Work diversion is perhaps the best known and most successful of these. Following a pilot scheme in Ayr such schemes have been introduced throughout Scotland. Under them alleged offenders who are considered to be likely to respond positively to social work assistance and who agree to participate are referred to a social work department rather than prosecuted in court. [See I. Willock, "Diversion to Social Work Assistance" (1987) 131 SCOLAG 124.] Under pressure from Scottish Women's Aid it is being increasingly accepted that diversion schemes are inappropriate in domestic violence or child abuse cases. Diversion may also be to outside agencies like Councils on Alcoholism or to detoxification centres for persons arrested for being drunk in public. The labour intensiveness and thus the expense of such centres means that regrettably there are only two such centres in Scotland. [See S. Lloyd and A. Taylor, "Alternatives to Custody for Drunken Offenders" (1985) 101 SCOLAG 24 and "Inverness gets new centre for drunken offenders" (1991) 179 SCOLAG 118.] Diversion may also take the form of Reparation and Mediation (recompensing the victim for the damage done) or a non-harassment agreement in neighbourhood disputes.

Notes

1.   There is considerable scope for diversion by the prosecuting authorities (the Procurator Fiscal) within the Scottish criminal justice system, although in comparative terms there is some overlap between the practice of police cautioning in England and Wales and the Procurator's decision not to prosecute or to give a warning. The Scottish system of fiscal fines was approved by the Royal Commission on Criminal Justice, who recommended that similar arrangements should be introduced in England and Wales (see para. 62 of the Commission's Report, and the extract above at p. 44).

2.   In England and Wales the Crown Prosecution Service (CPS) has the power to discontinue proceedings after the police have charged with an offence. Any such discontinuance as a matter of prosecution policy would

have to be on "public interest" grounds, but in practice only a small fraction of cases are discontinued on this basis. Such cases appear to be primarily those where the defendant was already charged with or sentenced for other more serious offences, or where the defendant had elected for jury trial in minor cases such as shoplifting and the cost was regarded as prohibitive: see M. McConville, A. Sanders and R. Leng, *The Case for Prosecution* (1991). The CPS is not therefore a significant institution for diversion in England and Wales, so that if police cautioning rates are low, there often follows a relatively high rate of conditional discharge after conviction: a late-in-the-day process of diversion by sentencers. In comparison, the Scottish Procurator Fiscal now has a significant range of diversionary options to consider, including referral to other agencies such as Social Work Departments.

3.   On the other hand, other prosecuting bodies in England and Wales do possess more significant diversionary powers. In particular, the Inland Revenue and Customs and Excise make use of "compounding", a procedure whereby offences comprising evasion of tax or duty are met with a "enhanced" penalty made up of the underpaid amount and an additional financial penalty. In practice, the unpaid money may be more effectively recovered by offering non-prosecution and avoidance of the stigma associated with court appearance and conviction. Ashworth has commented:

> "Is there any good reason why forms of compounding should not be applied to a wide range of economic offences – why it should not be a matter of routine for the shoplifter to be served with a notice requiring him to pay the court a sum equivalent to the value of the goods stolen (as well as returning the goods or their value to the shop)? Why should not the routine response to the offender who evades his fare on bus or train be to serve him with a notice to pay, say, treble the fare evaded? The advantages would appear to be the same as the advantages of demanding enhanced penalties from those who evade income tax, and the scope for their use would seem to be considerable." ("A Guide to Good Gatekeeping", 23 (1984) *Howard Journal*, pp. 74–5).

The policy in relation to compounding by the Customs and Excise was stated by the Treasury in the following terms:

> "The decision whether to prosecute or to offer to compound proceedings is taken on the merits of each case. The general factors taken into consideration are the gravity of the offence and the best interests of law enforcement and of the revenue. In view of the pressure on the courts and so on departmental resources, it is the Commissioners' policy to offer compounding whenever appropriate. If the offer is refused, they then proceed with the prosecution of the alleged offender." (Written Answer by Treasury Ministers, April 25, 1984, *Hansard*, House of Commons, col. 542)

See also: Lidstone, Hogg and Sutcliffe (1980); Report of the Keith Committee on *Enforcement of Revenue Legislation*, Cmnd. 8222 (1983), Michael Levi, *Regulating Fraud: White-Collar Crime and the Criminal Process* (1987); Customs and Excise Management Act 1979, section 152.

4.   Prosecution-initiated diversion is also to be found in a number of European criminal justice systems. A notable example is the Dutch "*transactie*", which operates alongside a system of prosecution waiver (which itself may be conditional or unconditional) in the Netherlands. As the name suggests, *transactie* is a kind of deal whereby the offender buys off prosecution but waives the right to trial; the offender pays a kind of fine (not exceeding the amount payable in a fine imposed as a sentence); although regarded formally as a transaction, this measure is regarded as a punitive and deterrent sanction for purposes of legal control under the European Convention on Human Rights (*cf. Öztürk v. Germany*, discussed at p. 15, above). The *transactie* may be used in relation to any offence except those punishable with terms of imprisonment of six years or more. Linking the level of the *transactie* fine with that of sentencing fines addresses the kind of concern expressed sometimes in England and Wales about cautioning, that it may in practice be more extensive in its impact than a formal sentence would have been. Prosecution waiver and *transactie* are significant responses to offending in the Netherlands, even in the area of serious crime ("*misdrijven*"). In 1989, out of 211,807 *misdrijven* which went forward to prosecution, 48 per cent were dealt with by waiver or transactie and about a third of these were dealt with by transactie. The average *transactie* sum was DG 389. For further information, see Brants and Field, above.

III. THE IMPACT OF THE BAIL DECISION ON THE PENAL SYSTEM

An important point in the pre-trial stage of the criminal justice process is the decision as to whether a defendant, once charged, should remain at liberty pending the trial or alternatively be remanded in custody (in the interest of protecting others, the defendant him or herself, or in order to guarantee the administration of justice). Remand in custody has implications for the prison system, in terms of management and resources, and alternatives to such remand have become a matter of urgency in recent years.

Bail Act 1976, s. 4(1), (2), (3), (4); Sched. 1, Parts I and II.

Bail for accused persons and others

General right to bail of accused persons and others.

4. – (1) A person to whom this section applies shall be granted bail except as provided in Schedule 1 to this Act.
(2) This section applies to a person who is accused of an offence when –

   (a) he appears or is brought before a magistrates' court or the Crown Court in the course of or in connection with proceedings for the offence, or

(b) he applies to a court for bail in connection with the proceedings.

This subsection does not apply as respects proceedings on or against a person's conviction of the offence or proceedings against a fugitive offender for the offence.
(3) This section also applies to a person who, having been convicted of an offence, appears or is brought before a magistrate's court to be dealt with under section 6 or section 16 of the Powers of Criminal Courts Act 1973 (breach of requirement of probation or community service order).
(4) This section also applies to a person who has been convicted of an offence of enabling inquiries or a report to be made for the purpose of enabling inquiries or a report to be made to assist the court in dealing with him for the offence.

SCHEDULE 1

Persons Entitled to Bail: Supplementary Provisions

Part I

Defendants Accused or Convicted of Imprisonable Offences

Defendants to whom Part I applies

1. Where the offence or one of the offences of which the defendant is accused or convicted in the proceedings is punishable with imprisonment the following provisions of this Part of this Schedule apply.

Exceptions to right to bail

2. The defendant need not be granted bail if the court is satisfied that there are substantial grounds for believing that the defendant, if released on bail (whether subject to conditions or not) would –

(a) fail to surrender to custody, or
(b) commit an offence while on bail, or
(c) interfere with witnesses or otherwise obstruct the course of justice, whether in relation to himself or any other person.

3. The defendant need not be granted bail if the court is satisfied that the defendant should be kept in custody for his own protection or, if he is a child or young person, for his own welfare.

4. The defendant need not be granted bail if he is in custody in pursuance of the sentence of a court of any authority acting under any of the Services Acts.

5. The defendant need not be granted bail where the court is satisfied that it has not been practicable to obtain sufficient information for the purpose of taking the decisions required by this Part of this Schedule for want of time since the institution of the proceedings against him.

6. The defendant need not be granted bail if, having been released on bail in or in connection with the proceedings for the offence, he has been arrested in pursuance of section 7 of this Act....

PART II

DEFENDANTS ACCUSED OR CONVICTED OF NON-IMPRISONABLE OFFENCES

Defendants to whom Part II applies

1. Where the offence or every offence of which the defendant is accused or convicted in the proceedings is one which is not punishable with imprisonment the following provisions of this Part of this Schedule apply.

2. The defendant need not be granted bail if –

    (a) it appears to the court that, having been previously granted bail in criminal proceedings, he has failed to surrender to custody in accordance with his obligations under the grant of bail; and

    (b) the court believes, in view of that failure, that the defendant, if released on bail (whether subject to conditions or not) would fail to surrender to custody.

3. The defendant need not be granted bail if the court is satisfied that the defendant should be kept in custody for his own protection or, if he is a child or young person, for his own welfare.

4. The defendant need not be granted bail if he is in custody in pursuance of the sentence of a court or of any authority acting under any of the Services Acts.

5. The defendant need not be granted bail if, having been released on bail in or in connection with the proceedings for the offence, he has been arrested in pursuance of section 7 of this Act.

Criminal Justice and Public Order Act 1994 sections 25 and 26

    25. – (1) A person who in any proceedings has been charged with or convicted of an offence to which this section applies in circumstances to which it applies shall not be granted bail in those proceedings.

    2. This section applies, subject to subsection (3) below, to the following offences, that is to say –

    (a) murder;

    (b) attempted murder;

    (c) manslaughter;

    (d) rape; or

    (e) attempted rape.

    (3) This section applies to a person charged with or convicted of any such offence only if he has been previously convicted by or before a court in any part of the United Kingdom of any such offence or of culpable homicide and, in the case of a previous conviction of manslaughter or of culpable homicide, if he was then sentenced to imprisonment or, if he was then a child or young person, to long-term detention under any of the relevant enactments.

    (4) This section applies whether or not an appeal is pending against conviction or sentence.

    (5) In this section –

        "conviction" includes –

(a) a finding that a person is not guilty by reason of insanity;

(b) a finding under section 4A(3) of the Criminal Procedure (Insanity) Act 1964 (cases of unfitness to plead) that a person did the act or made the omission charged against him; and

(c) a conviction of an offence for which an order is made placing the offender on probation or discharging him absolutely or conditionally;

and "convicted" shall be construed accordingly; and "the relevant enactments" means –

(a) as respects England and Wales, section 53(2) of the Children and Young Persons Act 1933;

(b) as respects Scotland, sections 205 and 206 of the Criminal Procedure (Scotland) Act 1975;

(c) as respects Northern Ireland, section 73(2) of the Children and Young Persons Act (Northern Ireland) 1968.

(6) This section does not apply in relation to proceedings instituted before its commencement.

26. In Part I of Schedule 1 to the Bail Act 1976 (exceptions to right to bail for imprisonable offences) –

(a) after paragraph 2, there shall be inserted the following paragraph –

"2A. The defendant need not be granted bail if –

(a) the offence is an indictable offence or an offence triable either way; and

(b) it appears to the court that he was on bail in criminal proceedings on the date of the offence."; and

(b) in paragraph 9, after the words "paragraph 2" there shall be inserted the words "or 2A".

Notes

1. The Bail Act governs the question of what should happen to a defendant while awaiting trial (although note that release from police custody without a warrant is covered by the Magistrates' Courts Act 1980, s. 43). Since 1976 there has been a presumption in favour of bail (*i.e.* release pending trial) and the use of recognisances (the defendant's promise to pay a sum of money if he absconds and is caught) was abolished, although sureties (such a promise by a third party) can still be used (see section 3). Under the Act, a failure to appear subsequently as required is an arrestable offence (sections 6, 7). At the same time, the legislation attempted to increase the level of protection for defendants: the decision relating to bail must be recorded; reasons must be given for refusing bail or the attachment of conditions to bail; and an unrepresented defendant who is refused bail must be informed that he has a right to apply to a higher court for bail (see section 5).

2. Schedule 1 to the Bail Act provides the legal justifications for a refusal of bail. The traditional reason for detaining a defendant at this stage has derived from the needs of the administration of justice: to ensure the defendant's appearance at the trial. But research carried out in the early 1970s suggested that, on the basis of police objections to the grant of bail, the bail decision was providing to a large extent for a system of preventive detention, intended to avoid further risk to the community or interference with police investigations (see Michael King (1971)).

3.   The 1994 Criminal Justice and Public Order Act has tightened the criteria for giving bail to those charged with serious violent or sexual offences with previous convictions and custodial sentences for such offences (section 25) and defendants charged with or convicted of offences committed while already on bail (section 26).

4.   Is it a matter for concern that a person is kept in custody before trial, on one of the grounds listed in the Bail Act, yet, although subsequently convicted, is not considered to merit a custodial sentence? In other words, if, in terms of the seriousness of the offence or need to protect the public, a prison sentence is not seen as necessary, can it be convincingly argued that it had been necessary to remand the offender in custody before trial? Is there an equation according to which only post-trial custody can justify pre-trial custody? (See: Rod Morgan, "Remands in Custody: Problems and Prospects", (1989) *Criminal Law Review* 481, at pp. 487–481.) Theoretically the decision as to bail or custody is distinct from that concerning sentence so that differing decisions as to custody at the two stages could be supported. But, if this is so, what is the juridical basis for section 67(1) of the Criminal Justice Act 1967? This provides:

> "The length of any sentence of imprisonment imposed on an offender by a court shall be treated as reduced by any period during which he was in custody by reason only of having been committed to custody by an order of a court made in connection with any proceedings relating to that sentence or the offence for which it was passed or any proceedings from which those proceedings arose..."

Naturally, this section is based upon an idea of fairness but the fact remains that the period of remand is being treated retrospectively and conveniently as part of a sentence of imprisonment. The rationale of this measure lies in expediency and pragmatism.

5.   Studies made of the decision-making process in bail hearings have revealed a number of causes for concern, related in particular to huge geographical variations in the policy adopted by magistrates as regards bail and custody (see B. Gibson, "Why Bournemouth?" (1987) *Justice of the Peace* 520), the speed and fairness of the proceedings, and the level of information available to magistrates.

M. Doherty and R. East, "Bail Decisions in Magistrates' Courts" (1985) 25 B. J. Crim. 251, pp. 262–264

Prospects for Reform in Bail Decision-Making
   Whilst it is clear that the bail rate has increased over the last 25 years the basic problem of the bail system remains. The nature of the system inhibits rather than guarantees informed and consistent decisions; as is clear from the Bail Act criteria for refusing bail, it is expected to be multi-purpose. Defendants can be remanded in custody if it is thought that they may fail to appear at the next hearing and also, for example, if they might commit further offences or obstruct the course of justice. At some point the risk of one or more of these may become unacceptable and a

remand in custody is ordered. The necessity of having regard to several matters makes for complexity in bail decision-making, which is increased by the fact that in relation to each and all of them numerous factors may have to be taken into account. In our study, in the 77 cases in which the police gave reasons for opposing bail, they made use of 21 different reasons and on average suggested two reasons per case. They concentrated their attention on the defendant's past and potential criminality and the needs of the criminal justice system. In the 89 cases in which defendant's representatives gave reasons as to why bail should be granted they presented an average of three reasons per defendant. They used a total of 24 different reasons which referred to factors broadly similar to those used by the police but with a greater emphasis on the defendant's circumstances.

The difficulties caused by the complexity of decision-making are compounded in several ways. The lay magistrates who make many of the bail decisions are amateurs who receive only limited training. Also, the nature of the proceedings is problematic. One of the most striking features of the operation of the courts was the rapidity of decision-making. Information was gathered on the amount of time spent on bail decisions in 209 (42 per cent) of the cases in the study. It was found that 62 per cent of the hearings lasted less than ten minutes and 96 per cent less than 10 minutes. There was a tendency for more time to be spent on the decision when bail was refused than when it was granted. But even in these cases 38 per cent were dealt with in less than two minutes and 87 per cent in less than 10 minutes. The main reason for such speed was that the two charge courts had a heavy work-load, dealing with an average of 60 cases between them each day. Also the participants in the court proceedings (magistrates, clerks of the court, solicitors, police office and probation officers) would often have other responsibilities that required their attention. The court proceedings are designed to ensure that cases are dealt with quickly and there is an expectation that the participants in the process will assist in this. The behaviour of the clerks of the court was instructive. When they made formal announcements, such as informing the defendant of a right to elect for trial by jury or when reciting the charges in the case, they speak very quickly. As to the police, they regularly use the same officers as presenting officers, thus allowing them to adapt to and assist the routine of the court. Similarly, the work of the prosecuting solicitor is carried out by a small number of solicitors, and the probation service regularly allocates the same few officers to discharge their responsibilities in the courts. Solicitors who act as defendants' representatives are more numerous but most of them are regular participants in such work. In these circumstances it is probably inevitable that a camaraderie develops between the participants, and this no doubt partially explains why so few of the hearings attended were markedly adversarial in character. Indeed, it must be observed that examples were noted of allegedly opposed sides assisting each other; for example when the police presenting officer gave details of the representations of the defendant's solicitor, who was unable to attend because she was appearing in another court.

In a situation where there is an expectation that cases are dealt with quickly, often in a non-adversarial fashion, it is perhaps not surprising that only limited information of a low quality is made available to the courts. The police and defendant's representatives are the main sources of information. Whilst, as mentioned earlier, they suggest reasons for the granting or refusing of bail these assertions are rarely scrutinised. The result is that decision-makers, often amateurs with limited training who are working under a time-pressure, have to make subjective decisions on the basis of limited unsubstantiated information. The quality of decision-making must thus be regarded as suspect with consequent problems of the type outlined in the introduction to this paper. Such a situation is far from ideal. To attempt to attain the ideal would require the introduction of a standardised system, in which good-quality information of as objective a character as possible would be scrutinised by well-trained decision-makers. The operators of the system would themselves require scrutiny and probably further guidance, so as to ensure the reasonable consistency of decisions.

Suggested reforms of the bail system have been made by numerous writers and some of their ideas could be utilised in the production of a system closer to the ideal outlined above. One suggestion that seems particularly worthy of consideration is the use of a scheme similar to the Manhattan Bail Scheme. In the Manhatten scheme defendants are asked to complete a questionnaire regarding their community ties. The information is checked and points are allocated depending upon the findings. Defendants with a high point score are thus indicated as being a better bail risk than others. As Davies pointed out, it is claimed that the use of the scheme in American cities "has resulted in four times as many defendants being released on bail, whilst the rate of bail-jumping has dropped from 3 per cent to 1.6 per cent. The judiciary and the police, after initial misgivings, have given the scheme their thorough approval." He went on to say that "The great argument in its favour is that it has been found to work well in practice" (Davies, 1969, p. 483). However, two British attempts to foster the idea have not fared well. First, in 1975, the Secretary of State in a Home Office Circular suggested that schemes should be introduced so as to supply courts with information on defendants' community ties. Such schemes were to be financed within existing resources. As King points out, only 36 out of 680 courts took up the suggestion and it appears that 12 of these schemes were operated by the police (King, 1981, p. 333). Secondly, in Camberwell Green, the Inner London Probation and After-Care Service, with the co-operation of the Vera Institute of Justice, set up an information-form scheme in the area. Roshier and Teff state that it "encountered much opposition from the police and Magistrates' Association and has not been developed" (Roshier and Teff, 1980, p. 113).

To consider the merits of such schemes in greater depth would achieve very little at present. This viewpoint is based on the premise that the legislators for and administrators of the bail system have not demonstrated real commitment to the idea of producing a bail system in which informed and consistent decisions can be made. Their approach seems instead to be based on concern about prison numbers and the financial cost of the system. For example, the recent legislative response to a basic problem with bail decisions, that of the quality and quantity of information, was virtually to ignore it. As was noted earlier, insufficient information is one of the circumstances in which the statutory presumption in favour of bail can be rebutted. The unwillingness of governments to commit resources to the bail system has been evident on a number of occasions. The suggested use of information forms carried the proviso that this was to be within existing resources. Also, King noted that there was an unchallenged assumption during the debates on the bill which later became the Bail Act 1976 that "no financial resources were available either for information verification schemes, or for the relief of the overcrowded conditions in remand prisons, or to provide more bail hostels" (King, 1981, p. 134).

C. Davies, "Imprisonment without Sentence", (1969) *New Society* 482; M. King, *The Framework of Criminal Justice* (1981); B. Roshier and H. Teff, *Law and Society in England* (1980).

Note

Doherty and East's study, based on a sample of almost 500 bail hearings in Cardiff Magistrates' Court over a six month period during 1981–1982, is pessimistic about the prospects for significant improvement in the quality of decision-making in bail proceedings. Some of the problems relating to the way in which the bail decision is reached were addressed by the Woolf

Report on prison disturbances, which considered the reasons for the high level of the remand prisoner population in England and Wales.

Prison Disturbances, April 1990: **Report of an Inquiry by Lord Justice Woolf and Judge Stephen Tumim, Cm. 1456 (1991), paragraphs 10.75–10.101**

i) The Remand Prisoner

10.75   We start our consideration of whether there are inmates in prison who should not be there, with the remand prisoner. Considerable efforts have been made by the various agencies which constitute the Criminal Justice System to try and reduce the number of persons remanded in custody and to limit the periods they spend on remand. However, much more still needs to be done.

10.76   Some successful initiatives are being tried locally. They need to be applied throughout the country. Other initiatives could be improved. The Courts could do more than they do at present to divert remand prisoners from custody.

10.77   The number of untried prisoners fell from 9,811 at the end of September 1988 to 8,366 in February 1990. But the main effect of this fall was not to relieve the pressure on the prisons, but to relieve drastically the pressure on the use of police cells to accommodate such prisoners.

10.78   Subject to what we have just said with regard to numbers, we fully agree with what was said by the Rt Hon John Patten MP, a Minister of State at the Home Office, during his keynote speech of September 11, 1989 to the 1989 International Half-way House Association. Mr Patten said:

> "The remand prison population has grown strikingly over the last decade. In 1979 it stood at around 6,100 whereas now, despite some recent improvements, it stands at about 10,700. This means that about a fifth of the prison population is made up of unconvicted and unsentenced prisoners. Not only has this growth contributed significantly to overcrowding in local prisons, but at times there has been a substantial and even more unwelcome overspill into police cells. This has placed an intolerable burden on the police, and provided totally unsuitable accommodation for defendants – all at great expense for the taxpayer. Overall a very poor bargain for everybody...
>
> Bail decisions are a matter for the Court and there will inevitably be many cases where bail has to be refused for good and proper reasons. On the other hand, people should be remanded in custody   only when this is absolutely necessary and for the shortest possible time."

10.79   The many initiatives which have been taken in recent years to try to tackle the problem created by the size of the remand population have on the whole been successful. Indeed the scale of their success suggests that there were, and almost certainly still are, a substantial number of people remanded in custody who should not be in prison. They come from areas where there is no alternative scheme in operation. They create an unnecessary handicap for the Prison Service. The problems created by the unnecessary remands need to be tackled from a number of different directions. Each involves co-operation between the Courts, the Crown Prosecution Service, the Probation Service and the Prison Service.

a) The Courts

10.80   From the discussions we have had with those who have provided evidence to the Inquiry, it is clear that insufficient status is given to whether or not to remand a defendant or to grant him bail. All too often, remands are dealt with hurriedly before the real business of the day. They can be dealt with by a single Magistrate or two Magistrates rather than a full Court. They can be dealt with hurriedly on Saturday morning.

10.81   It is often suggested that decisions about whether or not to grant bail in Magistrates' Courts depend on whether or not bail is opposed by the Prosecution. (It is partly because of this that, at the present time bail information schemes – to which we will refer – are structured on the basis of providing information to the Crown Prosecution Service.)

10.82   None of this is to criticise Magistrates. They usually have virtually no information on which they can differ from the bail submission made by the Crown Prosecution Service. This is a highly unsatisfactory situation. Magistrates would not regularly, if ever, sentence a defendant to imprisonment on the limited information which is usually available on a bail application. Yet frequently the question of whether or not to refuse bail has an important influence on the sentence which is eventually passed. The refusal of bail can result in a defendant, for example, losing his employment or his accommodation, both of which may be important considerations in determining his ultimate disposal.

10.83   We propose, therefore, that there should be a clear expectation that Magistrates should not make a final decision to remand a defendant in custody until they have received at least the information which will be available to the Crown Prosecution Service in those areas where a Bail Information Scheme is in operation. We would expect Magistrates to insist on more information than that which is made available at the present time to the Crown Prosecution Service where there is no Bail Scheme in operation. They should develop the practice of requiring a report on the community ties which the prisoner has.

10.84   In addition, we propose that Magistrates should attach considerable significance to whether or not the offence which the defendant is alleged to have committed is one which, if proved, would justify a sentence of imprisonment. While it is in order to grant bail irrespective of the likely sentence, to remand a defendant in custody for an offence for which he would never be sentenced to imprisonment can be questionable, unless there is some reasonable justification, such as possible interference with justice or a persistent failure to surrender to his bail or to comply with its terms.

10.85   We propose that information should be provided to Magistrates about where the defendant would be confined if bail was not granted and about what was the regime then available at that establishment for remand prisoners. In the majority of cases, remands from a particular Court will always be held in the same establishment. There should not be too much difficulty in keeping the Magistrates fully informed about that establishment and in drawing the Magistrates' attention to the fact that the establishment is overcrowded where that is the case. This is a subject to which we return later.

10.86   In their submission to the Inquiry, the Parliamentary All-Party Penal Affairs Group drew attention to the fact that the higher Courts do not give guideline decisions in bail applications (as they do in the case of appeals on sentence). The applications are dealt with in chambers by High Court Judges and so are not reported. This results in a failure to rectify any lack of consistency of approach in dealing with bail applications by the lower Courts. It also prevents the higher Courts laying down a policy on bail. The Group therefore recommends that there should be a review of the Bail Act 1976 or a mechanism established to enable guidance to be given by the High Court. There is substance in this point. We would propose that, in the first instance, consideration should be given by High Court Judges to adjourning some bail applications to open Court so that a reasoned decision can be given where an area of difficulty is identified and where guidance could be useful.

10.87   There is also a need to monitor vigorously the progress of cases involving defendants held in custody. Both the prosecution and the defence must be encouraged to reduce the period they need to prepare for trial to a minimum. The time limits which already exist need to be regularly reviewed to see whether they can be reduced. It is particularly important to have the shortest possible waiting time where a defendant is convicted but awaiting sentence. The experience of prisoners at Glen Parva and Pucklechurch, reported in Part I, is testimony to this.

b) Bail Information Schemes

10.88   These schemes featured prominently in the evidence of the Association of Chief Officers of Probation. The evidence records:

> "There has been a reduction in the remand population of 1,200. This has been influenced heavily by the Bail Information Schemes initiated by A.C.O.P. which, in the areas where they are in operation, have reduced custodial remands by 13 per cent."

10.89   A Bail Information Scheme operates through the Probation Service providing the Crown Prosecution Service with verified information about a defendant. It involves interviewing defendants either before the first Court appearance or before the second appearance. The resultant reports enable the Crown Prosecuting Service to take an informed view about whether to oppose bail. This in turn enables the Court to take an informed decision on whether to grant bail (assuming that the Court seeks to go behind and question the view of the Crown Prosecution Service).

10.90   Eight pilot schemes were monitored and co-ordinated by the Vera Institute of Justice throughout 1987. According to the evidence from the Association of Chief Officers of Probation, the findings were that Bail Information Schemes:

> "demonstrated their effectiveness by influencing the bail decision making process, in favour of bail, in a significant number of cases."

10.91   The scheme depends upon the co-operation of both the Crown Prosecution Service and the police. The expansion of the Court based schemes has been rapid. We propose that they should be established in all areas of the country.

c) Prison Bail Schemes

10.92   Prison establishments can also have a role to play in bail information schemes. Ideally, the schemes try to avoid an unnecessary remand in custody at the first Court appearance. Sometimes, however, there has been insufficient time to interview a defendant or to contact the source of information for verification. In either situation, there could be a remand in custody. Further work has to take place before the second Court appearance while the remand prisoner is in prison.

10.93   The work which is required during the intervening period can be conducted under a prison based scheme. The prison based scheme can take up from where the Courts based scheme may have left off, or it can play a primary role and, under it, defendants can be interviewed for the first time.

10.94   The schemes based upon the prisoners are still at an early stage. We propose that they should be expanded as rapidly as possible. Dr Mair's Home Office research on a scheme in Wormwood Scrubs showed the important contribution the schemes can make. Significantly, this research found that key information about the bail/remand decision was not available to the prison or the prisoner. The project found that the Court did not in every case, as it should have done, provide to the defendant a note on the reasons for refusal of bail.

10.95   To operate prison- based units will involve training. There is now a national training course which is available for probation staff. It should be extended to members of the Prison Service who can then play a key role in this valuable probation-led initiative.

d) Bail Hostels

10.96   Magistrates are handicapped if they are placed in the position where they have to choose between unconditional bail on the one hand and custody on the other. The availability of bail hostels or other accommodation arranged by the Probation Service can be significant in assisting the Magistrates to come to a decision to favour of granting bail. Unfortunately, there are at present, as the Government appreciates, too few bail hostels. Additional resources of over £36m in capital and revenue have been secured to provide 1,000 new bail places at approved hostels between April 1988 and April 1993. This will obviously result in an improvement. We propose that consideration be given to bringing forward this programme, to which we attach the greatest importance.

e) Special Hostels

10.97   We propose that more special hostels be established to cater for those with drugs or drink related problems. Many hostels are not in a position or are unwilling to accommodate this type of inmate. They have needs which could be catered for in special hostels by or in association with agencies in the community. The same is true of the mentally ill or the mentally disordered. They frequently cannot be placed in ordinary hostels, but could be accommodated in hostels which have psychiatric facilities.

10.98   If more people with these problems could be diverted from prison, this would be especially beneficial to the Prison Service because of the demands this type of inmate makes upon the Service. We recognise that there will not be savings of the same order as will accrue from diverting a person from prison to an ordinary hostel. It may, indeed, cost more. However, the additional benefit to the defendant who needs a place at a special hostel and to the Prison Service of that need being met outside prison, in our view justify any additional cost involved.

f) Secure Hostels

10.99   These are hostels which, as their name suggests, would provide a regime which would be more controlled and more secure than that provided at a normal hostel. They do not exist at present. There is by no means the same enthusiasm for secure hostels as there is for the other hostels to which we have already referred. The existence of secure hostels could encourage the use of conditions of detainment which would be close to those in a remand prison.

10.100   The Home Office on February 13, 1989 issued a consultation paper on Bail Accommodation and Secure Hostels. None of the probation organisations that responded to the discussion paper was in favour of secure bail hostels, though some would have been in favour of further research. They were concerned that the boundary between bail and remand in custody would be blurred by secure hostels.

10.101   We found convincing and would endorse the alternative approach which has been adopted in the Inner London Probation area and which was described to us by Mr Graham Smith, the Chief Probation Officer. He said that, within his probation area, there was a range of hostels which provided differing degrees of security. In his experience, without having any special category of hostel, it was possible in the Inner London area to identify a hostel which met the needs of any particular defendant who was a suitable subject to be granted bail on the condition that he or she resided at a hostel. It is important, if this approach is adopted, for the Magistrates in the case to be aware of the range of regimes available so they can name an appropriate hostel. In the Inner London area the Chief Stipendiary Magistrate told us that he would have welcomed more information about the choice of hostels which are on offer.

Note

The Woolf Report (at paragraph 10.96) reiterates concern about the small number of places at bail hostels. These hostels represent a further useful option, moderating the stark choice between unconditional bail and custody. Financing of bail hostels was first provided for in section 53 of the Criminal Justice Act 1972; in recent years there has been official approval but limited expenditure on the establishment of such hostels. For research into the operation of bail hostels, see: Frances Simon and Sheena Wilson, *Field Wing Bail Hostel: The First Nine Months*, Home Office Research Study No. 40 (1975); Karen White and Stephen Brody, "The Use of Bail Hostels", (1980) Crim L.R. 420; J. Pratt and K. Bray, "Bail Hostels – Alternatives to Custody?" (1985) 25 B. J. Crim. 160; H. Lewis and G. Mair, *Bail and Probation Work 11: The Use of London Probation Bail Hostels for Bailees*, Home Office Research and Planning Unit Paper No. 50, 1989.

Note

Ironically, although the regime for remanded prisoners is intended to be less harsh than that for convicted prisoners, the fact that many on remand are confined in overcrowded conditions in the local prisons means that their lot is often no better and sometimes worse (see Morgan and King (1977)). However, Morgan and King's study also suggested that conditions in separate remand centres for offenders under the age of 21 differed very little from those in the prisons themselves. Morgan and King's impression of the conditions for remand prisoners was based upon research carried out during the 1970s. The Woolf Report suggested that little had changed by the beginning of the 1990s.

Prison Disturbances, April 1990: **Report of an Inquiry by Lord Justice Woolf and Judge Stephen Tumim, Cm. 1456 (1991), paras. 10.47–10.56, 10.64**

Remand prisoners, unless and until found guilty, are presumed innocent. They are not therefore in prison as a punishment. The fact that prisoners on remand have to be presumed innocent has important implications for the Prison Service's role in relation to them.

10.48   The remand population is a significant part of the total prison population. Until recently it was an increasing part. The proportion of the total prison population made up of remand prisoners increased from 14 per cent in 1975 to 23 per cent in 1988, before falling to 22 per cent in 1989 and the first five months of 1990. This represents an increase from 5,600 remand prisoners in 1975 to 10,500 in 1989, falling to 10,100 in the first five months of 1990. The majority of these remand prisoners were awaiting trial (82 per cent of them in the first few months of 1990). The remainder are prisoners who have been convicted but are awaiting sentence.

10.49   Not all prisoners held on custodial remand are later given a custodial sentence. Criminal Statistics show that of those earlier remanded in custody who were tried at Magistrates' Courts in 1989, a quarter (26 per cent) were given non-custodial sentences and 12 per cent were acquitted. The remainder, the great majority, were committed for trial or sentence to the Crown Court. Even at the Crown Court, a later custodial sentence is by no means certain. Of those previously remanded in custody by Magistrates tried at the Crown Court in 1989, a quarter were either acquitted or were given a non-custodial sentence (6 per cent acquitted, 19 per cent given a non-custodial disposal). The remaining three quarters were given sentences of immediate custody.

10.50   The dramatic increase in the number of prisoners on remand is not primarily because of the increase in the number of prisoners remanded in custody. The number of receptions of untried and unsentenced prisoners in 1975 was 77,903 and in 1989 it was 77,435. The increase is primarily due to the duration of the period in custody. This in turn is linked to an increase in the proportion of those committed to the Crown Court (up from 15 per cent in 1979 to 21 per cent in 1989 – partly because more cases can be tried either way) and to an increase in the percentage of those convicted who are in custody (up from 12 per cent following the Bail Act 1976 to 22 per cent now).

10.51   The time spent in custody by remand prisoners is, therefore, affected by whether or not the case proceeds to the Crown Court. In 1989 in the Magistrates' Court, defendants remanded in custody throughout the entire proceedings spent on average seven weeks in custody. This was about half a week longer than in the three preceding years. The period may have increased slightly during 1990. In the Crown Courts, the national average time between committal and the start of the hearing for defendants remanded in custody was 10.1 weeks. In some cases this period was substantially longer. In 1989, 950 persons had been in custody for more than six months. There are some defendants who wait up to a year in custody before they are sentenced (there were 100 such defendants in 1989).

10.52   We have quoted these statistics because they show beyond peradventure why the Prison Service must have a clearly defined role as to remand prisoners. The figures make clear that it would be wrong to regard the Prison Service's role in respect of remand prisoners as being limited to making provision only for short term visitors. They also demonstrate how changes in what happens in one part of the Criminal Justice System (the Courts) affects another part (the Prison Service).

10.53   In Section 9 of this Report, attention is drawn to the prominent part played in many of the disturbances by remand prisoners. They are an unstable section of the prison population. This is connected with the conditions of their confinement.

10.54   It is beyond dispute that in the majority of prison establishments holding remand inmates, the regime for these inmates is wholly unsatisfactory. Because they are not in prison as a punishment, the regime for remands should be better than that for sentenced prisoners (if it needs to be of a different quality). Unhappily the position is all too often the reverse. Even where the regime for the sentenced prisoner is far from satisfactory, the regime for the unsentenced prisoner is still more impoverished.

10.55   The explanation for this travesty of justice is partly that it is the natural inclination of the Prison Service to devote proportionately more of its resources to the inmates who are the longest in custody. Frequently, because remand inmates are entitled to have daily visits, because they need to make preparations for their trial and because they are not required to work, the Prison Service appear to conclude that, on the whole, it is not worthwhile devoting resources to remands. In the language used at one of our seminars, they are allowed to sink to the foot of the pile.

10.56   It is necessary to redress the present unacceptable situation for remand prisoners. Section 11 of this Report deals with the way in which the Prison Service should accommodate the remand population and in Section 12 we refer to their management. However, in addition to what is said in those sections, we emphasise in the following paragraphs the special responsibility which the Prison Service has in relation to remand prisoners. It is and should be seen as a central part of the Prison Service's role....

10.64   It will be for the Prison Service to construct a statement which satisfactorily encapsulates the approach to be adopted. The policy which we would suggest that statement should reflect, however, may be summarised as follows. So far as this is reasonable, a remand prisoners' containment should reflect the following considerations:

      a) a remand prisoner is presumed innocent until found guilty. His custody should contain no more restrictions than those which are necessary to reflect the ground upon which he was refused bail under the Bail Act 1976;

      b) a remand prisoner should be enabled to prepare for his trial and to have access to lawyers, probation officers and the Court;

      c) a remand prisoner must be permitted to maintain his links with his family, friends and community;

      d) a remand prisoner should be enabled to attend to business and personal affairs, to preserve his employment and to proceed with any education or training;

      e) a remand prisoner should be encouraged to spend the period on remand constructively in accordance with his wishes. This should include access to exercise (including PE), education, training, work and religion;

      f) a remand prisoner should have access to welfare bodies, the Social Services and a bail unit.

Note

In Section 11 of the Report, a number of broad principles are enunciated in relation to the prison estate; the eighth of these concerns the accommodation of remand prisoners:

> unless they consent to different arrangements, wherever this is practical, remand prisoners should be accommodated in separate prisons or in separate units which are treated as separate prisons, from prisons or units occupied by convicted and sentenced prisoners.

Section 12 of the Report is also critical of the management of remand prisoners, and argues that the security classification for such prisoners is usually too strict: see in particular paragraphs 12.308–12.313.

IV THE DECISION AS TO PLEA

JUSTICE, *Negotiated Justice: A Closer Look at the Implications of Plea Bargains* (JUSTICE, 1993), pp. 1–4, 19–20

A survey of over 3000 crown court cases undertaken in February 1992 for the Royal Commission on Criminal Justice reveals that 90 per cent of barristers and more than 60 per cent of judges favour extending plea bargaining practices. In May 1992 the General Council of the Bar published the report of a working party chaired by Robert Seabrook QC which recommends plea bargaining as the "single most effective form of judicial intervention" to save court time and money. Given this apparent strength of support, JUSTICE has been prompted to take a closer look at the implications of such a system.

JUSTICE recognises the need to contain the rapidly rising costs of the criminal justice system. Plea bargaining is only one of many changes proposed in the Bar Council's report and in a November 1990 report from a working group on pre-trial issues, in attempts to ensure greater administrative efficiency in the criminal justice system. But whatever the administrative grounds for supporting so fundamental a change, the ultimate test is what effect it will have on the right to a fair trial.

Exchanging a benefit

Plea bargaining is a loose term covering a process which exchanges a "benefit" for a guilty plea. It can take several different forms. Certain plea bargaining practices are already well-entrenched in the English court system:

- the practice of "plea (or 'charge') negotiation" between the prosecution and defence. This frequently results in the prosecution agreeing not to pursue a more serious charge if the defendant pleads guilty to a lesser charge.
- the practice of agreeing the factual basis on which a guilty plea is presented to the judge for sentencing purposes. This may reflect less serious criminality on the part of the defendant than the evidence might suggest.
- the question of sentence discounts or reductions for a guilty plea. Although not automatic, it is well understood that in most cases a guilty plea should attract a lesser sentence than that following a conviction. This may lead to a reduction of around one-third of a custodial sentence, or a reduction from a custodial to a non-custodial sentence.

Fundamental to all these practices is an inducement or promise in exchange for a plea of guilty.

Seabrook proposals

The Seabrook report proposes to extend and formalise plea bargaining in two ways.

Formalised plea discounts

There should be graduated minimum discounts which would especially reward early pleas of guilty – for example, a 30 per cent discount in the length of a prison sentence for a plea at committal stage. The aim is to provide greater incentive to defendants to plead guilty. Both lawyers and defendants are said to be sceptical as to the extent to which the present informal plea discount is currently applied. The report states that there is often "a feeling that a judge has done little more than pay lip-service to the giving of credit for a guilty plea". Recent analysis of the judicial statistics for 1987–90 not only confirms this view but shows that in some courts pleading guilty might actually be a disadvantage. The findings suggest that in some 10 per cent of crown courts, those who pleaded guilty were at a disadvantage in terms of receiving a custodial sentence over those found guilty after trial. These factors, coupled with the risk of losing bail or, if in custody, losing the privileges of a remand prisoner, are said to provide little incentive to pleading guilty, especially at an early point in the proceedings.

Negotiation with the judge

This would have the same aim: to provide greater incentive to plead guilty by reducing the uncertainty over the sentence which would follow such a plea. This would mean the introduction of a formal sentence indication procedure in which the judge would be asked by defence counsel to give an indication of the sentence if the defendant pleaded guilty. Despite strong judicial disapproval in a long line of cases on the grounds that this could place "undue pressure" on the defendant, it is accepted that the practice does, in fact, occur at present. The Court of Appeal believes that "unnecessary visits" by defence counsel to the judge for a sentence indication continue "up and down the country" (*R v. Smith* 1990). Some practitioners disagree, saying that the majority of judges refuse to see counsel for this purpose.

There is nevertheless consensus that the present haphazard arrangements are undesirable.

The Seabrook report questions whether a system of sentence indication does, in fact, impose improper pressure on the defendant to plead guilty. So long as there are a number of procedural requirements to safeguard against impropriety, it sees nothing wrong with moving to formalise plea bargaining practices. It believes that many guilty defendants would plead guilty if they knew what the sentence would be.

Controversial issues

All forms of plea bargain can be viewed as sentencing devices. As such, they raise some basic moral and social questions. Even the offering of concessions to induce guilty pleas can be queried. Many believe there is no justification in any circumstances for giving a person who pleads guilty a lighter sentence than one who goes to trial. It has been argued that however open and regularised this bargaining may be, it is incompatible with a just sentencing system based on the principle that the punishment reflects what an offender has actually done.

At the same time, serious criticism has been levelled at the way plea bargaining practices can seriously undermine the adversarial model of criminal justice. It is said that in legal systems which are heavily reliant on guilty pleas, certain fundamental principles, such as the presumption of innocence and the burden of proof can be undermined. Under such systems, the focus is no longer on whether the prosecution has sufficient legal evidence to prove guilt; but rather on securing a plea from the defendant and hence saving time and money by avoiding trial. This can set up a culture of presumed guilt of those appearing in court.

These and other issues surrounding plea bargaining practices continue to provoke debate in many countries. In some, like the United States, plea bargaining is a key component of the administration of justice: 90 per cent of all criminal cases are routinely dealt with through systems of bargaining. In others, like Germany, negotiating pleas has been introduced only relatively recently (mainly for white-collar crime) and the question of plea bargaining has become a highly controversial subject. In France, where it is laid down that every case must be judicially scrutinised before conviction, there is no procedure for accepting a guilty plea. Although this may change following recent proposals, the idea of a negotiated outcome remains anathema.

Different legal structures affect the way that plea bargaining develops. One key difference in the United States is the role played by prosecutors. Not only are they able to recommend a sentence, but as full-time state employees their performance is judged largely by the number of convictions achieved and they therefore have a direct interest in the outcome of plea bargain negotiations. Critics of the American system say that the administration of criminal justice is largely determined by lawyers, with the courts making only the most perfunctory scrutiny of their actions.

Before looking at the detail of the Seabrook proposals, it is essential to consider the mischiefs that they are intended to rectify. The Seabrook report considers that the lack of incentive to plead guilty has two consequences:

- it contributes to the "cracked trial" syndrome where pleas of guilty to the offence charged or to alternative charges are entered at the last minute: at the door of the trial court or shortly before. Recent published figures show that the overall average rate of cracked trials is running at around one third of cases listed for trial at the crown courts.
- it results in "many guilty defendants" opting for jury trial. One of the stated aims of the proposed changes is to emphasise to these defendants that they run the risk of paying "a significant price" either for delaying a guilty plea or taking their chance before a jury.

Part 1 of this report considers the evidence on both these matters. It questions whether lack of incentives to plead guilty significantly contribute to these problems: in other words, whether plea bargaining will indeed contribute to greater efficiency.

Part 2 examines the pressures inherent in plea bargaining practices by looking at the practical implications of introducing formalised plea bargaining. It seeks to draw the line between acceptable inducement and improper pressure to plead guilty; whether, for example, the benefit of providing defendants with more informed choice is outweighed by greater pressure.

This report does not consider the particular issues surrounding complex fraud cases. This is a matter which is being considered separately in the context of JUSTICE's work on serious fraud.

Conclusion

Two arguments underpin the Seabrook report: that more and earlier pleas of guilty will increase the efficiency of the courts and that prior knowledge of the sentence on a guilty plea will benefit lawyers and their clients in the choices they have to make. Greater efficiency in courts and a sentencing system which can be more accurately predicted are legitimate aims of a fair criminal justice system; moreover, it is clear that they are aims which are at present some way from realisation.

However this report's attempt to analyse and dissect the components of an extended and formalised system of plea bargaining casts doubt on its claims to increase both efficiency and fairness. In Part 1 we pointed to poor administrative case management and the absence of effective pre-trial procedures as the main source of cracked trials. The substantial cost of abandoning 10,000 cases a year through directed acquittals is one of many examples of the inefficiency of the present system. Although we have not set out to identify particular areas of inefficiency, we are aware of the more obvious ones that require immediate attention: lack of pre-trial liaison between prosecution and defence, initial "over-charging" by the prosecution, late return of briefs and late contact generally between defence barristers and their clients. These suggest the need for administrative and management solutions rather than changes in substantive law; and moreover, the former are likely to produce more predictable and reliable savings than would extended plea bargaining practices, for example.

In Part 2 we looked to the practical and ethical consequences of increasing the incentives to plead guilty and to do so at an early stage. We pointed out the practical difficulties involved in both Seabrook proposals. In sentence indication practices, there are the problems of assessing culpability and putting forward mitigation at a time when the defendant is still overtly innocent of the charge. In particular, there is the problem of not having available a pre-sentence report as required by the 1991 Criminal Justice Act. There is also the likely effect that such a practice would have on the actual and perceived roles of the defence lawyers and the judge. In relation to a more formalised plea discount system, we highlight problems relating to the management of cases which would effectively make fixed and graded discounts an impractical question in many cases.

It is, however, the ethical problems that cause us most concern. First, incentives to plead guilty are not far removed from penalties for those who choose to go to trial. Second, the greater the incentive, the greater the pressure to plead guilty. In other words, a system which is designed to induce more and earlier guilty pleas will, we fear, change an incentive to a penalty, an inducement to a pressure.

There are likely to be a number of consequences of this. In terms of creating a penalty, we are particularly concerned at those passages in the Seabrook report which concentrate on ways of identifying guilt at an early stage and which seem almost to place a duty on defendants to save the courts' time by finding against themselves. This subtly undermines the presumption of innocence in the criminal justice system and the requirement that the prosecution prove its case. Indeed, it can rapidly lead to a system which becomes accustomed to looking for guilt and which penalises those who opt for jury trial.

In accepting the practice of a plea discount – albeit in more closely defined circumstances than at present – we acknowledge that the system already incorporates a degree of incentive to plead guilty. But we believe that to go further than this runs the risk of defendants being put under undue pressure to plead guilty. Indeed, some practitioners have expressed concern that just as safeguards have been introduced to protect suspects from being subjected to undue pressure at police stations, these proposals would create just such pressures at court. This would hardly be wise at the time when a Royal Commission has been established as a result of concern at the conviction of the innocent.

A further ethical concern is the likely impact of such practices on sentencing. Whatever the aims of sentencing, a minimum requirement in any rational system is that there is some degree of correspondence between the facts of the crime and the sentence. To sentence on the rigid basis of fixed and graded discounts or to indicate a sentence before the full facts (including mitigating circumstances) can be brought out, starts to undermine this requirement. Such practices would operate sometimes to the benefit of defendants and sometimes to their detriment; however, they would not operate in favour of justice or the public interest generally.

We are aware, from our own casework, of the anger and sense of unfairness generated by a system which does not permit accurate information on the likely outcome of a plea. We therefore fully support the call for more consistency in sentencing; and for better advice and information on the options and likely outcome to be available to defendants and their lawyers. We put forward proposals in a previous report Sentencing – A Way Ahead (1989). This recommended a system of detailed sentencing guidelines which would be drafted, monitored, evaluated and updated by a Sentencing Commission. We remain convinced that this is the best way forward.

Report of the Royal Commission on Criminal Justice, Cm. 2263, pp. 110–114

Sentence discounts, "cracked" trials, sentence "canvass" and "plea bargaining"

41. For many decades defendants who plead guilty in the Crown Court have been regarded by the Court of Appeal as usually entitled to a discount or reduction in their sentence. The usual range of discount is 25 per cent to 30 per cent. The primary reason for the sentence discount is to encourage defendants who know themselves to be guilty to plead accordingly and so enable the resources which would be expended in a contested case to be saved. A subsidiary reason, applicable in some types of cases, is to recognise that the defendant by pleading guilty has spared witnesses the trauma of having to give evidence at court.

42. Provided that the defendant is in fact guilty and has received competent legal advice about his or her position, there can be no serious objection to a system of inducements designed to encourage him or her so to plead. Such a system is, however, sometimes held to encourage defendants who are not guilty of the offence charged to plead guilty to it nevertheless. One reason for this is that some defendants may believe that they are likely to be convicted and that, if they are, they will receive a custodial sentence if found guilty after a contested trial but will avoid such a sentence if they plead guilty. The risk cannot be wholly avoided and, although there can be no certainty as to the precise numbers (see next paragraph) it would be naive to suppose that innocent persons never plead guilty because of the prospect of the sentence discount.

43. In the Crown Court Study defence barristers were asked: "An innocent defendant sometimes decides to plead guilty to achieve a sentence discount or reduction in the indictment. Were you concerned that this was such a case?" In 53 cases the defence barristers answered "Yes". Since the Crown Court Study was conducted over two weeks this appeared at first sight to mean that there were some 1,400 possibly innocent persons pleading guilty every year. Closer examination of these 53 cases showed, however, that there was little if any evidence that persons who were innocent of all the charges brought against them had pleaded guilty to one or more of these charges because of the sentence discount. It was clear that in many instances the defence barristers had misunderstood the thrust of the question they were asked. Thus in some cases the defendants were said to be not guilty only to one of several charges. In some cases too the barristers made it clear that they did not think that the client was innocent, only that he or she was claiming to be – sometimes in the face of considerable evidence to the contrary.

44. The position of the defence barrister is dealt with in the Bar's Code of Conduct as follows:

> "Where a defendant tells his counsel that he did not commit the offence with which he is charged but nevertheless insists on pleading guilty to it for reasons of his own, counsel must continue to represent him, but only after he has advised what the consequences will be and that what can be submitted in mitigation can only be on the basis that the client is guilty."

Defence barristers should and normally do advise clients that they should not plead guilty if they are not guilty, but that the decision is one for them.

45. Against the risk that defendants may be tempted to plead guilty to charges of which they are not guilty must be weighed the benefits to the system and to defendants of encouraging those who are in fact guilty to plead guilty. We believe that the system of sentence discounts should remain. But we do see reason to make the system more effective. In particular we believe that a clearer system of graduated discounts would help to alleviate the problem of "cracked" trials (see paragraph 13 above). The Crown Court Study showed that "cracked" trials were 26 per cent of all cases or 43 per cent of cases other than those listed as guilty pleas.[11] "Cracked" trials create serious problems, principally for all the thousands of witnesses each year – police officers, experts and ordinary citizens – who come to court expecting a trial only to find that there is no trial because the defendant has decided to plead guilty at the last minute. This causes in particular unnecessary anxiety for victims whose evidence has up to that point been disputed.

46. At present, the sentence discount is available at any stage until the beginning of the trial but the Court of Appeal has stated in terms that, other things being equal, an earlier plea ought to attract a higher discount and that late tactical pleas should not attract the same discount:

> "This court has long said that discounts on sentence are appropriate, but everything depends upon the circumstances of each case. If a man is arrested and at once tells the police that he is guilty and cooperates with them in the recovery of property and the identification of others concerned in the offence, he can expect to get a substantial discount. But if a man is arrested in circumstances in which he cannot hope to put forward a defence of not guilty, he cannot expect much by way of a discount. In between come this kind of case, where the court has been put to considerable trouble as a result of a

---

[11] Of the total of cases listed, 39 per cent were listed as guilty pleas, 26 per cent were listed as not guilty pleas but "cracked" (*i.e.* became guilty pleas), 31 per cent were actually contested before a jury and 3 per cent ended without a plea where the defendant was bound over or the charges were allowed to lie on the file.

tactical plea. The sooner it is appreciated that defendants are not going to get a full discount for pleas of guilty in these sorts of circumstances, the better it will be for the administration of justice."[12]

47. We agree with the view expressed by the Court of Appeal that, other things being equal, the earlier the plea the higher the discount. In broad terms, solicitors and barristers should advise their clients to that effect. Judges must, however, retain their discretion to deal appropriately with the particular circumstances of the individual case. Subject to these points, a system of graduated discounts might work broadly as follows:

- (a) The most generous discount should be available to the defendant who indicates a guilty plea in response to the service of the case disclosed by the prosecution.
- (b) The next most generous discount should be available to the defendant who indicates a guilty plea in sufficient time to avoid full preparation for trial. The discount might be less if the plea were entered only after a preparatory hearing.
- (c) At the bottom of the scale should come the discount for a guilty plea entered on the day of the trial itself. Since resources would be saved by avoiding a contested trial even at this late stage, we think that some discount should continue to be available. But it should be appreciably smaller than for a guilty plea offered at one of the earlier stages.

We do not think that clearer articulation of the long accepted principle that there should be greater sentence discounts for earlier pleas will increase the risk that defendants may plead guilty to offences which they did not commit. We would on the other hand expect that it would lead some who would at present plead guilty to do so earlier.

48. We believe, however, that still more could be done to reduce the incidence of "cracked" trials. As the Seabrook Committee argued, the most common reason for defendants delaying a plea of guilty until the last minute is a reluctance to face the facts until they are at the door of the court. It is often said too that a defendant has a considerable incentive to behave in this way. The longer the delay, the more the likelihood of witnesses being intimidated or forgetting to turn up or disappearing. And, if the defendant is remanded in custody, he or she will continue to enjoy the privileges of an unconvicted remand prisoner whereas, once a guilty plea has been entered, the prisoner enters the category of convicted/unsentenced and loses those privileges. Although this last disincentive can be removed, as we recommend below, the problem of last minute changes of plea can never be completely eradicated. We believe, however, that a significant number of those who now plead guilty at the last minute would be more ready to declare their hand at an earlier stage if they were given a reliable early indication of the maximum sentence that they would face if found guilty.

49. The defendant will be interested not so much in the discount on sentence that he or she might receive as the actual sentence and in particular whether it will be custodial or not. It used to be possible for defence counsel to ask the judge for an indication of the sentence that his or her client might receive if found guilty after a contested trial, as opposed to the sentence that might be passed if the plea were changed to guilty. But the discussion of likely sentences with judges is now severely constrained by the Court of Appeal's judgment in *R. v. Turner*.[13] According to this, judges may say that, whether the accused pleads guilty or not guilty, the sentence will or will not take a particular form. They must not, however, state that on a plea

---

[12] *R. v. Hollington and Emmens* (1986) 82 Cr. App. R. 281.
[13] [1972] W. L. R. 1093.

of guilty they would impose one sentence while on conviction following a plea of not guilty they would impose a severer sentence. The court took the view that this would be placing undue pressure on defendants, depriving them of that complete freedom of choice which is essential.

50. Many witnesses, particularly from the judiciary and the Bar, urged on us the desirability of reverting, in essence, to the system as it applied before the judgment in the case of *Turner*. The Crown Court Study also showed that, among the judges and barristers who responded, there was overwhelming support for change.[14] We do not support a total reversal of the judgment in *Turner*, since we agree that to face defendants with a choice between what they might get on an immediate plea of guilty and what they might get if found guilty by the jury does amount to unacceptable pressure. But the effect of *Turner* and related judgments appears to have been to make judges reluctant to discuss sentence with counsel at all. We think that there is a case for a change of approach. We recommend that, at the request of defence counsel on instructions from the defendant, judges should be able to indicate the highest sentence that they would impose at that point on the basis of the facts as put to them. A request for such an indication might be made at a preparatory hearing, at a hearing called specially for this purpose, or at the trial itself....

56. The availability of a sentence discount for a guilty plea and the practice of asking the judge to give an indication of the possible maximum sentence should not be confused with the discussions that commonly took place between the prosecution and the defence over charge. This is what is normally described as "plea bargaining", although it might be more accurate to call it "charge bargaining"; the defence may offer to plead guilty to a lesser charge than the one brought by the prosecution or the prosecution may offer to accept a plea of guilty to a lesser charge. We see no objection to such discussions, but the earlier they take place the better; consultation between counsel before the trial would often avoid the need for the case to be listed as a contested trial

57. As we have previously noted, it may be a disincentive to remand prisoners to plead guilty that, by doing so, they lose the privileges enjoyed by unconvicted prisoners. We recommend that the additional privileges enjoyed by unconvicted prisoners be extended to convicted prisoners awaiting sentence. We understand that this reform is already under consideration by the Prison Service.

58. We are also aware that Roger Hood's research provides evidence that the current system of sentence discounts, combined with the greater tendency of members of certain ethnic minority communities to maintain a plea of not guilty, puts black and other ethnic minority offenders at a greater risk of being sentenced to custody and serving longer sentences. We therefore support the recommendation made by Hood that the policy of offering sentence discounts should be kept under review. This means that it is essential for the Crown Court to monitor the ethnic origin of everyone who appears there. Only with information on all sentences, analysed by ethnic origin, would it be possible to detect whether sentencing patterns are being established which might be unfavourable to particular minority groups. The Home Office is exploring with the Lord Chancellor's Department the feasibility of introducing ethnic monitoring of all court outcomes and we welcome this development.

---

[14] Judges and barristers were asked whether "*Turner* should be reformed to permit full and realistic discussion between counsel and judge about plea and especially sentence". Close to 90 per cent of barristers and two-thirds of judges answered "Yes".

References

Report of a Working Party (Seabrook Committee) of the General Council of the Bar, "The Efficient Disposal of Business in the Crown Court", May 1992; R. Hood, *Race and Sentencing: A Study in the Crown Court* (Oxford University Press, 1992); *R v. Smith* [1990] 90 Cr. App. Rep.

Notes

1.   Negotiation about charges may affect the sentencing process in that sentencing opportunities are removed if a charge is dropped. This may also be regarded as a kind of "diversion of the offence" out of the criminal justice process. Negotiation about the plea – whether to plead guilty or not guilty – affects the sentencing process via the sentencing discount customarily awarded for a guilty plea. As the above extracts show, both types of negotiation are well established in relation to the more serious cases heading for the Crown Court; the problem is to achieve a balance between considerations of expediency on the one hand and justice on the other. The whole issue of sentencing discounts was brought to the forefront of discussion in the later 1970s with the publication of research by Baldwin and McConville (*Negotiated Justice*, 1977), the first thoroughgoing critical empirical research on the subject carried out in England and Wales. The authors were critical of existing accounts of plea discussions (R. Purves (1971); C. Davies (1970)) as being over-tolerant of the practice on the basis of little empirical research. In order to gain a more detailed picture of what was actually happening, Baldwin and McConville interviewed a sample of defendants from the Birmingham Crown Court about their own experiences. The authors were conscious of the limitations arising from their reliance on such sources (see their discussion at pp. 9–12) but concluded that "we can see no other satisfactory way of approaching the question of guilty plea negotiation than through the defendant himself. Since all informal discussions of this nature are, almost by definition, conducted *in camera*, formal observation is not possible.' In addition, so as to test the predictions made by defence counsel of the likely outcome of the defendants" cases, copies of all the committal papers relating to the sample were independently examined by two assessors (a retired Chief Constable and a retired Justices' Clerk) for their "expert" view of the likely outcome. Baldwin and McConville's overall conclusion was that the system in operation resulted in a certain level of pressure on defendants to plead guilty; the consequent risk of injustice in some cases could not, in their view, be morally tolerated, either on the basis of supposed remorse (now a largely discarded justification) or by reference to any gains in administrative expediency.

2.   The JUSTICE report was much less tolerant of plea negotiation than that of either the Seabrook Committee (a working party of the Bar Council) or the Royal Commission. The latter took up the two major proposals of the Seabrook Committee: that there be a system of "graduated discounts", which would give a greater reduction of sentence to those who pleaded guilty at an earlier stage; and that the trial judge should, if the defendant

requests it, be able to indicate the highest sentence he would impose at that particular point on the basis of the facts known to him then ("sentence canvass"). These proposals were intended to render the system of sentencing discounts more effective, in that they could help to reduce the number of "cracked trials" (contested cases which collapsed at the last moment) and give defendants a greater assurance that the discount would materialise. The system of graduated discounts has been embodied in the 1994 Criminal Justice and Public Order Act, section 48 of which places the discount principle on a legislative basis for the first time.

Criminal Justice and Public Order Act, 1994, section 48

48. – (1) In determining what sentence to pass on an offender who has pleaded guilty to an offence in proceedings before that or another court a court shall take into account –

(a) the stage in the proceedings for the offence at which the offender indicated his intention to plead guilty, and
(b) the circumstances in which this indication was given.

(2) If, as a result of taking into account any matter referred to in subsection (1) above, the court imposes a punishment on the offender which is less severe than the punishment it would otherwise have imposed, it shall state in open court that it has done so.

3. The JUSTICE report confronts these proposals with both ethical and practical arguments. Of the former, there is firstly the objection that the question of plea is not a relevant sentencing consideration: the sentence should reflect the nature of the offence and the defendant's character and situation at the time of the offence. Secondly, it is argued that the process of pre- sentencing negotiation undermines the adversarial nature of the British system of criminal procedure and compromises the presumption of innocence before conviction. Related to this argument is the misgiving that the "inducement" to plead guilty becomes institutionalised into a kind of pressure and seems "almost to place a duty on defendants to save the courts time by finding against themselves" (p. 20 of the JUSTICE report). Finally, it is argued, the "incentive" to plead guilty is tantamount to a penalty for those who choose to go on trial. The Royal Commission's Report does not squarely consider any of these ethical or policy objections, merely stating that "there can be no serious objection to a system of inducements" (p. 110, para 42).

4. The other main thrust of JUSTICE's criticism is that some of the mischief that the system of sentencing discounts sets out to remedy is the product of administrative inefficiency within the operation of criminal procedure itself – lack of pre-trial liaison between prosecution and defence, initial over-charging by the prosecution, late return of briefs and late contact generally between defence barristers and their clients: all of which suggest the need for administrative and management solutions. Some of these

criticism echo those of Baldwin and McConville in the 1970s. The Royal Commission considered some of these organisational and administrative problems and made a number of recommendations about pre-trial reviews and preparatory hearings, and listing arrangements. Earlier in its Report, it stated:

"We recognise that if the scheme for pre-trial preparation which we propose in outline is to be effective, a significant change in the working habits of both solicitors and barristers will be called for. But we refuse to share either the complacency of those who believe that the present system does not call for improvement at all or the scepticism of those who believe that although earlier and better preparation of cases is desirable in principle, it cannot be achieved in practice. It is true that attempted reforms have been frustrated in the past by the failure of practitioners to comply even with practice directions from the most senior members of the judiciary. But that is hardly a creditable argument against making a further and more determined effort to make them do what they ought." (p. 102; para 3)

At a later point in the Report, the Royal Commission commented:

"The Crown Court Study indicated that half the prosecution barristers and nearly one-third of defence barristers only received their briefs on the day before the hearing or the day of the hearing itself. This ... is an undesirable state of affairs, even if 95 per cent of prosecuting barristers and 93 per cent of defence barristers nevertheless said that they had had enough time to prepare for the case. In view of the widespread dissatisfaction with the system, we welcome the steps that are being taken, particularly through increasing computerisation ... and national listing guidelines to improve matters." (pp. 109–10; para. 38)

Reference: Michael Zander and Paul Henderson, *The Crown Court Study*, Royal Commission Research Study, No. 19.

However, even if the efficiency of pre-trial procedure is improved, this is unlikely to disturb the assumption of most participants in the system that plea negotiation and sentencing discounts are an integral part of the process; it would seem that the system of "incentives" to plead guilty has achieved a dynamic of its own (something which was also implied in Baldwin and McConville's earlier research).

5.   Critics of the Royal Commission's position on sentencing discounts point to its tendency to argue more on the basis of assumption rather than on research findings. Sanders and Young (1994), for instance, assert:

"... the Runciman Commission has simply made a value choice, expressing a preference for more crime control and less due process.

But ... empirical evidence should play a central part in informing one's choice of values....

... It was simply assumed that defendants were wasting everybody's time and money by delaying their pleas of guilty until the last moment. This crime control line of reasoning, that guilty persons will take advantage of due process protections in order to further their own interests and in seeking to avoid their just deserts, is not borne out in research findings on the operation of the criminal process." (Andrew Sanders and Richard Young, *Criminal Justice* (1994), pp. 347–348).

6.   Care should be taken in drawing any comparisons between plea negotiation at the level of magistrates' courts and Crown Courts since the context of the discussion is clearly very different, both as regards the nature of the offences and the possible outcome for defendants, and the personnel involved. However, an account presented by John Baldwin (1985) of the practice at Nottingham Magistrates' Court suggests that the pre-trial review provides a more visible environment for discussions about pleas and that these are carried out in a more careful and structured manner than is the case with plea negotiations in Crown Courts. Baldwin comments (1985, p. 108):

"... the robust and pragmatic approach adopted at pre-trial reviews in Nottingham seems to this writer well suited to the sort of cases heard in the lower courts where issues are often not black and white and where a full-blooded contest in the court may well be unnecessary or inappropriate. And, from the writer's own observations, it must be stressed that discussions at pre-trial reviews in Nottingham were almost always conducted in a seemly and proper manner. It is rather that there are serious dangers in the reliance that has to be placed under these procedures on the competence and integrity of the lawyers, particularly where difficult decisions about mutual disclosure of evidence need to be made. Supervision of the pre-trial review, in Nottingham and in other courts, is provided by a member of the court staff though this on the whole nominal. In the writer's view, the only satisfactory solution to the difficulties that seem inherent in the informality of the pre-trial review is to invite the defendant (and perhaps also the complainant) to attend so that they can satisfy themselves as to the procedures that are adopted."

It may be, therefore, that some useful lessons could be drawn from this area.

7.   It must be remembered that the phenomenon of plea negotiation is largely a response to an organisational problem: the inability of the court system to deal with the volume of cases being referred to it. Clearly, there may be other ways of dealing with this problem, such as the use of cautioning rather than bringing a case to trial, or advance disclosure of evidence so as to prevent a last-minute collapse of a case or a weak case being dealt with unnecessarily in court. Baldwin's study touches upon the

practice of advance disclosure, which has developed mainly on an informal basis, although section 48 of the Criminal Law Act 1977, which provides for disclosure of the prosecution case in summary trials, has now been brought into force (see as well the further study of advance disclosure by Baldwin and Mulvaney (1987)). One prosecutor (G. N. Barnett (1983)) has argued that pre-trial disclosures lead to an avoidance of trial in around 40 per cent of the cases originally set down for summary trial, which results in a substantial saving of time and money. But it would be misleading to suggest that there is likely to be a single, easily implemented solution to the formidable organisational problems of case-load and delay now facing the criminal courts in this country. Andrew Ashworth (1984) has commented that, "Almost all enquiries have concluded that the causes of delay are many and varied, and that no single practical change of policy could achieve immediate success ... The problem mainly concerns large urban courts and may call for different expedients in different areas" (pp. 70–1; see as well his discussion of what research has been carried out in this area).

8.   On pre-trial review in magistrates' courts see also: A. Mulcahy, I. Brownlee and C. Walker, *An Evaluation of Pre-Trial Review in Leeds and Bradford Magistrates' Courts*, (1993) 33 Home Office Research Bulletin 10; Andrew Sanders and Richard Young, *Criminal Justice* (1994), pp. 271–81. On the key role of defence lawyers in bringing about plea bargains, see M. McConville, J. Hodgson, L. Bridges and A. Pavlovic, *Standing Accused* (1994).

9.   For an account of plea negotiation in the Scottish criminal justice system, which has for a long time operated a different process of public prosecution, see S. R. Moody and J. Tombs (1982). It is of interest that, in Scotland, plea negotiation flourishes in the absence of any real sentencing discount, but an inducement to plead guilty may arise from the ability of the Procurator Fiscal to reduce or drop charges or alter his presentation of the facts to the court.

CHAPTER THREE

THE SENTENCING PROCESS

I. THE SENTENCERS

Under the British criminal justice system the sentencing function is the responsibility of the courts; in England and Wales this means the magistrates' courts, Crown Courts and the Criminal Division of the Court of Appeal. Yet the suitability of trial courts for a sentencing role has not gone unchallenged. As early as 1893, Sir Henry Hawkins (in the New Review) called for the setting up of a Sentencing Commission in response to concern about disparities in sentencing practice. The idea was debated during the 1894–5 session of parliament, but opinions were too divided to lead to any hope of practical reform. The proposals of Margery Fry (1944) for a "treatment authority" and the Howard League for "treatment tribunals" (*Howard Journal*, 1946–7) also encountered a sceptical reaction. Such demands for an injection of expertise into the sentencing process were reinforced by the mid-twentieth century shift towards a treatment model of criminal justice. However, since that time, there has been a conspicuous retreat from this approach and an increasing concern with due process, which has bolstered the courts' involvement in the sentencing process.

Although the responsibility of the courts for sentencing is now assured, it is generally accepted that sentencers at all levels should be fully informed about the nature and consequences of the measures which they have at their disposal. Change has therefore been in the form of educating the judges for sentencing purposes, and not in their replacement. It is important to bear in mind, however, the scope for mutual influence between judicial sentencers and other agencies in the criminal justice system; for example, the degree to which information provided by the probation service may influence the final sentencing decision or how far judicial notions of due process have infiltrated penal decision-making, in the prison system and elsewhere.

The first question to consider is whether sentencing is a specialist judicial function, or is it one to which some lay involvement is essential? The system of appointment to our criminal courts means that the sentencing function is carried out by a mixed body of professional lawyers – such as the Appeal Court and Crown Court judges and stipendiary magistrates in England and Wales – and lay justices, who sit in the magistrates' courts. What are the relative advantages and disadvantages of legally trained and lay sentencers?

Sir Leon Radzinowicz and Joan King, *The Growth of Crime* (1977), pp. 244–251.

What do we expect of those who pronounce sentence? Certainly fairness, freedom from prejudice or bias, from the kinds of attitude that lead, consciously or unconsciously, to improper discriminations. But at the same time we expect them to be aware of a wide range of issues; to be sensitive to the kind of person to be sentenced, what has influenced him in the past and is likely to influence him in the future, and to be aware of the various ways of dealing with him offered by the penal system, and of what each really implies.

Doubts about the ability of sentencers to carry out this double responsibility have clustered round a few main issues. Are they so remote from the majority of those they deal with, in age, in class, in associations, that they can neither judge fairly in terms of culpability nor deal with them effectively in terms of treatment, deterrence or protection? Does political bias, like the racial bias already demonstrated in certain contexts, seriously distort their decisions? Does a legal training help them in their role as sentencers, or does it make them more rigid and legalistic? Do they, at any point in their careers, learn how to sentence at all, let alone learn how to sentence as thoroughly as they learn how to weigh up the evidence of guilt or argue a case for prosecution or defence?

Predictably, the bits and pieces of findings so far available confirm that judicial benches are heavily weighted on the side of the middle and upper-middle class, the middle-aged to elderly, in many places the conservative side in politics, and with the notable exception of the English lay magistracy, of the legally trained.

Less clear and less uniform is the evidence on how, and how strongly, these features affect their sentencing....

... In many parts of the world it is taken for granted that those responsible for sentencing will always be lawyers. That is not the case in England where at least nine sentences out of ten are imposed by lay magistrates. Legal training should certainly help the sentencer in some respects: he should have learned to look at a case from different sides, to select the genuinely relevant issues, to weigh arguments, to reach decisions. On the other hand it is sometimes suggested that it makes him pedantic, detached from real life, more concerned with legal formulae than with genuine human problems. The lay magistrate, by contrast, is pictured as full of robust common-sense, more understanding both of offenders and of the everyday world. To compare them in terms of research is not easy. In England, for example, the lay magistrate is part-time, the stipendiary normally full-time, the laymen sit in groups, the stipendiary sits alone. If there are differences in their attitudes and sentencing, they may stem from such circumstances as these as much as from the fact that the general run of justices of the peace are not lawyers whereas the stipendiary magistrates are. In Canada, however, where the summary courts have all had full-time justices, mostly lawyers but some laymen, a small comparison has been possible. In that situation, at least, it is not the layman but the lawyers who come out best, as more confident, more likely to take account of a range of factors in the offence, less likely to be rigid in their sentencing, less vulnerable to pressures from those around them.

My own view is that sentencing is not a job for laymen. Such devices as "people's courts" appear to me highly dangerous. At least in the western world the moves are towards unified court systems, staffed from top to bottom by qualified lawyers. That has long been the position on the continent of Europe ... It has been introduced in some parts of the United States and there is strong pressure to bring it in elsewhere, especially in cities. There the neglect, squalor and corruption of summary courts, struggling against overwhelming odds, apart from the mainstream of legal protection, legal reform and penal provision in the superior courts, has driven reformers to the conclusion that only a unified system can offer the hope of equal justice and adequate resources at the bottom of the pile.

The English summary courts and the English lay justices seem to me the exception that proves the rule. They have evolved over centuries in the soil and climate of a highly individual nation, part of its strong traditions of local and voluntary responsibilities. Their jurisdiction has been extending rather than contracting even in the most recent decades. They deal with 98 per cent of criminal cases. In terms of expense the saving is immense. In terms of justice and of behaviour there are surprisingly few scandals. In terms of status and respect they still stand high: an invitation to join their ranks is still esteemed an honour. It is a system that does not easily transplant to other countries: it tends either to wither or become corrupt, as has happened in the States. Yet to uproot it whilst it still flourishes in its native soil would be wanton and wasteful. It may be that even there it will in time be starved, eroded by social change. If so it will become necessary to think again.

Notes

1.   Might it be argued that the above comment that "sentencing is not a job for laymen" is too categorical and influenced in particular by the North American experience? It should be noted that the trend towards "professional" sentencers is not universal (for instance, witness the adoption of lay "children's panels" in Scotland).

2.   Not unnaturally, the social and professional background of sentencers, as well as their political preferences, have excited speculation as to how such factors may influence sentencing decisions. A number of studies have been made of apparent disparities in sentencing practice and whether these may be explained by reference to the sentencers' own backgrounds and attitudes. For a discussion, see Roger Hood, *Sentencing in Magistrates' Courts* (1962) pp. 119–120 and L. H. Leigh and S. Brown, "Crimes in Bankruptcy", pp. 188–189, in *Economic Crime in Europe* (Leigh ed., 1980). Also see Roger Hood, *Sentencing the Motoring Offender* (1972). In this study, the magistrates' social background did not emerge as a significant factor in explaining disparity. But Hood did not rule out the possibility that different social backgrounds discriminate between sentences imposed for other types of offence.

3.   There are conflicting views on the appropriate age of sentencers. John Hogarth in his major Ontario study, *Sentencing as a Human Process* (1971), found evidence that younger magistrates tended towards extremes in sentencing decisions, while older members of the bench displayed more flexibility and moderation. On the other hand, there are convincing arguments that, as they move towards old age, sentencers may become too rigid in their views and out-of-touch with prevailing attitudes and the behaviour of younger people. Class bias is also notoriously difficult to assess and it is necessary to guard against over-ready assumptions about class sympathy. There is some evidence, for example, that "respectable" working-class magistrates may be relatively tough in dealing with working-class offenders. As regards the professional, legal background of sentencing judges, the disadvantages of a relatively narrow professional experience have to be weighed against the benefits of a training which inculcates objectivity in decision-making. In short, the available research does not enable us to

pronounce with any confidence on the optimum qualifications or experience for a good sentencer.

4.   In view of the central role of magistrates in our sentencing system it is perhaps surprising how little empirical research has been conducted in this area. A valuable recent study, however, is that of Ralph Henham, entitled *Sentencing Principles and Magistrates' Sentencing Behaviour* (1990). This study aimed, *inter alia*, to examine the relationship between the social background of magistrates, their sentencing objectives and their application of sentencing principles. Although the official aim in the recruitment of magistrates is to appoint a fair representation of all responsible groups in society, research findings suggest that this aim is not realised in practice. Henham found that the available figures reveal a "predominantly middle-class bias in the social class composition of the magistracy" (*ibid.* p. 83). But he warns against any simplistic assumption that this lack of social balance amongst magistrates is automatically reflected in their sentencing behaviour. Henham later concluded:

> "The results presented [here] demonstrate again the difficulty of finding any consistent associations between magistrates' social background characteristics and their sentencing behaviour. (See Hood (1972), pp. 140–1). However, the presence of some statistically significant relationships does indicate that it is an area which deserves close examination and that it is an important aspect of the overall sentencing process. The implication is simply that magistrates' approach to different sentences and sentencing principles is not explicable solely in terms of the influence of certain social background characteristics. This particular study did not attempt to investigate the influence of such factors in producing sentencing disparities whilst Hood's (*ibid.*, p. 140) study did attempt to take his analysis that one step further. It was concluded that differences in social background characteristics alone did not account for magistrates' sentencing disparity. Although the findings presented here would tend to support such a view from an empirical perspective they would also support the notion that the interrelationship of all significant variables is most crucial, particularly the influence of local bench policy" ((1990), p. 175).

Race and Sentencing

The treatment of ethnic minorities under the criminal justice system is a subject of much recent interest. (See Report of the NACRO Race Issues Advisory Committee (1986), *Black People and the Criminal Justice System*; G. Mair, "Ethnic Minorities, Probation and the Magistrates Courts" (1986) 26 B.J. Crim. 147 and I. Crow, "Black People and Criminal Justice in the UK." (1987) 26 *Howard Journal* 303). A recent NACRO briefing paper compiled statistics and research findings on this subject and voiced concern that the 16 per cent of prisoners in England and Wales from ethnic minorities represents more than three times their proportion in the general population (see NACRO (1991), *Race and Criminal Justice*). In particular, there is a need for more research into whether black prisoners have fewer previous convictions than white prisoners sentenced for the same offence type. A suggestion for reform which has been urged by NACRO is the alteration of recruitment and promotion policies so as to ensure that ethnic minorities are better represented in senior criminal justice posts. Their under-representation at present is a cause for disquiet.

To what extent can differential sentencing be seen as an explanation for the disproportionate number of black people in prison? McConville and Baldwin's research, "The Influence of Race on Sentencing in England" (1982), found no evidence of systematic bias along racial lines in Crown Court sentencing although, as they observe, this does not rule out the possibility of discrimination at earlier stages in the criminal justice process. (Also see I. Crow and J. Cove, "Ethnic Minorities and the Courts" [1984] Crim. L.R. 413; and I. Brown and R. Hullin, "A Study of Sentencing in the Leeds Magistrates' Courts: The Treatment of Ethnic Minority and White Offenders" (1992) 32 B.J. Crim. 41).

In a major piece of research, funded by the Commission for Racial Equality, Roger Hood attempted to overcome the methodological problems of earlier studies and to assess whether the criminal courts are guilty of discrimination against ethnic minorities when passing sentence.

Roger Hood, *Race and Sentencing* (1992), pp. 179–192

This study has confirmed what has for long been suspected, namely that, to a very substantial degree, the over-representation of Afro-Caribbean males and females in the prison system is a product of their over-representation among those convicted of crime and sentenced in the Crown Courts. The best estimate that it is possible to make from this study is that 80 per cent of the over-representation of black male offenders in the prison population was due to their over-representation among those convicted at the Crown Court and to the type and circumstances of the offences of which black men were convicted. The remaining 20 per cent, in the cases of males but not females, appeared to [be] due to differential treatment and other factors which influence the nature and length of the sentences imposed: two thirds of it resulting from the higher proportion of black defendants who pleaded not guilty and who were, as a consequence, more liable on conviction to receive longer custodial sentences....

... Furthermore, black defendants were at a disadvantage both because of decisions they made and decisions made about them during the processing of cases before they appeared for sentence. They were more likely to be remanded in custody by magistrates who committed them for trial, even taking into account the seriousness of the charges against them and other factors which might legitimately have had an effect on the decision whether to give bail. They were much less likely to have had a social inquiry report prepared on their background, mainly because a considerably higher proportion of them signified their intention to plead not guilty, but also because fewer who pleaded guilty were reported on, although, the reasons for this are not known.

Being already in custody, pleading not guilty, and not having a report were all associated with a higher probability of receiving a custodial sentence or with a lengthier sentence. And all of them, of course, limit the possibilities for effective pleas in mitigation. Those who have been in custody have less opportunity to show that they have been of exemplary behaviour or have sought to make amends by, say, entering regular employment since they were charged with the offence. Those who deny the offence cannot suddenly, on being found guilty, convincingly express remorse. For those without social inquiry reports there is often insufficient information on hand to put the offence in its social context and no opportunity to take advantage of a specific proposal from a probation officer for an alternative sentence to custody. It would appear, therefore, that ethnic minority defendants were inadvertently subjected to a form of indirect discrimination at the point of sentence due to the fact that they chose more often to contest the case against them. Because of the way that the system works to encourage guilty pleas through a "discount" on sentence, which has been shown to produce a substantial reduction, and because it is the policy of the Probation Service not generally to make social inquiry reports on those who intend to contest the case against them, black defendants obviously put themselves at greater risk of custody and longer sentences....

... This research has also revealed a rather complex pattern of racial disparities in the sentences imposed. It should be recognised that there was no evidence of a "blanket" race or colour discrimination against all ethnic minority defendants, male or female. In most respects, Asian offenders did not fare worse than whites nor did all Afro-Caribbeans. Whether they did or did not depended on a number of factors: the seriousness of the case, age, employment status, whether they had pleaded not guilty, and, above all, the court centre to which they had been committed for trial [and] the judge before whom they appeared for sentence, some of whom appeared to sentence a considerably lower proportion of black defendants to custody than would have been expected. At Coventry, for example, white defendants were much more likely to receive a custodial sentence than whites dealt with elsewhere in the West Midlands, particularly at nearby Birmingham. On the other hand, although blacks at Coventry more often got a custodial sentence than blacks at Birmingham, they were more leniently treated [than] either whites or Asians at Coventry.

Taking the total number of male cases dealt with over the whole of the West Midlands, and controlling for the nature of the offences and several other legally relevant variables, the apparent differences in the proportionate use of custody between white, black and Asian males dealt with by these courts was considerably reduced from eight percentage points to about two-and-a-half points. Thus, a relatively small difference remained. Depending on the basis of the comparison, a black offender had a probability of receiving a custodial sentence about five to eight per cent higher than a white offender. Asians, on the other hand, had about a four per cent lower probability. Given the number of cases which appeared before these courts in the course of a year, these differences were sufficiently large to be to the disadvantage of a considerable number of black defendants especially when combined with the longer sentences imposed on the higher proportion of them who had pleaded not guilty.

But does this amount to evidence of discrimination? Or, to put it another way: is the evidence consistent with a pattern of discrimination rather than a residue of unexplained variation?

It is true, of course, that no statistical study can control for all the variables which might affect differences between cases ... [but] ... It is difficult to imagine what other legally relevant variables not already taken into account could explain the fact that for every 100 black males sentenced to custody at Birmingham about 130 black males were given a custodial sentence at the Dudley courts, and even more at Warwick or Stafford.

It is therefore apparent that the failure to find a large overall difference in the use of custody for blacks, whites and Asians in the West Midlands as a whole was a product of the fact that by far the largest proportion of cases in the sample had been dealt with at Birmingham Crown Court, a court with no overall racial bias in its sentencing patterns as far as the use of custody was concerned.

Leaving Birmingham aside, there were substantial racial differences in the sentencing patterns of the other courts and it seems inconceivable that similar variations would not be found in other regions of the country. It would not need very many courts to behave as the Dudley courts and Warwick and Stafford appear to do, for it to have a considerable impact on the proportion of black offenders in the prison system: especially when one bears in mind that not only are they more readily sentenced to custody but, because they are more likely to contest the case, they have longer sentences to serve.

When one contrasts the overall treatment meted out to black Afro-Caribbean males one is left wondering whether it is not a result of different racial stereotypes operating on the perceptions of some judges. The greater involvement of black offenders in street crime and in the trade in cannabis, their higher rate of unemployment, their greater resistance to pressures to plead guilty, and possibly a perception of a different, less deferential, demeanour in court may all appear somewhat more threatening. And, if not threatening, less worthy of mitigation of punishment. It was significant that being unemployed increased the risk of a black male getting a custodial sentence, but not, in general, for a white or an Asian offender. In contrast, the better financial and employment status of the Asians and their more socially integrated households, when judged by white standards, as well as the fact that they were much more likely to be first-time offenders, may have meant that they were probably able to present themselves as less threatening, and more worthy of mitigation than either whites or blacks ... But without research which would allow the investigation of judicial attitudes towards, and perceptions of, racially related differences in crime patterns and in cultural responses to the criminal justice system, all this for the moment must remain speculation. It cannot be doubted that such a programme of research is now needed.

What conclusions of a practical kind can be drawn from this study? First, that the research has revealed a complex picture of the way in which race appears to have affected the pattern of sentencing. In doing so, it has led to some uncomfortable conclusions for those whose duty it is to sentence offenders. It will not be possible any more to make the claim that all the differences in the treatment of black offenders occur elsewhere in the criminal justice system. At least some of it occurs in the courts, and more often in some localities than others. Much will be achieved if judges recognise this. One aim of studying sentencing by empirical methods is to help stimulate reassessment of attitudes and judicial responses. Previous research has shown how unaware judges may be of their own practices, let alone those of their colleagues. It may be that some are not yet sufficiently sensitive to the way in which racial views and beliefs may influence their judgement.

[Also], there are obvious implications relating to the duty placed on the Secretary of State by Section 95(1)(b) [of the Criminal Justice Act 1991] to "publish such information as he considers expedient for the purpose of ... facilitating the performance ... [by persons engaged in the administration of criminal justice] ... of their duty to avoid discriminating against any persons on the grounds of race or sex or any other improper ground." To do this it will be essential for the Crown Court to monitor the ethnic origin of all persons appearing before them. If the self-reflection on sentencing performance mentioned above is to be achieved, information on sentencing dispositions, analysed by ethnic origin, should be communicated to each judge and to the court as a whole annually. Only then will it be possible to detect whether sentencing patterns which might prove to be unfavourable to any ethnic minority are becoming established. Judges may regard this as an unnecessary imposition, or even as a slight on their integrity and impartiality. But in all walks of public life, servants of the Crown are being expected to monitor their performance, both with regard to its quality and to its even-handedness with respect to ethnicity and gender. There can be no good reason for judges to be excepted from this demand.

Notes

1. Hood's findings make reference to the over-representation of Afro-Caribbean males and females amongst those convicted of crime at the Crown Court and to the type and circumstances of their offences. He notes (at p. 170) that a higher proportion of black people were charged with crimes which could only be dealt with on indictment at the Crown Court, especially robbery – of the type often characterised as "mugging". He raises the pertinent question why this sort of offence should be seen as necessarily more serious than grievous bodily harm, which is capable of being dealt with by summary trial. Furthermore, Hood points out that Afro-Caribbeans were also more frequently involved in the supply of drugs, such as cannabis, and that these convictions involved the police in a more active role in which they were not simply responding to complaints from the public. There can be little doubt that black offenders' involvement in such cannabis-related crime has a distorting effect on the Crown Court conviction rate of this section of the community and, in turn, on their rate of imprisonment.

2. Hood's findings that black defendants were more likely to be refused bail by magistrates is also a cause for disquiet, as is the fact that they were much less likely to have been the subject of a social enquiry (now termed "pre-sentence") report. In a monitoring exercise carried out by the West Midlands Probation Service in 1986, 222 reports which were presented by the probation service to the criminal courts in Birmingham were studied. The survey took a rather small sample (54 were on black and 169 on white defendants), but its findings are still of interest. Black defendants were found to be more likely to receive an immediate or suspended custodial sentence than white defendants, and were less likely to receive a non-custodial alternative, such as a fine or a community service order. Moreover, where a social enquiry report recommendation was made for a non-custodial sentence, it was less likely to be followed in the case of black defendants, than in that of white defendants. It was not possible to explain away such disparities of treatment by saying that black defendants were involved in more serious offences; on the contrary, it appeared that white defendants had committed a higher proportion of violent offences. Of those convicted of burglary, black defendants were much more likely to receive a custodial sentence (79 per cent, as opposed to 25 per cent of the white defendants). (See West Midlands Probation Service, *Birmingham Social Enquiry Report Monitoring Exercise*, 1987). For similar findings which suggest disparity of treatment for Afro-Caribbean and Asian offenders, see R. Voakes and Q. Fowler, *Sentencing, Race and Social Enquiry Reports*, West Yorkshire Probation Service (1989). This research found that Afro-Caribbean and Asian offenders were more likely to be given a custodial sentence than white offenders. For a very useful discussion of these and other empirical studies, see NACRO briefing, *Race and Criminal Justice* (1991).

3. In an earlier survey entitled *Black People and the Criminal Justice*

System (Report of the NACRO Race Issues Advisory Committee (1986)), it was stated (at paragraph 3.40–3.41):

"We do not think it satisfactory that the key agencies or representative bodies of those working in the courts have no policies on equal opportunities, racial equality and racial discrimination. All national professional bodies whose members work in the court setting, including the Magistrates' Association, the Bar Council, the Law Society and the Justices' Clerks Society, should adopt equal opportunities policy statements which would outline their opposition to inequality of treatment based on colour or ethnic origin, as well as the steps which are being taken to eliminate racial discrimination from their organisation and from their provision of services. These policies, once adopted, should be made public, particularly to local black organisations.

We were concerned at the apparent lack of initiative to recruit black people to all agencies working in the court setting, and in particular at the lack of a forthright lead from the Lord Chancellor's Department. We see this as one of the major priority areas for action."

More recently, a NACRO study, *Black People's Experience of Criminal Justice* (E. Smellie and I. Crow (1991)) reported that some progress has occurred since these strictures were expressed. It stated (at p. 25):

"The Home Office has issued a circular on race issues to magistrates' court committees and clerks to the justices. The Justices Clerks' Society has published its own excellent code of practice. In 1988, the Bar Council's Race Relations Committee commissioned a survey on racial disadvantage at the Bar. This showed that 6 per cent of all pupils are black. About 9 per cent of barristers practising for less than five years were black, but fewer than 1 per cent were silks. In 1984, black barristers were identified in 48 sets of chambers. The figure is now nearer 180. Since the 1970's, there has been some concern about the low numbers of black solicitors. This concern led to the setting up of the Society of Black Lawyers and the Law Society's own Race Relations Committee which since 1986 has pressed for change. It has drawn up a code of practice on racial discrimination, adopted by the Law Society, which governs service delivery, acceptance of instructions and instructing barristers as well as employment within solicitors' time."

For a detailed breakdown of the representation of ethnic minorities employed within the system, see NACRO briefing, *Statistics on Black People Working in the Criminal Justice System* (1992). This report used the term "black" to cover all non-white ethnic groups. It found that only one per cent of police officers was black and that, of these officers, 92 per cent were constables. The most senior black officer was a chief superintendent. Although merely two per cent of lay magistrates were black in 1987, some attempt was being made to improve upon this as five-and-a-half per cent of magistrates appointed in 1989 were black. However, in 1992, none of either the 76 stipendiary magistrates, or the 263 justices' clerks, was black. Of solicitors holding practising certificates in 1992, two per cent were black, whilst six per cent of practising barristers in 1988 were thought to be black. Just two per cent of assistant recorders, and one per cent of both recorders and circuit judges were believed to be black. Amongst the senior echelons of the judiciary, all were white in 1992. In the probation service, three per cent of maingrade officers in 1991 were black (or, at least, amongst those whose racial origin was identified). In 1992, there were no black chief probation officers or deputy chief probation officers. (The sources of all these statistics can be found in the NACRO (1992) report).

4.   In looking at the various studies which have investigated the treatment of ethnic minorities in the criminal justice system, it should be remembered that the *perception* of their treatment by members of these groups may be at least as important as whether there actually is any demonstrable proof of unequal treatment. This point is well made in the following extract.

Iain Crow, "Black People and Criminal Justice in the U.K.", *Howard Journal*, Vol. 26, 1987, pp. 311–312.

Although the information that is available about black people and criminal justice in this country is limited in several respects, one of the things the material does illustrate is the inter-relatedness of the criminal justice process. The interdependence of the criminal justice system is becoming increasingly recognised. It needs to be realised that this interdependence also extends to and effects the way black people experience the system. Thus, discrimination at one part of the process, direct or indirect, is likely to feed through to other parts and reinforce black people's perception of the whole system as racist. This can only have disastrous consequences. The research to date shows that undoubtedly policing is a major problem area. But there is no basis for complacency elsewhere in the system. Anti-racist policies need to be pursued by the courts, the probation services and the prison service as much as by the police. Surveys which have enquired into black peoples' views of criminal justice show that there is a lack of confidence in the U.K. criminal justice system. The quality of justice is not solely a matter of concern for black people, however: the importance of justice being seen to be manifestly fair and equal is something that concerns us all...

One of the main problems, as far as the criminal justice system is concerned is that it is almost wholly a white dominated structure and this is reflected in the way it is staffed. Whether one looks at the police, judiciary, magistracy, probation service or Boards of Visitors, ethnic minority representation is minimal and, where it does occur, is rarely found at the more senior levels. Clearly there are many problems to be overcome, not least the fact that suspicion of the criminal justice system makes it difficult for those from ethnic minority backgrounds to become part of it. Realistically, adequate ethnic minority involvement in the criminal justice system may take some time to achieve. But a more immediately achievable aim should be to give those who already operate the system an increased amount of training in working in a multi-racial society. Although some training along these lines already occurs, a recent report suggests that there is still much room for development (NACRO *Black People and the Criminal Justice System*, 1986).

White cultural dominance extends to the research itself. Much of what has been reported here is the result of data collected by white researchers and officials. What it fails to do, so far at least, is adequately comprehend black people's experience of the criminal justice process. For example, whether or not there is any objective proof of bias in sentencing, the reality for the young black person in a courtroom is that of being surrounded by white authority. The black community's knowledge of the criminal justice system is less likely to be found in academic journals. This article has highlighted the fact that, although research on ethnic minorities and criminal justice in the U.K. is increasing, there are still many respects in which it is inadequate. The lack of a black perspective is one of these inadequacies. What is needed is more research by black researchers and the incorporation of different strands of research, reflecting more adequately ethnic minority perspectives. It is also important to recall what was said at the beginning of this article: that black people have become impatient with research in other areas, often feeling that what is needed is not research but action. Future research on criminal justice matters should therefore be capable of being demonstrably related to developments in policy and practice. This need not dilute the quality of research. But, if research becomes seen as merely a substitute for action, this will engender cynicism among black people about it, decrease their inclination to co-operate in it and this, in turn, *will* affect the quality of the research and thus diminish its value.

One way in which both research and policy could be advanced significantly and soon is by the extension of ethnic monitoring. This should cover the staffing of criminal justice agencies, the way different ethnic groups are dealt with by those agencies and the availability of services for black offenders. There is no reason in principle why existing statistical series should not incorporate ethnic data in the same way they currently do age and sex. Individual courts and probation services could also benefit from maintaining ethnic records on a local basis.

Development of Education and Training Schemes

What degree of expertise or specialisation is required by sentencers? Naturally, the sentencer needs to be adequately informed about the nature and purpose of the measures at his or her disposal. In addition, one would hope he has an awareness of the overall values and aims of the penal system and the possible difficulties and consequences of adopting certain measures. More specifically, this involves questions relating to the justice of imposing particular penalties, and the likely personal and social effects on the offender. In this respect the sentencer is called on to display not only a knowledge of individual measures, but also some penological insight and awareness of how other sentencers might act in similar cases. While it is clear that lay sentencers cannot be assumed to have such a knowledge, it is equally true that practising lawyers may not come to the bench so qualified. Radzinowicz and King note:

> "It is only comparatively recently that criminal law has ceased to be a Cinderella of legal education. Criminology, though fast gaining recognition, is still an optional extra even for those planning to work in the criminal courts ... Yet some understanding of the factors affecting crime and the penal system is surely essential. So is some direct knowledge of penal institutions" ((1977), p. 251).

Training for magistrates has developed in a piecemeal fashion. From the 1920s the Magistrates' Association encouraged justices to undergo some measure of training, usually in the form of meetings, conferences and literature. But such schemes were not given a statutory basis until 1949, and training did not become compulsory for newly appointed magistrates until the beginning of 1966. A further stage in these developments, preceded by much debate during the late 1970s, was the introduction of compulsory refresher courses, eventually agreed to by the Lord Chancellor for all magistrates appointed after the beginning of 1980. (For a detailed account of these developments, see Sir Thomas Skyrme, *The Changing Image of the Magistracy* (1979), pp. 64–70).

The following extract by John Baldwin reports on some research which set out to assess the effectiveness of the compulsory training scheme for magistrates in the early 1970s.

John Baldwin, "The Compulsory Training of the Magistracy" [1975] Crim. L.R. 634–643.

The reliance of our legal system upon laymen is one of its highly distinctive characteristics. In the case of the lay magistracy, the individuals involved are no longer the untrained amateurs they once were. On the contrary, magistrates appointed in recent years are obliged, as a condition of their appointment, to attend a basic training course of some depth and intensity. It is not always appreciated that in any year almost a half of all those sentenced to terms of imprisonment are sent to prison by magistrates. Their very considerable powers are, then, indisputable. At a time when the administration of justice in magistrates' courts is being criticised on the grounds of bias, inconsistency, capriciousness and so forth, it becomes important to examine the compulsory training that magistrates receive and to explore ways in which it might be made more relevant to changing conditions. Somewhat surprisingly, remarkably little is known about the training that newly-appointed magistrates are given and it is the purpose of this paper to examine in some detail the basic training given to a sample of magistrates who were appointed in 1971 and 1972....

... At the risk of some oversimplification, it can be said that the main thrust of basic training is concerned not so much with legal and procedural matters as with the more general development of what is known as a "judicial approach", though some knowledge of court procedure, rules of evidence and sentencing options is required. Nothing of substance is known about how basic training courses are received by magistrates or indeed about how the training requirements are put into practice. This being the case, the present writer, under the auspices of the Institute of Judicial Administration and with the co-operation of the Lord Chancellor's Office and the Magistrates' Association, carried out a small-scale study investigating the reactions of a group of relatively recently trained magistrates to the basic training they had received.

[Baldwin goes on to give details of his survey, based on a nine-page questionnaire sent to a sample of 372 magistrates, appointed 1971–2, which included magistrates from 128 benches. The purpose was to seek the views of these magistrates on their experience of basic training, to gather information about their social characteristics, and to obtain their opinions on how basic training courses might be improved.]

The Findings

Turning to the replies to the questionnaires, three main results emerged from the analysis very clearly, and in the remainder of this article each of these findings will be discussed in some detail. First, there can be no doubt that, however one approaches the question, this sample of magistrates, taken as a whole, were well-satisfied with the basic training they had received; secondly, there appears to be a relatively widespread disregard of fundamental requirements of the basic training syllabus; and thirdly, there are enormous variations in the depth and variety of courses offered among benches and important differences in particular between urban and county benches . . . .

. . . [T]here can be little doubt that there is considerable scope for improving basic training courses if the magistrates' own views on training are heeded. It is important to bear in mind, when discussing their views, that the respondents were not on the whole a critical group. On the contrary, they tended to be by and large very enthusiastic about training and by no means dissatisfied with the training they had been given. This makes their comments, and particularly their opinions about the way their courses might have been improved, the more significant . . . . It is worth drawing particular attention to two points which were raised with relative frequency by respondents.

The first concerns the view expressed by many magistrates that more time could usefully have been devoted in basic training to sentencing exercises and to other particular exercises which are not at present a required part of basic training. This was indeed the most commonly suggested improvement . . . . Not all those responsible for ogranising training courses would perhaps agree on this point and there is certainly a danger that magistrates can participate in too many simulated exercises. There is nevertheless reason to believe that other forms of practical exercises than those concerned with sentencing may be no less valuable. As has already been noted, only a very small minority of respondents had had the opportunity of participating in these. Many magistrates indicated, for example, that they would greatly have welcomed the opportunity of participating in some form of "mock court" prior to adjudicating on the bench or in an exercise on fine enforcement. Furthermore, exercises concerned with the granting of bail could perhaps be particularly valuable. There is no doubt that more public criticism attaches nowadays to disparities and inconsistencies between courts in this regard than is the case for instance, with sentencing decisions. Almost one in three of the respondents spontaneously drew attention to practical exercises of this nature and there is little doubt that thought should be given to the more extensive use of this method of teaching than has hitherto been the case.

The second point worthy of special mention concerns the relative infrequency with which Justices' Clerks and senior Justices were freely available to engage in informal discussion with newly-appointed justices . . . . One in three respondents would have welcomed greater opportunity to discuss cases informally. Almost one in 10 of the magistrates reported that the Clerk or senior colleagues were never available for such discussion and a further one in three stated that they were available no more than occasionally. This is regrettable since informal discussion was seen by those who had been able freely to consult Clerks or colleagues as being one of the most beneficial forms of training, particularly in the first months of their appointments and it is certainly the case, at least as far as this sample of magistrates is concerned, that there is much to be gained from such discussion.

Suggestions as to possible improvements in basic training have, of course, been implicit in much of the earlier part of this paper. Perhaps the most important implication of the results of this relatively small-scale study can scarcely be stressed too strongly – this relates to the rather widespread non-observance in many areas of the basic requirements of training. It may be argued that since the vast majority of magistrates continue voluntarily to pursue further training courses, such defects are fairly quickly remedied. This is not necessarily the case, however, since not only is the timing of some aspects of basic training crucial but it should be remembered that further training courses fulfil purposes other than those important in basic training. As the administration of justice in magistrates' courts becomes increasingly complex and on that account alone raising fundamental questions about the adequacy of existing training requirements, it is regrettable that the relatively undemanding standards of the basic training syllabus should fail to be met on such a wide scale. Insofar as this failure reflects a lack of commitment in the provision of training, it can only lend weight to the arguments of those who see the magistracy as lacking the expertise and judicial temperament necessary to the equitable administration of justice.

Note

1. One of the important points to emerge from Baldwin's study is the rather reticent attitude of professional lawyers to the idea of training for sentencers. We shall return to this subject later. But consider the following, more recent assessment of magistrates' training and the role of justices' clerks.

A. J. Turner, "Sentencing in the Magistrates' Court", in *Sentencing, Judicial Discretion and Training*, **(C. Munro and M. Wasik eds., 1992), pp. 196–200.**

In January 1990 there were 28,660 lay magistrates and 64 stipendiaries in post in 550 petty sessional divisions, with the number of stipendiaries expected shortly to rise by a small number.

The aim in recruiting magistrates is to achieve a cross-section of all the responsible elements in society, though some studies have revealed an imbalance in class and occupations. Such results are not particularly surprising. The work is very demanding and involves a substantial commitment in terms of time and, in some cases, financial sacrifice. Furthermore, magisterial law is becoming more and more complicated, and this is by no means limited to sentencing. Clerks are there to advise, but justices must have the capacity to comprehend and apply that advice. Clearly, there needs to be a minimum intellectual standard.

Justices appointed since 1980 are subject to obligatory, continuing training. The Judicial Studies Board has produced a handbook containing guidance on possible topics and how to organise and run courses. However, the only subject which *must* be included in the further training (Stage 3) syllabus is chairmanship. Moreover, the minimum requirement for Stage 3 is only 12 hours in each triennium. The Criminal Justice Act 1991 alone requires a minimum of 11 hours' training, and for many justices this follows closely upon the extensive training provided on the Children Act 1989.

Responsibility for organising magistrates' training rests with magistrates' courts committees, of which there is one in every non-metropolitan county and metropolitan district, elected by the justices themselves and their training officers, usually justices' clerks. The only external control over the training programme is that the approval of the Lord Chancellor is required under section 63 of the Justices of the Peace Act 1979 for course expenses to rank for grant.

Thus it can be seen that the system of summary justice depends heavily on lay volunteers, of whom only the more recently appointed have to undergo any continuing instruction at all. Even then, the minimum required is very inconsiderable (apart from special cases like the Children Act 1989). There is almost total discretion vested in the courts committee and its training officer as to subjects and teaching methods, and there is little effective external control.

The only legally qualified officer required to be in post in a petty sessional division is the clerk to the justices. Neither statute nor rules state that he, or one of his qualified staff, must be in court when magistrates are adjudicating in criminal cases. However, it would be unthinkable nowadays for a lay bench to sit without a clerk, and it could justify an application for judicial review if it were ever to happen.

The "job description" of a justices' clerk as gathered from the various pieces of primary and delegated legislation which place duties or confer powers upon him, comprises an amalgam of judicial, advisory and administrative functions. Of these responsibilities, one might reasonably consider the advisory role to be paramount. However, the reality is that clerks to the justices are being pressured more and more to consider themselves as "managers" and "finance directors" of their courts, particularly with the commencement of cash-limiting in April 1992, and these days sit in court only infrequently.

Government responsibility for magistrates' courts passed on April 1, 1992 from the Home Office to the Lord Chancellor's Department. This may presage major change. Ultimately, it may lead to the creation of a new Ministry of Justice. Certainly, there are hopes that it will strengthen the independence of magistrates. The Home Office was (and remains) also responsible for the police, prison and probation services, whose interests can be different from those of the courts. It will be some time, however, before the future shape of the service, if it is to be radically changed, will become clear. It is understood that various administrative changes are being considered to accompany this move, including the establishment of a court inspectorate, a reduction in the number of courts committees, and the establishment of chief executives to advise those committees, who will probably be persons qualified to be clerks to the justices themselves. Whether this will result in justices' clerks reverting to a mainly legal role, or at least gaining more time to discharge their advisory duties, is, however, uncertain. I certainly hope so, but experience elsewhere in the public sector does not give cause for optimism. These days, there are few public servants belonging to one of the professional categories who do not have to participate in management and financial matters, whether or not they are qualified and competent to do so.

In practice, most sittings of magistrates' courts are delegated by clerks to the justices to court clerks. The minimum qualification required to act as a court clerk may come as a surprise to some readers. I cannot think of any other court of judicial tribunal in England and Wales which is not required to include, either as a member or as an advisor of its adjudicating panel, a professionally qualified lawyer. Such is the case in the magistrates' court, however, despite the importance of its work and the gravity of many of its decisions. This arises because the Diploma in Magisterial Law, a qualification peculiar to the service as the name implies, is deemed to be an adequate qualification. Upon passing the Diploma, which is about to be reduced to a two-year, part-time course, a court clerk is deemed sufficiently qualified to take any kind of court, without requiring anyone's approval save that of the Justices' Clerk under whose direction he works. Moreover, magistrates' courts committees can authorise a person to act as a court clerk on completion of only the first year of this course.

The failure to stipulate a professional qualification for court clerks (that is, as a solicitor or barrister) as a present or future goal within the service has been criticised by many people, but the Home Office has so far refused to move on this issue. After the Lord Chancellor's Department has taken over responsibility for magistrates' courts, the position may change. We shall have to see. The Home Secretary's statement to the House of Commons, in which the change of responsibilities was announced, however, made no mention whatsoever of legal standards. He preferred, instead, to concentrate on the organisation of the service and its internal management structure.

Continuing education is a vital part of any profession, particularly one which is concerned with a constantly changing subject. Here again, however, the position is disappointing. There is no *requirement* for further training for clerks outside the

Law Society's points system which applies, of course, only to solicitor court clerks. Staff training, in general, has been slow to develop within the service. Legal knowledge and skills training, too, have been left to local discretion and have consequently been patchy. Most courts now find themselves within consortia which have appointed one or more regional training and development officers, but the latter are *trainers* rather than *legal trainers* and they depend, in practice, on justices' clerks to provide legal knowledge courses.

Nor is there any external mechanism for review of performance of justices' clerks, or for court clerks. A few progressive courts committees may have implemented staff appraisal schemes of some sort, and these may include a review of training undertaken and an attempt to assess the quality of advisory work. In my experience, however, such arrangements are extremely rare. Even where they are claimed to exist, it is difficult to see how an essentially lay committee elected by the bench or constituent benches (assuming the courts committee involves itself directly) can effectively monitor legal standards.

As far as sentencing is concerned, many studies have revealed that, while some efforts may be made to achieve internal consistency, there is little or no interest in finding out about and making comparisons with sentencing practice in other divisions. Government and other publications which include sentencing statistics may reach some magistrates, but these merely provide information. The average clerkship these days has in excess of 100 magistrates, and the trend towards larger courts is continuing, mainly for reasons of economy. It is difficult to see how fundamental change in an area's sentencing practice can be effected unless a substantial number of the magistrates meet and agree upon it. That prospect is fairly remote.

The perception tends to be a local one, with low emphasis on consistency. This may be because "consistency" is associated with "rigidity." Many magistrates (and I am sure, judges), when challenged about lack of conformity in sentencing decisions, will quickly make the point that no two cases are exactly alike. There is also the prominence of moral assessment and the strong desire to do justice in the particular case. The "individualised approach" to sentencing is very firmly entrenched indeed. Even if, "uniformity of approach" were achievable in the magistrates' court, we would still need to ensure that sentencers attached the same degree of importance to all the important variable factors, or sentencing disparities would continue.

Notes

1. Turner's description of the organisation of magistrates' courts today paints a far from reassuring picture of such matters as the training of court clerks, the workload of justices' clerks, and the extent of quality assessment. The lack of external control over the training programme for magistrates is also a cause for concern.

2. How does the training of magistrates contrast with that of legally qualified sentencers in the higher courts?

The following extract provides useful background information on the setting up and subsequent development of the Judicial Studies Board.

The Rt. Hon. Lord Justice Glidewell, "The Judicial Studies Board", in *Sentencing, Judicial Discretion and Training*, (C. Munro and M. Wasik eds., 1992) pp. 165–170

The Board's Origins

In July 1978 a Working Party on judicial studies and information, under the chairmanship of Lord Justice Bridge, published its report. This recommended that there should be set up a Judicial Studies Board, which would have responsibility for the provision and content of training for newly-appointed judges, for refresher seminars for existing judges, and for the dissemination of information to the judiciary in other ways. Most of the recommendations in this report were accepted, and led to the setting up of the "old" Judicial Studies Board in April 1979 under the chairmanship of Mr. Justice Watkins, V.-C., as he then was. The other members of the board included circuit judges, recorders, magistrates, and academic lawyers.

The "old" Board was concerned only with the criminal jurisdiction, and thus solely with the provision of training, instruction and information for the full-time and part-time judiciary of the Crown Court. The Board's principal purpose from its inception was to try to reduce inconsistencies in sentencing in the Crown Court. However, the seminars also covered topical problems in criminal law and procedure and the proper conduct of criminal trials. There were also background talks on particular subjects such as probation and the mentally disordered offender, and visits to penal institutions....

... In 1985 the then Lord Chancellor, Lord Hailsham, decided that the time was ripe to expand the sphere of activity of the Judicial Studies Board. A new Board was therefore created on October 1, 1985, which was given the task of providing training for the judiciary both in the criminal field and in the civil and family jurisdictions. At the same time the task of supervising the training of magistrates was transferred to the Board, and the supervision of the training of tribunal chairmen and members was added to its responsibilities.

The Operation of the Board

The Judicial Studies Board today comprises a Main Board, which is concerned with matters of policy and planning and the making of recommendations to the Lord Chancellor. The first chairman of the Main Board (until 1989) was Lord Justice Mustill, who was largely responsible for formulating the general principles upon which it now operates. The executive functions of the Board have been delegated to four committees. The first is the Criminal Committee, under the chairmanship of a judge of the Queen's Bench Division. In effect it is the successor to the old Judicial Studies Board, and it is concerned with the training of full-time and part-time judges of the Crown Court. The second is the Civil and Family Committee, which is jointly chaired by judges of the Queen's Bench and Family Divisions, and has the task of training the judiciary in these fields. The third is the Magisterial Committee. It is chaired by a circuit judge, and advises the Lord Chancellor on the training of magistrates. Fourthly, there is the Tribunals Committee, which has a similar function with regard to chairmen and members of tribunals....

Judicial Training Activity

The main activity of the Criminal Committee consists in organising and running two kinds of seminars for the Crown Court judiciary. First, there are induction seminars. Attendance at such a seminar and attachment to an experienced judge for one or two weeks is compulsory before a newly appointed assistant recorder is permitted to sit for the first time in the Crown Court. Secondly, there are refresher seminars for experienced circuit judges and recorders. A judge or recorder normally attends such a seminar at five-yearly intervals. In 1990 there were four induction seminars and refresher seminars in total, each of three-and-a-half to four days' duration.

The Board also conducts occasional single-subject seminars. Thus in 1990 there was a conference on accountancy for judges conducting fraud trials, which was held on a Saturday at the Board's headquarters in London, and later repeated in Manchester.

The Board also gives assistance with the running of one-day sentencing conferences on each circuit. Each member of the full-time and part-time judiciary is required to attend such a conference each year on his or her circuit. The name "sentencing conference" is to some extent a misnomer, because like the Board's refresher seminars these conferences often also include talks on, or discussions about, matters relating to the conduct of criminal trials as well as sentencing.

The Board's criminal induction courses include a considerable amount of instruction and help in the proper conduct of a criminal trial. This includes a mock trial, which runs throughout the conference in two-hour sessions with adjournments for lectures and discussions on other matters. The participants in the trial are the trainees themselves, with tutor-judges stopping the action periodically and posing a question or making a comment on what the judge should do at the particular point. This has been refined over the years and is a most useful, as well as entertaining, teaching method. The induction courses also include a considerable input on sentencing.

At the refresher courses, sentencing occupies a large part of the total time. Altogether there is a major session on sentencing each day throughout the seminar. Normally the participants are asked to discuss what sentence they would pass to meet a particular situation, and the decision of the Court of Appeal, Criminal Division, on the particular case is then announced and discussed, not always uncritically. In addition, the refresher seminars normally include talks on sentencing generally, on newly decided cases or changes in legislation, on prisons, and from a Senior Probation Officer.

In the last two years the criminal refresher seminars have invariably also been addressed by a representative of the Home Office on the proposals which led to, and the provisions of, the Criminal Justice Act 1991. The inclusion of these talks in the seminars is, in its way, a novel departure. It has provided an opportunity for the judiciary to learn at first hand from the Home Office something of their thinking, and at the same time to give the response of a group of senior circuit judges concerned with the administration of justice in the Crown Courts to the proposals in the Bill. It would not be right to say that the Home Office has adopted all the comments which have been made, but certainly I believe that the wording of the Act does reflect some of the representations made by the judiciary.

In its last report to the Lord Chancellor, the Judicial Studies Board made it clear that it has no responsibility for making policy in the fields of substantive law or procedure. This is especially true in relation to criminal sentencing. The Board's task is to give the judiciary information about guideline decisions given by the Court of Appeal, Criminal Division, under the Lord Chief Justice, and about other directions and advice. However, when a group of 50 or so experienced Crown Court judges are together, discussing sentencing or related matters, it is inevitable that problems that have arisen will be highlighted and suggestions will be made. The seminars are thus a useful vehicle for receiving such suggestions, which can then be discussed by the Board and, when appropriate, relayed to the Lord Chief Justice.

The Board's Criminal and Magisterial Committees have considered the extent to which it will be possible to give guidance to the judiciary and magistracy on the provisions of, and application of, the principles in the Criminal Justice Act. The problem is, of course, that the final word on the interpretation and application of the Act will have to come from the Court of Appeal, Criminal Division, (if not the House of Lords). Thus any view which is expressed at a seminar organised by the Board before that stage is reached will inevitably be subject to possible later correction. Nevertheless the Board envisages giving such guidance both to the Crown Court judiciary and to the magistracy. . . .

Notes

1. The Report of the Working Party, referred to by Lord Justice Glidewell and chaired by Lord Bridge, entitled *Judicial Studies and Information* (1978) stated that:

> "the judge called on to pass sentence in the Crown Court needs not only to be thoroughly well-versed in the law and practice directly relevant to any sentencing problem which may confront him but also to be thoroughly well informed on the extremely wide range of topics which are in different degrees indirectly relevant to his choice of sentencing options. Newly appointed judges do not in all, and perhaps not in many, cases bring with them to the bench the full measure of these desirable qualifications derived either from their previous forensic experience or from their own private investigations and studies."

This seemingly unexceptionable conclusion, and its concomitant proposals for a modest programme of judicial training, met with hostility from some judges. A notable critic of the training proposals, Lord Devlin, expressed the view that they appeared to him:

> "... even on the assumption that judges should be penologically minded, as a dazzling manifestation of the unacceptable face of socialism, that is, an excessive zeal for setting up at public expense institutions for regimenting people into doing things which any sensible person does for his own benefit, at his own expense, and in his own way ... When sentencing I did not feel handicapped by my ignorance of penal theory and criminology; I have not from my slight subsequent acquaintance with them discovered to what use I could have put them ... To offer a new judge a little learning is a dangerous thing; penology can be no exception to the rule that wisdom drinks deeply or tastes not." (Patrick Devlin, *The Judge* (1979), pp. 37–40).

2. The role of the Judicial Studies Board today extends beyond the original concentration on providing information about sentencing matters to judges in the higher courts. Moreover, in addition to the four committees of the Board, an Ethnic Minorities Advisory Committee was established in 1991. This Committee was responsible for organising race awareness seminars for judges – a scheme which started in 1994. These seminars include practical exercises to tackle racial stereotyping and they provide judges with the findings of relevant research on this subject.

3. Despite the extension of the activities of the Board to other areas of law, such as Civil and Family, it still retains an important function in the training of full-time and part-time judges of the Crown Court. But how thorough is this training? The following article provides an interesting insight into the short courses being provided in 1990 for part-time judges.

Clare Dyer, "Making a Snap Decision", *The Guardian*, February 14, 1990

Four times a year 30 to 35 lawyers in their late thirties and forties gather for three-and-a-half days at a college or country house not far from London ... These are the latest batch of assistant recorders, embarking on a path which could lead eventually to a seat on the high court or circuit bench. Most of the new recruits are barristers but the courses, run by the Judicial Studies Board, generally include a few solicitors. Circuit judgeships have been open to solicitors since 1972, and the Courts and Legal Services Bill, now going through parliament, will open a possible path to the high court bench.

Many will never end up on the bench but all will spend at least a month each year as part of the army of part-time judges shoring up the justice system. "Casuals" outnumber full-time judges by two to one, handling nearly 10 per cent of High Court work and 25 per cent of crown court work, at a fraction of the cost of full-time judges. The system has a dual function: keeping the crown courts from collapsing under the weight of crime, while at the same time testing the fledgling Solomons' judicial qualities. After three to five years – one or two for Q.C.s – assistant recorders who measure up can expect promotion to recorder, a permanent part-time job. In choosing assistant recorders, according to the official booklet on judicial appointments, "the Lord Chancellor is looking for practitioners of at least 35 and below 50 years of age, who are of above-average ability and judged to be so by the professional community, are professionally and personally suitable to sit judicially, and who seem likely to qualify in due course for promotion to recorderships."

Their 15 or 20 years in practice have been spent as professional partisans, pleading their clients' causes. Now, within three-and-a-half days, they must be transformed into neutral arbiters, ensuring justice for both sides. A visit to a prison and a young offenders' institution, a week shadowing a crown court judge on the bench, and they are ready to be let loose on real defendants, with power to send them to prison for years.

Most have some experience in the criminal courts but many have long since moved on from crime to other types of work. Some have never set foot in a criminal court. On the first day, a high court judge tells them how to prepare for and conduct a trial, and how to sum up to a jury. Later they will practise summing up and pronouncing sentence.

Day two is the highlight of the course – a mock trial in which the novice judges play all the roles, including defendants, counsel, jurors, witnesses and even a heckler in the public gallery. Two young men are charged with causing actual bodily harm and grievous bodily harm after a punch-up at a bus stop. The victim, a teenager out with his girl-friend, has a fractured jaw and pelvis, bruising and lacerations. Trying to escape his attackers, he dashed into the road and was run down by a car. Whether the defendants are liable for the road injuries is one of the issues.

Everything that could go wrong in a trial does, and experienced circuit judges constantly interrupt the action to discuss how a judge should handle the problem. One juror can't read; another, who turns out to be a former policeman, is challenged by defence counsel; a third is related to one of the defendants. Prosecution and defence lawyers make deliberate mistakes, and there is a "trial within a trial" about whether a defendant's "character" – his previous record – can be put before the jury.

The third day focuses on sentencing exercises. As homework before their arrival, the trainees are given examples of real cases – actual bodily harm, theft, burglary, wounding carrying imitation fire-arms, using threatening behaviour and causing death by dangerous driving – and asked what sentences they would impose. These are marked and compared with what the Court of Appeal thought the appropriate punishment.

On one recent course, the results showed "huge variations", according to one novice. "My impression was that those who didn't practice in the criminal courts were much more likely than others to impose prison sentences and to imprison for longer periods. I suppose they're representing Joe Public." A leading sentencing expert, David Thomas of Trinity Hall, Cambridge, delivers a lecture on the principles involved . . . .

. . . Is it enough? "Absolutely not, it barely breaks the ice. You learn on the job. It's really all too short. The idea's good but it's a drop in the ocean." In 1972, a committee of the law reform group Justice suggested a three- to six-month training period. In 1978, an official working party chaired by Lord Justice Bridge (now Lord Bridge, the Law Lord) recommended a two-week programme for those with no experience of criminal work.

"I think the three-and-a-half-day course should be extended to three weeks" said one new assistant recorder. "You have to distinguish between people doing crime all the time and those who are not, who do need more practice. Anyone who has never done criminal work must find it quite difficult. Summing up is difficult because every word will be pored over with a view to an appeal.

"The course is good as far as it goes, but in spite of the best efforts of those involved it can only be described as amateurish. It's dipping a toe in the judicial waters."

One problem is that for the barristers, a three-week course paying them less than £100 a day instead of their usual £500 to £1,000 a day would mean a significant loss of income. Most regard sitting their 20 days a year as an assistant recorder at £179 a day as a sufficient professional sacrifice.

If they eventually become circuit judges, they will be asked to attend a more advanced refresher seminar, also lasting three-and-a-half days, every five years. Courses concentrate mainly on crime but training in civil and family law was introduced in 1985.

Notes

1. It is clearly a step in the right direction that novice judges receive some training, albeit rather basic, and that the views expressed by Lord Devlin would find little support today. However, it must be seriously questioned whether such short courses are sufficient and whether it would not be better to insist on more intensive training in criminal law, procedure and sentencing before lawyers (especially those who lack experience of the criminal courts) become part-time judges in the Crown Courts. At present, it is still difficult to defend the training arrangements against charges of amateurism.

2. Recently, the Judicial Studies Board was responsible for supervising the training in relation to the implementation of the Criminal Justice Act 1991. This training took the form of nationwide seminars and the use of information packs prepared by specialists and distributed by the Board.

3. For an interesting discussion of the Australian sentencing system, see Austin Lovegrove, "Sentencing Guidance and Judicial Training in Australia", in *Sentencing, Judicial Discretion and Training* (C. Munro and M. Wasik eds., 1992), pp. 207–28. Lovegrove reports that little progress has been made towards judicial training for sentencers, with the exception of New South Wales and, to a lesser extent, Victoria. But with the

backing of the Australian Law Reform Commission, programmes of judicial education may perhaps be developed. (For further reading, see the Law Reform Commission (Australia) Discussion Paper No. 29 (1987) and the same Commission's Report No. 44, *Sentencing* (1988)).

4.   The Woolf Report made the following plea for further information for sentencers about prison conditions.

Prison Disturbances, April 1990: **Report of an Inquiry by Lord Justice Woolf and Judge Stephen Tumim, Cm. 1456 (1991), pp. 258–9.**

Great strides have been made in recent years in training Judges and Magistrates who are responsible for passing sentences on offenders. The time spent on training is, however, still limited. Part of that training involves making some visits to prisons. High Court Judges and Court of Appeal Judges who sit in the criminal division are not required to make any visits to prison establishments, but many do. When Judges and Magistrates visit prisons, however, they may have little, if any, opportunity to learn the views of prisoners.

It is unlikely that more than a small minority of the judiciary had any real knowledge of the appalling conditions in local prisons which contributed to the disturbances in April 1990. The information about prison conditions available to those who pass sentences, and about what actually happens to those who are sentenced, is still modest.

This needs to be remedied. We propose Judges and Magistrates should be given general information about the conditions within prisons to which those whom they have remanded in custody or sentenced are sent. If the prison is overcrowded, this is something of which the sentencer should be aware. They need to know about the regime to which they are likely to be subjected.

Judges and Magistrates need to know the likely facilities for education, training and treatment. They should know what the prospects are of prisoners going to Grendon prison, or an open prison, or an overcrowded local prison, and what will happen to the prisoners while they are there.

Judges and Magistrates need also to know the cost implications of the actions which they propose to take. They should have the opportunity to take these into account, to the extent to which they consider this is appropriate, when deciding on whether a person should be deprived of his freedom.

Judges and Magistrates need also to be aware of the alternatives to imprisonment, how their success compares with imprisonment and the comparative costs....

... We propose that much of the information which we believe is needed and to which we have referred should be provided to the judiciary by the Prison Service. The Judicial Studies Board is already involved on a limited scale. It could provide the machinery for making available to the judiciary the additional information which we consider the Prison Service should provide.

Some sentencers still take the view that what happens to a prisoner after sentence and the state of our prisons are of no concern to them when deciding what course to take in relation to defendants who appear before them. Some Magistrates' clerks are still advising Magistrates to this effect. We would suggest that this approach is wrong and should be authoritatively stated to be wrong. To be provided with information does not interfere with the independence of the judiciary. Such information is needed in order to perform satisfactorily the sentencer's difficult and demanding task of deciding whether someone needs to be deprived of his or her liberty and if so for how long.

II. INFORMATION FOR SENTENCERS

Although judges and magistrates have sole responsibility for sentencing offenders, they are dependent on other professions for the provision of reliable information about defendants who either plead or are found guilty. (For an invaluable study of the process between conviction and sentence, see Joanna Shapland (1981)). For example, the prosecution will present a summary of the facts of the case to the court, dealing with background information about both the offence and the offender. (See "Practice Direction (Crime: Antecedents)" [1966] 1 W.L.R. 1184). The "antecedents" evidence will also include, where applicable, the offender's previous convictions. A convicted person is also entitled to make a plea in mitigation. This is an opportunity to make known to the court, either in person or through the defence lawyer, the offender's attitude to the crime, his individual circumstances, his feelings of remorse and any other mitigating factors. (For a useful study of the content of mitigating speeches, see J. Shapland, *ibid*).

There are also other types of specialist reports which may be available (where appropriate) to sentencers, such as medical and psychiatric reports. It is also worth noting that a recommendation was made in the Woolf Report ((1991), paragraph 10.156) that serious thought should be given to requiring the Prison Service to provide the sentencing court, as a matter or routine, with a report on the behaviour of remand prisoners while in custody. The idea behind this suggestion is to encourage good behaviour by remand prisoners and to permit their sentence to reflect this.

A major development in the sentencing system over the past thirty years has been the role of the probation service in providing background information about defendants to assist sentencers in the Crown Courts and, to a lesser extent, in the magistrates' courts. Until the Criminal Justice Act 1991 was enacted, these reports were known as social enquiry reports, but they are now to be referred to as pre-sentence reports. The following section explains the growth of social enquiry work by the probation service and an assessment of the changes brought about by the 1991 Act.

The Growth of Social Enquiry Reports

Since its origins in the late nineteenth century, the probation service has been involved in preparing reports for the courts but, until the 1930s, it was confined to the assessment of an offender's suitability for probation. But it was recommended, in 1936, by the Departmental Committee on Social Services in Courts of Summary Jurisdiction, that the social enquiry work of the service should also extend to cases where a probation order is unlikely to be made. The Criminal Justice Act 1948 gave effect to this suggestion by requiring the probation service "to inquire, in accordance with any directions of the court, into circumstances or home surroundings of any person with a view to assisting the court in determining the most suitable method of dealing with his case." (Schedule 5, paragraph 3(5)).

The practice of social enquiry was considered in detail by the Inter-departmental Committee on the Business of the Criminal Courts (The Streatfeild Committee, Cmnd. 1289 (1961)) which, in Part B of its report, encouraged this development in the sentencing process. (Although the Committee was chiefly concerned with the higher courts, its report was of interest to sentencing practice generally). It referred to the growing emphasis on the offender's social and domestic circumstances, particularly where he is young or without previous convictions, and it dealt with the scope and content of probation officers' reports (see paragraphs 332–47). How far was an officer to go in advising the courts as to the most suitable sentence? The Committee stated:

> "We have no doubt that where a probation officer is reporting to the court on an offender, whether before trial or after conviction, and feels able to offer a reliable opinion which may be relevant to the court's consideration, the court should have the benefit of this assistance and should welcome rather than resent it. It is material which will usually not be available to the court from any other source and may therefore be essential if the sentence is to be passed on adequate information ... It is not a recommendation, but an opinion proffered for the assistance of the court on one aspect of the question before it." (paras. 344 and 346).

The Morison Report, Cmnd. 1650 (1962), whilst concurring with the wider use of social enquiry reports, was more cautious than Streatfeild in relation to officers expressing opinions about offenders' likely responses to measures other than probation. It stated that:

> "even the most experienced probation officer, with his wide knowledge of offenders and their records, would we believe, find difficulty at present in making such forecasts ... officers are not now equipped by their experience, and research cannot yet equip them, to assume a general function of expressing opinions to the court about the likely effect of sentences" (para. 41).

Yet despite this plea for caution, a Home Office circular (28/1971) encouraged probation officers to express opinions not only on the likely response of offenders to probation, but also to other forms of disposal. A later Home Office circular (195/1974) directed that "if an experienced probation officer feels able to make a specific recommendation in favour of (or against) any particular form of decision being reached he should state it clearly in his report." (Also see circulars 19/1983 and 92/1986).

Some writers were far from happy with the idea of probation officers making recommendations as to sentence. (For an interesting criticism of this practice, see Brian Harris (1979)). It was also not unknown for judges to criticise probation officers' recommendations as "unrealistic" (see *Smith* and *Woolland* [1978] Crim. L.R. 758; and also *James* [1982] Crim. L.R. 59).

The influence of probation officers' recommendations over the eventual sentence of the court has been the subject of much research and debate. It appeared that such recommendations were followed in about 80 per cent of cases (see Thorpe (1979); Ford (1972); and Thorpe and Pease (1976)) and this certainly suggests a considerable influence over sentencing decisions. On the other hand, it could be argued that the recommendations of officers were often merely predicting or anticipating the likely choice of sentence by the court. (For a discussion of the interaction between officer and sentencer in decision-making, see Davies (1974), pp. 26–30). Despite the need for caution in interpreting the "take-up" rate of recommendations, it seems likely that officers did achieve a degree of influence over sentencing decisions. The research of Hine *et al.* (1978), which used a simulated sentencing exercise to separate the various types of information available to a sentencer, did find evidence of probation officers' recommendations influencing magistrates. (For a useful analysis of this and other relevant research, see J. Roberts and C. Roberts (1982)).

But despite the steady growth of social enquiry work, and its increasing influence over court decisions, there were many criticisms relating to both the length and content of reports, and to the lack of uniformity of practice in their preparation. The Government made it clear that a review of the role of social enquiry reports was intended in its White Paper, *Crime, Justice and Protecting the Public*, Cm. 965 (1990) (paras. 3.10–11), where it was stated:

> "The Government proposes that before a court gives a custodial sentence, for offences triable summarily or either way, it should be required to consider a report from the probation service about the offender. Social Inquiry Reports (SIRs) are already considered in a great many cases. In 1987, the probation service prepared 144,000 SIRs for the magistrates' courts and 60,000 for the Crown Court. But the Government's proposal means taking a fresh look at the purpose, content and format of these reports. The purpose of requiring the courts to consider a report by the probation service when a custodial sentence is contemplated will be to provide the court with detailed information about how the offender could be punished in the community, so that option can be fully considered. Its purpose will not be to make recommendations about sentencing or to be a plea in mitigation. National standards are needed. So the content of the report will have to include:
>
> - details of a programme of activities which might enable the offender to make reparation through community service or a supervision programme tackling the offender's problems;
> - a description of the restrictions on liberty which the programme would involve;
> - information about the nature of the offence and the offender's attitude to it;

– essential background information about the offender; and
– an assessment of the offender's ability and willingness to tackle his or her offending behaviour.

More probation service reports would be needed and this risks adding to delays. If reports are to be produced quickly, efficiently and economically then it makes sense to have a standard format. There may also have to be changes in the way the probation service provides reports. The Home Office will discuss with judges, magistrates and the probation service the guidance and training which will be needed to ensure that the reports prepared for the courts are well written and effectively presented, and the organisational changes which may be needed to prevent delays."

Until this change of direction was signalled in the White Paper, there were some suggestions that the probation service might play a more positive role in persuading sentencers to change their sentencing habits, and argue more persuasively for non-custodial alternatives in their reports. (See, for example, J. Roberts and C. Roberts (1982); Bottoms and McWilliams (1979); and A. Willis in J. Pointing (ed., 1986)). But since the Government's proposals were first announced, it was clear that a different role was envisaged for the new "pre-sentence" reports (as they were to be known). It was highly significant that the White Paper stated that the purpose of requiring a court to consider a report is not for the probation service to make recommendations about sentencing. It is clear from the wording of the Criminal Justice Act 1991 that reports are now to be of relevance to the court's assessment of the seriousness of an offence, as well as to the suitability of an offender for a community sentence.

Sections 3 and 7 of the Criminal Justice Act 1991 (as amended by the Criminal Justice Act 1993)

PART I

POWER OF COURTS TO DEAL WITH OFFENDERS

Custodial Sentences

[For the text of sections 1 and 2, see p. 177]

3. – (1) Subject to subsection (2) below, a court shall obtain and consider a pre-sentence report before forming any such opinion as is mentioned in subsection (2) of section 1 or 2 above.
(2) Where the offence or any other offence associated with it is triable only on indictment, subsection (1) above does not apply if, in the circumstances of the case, the court is of the opinion that it is unnecessary to obtain a pre-sentence report.

(3) In forming any such opinion as is mentioned in subsection (2) of section 1 or 2 above a court –

   (a) shall take into account all such information about the circumstances of the offence or (as the case maybe) of the offence and the offence or offences associated with it (including any aggravating or mitigating factors) as is available to it; and
   (b) in the case of any such opinion as is mentioned in paragraph (b) of that subsection, may take into account any information about the offender which is before it.

(4) No custodial sentence which is passed in a case to which subsection (1) above applies shall be invalidated by the failure of a court to comply with that subsection but any court on an appeal against such a sentence –

   (a) shall obtain a pre-sentence report if none was obtained by the court below; and
   (b) shall consider any such report obtained by it or by that court.

(5) In this Part "pre-sentence report" means a report in writing which –

   (a) with a view to assisting the court in determining the most suitable method of dealing with an offender, is made or submitted by a probation officer or by a social worker of a local authority social services department; and
   (b) contains information as to such matters, presented in such manner, as may be prescribed by rules made by the Secretary of State.

[For the text of section 6, see pp. 291]

7. – (1) In forming any such opinion as is mentioned in subsection (1) or (2)(b) of section 6 above, a court shall take into account all such information about the circumstances of the offence or (as the case may be) of the offence and the offence or offences associated with it (including any aggravating or mitigating factors) as is available to it.

(2) In forming any such opinion as is mentioned in subsection (2)(a) of that section, a court may take into account any information about the offender which is before it.

(3) A court shall obtain and consider a pre-sentence report before forming an opinion as to the suitability for the offender of one or more of the following orders, namely –

   (a) a probation order which includes additional requirements authorised by Schedule 1A to the 1973 Act;
   (b) a community service order;
   (c) a combination order; and
   (d) a supervision order which includes requirements imposed under section 12, 12A, 12AA, 12B or 12C of the Children and Young Persons Act 1969 ("the 1969 Act").

(4) No community sentence which consists of or includes such an order as is mentioned in subsection (3) above shall be invalidated by the failure of a court to comply with that subsection, but any court on an appeal against such a sentence –

   (a) shall obtain a pre-sentence report if none was obtained by the court below; and
   (b) shall consider any such report obtained by it or by that court.

[NB. Sections 3 and 7 have been amended further by the Criminal Justice and Public Order Act 1994, Schedule 9, paragraph 40 – see Note 2 below].

Notes

1. What is the effect of a court's failure to comply with the Criminal Justice Act 1991, s. 3(1)? Section 3(4) states that a sentence will not be invalidated by such non- compliance, but on appeal against such a sentence, the court shall obtain and consider a pre-sentence report (PSR).

2. A court must obtain and consider a Pre-Sentence Report before deciding whether the seriousness of the offence necessitates a custodial sentence (unless it is an offence triable only on indictment and it is clear from the circumstances that a pre-sentence report is unnecessary). A court must also obtain and consider a PSR before deciding whether to impose a probation order (with additional requirements), a community service order, a combination order, and a supervision order (with additional requirements).

For a discussion of the impact of the Criminal Justice Act 1991, in relation to Pre-Sentence Reports, see N. Stone, "Pre-Sentence Reports, Culpability and the 1991 Act", [1992] Crim. L.R. 558; M. Wasik, "Rethinking Information and Advice for Sentencers" in *Sentencing, Judicial Discretion and Training* (C. Munro and M. Wasik eds., 1992); B. Gibson, "Information and Pre-Sentence Reports", (1992) 89 Law Society Gazette 28; S. Nunn, "Pre-Sentence Reports – A Defence Perspective" (1992) *Justice of the Peace*, 755.

It should also be noted that the 1991 Act has been amended by the Criminal Justice and Public Order Act 1994, Schedule 9, paragraph 40. The new provisions permit courts to pass a custodial or a community sentence without obtaining a Pre-Sentence Report, if satisfied that a report is not necessary in all the circumstances.

3. Pre-Sentence Reports can still be presented by the court liaison officer rather than the actual writer of the report. Apart from stating that a PSR means a report in writing, made or submitted by a probation officer or social worker, containing information to assist the court in deciding on the suitable sentence for an offender, there is little in the Act to prescribe the actual form that reports should take. Section 3(5)(b) states that PSRs are to be presented in accordance with the rules laid down by the Secretary of State and, in 1992, national standards were published, setting out the requirements for probation officers and social workers preparing PSRs (see below). In *Okinakan* (1992) 14 Cr. App. R. (S) 453, decided before the national standards were introduced, Lord Justice Taylor stated that, as long as a report is in writing and made or presented by a probation officer or social worker, and contains the necessary information about the defendant, it is for the trial court to decide whether a report is adequate for sentencing purposes and complies with the Act. The appellant contended that the trial court was wrong to treat a social enquiry report (dated March 26, 1992) as an acceptable Pre-Sentence Report, on the grounds that it was out of date by the time of his trial in October 1992 and that, as a result, the presentation of the report did not comply with the Criminal Justice Act 1991, s. 3(5). The Court of Appeal rejected this argument, deciding that there had been no failure to comply with the Act.

4. The Streatfeild Committee recommended that social enquiry reports were to be ready on (or in the event of) conviction of an offender so as to avoid delays in sentencing. Despite the obvious advantages of this practice, it raised problems in preparing reports on those intending to plead not guilty. In the mid-1970s, the National Association of Probation Officers expressed its disapproval of the preparation of reports in such circumstances. A Home Office circular (1977) urged the probation service to reconsider, stressing the inconvenience and delays that would result (and the risk of more custodial remands pending reports). Although practice varied in relation to reports on not guilty pleas, since the mid 1980s in particular, the general approach of the probation service was not to prepare reports before the trial of those intending to plead not guilty. This led to defendants being sentenced in the absence of a report. This could also occur where a defendant made a late change of plea (to guilty) just before, or on the day of his trial. Since the Criminal Justice Act 1991, Pre-Sentence Reports will be mandatory in many cases where formerly a court might have proceeded to sentence without awaiting a report. The National Standards for the Supervision of Offenders in the Community (1992, Chap. 2, paras. 28–33) state:

"At the Crown Court there is need to ensure as few and as short adjournments as possible for PSRs to be prepared: the standard requires probation services to be able to prepare some PSRs at court, and to seek a common understanding locally with the judiciary about the commissioning of PSRs ... In preparing reports for the Crown Court, the objectives should be:

- to avoid, as far as possible, adjournments for reports, by preparing PSRs in advance of trial whenever sufficient notice of a guilty plea to the principal charge(s) in a case is given;
- where adjournment for a PSR is necessary, to prepare the report as expeditiously as possible, especially where the offender is remanded in custody, the trial judge wishes the report to be available quickly or there is any other reason for urgency, consistent with the requirements of this standard;
- to seek to operate these arrangements on a basis of mutual understanding with the judiciary and others in the criminal justice system, respecting, for example, trial judges' wishes and the professional advice of report writers as to the length of time needed for reports to be prepared to the requirements of this standard...

Probation services should make some provision at each Crown Court centre to write quickly PSRs which do not require a lengthy adjournment...

The preparation of PSRs in magistrates' and youth courts differs from the preparation of reports in the Crown Court: most significantly because it will normally be impracticable to provide dedicated PSR-writing teams in magistrates' or youth courts and, therefore, to respond very quickly to requests for short notice reports. Nevertheless, all reports should be prepared as expeditiously as possible – particularly, for example, in more straight-forward cases and those where the offender is remanded in custody awaiting sentence..."

The national standards contain reference to the possibility of preparing some reports, in writing, on the same day that they are requested (paragraph 29). It is also stated that, wherever possible, a "PSR requested on adjournment on a remand prisoner should ... be completed in seven days" (para. 32). Without a considerable increase in funding and resources, it might be questioned whether the probation service can meet this challenge and still provide reports of the requisite quality. This was certainly the fear of the National Association of Probation Officers. However, pre-sentence report pilot trials in the Crown Court were conducted in five regions, in 1991, to identify organisational implications of the new Pre-Sentence Report provisions. The pilot scheme, overseen by a National Steering Committee and evaluated by the Research and Planning Unit of the Home Office, did not find that the quality of reports necessarily suffers if speed and efficiency is increased. In the report of the pilot scheme, *Justice Informed* (Vol. I, 1992), it was stated that "instances of poor quality and incompleteness in report writing were not generally found to correlate with speed of production or other unusual factors and procedures introduced by the pilots. Poor quality when evident, seemed to be a function of variables *not* unique to this project" (p. 20). In *Justice Informed* (Vol. II, App. I) Loraine Gelsthorpe and Peter Raynor reported on their evaluation study of the quality of Pre-Sentence Reports in the pilot scheme. They concluded (at paras. 2.1–2.5):

"This study provides no general support for the view that faster reports are necessarily of lower quality than reports for which longer completion times are allowed. Regardless of completion time there are major variations in quality which require attention through quality assurance and training.

The only area in which fast-completion reports scored significantly lower than reports with longer completion times was in the discussion of offending behaviour, where they were less likely to give a clear account of the offence, an explanation of the offence or an evaluation of response to past sentences. This is not unimportant, as assessment of offending seems likely to be a major function of pre-sentence reports. Fast reports were also less likely to suggest community options which required consultation with a third party before presenting the report, and less likely generally to have a wide range of sources for the information they contained ... Fast reports were less likely to propose a probation order with additional requirements."

The following extract summarises the main conclusions and recommendations arising out of the pilot trials conducted in the five Crown Court centres (Birmingham, Bristol, Lincoln, Newcastle-upon-Tyne, and Southwark) between May and December 1991.

J. K. Bredar, "Justice Informed: The Pre-Sentence Report Pilot Trials in the Crown Court", Vol. I (1992), pp. 34–40.

Findings and Recommendations

All who participated in the pre-sentence report pilot trials learned much about the practical and organisational implications of the PSR provisions of the Criminal Justice Act 1991. The detailed findings and recommendations of local steering committees, government agencies, and groups participating from outside of government may be found in sections IV and V of this report. The National Co-ordinator has made certain key findings and recommendations which have national application, and they are set out here.

1. The Probation Service will be required to prepare more reports.

According to projections of the Home Office, the Probation Service will be required to prepare more than 20,000 additional reports per year from October 1992, when as a result of the Act preparation of pre-sentence reports will be mandatory in all summary and "either way" cases where custody is being considered, and in all types of cases (summary, "either way", and indictable only) where a significant community sentence is being considered. This would constitute an increase of more than 10 per cent in the total number of reports required, considering that the Probation Service prepared 193,920 total reports in 1990. More specifically, the pilots indicate that most of this increase in demand for reports will come in Crown Court cases where the offender is offering a not guilty plea (or no plea) before the day of trial, or where for some other reason a report cannot be prepared in advance of court proceedings. In such cases, reports will not have been prepared pretrial *but nonetheless will be required under the mandatory* provisions. Under former practice, reports were usually dispensed with in such circumstances. When the most important statistical comparison is made – that between the projected increase in Crown Court reports (at least 19,000) and the total of Crown Court reports prepared in 1990 (60,860) – the rate of increase for Crown Court reports is over 30 per cent. This is significant growth for which planning is required.

At the start of the pilot scheme, the Home Office projected that the new PSR provisions would require the preparation of 20,000 additional reports per year. In anticipation of this increased workload, the Probation Service sought and gained budgetary authority to appoint additional probation officers, and to fund their support (*e.g.* secretaries, etc).

2. Up to thirty per cent of all Crown Court pre-sentence reports will be requested on adjournment, and, the Probation Service will be required to prepare these adjourned reports according to VARYING timescales.

After implementation of the new PSR provisions, in most Crown Court cases the Probation Service will continue to be able to prepare pre-sentence reports pretrial and without time pressure. However, because reports will be mandatory in most Crown Court cases, there will be a substantial increase in the number of reports required on adjournment: 30 per cent of Crown Court reports will be sought on adjournment in some areas. With respect to these 30 per cent of Crown Court reports, the traditional Probation Service request for 21–28 days preparation time is not realistic in the new era of mandatory reports. When so many more reports will be required on adjournment, the needs and interests of others in the criminal justice process dictate that some of these reports be prepared quickly, to keep adjournments short. *In particular*, the important interests of unsentenced offenders remanded in custody must be kept in mind here. The Probation Service must offer a flexible position on timescale for adjourned report preparation....

3. At every Crown Court Centre the Probation Service must establish court-based capability to prepare some reports quickly.

To meet the demand for short-notice reports on adjournment, which will exist in every Crown Court Centre to varying degrees, each Crown Court Centre will require a court-based report writer or team of report writers. It would be most efficient if this new report writing responsibility was merged into the duties of already-present, court-liaison probation officers, with an appropriate increase in court-liaison staff to manage the additional workload. In some areas the demand for faster reports prepared at court will be substantial; in other areas it will be less. But the pilots indicate that there will be some demand for this service at every Crown Court Centre once reports are mandatory across a wide range of cases. The Probation Service in local areas will be required to gauge the local situation before determining the necessary size of their particular court-based teams.

Technological aids, such as fax machines and word processors, will be required by court team members if they are to consistently produce quality reports at short-notice.

4. Better communication between the Judiciary and the Probation Service is required.

If the production of mandatory pre-sentence reports is to occur without difficulty, there must first be better communication between the Judiciary and the Probation Service regarding the mechanics of report preparation....

5. There must be good quality control for pre-sentence reports.

As implementation of the Act will require some significant changes in the methods by which reports are prepared, the Probation Service must be doubly careful to monitor the quality of reports produced, particularly in early days under the Act, and particularly with reference to reports prepared at short-notice on adjournment. Experience teaches that it is during times of transition in policy and method that particular instances of bad practice "slip through the cracks," with consequent harm and unfairness in individual cases. Within the Probation Service quality control methods should be reviewed, redesigned if necessary, and made fully effective before changeover begins in October 1992.

6. Local "PSR Implementation Committees" should be established.

To facilitate the smooth implementation of the new provisions making pre-sentence reports mandatory in many cases, local "PSR Implementation Committees" should be set up in each Crown Court Centre. In both membership and remit, these committees should mirror the local steering committees established during the pilot trials. The committees should serve as the forum for resolution of inter-agency difficulties and friction points as the PSR provisions are implemented. These committees should operate for between six months and one year, meeting on a monthly basis...

7. Consistent provision of offence information by the Crown Prosecution Service to the Probation Service is essential.

To improve the quality of reports, and with special reference to those reports which must be prepared quickly, the Crown Prosecution Service should provide offence information to the Probation Service in connection with every Crown Court case. This information should be in the form of an "advance disclosure bundle" or a "committal bundle", and it should be provided at the time of, or immediately after committal. The pilots demonstrated conclusively that the receipt of this information by the Probation Service is essential to the consistent preparation of thorough and accurate pre-sentence reports....

8. The Prison Service should ensure that outside probation officers can gain immediate access to remanded offenders on whom short-notice reports have been ordered.

Before October 1992, the Prison Service should have in place, at every facility to which Crown Court defendants are remanded, a firm policy by which probation officers from outside of the prison will be assured immediate access to remanded offenders on whom short-notice reports have been ordered. This to permit interviews essential to the completion of PSRs....

9. Listing officers should avoid scheduling "not guilty" plea cases for the final days of part-time recorders' sitting periods....

10. Uniform national sentencing days and times should be established.

The Lord Chancellor's Department in conjunction with the Judiciary should establish uniform national sentencing days and times for the listing of adjourned sentencing proceedings.... Those who resist this concept must come to terms with the reality that sentencing adjournments will occur in as many as 30 per cent of all Crown Court cases from October 1992. Currently, sentencing adjournments probably occur in about 15 per cent of Crown Court cases.

11. The "Cracked trials" problem must be alleviated.

The "cracked trials" problem bedeviling British courts must be resolved. Some strategy must be adopted whereby the "day of reckoning" for defendants facing plea decision is advanced, from the day of trial to a point at least 10 days before trial. The proposals set out in Appendix H should be seriously considered by the Judiciary, the Lord Chancellor's Department and the Bar.

12. There should be better notification of guilty pleas from solicitors.

Solicitors should be required to immediately notify listing officers and the Probation Service when defendant clients change their intention as to plea. While many defendants only take the decision to plead guilty on the day of trial, others change their minds several days or weeks before the trial date, and listing officers and the Probation Service need to hear of this changed intention at the earliest possible stage....

13. The pilot trials could not and did not uncover all of the issues that probably will be presented upon national implementation of the PSR provisions. The National Steering Committee should be retained to address additional issues, should they arise....

Notes

1.   The term "cracked" trial, referred to in the report, describes the process where a defendant indicates an initial intention to plead not guilty, persists in this plea until right up to the trial, and then changes his plea to guilty (see Chapter 2 above). This practice causes obvious practical difficulties, particularly in view of the provisions (in the Criminal Justice Act 1991) which make Pre-Sentence Report preparation mandatory in a wide range of cases. For a useful discussion of the problem, and suggested strategies for "advancing the day of reckoning" for late plea changers, see James Bredar's report (*Justice Informed*, Vol. II, 1992, App. H).

2.   The Criminal Justice Act 1991 requires the probation service to prepare a far greater number of reports than was formerly the practice under the old social enquiry report system. The number of reports required on adjournment has also increased as we have seen. It is clear from the context of the 1991 Act, and its intended changes in sentencing and penal policy, that more than a change of name was envisaged with the introduction of Pre-Sentence Reports. The new reports are to represent as change of focus and approach. What guidance has been given as to their purpose, preparation and content? The national standards have addressed these questions recently. (See *National Standards for the Supervision of Offenders in the Community* (1992), Chap. 2.)

3.   What is the status of these national standards? They are issued by the Home Office to regulate standards of practice for the probation service in relation to the supervision of offenders in the community and the preparation of Pre-Sentence Reports. The probation service is "expected to follow the guidance and requirements in the standards or – should that become impossible at any stage – to ensure locally that sentencers are made aware of the situation" (*National Standards for the Supervision of Offenders in the Community* (1992), Ch. 1, para. 4). This same document also states that "in many respects, the standards lay down expected norms rather than outright requirements, with the clear onus on practitioners and managers to record and justify any necessary departures from these norms in individual cases" (*ibid.* Chap. 1, para 5).

4.   The national standards require that a clear, concise and jargon-free report is prepared, preferably no more than two pages in length. Some attempt to encourage standardisation is made by the suggestion of a consistent set of sections and headings in each report.

5.   A major shift in emphasis, as noted earlier, is the ending of the practice of probation officers making recommendations as to sentence. The report writer is reminded that the "sentencer in a criminal case has sole responsibility, after a finding of guilt, for imposing sentence and, therefore, for judging the seriousness of the offence(s) committed" (*ibid.* Chap. 2, para. 6). The writer of the report is urged to be impartial in the presentation of information and to present a balanced picture, reflecting accurately both the mitigating and aggravating aspects of the case. In short, reports are to be more concerned with facts than with opinions. The national standards

(*ibid.* Chap. 2, para. 3) require the report writer to: summarise the facts of the current offence(s) and to assess offence seriousness and the offender's attitude to the offence; provide relevant background information about the offender; and to propose, where relevant, the most suitable community sentence.

6. As a central principle of the Criminal Justice Act 1991 is the concept of proportionality in sentencing, with tighter control over judicial discretion, the seriousness of the offence now has even greater importance in sentencing decisions. Formerly, offence seriousness was not something which was addressed in the majority of social enquiry reports, but this has now changed radically. Henceforth, information on this subject will be required by sentencers, and probation officers will have to assist them. The national standards state that "in preparing a Pre-Sentence Report, the report writer should first consider the seriousness of the offence(s) at issue and the likely range of penalties, since this has a large bearing on the style and detail of the report that should be prepared" (*ibid.* Chap. 2, para. 9). This provisional assessment of offence seriousness by the report writer is "intended to ensure that the PSR is properly focused and addresses only those outcomes that are broadly likely" (*ibid.* Chap. 2, para. 10).

One difficulty with this change in emphasis is that probation officers may have a different conception of offence seriousness to that of the courts. (For an interesting analysis of this issue, see M. Wasik, "Rethinking Information and Advice for Sentencers", (C. Munro and M. Wasik eds., 1992), at pp. 185–91). What help will the report writers receive in evaluating offence seriousness now that they are to be involved with this question? They are told (rather lamely) by the national standards that "the seriousness of the offence depends on a wide range of factors, including the harm caused by the offence and the culpability of the offender" (Chap. 2, para. 13).

The following extract considers some of the problems faced by report writers in assessing offence seriousness.

N. Stone, "Pre-Sentence Reports, Culpability and the 1991 Act" [1992] Crim. L.R. 558, pp. 561–567.

If in post-1991 law sentencers are to interpret "circumstances of the offence" very narrowly, the PSR writer will make a very modest contribution. Reporters are wary of giving detailed accounts of crimes, conscious of their relative ignorance of what will be stated in court or negotiated between prosecution and defence. The report should not be simply repetitious or a re-statement of the obvious (for example in pointing out the vulnerability of an elderly victim, the breach of trust by an employee, the use of excessive force or gratuitous violence/damage, or the age difference between the perpetrator of unlawful sexual intercourse and the girl concerned). If the report does present new information, will this be an awkward, tangential contribution or a competing view which neither fits readily with the advocates' accounts nor can be easily tested or challenged?

It is possible to envisage the presentation of factual offence details which are not necessarily available to the court by other routes, though this may require a more careful than accustomed line of enquiry and perhaps greater foundation knowledge of criminal behaviour. In the context of the extent of planning, pre-meditation and skill of execution, examples might include whether the offender used any technical know-how in entering and starting a car taken without consent or in altering a credit card, and how this was acquired. In regard to the defendant's contribution to an offence, the report could address who was influential or played a particular role among a group of co-offenders, *e.g.* in embarking on a burglary or initiating an affray.

The latter example points to the probation officer's principal professional strength, not in tackling factual aspects of a crime's *modus operandi* but in throwing light on the mind, judgment, motives, anticipation/intent, reaction, emotions and mental state of the offender, before, during and after the crime. However, the further we go in exploring this "softer" data, the more unchartered the territory. First, it becomes increasingly difficult to distinguish between what constitutes "the circumstances of the offence" and what is merely "relevant in mitigation" under section 28. Culpability is an expansive concept which can encompass extent of temptation, method of exploitation used, availability of other courses of action, the anticipation of harm, the presence of "diminishing" factors such as provocation or other moral justifications, underlying stress, ignorance of the law, the offender's broader capacity for self-control and the extent to which the offending episode can be regarded as a behavioural aberration. The only obvious limiting boundary in the calculation of culpability is that we should not go beyond the offence itself into post-offence realms such as remorse, assisting the police and making restitution, though in practice this may prove a hard line to draw.

Secondly, the Court of Appeal's views on mitigation and aggravation are far less explicit in regard to somewhat shadowy, ephemeral or subjective aspects of the offender's thinking and emotions, in so far as these may have affected behaviour. Thirdly, these ingredients can be very hard to prove and their impact on the defendant's mood or judgment even more so. Without a great deal of extra inquiry we largely have to take the defendant's retrospective word for it. Fourthly, even if these factors are reliably clear, it can be difficult to know if their presence is of aggravating or mitigating effect. The use and impact of alcohol presents a key example of this kind of ambiguity.

Two examples may assist in illustrating the difficulties. The first concerns a 23 year old man with a substantial alcohol problem for which he has been receiving help in a residential recovery project, now convicted of a rather clumsy attempt to rob a petrol station by seizing a customer and pretending to have a knife. The probation report stated:

> "This offence occurred after Mr A had been abstinent for 11 weeks. He had been prompted to drink again because, despite his intentions not to become heavily involved in another relationship until he had re-established his life, he had become infatuated with a female friend and was depressed when she felt unable to respond. He estimates that he consumed alcohol totalling some 42 units or more during that day's binge and thus had difficulty in recalling either the details of his crime or what his intentions were."

Though the defendant's alcohol problem and some degree of intoxication is undoubted, how reliable and relevant is his account of unrequited love and is his culpability diminished because of his distressed and drunken state?

The second extract features the sequence of events, the defendant's role and his frame of mind. A 20 year old man with a difficult upbringing stands convicted of wounding a man whom he had confronted, believing that he had earlier threatened the defendant's younger brother. Another youth was involved in the assault but was not identified or prosecuted.

> "Mr B stated that he did not plan or anticipate the assault. By his account the

encounter became violent when his companion unexpectedly swung a dog chain at [the victim]. He said that he then hit [the victim] because 'something snapped' inside him, based on his earlier years in which he witnessed his brother being hit by their stepfather and had tried to protect him. The two brothers have always felt a strong bond of loyalty and [the victim] appears to have taken some of the brunt of Mr B's revived bad memories of their aggressive stepfather."

This may seem pertinent information but with what impact on culpability for what otherwise seems a relatively serious and unprovoked attack? Also the allegedly leading role of the co-offender in inflicting the more serious of the victim's injuries is virtually impossible to substantiate.

These problematic dilemmas are clearly visible – though not acknowledged – in the Home Office's recent training pack on the Act for the Probation Service which seeks to differentiate between factors affecting the seriousness of offence and those which mitigate but are unrelated to the offence. The guide characterises "attitude to the offence" ("has the offender shown any signs of guilt, remorse, concern for victim, or desire to make reparation?") as a factor affecting offence seriousness, while the defendant's age is identified merely as an unrelated mitigating factor. Alcohol or drugs as a feature of the offence is baldly offered as a factor affecting seriousness but without any explanation of their significance either way. We are told that a racial motivation for an offence amplifies seriousness but, whilst this may be a commendable feature of progressive sentencing principles in combatting racism, this may not necessarily accord with the current established sentencing consensus.

Intended or potential harm

The nature of harm intended or risked, as distinct from that caused by the defendant, is a further pertinent factor which can only be grasped either by the sentencer's surmise or the defendant's own admission and thus may become known to the court only through the PSR. This is a complex question in culpability and proportionality, not least because it is so intangible or speculative. If the defendant convicted of resisting a police officer tells the probation officer that he was actually trying to kick the officer in the testicles but missed, this somewhat transforms what might otherwise seem merely a truculent incident into an attempted assault of some seriousness. A further illustration arose in a probation report on a man aged 30, convicted of section 20 wounding after inflicting a cut on the victim's elbow with a metal bar in a neighbourhood row:

> "Mr C told me that after the victim swung at him he felt so angry that his intention was to knock him to the ground and inflict serious injury upon him to the extent that 'he'd need an ambulance'. But for the intervention of others he does not know what would have caused him to desist the attack. He still wishes that he had inflicted more grievous injury and claims that if he had his chance again he would 'make a better job of it'."

In addition to the light this extract throws on intent, it is also pertinent to issues of post-offence attitude, to be discussed later in this article. . . .

. . . This article has attempted to pose more awkward questions about the role of PSRs in the moral evaluation of criminal behaviour. My concern is that the probation officer is requested to interview the defendant in a private, relatively unhurried, in-depth encounter, having some of the ambience of the confessional, encouraging the defendant to be candid, open and trusting. Defendants can welcome this opportunity to speak because they can feel listened to, understood and respected in a way that may be missing from their other encounters with criminal justice professionals. Much may depend on skill, time availability, thoroughness, values and perceptions of the reporter who is increasingly trained and encouraged to "confront" or challenge offending and devise corrective intervention in the community. The written product of the encounter is difficult to challenge and its impact on the sentencer is even more difficult to assess. Little thought appears to have been given to the formidable problems of evidence in establishing factors relevant to seriousness. Should, for instance, the prosecution now be supplied reports in order to anticipate questions about the defendant's role in the offence? This would be a considerable departure from current practice. Will reporters be more routinely expected to attend court to give evidence to support their offence analysis?

Defendants usually conclude or are advised that it is in their interests to participate in enquiries or that the process is, at worst, of neutral weight, but some of the examples provided above suggest that this is not necessarily the case. As I have asked elsewhere, "can it be right for the defendant's culpability to be weighed more heavily as a result of this kind of voluntary self-disclosure, filtered through the judgment of the individual reporter?" What choice does the defendant have to decline to be interviewed? The Act is silent on the question of consent, as is the draft National Standards document. Only the Home Office's training guide refers, in the context of "good practice procedures", to obtaining the defendant's consent. If the defendant declines, a probation officer's written statement of explanation hardly seems to count as a report made "with a view to assisting the court in determining the most suitable method of dealing with an offender", as defined by section 3(5)(c), but the court can doubtless proceed without the benefit of a PSR. It is perhaps a regrettable omission that a defendant's participation is taken so much for granted, while the scope to question or challenge PSR writers is likely to remain so limited. The preference to be sentenced on the basis of the advocates' presentations may be a sensible option in some instances. Alternatively, will defendants become more circumspect in what they share with their reporter?...

... As the new law stands, the report is required simultaneously to undertake several burdens which are potentially neither entirely fair nor readily compatible.

Notes

1.   Stone raises some interesting issues about the evidential and due process implications of requiring report writers to assess offence seriousness. Further telling criticisms of the new Pre-Sentence Reports are made by Stephen Nunn in his article "Pre-Sentence Reports – A Defence Perspective" (1992) 156 *Justice of the Peace* (at pp. 755–7), in which he concludes that it is "likely that the relationship between the defence and the probation service will come under some pressure" as a result of the Criminal Justice Act 1991.

2.   Would it have been more appropriate for Pre-Sentence Reports to be considered only after the primary decision has been taken about the seriousness of the offence? Do you agree with Stone's conclusion that the Pre-Sentence Report is "required simultaneously to undertake several burdens which are potentially neither entirely fair nor readily compatible"?

3.   In view of the new sentencing philosophy of the Criminal Justice Act 1991, with its "just deserts" approach, the Pre-Sentence Report is now to take account of offence *seriousness*. On the other hand, it is also required to assess the *suitability* of an offender for the various community sentences. How is a Pre-Sentence Report writer to deal with the potential conflicts which may arise out of these two criteria for selecting community sentences? (For instance, where the sentence which reflects the defendant's culpability is not regarded as the most suitable penalty). In the absence of any statutory

guidance on this issue, Martin Wasik recommends that "the most coherent way of tackling the problem is to say that the most suitable community sentence should be selected, but provided this does not impose a more onerous burden upon the offender than is justified by the seriousness of the offence." (In C. Munro and M. Wasik eds., (1992) at p. 189).

III. SENTENCING DISCRETION AND LEGISLATIVE CONTROL

Traditionally, the English sentencing system has bestowed upon sentencers a wide discretion in their choice of sentence for a particular offender. Subject to fairly broad statutory and common law constraints, sentencers were able to deal with cases on an individual basis and to adopt whichever approach seemed most appropriate to deal with the case in question. Undoubtedly there is some intuitive appeal in the idea that two offenders committing similar crimes may be dealt with differently so as to reflect different purposes of punishment: for instance one may require a rehabilitative measure, whilst the other may be dealt with more aptly by a deterrent response. But the problem with this "free choice" approach is that it tends to produce indefensible disparities in practice and it inhibits the development of consistent and principled sentencing policies. In other words, sentencers have no coherent basis for choosing between the different philosophies (deterrence, rehabilitation, etc.) which underlie the alternatives available to them. Recently, however, with the passing of the Criminal Justice Act 1991, there has been an attempt to restrict judicial discretion and give priority to proportionality in sentencing: a sentence should primarily reflect the seriousness of the crime, with offenders receiving their "just deserts".

Much of the impetus for this tighter control of judicial discretion came from a growing dissatisfaction with disproportionate sentences, especially lengthy custodial sentences for non-violent offenders. Despite attempts by the Court of Appeal to persuade sentencers to pass shorter prison sentences, and to avoid custody for non-violent offenders wherever possible, there was little discernible improvement in prison conditions and overcrowding. The policy of persuasion and piecemeal legislation was not a successful method of inducing sentencers to change attitudes which were deeply ingrained, and the creation of a number of alternatives to the custodial sentence was similarly unsuccessful (see Chapter 5). As a result, there was little doubt that the traditional, "wide discretion" approach to sentencing failed to produce the required changes. Sentencing policy became too important to be left to judges and the Court of Appeal. An evaluation of these developments is provided in the extracts which follow.

A. Ashworth, "The Criminal Justice Act 1991", in *Sentencing, Judicial Discretion and Training* **(C. Munro and M. Wasik eds., 1992), pp. 77–83.**

The 1980s were characterised by a number of significant but apparently contradictory changes in sentencing. The Lord Chief Justice handed down several guideline judgments on sentencing, but the calls for greater consistency did not abate. The government voiced its support for judicial independence and judicial discretion in sentencing, and yet restrictions on custodial sentences for young offenders were introduced in 1982 and refined in 1988, and the parole system was manipulated so as to shorten many of the sentences imposed in court. The use of custody for juveniles and, eventually, for young adults began to decline significantly, whereas the number of long custodial sentences for adult offenders has greatly increased. Into the fast-flowing waters already subject to these cross-currents came the White Paper of 1990, *Crime, Justice and Protecting the Public*, followed by the publication of and the debates on the Criminal Justice Bill, and on July 25, 1991, the royal assent for the Criminal Justice Act.

There has been a plethora, some would say a surfeit, of Criminal Justice Acts in recent years. This one is different. It is not the usual rag-bag of minor reforms: it has general themes. In terms of changing the direction of sentencing, it is certainly the most important such statute since 1948, and perhaps the most important of the century. This is not to suggest, however, that it makes a clean break with the past on all issues. One of its features is to preserve a certain element of continuity in the English approach to sentencing policy and practice. For this reason, the outline of the Act's major provisions in this essay will seek to relate the new law to the system of which it will become part. It will focus less on the minutiae of the Act, which have received detailed consideration elsewhere and more on its major themes and their probable impact on English sentencing....

Sentencing and the Rule of Law

During this century, the English system has seen a constant process of adjustment and re-adjustment between law and discretion in sentencing, and between legislative and judicial guidance. For most of the century Parliament has contented itself with setting maximum penalties for offences, limiting the sentencing power of magistrates, and introducing new forms of sentence and abolishing others from time-to-time. Within the large reservoir of discretion left to courts by the legislature, the Court of Criminal Appeal began to enunciate principles of sentencing soon after its creation in 1907, and its successor the Court of Appeal (Criminal Division) has dealt with more and more sentence appeals in recent years. Reports of those decisions and commentaries on them by Dr David Thomas have greatly assisted the process of concretisation of principles and policies. In the last decade Lord Lane, as Lord Chief Justice, has begun to develop the guideline judgment as a major tool of policy-making, using it to set out a clear sentencing structure for certain offences, and occasionally to raise or to lower the general level of sentences for a particular type of crime. Thus during the 1980s, if not before, judicial precedents became a leading source of law for sentencers. The large area of discretion left by the legislature was to some extent being structured by the judiciary.

The legislature itself has, however, become more active. In the 1982 Criminal Justice Act three criteria for custodial sentences were introduced in respect of offenders under 21. Although it did not originate in a government proposal, the new framework of restrictions was accepted by Parliament. The courts had to apply the criteria, and the Court of Appeal had to deal with cases which turned on interpretation of the criteria. After early reluctance, a new realm of sentencing precedents developed. The criteria were tightened by the 1988 Criminal Justice Act, this time at the government's suggestion, and decisions on these statutory criteria are the most numerous group in any recent volume of *Criminal Appeal Reports (Sentencing)*. The legislature has also been active in imposing mandatory requirements on sentencers. The Drug Trafficking Offences Act 1986 forces judges through a complex series of decisions in all drug trafficking cases. Section 104 of the Criminal Justice Act 1988 requires a court of make a compensation order in all cases involving death, injury, loss or damage, or to give reasons for not doing so. These and other duties imposed on judges and magistrates serve to underline the increasing complexity of the task of passing sentence.

How should the increased technicality of sentencing be regarded? Some have attacked it, but it is essential that two distinct points be kept separate. One is that simplicity is an important ideal, which Parliament has sometimes failed to achieve. Some provisions on sentencing have not been well-conceived or well-drafted, giving rise to avoidable complexity. Sentencing is a hard enough task without that. But the other point is that there are other goals and values apart from simplicity. Decisions have to be made about the policies which are thought socially desirable. Compensation for the victims of crime is one which gained prominence in the 1980s. Depriving offenders, particularly drug traffickers, of the profits of their crimes is another. Such policies are too important to be left at the discretion of the court. A statutory framework is needed here if the "rule of law" values of certainty, consistency and predictability are to be achieved. This is not to excuse the over-complexity of some of the provisions. The point is that simplicity is merely one of a number of social values, and it may have to give way to some extent if other objectives are to be achieved.

Coinciding with the burgeoning amount of Court of Appeal guidance and increased activity of the legislature in sentencing matters, has been the development of the Judicial Studies Board. This betokens a far more serious-minded approach to sentencing than obtained at the beginning of the 1980s. The Board's functions are described elsewhere in this volume by Lord Justice Glidewell. One major function is that of keeping Crown Court sentencers up-to-date with new legislation and new decisions. This may be seen as recognition that sentencing is the most important function that the judge performs in the majority of criminal cases (especially where there is a guilty plea), and that it is a task with considerable social impact and public interest.

The Origins of the Act

The developments described above show that the amount of guidance for, and restriction on, sentencing by magistrates and judges has increased considerably in recent years. However, there were still sources of dissatisfaction for almost all parties involved. The Government became more and more concerned about the high use of custodial sentences. There had been success in the mid-1980s in securing a dramatic reduction in the numbers of juveniles sent into custody, from some 7,600 in 1981 to some 2,200 in 1989. The new opportunities for "intermediate treatment" seemed to have assisted this process of diversion. In the late 1980s the government called upon the probation service to produce "Action Plans" to divert young adult offenders (aged 18 to 20) from custody, and this now seems to have had some success. But for adult offenders the downturn in the use of custody was slow to come, small and not sustained. The Government began to tackle this by the "back door," increasing remission on short prison sentences and increasing the use of parole for short and medium-term sentences. This approach drew criticism from the judiciary, who argued that the sentences passed in court were being "devalued." The Government accepted the criticism to the extent of appointing a review committee under Lord Carlisle. That Committee reported in 1988 and its rec-ommendations, designed to restore meaning to sentences, were largely incorporated into the 1991 Act.

If the executive was to be denied its manipulation of remission and parole in the future, would the courts also change their ways and use custody more restrictively? Only weeks after the Carlisle Report, research revealed that in the Crown Court some 39 per cent of thefts from shops of goods valued at under £200 resulted in immediate custody. Some sentencers apparently took the view that custody had to be used for lack of suitable alternatives, and they argued for new measures in which they could have greater confidence. The Government's Green Paper of 1988 invited sentencers and others to propose new measures, and the Government itself was moving towards tougher and more demanding non-custodial sentences which would not be regarded as a "let-off" by the courts, by offenders or by the public at large.

A new sentencing policy was thus beginning to take shape. The Government called it the "twin-track" approach. Sentences for really serious crimes, particularly those involving violence, sex or drugs, would remain high. The Government and the judiciary seemed at one on this. However, for less serious offences, custody should be replaced by tougher forms of punishment in the community – demanding sentences, backed by more rigorous standards for enforcement and breach proceedings. The details were new, but the strategy was not. The idea of "bifurcation" of sentence levels had been identified by Professor A. E. Bottoms in 1977. The policy of introducing new types of non-custodial sentence had been tried before, in 1967 (suspended sentences), in 1972 (community service orders), and in 1982 (Schedule 11 probation orders), without any obvious restraining influence on the steady upward march in the use of immediate custody for adults. If there was to be a real impact on sentencing practice this time, something more was required than simply offering new types of sentence to the courts.

The Government had begun to reconsider its position on the so-called principle of judicial independence. During the 1980s the principle had sometimes been used to bolster the claim that judges should be left with maximum discretion on sentencing matters and that any legislative encroachment on this constituted a threat to judicial independence. This was and is a manifestly false claim. Parliament clearly has the power to legislate on sentencing mattes as it thinks fit, and no-one has ever claimed that there is unconstitutionality in the mandatory penalty for murder, or in the mandatory minimum disqualification period for drunk drivers. The true principle of judicial independence in relation to sentencing is indeed vital, and it is this: that judges and magistrates should be allowed to pass sentence in each case without fear or favour, without pressure of inducements. This has nothing to do with the amount of discretion which Parliament ought to leave to the courts. As the White Paper correctly concludes, "sentencing principles and sentencing practice are matters of legitimate concern to Government."

What were the sources of concern? One, as we have seen, was the over-use of custody for offences which were not particularly serious. Another was the consistency of sentencing. Although the White Paper signals the Government's admiration for the achievements of the Court of Appeal in developing guideline judgments, the fact remains that appellate guidance covers only a small part of the reservoir of judicial discretion. The guideline judgments had been much trumpeted in the areas to which they applied – drug trafficking, rape, incest and so forth. But if one starts by asking for what crimes the courts most frequently pass sentence, and one then enquires what guidance exists there, the picture is much less impressive. There is a smattering of appellate judgments, dealing with only some of the points, and leaving others entirely at large. This is still the case in respect of most non-custodial sentences and most cases of burglary, theft, handling and deception. Despite some improvements in recent years, the conscientious judge or magistrate who tries to seek out coherent guidance on how to approach such cases is likely to be disappointed. Indeed, some of the guidance which does exist may be said to encourage incoherence. A decision-making guide for magistrates, issued by the Judicial Studies Board, states that an essential step is for the court to decide what aim it wishes to achieve by its sentence, and then it lists such aims as deterrence, retribution, public protection, reform of the offender, and so on. If sentencers are being encouraged to set off in different directions, without any guidance on how to choose, what hope is there for consistency of approach?

In its White Paper the Government proposed to tackle the problem at two levels. First, it decided to establish proportionality or "just deserts" as the main rationale for sentences. The "cafeteria" system of allowing sentencers to pick and choose which aim to pursue should disappear, not least because, as the White Paper pointed out, the claims sometimes made for deterrence and rehabilitation are unsubstantiated. If there is a primary rationale, then at least a sentencer knows what issue has to be addressed if there is no other guidance available: how serious is this offence in comparison with others? The second approach is to introduce a statutory framework within which the courts, under the guidance of the Court of Appeal, should be left to develop more detailed principles. Parliament would lay down the *grandes lignes*, and the Court of Appeal would continue to hand down judgments which would provide lower courts with guidance about how to interpret and apply the framework.

Some had argued for the creation of a Sentencing Council to accomplish the necessary task of creating detailed guidance for magistrates courts and the Crown Court. For one thing, the Court of Appeal stands utterly remote from magistrates' sentencing and somewhat remote from the everyday business of the Crown Court. For another thing, the Court of Appeal's record suggests that its guidance tends to cluster round serious crimes and substantial prison sentences. However, the Government dismissed these arguments and preferred to speak of a continuing partnership between legislature and judiciary. The new legislative framework is therefore to be grafted on to the existing system of giving guidance. Much of what was said about existing practices above will therefore remain relevant in the years to come.

Notes

1.   Although English sentencers have enjoyed considerable freedom in the past, with few restraints on their exercise of discretion, there has been something of an international movement towards proportionality in sentencing and the development of stricter sentencing guidelines. For the background and practice in the United States, see D. J. Champion, *The U.S. Sentencing Guidelines: Implications for Criminal Justice* (1991) and M. Tonry, "The Politics and Processes of Sentencing Commissions", Vol. 37 *Crime and Delinquency*, (1991) pp. 307–29; for England, see R. J. Henham, *Sentencing Principles and Magistrates' Sentencing Behaviour* (1990), B. Hudson, *Justice Through Punishment: Critique of the Justice Model of Corrections* (1987), and *Sentencing Reform*, (K. Pease and M. Wasik eds., 1987).

The "guidelines" movement cannot be discussed in detail here but it can be noted that many countries have shown interest in creating a statutory framework for sentencing. In particular, the guidelines approach has been closely associated with the United States of America where, at federal as well as state level, such legislation has been introduced (see A. von Hirsch, K. Knapp and M. Tonry, *The Sentencing Commission and its Guidelines* (1987)). Sometimes this guidelines approach takes the form of a detailed numerical sentencing "grid" (such as the Minnesota system), but it can also be introduced in the non-numerical form of statutory sentencing principles. Certain European countries, such as Sweden, have introduced legislation of the latter type (see A. von Hirsch and N. Jareborg, "Swedish Sentencing Statute Enacted" [1989] Crim. L.R. 275). The advantage of statutory guidelines is that they can stipulate which of the often conflicting penal objectives is to have primacy in sentencing policy and this, in turn, can encourage the development of a more coherent body of sentencing law.

It is a valid criticism of "individualised" sentencing (or the "cafeteria" approach as it is referred to in Ashworth's article) that it can lead to indefensible disparities, with judges appearing to pursue their own personal sentencing philosophies, making consistency difficult to achieve. Failure to treat like cases as like is seen by some as a fundamental injustice. But not all writers agree that a "justice" approach to sentencing should lead inexorably to a restriction of judicial discretion. This point was made in a recent comparative study:

> "[Those who call for greater equality in sentencing] ... mean equality in sentencing policy between different criminal courts, or between different (panels of) judges at the same court. This is the equality that has received all the attention during the past two decades ... It is also the equality that figures most in academic research. Gradually an ideal of equality has been developed by means of which the margins of judicial discretion can be filled in. This idea has been considerably reinforced by an enormous increase in numbers of criminal cases requiring ever more judges, and increasingly giving rise to questions of equality in sentencing ... Of course, no one would dispute the injustice of sentencing that was completely dependent on the personality of the judge, and of course consensus exists on the necessity of treating equal cases as equally as possible, given the exorbitant context of criminal law and its consequences for the lives of ordinary people. The questions then arise: what are equal cases, what is equal treatment, and how unequal must a case be to warrant unequal treatment? Everyone recognises these questions, but the problem is that there are many different answers, and that such answers cannot be objectively tested ... This is closely linked to the fact that more or less equal circumstances may seem to exist at first sight, while there may still be other actual or individual circumstances that affect the subjective experience of punishment, and therefore the severity of a penalty in individual cases.

(See C. Kelk, L. Koffman and J. Silvis, "Sentencing Practice, Policy and Discretion" in *Criminal Justice in Europe* (P. Fennell *et al.* eds., 1995, p. 328)).

2.   Until the introduction of the Criminal Justice Act 1991 there were few statutory provisions which significantly restricted the discretion of sentencers in relation to adult offenders. There were (and still are) statutory maximum penalties for offences – often unrealistically high – and also restrictions on the sentencing powers of magistrates. But, within this very wide framework, sentencers have always enjoyed a good deal of freedom to manoeuvre. There is rarely such a thing as a "correct" sentence for a particular crime: murder is the only offence of any practical significance where the sentence is fixed by law (*i.e.* life imprisonment).

An interesting explanation of the meaning of judicial discretion in relation to sentencing decisions was given by his Honour Judge Christopher Stuart-White in a lecture delivered to a sentencers' training conference in 1989. The following extract is taken from his lecture.

Judge Christopher Stuart-White, *The Magistrate*, Vol. 45, (1989) p. 194.

Sentencing is, in one sense, a highly developed example of the exercise of judicial discretion. The sentencer is not seeking the answer to a "yes or no" question as is the magistrate who has to decide whether a defendant is guilty or not guilty. He is not even deciding where, on a single scale the answer should be found, as is the judge deciding the amount of an award of damages for personal injuries. The sentencer is making a very complex decision; he is deciding first what type of sentence should be imposed – should it, for example, be a fine or a conditional discharge? Should it be a community service order or a probation order? Should it be a custodial sentence, and if so should it be suspended.... And within those broad categories, he must refine the sentence and set it at the appropriate place on the scale. How much should be the fine? How many hours community service? How long should be the custodial sentence? And so on.

So sentencing really involves the ultimate "multi-choice question". What is more, it is the multi-choice question to which there is no one correct answer, though there are almost certainly a large number of incorrect answers.

Should all this cause us to be down- hearted? I suggest that it should not. If there were a "correct" answer to each sentencing problem that would mean not only that the sentencer could quite adequately be replaced by a computer, but more importantly, the result would be that the degree of injustice done in individual cases by the application of such "correct" answers would cause to pale into insignificance such injustice as occurs or appears to occur as the result of actual – or perceived – inconsistencies of sentence.

So each sentencing problem calls for the exercise of judicial discretion. For judicial discretion to be properly exercised what is required is an appropriate mixture of three elements: first, knowledge and understanding of the facts of the particular case – the facts relating to the offence and the facts relating to the offender; secondly, knowledge and understanding of the legal framework within which the sentence must be considered; and thirdly, the exercise of the sentencer's powers of judgment as to what is just and appropriate – powers acquired both by his experience of life and his experience on the bench.

It is this third ingredient which is the exercise of discretion; but unless it operates within the constraints of the other two ingredients it will not be judicial discretion.

The legal framework of sentencing decisions has itself a number of elements....

... Let us now turn to the final element – the exercise of judgment – the part that no computer can do for us.

We shall not even start to get that right unless we use a consistent approach to our task – preferably a logical and structured approach such as that suggested in the Judicial Studies Board's *Notes for the guidance of magistrates* or in the book *Decision making in magistrates' courts* by Barker and Sturges.

But, in addition to that, we must try not to exercise our judgment in a vacuum – in ignorance of what our fellow magistrates and judges are doing on the other days of the week, on other benches or in other areas or regions. That is the value of sentencing conferences and sentencing exercises. That is the value if they have one, and I think they can have, of sentencing guidelines agreed by benches in annual meeting, by counties or commission areas or by The Magistrates' Association which, as you know, has recently published a set of such guidelines. I suggest that the proper function of guidelines of this kind is to inform magistrates, to the extent that that is possible or practicable, about the sort of sentences that their colleagues throughout the country are *in fact* passing for particular types of offence and also about the sort of sentences that the Crown Court is passing for similar offences. I further suggest that it is not their function to prescribe what sentences magistrates *should* pass for any particular offence.

Such guidelines, whoever has prepared them, can be regarded as one of the tools – often a useful tool – in the sentencer's toolkit; but never as a blueprint for the sentence itself.

In this respect they are to be distinguished from guidelines laid down by the Court of Appeal, which is a superior court of record whose decisions the Common Law of England requires us to follow.

There has always been a problem of inconsistency – or perceived inconsistency – in sentencing and there always will be a problem unless and until magistrates and judges are replaced by a computer.

May I leave you with this thought: we should continue to strive to achieve consistency. It will not be a tragedy if we fail. It would be a tragedy if we were ever entirely to succeed.

Notes

1. It is a matter for debate as to what are the acceptable levels of inconsistency in sentencing practice. But the extent of sentencing disparity, both in magistrates' courts and Crown Courts, has long been a source of concern to many of those who have made a study of sentencing practice. For valuable recent studies of magistrates' courts, see H. Parker *et al.*, *Unmasking the Magistrates* (1989), R. Henham, *Sentencing Principles and Magistrates' Sentencing Behaviour* (1990), and Liberty, *Unequal Before the Law: Sentencing in Magistrates' Courts in England and Wales 1981–91* (1992).

2. In view of the relative paucity of information about Crown Court sentencing practices, it is disappointing that the pilot study of Ashworth *et al.*, entitled *Sentencing in the Crown Court* (1984), encountered the opposition of the then Lord Chief Justice and was not permitted to progress beyond the preliminary stage.

3. In order to encourage magistrates to aim for greater sentencing consistency, while retaining their discretion to do justice in individual cases, the Magistrates' Association issued sentencing guidelines for the most common offences in June 1992. (See the Magistrates' Association, *Sentencing Guidelines*, 1992). Although critics of such guidelines felt that this development might fetter the discretion of magistrates, the overall response to draft guidelines which were used for a short period prior to 1992 was very positive. The suggested sentences are to be viewed as the point from which sentencing decisions should commence, they are not to be used as a "blueprint for the sentence itself". The introduction of these guidelines shows a willingness on the part of the magistracy to confront the problem of disparity and to do something constructive about it.

The development of these guidelines is dealt with in the extract which follows.

**W. Wasik and A. Turner, "Sentencing Guidelines for the Magistrates' Courts",
[1993] Crim. L.R. 345, pp. 346–350.**

The Magistrates' Association's initiative was, therefore, a considerable step forward and was indicative of a wish to take the lead in generating greater consistency of decision making in the lower courts. The Association is a voluntary body, but nearly all magistrates choose to belong to it. Its views on criminal justice matters are widely reported in the press, and it operates as an influential pressure group. The 1992 Guidelines descend from two earlier documents, the Association's *Suggestions for Road Traffic Penalties*, which were first issued as long ago as 1966, and which have been regularly updated since, and the *Sentencing Guide for Criminal Offences (other than Road Traffic)*, issued in 1989. The latter were innovative and were hailed as "much more sophisticated" than the traffic penalty suggestions, representing "a significant stride towards consistency of approach." Use of the rather sensitive word "guidelines" was avoided in the title of these documents, and when the Committee that produced the 1989 Guide began its work its Chairman, Mrs Ann Rich, commented that to refer to these developments as guidelines "would not be right." The concern, presumably, was to avoid terminology that might arouse unease about possible diminution of sentencing discretion. Once produced, however, the 1989 guide was regularly referred to as "the Guidelines." Any reticence about the term seems now to have disappeared, and the 1992 version bears the title "Sentencing Guidelines" on its front cover....

... Clearly, then, these documents are important. Many benches, nonetheless, make minor or sometimes quite substantial adjustments to the Association Suggestions, and some prefer to stick to their own "in-house" bench norms. As this tinkering with the Suggestions demonstrates, they are at root no more than a voluntary code, having no legal force. As Ashworth points out, senior magistrates on the bench, the local clerk to the justices or the local liaison judge are in fact capable of exerting just as much influence over bench sentencing policy as the Magistrates' Association's Guidelines. The Suggestions for Road Traffic penalties have, however, received an important measure of appellate recognition and endorsement through reference being made to them in several appellate decisions. In those cases, where Crown Court sentences were being reviewed, the Court of Appeal had regard *inter alia* to the sentencing norm (as exhibited in the Suggestions) for the same offence tried summarily. The non-traffic Guidelines have not yet, to our knowledge, been similarly considered, but their production in 1989 was strongly encouraged by Lord Hailsham during his second term as Lord Chancellor (1979–87), and their use by the courts has required the sanction of Lord Lane, then Lord Chief Justice. The Guidelines are set out, or referred to, in leading practitioner works used in the magistrates' courts.

Disparity in magistrates' sentencing

It is important to realise that the main driving factor in the creation of the 1989 Suggestions was the perceived need to respond to widespread criticism of disparity in magistrates' sentencing. Mr John Hosking, the Chairman of the Association when the Suggestions were published, commented that his Association was "well aware of public concern about apparent inconsistency, and we are determined to try to reduce the extremes." In July 1989 Mr Douglas Hurd, then Home Secretary, told magistrates at a conference in York used to launch the Suggestions, that "local justice will be seen as injustice if its sentences differ considerably from those elsewhere."

We are aware of no systematic study subsequently undertaken to examine the impact of the Suggestions upon sentencing disparity in magistrates' courts. Certainly, later studies have identified continuing disparity. To some extent, however, this main thrust to "reduce the extremes" has been superseded by the shift in government thinking about sentencing policy in general, as embodied in the 1990 White Paper and the 1991 Act.

The Act came into force in October 1992. Between the enactment and commencement of the Act there was substantial training for magistrates, locally organised but based on the same specially commissioned pack, at least equalling in volume (a minimum of 11 hours was recommended) the preparation required for the Children Act 1989, which members of Family Panels had only just completed. The two sets of Magistrates' Association Suggestions have, in the light of the provisions of the 1991 Act, been extensively revised and amalgamated into one folder, together with applicable guidelines for compensation of victims who have incurred injury, loss or damage as the result of an offence.

One of the central aims of the new legislation (though not explicitly stated) is to reduce disparity, but by a more fundamental approach. Its emphasis on principles, giving primacy to "seriousness," has influenced considerably the design of the Guidelines. "Seriousness indicators" are dominant, and the prescribed factors and decision-making sequences aim to structure magistrates' thinking and approach to sentencing in the way the Act requires. The Guidelines provide only secondarily an indication of the presumptive penalty. This takes further the principle begun by the Suggestions that the way to consistency is not through indicated penalties to be adjusted according to the circumstances of the individual cases, but through uniformity of approach.

The Guidelines and the 1991 Act Sentencing Structure

The Guidelines were, then, issued in July 1992 with an eye to the provisions of the Criminal Justice Act, which were to come into force in October that year. They should be seen as an important attempt to improve consistency in the day-to-day sentencing of the lower courts, through the application of the philosophy of the 1991 Act.... More generally, though, the "Introduction and User Guide" to the Guidelines summarises their aim as being to improve "consistency of approach" and identifies the central task of the sentencer to be "how to assess the relative *seriousness* of each case and how to arrive at a *commensurate penalty*"....

... The Guidelines are obviously designed to be "user friendly," and they adopt a broad brush approach. No doubt this is for reasons of utility. A more detailed guide may be too cumbersome for convenient use in a court where sentencing lists are often long and time for thought and discussion may be consequently short. Important general information is given in the first three pages of the Guidelines. For each of the offences listed, the user is advised to ask how *serious* is the particular case to be sentenced compared with other offences of this type. Each offence is then set out on a single page which bears the commonly used name of the offence (*e.g.* "no insurance," "overloading") or relevant form of it (*e.g.* "theft from vehicle" or "burglary: non-dwelling"). A number of positive and negative "seriousness indicators" (typically three or four) are given for each offence, listed under plus and minus signs. These factors are much the same as "aggravating and mitigating factors" but, in line with the Act, they are confined to those matters which relate to the seriousness of the offence, which the court is bound to take into account under the Act's provisions, rather than to the mitigating circumstances of the offender, which the court may take into account in its discretion....

... The Guidelines user is then taken through a series of threshold decisions, or the ascending levels of the sentencing "pyramid," and is asked to consider whether a particular form of sentence is appropriate, given the key factor of the seriousness of the offence. A move upwards from a fine or a discharge to a community sentence has, under the Act, to be justified by the sentencer in terms of the "seriousness of the offence," whilst a move upwards to a custodial sentence must be justified either in terms of the "seriousness of the offence" or "protection of the public in cases of violent or sexual offences." This latter category is not of great importance in magistrates' jurisdiction. The guidelines start each time at the *base* of the pyramid and ask each of the threshold questions in turn. For each offence a "guideline fine" is suggested, but the introduction makes it clear that these are to be regarded as "starting points, not finishing points" and that "the proper approach is to consider all the facts in each individual case and then to decide whether, and by how much, the sentence should be higher or lower than the starting point...."

Notes

1. The development of sentencing guidelines by the Magistrates' Association is clearly to be welcomed. Is it right that the local clerk to the justices, senior magistrates, or the local liaison judge are capable of exercising an equal amount of influence over magistrates' sentencing decisions? Should the sentencing guidelines be given statutory force?

2. In his editorial comment in the Criminal Law Review, Professor Ashworth explains that magistrates have a particular need for their Association's guidelines as appellate decisions rarely have much relevance to the type of sentencing questions which are faced by the lower courts. He states (at [1992] Crim. L.R. 610):

> "Some have argued that the result of promulgating guidelines of this kind is that some magistrates follow them slavishly, and fail to exercise their judgment in individual cases. That is a response which the guidelines themselves may not be able to prevent, even though they state repeatedly that they provide 'starting points not finishing points'. It is a matter for those who direct the training of magistrates."

3. Wasik and Turner make reference to the sentencing "pyramid". This represents the decision-making process, with offence seriousness as the key concept, which starts at the base with a fine or discharge, moving upwards to community sentences, with a custodial sentence at the top. This is one way of viewing the guidelines for sentencing contained in the Criminal Justice Act 1991: the seriousness of the offence is the determining factor as to whether the sentencer moves "up" the pyramid in search of the appropriate or "proportional" sentence. (For the origins of this analogy, see A. Ashworth, "Non Custodial Sentences" [1992] Crim. L.R. 242).

There is nothing new about sentencers having to address the issue of offence seriousness. It is the pre-eminence of this criterion that is novel. It is surely correct to use the idea of proportionality as a guiding principle, rather than to rely upon nebulous notions of deterrence or rehabilitation which were formerly the basis of reductivist sentencing. Once a fair and consistent approach has been established, it is to be hoped that sentencing disparity will become less of a problem. The Magistrates' Association guidelines, taken in conjunction with the Criminal Justice Act 1991, are a step in the right direction.

How are other sentencers to arrive at an informed and principled decision?

There has to be a generally accepted "ranking" of offences in terms of seriousness. Within each type of offence there must also be a notional scale of seriousness: for instance, a crime such as robbery can range form an armed raid on a security van to a youth snatching a handbag from its resisting owner in the street (see *Clouden* [1987] Crim. L.R. 56). When there is more than one offender involved in the commission of the offence, the sentencer may also have to make distinctions between their levels of culpability; for instance, one offender may have planned the crime or exerted pressure on a co-defendant to participate. Finally, a wide range of mitigating and aggravating factors may affect the sentencer's assessment of offence seriousness (see below).

To assist sentencers to achieve consistency with one another, reference is sometimes made to a notional scale of penalties (or "tariff") which has been developed by the courts under the guidance of the Court of Appeal. The idea of a fixed "tariff" can be rather misleading, especially when sentencing is represented as a choice between "tariff" and "individualised" sentences. (In any case, the Criminal Justice Act 1991 has now overtaken this oversimplified view of sentencing decisions). But it is inevitable that some notional scale of penalties, based on established practices and applied with discretion, will be influential in determining the sentence of the court.

The role of the Court of Appeal in giving guidance to the lower courts is of considerable importance, although the precise jurisprudential nature of these decisions is still a matter for debate. It was observed in *De Havilland* [1983] Crim. L.R. 489 (at 490) that Court of Appeal sentencing decisions are "not authoritative in the strict sense". But with the increased reporting and citing of such authorities it is slightly pedantic to debate their precise normative value. One significant development has been the increase in number of "guideline" judgments of the Court of Appeal which are clearly regarded as binding by the lower courts. These decisions deal with a certain type of offence and explain the levels of sentence appropriate for the different manifestations of the crime, taking account of aggravating and mitigating factors. (For example, see *Billam* [1986] Crim. L.R. 347 (on rape); *Aramah* [1983] Crim. L.R. 271 (on importation of cannabis); *Stewart* [1987] Crim. L.R. 520 (on social security fraud); *Barrick* [1985] Crim. L.R. 602 (on theft in breach of trust)). But a major weakness of appellate guidance on sentencing, in general, is that it has tended to concentrate on more serious offences, with relatively little help offered to the lower courts in sentencing the more common property offences.

Aggravation and Mitigation

When a sentencer considers the seriousness of an offence, he must include any aggravating or mitigating factors in his assessment. For example, the Criminal Justice Act 1991, section 3(3)(a) states that "in forming any such opinion [about offence seriousness] ... a court shall take into account all such information about the circumstances of the offence ... (including any aggravating or mitigating factors) as is available to it." The decision whether to impose a custodial sentence, as opposed to either a financial or a community penalty, will turn on the important concept of offence seriousness: aggravating and mitigating factors will be relevant to this decision. So what are the well established aggravating and mitigating factors? If the offence was premeditated, as opposed to impulsive, it will tend to influence the court. Offences committed in breach of a position of trust will also tend to be regarded as more serious. For instance, a shop manager stealing from his employer can expect the court to view his conduct more severely than theft by a customer or someone else not in a position of trust. The behaviour of the victim might also be a relevant consideration, for example where the offender was provoked into committing an assault.

There are other mitigating factors which have no direct relevance to the issue of offence seriousness, such as whether the offender pleaded guilty, his previous good character, or indeed other personal circumstances which are presented to the court in either the mitigation speech or the pre-sentence report. These factors might lead to a reduction in the sentence which would otherwise have been imposed. The offender's personal circumstances which are unfavourable should not lead to an increase in the sentence, otherwise the penalty imposed would not reflect the seriousness of the crime.

Andrew Ashworth, *Sentencing and Criminal Justice* **(1992), pp. 122–123, 125–128.**

Some Preliminary Problems of Principle

The 1991 Act begins, then, by linking aggravating and mitigating factors to the seriousness of the offence. This means that the court's duty, under section 3(3)(a), is to take account of factors which bear on the harmfulness or potential harmfulness of the conduct, and the culpability of the offender. Taking account of section 28(1), it could also be said that the 1991 Act links aggravating factors to the primary rationale for sentencing – proportionality or desert – and yet insists on no such link for mitigating factors. Is this defensible in theory? Is it fair in practice? How, for these purposes, should aggravation and mitigation be defined?

It might seem strange to have proportionality as the primary rationale of sentencing, and then to have a list of aggravating and mitigating factors which included some based on considerations of deterrence, or rehabilitation, or some other purpose, which conflicts with the primary aim. However, this is not necessarily illogical. We have already observed, that it is possible to justify a sentencing system which has a primary rationale and which then allows certain other rationales to have priority in respects of certain types of crime or types of offender. The key requirement here is that the justifications be strong. Similarly, the notion that all aggravating and mitigating factors ought necessarily to be linked to the primary rationale must be rejected as too astringent a view, particularly in the context of a branch of the law so closely entwined with social policy and so politically sensitive as sentencing. It would seem odd and probably inconsistent if the core of aggravating and mitigating factors were not linked to the primary rationale, but there is no reason why additional factors should not be recognised. Everything depends on careful examination of the justifications for these factors.

One reason why the main aggravating and mitigating factors should be related to the primary rationale is that their status as such might be purely adventitious. One legal system may have separate offences of robbery and armed robbery, the latter defined so as to penalise robbery involving the use or threatened use of a gun. Another, such as England and Wales, might have a single offence of robbery, and might treat the use or threatened use of a gun as an aggravating factor. Similarly, some countries have a separate offence of sexual abuse by a person in a position of authority over the victim, whereas English law treats this factor as an aggravation of any sexual offence. It may therefore be a matter of legislative tradition whether such factors are part of the definition of the crime or are left to sentencing. Clearly, however, it should not affect the principle on which they are based. The definitions of offences should in general be coherent with the primary rationale of sentencing, and the same should apply to factors which could readily be treated as elements in the definitions of offences.

A third preliminary question concerns the practical relationship between aggravating and mitigating factors. It is often right to suppose that the opposite of a mitigating factor will count as aggravating (*e.g.* impulsive reactions may justify mitigation and premeditated behaviour may be aggravating), and this applies particularly where the two factors can be represented as extreme points on a spectrum. There may be other circumstances in which the absence of a mitigating factor should not count as aggravating. There has been some debate in England about the implications of the sentencing "discount" for pleading guilty: clearly a person who pleads not guilty and is convicted cannot receive this discount, and so the sentence will be higher than for someone who pleaded guilty to a similar offence. But does that mean that pleading not guilty and putting the prosecution to proof is an aggravating factor? It does mean that pleading not guilty has a potential cost; but in principle the person who is convicted after a not guilty plea should receive the normal sentence, not an aggravated sentence. In essence, there should be three notional responses to factors in each case – aggravated, neutral, and mitigated. These may simply represent points on a spectrum (*e.g.* between impulsivity and premeditation). But where the factor relates to the presence or absence of a single element (*e.g.* pleading guilty or not guilty), there is a question how they should be characterised. The wrong approach is to assume that the opposite or negative of a mitigating factor is necessarily aggravating; it might be neutral, as demonstrated by the theory of the discount for a guilty plea. For example, it is widely accepted to be an aggravating factor if the offence is committed against an elderly or a very young victim, but it would be absurd to claim mitigation on the basis that the victim was aged between, say, 20 and 50. That is simply a neutral factor....

... It is not difficult to think of a handful of aggravating factors which are well established in English sentencing practice: offences by groups or gangs, offences against young, elderly or otherwise vulnerable victims, offences involving the abuse of trust or authority, racially motivated offences, and offences involving planning or organisation. How do these possible justifications relate to the theory of proportionality? In relation to each of them, is the conduct more harmful, or are the offenders more culpable?....

... From this brief consideration of six general aggravating factors it is evident that the Court of Appeal has not tended to justify them in terms of their effect in increasing the seriousness of the offence. Instead, courts have usually adopted the terminology of deterrence, and have probably done so without reflecting on the different rationales of sentencing. It is true that in a carefully constructed theory of deterrence the concept of proportionality is important, since Bentham devoted a whole chapter to it and included such injunctions as "venture more against a great offence than a small one". However, deterrence is not the benchmark under the 1991 Act. The central concept is proportionality, and this is how any aggravating factor must be justified. The suggestion here is that each of the [general aggravating] factors is rightly regarded as increasing the seriousness of offences, even though the foundations of the "breach of trust" factor may be thought rather nebulous....

... The factors which have been recognised as mitigating sentences in England are a much more heterogeneous collection than the aggravating factors. The distinction between general mitigating factors and those relevant only to particular types of offence can be applied, of course, but it is merely one of several. Amongst the specific and general factors are some which reduce the harmfulness of the offence, and many more which reduce the culpability of the offender. There are also further distinctions to be drawn between mitigating factors relating to the seriousness of the offence, those relating to contributions to the criminal justice system since the offence, those relating to the wider social contribution of the offender, and those relating to the probable impact of the sentence....

... We can list as general mitigating factors such matters as the small amount of damage caused, the minor role of the offender and provocation received from the victim. Perhaps a less obvious factor would be an element of justification, as where the offender had a right to defend himself from attack but used excessive force in doing so. In this kind of case the harm done remains the same, but its context and social meaning are less serious than an offence with no colour of justification. Indeed, the same line of reasoning can be used to classify provocation as a general mitigating factor, emphasising the apparent wrong which caused the resentment and impulsive response of the offender.

The core of mitigation surely lies in the conditions personal to the offender which are treated as reducing culpability. It is hardly necessary here to construct an argument in favour of reduced culpability for those who fail to bring themselves within the narrow confines of criminal law defences such as insanity, duress, necessity, mistake of law, etc. Indeed, many of those defences are restricted tightly in the expectation that courts will award substantial mitigation of sentence where the circumstances fall just outside the legal requirements for a defence. As for the entrapment of the offender by the police or an *agent provocateur*, the English courts have declared that there is no such defence but that it ought to be a matter of mitigation in appropriate cases. Turning to cases where the offender has been under exceptional stress or emotional pressure, this will generally be regarded as mitigation, on the basis of reduced culpability. This is one of a number of factors regarded as insufficient to amount to complete defences to liability but appropriate for mitigation, which may be substantial in an appropriate case. An example might be the person who steals in order to provide comforts for a dying relative. Some legal systems might respond to cases of entrapment or of exceptional stress by granting a complete defence to liability, or at least reducing the class of offence. We are not concerned with those arguments here, we are concerned only to state that conditions which involve partial exculpation rather than total exculpation seem prima facie grounds for mitigation.

What about other matters personal to the offender? It is generally treated as mitigation where the offence was committed impulsively or suddenly: this lies at the opposite end of the spectrum from planning and premeditation, which are treated as aggravating, whereas an intentional but unplanned offence might perhaps be neutral. Where the offender is fairly young or fairly old, this may also be treated as a mitigating factor. The age of criminal responsibility is 10 in English law, and it is rare for anyone under 14 to be convicted of an offence. It is logical to suggest that offenders in their teens might be slightly less responsible than older offenders, being more impressionable, more easily led and less controlled in their behaviour. It might also be assumed that elderly people sometimes become less rational in their behaviour. In these cases, as in all others, we are concerned with general arguments and their foundations. Of course, much depends on the court's assessment of the facts in the particular case. Some young people can be deliberate and calculating in their offences, and some elderly people are thought sufficiently rational to govern major nations of the world.

Note

Section 28(1) of the Criminal Justice Act 1991 states that nothing in the relevant part of the Act "shall prevent a court from mitigating an offender's sentence by taking into account any such matters as, in the opinion of the court, are relevant in mitigation of sentence". As noted earlier, under section 3(3)(a) sentencers are required to take account of any mitigating or aggravating factors which are relevant to offence seriousness. Section 28 gives the sentencer a discretion to consider other mitigating circumstances which do not impinge upon the seriousness of the offence committed. This acknowledges that although proportionality is now to be the primary principle guiding the sentence of the court, other factors will still be relevant, such as the need to ensure the smooth running of the criminal justice system.

Another difficulty facing sentencers is the need to weigh the harm inflicted by an offender on his victim against the intent (or lack of it) with which the offence was committed. These problems are starkly illustrated by recent controversial cases which are discussed in the following article.

David Thomas, "Why the Sentence Fits the Crime", *The Guardian*, March 22, 1994.

Shoplifter Andrew Bray was sentenced to five years in prison last week for the manslaughter of Jonathan Roberts, the 17-year old shop assistant who tackled him. The next day Stephen Doyle, a heroin addict whose victim, policewoman Leslie Harrison, survived a stab wound in the chest, was sentenced to 15 years. Mr Justice Drake, the judge in the first case, complained publicly that he was unable to pass the sentence he thought was right, even though the law allows a life sentence. The public are once more puzzled by what looks like crazy sentencing.

There are logical explanations. The sentencer's task is to punish the offender according to his culpability, not to find a sentence which will somehow make good the damage he has done. As the Lord Chief Justice, Lord Taylor, said in a recent case, human life cannot be restored, or its loss measured, by the length of a prison sentence; no term of months or years imposed on the offender can reconcile the victim's family to their loss or cure their anguish.

Two elements are involved in assessing culpability – the harm the offender has caused and his state of mind when he committed the crime. In a case of attempted murder, like the policewoman's stabbing, the prosecution must prove that the offender actually intended to kill the victim. Long sentences are normally passed, unless there is extraordinary mitigation.

In cases of involuntary manslaughter, death results from an unlawful act which was not intended to cause serious harm (if such harm had been intended, the verdict would have been murder). Bray said he wanted only to get away from Jonathan Roberts, and had not intended him serious harm. According to a pathologist's report, Jonathan would have survived Bray's blows, but was knocked unconscious and choked on his own vomit.

The harm is extreme, but the intention may be only to commit a relatively minor assault. In one recent case, the defendant hit an elderly man, who struck his head as he fell to the ground. The defendant, who had not started the fight, was charged with common assault. The prosecution dropped the charge at the magistrates' court and the defendant was bound over to keep the peace. When the victim died three months later he was charged with manslaughter and sentenced to two years in prison.

At the other extreme, an offender who goes out to commit a dangerous crime such as armed robbery, and causes death unintentionally when his shotgun goes off by accident, can expect a very different sentence – 16 years in one recent case.

The principle on which these sentences are based – and it is not a new one – is clear. The court takes the conduct of the defendant as a starting point, paying particular attention to his state of mind, and imposes a sentence based on the gravity of that conduct but including an additional element to reflect the fact that death has been caused, albeit unintentionally.

In the armed robbery case, the Court of Appeal thought that the sentence for the robbery on its own would have been 13 years. The fact that the victim had been accidentally killed (the defendant severed his own finger in the blast) justified an extra three years.

Cases where death results unexpectedly from what would otherwise have been a relatively minor assault are not uncommon, and the courts have established conventional sentencing practices to deal with them. In a recent case, the defendant punched a man who had been shouting obscenities. The man tripped over a kerbstone and fell to the ground, banging the back of his head.

The Appeal Court said that where there was a single blow of moderate force, no provocation and an immediate admission, the starting point would be twelve months. If the assault was gratuitous and unprovoked, more than one blow struck, and the offender susceptible to outbreaks of violence, a longer sentence would be right.

In the most recent Court of Appeal case, two men who had been drinking started to fight. One threw a chair at the other and hit him with a bottle. The other seized his assailant by the throat and tried to punch him. Death was caused by pressure applied to the throat. The jury acquitted the defendant of murder. The Appeal Court reduced his sentence from four years to two-and-a-half.

Against this background, the options available to Mr Justice Drake were limited. A judge is not free to sentence simply according to his own views of the relative gravity of different crimes. If he were, there would be unacceptable disparities in sentencing. The judge must sentence within the statutory framework provided by Parliament, and in the light of general principles followed by all judges.

The most important is that the offender must be sentenced for the offence of which he has been convicted, not for an offence of which some people think he may be guilty but which cannot be proved. If an accused is acquitted of murder by the jury, or his plea of not guilty to murder is accepted by the prosecution, the judge must sentence on the basis that he did not intend to cause serious injury. If the defendant has pleaded guilty, he should normally be given some credit in the sentence for that.

Has the Court of Appeal got it badly wrong, as Mr Justice Drake seems to imply? In another case last Friday, he said: "If, as a result of the publicity, the Court of Appeal has another look at this matter or politicians insist in some way on higher sentences, I shall be delighted." The idea that an offender should be sentenced simply on the basis of the harm he has done, without regard to his intentions, went out of fashion hundreds of years ago. The principles for dealing with involuntary manslaughter have been in place for decades.

The Law Commission is about to publish proposals for reform of the law of involuntary manslaughter. Lawyers will be surprised if it does not propose restricting the scope of the crime to exclude minor assaults which unexpectedly and unintentionally cause death. Should the Appeal Court reconsider the guidance it has given in cases of this kind over the last 30 years?

No sentence which could be passed will ever satisfy the conflicting expectations of the bereaved relatives for a sentence which properly recognises their loss, and of the defendant for a sentence which does not unfairly punish him for the unintended consequences of his action. It may be that the compromise the Court of Appeal has found, through years of experience of similar cases, is the best that can be achieved.

Notes

1. It is difficult to fault the logic of Dr Thomas' arguments. But the defendant Bray, whilst attempting to escape from the scene of his earlier crime, knocked his victim unconscious and caused his death. The judge may be forgiven for thinking that the Court of Appeal could do well to reconsider the appropriate level of sentence in such cases. In particular, it might be considered whether using violence to escape apprehension by a member of the public ought to be an aggravating factor (as it surely would be to assault a policeman in similar circumstances). There is a social value in members of society trying to prevent crime, rather than simply taking no notice, and the sentence imposed on Bray fails to reflect this consideration. It also fails to take account of the vulnerability of his victim (Jonathan Roberts was merely seventeen years old).

2. The above examples show how difficult it can be to assess the seriousness of the offence and also which factors should be regarded as aggravating or mitigating in relation to offence seriousness. This key concept, on which the Criminal Justice Act 1991 is based, will be considered further below.

But before assessing the new legislative framework for sentencing decisions, it is interesting to look at how the considerable changes to the sentencing system came about. It was once thought that sentencing policy was the preserve of the Court of Appeal and the judiciary, whilst penal policy was a matter for the executive. Was there any constitutional justification for the Court of Appeal's control over sentencing policy? Can legislative restrictions on sentencing discretion be regarded, in any sense, as unconstitutional? Although some parts of the following extract are now a little outmoded, it raises a number of interesting issues which are germane to this discussion.

A. Ashworth, "Judicial Independence and Sentencing Reform", in *The Future of Sentencing* (D. A. Thomas, ed., 1982), University of Cambridge, Occasional Papers No. 8, pp. 46–52.

Are Executive Attempts to Influence the Judiciary Unconstitutional?
    Like many other constitutional matters in England, the proper relationship of the legislature, the judiciary and the executive on matters of sentencing has never been defined. Certainly it must be unconstitutional to "pack" the bench with sentencers of a particular persuasion, or to attempt to exert influence over the sentence in a particular case. There has often been acrimonious debate over the power of the executive to review sentences passed by the courts, but the debate has invariably been over the *way* in which executive review is carried out rather than over the constitutionality of this power. Moreover it is difficult to speak of a separation of powers in a system which has, in the Lord Chancellor, a figure who is both a member of the government and head of the judiciary. In his judicial capacity the Lord Chancellor has from time to time offered advice on sentencing policy to the magistracy; to what extent he might do the same for the judiciary has not been

tested. The present relationship between the executive and the judiciary may be found expressed in this passage from the report of the House of Commons Expenditure Committee (Session 1977–8, H.C. 662)

> "The starting point of our discussion must be recognition of the constitutional position of the judiciary as independent of the executive arm of the government and the legislature. This means that it would not be appropriate for the Home Office to tell the judges what to do, even if the result of judicial activity were to threaten the breakdown of the prison system, which is very nearly what has occurred." (para. 37)

This suggests that the proper role of the executive is to "service" the courts, providing facilities and information and ensuring that (subject to the exercise of executive review, through the parole system or the prerogative of mercy) the sentence of the court is duly carried out. Thus, for example, the Expenditure committee stressed the importance of reserving custodial penalties only for those "whose behaviour seriously menaces society and threatens personal safety", and of not imprisoning those who are young enough to "grow out" of their criminal behaviour or whose offences are more of a nuisance than a menace (para. 237). But when they came to the implementation of this policy, the inhibiting effect of the taboo [sc. the principle of judicial independence in relation to sentencing policy] showed itself:

> "It is the courts who decide into which of the various categories described the offender fits, in the light of his offence and his previous behaviour. The Sub-Committee firmly believe in the principle of judicial independence and accept its consequences in terms of our recommendations. At the same time we feel that more could be done to *acquaint* the courts at all levels with reliable information about the availability of accommodation in custodial institutions which we feel might *help* them in making their decisions. We also believe that relevant *information* about the alternatives to imprisonment should also be *supplied* to the courts . . .' (para. 238).

The words which I have underlined show the practical limitations imposed by the taboo: the executive may strive to provide all sentencers with the maximum information about alternatives to custodial sentences, but it must not tell the courts what to do. The report does, however, accept the importance of *persuading* the courts to impose shorter sentences of imprisonment, and adds:

> "It is our view that for a small but significant proportion of cases which come before the courts there can be no clear-cut reasons for choosing imprisonment for deterrent, retributive, containment or rehabilitative reasons. We wish the courts to be more aware of these considerations, and to choose, for cases which fall within this margin, non-custodial rather than custodial sentences." (Para. 32).

The practical implications of "wishing the courts to be more aware . . ." remain obscure: in effect, this is a policy recommendation without much hint of how it might be implemented, save by "informing" the courts of the Committee's reasoning. The Home Office itself has been more bold. It ensured that a copy of the Advisory Council's interim report on *The Length of Prison Sentences* was sent to every judge and every bench of magistrates in the country, and that report contained some direct advice to sentencers:

> "Given, however, that there is no reason to suppose that longer sentences have a greater impact upon the prisoner than shorter ones, the general rule which we *advocate* for all courts to follow is to stop at the point where a sentence has been decided upon and consider whether a shorter one would not do just as well." (HMSO 1977, para. 12).

"We think that the time has come when the courts should be *invited* to make their contribution towards a solution of this problem [sc. overcrowding in prisons]." (para. 16).

Although the effect of the taboo is apparent from the deferential tone of a later remark – "we are encouraged to believe that the judges who sit in the Court of Appeal, Criminal Division, will be sympathetic to our overall approach" (para. 18) – this interim report and the Home Office's action in distributing it to all sentencers assume a more active role for the executive than merely "servicing" the courts. This raises two further questions: if the government has a sentencing policy which it wishes the courts to adopt, (a) is it constitutionally proper to attempt to influence the courts through executive rather than legislative channels; and (b) is this method likely to be less, equally or more effective?

Is Legislative Curtailment of the Judicial Sentencing Discretion Unconstitutional?

Almost everyone would answer this question in the negative; attempts by the legislature to "interfere with" the sentencing discretion have invariably been attacked in England as unwise and unpractical, but it would be unusual to argue that such attempts are strictly unconstitutional. Thus the limitations imposed on English sentencers by section 3 of the Criminal Justice Act 1961 and, for a few years, by the Criminal Justice Act 1967 (mandatory suspension of certain short sentences), were vigorously attacked from many points of view – but not their constitutional status. Yet the taboo only grudgingly stops short of legislative intervention, and this raises the question of what is the proper separation of functions between legislature and judiciary on matters of sentencing. On this there is much to commend the view of Sir James Fitzjames Stephen that if the judiciary took upon themselves the task of formulating principles of sentencing, "they would be assuming a power which the constitution does not give them." Of course it might be retorted that the British constitution is so vague that it frequently "does not give" a power which had been traditionally exercised by a particular body. But the substantive point is surely that matters of general policy should be for the legislature, whilst the proper function of the courts is to carry out those policies in the varying circumstances of individual cases. This is the view which is hardly ever questioned in relation to the criminal law itself or to such matters as social welfare legislation – who would argue that the development of policy in these areas should be for the courts alone? – and it is difficult to see why sentencing should be different. The creation and alteration of sentencing policies and priorities should be for Parliament, whereas the true role of the courts is the loyal individuation of those policies. Whether the courts should be left a greater or lesser degree of discretion for their task of loyal individuation may well depend on questions of practicality, but the constitutional principle is surely clear.

This principle is not reflected in the present separation of functions in England. The courts have assumed the very power which Stephen maintained they do not possess ... This is not to imply that the courts are to blame for this usurpation. On the contrary, it is inevitable that a court which gives reasoned judgments on appeals against sentence will draw upon broad principles. If no such principles are laid down, they will surely develop over a period of time. This is how the courts developed the English common law over the centuries, and it is also how they have developed principles of sentencing since the creation of an appeal court in 1907. Parliament's desultory forays into sentencing policy have, by comparison, been rather insignificant and not conspicuously successful ... It is thus fair to say that in England the legislature has delegated or even abdicated its policy-making function on sentencing to the judiciary, save on a few peripheral issues. Whether one judges this to be a good thing or a bad thing might depend less on notions of constitutional purity than upon the acceptability of the policies evolved by the courts ... [Ashworth goes on to suggest that there is a gap between official, Home Office policy and the actual policy pursued by the courts] ... And the existence of such a gap can only call into question the continuing wisdom of delegating the policy-making function to the courts, which in turn raises questions about possible alternative approaches.

Can All Attempts to Fetter Sentencing Discretion Be Dismissed As Unpractical?

Whilst the taboo does not strictly exclude legislative intervention on constitutional grounds, it certainly does so on practical grounds. My version of the taboo might be though extreme, since it excludes *all* attempts to fetter the discretion. But it is important to gain acceptance for the view that some legislative attempts might be worthwhile: once that is accepted, the discussion can move forward.

We might begin by enquiring why the discretion to select a sentence is so highly valued. In this connection, two distinctions should be noticed. One is the distinction between variations to reflect the circumstances of a particular case and variations to reflect the sentencer's own preferences. The purpose of discretion is certainly to allow the sentencer to select the sentence which he believes to be most appropriate in the individual case, considering both the facts of the case and any reports on the offender's character. The purpose of discretion is surely not to enable individual judges and magistrates to pursue personal sentencing preferences. Whether a system of sentencing can successfully promote the former whilst controlling the latter may depend on the strength of collegiate pressures among sentencers and the operation of the appeals system ... A second distinction is that between choosing which policy to apply, and choosing how best to implement a given policy in an individual case. It may be strongly argued that it is essential to preserve a judicial discretion to individuate a given policy by applying it to a particular case, and it might be found that for some classes of case the courts must in effect be left to select the appropriate approach – because of the difficulty of laying down criteria in some areas of sentencing. But the principal arguments in favour of discretion merely support discretion to select the appropriate way of implementing the given policy in a particular case, not a discretion to select the policies to be applied.

The sheer multiplicity of possible legislative techniques for fettering the sentencing discretion makes it inherently unlikely that every one can be dismissed as unpractical. Even the approach of listing guidelines and policies, in the manner of the Model Penal Code, has been used by the English legislature in other fields of judicial discretion. And whilst section 3 of the Criminal Justice Act 1961 and the mandatory suspension of certain short sentences might be conceded to be "failures" in legislative intervention (although arguments could be ranged on both sides), the provision that a court must disqualify a drunken driver for at least one year unless there are "special reasons" for not doing so shows that legislative intervention can be successful. The aim was to reduce disparity in sentencing and to ensure strict control over the category of cases in which disqualification was not ordered, and this aim has been achieved. There may well be other areas of sentencing which could be amenable to this legislative technique: if parliament is clear about the desired policy and doubtful whether that policy would be consistently implemented if the courts were left with an unfettered discretion, this is one of the approaches which should be considered. It is therefore submitted that *all* attempts to fetter sentencing discretion cannot be dismissed as unpractical, and that the question should remain open for discussion in relation to each particular type of problem.

Would the Fettering of Sentencing Discretion Inevitably Lead to Injustice?

To an extent the "injustice" argument is merely a consequence of the high value placed upon the existence of discretion in sentencing. Since discretion allows the court to impose a sentence appropriate for the individual offender, the removal of discretion is seen as inevitably leading to some inappropriate sentences and thus to injustices against offenders. Whilst that is an understandable line of reasoning, it neglects some important points. First, the fettering of discretion does not necessarily mean the complete removal of discretion. Thus, returning to the different senses of discretion distinguished earlier, the legislature might enunciate certain general principles whilst leaving the courts to apply them in individual cases. Secondly, it is fair to assume that any sentencing system will produce some anomalous results which might be described as injustices. It is surely wrong to suggest that the fettering of discretion will cause injustice to individuals, with the implication that to leave an unbridled discretion would never produce injustice. It may well be true that some legislative methods of fettering discretion, such as the mandatory suspension of short prison sentences, produce more anomalous results than would an unfettered discretion. But that is no reason for opposing all fettering of discretion; each proposal must be viewed on its merits. Thirdly, the very concept of injustice raises difficult questions. Is it not impossible to evaluate the justice or injustice of particular sentences without some conception of the proper aims of sentencing? Could it not be the case that those who cry "injustice" are supporting aims which differ from those of the system as a whole? Or, on a slightly lower plane, is it not possible that a particular legislative fetter on sentencing could produce more sentencing decisions in accord with the legislature's policy than an unfettered discretion – thus illustrating the difference between the legislature's view of justice in sentencing and the view of the critic? The criteria upon which any "injustice" argument is based must always be thoroughly explored.

Notes

1.   For a thorough examination of the constitutional basis of judicial independence, and its relevance to the sentencing function, see Colin Munro, "Judicial Independence and Judicial Functions", in *Sentencing, Judicial Discretion and Training* (C. Munro and M. Wasik eds., 1992). Munro concludes that judges should not "cease to play any role in the determination of sentences. But any defence of their participation will have to be advanced on some ground such as their special expertise or particular experience, and the participation of others should be debated on its merits.... A judicial monopoly should never again be advocated on the bases of mis-understandings of legal history and misrepresentations of constitutional theory". (at p. 32).

2.   For a contrasting view to Ashworth's, see David Thomas' essay "The Justice Model of Sentencing – Its Implications for the English Sentencing System" (in *The Future of Sentencing* (D. A. Thomas ed., 1982)).

3.   The government eventually lost patience with the senior judiciary's failure to bring about any effective changes in sentencing practice. Repeated pleas for shorter sentences, and for avoiding imprisonment wherever possible for less serious property offences, met with very little success. It became increasingly apparent that more direct legislative intervention into sentencing policy and practice was required. The traditional objections to such a course of action have been noted above – the "taboo" as Ashworth called it – but a number of circumstances combined to override these objections. The continuing crisis in British prisons (which resulted in serious rioting in 1990), the failure of piecemeal legislation introducing measures like the partly suspended sentence, and an international movement towards stricter

guidelines for sentencers, all helped to create a climate in favour of more systematic legislative intervention. In 1990, the government revealed its plans for a radical reform of sentencing practice in its White Paper, *Crime, Justice and Protecting the Public*. Its aim was to establish a clearly defined set of principles for sentencers and, as such, it broke new ground.

Crime, Justice and Protecting the Public, (1990) White Paper, Cm. 965, paragraphs. 1.6, 1.15, 2.1–2.9, 2.16–2.17, 2.19–2.20, 3.9.

1.6 The aim of the Government's proposals is better justice through a more consistent approach to sentencing, so that convicted criminals get their "just deserts". The severity of the sentence of the court should be directly related to the seriousness of the offence. Most offenders can be punished by financial penalties – by paying compensation to their victims and by fines. When offences are too serious to be properly punished by financial penalties alone, the courts have a choice of community penalties, such as probation or community service, or of custody. A community penalty, like custody, can restrain an offender's liberty and freedom of movement, though obviously to a lesser extent than prison. The legislation will give guidance in general terms on when these punishments should be used. The Government expects the Court of Appeal will wish to give more detailed guidance to the courts as it interprets the legislation.

1.15 These changes are aimed at getting a coherent framework for the use of financial, community and custodial punishments, decisions on releasing long term prisoners on parole, and the arrangements for supervising offenders in the community, whether as a sentence or on release from custody. This should provide a more consistent approach, so that victims are compensated, the public protected and offenders receive their just deserts.

2.1 The Government's aim is to ensure that convicted criminals in England and Wales are punished justly and suitably according to the seriousness of their offences; in other words that they get their just deserts. No Government should try to influence the decisions of the courts in individual cases. The independence of the judiciary is rightly regarded as a cornerstone of our liberties. But sentencing principles and sentencing practice are matters of legitimate concern to Government, and Parliament provides the funds necessary to give effect to the courts' decisions.

2.2 The sentence of the court prescribes the punishment for criminal behaviour. Punishment in proportion to the seriousness of the crime has long been accepted as one of the many objectives in sentencing. It should be the principal focus for sentencing decisions. This is consistent with the Government's view that those who commit very serious crimes, particularly crimes of violence, should receive long custodial sentences; but that many other crimes can be punished in the community, with greater emphasis on bringing home to the criminal the consequences of his actions, compensation to the victim and reparation to the community.

A new legislative framework for sentencing

2.3 The Government proposes a new legislative framework for sentencing, based on the seriousness of the offence or just deserts. Other common law jurisdictions, for example, in the United States, Canada and Australia, are moving in this direction or are thinking of doing so. So far, Parliament has given little guidance to the courts on sentencing, beyond setting the maximum penalties for offences. The main guidance on sentencing has come from the Court of Appeal, which has increasingly emphasised the need for the courts to take account of the seriousness of the individual offence, and the aggravating and mitigating circumstances, if justice is to be done and to be seen to be done. The recent guidelines judgements, such as those on rape, incest and drug trafficking, have provided much clearer guidance on how sentencing decisions should be reached, as well as advice on the sentences suitable for the varying degrees of seriousness of an offence. To achieve a more coherent and comprehensive consistency of approach in sentencing, a new framework is needed for the use of custodial, community and financial penalties.

2.4 Punishment can effectively denounce criminal behaviour and exact retribution for it. The sentence of the court expresses public repugnance of criminal behaviour and determines the punishment for it. If the punishment is just, and in proportion to the seriousness of the offence, then the victim, the victim's family and friends, and the public will be satisfied that the law has been upheld and there will be no desire for further retaliation or private revenge.

2.5 Some forms of punishment, such as imprisonment, can effectively protect the public from further offences by an offender for a period of time. The offender may also be required to pay compensation to the victim or make some reparation to the public. The responses to the Government's Green paper "Punishment, Custody and the Community" showed there was widespread support for the priority given in the Criminal Justice Act 1988 to compensating victims. There is considerable support, too, for community service, when the offender has to make reparation to the public through unpaid work.

2.6 Reforming offenders is always best if it can be achieved. It is better that people should exercise self-control than have controls imposed upon them. This needs self discipline and motivation. Many offenders have little understanding of the effect of their actions on others. Compensation and community service can bring home to offenders the effect of their behaviour on other people. The probation service tries to make offenders face up to what they have done, to give them a greater sense of responsibility and to help them resist pressure from others to take part in crime. Voluntary organisations have a long tradition of helping offenders to turn away from crime.

2.7 It was once believed that prison, properly used, could encourage a high proportion of offenders to start an honest life on their release. Nobody now regards imprisonment, in itself, as an effective means of reform for most prisoners. If there is continued progress against overcrowding in prisons, the recent reforms should enable better regimes to be developed, with more opportunities for education, and work, and so a greater chance of turning the lives of some inmates in a positive direction. But however much prison staff try to inject a positive purpose into the regime, as they do, prison is a society which requires virtually no sense of personal responsibility from prisoners. Normal social or working habits do not fit. The opportunity to learn from other criminals is pervasive. For most offenders, imprisonment has to be justified in terms of public protection, denunciation and retribution. Otherwise it can be an expensive way of making bad people worse. The prospects of reforming offenders are usually much better if they stay in the community provided the public is properly protected.

2.8 Deterrence is a principle with much immediate appeal. Most law abiding citizens understand the reasons why some behaviour is made a criminal offence, and would be deterred by the shame of a criminal conviction or the possibility of a severe penalty. There are doubtless some criminals who carefully calculate the possible gains and risks. But much crime is committed on impulse, given the opportunity presented by an open window or unlocked door, and it is committed by offenders who live from moment to moment; their crimes are as impulsive as the rest of their feckless, sad or pathetic lives. It is unrealistic to construct sentencing arrangements on the assumption that most offenders will weigh up the possibilities in advance and base their conduct on rational calculation. Often they do not.

2.9 The Government's proposals therefore emphasise the objectives which sentencing is most likely to meet successfully in whole or in part. The first objective for all sentences is denunciation of and retribution for the crime. Depending on the offence and the offender, the sentence may also aim to achieve public protection, reparation and reform of the offender, preferably in the community. This approach points to sentencing policies which are more firmly based on the seriousness of the offence, and just deserts for the offender....

Implementing the new sentencing framework

2.16 The legislation will be in general terms. It is not the Government's intention that Parliament should bind the courts with strict legislative guidelines. The courts have shown great skill in the way they sentence exceptional cases. The courts will properly continue to have the wide discretion they need if they are to deal justly with the great variety of crimes which come before them. The Government rejects a rigid statutory framework, on the lines of those introduced in the United States, or a system of minimum or mandatory sentences for certain offences. This would make it more difficult to sentence justly in exceptional cases. It could also result in more acquittals by juries, with more guilty men and women going free unjustly as a result.

2.17 The Government hopes that the Court of Appeal will give further guidance, building on the legislative framework. It has already done so on sentencing young offenders, interpreting the provisions in the Criminal Justice Acts of 1982 and 1988. More than one type of sentence may be suitable for a particular type of offence. The types of sentence imposed for violent and property crimes are likely to overlap, so that some less serious violent crimes receive penalties similar to those for the middle range of property crimes. Even within a single offence, there is a wide range of culpability, according to the circumstances, the vulnerability of the victim and the degree of provocation....

2.19 Injustice is more likely if the courts do not focus on the seriousness of the offence before them when they sentence. In the new sentencing framework, a court's sentence usually should be the outcome of a sequence of questions. How serious is this offence? Is it more or less serious of its kind and are there mitigating factors? Can some compensation be given to the victim? Will financial penalties be adequate? If not, how much restraint on liberty is needed to punish this crime? If some restraints are justified, is community service, probation or another penalty most suitable for this offender? If community service, how many hours should be ordered? If probation, are additional requirements needed? Is the offence serious enough to justify a combination of financial and community penalties? Is the offence so serious that only a custodial sentence is justified? If so, how long a sentence is necessary to punish this offence? And, once these questions have been resolved, is a longer sentence needed from the Crown Court to protect the public from serious harm from an offender who has been convicted of a number of violent or sexual offences?

2.20 The Government will look to the Judicial Studies Board to make arrangements for training sentencers to give effect to the new sentencing policies and the more detailed interpretation of the legislation by the Court of Appeal. The new legislative provisions, the maximum penalties for each offence, the guidance from the Court of Appeal and the Attorney General's new power to refer over-lenient sentences for very serious offenders to the Court of Appeal, should all contribute to the development of coherent sentencing practice, which can be disseminated to the courts by the Judicial Studies Board. Against this background, the Government see no need for a Sentencing Council to develop sentencing policies or guidance....

Proposed legislative provisions on the use of custody....

... 3.9 The Government intends to introduce legislation which would require a court, before it gives a custodial sentence, to be satisfied that the offence for which the offender has been convicted by the court is so serious that only a custodial sentence is justified or that a custodial sentence is necessary to protect the public from serious harm. The length of a custodial sentence should be justified by the seriousness of the offences for which the offender has been convicted or which have been taken into consideration by the court. The court should give reasons why it considers a custodial sentence is justified.

Notes

1. The White paper makes it clear that, whilst not wishing to interfere in individual sentencing decisions, "sentencing principles and sentencing practice are matters of legitimate concern to Government."

2. In proposing a new legislative framework for sentencing based on proportionality (or "just deserts"), the White Paper explicitly rejected a deterrent approach as the correct method of deciding on the type and length of sentence. This signified quite a dramatic departure from traditional sentencing practice.

3. A useful discussion of the White Paper can be found in M. Wasik and A. von Hirsch, "Statutory Sentencing Principles: The 1990 White Paper", (1990), 53 Mod. L.R. 508. The authors state (at pp. 509–10):

> "The White Paper would make proportionality the main guiding criterion for deciding the severity of sentence. We agree with this approach for reasons that have been detailed elsewhere. Suffice it to say that proportionality is the criterion used in everyday life in evaluating the fairness of penalties and – since punishment by its very nature conveys blame – its severity should be allocated according to the blameworthiness of the criminal conduct....
>
> ... The proportionality principle can also provide useful guidance for sentencers. It is possible for courts to make judgments about the seriousness of criminal acts, and to grade penal responses accordingly. The judge, using his or her skill in legal arguments, can compare the harmfulness and culpability of a given type of criminal act with those of other types of criminal behaviour, and compare the severity of the proposed sentence with other sanctions. It is much harder for sentencers to estimate the rehabilitative, incapacitative or deterrent effects of a penalty – as those effects are largely uncertain, even to those who may profess some expertise in these matters, such as criminologists.
>
> The White Paper proposes to keep the power to decide the severity of sanctions for the various offence categories where it traditionally has been, with the judiciary. Proportionality is to be supplied as the guiding principle, but not as a formula. It is the courts which would decide the deserved severity of penalties for this or that type of crime, and would decide when circumstances of mitigation or aggravation were present in particular cases."

4. In another assessment of the White Paper by Paul Cavadino, "The White Paper – Will it Achieve its Objectives?" (1990) 80 *Prison Service Journal* 5, the author concludes (at p. 18):

"Overall, the White Paper includes many positive proposals, some of which will undoubtedly help to achieve its aim of cutting the unnecessary use of prison. Yet if the White Paper's strategy is to succeed, it must counteract the increase in prison numbers resulting from the parole changes, the danger of the new combined orders 'slipping down the tariff' and the prospect of a large increase in the numbers imprisoned for breach of community penalties. This requires much more detailed guidance to sentencers than the Court of Appeal has hitherto shown itself able or willing to give.

At present the more frequent the type of case, the less relevant guidance is likely to exist. In recent years the Court of Appeal has produced a plethora of guideline judgments on sentencing for serious violent and sexual offences, robbery and drug trafficking. Yet judgments containing guidance on less serious assaults, thefts, burglary and criminal damage are much harder to find. Moreover, as the sentence was probably unusually high in the first place, such judgments are often of little use in the average case. There is therefore a powerful argument for a Sentencing Council which would develop detailed guidance to be issued as practice directions, on sentencing in everyday criminal cases."

5. A further critique of the White Paper in the same journal raises slightly different issues. See Derek Williamson, "Questions of Punishment" (1990) 80 *Prison Service Journal* 18. He observes (at p. 20):

"The final and underlying question has little to do with punishment and whether it should become the focus of sentencing decisions. Far more fundamental is the question of whether it remains appropriate for crime, its effects and the elaborate systems for handling these to continue to be dealt with in semi-isolation from normal society. Admittedly, the White Paper recognises that the community and other bodies should be drawn increasingly into such fields as crime prevention, victim support and providing positive opportunities for offenders. But the White Paper stands firmly in that tradition which draws a sharp distinction between offenders and non-offenders, which fails to acknowledge that social and life conditions are experienced unequally, and which fails to recognize that the kind of society we create through social policy and legislation may contribute, sometimes in quite direct ways, to a persistent and endemic undercurrent of crime and/or other anti-social behaviour. Only when we begin to move away from the simplistic notion of a basically 'good' society against which a minority offend, and begin to try to understand and deal with crime as integral to that society, will we begin to make sufficient progress. The White Paper is light years away from such an approach."

Similar reservations about over-reliance on proportionality were expressed in a comparative study of Dutch and English sentencing practice by C.

Kelk, L. Koffman and J. Silvis, entitled "Sentencing Practice, Policy and Discretion" (in *Criminal Justice in Europe* (P. Fennell *et al.* eds., 1995)). In relation to the Dutch system it was stated:

> "We are not suggesting that a certain level of punishment is not indicated for certain types of offences committed in comparable circumstances. Such levels will be largely based on accepted practice. However, this severity scale is not the only determinant. There must also be scope for the special normative aspects of a case; a penalty may be excessively severe in some circumstances, if the offender has already been 'punished' (been injured for example) or if there is a deplorable family background, or serious illness. In such cases the best remedy, with most behavioural effect, could well be a fine or a community service order, rather than a custodial sentence. Such special aspects could result in moderation of what is, at first sight and according to the directives, a justified penalty in the given circumstances. Moderation could mean a less severe sentence, or a different type of penalty. In the traditional terminology of criminal law, this means the following: retribution, the essence and legal basis of all punishment, may very well justify a certain sentence, but different purposes of punishment, principles of humanity and subjective experience may all serve to undermine retribution."

IV. CRIMINAL JUSTICE ACT 1991: A STATUTORY FRAMEWORK FOR SENTENCING

The Criminal Justice Act 1991 represented a major development in sentencing law and practice. It did not ring the knell for sentencers' discretion, but it sought to curb the freedom of sentencers to pursue their own personal approaches to sentencing, based on their own perception of individual cases. The 1991 Act reflected the policy set out in the 1990 White Paper (discussed above), and established proportionality, or just deserts, as the guiding principle for sentencers. Although certain aspects of the new Act were not without problems, it was surprising that the Government responded so quickly to criticisms by amending parts of it before the Act's effects could be fully assessed. It seemed rather premature to start tinkering with such a carefully constructed piece of legislation. Some parts of the 1991 Act are dealt with in this section, in relation to the enactment of statutory principles for sentencers. Later sections of the book consider the Act in relation to imprisonment and release from prison, community sentences, and financial orders.

The following extract gives the text of some key provisions of the 1991 Act. It should be borne in mind that there have been some amendments to these provisions notably under the Criminal Justice Act 1993, which will be discussed later.

Criminal Justice Act 1991

PART I

POWERS OF COURTS TO DEAL WITH OFFENDERS

Custodial sentences

1. – (1) This section applies where a person is convicted of an offence punishable with a custodial sentence other than one fixed by law.

(2) Subject to subsection (3) below, the court shall not pass a custodial sentence on the offender unless it is of the opinion –

(a) that the offence, or the combination of the offence and one other offence associated with it, was so serious that only such a sentence can be justified for the offence; or

(b) where the offence is a violent or sexual offence, that only such a sentence would be adequate to protect the public from serious harm from him.

(3) Nothing in subsection (2) above shall prevent the court from passing a custodial sentence on the offender if he refuses to give his consent to a community sentence which is proposed by the court and requires that consent.

(4) Where a court passes a custodial sentence, it shall be its duty –

(a) in a case not falling within subsection (3) above, to state in open court that it is of the opinion that either or both of paragraphs (a) and (b) of subsection (2) above apply and why it is of that opinion; and

(b) in any case, to explain to the offender in open court and in ordinary language why it is passing a custodial sentence on him.

(5) A magistrates' court shall cause a reason stated by it under subsection (4) above to be specified in the warrant of commitment and to be entered in the register.

2. – (1) This section applies where a court passes a custodial sentence other than one fixed by law.

(2) The custodial sentence shall be –

(a) for such term (not exceeding the permitted maximum) as in the opinion of the court is commensurate with the seriousness of the offence, or the combination of the offence and other offences associated with it; or

(b) where the offence is a violent or sexual offence, for such longer term (not exceeding that maximum) as in the opinion of the court is necessary to protect the public from serious harm from the offender.

(3) Where the court passes a custodial sentence for a term longer than is commensurate with the seriousness of the offence, or the combination of the offence and other offences associated with it, the court shall –

(a) state in open court that it is of the opinion that subsection (2)(b) above applies and why it is of that opinion; and

(b) explain to the offender in open court and in ordinary language why the sentence is for such a term.

(4) A custodial sentence for an indeterminate period shall be regarded for the

purposes of subsections (2) and (3) above as a custodial sentence for a term longer than any actual term.

Community sentences

6. – (1) A court shall not pass on an offender a community sentence, that is to say, a sentence which consists of or includes one or more community orders, unless it is of the opinion that the offence, or the combination of the offence and one other offence associated with it, was serious enough to warrant such a sentence.

(2) Subject to subsection (3) below, where a court passes a community sentence –

(a) the particular order or orders comprising or forming part of the sentence shall be such as in the opinion of the court is, or taken together are, the most suitable for the offender; and

(b) the restrictions on liberty imposed by the order or orders shall be such as in the opinion of the court are commensurate with the seriousness of the offence, or the combination of the offence and other offences associated with it ...

Notes

1. The following commentary on these legislative provisions, which came into force on October 1, 1992, appeared in the Editorial: "Face the 1991 Act" [1992] Crim. L.R. 229, in which Andrew Ashworth wrote:

"[I]t can be claimed that the 1991 Act differs from its predecessors in one significant respect: its sentencing provisions have some fairly coherent themes. This is not to overlook the problems of the 1991 Act, one of which is that its themes do not emerge clearly from the wording of the legislation. The Act does not begin with a clear enunciation of principles: that is not the English way, although on this occasion it would have helped immensely with interpretation. Instead, the principles have to be inferred from the legislation, supplemented by reference to other documents. The leading principle is proportionality. Sentences should be calculated on the basis of what the person deserves for the offence committed, and not lengthened for any supposed deterrent or rehabilitative reasons, although there is a limited exception for 'public protection' sentences. The notion of proportionality promoted by the Government is the 'twin-track' approach, which involves less resort to custody for non-serious offences but longer custodial sentences for serious crimes ... The Act is designed to encourage greater resort to non-custodial sentences by introducing statutory restrictions on custody, by making available tougher 'community orders', and by fostering the notion of punishment in the community."

2. Section 1(2) of the 1991 Act states that a court is not to impose a custodial sentence unless it is of the opinion that the offence was so serious that only such a sentence can be justified; or, in cases of violent or sexual offences, that only such a sentence would be adequate for the purposes of

public protection. This sub-section shows that although proportionality is now to be the guiding sentencing principle, courts are not precluded (albeit in limited circumstances) from imposing a sentence to incapacitate a violent or sexual offender from whom the public requires protection. Deterrent sentencing *per se* is not permitted under these provisions if this would involve passing a sentence which would be disproportionate to the seriousness of the offence. However, the desert approach may have a deterrent effect on would be offenders as a by-product of its consistency and its concentration on offence seriousness.

The length of a prison sentence, under section 2, is now, primarily, to reflect the seriousness of the offence which has been committed. Similarly, section 6(2)(b) provides that restrictions on liberty imposed by a community sentence are to be "commensurate" with the seriousness of the offence in question. Also in relation to the fixing of fines, section 18(2) (as amended by the Criminal Justice Act 1993, s. 65(1)) states that "the amount of any fine fixed by a court shall be such as ... reflects the seriousness of the offence."

3.   An important aim of the 1991 Act was to provide a framework for sentencing decisions: not to abolish discretion, but to ensure that discretion was exercised according to consistent principles. Since the Act, the sentencing framework consists of four basic levels of sentence; discharges, fines, community sentences and custody. The concept of offence seriousness is the determinant of whether an offender will require a more severe penalty than either a discharge or a financial penalty. If it is warranted by the seriousness of the offence, a community sentence may be passed (see section 6(1)) instead of one of these lesser measures. In turn, custody may be imposed where the court decides that the offence is so serious that only such a sentence can be justified (subject to the exception discussed earlier).

4.   The relevance of an offender's previous convictions to the sentencing decision raises an issue of considerable importance. It is accepted that, in relation to most types of offence, an offender who has no previous convictions (or at least very few) should be allowed some mitigation of sentence. On the other hand, it was also well established that it is wrong in principle to pass a sentence which is disproportionate to the gravity of the offence, as a means of punishing the offender for his previous record. (See *Queen* (1981) Cr. App. R(S) 245 where the Court of Appeal reduced the sentence in a case involving theft and deception because the trial court had clearly sentenced the defendant on the basis of his bad criminal record). Thus, a bad record should not be regarded as an aggravating factor. This idea is sometimes expressed in terms of the "ceiling" principle of sentencing: that the facts of the present offence set a limit beyond which the sentencer should not go, regardless of the criminal record of the offender. Yet in practice, this principle has done little to prevent sentencers from sentencing offenders on the basis of their bad criminal records. In short, law and practice have tended to diverge on this point. This is acknowledged by Andrew Ashworth (1982) in "Reducing the Prison Population in the 1980s:

The Need for Sentencing Reform", in *A Prison System for the 1980s and Beyond* (NACRO) where he states (at p. 7):

> "This is where the English sentencing system, with all its principles, comes to grief. Ceilings are vague and elastic, and sometimes astoundingly high. For example, in *Gilbertson* [1981] Crim. L.R. 63 the Court of Appeal held that a sentence of twelve months imprisonment was a proper sentence for two crimes of theft from shops, to a total value of less than £10, by a woman with 14 previous convictions for similar offences; in *Harrison* [1979] Crim. L.R. 262 the Court held that three years imprisonment was appropriate for a single burglary of a dwelling (in which, incidentally, nothing was stolen) by an offender with a long record of similar offences. Decisions such as these, from the Court whose function is to give guidance to sentencers, illustrate how a principle which is sound in theory may be subverted in practice. Indeed, it is almost as if some 'ceilings' have been raised simply in order to punish persistence severely."

For a more recent discussion of this subject by the same author, see Ashworth, *Sentencing and Criminal Justice* (1992), ch. 6, where (at p. 150), Ashworth makes the point that unless clear guidelines are established for particular offences, the "proportionality constraint becomes weak, sufficient only to exclude grossly disproportionate sentences." He also poses the question whether there can "even be agreement as to when a sentence is grossly disproportionate?"

Under the Criminal Justice Act 1991, it was intended to restate the principle referred to earlier that an offender should be sentenced on the basis of the seriousness of his offence; whilst a good record may result in some mitigation, a poor record is not an aggravating factor. Of course, a bad record can result in a "progressive loss of mitigation" (see Ashworth, 1992, *ibid.* p. 151) under this system, so it is not accurate to say (as some critics did) that, under the 1991 Act, an offender's previous record could not be taken into account. The relevant provision stated:

> **29.** – (1) An offence shall not be regarded as more serious for the purposes of any provision of this Part by reason of any previous convictions of the offender or any failure of his to respond to previous sentences.
>
> (2) Where any aggravating factors of an offence are disclosed by the circumstances of other offences committed by the offender, nothing in this Part shall prevent the court from taking those factors into account for the purpose of forming an opinion as to the seriousness of the offence.

The Home Office general guide which accompanied the Act stated (at para. 2.25) that the Act "does not allow the penalty for a given offence to be increased beyond what its seriousness requires simply because the offender has an extensive previous record, or because he has continued to commit offences in spite of having been given community or custodial sentences in the past." However, the circumstances of other offences committed by the offender (either in the past or at the same time as the present offence) "may be relevant as aggravating factors of a particular offence, and the Act allows them to be taken into account in this way. If, for example, an offender convicted of an assault against a member of the ethnic minorities has also been convicted of spraying racist graffiti, that fact could be taken into account in concluding that the assault was racially-motivated and therefore more serious."

On the face of it, there seemed to be little that was contentious about section 29 of the 1991 Act. The legislation as a whole represented a clear endorsement of the proportionality principle, so it was logical that previous convictions were not to be treated as an aggravating consideration (despite views to the contrary of many sentencers in practice).

In *Bexley* [1993] 1 W.L.R. 192, the Court of Appeal considered the true construction of section 29 of the Criminal Justice Act 1991. In this case, the offender had been sentenced to two years' imprisonment after pleading guilty to nine offences of dishonesty (relating to theft of credit cards and cheque books) and asking for 39 other offences to be taken into consideration. However, the judge indicated that, in sentencing B, he had taken into account the fact that the offender had a number of previous convictions. The Court of Appeal (at p. 197) stated clearly that the judge made an error in doing so. Accordingly, the Court substituted a sentence of 12 months' imprisonment. Of particular interest is the statement of Lord Chief Justice Taylor in relation to section 29. He stated (at p. 194–5):

"Subsection (1) prohibits the sentencing court from regarding an offence as more serious simply because the offender has previous convictions. This prohibition applies, whether the previous convictions are for different classes of offence or even the same class of offence as that before the sentencing court. It embodies the principle established in case law before the Act of 1991 that an offender who has been punished for offences committed in the past should not in effect be punished for them again when being sentenced for a fresh offence: see, e.g., *Queen* (1981) 3 Cr. App. R(S) 245 and *Bailey* (1988) 10 Cr. App. R(S) 231. But section 29(1) goes further.

The criterion for deciding whether only a custodial sentence can be justified is the seriousness of the offence or its combination with one other: section 1(2)(a). So the sentencer must focus attention on the seriousness of that offence or that combination. The approach, commonly adopted before the Act, of regarding the instant offence as more serious and deserving of custody because it repeated previous offending which had been treated more leniently is now forbidden. Thus the second limb of section 29(1) expressly provides the failure of the offender to respond to previous sentences is not to be regarded as rendering the instant offence more serious. It follows that familiar sentencing remarks before the Act such as. 'You have a long history of committing offences of this kind', or 'You have been given every chance, fines, probation, community service, and here you are again', will no longer be appropriate. They would be statutorily irrelevant as indicators of seriousness in the instant offence. So much is clear from section 29(1)."

Surprisingly, perhaps, section 29 encountered considerable hostility. The main thrust of the criticism directed towards it was that this provision imposed too great a restriction on sentencers' discretion. It is also fair to state that the language of section 29 might have been more carefully chosen to express its true purpose. An interesting account of section 29 and its revision can be found in an article by M. Wasik and A. von Hirsch, entitled "Section 29 Revised: Previous Convictions in Sentencing" [1994] Crim. L.R. 409 where the authors refer to criticisms of section 29 made by Lord Chief Justice Taylor (at p. 412):

"In a March 1993 speech to the Law Society of Scotland, the Lord Chief Justice referred to the Act as an 'ill-fitting straitjacket' ... While the speech was widely construed as an attack on section 29, a close reading suggests that the main target was not section 29 as such, but rather the so-called 'two offence rule' (now also a victim of the 1993 Act amendments), which restricted the number of associated offences which could be weighed by the court when deciding whether the offending was so serious that only a custodial sentence could be justified for it. It is not disputed, however, that section 29 could have been much better drafted."

Whatever the true interpretation of Lord Taylor's comments may have been, his attack on the 1991 Act can hardly have inspired confidence in it. (For the text of his speech, see "Judges and Sentencing" [1993] Jo. of the Law Soc. of Scotland, 129–31). Further criticisms were made, almost simultaneously, by David Thomas, a leading expert on the sentencing system. (See David Thomas, "Law That's Hard to Judge", *The Guardian*, March 30, 1993), who concluded that "urgent action [was] needed to remedy the deficiencies of the Criminal Justice Act 1991."

Criminal Justice Act 1993

Faced with such criticisms by judges, magistrates and some commentators, it would have surprised no-one if a review of certain provisions of the 1991 Act had taken place. What was surprising was the speed with which it was decided to make major statutory amendments to the new law. The Criminal Justice Act 1991 had been in force for only eight months by the time the then Home Secretary, Kenneth Clarke, announced the government's decision in May 1993 to abolish the system of income-related unit fines and to make changes to other central provisions. This swift response was applauded by some as a triumph of common sense, but was criticised by others as "bowing to the law and order vote" and pressure from sentencers.

Section 66(6) of the Criminal Justice Act 1993 was included to replace section 29 of the 1991 Act with a new section 29, which now states:

(1) In considering the seriousness of any offence, the court may take into account any previous convictions of the offender or any failure of his to respond to previous sentences.

(2) In considering the seriousness of any offence committed while the offender was on bail, the court shall treat the fact that it was committed in those circumstances as an aggravating factor...

The effects of this specific amendment to the 1991 Act are considered in the extract which follows. (More general criticisms of the government's hasty amendments, are included in a later extract).

Martin Wasik and Andrew von Hirsch, "Section 29 Revised: Previous Convictions in Sentencing" [1994] Crim. L.R. 409, pp. 412–418.

The new section 29(1) provides: "In considering the seriousness of any offence, the court may take into account any previous convictions of the offender or any failure of his to respond to previous sentences." It may be argued that, on the face of it, this subsection now gives complete discretion to sentencers to take account of an offender's previous convictions whenever, and to whatever extent, they wish. If this view is correct, it would entail the abandonment of the theory of progressive loss of mitigation. In this article, however, we claim that the new section 29(1) does *not* confer unfettered discretion upon sentencers, nor was it intended to do so. We argue, in contrast, that section 29(1) is best understood as (1) giving continued statutory force to the principle of progressive loss of mitigation and (2) permitting aggravation of sentence on account of the record only in certain fairly narrowly defined situations.

The new section 29(1): no wide discretion
The new section 29(1) should not be seen by the courts as conferring an unfettered discretion. There are two reasons for this view:

(i) The subsection states that the court may have regard to previous convictions and previous failures to respond "in considering the seriousness of the offence." It is clear, then, that "seriousness" is the key concept in the new section 29(1), as it is in the 1991 Act as a whole. If Parliament had intended to confer a wide discretion on sentencers, it would surely not have used "seriousness" as the limiting consideration in the subsection. To underline the point that section 29(1) does not confer a general discretion, its language may usefully be contrasted with section 28(1), referred to above, which is *not* related to seriousness and which clearly *does* confer a general discretion. If the new section 29(1) conferred a general discretion to use cumulative sentencing on those who have criminal records, it would be impossible to reconcile it with the key provisions of the 1991 Act which set out the framework of proportionality (particularly sections 1, 2 and 6).
(ii) Our interpretation is, we believe, bolstered by the legislative history of the 1993 Act. During the course of the passage of the Criminal Justice Bill 1993 through Parliament a Private Members Bill was tabled with the intention of substituting section 29(1), but inserting a proviso that when the court passed a more severe

sentence by reason of an offender's previous convictions, that sentence should still be proportionate to the seriousness of the offence. That Bill was subsequently withdrawn, as was an Opposition amendment tabled in identical terms. In moving the amendment, its sponsor Mr Michael said that:

> "The danger is that, if we do not write into the law a limiting principle of proportionality we could return, not to the position before the 1991 Act, *which is what the minister intends*, but to a more punitive sentencing framework, under which some offenders could be given sentences out of all proportion to what they deserve." (emphasis added)

After appropriate assurances from the government minister, the amendment was withdrawn. The assumption must be that the government believed the subsection already to achieve that effect. We infer that it was the government's purpose to restate in clearer language than the original section 29(1) had achieved, the principle of progressive loss of mitigation. Subsequent to the passage of the 1993 Act, we find support for our interpretation of section 29(1) in the words of Lord Taylor C.J., given in a speech to NACRO in November, 1993. He began by stating that, notwithstanding the 1993 Act changes, "the philosophy of the Criminal Justice Act 1991 as it was originally envisaged still holds good." He continued:

> "That is not to say that the rule which the courts have evolved long before the Criminal Justice Act should be ignored – namely that a person should not be sentenced a second time for offences which have already been punished in the past. That is a basic principle of judicial precedent and I see no conflict between that and having regard to previous record and to previous sentences which have been imposed on the offender. Now, it seems to me, the balance is right. The court will approach the question of seriousness, of course, by looking primarily at the instant offences which have to be dealt with, but looking at them not in a vacuum or in blinkers but against a previous history."

Lord Taylor's language here is clear enough: section 29 is meant neither to reject the progressive loss of mitigation principle nor to confer an unrestricted discretion in dealing with the record.

Recidivism *per se* does not constitute a "failure to respond"

As we have seen, as well as referring to previous convictions, section 29(1) speaks also of the "failure of [the defendant] to respond to previous sentences." It has been suggested by Ashworth and Gibson that it is *this* part of section 29(1) which potentially is the most troublesome. We think however, that the reference to "failure to respond" can, and should, be construed more narrowly. Naturally, there must be *some* circumstances where "failure to respond" matters, for otherwise that phrase would not have been included in the subsection. We will suggest below what those circumstances might be. However, we feel that the phrase does not constitute any general, open-ended invitation to inflate the sentences of recidivists.

The language of the subsection makes clear that "failure to respond" is relevant only "in considering the seriousness of the offence." Conventionally, cumulative sentencing has had little to do with offence seriousness. It has been linked to concerns of individual deterrence, rehabilitation or dangerousness. Sentencers identified an offender's "failure to respond" to sentences in the past, and concluded that since these had not "worked," something stronger was needed this time to make the penalty "bite." While this may be coherent in a sentencing system based chiefly upon deterrence or incapacitation, it is not coherent in a sentencing system based on offence seriousness. In such a system, the offender's failure to respond should only be regarded as relevant where it impinges upon the offender's *culpability*. "Failure to respond" to non-custodial sentences was one ground upon which a custodial sentence could be justified in the law which applied to young offenders before the 1991 Act. It was narrowly interpreted by the courts and found no place in the 1991 legislation, as being inconsistent with the Act's desert rationale.

It might be argued, against our view, that to reoffend is a kind of "defiance" of the court, or of the legal system, which makes the fresh lapse more culpable than it would otherwise be. We disagree. First, we think that while occasionally reoffending may contain an element of defiance, this is far from generally the case, and should not ordinarily be seen as a flouting of the court's authority. People reoffend for all kinds of reasons (economic and social circumstances, lack of personal control, fecklessness, boredom) which have nothing to do with defiance of the court. Secondly, we think the general claim that "defiance" is a culpable act warranting more punishment, is misguided in endowing the sentencer with an authority in the judicial role far beyond that which is appropriate in a modern democracy. In English law, cases of defiance in the face of the court are appropriately dealt with by way of a circumscribed offence of contempt of court. To suggest that the mere fact of reoffending exhibits punishable defiance is, we think far too wide a proposition.

Our conclusion here is again bolstered by the Lord Chief Justice's speech to NACRO. There, he gave the example of a female offender with a history of many minor shoplifting offences, who had been given a prison sentence of 12 months suspended for two years for burglary and for taking part in a robbery. During the period of the suspended sentence she committed another minor offence of shoplifting. Explaining that imprisonment was "not justifiable" for this new offence, Lord Taylor C.J. pointed out that even where an offender *has* offended during the currency of a previous sentence, the current offence still operates as a ceiling of "seriousness" which cannot be exceeded. In his words: "the triviality of the type of offence – notwithstanding the background of previous offending, *notwithstanding that it was committed during the period of suspension* – simply did not justify [imprisonment]."

When the criminal record is relevant under the new section 29: four situations

When does the new section 29 permit an adjustment of sentence on account of the criminal record? We see four kinds of situation where it does. The first two were recognised by the old section 29 as well as by the earlier law: progressive loss of mitigation and culpability-enhancing factors specifically disclosed by the record. The second two were recognised before the 1991 Act, had been placed in doubt by the former section 29, and have now been revived by the new section 29. These are: crimes committed on bail and crimes committed in breach of penal orders. Let us take each of the four in turn.

(i) Progressive loss of mitigation

The 1991 Act actually provided somewhat uncertain authority for the Court of Appeal's long-standing doctrine of progressive loss of mitigation. The old section 29 did not address mitigation at all, and merely limited the extent to which prior offending could be deemed an aggravating ground. Section 28 (dealing with mitigation personal to the offender) could be invoked, but was discretionary; the individual judge was not required to invoke personal mitigating grounds. By explicitly authorising the court to take previous convictions into account in determining the seriousness of the offence, the new section 29(1) provides clearer statutory authority for progressive loss of mitigation.

Section 29(1) provides that the court "may" consider previous offending. However, this cannot – for reasons we have outlined earlier – be construed as meaning that the court has free discretion to grant or deny mitigation to those not having a criminal record. Rather, the "may" reflects that, read within the context of the 1991 Act as a whole, mitigation is more appropriate in some cases than in others. When, then, would it be appropriate? The Court of Appeal's earlier jurisprudence suggests that normally the first offender, or the offender with only a modest record, should receive a discount from his sentence. This principle should be continued – it reflects the idea of a degree of tolerance for human fallibility, of which we have spoken earlier. Repetition after a certain number of prior convictions exceeds any bounds of ordinary fallibility, so that the discount should then be lost. However, mitigation for first offenders might not be applicable to the most serious crimes, such as aggravated forms of assault. Where the gravity of the offence is great enough, even a first offence would seem to fall outside the scope of ordinary human fallibility – which we have suggested to be the basis of the doctrine.

(ii) Special culpability: aggravating factors disclosed by the record

A second ground for sentence adjustment – pointing towards aggravation of sentence – is where the circumstances of past offences reveal something that reflects specifically on the offender's present culpability. This was formerly dealt with by the old section 29(2). It is a situation where the record *does* affect the seriousness of the current crime, and may thus properly be recognised under the new section 29(1). An example is where a perusal of the circumstances of the previous offending shows a pattern of racial motivation. In this context, an aggravating feature of the latest offence is revealed, which would not otherwise have been apparent to the sentencer. The latest offence can thus properly be regarded as more serious, in the light of the enhanced culpability. Ashworth and Gibson point out that the new section 29 may be deficient in making no express provision for this type of case, and that the wording of section 3(3)(a) of the Act might be taken to prevent a court from investigating the *circumstances* of earlier offences for this purpose. Such an interpretation would lead to the bizarre result that the paradigmatic case where prior offending *is* relevant to the seriousness of the latest offence would be excluded from consideration by the court. We do not think that the new section 29 should be so construed.

(iii) Crimes committed on bail

Prior to the 1991 Act, the case law, as confirmed in *Baverstock*, permitted an increase in sentence if the crime was committed on bail. The old section 29, however, did not seem to recognise this situation. The new section 29(2) explicitly does, thus reviving the earlier cases.

When, and why, does committing a crime on bail make it worse? We have been unable to find any articulation of the rationale in the Parliamentary debates on the sub-clause which became section 29(2). It seems to us that the best reason for the rule in section 29(2) is that the offender who commits a further offence while he is on bail commits that offence in *breach of trust*. Breach of trust is a well-established aggravating factor in sentencing, and bail might be viewed as an arrangement where the defendant is entrusted with his liberty in exchange for certain undertakings. However, we do not think that the breach of trust makes the new offence *greatly* more serious, since on desert principles the predominant consideration should be the degree of harmfulness and culpability of the actual criminal conduct. The breach of trust involved in a shoplifting committed on bail may make that crime somewhat worse, but shoplifting (even when involving such a breach) remains a minor crime; it should not be treated as an offence on a wholly different scale of seriousness, only because it took place when the offender was on bail. We further think that "shall" in section 29(2) is better read as "shall ordinarily," thereby permitting the courts to establish types of cases (say, when the current offence is of a different nature from the prior one) in which a sentence increase would not be appropriate.

(iv) Breach of penal order

A fourth situation relates to what may be regarded as true cases of "failure to respond": namely, where the offence is committed by an offender who is at the time subject to a specific penal order. In *Bexley*, Lord Taylor C.J. pointed to the anomaly that the courts under common law principles were entitled to regard an offence committed on bail as being more serious, but that the original section 29 required them to ignore the fact that the offender was in breach of an earlier sentence. We accept that there is an analogy between an offence committed on bail and an offence committed during the currency of a penal order, since both involve an element of breach of trust. Where the relevant penal order has lapsed, however, later reoffending does not constitute a breach and, in our view, ought not to be regarded as a "failure to respond." A sentence should not be seen as a directive to behave well, valid indefinitely.

Again, however, in line with our comment on offences committed on bail, we think that even where a new offence places an offender in breach of a penal order, it is the inherent seriousness of the *new* offence which should be the driving factor in sentencing. Such an approach has been enjoined by the Court of Appeal in a line of appellate decisions in cases where courts have dealt with a fresh offence committed during the currency of a suspended sentence. The principal relevance of an offender's failure to comply with the requirements of a *community sentence* should lie elsewhere, in assisting the court to determine, under section 6 of the 1991 Act, the offender's "suitability" for a particular form of community sentence on a future occasion. The record of prior offending may suggest that certain types of community dispositions are less, or are more, suitable for this offender. This matter, however, bears upon the form of the community order, rather than upon the severity of the sentence.

Notes

1. The authors' arguments represent a well reasoned effort to salvage something from the wreckage of the original section 29, by attempting to view the revised section in the context of the overall philosophy of the 1991 Act. There is certainly much to recommend their position. But, taken literally, the new section 29 is a radical change. It permits the court to "take into account any previous convictions of the offender or any failure of his to respond to previous sentences" when considering the seriousness of the offence. It will require guidance from the Court of Appeal to determine the extent of these changes introduced by the new section.

2. Other amendments to Part 1 of the 1991 Act were made by section 66 of the Criminal Justice Act 1993, as follows:

> **66.** – (1) In section 1 of the Criminal Justice Act 1991 (restrictions on imposing custodial sentences), the following shall be substituted for subsection (2)(a) –
> "(a) that the offence, or the combination of the offence and one or more offences associated with it, was so serious that only such a sentence can be justified for the offence; or"
>
> (2) In section 2 of the Act of 1991 (length of custodial sentences), in subsections (2)(a) and (3), for the word "other" there shall be substituted "one or more".
>
> (3) In section 3 of the Act of 1991 (procedural requirements for custodial sentences), in subsection (3)(a), the words "or (as the case may be) of the offence and the offence or offences associated with it," shall be inserted after the word "offence".

(4) In section 6 of the Act of 1991 (restrictions on imposing community sentences) –
    (a) in subsection (1), for the words "other offence" there shall be substituted "or more offences"; and
    (b) in subsection (2)(b), for the word "other" there shall be substituted "one or more".

(5) In section 7 of the Act of 1991 (procedural requirements for community sentences), in subsection (1), the words "or (as the case may be) of the offence and the offence or offences associated with it," shall be inserted after the word "offence".

In order to encourage sentencers to focus on the seriousness of the offence in deciding whether an offender should be given a custodial sentence or a community sentence, sections 1 and 6 of the 1991 Act restricted sentencers to taking account of a maximum of two offences. Sentencers were intended to concentrate on passing a sentence which reflected the gravity of the offence committed "or the combination of the offence and one other offence associated with it" (See subsections 1(2)(a) and 6(1)). Why was there a "two offence" rule when sentencers were expected to concentrate on the seriousness of a particular offence? This was perhaps to help sentencers deal with borderline cases. For example, a case which was borderline between a prison sentence and a community order might be resolved in favour of the former due to the "two offence" rule. (Of course, the offences, assessed individually would still have to be relatively serious to permit a custodial sentence in this example). Despite the good intentions of this rule, it was capable of operating in an arbitrary way with the outcome depending on how the charges could be framed by the prosecution, rather than on the inherent seriousness of the offence.

Some of these problems with the 1991 Act (including the "unit fine" experience which is discussed in Chapter 5) could perhaps have been resolved by means of appropriate guidance and a little tolerance. But, as we have seen, considerable hostility towards certain central provisions of the 1991 Act led to precipitate legislative action; or, as Ashworth and Gibson more forcefully argue in a recent article, "policies based on mature reflection, consultation and research findings were abandoned in an instant, in one of the most remarkable *volte-faces* in the history of penal policy in England and Wales". The following is an extract from their critique of the 1993 amendments, in which they assess the extent of the changes to the 1991 Act.

Andrew Ashworth and Bryan Gibson, "Altering the Sentencing Framework", [1994] Crim. L.R. 101–106.

1. Multiple offences

Section 1(4A) of the Criminal Justice Act 1982 (as amended by s. 123 of the 1988 Act) provided, *inter alia*, that an offender under 21 could not be sentenced to detention unless the offence was "so serious that a non-custodial sentence for it cannot be justified." This was interpreted to mean that, in cases where a court was sentencing an offender for two or more offences, it could only impose detention if at least one of the offences, taken individually, was "so serious that a non-custodial sentence for it cannot be justified." It was not permissible, the Court of Appeal finally held in *Davison*, to aggregate several less serious offences and to decide that taken as a whole they merited custody. One effect of this was that offenders who committed several offences of moderate or low seriousness would not lose their liberty: custody was reserved for particularly serious offences, and others had to be dealt with in the community. The Government's intention was originally to apply this policy to offenders of all ages in the 1991 Act, but the policy came under attack from sentencers who believed that it left them with insufficient powers to deal with people who committed a large number of offences before being caught. The Government made a small concession to this view, abolishing the "one offence" rule of the 1982 Act and replacing it with the "two offence" rule in the 1991 Act. Thus, in deciding whether a case was serious enough to warrant a community sentence, and in deciding whether a case was so serious that only a custodial sentence could be justified, a court was allowed to aggregate any two (but only two) of several associated offences for which the offender was being sentenced.

Section 66(1) of the 1993 Act abolishes the "two offence" rule, and provides that courts may now consider "the offence, or the combination of the offence and one or more other offences associated with it," when determining whether the case meets the criterion for a community sentence or for custody. The effect is to reverse the previous policy, in the sense that there is no longer any barrier against sentencers lumping together a series of minor offences and deciding that, taken as a whole, they merit custody. However, whether this is the correct approach in a given case will depend very much on the facts of the offences and the relationship between them. Thus the court must be satisfied that the offences can be said to increase the seriousness of one another, and that it would not be appropriate simply to give a nominal sentence for some of the offences. Moreover, the common law rules on concurrent and consecutive sentencing still apply, as does the provision in section 28(2) of the 1991 Act that "nothing in [the Act] shall prevent a court ... in a case of an offender who is convicted of one or more other offences, from mitigating his sentence by applying any rule of law as to the totality of sentences." As formulated in the classic work by Dr David Thomas, the totality principle is that:

> "the aggregate sentence should not be longer than the upper limit of the normal bracket of sentences for the category of cases in which the most serious offence committed by the offender would be placed. This formulation would allow an aggregate sentence longer than the sentence which would be passed for the most serious offence if it stood alone, but would ensure that the sentence bore some recognisable relationship to the gravity of that offence."

This principle, distilled from Court of Appeal decisions and preserved by the 1991 Act, makes it clear that the abolition of the "two offence rule" by the 1993 Act does not remove all restrictions on courts when sentencing for multiple offences. An overall notion of proportionality still governs.

Two cases decided before the 1991 Act may be used to illustrate the change. In *Choudhary (1992)* a young man of 19 pleaded guilty to four offences of theft, with 136 taken into consideration. He had used a stolen credit card to defraud his employers, in small amounts of £20 or £30, up to a total of £3,000. The Court of Appeal quashed the sentence of detention on the ground that no individual offence was sufficiently serious. Under the 1993 Act a court would be permitted to aggregate these offences and to sentence him in relation to the £3,000, bearing in mind the totality principle. In the somewhat similar case of *Clugston (1992)*, in which an adult had obtained over £5,000 by some 100 transactions of £50, the court had aggregated the offences and imposed a sentence of three years' imprisonment, upheld by the Court of Appeal. Although the judgment does not mention the totality principle, the Court was presumably satisfied that the sentencer had complied with it. This, the "common law" approach, will apparently now prevail.

What, if anything, remains of the 1991 Act on multiple offences? The various decisions in which it had been sought to whittle down the effect of the "two offence" rule by invoking section 29(2) of the 1991 Act will no longer be relevant, since the original section 29(2) has been repealed. But the concept of an "associated offence," introduced by the 1991 Act, remains central. Courts can only combine the offence with "one or more offences associated with it" for the purposes of assessing seriousness. Section 31(2) of the 1991 Act states that an offence is associated with another if:

> "(a) the offender is convicted of it in the proceedings in which he is convicted of the other offence, or (although convicted of it in earlier proceedings) is sentenced for it at the same time as he is sentenced for that offence; or (b) the offender admits the commission of it in proceedings in which he is sentenced for the other offence and requests the court to take it into consideration in sentencing him for that offence."

Paragraph (b) is a straightforward reference to offences t.i.c., but the wording of paragraph (a) needs careful interpretation. Thus it was held in *Crawford* (1993) that when a person is sentenced for an offence committed within the operational period of a suspended sentence, the original offence for which the suspended sentence was imposed cannot be treated as an "associated offence." He is not convicted of it in the present proceedings, and neither does the court sentence him for it in the present proceedings – it merely activates a sentence already imposed. The position is different, however, where a court deals with an offender for breach of a conditional discharge as well as for the new offence. If a court revokes the conditional discharge and imposes a sentence for the offence in respect of which the conditional discharge was originally imposed, this does amount to sentencing the offender for that offence, and so it becomes an "associated offence" within paragraph (a). This would apply equally in cases where a new sentence is passed following the revocation of a community sentence under the 1991 Act.

2. Previous convictions

... The effect of section 66(6) of the 1993 Act is to substitute a new section 29 in the 1991 Act. The principal provision on previous convictions is now that "in considering the seriousness of the offence, the court may take into account any previous convictions of the offender...." It is far from clear in what way this alters the previous law. Even if the government's intention was that courts should be free to treat a bad record of previous convictions as an aggravating factor for sentencing purposes, that is not what these phrases in the new section 29(1) actually say. The Court of Appeal has in many decisions stated that previous convictions should be taken into account: a good record mitigates, a repeat offender progressively loses mitigation, but the current offence should be regarded as setting a "ceiling" beyond which the sentence cannot properly go. The Lord Chief Justice has stated extra-judicially that in his view these principles are preserved by the new section 29(1), and one might therefore expect this interpretation to be confirmed in an early Court of Appeal decision.

... The most far-reaching and least ambiguous change wrought by the new section 29 concerns previous sentences. The old section 29(1) stated that an offence should not be regarded as more serious by reason of any failure of the offender to respond to previous sentences. The new section 29(1), substituted by section 66(6) of the 1993 Act, provides that "in considering the seriousness of an offence the court may take into account ... any failure of [the offender] to respond to previous sentences." It is doubtful whether any court would be impressed by the logical argument that response to previous sentences has nothing to do with the seriousness of the present offence – although it is, in fact, exceedingly difficult to see how it does. Whatever the niceties, Parliament clearly intended to reverse the 1991 Act's prohibition on taking such matters into account.

The new section 29(1) refers to "response to previous sentences": this implies that the offender must have been sentenced at least twice before. What counts as a "sentence" for this purpose? The new section 29(3) provides that a probation order or conditional discharge made before October 1, 1992, is to be treated as a sentence. Such orders made since 1992 clearly are sentences. However, the new section 29(3) excludes absolute discharges, and it makes no reference to the status of a compensation order made as the sole order on conviction.

What may be regarded as a "response" to previous sentences? Presumably any conduct following the imposition of the penalty may be regarded as a response. On this view, not only is a breach of or failure in relation to a community order a "response," but reconviction (and perhaps even other behaviour falling short of criminality or conviction) after the termination of such an order might also be a "response." The breach of a suspended sentence is a "response," thus overturning the effect of decisions which have held that the fact that an offence is committed in breach of a suspended sentence does not render it more serious. If these are indeed the implications of the new section 29(1), then the reference to "response to previous sentences" may turn out to be far more important in practice than the opaque provision on previous convictions....

... Thus the notion of proportionality to the seriousness of the current offence, so pivotal to the scheme of the 1991 Act, has been weakened. Prisons and young offender institutions may once again fill with people who have been sentenced on their record, rather than for a serious offence. The old cumulative notion – a fine last time, a community sentence this time; community sentence last time, custody this time – seems to be back in full vigour. Even if the law on previous convictions continues to be interpreted in line with common law principles, the reintroduction of the phrase "failure to respond to previous sentences" may be treated as a clear invitation to sentence offenders on their record....

[The authors then consider the new section 18 which they argue "risks returning the system of fining to its former diversity and indiscipline"].

Notes

1.   The authors conclude by suggesting (at p. 109) that those responsible for the 1993 amendments may well have had diverging aims. Whilst sentencers wanted a return to less restricted discretion, the government wanted to be seen to be getting "tough".

2.   There can be little doubt that the new provisions under the Criminal Justice Act 1993 undermine the central principles of the 1991 legislation, but it is too soon to assess the extent to which they have done so. Ashworth and Gibson are not optimistic (at p. 109):

> "Many of those convicted of offences of moderate seriousness can much more easily be sentenced to custody as a result of the recent changes: the loosening of restrictions on sentencing for multiple offences, the opaque provision on previous convictions, the invitation to take account of 'failure to respond' to previous sentences, the apparently mandatory aggravating effect of committing an offence whilst on bail, the legislative abandonment of unit fines in favour of a

system which may produce more fine default, and the revised version of the Magistrates' Association's sentencing guidelines with their sometimes high 'entry points'. The coming months will be a stern test of sentencers' commitments to the basic principle of the 1991 Act that sentences should be kept in proportion to the seriousness of the current offence."

V. APPELLATE GUIDANCE AND THE FORMULATION OF PRINCIPLES

Introduction

A distinctive feature of our sentencing system has been the central involvement of the Court of Appeal in formulating sentencing policy (for example, see *Bibi* (1980) 71 Cr. App. R. 360). One might have expected sentencing and penal policy to be more closely co-ordinated and compatible, but this has not been the case in the past. Penal policy has been a matter for the executive and, occasionally, Parliament; the formulation of sentencing policy and principles was the province of the Court of Appeal. This separation was sometimes defended, not entirely convincingly, as the hallmark of judicial independence. Of course, there are good reasons why judges should be impartial and enjoy freedom from interference in individual cases. But this hardly explains why sentencing policy should be left exclusively to the judiciary. Sentencing policy is not based on strictly legal criteria, as it involves matters of social and penal policy, philosophy and economics. This was certainly the opinion expressed in the White Paper, *Crime, Justice and Protecting the Public* (1990, at p. 5) where it was stated that "sentencing principles and sentencing practice are matters of legitimate concern to Government, and Parliament provides the funds necessary to give effect to the courts' decisions." It can be argued that there was no particular constitutional reason for the Court of Appeal's influence on sentencing policy, and that it developed in the absence of any other body.

The Court of Appeal, in its capacity of giving guidance to lower courts (as opposed to its function of altering sentences in individual cases), has been open to a number of criticisms. There has been uncertainty over the precedent value of its decisions. Where decisions are delivered extemporaneously, and from more than one division of the Court, it is clear that consistency will be elusive. On more general matters of sentencing policy, it is perhaps unwise to regard individual decisions as binding or to rely on the precise wording of judgments. It is safer, if referring to precedent, to rely on a line or pattern of cases which, taken together, may identify a particular sentencing policy. But some appellate judgments are clearly intended and treated as more definitive. Where the Court interprets a statutory provision (*e.g.* see *Bexley* [1993] 1 W.L.R. 192 on the meaning of section 29, Criminal Justice Act 1991) there is no reason why it should not be binding. Also, the Court of Appeal's "guideline" judgments – which deal with a certain type of offence and explain the levels of sentence appropriate for the different forms it can take – are clearly regarded as binding by the lower courts. (For example, see *Billam* [1986] Crim. L.R. 347 on rape; or *Aramah* [1983] Crim. L.R. 271 on importation of cannabis).

A number of factors have combined to increase the importance of previous sentencing decisions of the Court of Appeal. Decisions are more widely reported today and there is even a separate branch of the Criminal Appeal Reports devoted to sentencing decisions, in addition to the excellent case and comment section in each edition of the Criminal Law Review. Sentencing law has become a more central area of legal education and research. As we have seen, it is also an area of much recent legislative activity (too much in the opinion of many), and these new provisions, which are often complex, need to be interpreted by the Court of Appeal. Accordingly, it is not surprising that appellate decisions on sentencing are more regularly cited today. On the other hand, there is still a suspicion that many sentencers in the lower courts do not adhere to the appellate guidance which is available. This may be due to lack of knowledge on their part, or it could be that some sentencers do not agree with the Court of Appeal (as in *Johnson* [1994] Crim. L.R. 537), or find its guidance to be impractical.

This may look like professional deviance, but there are reasons why the sentencer may find appellate pronouncements less than helpful. Appellate decisions have tended to concentrate on more serious crimes and the appropriate length of custodial sentences. This is inevitably going to occur in an appeal system where the bulk of cases concern offenders claiming that their sentence is too severe. (The system of appeal against lenient sentences will be dealt with below). The result of this, however, is that the more common the crime is, paradoxically the less attention it has received by the Court of Appeal. More guidance is needed for the lesser offences and the use of penalties other than the custodial sentence. Although this is starting to occur more frequently today, it must be questioned whether the appellate system is the most effective and comprehensive method of providing advice to the lower courts on sentencing policy and practice. This is one reason why some commentators, notably Andrew Ashworth, have called for the setting up of a sentencing council or commission to undertake more general guidance to sentencers.

Despite the increasing importance of precedent in sentencing law, and the enactment of ever more legislation on the subject, there is still perhaps a feeling amongst many sentencers that their discretion should not be unduly restricted by too much law. This may well account for the antipathy of many sentencers towards appellate decisions and also for their active hostility to legislative intervention. If this analysis is correct, it may well explain the unrest which followed the introduction of the Criminal Justice Act 1991. The determination of the judiciary and the magistracy to resist restrictions on their long established discretion should not be under-estimated.

Appeals Against Lenient Sentences

Until 1988, the appeal system relating to sentences was one-sided. An offender has been able to appeal against a too severe sentence since 1907. There was formerly no corresponding system of appeal by the prosecution against sentences which were perceived as unduly lenient. Given the diversity of approaches of sentencers, and the considerable discretion which was traditionally enjoyed by them, it is not surprising that individual cases of excessive leniency occurred. Whether such isolated cases were a sufficient justification to introduce a new system of prosecution appeal, or whether this reform was more a matter of political opportunism and expediency, is a matter for debate. The introduction of this new right of appeal undoubtedly had its fervent supporters and the case in favour of it is strongly made in the following extract.

J. R. Spencer, "Do We Need a Prosecution Appeal Against Sentence", [1987] Crim. L.R. 724–736.

The Arguments in Favour

According to my reckoning there are at least seven arguments in favour of a prosecution appeal against an over-lenient sentence, and all of them are strong. The first six are different ways of saying that something needs to be done to correct an aberrant under-sentence, because aberrant under-sentences are mistakes, mistakes are bad, and the legal system needs to be able to correct its mistakes. The seventh concerns the role of the Court of Appeal in shaping sentencing policy.

(i) deterrence The fact that the court of trial can under-sentence, and nothing can be done about it if it does, blunts the deterrent effect of the criminal law. The immoral and calculating citizen will always have two things to weigh against the threat of punishment which the law holds out. The first is the chance of not getting caught by the police. The second is the chance of getting improperly acquitted if he is. The absence of a prosecution appeal on sentence adds to these considerations a third: the chance of an appeal-proof "let off" even if he is caught and prosecuted to conviction.

(ii) outrage to the victim There can be no doubt about the sense of outrage which victims of offences often feel when the criminal who has been caught and convicted gets an undeserved let-off. Their natural desire for vengeance is frustrated, and the bottom is knocked out of their belief that the law protects the innocent and punishes the guilty; it is as they had gone to the police station to report an offence, only to find the criminal dressed in uniform sitting behind the desk. These feelings may not be fully appreciated by lawyers, because in England prosecutions are arranged in such a way that practising lawyers have little contact with victims of crimes except as witnesses in court....

(iii) demoralising to the police Catching criminals and collecting evidence against them is hard and exacting work. When the police have caught a criminal at the cost of a lot of time and trouble, and have collected the evidence to secure a conviction at the cost of further time and trouble, their efforts are set at nought if the offender is given an unjustified let-off. Resilient as the police may be, they would have to be superhuman not to find this demoralising.

(iv) injustice to those who were appropriately sentenced Inadequate sentences which go uncorrected on appeal are unjust to those who were appropriately sentenced, who must smart whilst other men who are equally wicked, equally caught and

equally convicted go free. The unfairness of an over-lenient sentence to a person who received an appropriate sentence is particularly obvious when both offenders were involved in the same crime, and where this happens the one who received the appropriate sentence may try to appeal on the ground that the disparity makes his sentence unfair. Time and again the Court of Appeal has accepted that the situation is an unjust one, but as the law stands there is nothing sensible which it can do about it . . . .

(v) undermining public confidence in the administration of justice and the authority of the courts In this country the papers, radio and television are free to make a fuss if they dislike a decision of the courts. They can and frequently do protest about sentences which they believe to be inept, and when they do so, an inevitable and unfortunate consequence is a dent in the authority of the individual judge and of the courts in general. If the outcry is about a sentence which is too severe the Court of Appeal can intervene to quash the offending sentence and substitute one which makes more sense. Then, provided the media reports this too, public confidence in the machinery of justice is to that extent restored. The reversal will not restore, as such, the damaged authority of the aberrant judge; but the public will at least tolerate his continued presence on the bench more willingly if they see that his mistakes can be corrected on appeal. If the outcry is about a sentence which is outrageously lenient – six months' suspended imprisonment for a bad rape, for example – nothing useful can be done in response to the fuss . . . .

(vi) public danger The fact that there is no prosecution appeal against an inadequate sentence sometimes means that a dangerous offender is prematurely released on society when he needs to stay locked up for the protection of the public. The most striking case is where a dangerous person carries out a deliberate killing for which he is convicted of manslaughter rather than murder because of the defence of diminished responsibility – and instead of giving him a life sentence, which is usually what is called for, the judge imposes a short fixed term of imprisonment . . . .

. . . Mandatory sentences stop this sort of thing, but they are unjust because they are inflexible, and that is why we have largely abandoned them. A mandatory life sentence survives as the penalty for murder, where it causes all sorts of problems; and the main reason why we cannot get rid of it is the fear of dangerous men being prematurely released as the result of irrationally lenient sentences.

(vii) hindering a rational sentencing policy The Court of Appeal can only make a pronouncement when it has a case before it, a case can only get before it when a defendant appeals. The result, as Andrew Ashworth tells us, is

> "... a lop-sided set of precedents. The Court hears appeals only against sentences which are thought by the offender to be too severe, with the result that there are myriad precedents on the aggravating features of serious offences but very few decisions at all on non-custodial sentences or the least serious kinds of manslaughter, rape and robbery. It is hardly too much to say that the more frequent the type of case, the less appellate guidance there is likely to be."

In recent years the Court of Appeal has struggled to get round this difficultly by issuing "guideline judgments," in which the appropriate sentence is discussed for a range of hypothetical facts less serious than the case before the court. But even here, it has been suggested that the Court of Appeal's palate is so affected by a continuous diet of heavy sentences that the guidance is sometimes over-severe . . . .

Arguments against a Prosecution Appeal on Sentence

The arguments which I have so far heard against a prosecution appeal against over-lenient sentences also number seven. Predictably, I think they are all extremely weak.

(i) there is no problem The first is that no prosecution appeal is needed because judges never really impose over-lenient sentences: the media just whips up groundless public hysteria, because it fails to grasp the facts, or misunderstands the sentencing process, or both...

... Of course the newspapers sometimes get things wrong. But even if they invariably did so, there are some people who unquestionably know the facts and who are convinced that undersentencing is a genuine problem. The Lord Chancellor is one, because those who are offended by the lenity of a particular sentence often complain to him, and he then investigates the matter. In a Parliamentary debate Lord Hailsham L.C. said this:

> "Having had week by week and year by year an increasing volume of complaint, I can say ... that although most of the complaints are without foundation ... I am still left with the conviction that there is an irreducible minimum of cases where public opinion is right and the grandees of the legal profession have not been right."

(ii) a prosecution appeal against sentence would undermine the independence of the judiciary At first sight this is an objection even more preposterous that the last. What is proposed is that the sentencing decisions made by the judiciary should be reviewable by the judiciary – not by the Home Secretary, the Parole Board, an ad hoc committee of right-wing M.P.s, Women Against Rape or the editor of *The Sun*. How would a power in the Court of Appeal to reverse a sentence because it is excessively lenient undermine the independence of the judiciary – any more than it is undermined by the existing power to review sentences which are excessively severe?...

(iii) it would lead to a general increase in severity, and make prison overcrowding even worse It is likely that the number of sentences actually increased by the Court of Appeal would be small, but the effect of them could go further. It has already been mentioned that the criminal statistics reveal certain gaps between what the Court of Appeal says the average sentence for an offence should be, and the average sentences which are actually imposed. One reason for this could be that some trial judges dislike their decisions being appealed, and, secure in the knowledge that a decision can be appealed if it is too severe but not if it is too lenient, they borrow a Christmas slogan from the Department of Transport and "stay low."...

(iv) it would over-burden the Court of Appeal Whether a prosecution right of appeal on sentence would overburden the Court of Appeal depends on three things: first, how much new work would be generated, secondly, whether any of the existing work would disappear as an incidental side-effect, and thirdly, whether the state would provide extra resources if there was a net increase in work. As to the third factor, we can only guess. The amount of work generated would depend on the details of the scheme....

(v) "it would be a complete departure from our tradition that the prosecutor takes no part, or the minimum part, in the sentencing process"....

(vi) it would put the defendant in double-jeopardy....

... But this is to misunderstand the principle against double-jeopardy. This principle means two things. The first is that it is wrong to punish a man twice for the same offence. A prosecution appeal against an over-lenient sentence does not offend against the principle in this sense, because a person is not punished twice when, before anything has been done to him, an adequate punishment is ordered to replace an inadequate one or no punishment at all. The second aspect of the principle is that we do not allow a man to be put in peril of conviction twice. That means we do not allow the prosecution to make repeated attempts to prove an accused person guilty when he has been acquitted on the merits, even if we suspect he was wrongly acquitted, because multiple attempts to establish guilt gradually exhaust the resources of the defendant, and create an ever-rising chance of his being convicted for something he has not done. A prosecution appeal against inadequate sentences does not offend against the double-jeopardy rule in this sense either. The defendant, by definition, has already been found guilty. The appeal court is not overturning his acquittal, but examining the abstract evaluative question of what sentence it is appropriate to impose in the light of his conviction....

(vii) it is cruel to the defendant to take his unexpected windfall away The argument goes like this. The defendant has experienced joy and relief. He has, perhaps, gone back to his home and family. It is really too unkind – "sheer cruelty," Lord Wigoder has called it – to tell him it was all a dreadful mistake and he must go to prison after all. This argument is very odd. The prosecution would have to give notice of the appeal, so the final outcome would hardly come as a complete surprise. The outcome would be painful for him; but if the proper sentence is a heavy one, it is painful when he receives it at the trial; and nobody in their right mind suggests that for this reason he should not get it there. But now it is seriously suggested that there is something special about the extra pain involved in taking away from him, when he is unquestionably guilty, the boon which he should never have had, and which it is mischievous to the public that he should keep....

Notes

1. Despite the many valid points made in his article, Spencer's reliance on the deterrent argument is far from convincing. There is little empirical evidence to support the supposed deterrent effect of more severe penalties. If he wished to rely on arguments of deterrence, he might have referred more appropriately to general, rather than individual deterrence. The threat of prosecution and conviction, and the publicity attendant upon these, is just as likely perhaps to deter individual offenders. To suggest that the random possibility (arguably remote) of receiving a lenient sentence will enter into the would be criminal's calculations is a little fanciful. Certain other of Spencer's arguments, notably the "demoralising" effect that lenient sentences have on the police, also do not advance his general argument significantly.

2. Spencer is on surer ground when he observes that inadequate sentences are an injustice in terms of failure to observe the proportionality principle.

3. Whatever the merits of a prosecution right of appeal against lenient sentences, this innovation was introduced under section 36 of the Criminal Justice Act 1988 which came into force in February 1989. Section 36 states:

> "(1) If it appears to the Attorney-General –
>   (a) that the sentencing of a person in a proceeding in the Crown Court had been unduly lenient; and
>   (b) that the case is one to which this Part of the Act applies,
>
> he may, with the leave of the Court of Appeal, refer the case to them to review the sentencing of that person; and on such a reference the Court of Appeal may –
>   (i) quash any sentence passed on him in the proceeding; and
>   (ii) in place of it pass such a sentence as they think appropriate for the case and as the court below had power to pass when dealing with him..."

The main purpose of the new Attorney-General's Reference procedure was to restore the public's confidence in cases where it was felt that the sentence was clearly too lenient, by permitting the case to be reconsidered by the Court of Appeal. The White Paper, *Crime, Justice and Protecting the Public* (1990), also expressed the hope that this new provision would play a part in contributing to the development of a coherent sentencing practice (see para. 2.20). However, it was arguably unrealistic to expect this new procedure to facilitate the development of detailed sentencing guidance.

The Attorney-General's Reference Procedure

The Court of Appeal must give leave before a reference can be made by the Attorney-General, under section 36, in cases where he considers that the offender received an unduly lenient sentence, or where he considers that the judge erred in law as to his sentencing powers (see section 36(2)). The offence for which sentence was passed must be triable only on indictment (section 35(3)(a)), or one which is triable either way and specified in an order made by the Home Secretary by statutory instrument (section 35(4)). The Home Secretary recently extended the reference procedure, by means of the Criminal Justice Act 1988 (Reviews of Sentencing) Order 1994, to cover certain sexual, violent, and child cruelty offences which are triable either way. (For a recent minor amendment to section 35 of the 1988 Act, see para. 34 of Schedule 9 to the Criminal Justice and Public Order Act 1994.)

The reference procedure has been used more extensively than was forecast by many, and it can be claimed that "it has gone some way to meeting the objectives of those who supported its introduction [by providing] a route to a judicial analysis of a sentence alleged to be unduly lenient" (David Thomas [1993] Crim. L.R. 228). Thomas adds: "The fact that the majority of cases referred have concluded in an increase in the sentence is probably best explained as the result of a careful selection process; there has certainly been no assumption by the Court that the decision to refer will inevitably lead to an increase."

In an early case under the new provision, the Court of Appeal took the opportunity to explain its approach to these appeals. In *Attorney-General's Reference (No. 4 of 1989)* [1990] Crim. L.R. 438; 11 Cr. App. R(S) 517, a reference was made to the Court of Appeal as a result of an offender receiving 18 months' imprisonment suspended for two years for two counts of incest and two counts of indecent assault. For such serious offences, the sentence did appear lenient at first sight, but was it unduly lenient having regard to the many mitigating circumstances that were said to be present here? The Court of Appeal thought not, and explained that the proper construction of section 36 was that the Court could only increase a sentence which it felt to be *unduly* lenient. It was not Parliament's intention to subject offenders to the risk of having their sentences increased merely because in the opinion of the Court of Appeal the sentence was less than it would have imposed. A sentence should only be regarded as unduly lenient if it fell outside the range of sentences which the judge, applying his mind to all the relevant factors, could reasonably consider appropriate. (Also see *Attorney-General's Ref. (No. 1 of 1994)* [1994] Crim. L.R. 764). In making this assessment, regard must be had to reported cases and to guidance given by judgments of the Court of Appeal. On the other hand, it had to be remembered that the trial judge was particularly well placed to assess the weight to be given to various competing considerations and that leniency was not *per se* a bad thing. Even where the Court does consider a sentence to be unduly lenient, the Court has discretion whether to exercise its powers under section 36. For example, the Court might decline the opportunity to increase an unduly lenient sentence where, in view of events since the trial, it appears that the sentence could be justified, or where it would be unfair to the offender or detrimental to others to do so.

The Court gave further guidance on the application of section 36 in *Attorney-General's Reference (No. 5 of 1989)* [1990] Crim. L.R. 278. In this case the offender pleaded guilty to causing death by reckless driving. His vehicle collided with an oncoming car, killing one of its passengers, after the offender had driven dangerously for about four miles and had ignored a friend's warning to slow down. The original sentence of a £2,500 fine and three year disqualification from driving was increased by the Court, which stated that it was plainly a case where a custodial sentence was required and it held that the proper sentence was 21 months' detention in a young offender institution. The disqualification was unaltered, but the fine was quashed. The Court explained that there had been an error in principle by the Crown Court. It was not a case which could be adequately dealt with by a fine; the only proper sentence was one of immediate custody in view of the aggravating factors involved such as persistently bad and potentially lethal driving. The Court stated that it was not a borderline case and that public confidence in the judicial system would be damaged if the sentence was not altered.

Another principle established by the Court in relation to the reference procedure is that, if a sentence is to be increased, the Court may allow some reduction of the correct sentence to take account of the "double jeopardy" factor. The offender will have been sentenced, in effect, twice and may also have thought after his trial that he had avoided imprisonment, only to find that an immediate custodial sentence is later imposed upon him by the Court of Appeal. In *Attorney-General's Reference (No. 19 of 1992)* [1993] Crim. L.R. 82, a man was sentenced to nine months' imprisonment, suspended for 18 months, for a number of buggery offences against his non-consenting wife. The Court held that this was clearly an unduly lenient sentence and increased it to four years' immediate imprisonment. However, Lord Taylor C.J. explained that in arriving at this sentence, the Court had made allowance for the fact that the offender had been sentenced on a second occasion, with the stress this involves, and was now being given a sentence of immediate imprisonment after having thought that he had escaped such a penalty.

Also in *Attorney-General's Reference (No. 13 of 1992)* [1993] Crim. L.R. 544, the offender was convicted of aggravated burglary and wounding with intent to cause grievous bodily harm and there were a number of aggravating factors present. The Court held that the original sentence of six years' imprisonment was unduly lenient and that an appropriate sentence would be in the order of ten years. However, it took into account the double jeopardy inherent in the Attorney-General's reference procedure, and imposed a sentence of nine years' imprisonment.

It is apparent that the Court of Appeal regards its main function, under section 36, as being to correct sentences which are either excessively lenient or where the original sentence had involved some error of principle which would affect public confidence in the judicial system. It does not see its role under the reference procedure as primarily one of providing guidance to lower courts on the appropriate level of sentences for particular offences. This attitude has been criticised by commentators, and it has been argued that the Court should give a clearer indication as to what it thinks the correct sentence should have been in all cases under the reference procedure. In his commentary on *Attorney-General's Reference (No. 22 of 1991)* [1993] Crim. L.R. 227 at p. 228, David Thomas argued:

> "The second factor limiting the usefulness of decisions on References are the principles adopted by the Court in exercising its powers to substitute a more severe sentence. The first is that a sentence will not be increased unless it is 'unduly lenient' in the sense that it falls outside the bracket which a sentencer could reasonably consider appropriate, taking all relevant considerations into account. The second is that when the Court does increase a sentence which it considers to be unduly lenient, the sentence substituted by the Court is not necessarily the sentence which it considers that the trial judge should have passed; the final sentence incorporates a discount to compensate the offender for the 'double jeopardy' element in facing the prospect of being sentenced a second time. The result is that the decision of the court not to interfere with a sentence does not necessarily mean that the original sentence was right, and the decision to impose a more severe sentence does not necessarily indicate what the proper sentence would have been at first instance. While the two principles adopted by the Court are based on fairness to the offender, there seems to be no obvious reason why the Court should not state, when giving the judgment on a Reference, what it considers the trial judge should have done, whether or not it substitutes that sentence itself. This would ensure that the best use is made of the full examination of the relevant considerations and principles which is typically found in judgments on References."

If the Court of Appeal were to follow Thomas' suggestion, as it did recently in *Attorney-General's Reference (No.s 17 and 18 of 1994)* [1994] Crim. L.R. 955, it would certainly be in keeping with the view expressed in the White Paper ("Crime, Justice and Protecting the Public", 1990, para. 2.20) that the reference procedure could contribute to the development of a coherent sentencing framework. The extent to which it has in fact made such a contribution was examined recently in an article by Ralph Henham, "Attorney-General's References and Sentencing Policy" [1994] Crim. L.R. 499. He concludes (at p. 512) that the reference procedure has made only "a very limited contribution to the development of sentencing principles and practice." He argues that the category of cases which are referable should be extended to cover most dishonesty offences and all drug offences. Henham also argues (at p. 512) that:

> "a major problem lies in the perceived role of the Attorney-General's reference procedure as a corrective to judicially created sentencing anomalies rather than a significant part of a wider sentencing framework reflecting an agreed sentencing policy ... [T]he reference procedure has enormous potential for providing consistent and useful sentencing guidance if it were to be regarded as part of a co-ordinated sentencing strategy by the judiciary."

The Case for a Sentencing Council

It could be argued that one of the obstacles in the way of the development of a coherent sentencing strategy has been the Court of Appeal itself. Traditionally, insufficient guidance has been given to the lower courts in relation to sentencing less serious offenders. Where guidance has been given, it has sometimes been unrealistic or out of touch with sentencing practices in the lower courts. Some have called for a more expert sentencing council or commission to be established, and given the responsibility for providing sentencers with guidance and keeping them abreast of relevant statistical and penological information. Professor Andrew Ashworth is a leading proponent of such a reform and he has put forward this idea on a number of occasions. An early formulation of his proposal can be found in his NACRO lecture, "Reducing the Prison Population in the 1980s: The Need for Sentencing Reform" (1982), in which he stated:

> "What is needed is a body which can consider sentencing practice from all these points of view, can instigate research which will provide systematic knowledge about the reasoning of judges and magistrates, and can then reformulate sentencing policy so that it is no longer reliant on custodial measures. The question of policy just outlined must be tackled by whatever body is assembled for the purpose. The Court of Appeal, I submit, is not the appropriate body. It lacks a wider appreciation of penal policy, and it is imperfectly informed about sentencing practices in the lower courts ... My proposal is for a sentencing council, chaired by the Lord Chief Justice himself and

producing recommendations which would be issued as practice directions ... Its membership should draw on persons with considerable
experience of the penal system, from magistrates, to a circuit judge
sitting in second- and third-tier centres, to a probation officer, a prison
governor, a Home Office official and an academic ... it would be
essential that there should be a number of sentencers who fairly
represent the range of English courts, so as to bring a wider experience
than a few senior judges can muster." (For a more detailed discussion
by the same author, see A. Ashworth, *Sentencing and Criminal Justice*
(1992), pp. 320–328).

Although such a proposal is not without its difficulties, it does offer some
distinct advantages over the present system. A sentencing council could
incorporate a wider field of expertise and experience than an appellate
court. It could perform an advisory role which is not fettered by the
appellate process and is not dependent on a particular issue being raised by
either the offender of the Attorney-General. Accordingly, the council would
be able to provide guidance in relation to all types of offence, and both
custodial and non-custodial penalties. Despite these potential advantages,
the Government rejected the case for this innovation in its White paper
(1990, see para. 2.20), where it stated that it could see "no need for a
Sentencing Council to develop sentencing policies or guidance".

Ashworth's call for the setting up of a sentencing council has been taken
up by reform groups in the criminal justice system. For example, see the
Prison Reform Trust's report entitled "The Case for a Sentencing Council",
discussed in the *Howard Journal*, Penal Policy File No. 42 ((1991) at p.
240), in which the Prison Reform Trust advocated a national commission
to plan sentencing policy. In addition, the Labour Party supported the
sentencing council idea at the time of the 1992 election.

In view of the obvious hostility of the judiciary to such a scheme, which
would involve the creation of an extra-judicial authority of considerable
influence over sentencing policy, it is unlikely that Ashworth's interesting
suggestions will come to fruition. Moreover, not all leading academics
support Ashworth's proposals, as is clear from the following short article
written by David Thomas in 1990.

David Thomas, "Penalties Without a Plan", *The Times* February 13, 1990.

The rejection in the White Paper on criminal justice last week of a sentencing
council will disappoint a growing number of pressure groups who believe such a
body would provide the answers to two of the most pressing problems of the
criminal justice system: the growth of prison numbers and disparity of sentences
imposed on offenders.
    But what is the basis of this belief? A sentencing council is something of a
penological unicorn; many have heard of one, but nobody has seen one in action.
Not one Commonwealth jurisdiction, whose sentencing laws resemble those here,
has set up such a council, and the experience of American jurisdictions, which

have appointed sentencing commissions in a very different context, indicates that expectations are not always fulfilled.

In some cases, the different backgrounds of the various commissioners lead to fundamental disagreements, which have made coherent policies impossible to achieve. In others, the guidelines of commissions have been vetoed by the legislature. Some of the guideline systems that took effect, such as those of Pennsylvania, would not satisfy supporters of a sentencing council; they specify wide judicial discretion subject to mandatory minimum sentences. The only state system (in Minnesota) regarded as reasonably successful relies on a crude grid, which groups cases simply by reference to the legal definition of the offence and "criminal history score", calculated on the number of previous convictions.

The more sophisticated system produced by the United States Sentencing Commission for the federal criminal courts avoids some of these criticisms. But it mostly produces sentences much more severe than would be passed here for equivalent offences.

How would a sentencing council work? Assuming agreement on who should appoint its members, there would doubtless be a judge as chairman and representatives of interested constituencies, both from the police and probation service. Unanimity would not necessarily come easily.

What form would the guidelines take? Would the commission have to provide detailed instructions for every conceivable case, or broad general principles leaving much to the interpretation of the sentencer? And, most crucial, there is the question of what authority the guidelines would have and how they would be promulgated. Advisory guidelines, which were not legally binding, might be published by the council (rather as the Criminal Injuries Compensation Board publishes suggested starting points for compensation in personal injury cases). But these would have limited effect if sentencers were free to ignore them.

Mandatory guidelines, which sentencers were bound to follow would necessarily be promulgated as statutory instruments, requiring parliamentary approval.

Given the high level of political interest they would generate, it is easy to imagine the difficulties they would encounter in this process, with the result that the council would tailor its guidelines to a shape that would find political favour.

But whatever their form, the practical effect guidelines would have would depend, ultimately on the extent to which they attracted the support of the higher judiciary. Sentencing commissions in the American jurisdictions have been created to fill a void left by the reluctance of American appellate courts to take sentencing seriously; few American jurisdictions have any significant tradition of appellate review of sentences or accumulated case law on sentencing. But a sentencing council in England would be a direct competitor of the Court of Appeal, which would always have the last word.

Advisory guidelines would depend entirely for their effect on being adopted by the Court of Appeal; mandatory guidelines would require interpretation and application to particular cases. So if senior judges were implacably opposed to a sentencing council or to its guidelines, there is not much hope of its achieving the objects it proponents seek.

The Court of Appeal is a familiar institution whose strengths and deficiencies can be assessed on the basis of evidence: the sentencing council is an unknown quantity; the ambitious claims made for it owe everything to hope and nothing to experience.

There is undoubtedly a need for a more considered approach to the development of a coherent sentencing policy, which cannot be achieved by direct parliamentary legislation. But evolution rather then revolution may be the best way to get it.

In the past 10 years, the Court of Appeal has taken initiatives in formulating sentencing policy and not all its guidance has been focused on custodial sentences for serious crimes. The guidelines dealing with social security fraud, in particular, show that the court is capable of tackling offences on the borderline between custodial and non-custodial sentences, and in lowering as well as raising sentence levels.

Yet there is a major obstacle to the development of a coherent sentencing policy in this way: Parliament's insistence on constant changes in the statutory framework under which sentencers operate; one statute follows another almost before the ink is dry, and the intervals between the invention of one form of sentence and its replacement by another are constantly reduced.

What is needed more than anything is a moratorium on sentencing legislation, so that coherent strategies can be developed within a settled framework. Unfortunately, the White Paper leaves no hope of that.

Notes

1.   There is no denying the strength of Dr Thomas' argument that there has been too much recent legislation on sentencing, which can only lead to greater confusion on the part of sentencers. The recent example of the hasty amendments to the Criminal Justice Act 1991, by the 1993 legislation, is a stark illustration of this point. Many of the political and practical problems which would beset a sentencing council are also correctly identified in Thomas' article.

2.   Thomas' arguments are less convincing in respect of his belief that the Court of Appeal is capable of providing the sort of guidance which will lead to the development of a coherent sentencing policy. Furthermore, the Court of Appeal is clearly incapable of performing the wider functions of the mooted sentencing council.

3.   Ashworth argues that it is not a fair comparison to look at the United States' experience of sentencing commissions when assessing the proposal which he has put forward for this country. He is undoubtedly correct in this assertion, as the United States' schemes, and the general milieu in which they operate, are different in many ways. Nevertheless, proposals for this country are bound to be tainted by criticisms which have been levelled (rightly or wrongly) at the U.S. schemes. For an interesting critical discussion of sentencing commissions in the United States, see Albert Alschuler, "The Failure of Sentencing Commissions", *New Law Journal* (1991) pp. 829–30. (For further details on the different forms that sentencing guidance and guidelines can take, see *Sentencing Reform* (K. Pease and M. Wasik eds., 1987) especially Chapter 3 by M. Tonry, "Sentencing Guidelines and Sentencing Commissions – The Second Generation", and Chapter 4 by A. von Hirsch, "Guidance by Numbers or Words? Numerical Versus Narrative Guidelines for Sentencing").

CHAPTER FOUR

IMPRISONMENT

I. INTRODUCTION

Imprisonment is now clearly seen as a penal measure of last resort. Section 1(2) of the Criminal Justice Act 1991 (as amended) states that a court is not to impose a custodial sentence unless it is of the opinion that the offence (or the combination of the offence and one or more offences associated with it) was so serious that only such a sentence can be justified; or, in cases involving violent or sexual offences, that only such a sentence would be adequate for the purposes of public protection. (The restrictions on the use of custodial sentences are discussed further in the following section of this chapter). Thus the seriousness of the offence is now, in most cases, to be the crucial determinant of whether an offender will be sentenced to imprisonment and there is a greater onus on sentencers to explain and justify the imposition of such a sentence (see the Criminal Justice Act 1991, section 1(4)).

With the virtual extinction of capital punishment, imprisonment has become the ultimate sanction within the system of criminal law, so that at the same time the measure has a large symbolic significance within the penal system as a whole. It is also, despite attempts to restrict its use and the development of a number of non-custodial measures, an institution of considerable quantitative significance (see the final section of this chapter). During the earlier part of this century, imprisonment evolved from a mainly short-term measure of penal confinement into a longer-term institution designed to effect the reform or deterrence of criminals. More recently, despite its pre-eminence in the general penal scheme, the institution of imprisonment has experienced a highly critical assessment; and, on the part of those actually administering the system, there has been an increasingly less sure sense of its functions and objectives. (For a detailed discussion, see C. Harding *et al.*, *Imprisonment in England and Wales – A Concise History* (1985), pp. 187–95).

The Prisons Act of 1877 brought all prisons in the country under direct central control, while the 1898 Act made this control the province of the Home Office rather than Parliament. Post-war legislation has not substantially affected the content of a prison sentence, which is largely determined by the Prison Rules, but has rather been concerned with the way in which the sentencer chooses imprisonment in the first place. The replacement of the Prison Commission by the Home Office's Prison Department has consolidated Home Office control, making the prison system, in the view of some commentators, less "open" than had previously been the case to outside criticism and influences. Although earlier prison officials, such as Sir Edmund Du Cane, may have appeared to be autocratic and overbearing, they were far from being anonymous administrators and were fully involved in academic and public debate about penal theory and practice. The prison system within the last 100 years has taken on a more monolithic character and has become much more the subject of slow-moving policy and much less affected by individual initiatives such as those of Alexander Paterson. The prison system experienced a contraction in the later years of the nineteenth century and the first years of this century, with a much reduced population of inmates and a number of prison closures (see Harding *et al.* (1985), pp. 195–199 for details). In contrast, since 1945 there has been a steadily rising population and since the 1960s, a programme of rebuilding and new prisons.

The regime of imprisonment – the prisoner's experience while serving his term – is based upon Home Office policy. Major shifts in policy have been brought about by particular Committee investigations and reports rather than as a result of Parliamentary initiatives. The Gladstone Committee's Report in 1895, despite the Committee's limited terms of reference, was in fact a prospectus for major change and signalled a shift towards the use of reformative methods within the sentence of imprisonment. More recently, the Mountbatten Report (*Report of the Inquiry into Prison Escapes and Security*, Cmnd. 3175 (1966)) shifted the emphasis towards security and control, while the May Committee, while actually enquiring into the prison services (Cmnd. 7673 (1979)), acknowledged the limits of what could be achieved by way of reform in the context of imprisonment and put forward "positive custody" as the objective of the Prison Service. The prison regime over the last century has therefore evolved largely as a response (and sometimes slowly) to such seminal statements in the reports of departmental committees and committees of enquiry. The most important recent inquiry into the prison regime, set up as a result of the riots of 1990, is the Woolf Report (Cm. 1456 (1991)). This major report, which was favourably received right across the political spectrum, will be looked at later in this chapter.

II. PASSING A CUSTODIAL SENTENCE

Before looking at the organisation of the prison system and the prison regime, it is useful to consider the legal restrictions on the use of custodial sentences. In the past, various exhortations were made to sentencers to regard a prison sentence as a last resort, to be used when the repertoire of non-custodial measures had been tried to little or no apparent effect, or when the offence was a very serious one. However, this did little to stem the (virtually) inexorable rise in the prison population, nor did it curb the apparent enthusiasm of many sentencers for using custodial sentences for recidivist property offenders. The restriction on the use of custodial sentences laid down by section 1(2) of the Criminal Justice Act 1991 represents an attempt to provide a more structured framework for the exercise of sentencing discretion. Opinions differ as to how much of a change was actually brought about by the 1991 Act in this context. In the words of David Thomas ([1992] Crim. L.R. 232):

> "According to one view, Part I of the Criminal Justice Act 1991 is a landmark in the history of sentencing; another view is that it is a largely irrelevant exercise in teaching grandmother to suck eggs. The principle around which the rules relating to custodial sentences are said to have been constructed, the principle of 'just deserts', is not new; it has been the basis of judicial practice for years ... There is no particular objection to the translation of established common law principles into statutory form, as long as the process is accomplished skilfully and does not result in creating more problems than it solves ... It is important to realise that the provisions of the Act regulating the use of custodial sentences will not in themselves change either the use of custodial sentences or the length of sentences to any degree."

The Criminal Justice Act 1991 (section 1(2)) states that a court shall not pass a custodial sentence on an offender unless it is of the opinion –

(a) that the offence, or the combination of the offence and one or more offences associated with it, was so serious that only such a sentence can be justified for the offence; or
(b) where the offence is a violent or sexual offence, that only such a sentence would be adequate to protect the public from serious harm from him.

Under section 2(2) it is also stated that a custodial sentence, which is not fixed by law, shall be:

(a) for such term (not exceeding the permitted maximum) as in the opinion of the court is commensurate with the seriousness of the offence, or the combination of the offence and one or more offences associated with it; or
(b) where the offence is a violent or sexual offence, for such longer term (not exceeding that maximum) as in the opinion of the court is necessary to protect the public from serious harm from the offender.

This broad statutory framework has left much to be determined by the courts. The central concept is that of offence seriousness, but there is no definition provided by the Act of what it means. When is an offence, or the combination of an offence and one or more offences associated with it, so serious that only a custodial sentence can be justified? The earliest indication of the meaning of this term could be derived by analogy with section 1(4) of the Criminal Justice Act 1982, which introduced statutory criteria for the imposition of custodial sentences on offenders aged under 21. In

Bradbourn (1985) 7 Cr. App. R.(S) 180 at 183, Lawton L.J. stated in the
Court of Appeal that the phrase "so serious that a non-custodial sentence
cannot be justified" – which was the key phrase under the 1982 Act, section
1(4A)(c) – refers to:

> "the kind of offence which when committed by a young person would
> make right-thinking members of the public, knowing all the facts, feel
> that justice had not been done by the passing of any sentence other
> than a custodial one. We think that it is as good guidance as we can
> give to courts and that any attempt to be more specific would only
> add to the difficulties of courts and not help them."

Although this provision under the 1982 Act was repealed by the Criminal
Justice Act 1991, the obvious similarities in language between these statutory
criteria for custodial sentences make it worth considering decisions on the
1982 Act as a starting point. Shortly after the introduction of the 1991 Act,
the Lord Chief Justice considered the meaning of section 1(2)(a) in the
Court of Appeal in *Cox* [1993] 1 W.L.R. 188. Lord Taylor observed that,
despite differences in the wording of section 1(4A) of the 1982 Act and
section 1(2)(a) of the 1991 Act, Lord Lawton's formulation (quoted above)
was appropriate to any consideration of the expression "so serious that
only such a sentence can be justified for the offence" and should be adopted.
So, in determining the criteria for custody, this definition is now applicable
to both young and adult offenders. (Also see *Winterton* [1993] Crim. L.R.
322).

But how useful is this appellate guidance on the interpretation of section
1(2)(a) of the 1991 Act? It is worth considering the case of *Keogh* [1993]
Crim. L.R. 895 in attempting to answer this question. The appellant pleaded
guilty to obtaining property by deception in a DIY store. Having selected
a car alarm worth £35, he concealed it under a carrier bag in his trolley
before asking the shop assistant whether he could exchange the alarm for
other goods. He was allowed to do so, but was then apprehended by
the store detective. The trial court imposed a sentence of one month's
imprisonment for this offence. (It may well have been influenced by the fact
that the appellant was, at the time of the offence, subject to a suspended
sentence for unlawful wounding). The Court of Appeal held that a short
custodial sentence was appropriate for this type of shoplifting offence. One
might have thought that this was a case where the offence was not so
serious that only a custodial sentence could be justified, in view of the
relatively modest value of the goods and the absence of any real planning.
However, the Court was of the opinion that, in relation to this sort of
offence, the test adopted in *Cox* was satisfied. The Court evidently felt that
right thinking members of the public, knowing all the facts, would not feel
that justice had been done if any sentence other than a custodial one had
been imposed. But if this is a correct interpretation of section 1(2)(a), it
suggests that the criterion of seriousness will easily be satisfied so as to
justify a custodial sentence under the Act. Indeed, it becomes difficult to

think of offences which are not so serious that only a custodial sentence could be justified. (Also see *McCormick* [1994] Crim. L.R. 612).

Further criticism of the appellate guidance, or lack of it, under section 1(2)(a) was made in a recent editorial in the Criminal Law Review ([1994] Crim. L.R. 153–5). It states (at p. 154):

> "It is worth raising the question whether such a sweeping test [i.e. *Bradbourn*] is the best we can do, especially when the results of the cases often seem difficult to reconcile and afford little guidance to the lower courts. How much sense does the test make as it stands? Could a more effective test be formulated?
>
> In asking whether the test makes sense, one could ruminate on whether such an important decision as "custody or not" should be taken by reference to the feelings of the people regarded by judges and magistrates as "right thinking". For example, how well informed are these people about the nature and function of other forms of sentence? Or is the wording of the test merely a camouflage for the personal views of the magistrates or judges themselves? But even if it is accepted that we should properly take this decision on the basis of the views of "right thinking members of the public" ... what evidence exists about these views? Of course, a court does not go out and conduct a poll, even a straw poll, in reference to the facts of each case. The court is assumed to know what right-thinking people think ..."

The editorial then goes on to criticise the *Keogh* decision in particular and to question whether right thinking members of the public would, in reality, have considered it an injustice if the defendant had not been given a custodial sentence. As an alternative approach, the editorial commended Lord Lane's statement in *Stewart* [1987] Crim. L.R. 520, in relation to social security frauds and the possibility of avoiding custodial sentences, where he stated that such offences were at least "non-violent, non-sexual and non-frightening". The editorial continues (at pp. 154–5):

> "Leaving aside residential burglaries, which raise separate issues, would it not be fair to argue that most small-value thefts, deceptions and other purely property offences should not result in a custodial sentence? ... Of course it would be foolish to suggest that courts should adopt a *rule* that no pure property offence of less than, say, £200 should result in imprisonment. But is there not good sense in considering a judicial *principle* or *presumption* that pure property offences below a certain value should not result in a custodial sentence, unless the court can establish that one or more aggravating factors justify a departure in the particular case? This would be one way of ensuring the courts articulate some distinct reasons – rather than vague references to right-thinking people – which can be connected to recognised sentencing principles.
>
> Of course some discretion should be retained. Of course, the proposed

test would not solve everything: it would be but a small development
in a field that must continue to develop as experience accumulates.
Perhaps an even better test could be found. The Court of Appeal
should begin to move away from the *Bradbourn* test if lower courts are
to be given guidance, and if the deprivation of liberty is not to be
ordered for offences so far down the criminal calendar."

In view of *Keogh*, it would seem that the custody "threshold" under the
1991 Act is somewhat lower than was anticipated at the time of its
enactment. This is so not only in relation to relatively trivial property
offences (as in *Keogh*), but also in relation to minor assaults. In the recent
case of *Fenton* [1994] Crim. L.R. 464, a motorist who pushed another road
user in the chest was given a sentence of 14 days' immediate imprisonment.
The Court of Appeal was of the view that this type of assault by one
motorist upon another did meet the statutory criteria for a custodial
sentence, so as to merit an actual period of custody. (The Court substituted
a sentence of seven days' imprisonment). It is possible to understand the
Court's wish to underline the importance of deterring motorists from
resorting to any acts of violence or aggression, but the actual decision in
this case is a little difficult to justify. Can it truly be said that the offence
in *Fenton* was so serious that only a custodial sentence could be justified?
Even applying the rather vague test laid down in *Bradbourn*, it is hard to
believe that right-thinking members of the public would feel an injustice
had occurred if the defendant had been given a non-custodial sentence.
An alternative ground for justifying custody, under section 1(2)(b), is if
the court, in dealing with a violent or sexual offence, thinks that only such
a sentence would be adequate to protect the public from serious harm from
the offender. It should also be noted that section 2(2)(b) enables the court
to pass a longer custodial sentence than would otherwise be permissible,
where the offence is a violent or sexual one, if it thinks that this is necessary
to protect the public from serious harm from the offender. At first sight it
is hard to see the value of section 1(2)(b). If the offence is a violent or
sexual one, it might be thought that it is likely to be so serious that only a
custodial sentence can be justified. The crucial difference in section 1(2)(b)
is that it is not based on desert or proportionality, which is the main
philosophy underlying the Criminal Justice Act 1991, but rather it is based
on the aim of incapacitating the potentially dangerous offender. This
obviously involves a prediction by the court as to who is likely to pose a
serious threat to the public in the future. The section 1(2)(b) justification
for a custodial sentence is unlikely to be widely used in comparison with
the use made of section 1(2)(a). (On the meaning of "violent offence" for
the purposes of the Act, see the contrasting cases of *Cochrane* [1994] Crim.
L.R. 382 and *Murray* [1994] Crim. L.R. 383).
An important case on the meaning of a "sexual offence" or a "violent
offence" under the Act is *Robinson* [1993] 1 W.L.R. 168. The appellant,
aged 16, forced his way into the house of an 87 year old woman and

attempted to rape her. He also demanded money, which she did not have, and then made his escape. The appellant received a sentence of eight years' detention in a young offender institution under the Children and Young Persons Act 1933, s. 53(2). The Court of Appeal was asked to rule whether attempted rape was a "sexual offence" or a "violent offence". The Court held that although the offence was indicted under the Criminal Attempts Act 1981, it was properly regarded as an offence under the Sexual Offences Act 1956. Thus it was correct to conclude that attempted rape was within the definition of a "sexual offence" for the purposes of the Criminal Justice Act 1991. Also, as the victim in this case did in fact suffer physical injury as a direct result of the attempted rape, it came within the definition of a "violent offence" for the purposes of the Act (see section 31(1)). The Court concluded that the sentence of eight years' detention was right for such an appalling offence committed against a woman of nearly 90 years old, who was alone in her home at night.

A new and comprehensive definition of "sexual offences" for the purposes of the Criminal Justice Act 1991 has been provided by the Criminal Justice and Public Order Act 1994, Schedule 9, paragraph 45. (This replaces the definition contained in section 31(1) of the 1991 Act). This definition should help to clarify a situation such as that which occurred in *Robinson*.

III. TYPES OF PRISON SENTENCE

In terms of prison regime, there is now a single generic sentence of imprisonment for offenders over the age of 21. Different species of imprisonment in the form of penal servitude and imprisonment with hard labour were abolished by the Criminal Justice Act 1948 (see Harding *et al.* (1985), pp. 205–10 for details of these forms of imprisonment). For adult offenders, a determinate prison sentence is the normal form that the custodial sentence takes. (The most common custodial sentence for those under 21 years of age, *i.e.* detention in a young offender institution, is looked at in Chapter 6). However, there are different types of prison, principally according to their holding function and degree of security (see below).

Life imprisonment, which is an indeterminate sentence, requires further discussion. A life sentence does not usually mean incarceration for life in a literal sense; it is an indeterminate sentence, for which the release date of the offender is not fixed at the time of sentence, but is decided upon by the parole authorities. It is necessary to distinguish between mandatory and discretionary life sentences. Section 1(1) of the Murder (Abolition of Death Penalty) Act 1965 provides that "a person convicted of murder shall ... be sentenced to imprisonment for life." Therefore, life imprisonment, since the abolition of the death penalty, is the mandatory sentence for murder. There is no sentencing discretion in dealing with a convicted murderer and, as a result of this, the offender has no right of appeal against the mandatory sentence. The judge can make a recommendation, when passing a life sentence for murder, as to the minimum period that the offender ought to serve in prison before being released on licence (see section 1(2) of the Murder (Abolition of the Death Penalty) Act 1965).

In contrast to the crime of murder, there are a number of offences for which life imprisonment is a discretionary alternative to other types of sentence. In these cases it is the specified maximum penalty, but its use is not, of course, mandatory. These offences include: manslaughter, wounding or causing grievous bodily harm with intent, destroying or damaging property with intent to endanger life, rape, robbery, and aggravated burglary. In what circumstances will a life sentence be appropriate in cases other than murder? A useful starting point is the case of *Hodgson* (1967) 52 Cr. App. R. 113, which involved an appeal against three sentences of life imprisonment in respect of two acts of rape and one of buggery committed against two women late at night in public places. The Court of Appeal decided that an indeterminate life sentence was justified in this case as the following conditions were satisfied (per Mackenna J, at p. 114):

> "A sentence of life imprisonment is in our opinion justified: (1) where the offence or offences are in themselves grave enough to require a very long sentence; (2) where it appears from the nature of the offences or from the defendant's history that he is a person of unstable character likely to commit such offences in the future; and (3) where if the offences are committed the consequences to others may be specially injurious, as in the case of sexual offences or crimes of violence."

This statement is still of relevance today (see *O'Dwyer* (1988) 86 Cr. App. R. 313), despite some refinement in later cases. It does raise problems of definition, however, in relation to which offences are considered "grave enough" and what amounts to an unstable character so as to warrant a life sentence. There are also problems of prediction in relation to dangerous offenders: *i.e.* how predictable is it that an "unstable" offender is likely to commit serious offences in the future? The available evidence does not really support the view that the courts are able to predict future offending with any degree of precision. (For a valuable discussion, see Jean Floud, "Dangerousness and Criminal Justice", (1982) 22 B.J. Crim. 213).

In *De Havilland* (1983) 5 Cr. App. R.(S) 109, it was stated that although it is normal practice for a judge to make reference to medical evidence before passing a life sentence (for rape in this case), he may nevertheless pass such a sentence without medical evidence. The ultimate responsibility lies with the judge and not the doctor. However, the judge should not pass a life sentence for rape unless he is satisfied on all the evidence, including any medical evidence, that he is dealing with an offender of unstable character who is likely to commit such offences in the future and be a danger to the public for an unpredictable and indefinite period of time. In *Blackburn* (1979) 1 Cr. App. R.(S) 205, by way of contrast, the appellant was convicted of conspiracy to rob, and was found in the possession of a sawn-off shotgun and other incriminating articles. It was held, in substituting an eight year determinate sentence for his sentence of life imprisonment, that a life sentence should not be imposed unless the judge is satisfied, on medical evidence, that the offender is suffering from some mental instability which makes him a danger to the public.

The sentencing principles in relation to discretionary life sentences must now also be read in the light of the Criminal Justice Act 1991. Section 2 of the Act deals with the length of custodial sentences imposed by the courts and this covers discretionary life sentences as well as determinate sentences. As a life sentence will rarely be justifiable under section 2(2)(a), it will normally only be justified under section 2(2)(b) "where the offence is a violent of sexual offence [the sentence shall be] for such longer term ... as in the opinion of the court is necessary to protect the public from serious harm from the offender."

To return to the issue of the mandatory life sentence for murder, we can see that this rule has attracted a great deal of criticism and debate. In a system which confers sentencing discretion on judges, and generally eschews the notion of fixed penalties for serious offences, it is regarded by some as an anomaly to have the mandatory sentence for murder. Others argue that in view of the heinous nature of this particular crime, it would damage public confidence in the judicial system if murderers received anything other than a sentence of life imprisonment now that the death penalty is no longer available. This subject was considered in detail by a House of Lords Select Committee in its report, *Murder and Life Imprisonment* (1988–9), H.L., Paper 78.

House of Lords Select Committee, *Murder and Life Imprisonment*, (1988–9), H.L., Paper 78, pp. 33–36.

The arguments for and against the retention of the mandatory sentence
Murder is a uniquely serious offence
108A. It is said that murder is a uniquely serious offence in that typically it consists in intentional and unprovoked killing of another human being and that it follows that it should attract a distinctive penalty in order to mark the revulsion with which society regards it. This fixed penalty should remain for denunciatory reasons.
108B. The counter-arguments are as follows:

   (i) Not all murders are "uniquely serious...."
   ... Some cases of murder will be less grave than some cases of attempted murder, or of manslaughter, or of causing grievous bodily harm with intent. The organisation JUSTICE has examined in some detail over 200 cases over the last 30 years and concluded that the circumstances giving rise to murder vary infinitely so that the relative heinousness of the crime covers the whole spectrum from the tragic mercy killing to the most sadistic type of sex murder of young children.

   (ii) The definition of murder is not and, if the Committee's recommendations are accepted, will not be confined to intentional killings. A jury's verdict of guilty of murder does not necessarily mean that they were satisfied that the defendant intended to kill.... If the intentional and unprovoked killings are to be regarded as "uniquely serious" the definition of murder ought to be limited to such killings.

(iii) Even intentional killings which are "unprovoked" in the legal sense vary greatly in their gravity. At one extreme, the "mercy killing" is intentional and unprovoked. Between such a killing and the most wicked murders there are many degrees of culpability.

(iv) The alleged "unique" quality of a life sentence for murder is undermined by the availability of that sentence for other offences.

Erosion of the distinction between murder and manslaughter

109A. The distinction between murder and manslaughter – which is to continue in the law – becomes meaningless if there is no difference in the sentencing powers available to the court; and the mandatory sentence is the only way of making such a distinction....

109B. The counter argument is that the court has regard to the "theoretical gravity" of the offence of which the offender has been convicted as well as the maximum sentence and the actual facts in fixing the sentence. If, of the two co-defendents in a joint enterprise, a jury were to convict A of murder and B of manslaughter, a judge with a discretion would naturally impose a more severe sentence on A than on B to mark the greater gravity of the offence committed by A. On the other hand, JUSTICE states that:

"some murders are less heinous than some manslaughters, and a legal system which does not reflect this in the sentence is plainly defective".

Retribution

110A. The Crown Prosecution Service argued that life imprisonment is the appropriate retributive sentence for murder.

"In cases where the accused is proved to have the necessary intent as reformulated [by the CPS's proposal], it is only right in our view that he should suffer the most severe penalty which a civilised society can impose on him, namely imprisonment for life in all cases".

110B. The counter argument is that, as a retributive sentence, mandatory life imprisonment fails to recognise that, however the intent is formulated, the requirements of retribution for murder are variable. The Lord Chief Justice took the view that the revulsion of society is marked by the verdict of guilty of murder rather than by the imposition of a penalty. Another view is that the stigma which ought to attach to any particular murder varies according to the circumstances and should be marked by a sentence appropriate to those circumstances. Retribution demands a variable sentence....

Protection of the public

111A. The mandatory sentence is necessary for the protection of the public. Offenders convicted of murder include a significant proportion who may kill again.

"A person who has killed once has demonstrated by his actions that he is capable of killing again."

Ten murderers who have been released since 1968 were convicted of a further homicide; and four of these were so-called "domestic" murders.

111B. The counter arguments are as follows:

(i) Many murderers are not generally dangerous. This was asserted by Dr Thomas who pointed out that, during a ten-year period when 6,000 persons convicted of homicide (including manslaughter) were at large, only six persons previously convicted of murder committed a second murder – and several of these were committed in prison....

(ii) The opinion of the Lord Chief Justice is that the problem of dangerousness arises in a more acute form in relation to offences other than murder. Rapists and arsonists may be much more likely to commit the same sort of offences than a murderer; and they are dealt with by passing a life sentence or a sentence which is somewhat longer than would have been necessary without the element of risk. The abolition of the mandatory sentence would involve only a slightly increased risk....

Public confidence in the criminal justice system

112A. The Crown Prosecution Service argued that public confidence in the criminal justice system would be eroded if the penalty for murder became discretionary. They believed that

".... the public favours a strong reaction to the deliberate taking of one life by another, and to allow individual judges the power to determine the appropriate sentence would often lead the public to question why a particular judge adopted a particular course of action".

112B. The counter argument is that the reaction of the public to the deliberate taking of life varies greatly according to the circumstances. In the case of the Maw sisters the sentence of three years imprisonment on two young women who had deliberately killed their drunken father was harshly criticised for its severity, and in the case of one of them, reduced on appeal to six months; and the Thompson sisters, who shot their tyrannical father as he lay in bed having an epileptic fit and were given a two year suspended sentence, seem to have attracted nothing but public sympathy. The public seems to be well able to recognise powerful mitigation, even in the case of deliberate killing. In the former case the defendants were found to be acting under provocation, in the latter to be under diminished responsibility; but there may well be similar cases where the jury is unable to find these defences to be made out....

The difficulty of establishing the appropriate length of a determinate sentence

113A. The abolition of the mandatory sentence would present peculiarly difficult sentencing problems for the trial judge. Because the sentence has always been fixed in law there are no precedents to guide the judge in imposing a determinate sentence for murder....

113B. The counter argument is that the Court of Appeal would soon establish appropriate principles of sentencing for murder as it has for other offences....

Deterrent effect of the life sentence

114A. The mandatory life sentence is, or may be, a valuable deterrent. The CLRC in 1980 pointed out that the scheme, which had been introduced by the 1965 Act, had then only been in operation for 14 years and

"it may be too soon to draw any firm conclusions whether the mandatory sentence has any special value as a deterrent"

The CPS think there is inevitably an element of deterrence in the mandatory sentence, particularly because of the existence of the life-long liability to recall.

114B. The counter argument is that the fact that the life sentence is mandatory actually reduces any deterrent value a life sentence may have. It dilutes what should be the awe-inspiring nature of the life sentence. Because many murderers receive unnecessary life sentences, the average time served is reduced, giving credence to the common belief that "life" means nine years. If the life sentence became discretionary, the average time served by lifers would be substantially increased. The passage of time will not affect the impossibility of proving whether the mandatory sentence has a deterrent effect or not: there is no material on which to base an assessment of the effect of giving the judge a discretion....

Inappropriate verdicts of manslaughter

117. Finally, the Committee were impressed by the argument put forward by Victim Support, that the existence of the mandatory life sentence led to inappropriate verdicts of manslaughter. Many families of murder victims felt that "somebody being charged and found guilty of murder does imply and represent an appropriate recognition of the crime that has actually happened". Dr Wright, a consultant psychiatrist and a member of the Parole Board, also argued forcefully that the defence of diminished responsibility was stretched in order to avoid the mandatory life sentence "in cases where it would be manifestly absurd and unjust for such a sentence to be imposed".

Opinion of the Committee

118. The Committee agree with the majority of their witnesses that the mandatory life sentence for murder should be abolished. Among the considerations which carried most weight with the Committee was the weight of judicial opinion in England and Wales. The Lord Chief Justice and 12 out of 19 judges of the High Court and the Court of Appeal were in favour of a discretionary sentence. The Committee also note that the great majority of judges who took part in the vote in the House of Lords in 1965 were in favour of the discretionary sentence....

Notes

1. The Select Committee could find little to justify the continuation of the mandatory life sentence for murder and, accordingly, supported the abolition of this fixed penalty. For a more recent discussion of the subject, see the Report of the Prison Reform Trust, Committee on the Penalty for Homicide (1993). Attempts were made in the House of Lords, during the passage of the Criminal Justice Bill (which became the Criminal Justice Act 1991) to abolish the mandatory sentence for murder. This gallant effort was defeated in the House of Commons.

2. It is a valid point that public opinion should not be advanced as a reason for maintaining the fixed penalty for murder. In addition to the instances cited in the Select Committee's report (at para. 112B), we can also consider cumulative "provocation" cases where repeatedly victimised women have killed their tormenters in circumstances which do not fall within the legally recognised defence of provocation. (For example, see *Thornton* [1992] 1 All E.R. 306; and consider *Ahluwalia* [1993] Crim. L.R. 63). The public are well able to understand the mitigating factors present in such cases and may find it difficult to accept the inflexible approach of the law.

IV. Arrangements for Early Release of Prisoners

Because of the inexorable rise in the prison population in the modern era, and the concomitant overcrowding of many penal institutions, successive governments have come to rely increasingly on early release mechanisms to manage the penal crisis. Governments have been wary of attempting to restrict judicial discretion so as to force sentencers to pass shorter prison sentences and to avoid custodial sentences for non-violent offenders. Attempts to persuade sentencers to follow such a course (see *Bibi* [1980] 1 W.L.R. 1193) by the Court of Appeal also met with a lack of success. The creation of non-custodial alternatives, such as the suspended sentence (see Chapter 5), failed to bring about the intended effect of reducing the prison population. Thus, legislative and judicial iniatives failed to provide any significant or lasting remedy for prison overcrowding. A great virtue of remission and parole, so far as governments are concerned, is that these early release procedures do not depend upon the courts' sentencing decisions. This enabled the executive to impose some restriction on the prison population without being accused of interfering with sentencing discretion. (Although, in 1981, a revolt was threatened by some senior judges when the Government planned to extend the early release of prisoners in response to serious overcrowding in prisons).

It should be emphasised that this policy was one of "managing" a crisis, rather than dealing with its root cause: namely, the sentencing practices of the courts in relation to both the use and length of custodial sentences. It also enabled governments to publicly appear "tough" on crime by stating that places in prison will always be found for those that the courts consider it necessary to send there, whilst (less publicly) relying on a system of early release of prisoners to prevent the prisons bursting at the seams. To achieve these aims, several changes were needed to these early release procedures until finally they were altered once more by the Criminal Justice Act 1991. A brief historical introduction follows and then the new provisions under the 1991 Act will be considered.

Historical Background

First authorised in the Prison Act 1898, remission (or, rather its loss) evolved as an important sanction in connection with the maintenance of prison discipline. A prisoner would receive a remission of one-third from any custodial sentence imposed by the court as a reward for his "industry and good conduct" (*e.g.* see Prison Rules 1964 (as amended), (S.I. 1964 No. 388), Rule 5(1), (2) and (4)). In August 1987, the period of remission was increased to one-half for those serving prison sentences of twelve months or less. There can be little doubt that despite the original rationale of remission being to help maintain order in prisons, it became a crucial means of managing overcrowding.

In 1965, the White Paper *The Adult Offender* proposed that a prisoner who had responded well ought to be able to earn a further period of freedom on parole. This proposed reform was justified on rehabilitative grounds in the White Paper:

> "A considerable number of long-term prisoners reach a recognisable peak in their training at which they may respond to generous treatment, but after which, if kept in prison, they may go downhill ... These arrangements would afford the strongest incentive to reform and greatly assist the task of prison administration."

The scheme was not in fact limited to long term prisoners, as it applied to all determinate sentence prisoners who had served at least twelve months in prison after sentence. The idea of a parole scheme commanded wide support, but there was some debate as to which body should decide upon this early release on licence. The Government favoured a wholly administrative system with much power vested in the Home Secretary. In response to criticism, a compromise was reached with the establishment of the Parole Board and local review committees. The Home Secretary was still able to exercise a veto even where he received a positive recommendation from the Parole Board, but he could not grant parole without a positive recommendation from the Board.

Criminal Justice Act 1967, s. 59(1), (3), (6); s. 60(1) (as amended by section 33 of the Criminal Justice Act 1982) (4); s. 61(1); s. 62(1), (2), (3); Sched. 2, para. 1(a)–(d).

59. – (1) For the purpose of exercising the functions conferred on it by this Part of this Act as respects England and Wales there shall be a body to be known as the Parole Board and for the purpose of exercising those functions as respects Scotland there shall be a body to be known as the Parole Board for Scotland, each body consisting of a chairman and not less than four other members appointed by the Secretary of State...

(3) It shall be the duty of the Board to advise the Secretary of State with respect to –

  (a) the release on licence under section 60(1) or 61, and the recall under section 62, of this Act of persons whose cases have been referred to the Board by the Secretary of State;
  (b) the conditions of such licences and the variation or cancellation of such conditions; and
  (c) any other matter so referred which is connected with the release on licence or recall of persons to whom the said section 60 or 61 applies....

(6) The Secretary of State may by rules make provision –

  (a) for the establishment and constitution of local review committees having the duty of reviewing at such times or in such circumstances as may be prescribed by or determined under the rules the cases of persons who are or will become eligible for release under section 60 or 61 of this Act and reporting to the Secretary of State on their suitability for release on licence; and

(b) for the interview of such persons by a member of any such committee (not being a prison officer);

and rules under this subsection may make different provision for different cases.

60. – (1) The Secretary of State may, if recommended to do so by the Parole Board, release on licence a person serving a sentence of imprisonment, other than imprisonment for life, after he has served not less than one-third of his sentence or twelve months thereof, whichever expires the later ....

(4) A person subject to a licence under this section shall comply with such conditions, if any, as may for the time being be specified in the licence.

61. – (1) The Secretary of State may, if recommended to do so by the Parole Board, release on licence a person serving a sentence of imprisonment for life or a person detained under section 53 of the Children and Young Persons Act 1933 (young offenders convicted of grave crimes), but shall not do so in the case of a person sentenced to imprisonment for life or to detention during Her Majesty's pleasure for life except after consultation with the Lord Chief Justice of England together with the trial judge if available.

62. – (1) Where the Parole Board recommends the recall of any person who is subject to a licence under section 60 or 61 of this Act, the Secretary of State may revoke that person's licence and recall him to prison.

(2) The Secretary of State may revoke the licence of any such person and recall him as aforesaid without consulting the Board, where it appears to him that it is expedient in the public interest to recall that person before such consultation is practicable.

(3) A person recalled to prison under the foregoing provisions of this section may make representations in writing with respect to his recall and shall on his return to prison be informed of the reasons for his recall and of his right to make such representations ....

SCHEDULE 2

PROVISIONS AS TO PAROLE BOARD AND LOCAL REVIEW COMMITTEES

The Parole Board

1. The Parole Board shall include among its members –

(a) a person who holds or has held judicial office;

(b) a registered medical practitioner who is a psychiatrist:

(c) a person appearing to the Secretary of State to have knowledge and experience of the supervision or after-care of discharged prisoners; and

(d) a person appearing to the Secretary of State to have made a study of the causes of delinquency or the treatment of offenders.

[Also see *Re Findlay and others* [1984] W.L.R. 1159, H.L.]

Notes

1.   Despite references in the White Paper *The Adult Offender* to the rehabilitative potential of the new parole system, the timing of its introduction was significant. Parole – early release on licence – was introduced in the Criminal Justice Act 1967, at the same time as the suspended sentence, for the main purpose of dealing with the serious problem of a rapidly increasing prison population. So parole was seen as having both pragmatic and penological functions: to reduce the prison population, and to release prisoners at an optimum point in their sentence from a corrective point of view. It undoubtedly was effective in reducing the numbers who would otherwise have been in prison, but whether it was a success in penological terms is much more open to question. A Home Office Research Study (No. 38, 1977) by Nuttall *et al.* carried out in the early 1970s provided:

> "no evidence that parole serves to reduce the rate of reconviction within two years of release. However, an analysis at six months from release ... could imply that parole does have an effect in reducing reconviction during the currency of the licence." (But, *c.f.* the case of *Darby* [1987] Crim. L.R. 280).

2.   The amendment of section 60(1) of the Criminal Justice Act 1967, by section 33 of the Criminal Justice Act 1982, allowed the minimum qualifying period for parole in relation to fixed sentence prisoners to be revised from time to time. In July 1984 it was reduced from twelve to six months and, as a result, the number of prisoners eligible for parole increased sharply. This reform of 1984 was generally welcomed as it tackled a problem which had been commented on frequently that, prior to this change, short term prisoners were at a disadvantage to longer term prisoners in relation to parole eligibility. But, despite the lack of critical comment at the time of this reform in 1984, it was later to lead to much concern about the operation of the parole system and its effect on the sentences given by the courts. In particular, there was disquiet amongst the judiciary about a parole rate of 75–80 per cent for prisoners serving less than two years. Far from being a privilege to be earned, parole was becoming almost an entitlement of prisoners.

3.   We have seen earlier that the decision-making procedure for parole was established to achieve a compromise between the different views as to where responsibility should lie. A useful explanation of the working of the "tripartite" system (*i.e.* the local review committees, the parole board, and

the Home Secretary) can be found in the report of the Carlisle Committee, *The Parole System in England and Wales*, Cm. 532 (1988) (paras. 113–143).
4. The Carlisle Committee (1988), set up to review the working of the parole system, was convinced of the need for major changes to our early release procedures. The findings of this Committee were largely reflected in the 1990 White Paper, and in turn, in the Criminal Justice Act 1991.

It is clear that the Carlisle Committee received evidence of a highly critical nature from members of the judiciary. The report states (at para. 160):

> "The judicial criticisms at their most blunt were that instead of being a narrowly selective system for certain medium and longer term prisoners, as originally envisaged, parole had become a convenient executive tool for wholesale interference with sentences in order to ease the pressures on the prisons. Moreover the operation of the minimum qualifying period was destroying proportionality between the sentence passed and the time served, since many prisoners receiving different sentences were being released on the same date. Parole processes were not, and could not readily be, as satisfactory as the procedure in open court at the time of sentence."

Having reviewed the strengths of the parole system (at paras. 182–5) and having made the point that over a twenty year period parole enabled over 120,000 prisoners to be released from custody at an earlier stage than would otherwise have been possible, the Committee then went on to consider the weaknesses of the system (at paras. 186–94). These included the criticism that it is wrong in principle, and unworkable in practice, to attempt to operate a selective parole system for prisoners sentenced to short periods of imprisonment. Secondly, the Committee shared the concern of many judges that the parole system was undermining the notion of proportionality in sentences (see above). The Committee also expressed its concern about the delay which seemed to occur under the parole system and it also accepted the criticisms which were made about the excessive secrecy of the system. It stated that the "lack of any reasons for negative decisions is particularly hard to justify" (paragraph 193). Finally, the Committee remarked (at paragraph 194),

> "We endorse the views which have been put to us that the introduction in 1987 of 50 per cent remission for those serving 12 months or less has, like the introduction in 1984 of section 33 parole, created an unacceptable disparity between what sentences say and what they mean. This has highlighted the fact that parole and remission, taken together, have created over the years an increasing unreality in the criminal justice system, and handed to the executive too much control over the length of custodial sentences served."

As stated earlier, the proposals put forward by the Carlisle Committee were taken up by the Government in its White Paper (1990) *Crime, Justice and Protecting the Public.*

White Paper, *Crime, Justice and Protecting the Public*, Cm. 965 (1990), paragraphs 6.10–6.11, 6.18, 6.22–6.26.

Government Proposals

6.10 The Government therefore proposes legislation to establish new arrangements for supervised early release based upon the Carlisle Committee's recommendations. The arrangements for early release would aim to encourage and help prisoners to live a more law abiding life when they leave prison. Preparations for release should begin in prison and this will need the active co-operation of the prisoner. Dangerous and unco-operative prisoners serving determinate sentences may have to be held in custody for most of their sentence to protect the public. The aims are therefore:

- protection of the public;
- prevention of re-offending; and
- successful re-integration of prisoners into the community.

6.11 The new system will restore more meaning to the sentence given by the courts. Remission will be abolished. All prisoners will still be released before the full term of the sentence as expressed in court, but

(i)   all prisoners will be at risk of being returned to prison up to the end of their sentence if convicted of a further imprisonable offence: at present the sentence expires when the offender is released on remission.

(ii) all prisoners will spend at least half the sentence in prison: the present minimum period is a third for those serving sentences of more than a year.

(iii) additional days spent in prison could be ordered for misconduct, effectively replacing the present sanction of loss of remission.

(iv) prisoners serving sentences of under 4 years will spend 50 per cent of their sentence in custody. It is very difficult to give proper considerations to individual parole decisions for those serving comparatively short sentences and it is better therefore that discretionary early release should end.

(v)   there will be a selective system of parole for prisoners serving sentences of 4 years or more. The Carlisle Committee recommended that the selective arrangements should apply to sentences of over 4 years. Many offenders given sentences of exactly 4 years have, however, been convicted of serious sexual and violent crimes. The Government believes that careful and individual consideration is needed before such prisoners can be released early from custody, and therefore proposes that all sentences of 4 years or more should fall within the selective scheme.

(vi) all prisoners sentenced to imprisonment of a year or more will be supervised on release until three-quarters of their sentence: supervision cannot be a guarantee against re-offending, but it offers a bridge between prison and total freedom in the community which can help protect the public as well as support the offender ....

... 6.18 In future, the Parole Board will take most parole decisions, while continuing to advise the Home Secretary on a small number of the most serious cases. In the last few years, about 24,000 parole cases have been reviewed each year. The Local Review Committees considered all of them, and about 16,500 were decided on the basis of their advice. The Parole Board considered the remaining 7,500. In future, the Board will not be involved in decisions to release prisoners sentenced to under 4 years and its workload is likely to be about 4,500 cases a year. Given the substantial reduction in the number of parole cases, the Government agrees with the Carlisle Committee's recommendation that Local Review Committees will not be needed.

... 6.22 Clear and published criteria for parole should become the linchpin of an integrated parole system, linking the decision to release, arrangements for taking that decision, the conditions of the licence and the arrangements for supervision in the community. The Government considers the decision on whether to release on parole should be based on the answers to three questions:

(i)   Is the prisoner likely to commit further serious offences, while under supervision?

(ii) Would his early release sometime after half his sentence rather than after two thirds significantly increase the risk of serious harm to the public?

(iii) Is he willing to co-operate with his supervisor and is it likely that extended supervision in the community would reduce the risk of his re-offending in future?

In answering these questions, the Parole Board would need to take into account the prisoner's offence and criminal history, his record in prison, his behaviour and response to training, his earlier responses to probation supervision, his home circumstances and employment prospects, medical reports, and any other available indicator of the likelihood of his re-offending and the consequent risk to the safety of the public. They would need to be satisfied with the proposed release plan.

6.23 The Government believes that these criteria are sufficiently stringent to replace the present restricted policy on parole for those sentenced to more than five years for an offence involving drug trafficking, sex, arson or violence, which was introduced in 1983. The proposed criteria, which focus on the risk of serious harm to the public, make it likely that many offenders convicted of violent crime will not be released on parole. However, there will be some offenders whom the Parole Board will judge may be released with little or no risk. In assessing the risk of serious harm to the public, the Government believes that a small risk of violence should carry more weight in the parole decision than a larger risk of further property crime. This could be made clear in a general policy direction, given by the Home Secretary to the Board.

The parole decision-making process

6.24 The arrangements for making the parole decision should, so far as possible, be equitable and fair and be seen to be so; they should be simple and easy to understand for all parties; delays should be avoided. The system should be cost effective and not place unreasonable burdens on the prison and probation services in making it work.

6.25 The Government agrees with the Carlisle Committee's view that the parole decision-making process should be made more open. This will be easier if there are published criteria for the parole decision, since the reports prepared for the Board and the Board's own decisions should focus on the criteria. The Government also agrees that there is no need for formal hearings by the Parole Board, with legal representation, nor for the decision to be made subject to due legal process, with the inevitable complexities and prospects of delay.

6.26 The Government will give further consideration to the detailed arrangements for making the parole decisions in future, with the aim of moving towards disclosing reports made to the Board and the Board giving reasons for its decisions. The Government believes that greater openness could improve the quality of decision-making. It would encourage a careful weighing of the evidence and arguments linked to the parole criteria. A detailed record of earlier decisions is likely to help future decisions and to encourage the development of clear policies and a consistent approach to parole decisions. This is particularly important because decisions are taken by panels of members of the Board. However, there is a risk that openness could lead to less full and telling reports and so to less well informed decisions. Disclosing reports is likely to fuel demands for even more disclosure and the information could be used to contest adverse decisions through judicial review and any other available means. On balance, the Government believes that the likely benefits of greater openness outweigh its disadvantages.

Notes

1. The White Paper recommended a system of early release for all prisoners, whilst doing away with the distinction between parole and remission. For those sentenced to less than four years in prison, release would be automatic after serving 50 per cent of the sentence. For prisoners sentenced to 4 years or more, the parole decision would be selective – careful and individual consideration is needed before such offenders can be released early. For these longer term prisoners, parole only becomes automatic after two-thirds of their sentence. It was also proposed that in all cases (apart from those serving less than twelve months), offenders would be supervised, on release, until three-quarters of their sentence.

2. This attempt to remedy the "unacceptable disparity between what sentences say and what they mean" was, generally, greeted with enthusiasm. However, these proposals would clearly lead to an increase in the prison population if they were not accompanied by a change in the pattern of custodial sentencing by the courts.

3. The proposals of the Carlisle Committee and the White Paper (1990) formed the basis of Part II of the Criminal Justice Act 1991. The Act also made alterations to the arrangements for release of prisoners serving discretionary life sentences. The key provisions are given below.

The Criminal Justice Act 1991, Part II, Early Release of Prisoners, sections 33–5, 37–9.

New arrangements for early release

33. – (1) As soon as a short-term prisoner has served one-half of his sentence, it shall be the duty of the Secretary of State –

>   (a) to release him unconditionally if that sentence is for a term of less than twelve months; and
>   (b) to release him on licence if that sentence is for a term of twelve months or more.

(2) As soon as a long-term prisoner has served two-thirds of his sentence, it shall be the duty of the Secretary of State to release him on licence.

(3) As soon as a short-term or long-term prisoner who –

>   (a) has been released on licence under subsection (1)(b) or (2) above or section 35 or 36(1) below; and

(b) has been recalled to prison under section 38(2) or 39(1) below,

would (but for his release) have served three-quarters of his sentence, it shall be the duty of the Secretary of State to release him unconditionally.

(4) Where a prisoner whose sentence is for a term of less than twelve months has been released on licence under section 36(1) below and recalled to prison under section 38(2) below, subsection (3) above shall have effect as if for the reference to three-quarters of his sentence there were substituted a reference to one-half of that sentence.

(5) In this Part –

"long-term prisoner" means a person serving a sentence of imprisonment for a term of four years or more;

"short-term prisoner" means a person serving a sentence of imprisonment for a term of less than four years.

34. – (1) A life prisoner is a discretionary life prisoner for the purposes of this Part if –

(a) his sentence was imposed for a violent or sexual offence the sentence for which is not fixed by law; and

(b) the court by which he was sentenced for that offence ordered that this section should apply to him as soon as he had served a part of his sentence specified in the order.

(2) A part of a sentence so specified shall be such part as the court considers appropriate taking into account –

(a) the seriousness of the offence, or the combination of the offence and other offences associated with it; and

(b) the provisions of this section as compared with those of section 33(2) above and section 35(1) below.

(3) As soon as, in the case of a discretionary life prisoner –

(a) he has served the part of his sentence specified in the order ("the relevant part"); and

(b) the Board has directed his release under this section,

it shall be the duty of the Secretary of State to release him on licence.

(4) The Board shall not give a direction under subsection (3) above with respect to a discretionary life prisoner unless –

(a) the Secretary of State has referred the prisoner's case to the Board; and

(b) the Board is satisfied that it is no longer necessary for the protection of the public that the prisoner should be confined.

(5) A discretionary life prisoner may require the Secretary of State to refer his case to the Board at any time –

(a) after he has served the relevant part of his sentence; and

(b) where there has been a previous reference of his case to the Board, after the end of the period of two years beginning with the disposal of that reference; and

(c) where he is also serving a sentence of imprisonment for a term, after he has served one-half of that sentence;

and in this subsection "previous reference" means a reference under subsection (4) above or section 39(4) below made after the prisoner had served the relevant part of his sentence.

(6) In determining for the purpose of subsection (3) or (5) above whether a discretionary life prisoner has served the relevant part of his sentence, no account shall be taken of any time during which he was unlawfully at large within the meaning of section 49 of the Prison Act 1952 ("the 1952 Act").

(7) In this Part "life prisoner" means a person serving one or more sentences of life imprisonment; but –

(a) a person serving two or more such sentences shall not be treated as a discretionary life prisoner for the purposes of this Part unless the requirements of subsection (1) above are satisfied as respects each of those sentences; and

(b) subsections (3) and (5) above shall not apply in relation to such a person until after he has served the relevant part of each of those sentences.

35. – (1) After a long-term prisoner has served one-half of his sentence, the Secretary of State may, if recommended to do so by the Board, release him on licence.

(2) If recommended to do so by the Board, the Secretary of State may, after consultation with the Lord Chief Justice together with the trial judge if available, release on licence a life prisoner who is not a discretionary life prisoner.

(3) The Board shall not make a recommendation under subsection (2) above unless the Secretary of State has referred the particular case, or the class of case to which that case belongs, to the Board for its advice....

37. – (1) Subject to subsection (2) below, where a short-term or long term prisoner is released on licence, the licence shall, subject to any suspension under section 38(2) below or, as the case may be, any revocation under section 39(1) or (2) below, remain in force until the date on which he would (but for his release) have served three-quarters of his sentence.

(2) Where a prisoner whose sentence is for a term of less than twelve months is released on licence under section 36(1) above, subsection (1) above shall have effect as if for the reference to three-quarters of his sentence there were substituted a reference to one-half of that sentence.

(3) Where a life prisoner is released on licence, the licence shall, unless previously revoked under section 39(1) or (2) below, remain in force until his death.

(4) A person subject to a licence shall comply with such conditions (which shall include on his release conditions as to his supervision by a probation officer) as may for the time being be specified in the licence; and the Secretary of State may make rules for regulating the supervision of any description of such persons.

(5) The Secretary of State shall not include on release, or subsequently insert, a condition in the licence of a long-term or life prisoner, or vary or cancel any such condition, except –

(a) in the case of the inclusion of a condition in the licence of a discretionary life prisoner, in accordance with recommendations of the Board; and

(b) in any other case, after consultation with the Board.

(6) For the purposes of subsection (5) above, the Secretary of State shall be treated as having consulted the Board about a proposal to include, insert, vary or cancel a condition in any case if he has consulted the Board about the implementation of proposals of that description generally or in that class of case.

(7) The power to make rules under this section shall be exercisable by statutory instrument which shall be subject to annulment in pursuance of a resolution of either House of Parliament.

Misbehaviour after release

38. – (1) A short-term prisoner –

(a) who is released on licence under this Part; and
(b) who fails to comply with such conditions as may for the time being be specified in the licence,

shall be liable on summary conviction to a fine not exceeding level 3 on the standard scale.

(2) The magistrates' court by which a person is convicted of an offence under subsection (1) above may, whether or not it passes any other sentence on him –

(a) suspend the licence for a period not exceeding six months; and
(b) order him to be recalled to prison for the period during which the licence is so suspended.

(3) On the suspension of the licence of any person under this section, he shall be liable to be detained in pursuance of his sentence and, if at large, shall be deemed to be unlawfully at large.

39. – (1) If recommended to do so by the Board in the case of a long-term or life prisoner who has been released on licence under this Part, the Secretary of State may revoke his licence and recall him to prison.

(2) The Secretary of State may revoke the licence of any such person and recall him to prison without a recommendation by the Board, where it appears to him that it is expedient in the public interest to recall that person before such a recommendation is practicable....

Notes

1.   Section 149 of the Criminal Justice and Public Order Act 1994 amends section 32 of the Criminal Justice Act 1991 (which provides the constitution and basic functions of the Parole Board). The new section 32(1) now provides that "the Parole Board shall be, by that name, a body corporate and shall be constituted in accordance with, and have the functions conferred by, this Part".

2.   The complex arrangements for early release under the 1991 Act are discussed lucidly in the following article:

Martin Wasik, "Arrangements for Early Release" [1992] Crim. L.R. 252–254, 256–258.

Outline of the New Scheme

The Act abolishes the long-established distinction between remission and parole, and puts in its place the single concept of early release. The abolition of remission requires that disciplinary offences in prison, formerly sanctioned by loss of remission, are now to be dealt with by the award of additional days in custody.

Adult determinate sentence prisoners will fall into one of three categories. For an offender serving a sentence of less than 12 months, release will be automatic after half the sentence has been served. There will be no supervision on licence. Then a distinction needs to be drawn between "short term" prisoners (those serving terms of twelve months or more but less than four years) and "long term" prisoners (those serving four years or more). For the short term prisoners, release will be automatic after serving half the sentence, but there will be supervision under licence by a probation officer for these offenders, which will last until the three-quarter point of the sentence. Failure by a short term prisoner to comply with the conditions of a licence is made a summary offence punishable by a fine, but it may also be dealt with by termination of the licence and recall to prison. Previously, failure to comply was not an offence, and was dealt with by the Parole Board rather than the courts. For the long term prisoner, there may be discretionary release at a point somewhere between one half and two thirds of the sentence, to be determined in accordance with a recommendation made in each case by the Parole Board. Supervision on licence will last from that point of release until the three quarter point of the sentence. In the event of breach of licence conditions by a long term prisoner, the Secretary of State may revoke the licence and recall the prisoner to custody, where it appears expedient to do so. This may be done with or without the recommendation of the Parole Board. A breach of licence by a long term prisoner may not be dealt with by way of a fine.

For both short term and long term prisoners, in the case of commission of a further offence punishable with imprisonment during the period from the date of release until the expiry of the full term of the sentence, the sentencing court "may, whether or not it passes any other sentence on him, order him to be returned to prison." This arrangement differs from that under the Criminal Justice Act 1967, in that the prisoner will remain at risk of being required to serve out the full term of the sentence if he commits the new offence either during the period under supervision or in the period from the end of supervision until the expiry of the full term of the sentence. It should also be noted that the offender may be returned to prison to serve the unexpired portion of the sentence even if he is convicted after that period has expired, so long as the offence was committed during it. The order to serve the unexpired part of the sentence is regarded as a sentence of imprisonment and may be ordered to run concurrently or consecutively to any custodial sentence imposed for the new offence . . . .

The Decision-Makers

The Parole Board will continue in place but it will have a much reduced workload (a reduction from 24,000 to 4,500 parole applications per year was the estimate given in the White Paper), since there will remain a discretion to be exercised over release on licence only in respect of prisoners serving sentences of four years or more. The White Paper envisaged that the membership of the Board could thereby be reduced and that the Board could sit in panels of three with a quorum of two, rather than in panels of four, which is the norm at present. Criteria for appointment of persons to the Board are unchanged.

The relationship between the Parole Board and the Secretary of State will be somewhat affected by the Act, but the exact position is not yet clear. The Board will continue to make recommendations on early release to the Home Secretary. The Home Secretary will not be able to release an offender without a recommendation from the Board but, as at present, will not be bound to follow the Board's positive advice. The Carlisle Committee recommended that the Home Secretary should no longer be responsible for individual parole decisions and that the Board should have full responsibility for them, but this was not fully accepted by the government. The Home Secretary's "veto," the exercise of which has increased in recent years is, therefore retained. Section 50 of the Act, however, enables the Home Secretary to make an order giving the Parole Board a decision-making power in certain classes of cases. This may be done, after consultation with the Board, by statutory instrument. The Home Secretary has indicated that it is his intention initially to delegate to the Board the final decision in cases where the prisoner is serving a sentence of less than seven years, but to retain the final decision for those serving seven years or more. There is also an exception with respect to discretionary life sentences imposed for a violent or sexual offence, where the Board is given the final say by the Act, section 34 directing the Home Secretary to release such prisoners upon recommendation by the Board. More generally, section 36 confers on the Home Secretary a broad power to release any prisoner on compassionate grounds. There is no requirement in the Act for securing the Board's agreement in such a case, though consultation with the Board is required if the prisoner is serving a long-term or life sentence.

Local review committees, which currently form the lowest tier of the parole machinery, are in fact responsible for most of the decision-making within the system. Two thirds of parole decisions, made mainly in respect of short-term sentences, are made by them alone. The changes outlined above mean that there will no longer be work for them to do, and they are abolished by the Act, once the transitional arrangements for dealing with prisoners sentenced before the new system comes into force have been completed....

... A thoroughgoing application of the desert model might well involve the abolition of early release arrangements altogether, since the sentence to be served should be proportionate to the seriousness of the offence committed. A modified version, which accepted the benefits of releasing offenders under supervision, would require a specified proportion of custodial sentences to be given over to supervision rather than incarceration. Some features of the modified version may be seen in the changes brought about by the 1991 Act. Subject to their good behaviour in custody, many more prisoners than before will know at the time of sentence what their actual date of release will be. There will be much greater correlation for short-term prisoners between the sentence imposed and time actually served. On the other hand, and running contrary to desert constraints, considerable discretion over the release date for long-term prisoners will remain in the hands of the executive. The exercise of that discretion may well serve to increase the effective sentence length of offenders convicted of violent or sexual offences, in respect of whom the sentencer is also permitted by the Act to depart from the normal proportionality requirements. The sanctions for breach of licence and for the reinstatement of the unexpired part of a sentence upon commission of a further offence are more severe than would be appropriate under a desert model, and are clearly designed to achieve a deterrent effect.

Early Release Mechanisms and Procedural Fairness

An important criticism of the parole system has been its procedural shortcomings and secrecy. To what extent are matters improved under the 1991 Act scheme? It is not possible to give a comprehensive answer yet since, as with so many of the Act's provisions, we await detailed rules to emanate from the Secretary of State, in this context under section 32(5) of the Act, to fill in the bare framework of the statutory scheme. The indications so far, however, are that not a great deal will change and there is a risk that the interests of offenders may be less well protected than before. The lack of any requirements that prisoners be given reasons for parole refusal has been a target for much criticism in the past. The practice of not giving reasons has been upheld by the courts, and there is nothing in the Act, on the face of it, to change that position. There have been undertakings by the government in the course of debates on the Act, however, to introduce administrative arrangements for the giving of reasons for early release decisions, both positive and negative. Lack of access to parole decision makers has also been criticised, and section 32(3) of the Act merely provides for a member of the Parole Board to interview the prisoner "if in any particular case the Board thinks it necessary," but prisoners will have no right to an interview. This may be contrasted with the position prior to the Act when all prisoners were interviewed by a member of a local review committee. Again, however, indications have been given by the Home Office that interviews with prisoners will be routinely conducted, and it may be that this is one role which parole assessors might play. There will continue to be no right of representation before the Parole Board, and no right of appeal against an adverse decision. If, however, as a result of the rules to be issued by the Secretary of State, statutory criteria for the granting of parole are introduced and the giving of reasons by the Board is made a requirement, judicial review of the Board's decisions would become a more practical possibility.

A more judicial procedure in respect of discretionary life sentence prisoners is introduced by the Act (see further below), consequent upon the strictures of the European Court of Human Rights.

Life Sentences

The procedure for determining the time to be served by life sentence prisoners turned out to be one of the most controversial issues which arose during the course of the Bill's passage through Parliament. In the event, the procedure with respect to discretionary life sentences was overhauled, as a result of amendments moved by the House of Lords at a late stage. These were based upon criticisms of existing procedures made by the European Court of Human Rights in *Thynne, Wilson and Gunnell.* On an application made by three discretionary life sentence prisoners, the Court had heard described a procedure whereby the period of time which it was thought appropriate for the offender to serve, to satisfy the demands of general deterrence and retribution ("the tariff"), was communicated privately to the Home Secretary by the trial judge and the Lord Chief Justice. The Home Secretary, in determining when the public interest would permit the offender's release, would then fix the duration of any additional period to be served by the offender. The Court held, in criticising this arrangement, that discretionary life sentence prisoners had a right to have their sentences reviewed as soon as the "tariff" period had expired. It was also said that the Parole Board was a body insufficiently judicial in nature to perform this function.

Section 34, which applies to discretionary life sentence prisoners, states that in a case other than murder, where a life sentence has been imposed for "a violent or sexual offence" and the sentence makes such an order, after a term specified by the sentencer has expired has expired the life sentence prisoner's case must be referred to the Parole Board. In these special circumstances the panel must be chaired by a judicial member of the Board and include a psychiatrist member. The prisoner will be entitled to appear before the panel and to legal representation for which legal aid will be available. The Board shall not direct release until satisfied that it is no longer necessary for the protection of the public that the prisoner should be confined. In such a case the Board's decision is final and the Home Secretary has no opportunity to exercise the veto. If the Board is not so satisfied, the prisoner has the right to have his case referred to them again subsequently every two years. The term to be specified by the sentencer should be fixed in accordance with the seriousness of the offence, but also having regard to the period in prison which a person serving such a term as a determinate sentence might actually serve.

The system for those given mandatory life sentences, on the other hand, continues as before. After extensive debate in Parliament, and in spite of the recommendation in the Report of the House of Lords Select Committee on Murder and Life Imprisonment, the fixed penalty for murder was retained, together with the procedures relating to determining the date of release of those offenders. The Parole Board can recommend release only if the Home Secretary has referred the case to the Board for its advice. If the Board advises release the Home Secretary may release the life sentence prisoner on licence, after consultation with the Lord Chief Justice and the trial judge if available. The system, much criticised, is preserved by section 35(2). It seems that a discretionary lifer in respect of whom the sentencer declined to make a recommendation under section 34, or a discretionary life sentence which fell outside the definition of section 34, would also have his release date fixed under the old rules.

When a life sentence prisoner is released on licence, the licence remains in force for the rest of the offender's life.

Notes

1. For further explanations of the new statutory early release provisions, see Chapter 5 in M. Wasik and R. Taylor, *Criminal Justice Act 1991* (2nd ed., 1994); and R. Leng and C. Manchester, *A Guide to the Criminal Justice Act 1991* (1991, Chapter 5).

2. The original rationale of the parole scheme suggested that it was, in part at least, a rehabilitative measure, offering prisoners the chance of early release at the stage of their incarceration when the sentence was supposed to have had a beneficial effect (see the White Paper *The Adult Offender* Cmnd. 2852, (1965) para. 5, discussed earlier). Whether parole was ever capable of fulfilling this rather idealistic goal is a matter for debate, but it seems that this philosophy was soon overtaken by more pragmatic aims, such as coping with the ever increasing prison population and the failure to change the sentencing patterns of the courts to any significant degree. (For a useful discussion of the policies which influenced the development of parole during the early years of the scheme, see N. Morgan, "The Shaping of Parole in England and Wales" [1983] Crim. L.R. 137). What is the rationale of parole today? Is the system of early release simply a method of reducing prison numbers whilst still appearing to be "tough" on criminals by using lengthy custodial sentences? Martin Wasik is correct in his observation (*op cit.* p. 254) that the new Act does not provide "a coherent philosophy underpinning the system of early release"; and, to some extent, its provisions do not appear consistent with the principle of desert which predominates in other sections of the Act.

3. Are the 1991 Act provisions likely to lead to improvements in procedural fairness in relation to early release decisions? A particular concern since the introduction of parole in this country has been that the decision-making bodies were under no obligation to explain a refusal of parole. This issue was tested in *Payne v. Lord Harris of Greenwich* [1981] 1 W.L.R. 754, where the Court of Appeal, while stating that these decisions must be arrived at fairly, refused to find an obligation to provide reasons. Lord Denning simply stated that "in the interests of society at large – including the due administration of the parole system – it would be best not to give [reasons]". In *R v. Parole Board, ex parte Bradley* [1991] 1 W.L.R. 134, which dealt with an application for judicial review of the Parole Board's decision to refuse release on licence and its refusal to give reasons, the *Payne* decision was applied. (However, the *Payne* decision was distinguished more recently in *R v. Parole Board, ex parte Wilson* [1992] 1 Q.B. 740).

There is nothing explicit in the 1991 Act to suggest that the old secrecy is now a thing of the past, but it will be remembered that the White Paper (1990, para. 6.26) stated:

"The Government will give further consideration to the detailed arrangements for making the parole decisions in the future, with the aim of moving towards disclosing reports made to the Board and the Board giving reasons for its decisions. The Government believes that greater openness could improve the quality of decision-making."

It seems that this progress is to be achieved by administrative measures rather than by legislative provisions. A prisoner refused parole will continue to lack the right of appeal.

4.   It appears that prisoners do not have a right to a personal interview with a Parole Board member under the Act's provisions. Section 32(3)(b) states merely that "if in any particular case the Board thinks it necessary to interview [the prisoner] ... before reaching a decision, the Board may authorise one of its members to interview him." In addition, section 32(5) enables the Home Secretary to make rules affecting the proceedings of the Parole Board "including provision authorising cases to be dealt with by a prescribed number of its members...." One can appreciate why it suited the Government to make administrative arrangements regarding these matters, rather than bestow positive rights upon prisoners, but do these new procedures truly suggest a new spirit of openness?

5.   The Act does not alter the system in relation to prisoners serving mandatory life sentences. Section 35(2) states that "if recommended to do so by the Board, the Secretary of State may, after consultation with the Lord Chief Justice together with the trial judge if available, release on licence a life prisoner who is not a discretionary life prisoner." However, some minor improvements to the system were made as a result of the decision in *R v. Secretary of State for the Home Department, ex parte Doody* [1993] 3 W.L.R. 154, which involved an application for judicial review of the Home Secretary's decision in relation to a mandatory life prisoner. The House of Lords granted a declaration in the following form (*per* Lord Mustill, at p. 175):

"1. The Secretary of State is required to afford to a prisoner serving a mandatory life sentence the opportunity to submit in writing representations as to the period he should serve for the purposes of retribution and deterrence before the Secretary of State sets the date of the first review of the prisoner's sentence.

2. Before giving the prisoner the opportunity to make such representations, the Secretary of State is required to inform him of the period recommended by the judiciary as the period he should serve for the purposes of retribution and deterrence, and of any other opinion expressed by the judiciary which is relevant to the Secretary of State's decision as to the appropriate period to be served for these purposes.

3. The Secretary of State is obliged to give reasons for departing from the period recommended by the judiciary as the period which he should serve for the purposes of retribution and deterrence."

It was also announced to Parliament by the Home Secretary, in April 1993, that prisoners serving mandatory life sentences are to be given access to reports prepared for the Parole Board and will be given reasons for decisions reached by the Board and by ministers about their release dates (see *Howard Journal*, (1993), p. 157). There will be some exceptions, however, to full disclosure to safeguard the interests of third parties, or the welfare of prisoners, or where disclosure would not be in the public interest.

These minor reforms in relation to mandatory life prisoners have satisfied very few people and there is still considerable pressure for further change. Until the distinction between mandatory and discretionary life sentences is ended it is difficult to see how major progress can be made. This point was addressed in an interesting recent article by Lord Windlesham, "Life Sentences: Law, Practice, and Release Decisions, 1989–93" [1993] Crim. L.R. 644, in which the author concludes (at pp. 658–659):

> "The Lords has twice agreed to legislation making life imprisonment the maximum rather than the mandatory penalty for murder ... once the final objective is achieved, everything will fall into place. Life sentences for murder would become less frequent than they are now, being reserved for cases where there was a clear risk of repeat offending, or where the crime was so serious that no other sentence would suffice. Public opinion would recognise imprisonment for life as the most severe penalty permitted by law in a civilised state, appropriate for the gravest crimes committed by the most dangerous people. The separation of mandatory and discretionary categories of offender, and the nomenclature, would disappear. All life sentences would be passed at the discretion of the court ..."

In support of this view, reference can also be made to a NACRO briefing paper of 1991, in which it was revealed that the United Kingdom has more "lifers" than all the other Western European countries combined. The major reason for this startling fact appears to be the existence of the mandatory life sentence for murder; a fixed term is not available as an alternative for the vast majority of life sentence prisoners.

Pressure for reform is also being maintained by cases against the Government being taken to the European Court of Human Rights. Edward Wynne, serving life for murder, argued (in February 1994) that the system for deciding the effective length of murderers' sentences is in breach of the European Convention on Human Rights. Such actions help to support the case for an independent review body to determine mandatory life prisoners' release dates.

However, a further recent development should be noted. On December 7, 1994, the Home Secretary (Michael Howard) referred to lifers "for whom the requirements of retribution and deterrence can be satisfied only by their remaining in prison for the whole of their life", subject to the periodic review of such cases. Mr Howard appeared to admit, by means of this statement, that there is a group of prisoners who are never going to be released from prison. Although this public admission is preferable to the secret marking of a prisoner's file with the label "natural life", it has led to renewed criticism of the Home Secretary's role in the sentencing system.

6.   In relation to discretionary life prisoners, the pre-Act procedures had already been subjected to criticism by the European Court of Human Rights in *Thynne, Wilson and Gunnell v. United Kingdom* (1991) 13 E.H.R.R. 135. In this case, three U.K. applicants complained of a lack of judicial procedure to review the lawfulness of their continued detention under discretionary life sentences of imprisonment, invoking Article 5(4) of the European Convention. (This states: "Everyone who is deprived of his liberty by arrest or detention shall be entitled to take proceedings by which the lawfulness of his detention shall be decided speedily by a court and his release ordered if the detention is not lawful"). It was stated (at pp. 140–141):

> "While it is true that all life sentences often involve both punitive and security elements, the discretionary life sentence belongs to a separate category because the sentencing court recognises that the mental stability or dangerousness of the accused may be susceptible to change over the passage of time ... The Commission further observes that the domestic courts have openly stated that a discretionary life sentence is composed of a punitive element ... and a security element based on the need to protect the public ... In addition, had it not been for the presence of mental instability and dangerousness, the applicants would have received a determinate sentence under the law of the United Kingdom leading to an earlier release date ... Against the above background the Commission considers that once the notional 'tariff' period has been served by the applicants the justification for continued detention depends on whether they remain a danger to the public ... It follows that the applicants are entitled under Art. 5(4) to have the lawfulness of their detention reviewed at the moment of any return to custody following release or at reasonable intervals during the course of their imprisonment. As the Commission has emphasised ... Art. 5(4) does not apply in this way to ordinary sentences of life imprisonment or other determinate sentences. The Commission has therefore considered whether this entitlement should only arise in these cases following the expiry of the 'tariff' or punitive element in their sentences. It does not, however, find it possible to limit the application of Art. 5(4) in this way because of the uncertainty surrounding the length of the 'tariff' period ... Accordingly the guarantee in Art. 5(4) must be considered to apply throughout the whole of the applicant's imprisonment...."
> [The Commission concluded that Art. 5(4) had been violated in relation to each of the applicants].

This decision necessitated a re-evaluation of the parole procedures for discretionary life prisoners culminating in section 34 of the Criminal Justice Act 1991 (see above). This section applies to a life prisoner if –

(a) his sentence was imposed for a violent or sexual offence the sentence for which is not fixed by law; and

(b) the court by which he was sentenced for that offence ordered that this section should apply to him as soon as he had served a part of his sentence specified in the order.

Under this section, the prisoner has the right to have his case referred to the Parole Board after having "served the relevant part of his sentence" (section 34(5)). Under the Parole Board Rules (1992), provision was made for special Discretionary Lifer Panels to hear such cases, and the prisoner will have a right to appear before the panel and have access to reports which are to be considered by the panel. The prisoner is also entitled to prompt notification, in writing, of the panel's decision and this includes notification of reasons for the decision.

The sentencer may decide not to specify a part of the sentence in accordance with the provisions described above, in which case the prisoner is not covered by the section 34 procedure. However, failure to specify such a period must now be regarded as an exceptional course of action for a judge. In a *Practice Direction (Crime: Life Sentences)* [1993] 1 W.L.R. 223, Lord Taylor C.J. stated in the Court of Appeal:

"1. Section 34 of the Criminal Justice Act 1991 empowers a judge when passing a sentence of life imprisonment – where such a sentence is not fixed by law – to specify by order such part of the sentence ("the relevant part") as shall be served before the prisoner may require the secretary of State to refer his case to the Parole Board.

2. Thus the discretionary life sentence falls into two parts: (a) the relevant part which consists of the period of detention imposed for punishment and deterrence, taking into account the seriousness of the offence and (b) the remaining part of the sentence during which the prisoner's detention will be governed by considerations of risk to the public.

3. The judge is not obliged by statute to make use of the provisions of section 34 when passing a discretionary life sentence. However, the judge should do so, save in the very exceptional case where the judge considers that the offence is so serious that detention for life is justified by the seriousness of the offence alone, irrespective of the risk to the public. In such a case, the judge should state this in open court when passing sentence.

4. In cases where the judge is to specify the relevant part of the sentence under section 34, the judge should permit counsel for the defendant to address the court as to the appropriate length of the relevant part. Where no relevant part is to be specified counsel for the defendant should be permitted to address the court as to the appropriateness of this course of action.

5. In specifying the relevant part of the sentence, the judge should

have regard to the specific terms of section 34 and should indicate the reasons for reaching his decision as to the length of the relevant part.

6. Whether or not the court orders that section 34 should apply, the judge shall not, following the imposition of a discretionary life sentence, make a written report to the Secretary of State through the Lord Chief Justice as has been the practice in recent years."

The Parole Board is not to recommend the release of a discretionary life prisoner unless it is "satisfied that it is no longer necessary for the protection of the public that the prisoner should be confined" (section 34(4)(b)). Under section 34(3)(b), it is clear that the decision concerning release is for the Parole Board to make, and if it directs a prisoner's release under this section, it is "the duty of the Secretary of State to release him on licence."

7. For the first case involving an appeal against the length of the period specified under section 34 of the CJA 1991, see *R v. H* [1994] Crim. L.R. 140. (Also see *Willsher* [1994] Crim. L.R. 769).

For a useful discussion of the development of parole for life sentence prisoners, see Nicola Padfield, "Parole and the Life Sentence Prisoner", (1993) 32 *Howard Journal* 187.

V. The Organisation of the Prison System

A useful, though now slightly dated, description of prison organisation can be found in M. Fitzgerald and J. Sim, *British Prisons* (1982).

Mike Fitzgerald and Joe Sim, *British Prisons* (2nd ed., 1982) pp. 29–32.

The prison system includes not only individual prison establishments, prisoners and staff. There is also an important centralised administration which organises the service and which has a direct impact and influence on the day to day life of the institutions. It is on this central department (the Home Office in England and Wales, and the Scottish Office in Scotland) that we depend for information about the prisons...

Constitutionally, Parliament is responsible for the prisons. In England and Wales the Home Secretary, and his or her junior minister, have a direct responsibility for the work of the Prison Department which is presently housed in the Home Office....

The Home Office in general, and the Prison Department in particular, is notorious for denying access to information. This has serious consequences not only for outsiders interested in the prisons, but also for prisoners, who find it almost impossible to have their complaints and requests listened to, and acted upon....

In 1980, in response to the criticisms levelled by the May Report the Home Secretary announced changes to the system of inspection of the prisons. The Chief Inspector of Prisons is to remain a Home Office civil servant, but the inspectorate will no longer be located within the Home Office. The inspectorate is to publish an annual report, reporting directly to the Secretary of State on prison conditions, the treatment of prisoners, and "such matters as the Secretary of State may direct". The system of inspection falls well short of the independent inspectorate recommended by May, and will do little to raise the shroud of secrecy which veils the prison system.

For purposes of administration, England and Wales are divided into four regions,

Northern, Midlands, South-Eastern and South-Western. Each region is headed by a regional director, and three more deputies. The region is responsible for the application of national penal policy, for the proper functioning of individual establishments, and a number of specialist tasks, including the allocation of prisoners to particular prisons.

Each prison establishment is formally controlled by a governor, who usually has a deputy and a number of assistant governors. It is the governor who is responsible for the day-to-day running of the establishment and for the maintenance of:

> "Security, good order and discipline, for the effective co-ordination of the work of all members of its staff, for the regime of the establishment, and the treatment and training of persons in its custody, and for the proper use of public money, materials and premises."

... Responsibility for Scottish prisons rests with the Secretary of State for Scotland, and his or her junior minister. The system is centrally organised and administered by the Scottish Home and Health Department within the Scottish Office based in Edinburgh ... As in England and Wales, responsibility for the day-to-day running of individual establishments rests with a governor, usually assisted by a deputy and a number of assistant governors....

Relationships in the prison system are rigidly hierarchical. Policies and decisions made at the centre are handed down to those in individual establishments for implementation. Not surprisingly, central directives often meet with hostility and resentment from prison staff, who have been increasingly critical of the central prison departments. And as we have already indicated, a major source of conflict in the prison system is the struggle within the prison service, particularly between staff in headquarters, regions and individual establishments....

Notes

1. The bureaucratic and secretive nature of the prison system has been a subject of critical comment since its nationalisation in 1877; see generally Stan Cohen and Laurie Taylor, *Prison Secrets* (1978), who commented (at p. 2):

> "the enlightened welfare state, with its notions of public accountability, the growth of documentary exposé journalism, the influence of the few social scientists who have looked at prisons, have created a climate in which the desire to know what is going on, if only in the name of justice and civil liberties, has become much stronger."

The authors then went on to discuss the "apparatus of secrecy" which, in their view, permeated every area of a prisoner's life at that time. One reaction to this aspect of the prison system has been the development of a movement to enunciate and protect the legal rights of prisoners. The subject of prisoners' rights has developed considerably in recent years into a discrete area of study dealt with in its own quite specialised literature. For this reason, it is not appropriate to discuss the subject here in any depth in a work which deals more generally with many other aspects of imprisonment. For those who wish to pursue this subject further, the following works can be consulted: S. Livingstone and T. Owen, *Prison Law – Text and Materials* (1993); the Prison Reform Trust's *Working Guide to Prison Rules* (1993); G. Richardson, *Law, Process and Custody: Prisoners and Patients* (1993);

and G. Treverton-Jones, *Imprisonment: The Legal Status and Rights of Prisoners* (1989).

2. The system of inspection of prisons, initiated in the middle of the nineteenth century (see Harding *et al.* (1985), p. 145 *et seq.*) is an important means by which the internal operation of the prison system may be scrutinised by the responsible government department (the Home Office). But, especially since the prison administration became the responsibility of a department of the Home Office, doubts have been raised as to the independence of an inspectorate which reports to the Home Secretary. The May Committee, in its Report on the Prison Services in 1979, recommended a more independent system of inspection.

Report of the Committee for Inquiry into the United Kingdom Prison Services, Cmnd. 7673 (1979), Chapter 5 *et seq.*

... We accept that in both theory and practice no inspection can be independent of Parliament, and thus generally in practice cannot be independent of government: we also accept that both in theory and practice no inspection carried out by a member of the Home Office can be independent of that government department nor thus of a prison service which also forms part of it. Nevertheless we have no doubt that the prison service would benefit from and that public sentiment requires that as many aspects of government, which includes the prison service, should be opened up to as wide an audience as possible. We therefore think that there should be a system of inspection of the prison service which although not "independent" of it in either of the senses canvassed in the Home Office paper, should nevertheless be distanced from it as far as may be practicable.

5.62 In so far as the in depth inspections hitherto carried out by the Chief Inspector and his Department of particular establishments are concerned, we think that in future these should be carried out by the regional directors. This should be a part of their operational management duties and their reports should be to the Director of Operations. They should make these inspections, either of a whole establishment, or a particular part of it, as frequently as they think necessary and they should be given the resources to do so. We do, however, recommend that there should be constituted within the Home Office an independent department to be called the "Prisons Inspectorate", headed either by someone independent of the civil service entirely or by a senior ex-governor as the Home Secretary may decide, with the post of HM Chief Inspector of Prisons, holding the same rank between that of Deputy and Assistant Under Secretary of State as will be held by the Deputy Chairman and Director of Operations. This department should not be a big one, but it should contain people with relevant prison service experience as well as such others as the Home Secretary thinks appropriate. HM Chief Inspector of Prisons and his staff should be available to make *ad hoc* inspections of any incident which may occur at the request of the Home Secretary: they should be empowered to set out unannounced and make an inspection of a particular establishment or a particular part of an establishment as and when they think it necessary or desirable to do so: they should also make inspections of more general aspects of the work of the prison service – for instance, of accounting procedures, or into questions of quarters, or into particular aspects of security or control. We recommend that except where security considerations dictate otherwise the reports of HM Chief Inspector of Prisons should be published and laid before Parliament and that each year his Department should also make a general report on the whole prison service, in so far as they have seen it during the year, which should be included in that year's Report of the work of the Prison Department. We do not anticipate that the Prisons Inspectorate should deal with particular grievances, either of prison staff or of inmates, unless one or more of these suggest that an inspection of one or other of the types that we have described should be made...

Following this recommendation, a new prison inspectorate came into being at the beginning of 1981, and was placed on a statutory basis by section 57 of the Criminal Justice Act 1982. The inspectorate's functions, detailed in a "charter" (see the Annual Report of the Chief Inspector of Prisons Cmnd. 8532 (1981)), include the inspection of and reporting on conditions, treatment of prisoners and facilities in prison establishments, and the regular inspection of individual establishments. The inspectorate is part of the Home Office but separate from the Prison Department. The reports, in the view of Rod Morgan (Chapter 7 in M. Maguire, J. Vagg and R. Morgan eds., 1985), have been

> "no public relations exercise; if the measured language is decoded, the reader is drawn to the conclusion that the Prison Department does not make the best of a bad job and that conditions for prisoners are not simply the result, as successive Home Secretaries would have us believe, of too many prisoners and too few resources" (p. 122).

3.   After the worst series of prison riots in the history of the British penal system, in April 1990, the Home Secretary set up a departmental Inquiry (or Judicial Inquiry) to investigate these events. This Inquiry was conducted by Lord Justice Woolf and its findings will be considered in detail later. Lord Woolf acknowledged that this Inquiry led him into a consideration of matters of prison management and organisation, which were also the concern of HM Chief Inspector of Prisons. He stated (at paras. 2.13–2.15):

> "When I was first appointed, I hoped that my task could be confined primarily to fact finding. But it quickly became clear to me that this was impossible if I was to produce a report which would explain why the disturbances took place and which would make useful recommendations. There were underlying issues relating to the management and operation of prisons which needed to be examined if there was to be any prospect of reducing the risk of such riots in the future.
> I was aware that HM Chief Inspector of Prisons, His Honour Judge Stephen Tumim, had given considerable thought to these issues. His authoritative and independent reports are highly respected. At the time of my appointment, he was already undertaking an examination of the very serious problem of suicide in prisons which would involve an examination of some of the issues with which I would be concerned. (This report was published on 19 December 1990). The Chief Inspector had at his disposal a fund of experience and expertise on a wide range of prison matters. It made clear and obvious sense that I should have the benefit of his help in considering the wider aspects of this Inquiry.
> ... The Home Secretary wrote ... agreeing with my proposal that

Judge Tumim should be joined to the Inquiry once I had completed the first part of the Inquiry in relation to the facts of the individual disturbances and before I moved to the second part involving consideration of the wider issues."

Although Judge Tumim's five year term as Chief Inspector of Prisons was due to end in 1992, it was decided by the Home Secretary that Tumim will continue in this role until October 1995 as he had successfully demonstrated how an independent inspectorate should serve the public interest. It is certainly true that many reports of the HM Prison Inspectorate are critical in nature (*e.g.* "A Short Inspection at Strangeways (Manchester)", 1992). A series of recent reports (reviewed in the *Howard Journal* (1993) Vol. 32, pp. 162–4) also give cause for disquiet: especially those relating to Wymott Prison (drug problems, gangland culture, poor morale and low staffing); Acklington Prison (poor communication by middle management, worsening inmate attitudes and behaviour, serious violence between prisoners, dirty and vandalised living units); Lewes Prison (poor regime, squalid conditions, bad visiting facilities and prisoners confined to cramped cells for long periods); Long Lartin (lack of staff confidence, drug problems amongst prisoners, as well as "no-go areas" in living units and other intimidation by inmates); Bullwood Hall Prison and Young Offenders Institution (racism amongst inmates, management failure, too much time in cells and routines designed for staff convenience rather than good management).

In HM Chief Inspector of Prisons' Annual Report (*Report of Her Majesty's Chief Inspector of Prisons April 1991–March 1992*, H.C. 203), Judge Tumim stated that during the period covered by the report, the Inspectorate had carried out 18 full inspections and 19 short inspections, with an additional seven unannounced or "short notice" visits being made. Predictably, the standards within the various institutions were found to be very uneven, but particular concern was expressed about Lewes Prison (see above) and the regime for young offenders at Feltham. More recently, numerous other reports have been published as a result of prison inspections. These reports are available from the Home Office Library and they are reviewed in the *Howard Journal* (1994) Vol. 33, pp. 86–8. This recent batch of inspections is of particular interest as it includes an inspection of "The Wolds", which is a purpose-built remand prison and the first custodial institution to be contracted out of the prison service. In September 1993, the government announced plans to privatise ten per cent of prisons in England and Wales, with perhaps eight private prisons by the end of 1994. (These developments are discussed later in this chapter).

4.   Further accounts of the structure and organisation of the prison system can be found in the extracts which follow.

Genevra Richardson, *Law, Process and Custody: Prisoners and Patients* **(1993), pp. 9–11.**

The formal management structure of the Prison Service, excluding for the moment the question of privatisation, can be used to illustrate the application of the traditional concept of ministerial responsibility. The Prison Act 1952 makes the Home Secretary responsible for the maintenance and organisation of prisons and requires him (we have yet to have a female Home Secretary) to report annually to Parliament. It also gives him the power to appoint prison personnel and to issue rules for the management of prison establishments. Thus, in the words of the Woolf Inquiry, "the Home Secretary, assisted by one of his junior ministers, is directly responsible and accountable to Parliament for all aspects of the Prison Service work".

In practice the Home Secretary acts through the Director General of the Prison Service, who chairs the Prisons Board. The Board is not a statutory body but was created within the Prison Department of the Home Office to monitor the performance of the Prison Service and to act as a consultative forum. Over the last 20 years the structure of senior management within the Prison Service has been regularly reviewed and reorganised ... Here it is necessary merely to note that at present the Board has nine members, three of whom possess operational as well as policy responsibilities. Between these three directors and the individual establishments there are 15 area managers, each of whom is responsible for approximately nine establishments. Each individual establishment has a governor appointed by the Home Secretary who, by section 7 of the 1952 Act, is made responsible for good order and discipline within the prison. Other duties, including the hearing of disciplinary charges and the hearing of complaints brought by prisoners, are outlined in the Prison Rules. Section 4(2) of the Act, however, makes the Home Secretary responsible for insuring "that the provisions of this Act and of any rules made under this Act are duly complied with". Thus, although a governor can be held directly responsible to the courts for the way in which he or she exercises certain of his or her powers, governors are generally regarded as the servants or agents of the Home Secretary, and act under his direction. In 1984 a new management framework for the accountability of individual establishments was introduced, requiring an annual "contract" to be drawn up between each governor and his or her area manager. These contracts are intended to define the function and goals of each prison establishment. Thus, whatever the merits of the present system, it is evident that a formal line of responsibility extends out from the Home Secretary, through the Director General and the Board, via the area managers, to the governors of individual establishments.

While the above account suggests that the Prison Service can be viewed as an arm of the Home Office, many tasks within the criminal justice system are entrusted to agencies which do not formally constitute part of a central government department. Indeed it is now clear that the Prison Service itself is to be devolved from the Home Office to be transformed into a "Next Steps" executive agency. Such developments aside, however, many fringe organisations already exist, performing statutory functions within the criminal justice system. In recognition of this phenomenon, the doctrine of ministerial responsibility extends beyond the strict limits of the central government department itself to cover agencies which, while not formally part of the department, are none the less within its patronage and sphere of influence. The responsible minister is typically given some direct means of control over such fringe bodies, the power to issue regulation, for example, or to make appointments, to call for inquiries or to withhold finance, and in return is responsible to Parliament for the performance of the agency. The Home Secretary, for example, is responsible to Parliament for the activities of the Parole Board as is the Secretary of State for Health responsible for the Mental Health Act Commission.

Thus, in formal constitutional terms, Parliament creates and empowers the various public agencies operating within the criminal justice system and achieves oversight of their operations primarily through the device of ministerial responsibility. Indeed, despite the scepticism of numerous observers in whose eyes the concept has long since ceased to command respect, ministerial responsibility is still regarded as crucial to the constitutional propriety of the agencies. When the creation of a prison ombudsman was considered by the May Inquiry the Home Office argued strongly that such a figure would interfere with the Home Secretary's direct responsibility to Parliament. More recently, the Woolf Inquiry has been at pains to emphasise that its favoured "structured stand-off" between the Home Secretary and the Director General of the Prison Service would in no way diminish the Home Secretary's responsibility to Parliament. Whatever its efficacy, however, ministerial responsibility is clearly insufficient on its own to render the various actors within criminal justice accountable to the public through Parliament. Accordingly, Parliament has created a variety of specialised agencies entrusted with the task of overseeing specific aspects of the system.

Within the custodial sphere these watchdog agencies include, for prisons, Her Majesty's Chief Inspector of Prisons, boards of visitors, the Parliamentary Commissioner or Ombudsman, and the new independent complaints adjudicator; and for hospitals, the Mental Health Act Commission and the Health Services Ombudsman. With the exception of the independent prison complaints adjudicator, each is set up by statute with specific powers and responsibilities ... Each, with the exception of boards of visitors and the complaints adjudicator, has a duty to report to Parliament, directly in the case of the Parliamentary Commissioner, and via the relevant minister in the other cases.

Note

For a detailed work on the subject of prison governors, see P. Waddington, *The Training of Prison Governors – Role Ambiguity and Socialisation* (1983). On prison management and discipline, see M. Maguire *et al.*, *Accountability and Prisons* (1985), especially parts 1 and 4.

Categories of Adult Penal Establishments

Although the statistics quoted are now a little out-of-date, the following brief description of the different categories of penal institutions for adult offenders is useful.

G. Treverton-Jones, *Imprisonment: The Legal Status and Rights of Prisoners* (1989), pp. 14–16.

Within the penal system there is a wide range of institutions, of which the most important are set out below. It should be noted that more than one category of prison can be contained within the same establishment. The most striking example is that of Wormwood Scrubs Prison, which houses a local prison, a long term training prison, facilities for category "A" prisoners (*i.e.* those of a maximum security establishment), and a remand centre.

(i) Local and training prisons

Every adult prison other than remand centres falls into one of these two basic categories. Upon conviction, the prisoner is received into a local prison, usually sited in a large or medium-sized town, and often constructed in the nineteenth century, which serves the local network of courts. At local prisons the categorisation and medical examination and treatment of prisoners is effected.

The great majority of sentences should be served in training prisons, which may be open or closed establishments. In 1987 there were 27 adult male local prisons, and 48 male training prisons, of which 38 were closed, and 10 open. The general policy of the Prison Department is to try to ensure that prisoners are sent to training prisons within their home area. The prisons themselves are usually more modern than local prisons, with better facilities.

(ii) Dispersal prisons: category "A" prisoners

Approximately one per cent of all prisoners belong to category "A", *i.e.* those whose escape would be highly dangerous to the police, the public, or the security of the state. Those prisoners are dispersed among the population of seven prisons and are held in conditions of maximum security.

(iii) Open prisons

An open prison is designed with no physical barriers to prevent inmates from escaping. Obviously, therefore, open prisons are suitable only for those who present a minimal security risk, and are unlikely to abuse the freedom which they obtain, or the trust which is placed in them. Moreover, due to concern amongst members of a community in which an open prison is to be sited, the Prison Department is often requested at planning application hearings to undertake to restrict the type of prisoner (*e.g.* to exclude violent and sexual offenders) to be held in such an institution.

(iv) Women's prisons

There is a surprisingly large discrepancy between the numbers of men and women in prison. The daily average prison population in 1986 was 46,770 of whom only 1,607 were women. Whereas there are over 60 closed penal establishments for males, there are only five such institutions for females.

(v) Industrial prison

Coldingley prison in Surrey, opened in 1969, is Britain's only industrial prison, in which the regime and conditions are intended so far as possible to be comparable to those in industry outside.

(vi) Psychiatric prison

Grendon Underwood prison, near Aylesbury, was opened in 1962 as Britain's first psychiatric prison, and exists to treat those prisoners with psychiatric or personality disorders who are nonetheless serving conventional prison sentences. Its regime and conditions differ markedly from any other institution in the country.

(vii) Special hospitals

Technically these are not part of the penal system, and are therefore beyond the scope of this book. There are a number of secure special hospitals for those persons who have been made the subject of various orders under the mental health legislation, or have been transferred to such hospitals by the Secretary of State.

Notes

1.   For the most recent statistics relating to prison service establishments, see the *Report on the Work of the Prison Service April 1991–March 1992*

(Cm. 2087). The total prison population in March 1992 was 47,746, which includes 1,882 prisoners in police cells. This total represents an increase of 2,640 prisoners since the previous annual report. For a comment on the more recent increase, see the Prison Reform Trust, *Prison Overcrowding: A Crisis Waiting in the Wings* (1993). Also of interest is the *National Prison Survey 1991: Main Findings*, by R. Walmsley, L. Howard and S. White (HORS No. 128), which revealed a prison population considerably more youthful than the general population, with a disproportionate representation of members of ethnic minorities. The Survey found that just over a half of prisoners had their own cell, with 29 per cent sharing with one other prisoner. There is still a small, but disturbing number of prisoners who share a cell with more than one other inmate.

[Note: By early 1995, the prison population had risen alarmingly to 51,243].

2.   The following extract provides a useful but more impressionistic account of prison organisation. (Once again, the statistics are now slightly out-moded – see above reports).

Vivian Stern, *Bricks of Shame* (2nd ed., (updated) 1993), pp. 18–22.

On June 30, 1987 there were 10,669 men and women in prison untried or unsentenced. There were nearly 300 civil prisoners, that is, people who have not made their maintenance payments, are in contempt of court, or are held under the Immigration Act. The other four fifths of the prison population there on that date were serving a sentence imposed by a court.

A substantial minority of young and older alike was serving what are considered in England and Wales to be short sentences. 40 per cent had been sentenced to eighteen months or less. A range of activities – burglary, theft, criminal damage, arson, driving under the influence of drink – accounted for over 20,000. Just over 12,000 were there for offences involving violence, 2,300 for sexual offences and 3,500 for drug-related offences.

The June 30, 1987 snapshot gives one picture of the prison population. A look at the flows in and out in the course of a year – receptions and discharges in prison language – gives quite another. Just over 86,000 people actually came into custody under sentence during 1987. Over 52,000 of these were serving sentences of eighteen months or less and about 16,000 three months or less. Nearly 19,000 people went to prison in 1987 for not paying a fine for periods that can range from two to 345 days.

At the other end of the scale there are the long-sentence prisoners. On June 30, 1988 about 4,100 people were serving more than ten years. Some of these are life-sentence prisoners – a steadily growing proportion of the population. Over 2,300 on any one day are serving life sentences, that is about 5 per cent of the prison population in England and Wales. In Northern Ireland the picture is very different – there over a quarter of the sentenced prison population is serving a life sentence.

So the prison system does much more than carry out the sentence of a court to deprive someone of liberty. It holds the untried, the unsentenced, the civil prisoners. It acts as a social service, a hospital, a place where reports are written, an educational establishment for people under school-leaving age, a nursery for mothers and their young babies, and a drug-rehabilitation facility (in 1987–8 2,600 prisoners were dependent on drugs when they were received into custody). It contains prisoners whom many other prisoners would like to injure because of the nature of their offences, and prisoners who want to injure or kill themselves. Between April 1987 and March 1988 a thousand prisoners injured themselves intentionally and 310 attempted suicide. Another thirty-seven succeeded.

The way the prison service organises itself reflects to some extent the many different jobs it has to do. It has to cope with sentenced prisoners, convicted of a range of crimes from the most trivial to the unspeakably heinous. It holds unsentenced prisoners who have to be brought to court, and ideally be kept separate from sentenced prisoners. It has men and women who have to be held separately. It has young offenders, who should not be housed with adult offenders.

In dealing with sentenced prisoners the main sifting process is categorisation. Sentenced prisoners are categorised according to how much of a security risk they are into security categories A, B, C and D. A is the highest and prisoners in Category A are those for whom escape would be highly dangerous to the public or the police or the security of the State. At the other end of the scale Category D is used for prisoners who are unlikely to escape, and if they do the public will not be endangered. Normally Category D prisoners are held in open prisons, that is, prisons where there is little physical security to keep the prisoners in. All prisoners in open prisons are Category D. If they abscond (the Prison Department word for escaping from an open prison) they are recategorised up again to Category C or even B.

Women are kept separately from men so this means a separate part of the organisation. Although the population of women is increasing much faster than the population of men – an increase of 25 per cent between 1977 and 1987 compared with 16 per cent for men – the numbers involved are very much smaller. Thus women in prison tend to be the neglected area of penal policy, barely mentioned in official reports. A Home Office research report notes "virtually all the published accounts of research on adult prisons and prisoners in England and Wales since 1970 relate to males". The House of Commons Expenditure Committee under its chairman of the time, Janet Fookes, MP, started an inquiry into women in the penal system but it was interrupted by the 1979 General Election and dropped.

In the women's prison system eight establishments are provided for sentenced women as well as a top-security separate wing in Durham men's prison and three remand centres which take women. Babies also have their place in prison. Three of the women's prisons. Holloway, Styal and Askham Grange, have mother and baby units which can cater for thirty-nine mothers with their babies at any one time. Babies can stay in Holloway and Styal until they are nine months old and in Askham Grange up to eighteen months old. After reaching those arbitrary ages they have to be separated from their mothers and placed elsewhere, usually in care or with relatives.

Women prisoners are in many respects the poor relations – not only in the relative neglect of their problems. They also pay the price of their small numbers and the consequent small number of prisons they can go to by being placed frequently hundreds of miles from their homes. For instance women in Holloway or Durham can come from almost anywhere in England and Wales or from Northern Ireland.

Organising prisoners awaiting trial or sentence is focused around getting the right prisoner to the right court on the right day, so location is very important. Such prisoners are kept in remand centres such as Pucklechurch or Risley (nick-named Grisly Risley) or in local prisons like Birmingham, Leeds or Wormwood Scrubs. There is little time for anything else, so those prisoners not going to court spend sometimes as many as twenty-three hours of the day locked in their cells.

These organisational factors produce one of the major scandals of the prison system: the holding, often for long periods, of nearly 11,000 remand and unsentenced prisoners – people not convicted of any offence or not sentenced to prison – in the worst conditions the prison system has to offer. The privileges granted to remand prisoners – that they are allowed to wear their own clothes, have more frequent though shorter visits and letters, a greater variety of articles sent in by relatives and friends, and are not obliged to work – in no way compensate for the overcrowding they are subjected to.

The position of remand prisoners has aroused particular parliamentary concern. In 1981 the House of Commons Home Affairs Committee declared that:

> Cell sharing, long periods locked up, and, for the majority, all the considerable disadvantages of the old Victorian prisons ... would be intolerable enough when inflicted on persons found guilty of an offence, but for the many persons still awaiting trial, and innocent before the law, these experiences are completely insupportable.

Seven years later, nothing has improved for remand prisoners. The Chief Inspector inspected Risley Remand Centre in 1988 and was obviously shocked by what he found. He concluded:

> Male inmates remanded to Risley enter an institution which is profoundly depressing. Apart from the times when they are being processed either to or from court or to see relatives or legal advisors, they are for most of the time forgotten people.

Remand prisoners not in remand centres are no better off. They are cheek by jowl in the overcrowded local prisons with a variety of prisoners: those serving short sentences, civil prisoners, young people awaiting allocation. Local prisons, or locals as they are known, are the gateway to the system, the warehouse for those serving short sentences whom there is no time to place elsewhere, the "sin bins" for disruptive prisoners from long-term prisons, as well as the overflow when other parts of the system are full. Out of the locals, some prisoners are transferred to training prisons – the usually less crowded, more recently built part of the system, often in a rural area – where there are more facilities. Prisoners who are deemed to need high security, and are invariably serving long sentences, usually go to the top-security prisons, described as dispersal prisons, where the level of security is the most oppressive but the physical conditions are some of the best the prison system has to offer.

Young men under twenty-one are destined for a different part of the system yet again, the young offender system. Run by a different group of officials in the Home Office and with its own rules and regulations, the young offender system contains young offender institutions, the former youth custody centres and detention centres with every appearance of prison except the name.

So, spending time in prison can mean many different experiences – being locked up with two other young men in a smelly cell for most of the day, waiting seven weeks to go to court for trial and then being released and given a community service order, bringing up a newborn baby in the mother and baby unit of Holloway, coping with mental illness in a prison hospital, working in the greenhouses of an open prison and sharing a dormitory with the most middle-class elements of the prison population, learning how to survive the bullying and intimidation in a dormitory in a young offender institution, or settling down for a long spell in an electronically controlled, not over-crowded, top-security prison on the Isle of Wight.

Notes

1. Although it is true to say that "women in prison tend to be the neglected area of penal policy", there has been more attention devoted to this subject in the recent literature. For example, see S. Casale, *Women Inside* (*the experience of women remand prisoners in Holloway*) (1989); and P. Carlen, *Alternatives to Women's Imprisonment* (1990).

2.   The problem of suicide and self-injury in prisons is also referred to in Vivien Stern's extract. It is a matter for serious concern that the suicide rate in prisons in England and Wales is four times that of the general population. This problem clearly has implications for prison management, staff training, physical conditions and medical and psychiatric care of prisoners. For a recent in-depth study of this subject, see Alison Liebling, *Suicides in Prison* (1992). The author summarises some of her findings as follows (at pp. 240–241):

> "Briefly, four limitations in current policy and its implementation were reported by the staff: poor communication and co-operation between departments within establishments, particularly between the hospital and the discipline staff on the wings; staff suspicions about the purposes and usefulness of instructions which were clearly intended to 'protect the Department at inquests', the application of a blanket set of procedures to widely differing types of establishment; and the lack of resources such as training and staff.
>
> The problem of communication and co-operation was clear: three-quarters of the uniformed staff reported serious difficulties between the wings and the hospital. Prison staff were thought by hospital staff to be making inappropriate referrals to the hospital, occasionally inundating them with 'non-medical' problems. Staff on wings reported inadequate feedback once referrals had been made. Disagreements inevitably arose as the whether or not the inmate was a 'suicide' or medical problem. Temporary respite in the hospital, followed by a swift return to the wing was seen as an inadequate response to wing staff's fears about the inmate's safety. Prison officers felt that the hospital did not share information or opinions with the wing on the inmate's return. . . .
>
> . . . At the time of the research few of the staff had received either local or national training in suicide prevention. Those that had felt that it had not answered their own queries about suicide attempts, nor had it allayed their fears that some of the responsibility for suicide prevention inevitably rested with the officers, and yet they had no influence over decisions about the inmate's risk categorisation or location."

On this subject, also see *Report of a Review by HM Chief Inspector of Prisons on Suicide and Self-Harm in Prison Service Establishments in England and Wales*, Cm. 1383 (1990). As well as reviewing existing practice Judge Tumim's report made 123 specific recommendations which include: more psychiatric and nursing training; psychiatric training for medical officers; improvements to staffing levels and prisoner accommodation; avoiding prison remands for very young offenders.

3.   Stern refers also to the problem of long-term prisoners. Once again, reference can be made to more specialised literature on this subject: see *Problems of Long-Term Imprisonment* (A. Bottoms and R. Light eds., 1987); S. Cohen and L. Taylor, *Psychological Survival* (1972); Report of the

Control Review Committee, *Managing the Long-Term Prison System* (1984); Report by the Research and Advisory Group on the Long-Term Prison System, *Special Units for Long-Term Prisoners: Regimes, Management and Research* (1987); R. Walmsley (ed), "Managing Difficult Prisoners: The Parkhurst Special Unit" (Home Office Research Study 122 (1991)).

4.   The security categories referred to by Vivien Stern were introduced as a result of the *Mountbatten Report on Prison Escapes and Security*, Cmnd. 3175, (1966); see Harding *et al.* (1985, pp. 224–6). Although the Mountbatten Report recommended the setting up of a single maximum security prison on the Isle of Wight, it was thought that such a concentration of prisoners of that kind would be unmanageable and a number of "dispersal" prisons were used instead. (For an account of conditions in Peterhead Prison and Barlinnie Special Unit in Scotland, see Jimmy Boyle: *A Sense of Freedom* (1977)).

The following extract discusses the reasons underlying the review of security arrangements during the 1960s and the arguments concerning the policy of dispersal of high-risk prisoners.

J. E. Thomas, "Policy and Administration in Penal Establishments", in *Progress in Penal Reform*, (Louis Blom-Cooper ed., 1974), pp. 61–64.

The author refers to a sense of crisis within the prison service which led to the setting up of the Mountbatten Inquiry....

... Three events in the 1960s provided the catalyst. The first was the abolition of capital punishment. Most murderers conform and collude with their imprisonment because of their hope of release. But after abolition, some murderers were imprisoned for offences of such gravity that it is highly unlikely that they will be released for a very long time, if at all. Unless present policies change, their numbers in prison will continue to rise. The second factor was the commission of crimes of such novelty, and on such a scale that the perpetrators were awarded very long sentences. Included among these were the "great train robbers", and certain spies. The third event was the escape of some of these prisoners from institutions where attention to matters of security had become lax. These escapes drew the attention of the community to the fact that the escape rate was very high, and that, confronted by prisoners who saw no advantage in collaborating with the staff, no prison was secure. And so, in 1965, the Mountbatten Inquiry took place....

... Mountbatten recommended that a special security prison should be built to house what he defined as Category "A" prisoners. These are prisoners who because of violence or "security considerations" must in no circumstances be allowed to get out. This recommendation was accepted. But two years later, the Advisory Council on the Penal System reviewed the problem of long-term prisoners, and recommended that, instead of "concentrating" high risk prisoners in one institution, they should be "dispersed" to a number of prisons which would have special security arrangements including dogs, floodlights, and closed-circuit television. This is now prison-department policy.

The dispersal of Category "A" prisoners has a certain amount to commend it. Some reformers believe it to be undesirable to concentrate such prisoners because they would be labelled as outcasts, and marked as beyond redemption. While they are part of a fairly normal prison group, they will avoid such a stigma. It is argued too that the tensions generated by the concentration of this group in an institution would be immense, not only on inmates, but on staff. Dispersal, however, has even worse effects.

The problem of the "A" prisoners should be important, but relatively minor. The dispersal policy makes it a problem that affects the entire prison system, and justifies its inclusion in this discussion of major issues. One lesson that prison staff learned from the events of the 1960s is that, above all, an "A" prisoner must not be allowed to escape. Naturally, in the dispersal prisons there is elaborate "perimeter security". It is claimed that, if this security is sound, then there can be freedom inside. In the traditional prison this cannot be so, since the design of the Victorian prison, within which most of these prisoners are located, militates against such as assertion. At the time when these prisons were built, security was based on a system of separation in individual cells. Prisoners cannot be allowed that great freedom which is envisaged.

There is an even more unpleasant effect of dispersal. It is that prisoners who are not "A" men are being subjected to unnecessary constraint, since it is impossible to compartmentalise the treatment of different groups within the same prison. This fact, which necessitates a variety of institutions with specialised functions, is the basis of any classificatory system. The effect is manifestly unjust. According to the 1971 Annual Report of the Prison Department, there are six dispersal prisons with a total population of 3,393, of whom some 10 per cent are category "A". This means that some 90 per cent of the inmates of these prisons are under unnecessarily oppressive security conditions.

The effect is actually even more widespread than that. If a specially designed prison were brought into service, then the problem of containing this group would be defined as a limited, highly specialised matter. Instead, dispersal not only affects six prisons, but also tends to generate a sense of crisis throughout the entire prison system. There is an emphasis on security which, in respect of most prisoners, is excessive. There are new roles for staff, dog handling which some regard as a particularly offensive technique, and security work. These have strengthened the emphasis on security.

The unpleasantness of the fact that there are now men who will spend most of their lives in prison cannot be avoided by suggesting that they are the same as ordinary prisoners. They are quite extraordinary; their sentences are extraordinary, their needs are extraordinary, and their treatment should be extraordinary. Failure to accept this will provoke more of those crises in prisons, which have already begun. The building of a special prison would go some way to allowing the Prison Service to develop methods of training and treatment both for "A" prisoners and for the rest – that is the bulk of the penal population . . . .

Notes

1. After the serious prison disturbances of 1990, the Woolf Inquiry was set up (see earlier) and the resulting report (in 1991) commented on the problems of security and categorisation of prisoners. The Report states (paras. 9.38–9.40):

> "There are undoubtedly within the prison system of this country a number of prisoners who, given the opportunity and whatever the conditions within the prison, would seek either to escape or to be disruptive. No improvement in the conditions of containment will alter this situation.
>
> For this group of prisoners, a reasonable and effective degree of security is needed. The prison system has to be managed in a way which will enable the required degree of security and control to be provided.

But even for these prisoners, it is important that a proper balance is struck. No more security safeguards should be applied than are strictly required. No more control should be exercised than is necessary. Excessive security and control have the opposite effect to the ones desired. Prisoners will feel unnecessarily oppressed. They will feel a genuine grievance which will attract sympathy and support from their fellow inmates...."

2.   For further details on the Mountbatten Report's reception and developments since that time, see R. Walmsley's "Special Security Units" (Home Office Research Study No. 109, 1989). The author states (at pp. 63–64):

"The initial size and subsequent growth of the Category A population deserves special mention. Mountbatten argued in December 1966 that his fortress prison should be built for 120 men and that such an institution would eliminate any immediate need for a second prison. He clearly envisaged the initial Category A population being about 100 strong. In fact it started (mid 1967) at almost 150 and passed 200 in mid 1970. At the end of 1987 it stood at about 375. This raises the question whether from the start Category A was restricted to those Mountbatten had in mind, and whether in the last twenty years the criteria have become more lax. One dispersal governor said that he was convinced that Category A extends much wider than Mountbatten intended ... But Category A section at prison service headquarters are convinced that the criteria for entry into Category A have in fact become tighter and that many of the original Category A men of 1967 would not be so classified now. They argue that there are many more men now coming into the prison system whose escape would be 'highly dangerous to the public or police or to the security of the state' .... Perhaps the main lesson to be drawn from the discrepancy between Mountbatten's expectations and what has happened since is that predictions relating to the prison population are extremely difficult to make and often incorrect."

3.   Like most institutions, the prison system manages its subjects by means of a process of classification and the organisation of the prisons – with institutions for young and adult, male and female offenders; the division into remand centres, local and training prisons, and special security units – reflects this business of classification. Since the nineteenth century the classification of prisoners has been a science in its own right (consider, for example, the complex grading of prisoners serving the former sentence of penal servitude, through the "progressive stages" system: Harding *et al.* (1985) pp. 205–7) and remains the principal determinant of the prisoner's inmate career. Such classification is carried out by the prison authorities themselves upon their reception of the prisoner and it is a matter outside the purview of the sentencer. The whole process reflects a mixture of penological and administrative concerns, but some commentators feel that

it is the latter and in particular the question of security, which tends to predominate. (For instance, see M. Fitzgerald and J. Sim, *British Prisons* (2nd ed., 1982), pp. 43–5).

4. Prison management and organisation changes over time to reflect changing attitudes to prisoners. But as regimes have become less authoritarian in some respects, this has increased the opportunity for prisoners to mix with one another and it has also increased the likelihood of violent behaviour and disturbances. In turn, this has created new problems for prison management and its task of maintaining control.

The developments in post war prison management are considered in the following extract.

J. Ditchfield, *Control in Prisons: Review of the Literature*, 1990, Home Office Research Study 118, pp. 148–52.

Other types of prison management developed in the post war era. Of particular importance was the type which Barak-Glantz called the "bureaucratic-lawful" model. Barak-Glantz used this rather ugly term to denote a style of management in which prison policy and practice was increasingly determined by central authority and increasingly laid down in terms of general rules and regulations. Under this system, the warden or governor's role changed from that of being a "singular ruler" to that of being a "prison manager", whose essential job was to ensure that these various rules and regulations were being properly enforced. Thus his own personal power was significantly reduced in favour of central direction.

The powers of discipline staff were also affected be the growth of central authority. In the traditional prison – in both England and the United States – uniformed staff had been part of the prison's chain of command and relatively free from competing sources of authority, such as (internally) professional groups and (externally) courts, civil rights groups and judicial review etc. Their function was one of straightforward custody, and because of their ability to reward or punish inmates, they were able to exercise a certain amount of informal power *vis-à-vis* the inmate community. With the development of the rehabilitative ideal, their role became more ambiguous. Their function of custody was still pre-eminent, but, in addition, they had to contend with the officially approved policy of providing elements of treatment and training as well, a requirement which some discipline staff felt to be at variance with their custodial role (and for which they felt themselves to be inadequately trained), and which also tended to bring them into conflict with professional staff as well (*i.e.* the welfare task).

One response was the development of their own countervailing power through the growth of unions and bureaucracies and an increasing willingness to use them in furthering their own aims and interests – occasionally using industrial action if necessary. A frequent target for such action was the "treatment and training" requirement itself, and inmates became well aware that, whatever the aims and ambitions of management might be, the staff had it in their power to thwart their realisation if necessary.

In England, the development of the "bureaucratic-lawful" approach to prison management exacerbated these tendencies. Centralisation of power, increased accountability of personnel to management and central authority, the increased importance of centrally determined rules, regulations and policy directives, the greater role of judicial review within the disciplinary system, etc, entailed a further shift of power away from discipline staff (and to some extent local management) in favour of central authority and headquarters administrative staff.

These same developments meant that the prison service needed to adopt a more systematic approach towards the delivery of inmate programmes and activities and the provision of facilities. Their realisation also required a better trained discipline staff and one that was prepared to be more flexible in its working methods. But to achieve this (particularly in an era of severe budgetary restraint) also required the reassertion of full control by local management so that staff organisations could no longer effectively "veto" their implementation.

The policy of Fresh Start was one of the Home Office's responses to this situation. One of the aims of introducing a new unified grading system for uniformed staff and governors (with contractual working arrangements, the introduction of flexible working methods, including group working, and the elimination of automatic overtime) was the reassertion of managerial authority at the local level and the containment of union power.

However, the implementation of this policy and the resistance of staff unions, both nationally and at the local level (including industrial action at particular prisons) initially produced a volatile situation with regard to inmate control. Inmates feared that industrial action by staff could quickly lead to a deterioration in their conditions of imprisonment – long lock up periods, curtailment of visits, reduced association etc – and that their welfare would be the first victim of any power struggle between staff and management. These apprehensions produced a very unstable situation indeed, and while the causes of the riots in English prisons in 1986 were many and various, there is no doubt that they were one of the major contributing factors.

Barak-Glantz argued that the "bureaucratic-lawful" style of management had developed as a response to the general bureaucratisation of public institutions after the war, when state legislatures had called for the establishment of formal chains of command and accountability similar to those of other government departments .... In the US, this process was aided by the extension and enforcement of constitutional rights, and in Britain, by increased judicial review and referral to the European Court of Human Rights. This meant that the treatment of prisoners could no longer be regarded as being outside the scope of normal judicial processes and constitutional safeguards but increasingly had to be compatible with them.

But other pressures also contributed to the development of the bureaucratic-lawful model. For example, prisons, particularly in the post war period, became much more "permeable" to outside influences. The widespread possession by inmates of radios, daily access to TV and newspapers, more frequent visits from friends and relatives meant that prisoners could easily keep in touch with events going on outside the prison. The inmate was therefore in the position of constantly being able to monitor and compare his treatment with the treatment of other prisoners (and other people), of being aware of his "entitlements" as a member of modern society, and of being able to rapidly detect any departure from its principles of equity and universal treatment.

Barak-Glantz's "bureaucratic-lawful" model of prison management is simply a generalised or "idealised" description of actual prison organisation. No prison exactly corresponds to this description, but many approximate to it in terms of their reliance on common rules and procedures, their accountability and their limited autonomy. If the term is understood in this generalised sense, then it is possible to argue that the "bureaucratic-lawful" model of prison management has become the dominant model of prison management – at least in England, where, unlike the US, it has not had to compete with a variety of other models.

This has important implications for prison management. The modern "bureaucratic-lawful" prison tends to be distrustful of informal inmate leaders and informal inmate power. This is because its legitimacy is based on its perceived ability to be able to deliver and enforce common standards of treatment for all groups and individuals in its charge. Thus it cannot allow situations to develop where it becomes unduly dependent on the goodwill of particular inmates (or groups of inmates) to maintain control.

Nor can the "bureaucratic-lawful" prison allow itself to become too dependent on the personalities or charisma of particular governors to help maintain control – at least to the same extent as in some traditional prisons. This is because the authority of such governors (whether exercised in an "authoritarian" or "liberal" sense) was to some extent dependent on their ability to wield a certain amount of "arbitrary" power. For example, it required them to be able to exercise considerable discretion in the interpretation and enforcement of prison rules and regulations – and thus to be free from too much central direction or oversight. Under the "bureaucratic-lawful" system, the scope for such arbitrary action is (almost by definition) limited, being increasingly circumscribed by centrally agreed norms, standards, rules of procedure etc.

This is not to maintain that governors' personalities (and therefore changes in governor) no longer affect control. They do, and to the extent that the modern governor can and does alter a prison's regime, then the same potential for disorder exists as in the traditional prison. It is rather the case that the modern bureaucratic-lawful prison does not allow the same scope for changing or modifying its regime as the traditional prison. Indeed, one of the components of the accountable regimes approach has been an attempt to define and agree the tasks of senior management in such a way that a large element of continuity is maintained between incoming and outgoing governors, and hence to minimise a possible source of disruption in prison communities. Such an innovation would not have been possible without the development (at a central level as well as a local level) of the "bureaucratic-lawful" type of approach to prison management.

Because the "bureaucratic- lawful" style of management tries to avoid situations developing in which it becomes unduly dependent on the goodwill of particular inmates (or groups of inmates), it is unusually reliant on the professional quality of its management as a whole (its "management team") for maintaining control. Moreover, it is a system in which a great deal of responsibility is delegated to governor grades and professional staff for day to day running of the prison. A great deal of this work consists of interpreting and enforcing the large (and growing) body of rules, regulations and procedures etc, that govern the conditions and treatment of prisoners in its care – and of explaining and justifying instances where these entitlements cannot be met. This, in turn, requires for its success high standards of coordination, communication and administration by management staff.

During the seventies and eighties, the development of the "bureaucratic-lawful" model of management coincided with increasing criticism of the treatment or rehabilitative philosophies of imprisonment. During this period there was an increasing reluctance to accept the idea of crime being a form of "disease" capable of "treatment" or "cure". Moreover, the success of treatment in rehabilitating offenders – *i.e.* in actually keeping them out of prison – was also being questioned. There was a feeling that it would be better to forget these ideas of cure and rehabilitation, and to concentrate instead on such "neutral" aims as normalising prison environments, ensuring equity of treatment for offenders, and providing inmates with better facilities and conditions. These ideas were common to a number of approaches to penal reform, but found particular expression in the "humane containment" approach.

The growth of the "bureaucratic-lawful" prison facilitated this development to some extent, because its emphasis on universal rules and regulations coincided to some extent with the importance they attached to observing the proper forms and procedures etc. However, the implications of these changes in penal philosophy for control are difficult to assess. While it is possible to recognise that some of the aims and assumptions of the treatment approach may have been impracticable, there has also been a growing feeling that the real value of such ideas has been their capacity to structure staff and inmate relationships with a set of common aims and purposes. Without such common aims and purposes, the maintenance of control in the future may be more difficult than would otherwise have been the case.

Notes
1. The change in philosophy, from rehabilitation and treatment to "humane containment", will be looked at more closely in the section (below) on the prison regime. But it is interesting to reflect that despite the lack of success of the rehabilitation ideal within prisons, the rejection of this philosophy has created something of a vacuum in official aims which may have made the management of prisoners even more difficult for the prison authorities.
2. For further details of the article referred to in the above extract, see I. Barak-Glantz, "Towards a Conceptual Scheme of Prison Management Styles" (1981), *The Prison Journal*, Vol. 61, No. 2, Autumn-Winter.
3. For a detailed discussion of staff structure and recruitment, and indus-trial relations within the prison service, see the Woolf Report ((1991), section 13). The "Fresh Start" initiative, referred to in the extract, was launched in 1987 in an attempt to improve staff/management relations, improve job satisfaction and to reorganise the working arrangements of prison officers. Despite the good intentions of this reform, it also led to further industrial relations problems.
4. In response to the recommendations of the Woolf Report, the Govern-ment produced a White Paper, *Custody Care and Justice*, Cm. 1647 (1991) to reveal its plans for the Prison Service.
5. It is, of course, an easier matter to identify the need for change than it is to produce tangible progress. The need for security and control within prisons will always make it difficult for prison officers to perceive their role in more constructive terms. For an interesting discussion of the reasons for the lack of change in the role of prison officer, see J. E. Thomas, *The English Prison Officer Since 1850* (1972). The author states (at p. 6):

> "The question with which this analysis is concerned is why the structure, and organisation culture, of the prison staff remains essentially the same as it was in 1877. This question can only be answered by examination of the primary task, which I have suggested is *control*. The stability of the staff structure is an indication of the persisting priority of this task, in spite of all pressures to change it. The prisoner population, for the most part, does not wish to be locked up. Therefore, in the total prison community, which includes the staff, there is not likely to be a universal consensus of agreement about behaviour which might result in an acceptance of the desirability of 'good order'. In a community which at times might see no virtue in 'good order', it is necessary to use coercion. Because of these differing attitudes to 'good order', and because of the existence of a coercive atmosphere, staff and inmates are in a relationship of hostility, potential, or actual. The degree and expression of this hostility will clearly vary from prison to

prison, and from time to time. As a generalisation it may be said that the staff can never expect maximum co-operation from the inmates in the achievement of the institutional task."

6.   Despite much talk of reform and improvement of penal conditions, problems of overcrowding still persist in prisons. Many local prisons continue to heavily exceed their official capacity, and, in February 1995, the prison population stood at 51,243. Because of this degree of over-crowding, the Government's intention to improve conditions (particularly its commitment to ending "slopping out") is being hampered. In figures published by the Howard League in February 1994, Britain still had the highest rate of imprisonment in western Europe. In the year 1993–4, assaults on prison staff rose by 20 per cent and violence between inmates also increased.

7.   The average cost of keeping a prisoner in jail in the financial year 1991/2 was £442 per week. In the maximum security dispersal prisons the cost was £807 per week, whereas it cost a more modest £316 per week to keep a person in an open prison. In local prisons and adult remand centres, the cost of imprisonment was £437 per week. For some reason, the cost of incarcerating a female prisoner was much higher – £629 per week. Staff costs represented around three-quarters of the net operating costs in penal establishments. (For further details, see *Report on the Work of the Prison Service* 1991/2, Cmnd. 2087 (1992)).

8.   On April 1, 1993, the Prison Service became an executive agency, following the report by Sir Raymond Lygo on the management of the Prison Service. One task for the new executive agency is the development of the "privatisation" policy (see below), as was made clear by the Home Secretary at the time of the introduction of the agency. (See Prison Service News Release, February 1, 1993). The Home Secretary stated that "the public sector Prison Service no longer has a monopoly, and over the next few years [he envisaged] an increased role for the private sector in managing prisons to provide a source of competition and new ideas." (The goals of the new Prison Service Agency are set out in a *Framework Document* which was published to coincide with the change of status of the Prison Service on April 1, 1993).

Prison Privatisation

As part of the political philosophy of the Conservative governments of the 1980s, the privatisation of state-run institutions became a central issue. Once some of the more lucrative and obvious targets for denationalisation had been exhausted, it was perhaps inevitable that the same philosophy would be applied to state-run services and even the criminal justice system. Since its Green Paper of 1988 (*Private Sector Involvement in the Remand System*), the government has shown enthusiasm for a policy of prison privatisation. At the time of the Prison Service's change of status to an executive agency (see above), the Home Secretary expressed the view that the element of competition provided by an increased role for the private sector will serve to raise standards throughout the prison system.

But apart from the rhetoric of "competition" and "efficiency", what has the policy of privatisation to offer the penal system? Is the policy truly concerned with making lasting improvements to the prison system? More fundamentally some critics of this policy object to the idea of the involvement of private enterprise in the penal system. The punishment of offenders is carried out on behalf of the state and any suffering inflicted on offenders gains its legitimacy by virtue of the fact that the punishment is deserved and that it is carried out by state-run institutions. Once the idea of profit-making is introduced, is there not a danger that the system of imprisonment will lose some of its legitimacy and integrity?

Some of the arguments for and against privatisation in the penal system are considered in the following extract.

M. Ryan and T. Ward, *Privatisation and the Penal System* **(1989), pp. 69–77.**

Opponents of privatisation use a lot of ... rhetoric, but they never seem able to say with any precision *why* the private administration of prisons would threaten the "essence" of the state. It is important to remind ourselves here that we are not discussing the legislative and judicial *allocation* of punishment, but only its *delivery*. As we have seen, there is nothing very new (or very archaic) about entrusting the delivery of punishment to private agencies.... So what is special about prisons?

The most plausible answer to this question, in our view, is that prisons rely *directly* upon the organised use of force. Non-custodial supervision is backed by the threat of force but (at least in the British system) force is rarely used in the actual administration of the sentence. Reformatories and approved schools did rely on the direct use of force to a certain extent, but this could be legitimated by an analogy with other private agencies, *i.e.* parents and non-penal schools. The degree of coercion required to run a prison, on the other hand, is far more substantial and would amount to a significant delegation of that "monopoly of the legitimate use of force" which Weber defined as a fundamental characteristic of the modern state....

... The potential for abuse is a strong reason for proceeding with caution before entrusting to *any* agency, public or private, powers to use force which it has not previously possessed. It is not, by itself, sufficient to render privatisation absolutely inadmissible, but it is a ground for insisting that only fairly weighty reasons could justify the risks which privatisation entails.

Profit and ethics

Many people, ourselves included, feel that it is morally repugnant to punish people – that is, to engage in the deliberate infliction of suffering – for the sake of profit, in much the same way that it is repugnant for mercenaries to kill people for profit. What is unjust about private prisons, according to this view, is not (or not only) the punishment inflicted on the inmates, but the rewards that accrue to penal entrepreneurs. The advocates of privatisation would retort that most of the people who work in the state penal system are paid for their labour, and "that is just another profit motive". This argument ignores the distinction between those who sell their labour power (and may have very limited choice about whom they sell it to) and those who own and control capital; and it also ignores the fact that many of those who engage in the distasteful business of inflicting pain do so not simply for economic reasons, but in the hope of mitigating the full impact of what they see as a regrettable social necessity. To equate their contribution with that of corporate executives and shareholders who are simply out to make a "fast buck" seems to us to be highly misleading....

But the moral case against privatisation is also bound up with the moral argument against the present excessive level of punishment. We agree with Nils Christie that the overriding moral imperative in the field of punishment is to reduce the level of pain infliction as far as possible. It is compatible with that goal to pay those whose job it is to inflict pain a reasonable wage, but not to create arrangements by which people get rich in direct proportion to the quantum of pain they inflict....

Prison Discipline

... One of the main problems to emerge both from the American experience of private prisons and the British experience of private juvenile institutions is the danger that such institutions may abuse their disciplinary powers and particularly their power to determine or influence an inmate's date of release.....

... Alongside the formal disciplinary system, moreover, there exists an "informal" or "shadow" system whose sanctions include segregation "in the interests of good order and discipline", withdrawal of privileges, transfers to other prisons, etc. If managers and staff find the formal system not to their liking, they may turn to these measures instead. Finally, it is not unknown for prison officers to resort to illegal violence as a means of punishment and control. If every possible check were employed against abuse of lawful methods – by severely restricting and monitoring the use of informal sanctions and paying the contractor nothing for detaining prisoners beyond their earliest dates of release – this could lead to acts of brutality by frustrated officers. In short, while it is difficult if not impossible to subject the disciplinary methods of any prison to thorough external control, in the case of private prisons the possibility of vested interests, and the conflict between outside supervision and the independence of a private body, pose additional problems.

Effects on the system

John Lea, Roger Matthews and Jock Young have argued, on the basis of research on the US juvenile justice system, that privatisation would lead to "the construction of a two-tier system of punishment", with private institutions creaming off the less serious and more tractable offenders. The dangers inherent in this process are, first, that the prisoners who are left in the public sector are defined as a "hard core" for whom nothing can be done; and secondly that the private sector is able to make spurious claims to greater efficiency and humanity....

Max Taylor and Ken Pease, two of the more sophisticated advocates of privatisation, see the possibility of such spurious claims to greater efficiency as one of the main dangers their proposals must avoid. They suggest the ingenious but unrealistic solution that private contracting should initially be restricted to sentenced prisoners serving 18 months or more. Even before the Green Paper was published, it should have been obvious (particularly to two writers who set great store by their political realism) that no government, and no contractor, was likely to run the risks inherent in conducting an *experiment* in privatisation at the deep end of the system.

Two more advocates of privatisation, Roger Hall and Neville Woodhead, have argued that it would achieve genuine savings because making each prison a separate economic unit would promote better financial management. They argue that while in theory it would be possible to introduce a more decentralised and efficient managerial system without resorting to privatisation, the Home Office's record is such as to make this unlikely....

Accountability

At first sight the issue of accountability is one where the advocates of privatisation appear to have a strong case. The great merit of privatisation, it is argued, is that it separates out the day to day administration of prisons from the Home Office's responsibilities for supervising them and upholding standards. At present the Home Office not only runs prisons, it also appoints the lay Boards of Visitors which act both as watchdogs and disciplinary tribunals, while the Inspectorate of Prisons forms part of the Home Office and is mainly staffed by seconded prison governors. Privatisation would at least go some way towards breaking this monopoly. As the *Independent* (July 26, 1988) put it in an editorial on the government's Green Paper:

> it is not in human nature to impose the most exacting standards on oneself. It is much more likely that the Home Office will develop into the tough regulatory body needed by British prisons if it is not also running them....

... Some opponents of privatisation weaken their case, however, by their readiness to take at face value the prevailing constitutional fictions about the accountability of *public* prisons. J. E. Thomas, for example, passionately affirms that "we cannot sweep aside the compelling legal and moral reasons for holding on to our responsibility and accountability for our prisoners". But what does this "responsibility and accountability" really amount to? The fact is that "our" elected representatives play only a very limited role in formulating penal *policy* – a role which they would still play after privatisation – and their (let alone "our") responsibility for what happens in individual prisons is negligible. Admittedly the Home Secretary is accountable to Parliament in the narrow and literal sense that s/he can be required to give an account of what happens in prisons, and it will be important to ensure that if prisons are privatised the Home Office, as the ministry responsible for maintaining standards, is required to make the same kinds of information available ("commercial confidentiality" notwithstanding). But if all the penal lobby is concerned with is preserving the existing forms of accountability, it is far from clear why this should lead it to oppose privatisation root and branch.

What is missing, not only from the privatisation debate but from the debate about prisons generally, is any adequate model of what genuine democratic accountability applied to prisons would look like. The unique characteristics of prisons make this a very complex question which we cannot discuss adequately here. Among the issues which need to be explored are: the prospects for developing a degree of internal democracy, involving prisoners and prison officers (the example of the Barlinnie Special Unit in Scotland is important here); the formulation and enforcement of minimum standards; the integration of prison medicine and education into the outside system of educational and medical administration; the role of local authorities (the Left has sadly failed to extend the police accountability debate to prisons); and the reform of Boards of Visitors, stripping them of their disciplinary functions and perhaps placing them under the auspices of local rather than central government. Related to this is the issue of legal accountability: the creation of a range of legally enforceable rights for prisoners.

There is, in theory, no reason why any of these forms of accountability should not apply to private institutions as well as to public ones. As Roger Matthews points out, the difference between a public and a private body may be of minimal significance if both have identical forms of accountability. What this argument overlooks, however, is that it is precisely the *lack* of public accountability in the private sector – viewed as freedom from "red tape" and political pressures – which is alleged to enable it both to save money and to pursue new managerial solutions to the prison crisis...

Notes

1. The authors conclude (at p. 82) that they have "a number of ethical and political objections to the private management of prisons", although they point out that there is no logical reason why the relationship between punishment and the state should be fixed and unchanging. It is clear from the Government Green Paper, *Private Sector Involvement in the Remand System* (1988), that the United States' experience of private involvement in the prison system was regarded as self-evidently a successful policy and many important questions were left unanswered (or were not asked). For a more critical approach, see Robert Porter's article, "The Privatisation of Prisons in the United States: A Policy that Britain Should Not Emulate", (1990) Vol. 29 *Howard Journal*, 65. The author states (at p. 79), after reviewing the U.S. experience:

> "It certainly would seem that there is a real commitment to the notion of privatisation. This commitment to change is, however, both ill-founded and misplaced. The American experience with private involvement in corrections has not been so satisfactory as to warrant easy acceptance. Indeed the involvement of the private sector in corrections is really still in its infancy. At least Britain would do better by standing back and monitoring the experiment for longer ... Using a more cautious approach, it might be possible to avoid adopting some of the difficulties and problems experienced in the United States ... [D]uring this breathing space, the government might realise that the symbolic question warrants much greater consideration than it seems to have been given so far. The bottom-line is that in this fundamental area of the administration of justice it is the government that should and must carry out these functions. At best the privatisation debate demonstrates an awakening to the unacceptable state of British prisons. Privatisation itself should not be hailed as the cure-all for this situation."

2. For a more favourable approach to the idea of privatisation, see M. Taylor and K. Pease, "Private Prisons and Penal Purpose", Chapter 8 in *Privatising Criminal Justice* (R. Matthews ed.). The authors make the valid point that the state-run penal system is "a disastrous mess" and, therefore, we should be receptive to ideas of improvement and progress. They state (at p. 183):

> "If one were to search for an instance of a State monopoly which has failed, one would not need to look beyond the Prison Service. It confines citizens and aspires to direct them towards a good and useful life. In fact conditions give the lie to the aspiration. They are more likely to brutalise than to improve. It is against the backcloth of this failure that we must consider privatisation."

Taylor and Pease list the possible advantages which, in their opinion, privatisation could offer (see pp. 191–192). In particular, they see the development of a new scheme as capable of challenging the "institutional inertia of public prisons". A policy of privatisation might provide a commercial incentive to develop penal regimes which might be less negative and more reform-oriented. However, the authors go on to warn that (at p. 192):

> "If prison privatisation takes place as an unthinking copy of North American practice, the situation in the UK will probably become worse. If it takes place without strong insistence on standards and on rewards for success in reconviction terms, the situation will probably become worse. If it takes place with no restriction on the triviality of offences which consign one to a private prison, the use of imprisonment will increase, and the private facilities will gain a spurious reputation as offering value for money. In short, the potential advantages which private prisons offer are specific to a narrow range of possible schemes. Our advocacy of such schemes is therefore a high-risk strategy. If all the right elements are not in place, privatisation will have entered our penal system to no good effect. We will have opened our gates to a particularly unpleasant Trojan Horse. Our fear is that liberal and radical lobbyists will oppose privatisation *per se*. The scheme introduced would then be a primitive and unsatisfactory version, and an opportunity would have been lost. Anyone who thinks that criticism of privatisation in principle will delay its introduction to our prisons in misguided."

3.   Prison privatisation progressed from an issue for debate to reality in April 1992 with the opening of the Wolds, a purpose-built remand prison run by "Group 4 Remand Services", with Stephen Twinn as director. The capacity of the Wolds is 320 and it is not to be used for high-risk (provisional Category A) remands. The new prison opened with a commitment by its owners to have prisoners out of their cells for up to 14 hours per day. A Home Office Controller was expected to monitor the performance of the prison administration and to investigate complaints. The Wolds, which has its own Board of Visitors, was also inspected by H.M. Chief Inspector of Prisons in 1993. The ensuing report found that although prison conditions were of a high standard, many inmates were in a state of inertia and there was found to be a significant drug problem within the prison. It is interesting (in view of the warning given by Taylor and Pease, above) that the contract for running the prison did not require the contractor to help prisoners lead useful lives. (In addition to the Chief Inspector's report, see the report of the National Audit Office, *Wolds Remand Prison*, H.C. 309, 1993–4).

The progress of the Wolds was also considered in the Prison Reform Trust's report: *Wolds Remand Prison Contracting-Out: A First Year Report.* Despite finding positive aspects to the new regime, such as the physical conditions and the amount of time spent by prisoners out of their cells, the report also expressed some concern, notably about the drugs problem within the prison. There was also concern that, given the amount of "leisure" time enjoyed by prisoners, there was relatively little for them to do of a constructive nature. The Prison Reform Trust's report also commented on a lack of accountability as evidenced by the fact that the Home Office controller's reports are not published and the financial details of the contract are secret.

4.   Despite the mixed reaction to the Wolds, and the unproven claims for its early promising performance, it is clear that the government intends to press on with its policy of privatisation. On September 3, 1993, it announced long-term plans to privatise one in ten prisons in England and Wales, with the intention that there will be eight private prisons by the end of 1994. (See *The Guardian*, September 3, 1993). Doncaster is the most recent private prison to be opened (in June 1994), built at a cost of nearly £80 million. The contract for running Doncaster was awarded to an American company, "Premier Prison Services". Due to low staffing levels and the inexperience of many of the prison officers, the prison has experienced a number of difficulties since it opened.

VI. THE PRISON REGIME

Report of the Departmental Committee on Prisons (Gladstone Committee), C. 7702, (1895), para. 25.

... Sir Godfrey Lushington thus impressively summed up the influences under the present system unfavourable to reformation: "I regard as unfavourable to reformation the status of a prisoner throughout his whole career; the crushing of self-respect, the starving of all moral instinct he may possess, the absence of all opportunity to do or receive a kindness, the continual association with none but criminals, and that only as a separate item amongst other items also separate; the forced labour, and the denial of all liberty. I believe the true mode of reforming a man or restoring him to society is exactly in the opposite direction of all these; but, of course, this is a mere idea. It is quite impracticable in a prison. In fact the unfavourable features I have mentioned are inseparable from prison life." As a broad description of prison life we think this description is accurate; we do not agree that all of these unfavourable features are irremovable. Already in many respects and in individual cases they have been modified, and we believe that this modification can be carried much further in the direction of the treatment adopted and practised by the best of the existing reformatories. We think that the system should be made more elastic, more capable of being adopted to the special cases of individual prisoners; that prison discipline and treatment should be more effectually designed to maintain, stimulate, or awaken the higher susceptibilities of prisoners, to develop their moral instincts, to train them in orderly and industrial habits, and whenever possible to turn them out of prison better men and women, both physically and morally, than when they came in. Crime, its causes and treatment, has been the subject of much profound and scientific inquiry. Many of the problems it presents are practically at the present time insoluble. It may be true that some criminals are irreclaimable, just as some diseases are incurable, and in such cases it is not unreasonable to acquiesce in the theory that criminality is a disease, and the result of physical imperfection. But criminal anthropology as a science is in an embryo stage, and while scientific and more particularly medical observation and experience are of the most essential value in guiding opinion on the whole subject, it would be a loss of time to search for a perfect system in learned but conflicting theories, when so much can be done by the recognition of the plain fact that the great majority of prisoners are ordinary men and women amenable, more or less, to all those influences which affect persons outside.

Notes
1.   The Report of the Gladstone Committee, overriding the doubts of one of the senior Home Office officials, Sir Godfrey Lushington, inaugurated the era of the prison as a "training" institution. This was based on penological optimism which envisaged the possibility that, through the experience of a constructive regime within the prisons, criminals could be reformed, in the sense of being nurtured away from their law-breaking propensities. The work of Sir Alexander Paterson, appointed Prison Commissioner in 1922, initiated a period of penal reform, in terms of better conditions for prisoners and more enlightened regimes. At least some effort was made to translate the optimism of the Gladstone Committee – "that prison treatment should have as its primary and concurrent objects deterrence and reformation" – into practical reality.
2.   Rule 1 of the Prison Rules states:

> "The purpose of the training and treatment of convicted prisoners shall be to encourage and assist them to lead a good and useful life."

Rule 2(3) provides:

> "At all times the treatment of prisoners shall be such as to encourage their self-respect and a sense of personal responsibility..."

(Section 47(1) of the Prison Act 1952 empowers the Secretary of State to make rules for the regulation and management of prisons. The Prison Rules (1964, as amended) are issued under this Act).

But how realistic is it to expect that offenders can be assisted to lead a good and useful life within custodial institutions? When many prisons suffer from overcrowding and poor conditions, and prisoners spend long periods locked up in their cells with little access to constructive work or recreation, it is unlikely that the ideals of the Gladstone Committee can be upheld. As we noted at the start of this chapter, since the second world war the prison system has steadily moved towards a state of crisis. A mood of penal pessimism set in, characterised by a growing disenchantment with the idea of prisons as reforming institutions, supported by high reconviction rates for those who had experienced incarceration. In the words of two modern writers (Taylor and Pease (1989), p. 184):

> "Prisons as we know them mock the aspiration of the first Prison Rule, to enable prisoners to lead a good and useful life. The rhetoric of 'humane containment' has come to signify the limits of what is hoped for, and itself is belied by the reality of warehousing of prisoners. A casualty of the process has been the hope of rehabilitation. Pessimism prevails ... The emphasis in the prison building programme is on new establishments rather than the provision of the necessities of decency,

notably the provision of integral cell sanitation. This is not consistent with the aspiration to change people. It is consistent with a tolerance of their degradation."

The shift in mood from the days of penal optimism to a less ambitious realism in the 1970s, can be seen in the extract which follows.

Report of the Committee of Inquiry into the United Kingdom Prison Services (May Committee), Cmnd. 7673 (1979), paras 4.25–4.31, 4.36, 4.45–4.48.

4.25 We take it as axiomatic that imprisonment is bound to remain as the final sanction for imposing social discipline in our community under agreed rules of law. For the reasons which will appear hereafter, we are forced to the conclusion that it should be used as little as possible.

4.26 If Rule 1 is to continue to set out the objectives of the prison service, then we think it should be re-written and we suggest the following for contemporary purposes:

"The purpose of the detention of convicted prisoners shall be to keep them in custody which is both secure and yet positive, and to that end the behaviour of all the responsible authorities and staff towards them shall be such as to:
(*a*) create an environment which can assist them to respond and contribute to society as positively as possible;
(*b*) preserve and promote their self respect;
(*c*) minimise, to the degree of security necessary in each particular case, the harmful effects of their removal from normal life;
(*d*) prepare them for and assist them on discharge"....

4.27 We think that the rhetoric of "treatment and training" has had its days and should be replaced. On the other hand, we intend that the rhetoric alone should be changed and not all the admirable and constructive things that are done in its name.

4.28 Secondly, we hope that by suggesting this alteration to Rule 1 we make it clear that in our view mere "secure and humane containment" is not enough. Prison staff cannot be asked to operate in a moral vacuum and the absence of real objectives can in the end lead only to the routine brutalisation of all the participants. There may be ample room for argument about the extent to which imprisonment should be used, but there can be no neutrality about it once it is imposed. We think that there both can and should be purposive objectives in imprisonment, but we do not feel that realistically they can be set any higher than we have just suggested.

Regimes

4.29 We now turn – concentrating principally on prison establishments – to consider briefly the nature of the regimes which we think should be established and operated to give life and effect to the new spirit embodied in the proposed new Rule 1 which we hope may help in part to rejuvenate and settle the prison service.

4.30 No prison routine is so sterile, degrading and harmful to the prisoner, and equally barren for the staff who have to operate it, than one in which the inmate is locked in his cell for a substantial part of the day and only released perhaps for the statutory one hour's exercise.

4.31 We think that a concerted effort should be made by both management and staff alike to ensure that as many inmates as possible are out of their cells and occupied for as much of a full working day as possible....

4.36 In England and Wales, the provision and use of educational facilities within establishments has been much more successful, much of the expansion occurring in recent years. As a result, relatively substantial educational and library facilities have been provided in most establishments. These have catered for academic courses in all subjects and of every standard, vocational training in many fields and courses to fit inmates for work at various trades in the construction industries. Recently increased attention has been paid to education and training in social skills but this has so far only been on a relatively small scale. We think that this can and should be enlarged substantially. Education has always been voluntary for inmates, except for those below school-leaving age. One further point, however, is important: most of the courses and classes are arranged to take place in the evenings to avoid interfering with work regimes which, as we have already mentioned, have however been sadly deficient....

Positive Custody

4.45 Although we hope that what we have said so far in this chapter indicates the general direction in which we think penal establishments may best move, we wish to emphasise some more general themes. This is both to make them explicit and to stress how we intend what follows in this report to be read and interpreted in the light of them.

4.46 Above all, we repeat that in putting "treatment and training" and "humane containment" aside, the last thing we intend is to suggest nothing should take their place. On the contrary, we fully appreciate that every community, whatever its nature, requires a suitable ethic. As will have been seen from our suggested redraft of Rule 1 in paragraph 4.26 we think that what we envisage might be best described as "positive custody". That is, it has to be secure and it must carry out all the intentions of the courts and society, in that respect. On the other hand, penal establishments must also so far as possible be hopeful and purposive communities and not be allowed to degenerate into mere uncaring institutions dulled by their own unimaginative and unenterprising routines.

4.47 We feel fortified in recommending such an approach because the prison services in the United Kingdom have historically displayed by any account a remarkably flexible and compassionate response to their tasks and charges. We therefore have no doubt they are capable of rising, in so far as that is necessary, to what we intend.

4.48 We also think that they need support from an informed and interested public. We have therefore throughout the report repeatedly sought to consider how the public might best be involved. We consider that the management of penal establishments must be consistently characterised by an openness of approach and mind not only to all the staff but to all public requirements and proper inquiries, as well as to the interests of inmates. We appreciate this is easier to say than to describe in detail or to maintain in all respects. However, we think it should nonetheless be the governing principle. Over time we would expect this to help the services themselves to be more understood because they have explained and shared their problems more with the outside world. We anticipate, too, that it should bring about changes for inmates, for example, in dismantling supererogatory elements of control, such as some aspects of censorship. In the same way we would want to see the dominant attitude of everyone in the services to be one of active search for development and change, and concerned to enable these to happen. We hope that this report will provide the opportunity to release fresh energies and initiatives rather than to support constricted views and offer impediments to development.

Notes

1. "Positive custody", advocated by the May Report, may strike many as simply making the best of what is already there: the idea that some people

have to go to prison and that they should be held humanely and with the minimum risk of disruption and institutionalisation. In this respect, the May Report received a critical reception for recognising the problems and disadvantages of imprisonment and then putting forward lame solutions. Fitzgerald and Sim ((1980), pp. 82–83) castigated the May Committee for "legitimising crisis", arguing that the Report:

> "represents a shift from 'warehousing' which simply involves storing people, to 'zookeeping' where some limited consideration is given to the state of the stored. While the term 'positive custody' may be new, it quickly became apparent that the ideas behind it are not. It is simply a statement of Home Office policy ... For the May Report uncritically to accept and legitimate such policies is wholly irresponsible."

For a further detailed criticism of the approach adopted by the May Committee, see R. King and R. Morgan, *The Future of the Prison System* (1980).

2.   It has often been stated that offenders are sentenced to imprisonment *as* their punishment and not *for* punishment; *i.e.* once inside, they are not meant to be subjected to a "deliberately painful or humiliating way of life" (see *Sentence of the Court*, 1979, para. 110). But with many prisoners living in conditions which were worse than over a century ago, with penal conditions and overcrowding being condemned by prison governors and politicians of all major parties, the 1980s heralded a period of deep-rooted dissatisfaction with prison regimes and conditions. One expert on the history of imprisonment described this disquiet in the following way (see A. Rutherford (1984) p. 101):

> "Concern in England about the level of prison crowding and its consequences reached a peak in the early 1980s. The phrase 'affront to a civilised society' was used by both the head of the prison system and by the Home Secretary to describe conditions in local prisons. Prison governors publicly complained about the condition of the institutions for which they were responsible. In a much publicised letter to *The Times* (November 19, 1981), the governor of Wormwood Scrubs stated that he could no longer tolerate the inhumanity of the system within which he worked. The reports of Her Majesty's Chief Inspector of Prisons, which began to appear in 1982, substantiated the scale of the problem. In Gloucester Prison, inspected in March 1981, 253 men were found in 112 cells designed for individual use. The Chief Inspector observed: 'The consequence of this policy of overcrowding is that conditions are so cramped in the multiple occupancy cells that, even when some items of furniture are removed, the remaining floor space does not allow two men to pass each other without difficulty ... They must eat in their cells and there is no means of sanitation other than a chamber pot ... We consider these conditions to be deplorable and degrading both for the inmates and for the staff who work on the

wings.' At Leeds Prison, 1,200 prisoners were 'jammed' into 520 cells designated for one person and 18 larger cells ... the report on [this] prison commented on the 'daily miracle in juggling numbers and processing people ... The prison is a humane, efficient conveyor belt, but we consider it highly undesirable that a prison should have to function like a production line.' "

Prison conditions and the treatment of inmates were also heavily criticised in the following extract.

Larry Gostin and Marie Staunton, "The Case for Prison Standards: Conditions of Confinement, Segregation and Medical Treatment", Chapter 5 in *Accountability and Prisons* (M. Maguire, J. Vagg and R. Morgan, eds., 1985).

Our working assumption is that the punishment intended by a prison sentence is simply deprivation of liberty. Minimally, society is entitled to expect that deprivation of liberty does not cause the individual any lasting harm of a physical or psychological kind. We shall argue that the most effective way to enable the development of a positive right, which we call *protection from harm*, is through the establishment of minimum standards of confinement and treatment, debated and agreed by Parliament and open to review by the courts.

In the first half of the paper, we highlight a number of areas in which the development of a set of agreed standards is a matter of some urgency. After a few illustrations of the unsatisfactory nature of conditions of confinement in general, we argue that groups concerned with prisoners' rights should pay particular attention to two specific areas; segregation and medical treatment – the latter with particular regard to the treatment of mentally disordered offenders. We then outline ways in which standards could be introduced and how they could be monitored so that any violations are remedied.

Criticism of the conditions under which prisoners are held have come not only from voluntary organisations advocating prison reform but also from those administering and inspecting prisons. For example, there is widespread acceptance that conditions in local prisons in London are intolerable. In a reply to Jo Richardson MP in August 1983, the Home Office stated:

"It is very much regretted that our Victorian local prisons in London (which were originally designed to take a much lower number of prisoners than they hold today) are overcrowded to the point where there is difficulty in providing all the amenities we would wish to be available."

A Report of HM Chief Inspector of Prisons put the same point more forcefully:

"Although Wormwood Scrubs is less overcrowded than other prisons which we have seen recently we nevertheless consider that it is such that, other than in D Hall, prisoners are not being held in conditions which ensure respect for human dignity."

A month earlier, in January 1983, the Governor of that prison had resigned, graphically describing conditions there as "a penal dustbin full of overcrowded cattle pens".

While the physical conditions in which convicted and unconvicted prisoners are held have been widely condemned, the courts have failed effectively to provide a remedy. The case of the Nahar brothers (1983) illustrates this well, as it involves conditions of confinement – in police cells – worse even than those existing in any

British prison. If the courts are unable to remedy such an extreme situation, there is little hope that they will act effectively on general prison conditions. The Nahar brothers were remanded in custody in Camberwell police cells and applied to the Divisional Court for *habeas corpus* on the basis that conditions under which they were held were inhuman and degrading and therefore that their detention was unlawful.

> "The two applicants were in a cell six feet by eight feet. The cell had no windows, the applicants were permitted no exercise outside their cells in the cell area. The cell was lit by one weak light bulb and ventilation was provided by two ventilators near the ground." (*Nahar* 1983)

The court held that although there must be some minimum standard which could render detention unlawful, neither the Imprisonment (Temporary Provisions) Act (1980) which provided for remands in police cells, nor the European Convention on Human Rights assisted in defining that standard. The applications were refused without the court itself suggesting any appropriate standard.

The effects of inadequate treatment and conditions may go far beyond physical discomfort. The repeated transfer of remand prisoners is an effective denial of the few rights which the Prison Rules and Circular Instructions specifically allow them because of their unconvicted status – to have their own food and clothes and access to their own doctors. In 1983, Mr T was transferred twenty times to a variety of prisons and police cells between the New Forest and Leamington Spa. He was in effect denied his visiting rights during that period: his wife had great difficulty in both tracking him down and in travelling to different parts of the country to visit him (NCCL casefile).

Every year the National Council for Civil Liberties' team of legal volunteers answers about 2,000 letters from prisoners. Complaints refer *inter alia* to damp, cold, lice, poor toilet facilities, overcrowding, lack of exercise, and difficulty in seeing a doctor or obtaining appropriate medical treatment. It is clear from this list that the physical conditions of imprisonment are only one aspect of the privations of prison life as perceived by prisoners. The lack of visits, inability to establish any privacy or territory of their own, lack of access to education, the perceived unfairness of loss of privileges or the operation of Rule 43 not only make conditions more difficult to bear but may lead to destructive behaviour. Similarly, sudden changes of policy ... not only lead to many requests for NCCL help by prisoners and their families but also to an increase in the tension in prisons. And the frequent movements between cells or between prisons can have a deleterious effect upon a prisoner's mental state, as illustrated by this account of imprisonment in 1983:

> "My mental state was very bad. Once you are settled you go to a cell and if you know you have to stay there you can make it as comfortable as possible, try to keep it clean, wash the walls because in some of the cells walls are impossible to look at, get your own plate, fork, knife – they are yours, they are clean. You even keep some bread and butter inside so if you are starving in the evening, a slice of bread and butter can calm your stomach. But when you are moving like that you are always in a new place, you never know where you are going." (Mr M, NCCL casefile 1984)

Notes

1. Despite assurances by the May Committee that it was not intending to create a "moral vacuum" by its rejection of treatment and training within prisons, it was far from clear, as the 1980s progressed, what the "suitable ethic" for prison regimes was supposed to be. The Report predicted – accurately, as it turned out – that without a proper sense of purpose and

direction the likely result would be "the routine brutalisation of all the participants" (May Report, para. 4.28).

2. In the Spring of 1986, prison governors complained directly to the Prime Minister about worsening conditions, prison officers refused to work overtime in furtherance of their dispute with the Home Office, and serious disturbances occurred in eighteen prisons. Further disturbances and damage resulted in other prisons and remand centres in the years which followed. But the most serious prison "rioting" occurred in April 1990. These events are described in the following account.

Vivien Stern, *Bricks of Shame*, (2nd ed., (updated) 1993) pp. 249–53.

The years since 1989 have been ones of hectic development in the history of Britain's prisons. We have seen highly publicised and deeply shocking events which have led to wider public discussion of prison matters than ever before. Changes in prison organisation and management have come more rapidly than once seemed possible. The squalor in which prisoners lived and prison staff worked has been much reduced. Most significant of all, perhaps, is the way understanding has spread that imprisonment is an ineffective method of dealing with crime.

What brought these changes about and where are they leading us? This chapter will try to answer these questions.

The catalyst for change was the terrible outbreak of violence and destruction at Strangeways prison, Manchester, in April 1990. This book began with a description of the disturbances of 1986 and the damage they caused. After 1986 and the post-mortem on it, from which little was learned, all those involved wondered how long it would be before there was another flare-up. The tensions caused by overcrowding, long hours locked up with two others and an overflowing slop bucket, and the routinised lack of respect for individuals would surely be ignited by some spark and explode. No one would have advocated riot as a way of achieving change. Everyone would have wished the warnings had been heeded. They were not.

On April 1 in the chapel at Strangeways prison the worst finally happened. Three hundred and nine prisoners were attending the Church of England service that morning. It was conducted by the prison chaplain, Noel Proctor, with help from a Church Army Chaplain. There were more staff on duty than usual, fourteen instead of eight, because of rumours of impending trouble...

... Prisoners started attacking prison staff with table legs, fire extinguishers, fire buckets, hymn books. A set of keys was ripped away from a prison officer. Most of the staff retreated as they had been told earlier to do in such circumstances....

... By noon the rioting prisoners had control of most of the prison. The staff had left the wings. One group of prisoners not involved in the riot was then in serious danger. These were the ninety-seven prisoners separated from other prisoners for their own protection under Rule 43 of the Prison Rules. Now they had no protection. The staff had left and the rioting prisoners had keys to wings where the prisoners on Rule 43 were living.

The following day reports appeared in the press suggesting that between twelve and twenty prisoners had been killed. Suggestions of castration and mutilation were also made. Fortunately, these reports were not true. But the truth was grim enough....

... Prisoners occupied the prison for the next twenty-three days. Television crews from around the world set up camp outside. Until April 9 a police helicopter circled overhead at night, playing loud music to keep the prisoners awake. The rioters broke through on to the roof and entered into a shouted dialogue with the world's press. During the twenty-three days prisoners were gradually evacuated as they asked to leave or gave up the protest. By April 7 only twenty-one were left. The Strangeways riot ended on April 25 when an operation was mounted to dislodge the last five prisoners from the roof.

Altogether, 147 prison staff were injured in the course of the riot. One prisoner received injuries and subsequently died. Forty-seven other prisoners were injured. Damage estimated at £60 million was done to the fabric of the prison (although it was due for refurbishment costing tens of millions of pounds). The rioters were taken to court and trials took place in 1992 and 1993. Many received further prison sentences, some of up to ten years, for their part in the disturbance. One of the rioters, a young man aged nineteen who had been in Strangeways awaiting trial, killed himself at Hindley prison two months after the riot ended.

The events at Strangeways sparked off disturbances elsewhere. In all, there was trouble at eighteen prisons, some of it serious. Prison administrators in other countries, watching the riot on their television, became anxious. Imprisonment – the nature of it, the purpose of it – became a talking-point as never before.

For the prison service in England and Wales the riot was a watershed. For penal reform the end of April 1990 was a dangerous moment. Change now had to come. but in what direction? There were conflicting pressures. Some people felt the right response would be a crack-down, greater control, more security technology, better riot gear for prison staff, no more occasions when over three hundred prisoners gathered together with fourteen staff in charge. Many felt that law, order and authority had been mocked by the spectacle of prisoners on the roof performing for the cameras of the world. Respect for authority needed to be reasserted.

Fortunately, five days after the riot began, the Home Office took an important decision. A judicial inquiry was to be set up. And then occurred an event of extraordinary good fortune for the prison service of England and Wales and the cause of humane treatment of prisoners everywhere. The first senior judge approached and prepared to conduct the judicial inquiry was Lord Justice Woolf (now Lord Woolf). He was highly regarded, a thoughtful, liberal-minded judge, ready to claim a role for the law in protecting the human rights of individuals.

On April 5, while the prisoners were still in control of Strangeways prison, Lord Justice Woolf was appointed to inquire into the events leading up to the disturbance at Manchester. After violence had broken out at other prisons the following weekend, the terms of reference were extended to there as well on April 10. The final terms of reference were:

> To inquire into the events leading up to the serious disturbance at HM Prison Manchester which began on April 1, 1990 and the action taken to bring it to a conclusion, having regard also to the serious disturbances that occurred shortly thereafter in other prison establishments in England and Wales.

Here was another point where the endeavour could have gone badly wrong. The terms of reference lend themselves to a broad interpretation – or to a narrow one. A consideration of "the events leading up to the serious disturbance" could have been restricted to why the prisoners were in a mutinous frame of mind in Manchester prison in March 1990, why the staff were not prepared, why prisoners coming to the chapel were not searched and the chair legs they brought with them were not found, why the walls and doors were not stronger, and why prisoners in other prisons were not locked up immediately news of the riot got out.

Lord Justice Woolf saw it differently. The terms of reference were taken in their widest sense. "The events" became a history of the prison service in recent years, the living conditions of prisoners, the relationships between all the actors in the drama of imprisonment and the role of the wider criminal justice players. The Woolf Inquiry became, in all but name, the much-needed and long-overdue Royal Commission into prisons in England and Wales. The first part of the inquiry concentrated on the disturbances and the events leading directly to them. For the second part, the wider analysis, Lord Justice Woolf was joined by Judge Stephen Tumim. Stephen Tumim had been Her Majesty's Chief Inspector of Prisons since 1987. In that role he had been responsible for producing a corpus of detailed analysis and criticism of prison conditions unparalleled anywhere in the world.

Notes

1. The events of April 1990 represented the worst outbreak of prison rioting in British penal history. The six most serious disturbances were at Manchester (Strangeways), Glen Parva (Young Offender Institution), Dartmoor, Cardiff, Bristol, and Pucklechurch (Remand Centre).

2. The departmental (or judicial) inquiry headed by Lord Justice Woolf was given the freedom to interpret its terms of reference in the way that it saw fit, and Woolf was given considerable assistance by expert assessors, lawyers, prison governors and various other bodies. As noted earlier, he was also able to enlist the help of Judge Stephen Tumim for the second part of the inquiry.

3. Without going into detail about conditions in all of the institutions where rioting occurred in April 1990, it is clear that Strangeways suffered from many of the problems already referred to in this chapter. Woolf reported (at para. 1.21–1.22):

> "The prison was overcrowded. The certified normal accommodation for the whole of Strangeways was 970. The total population on April 1, 1990 was 1,647. In the past, the prison population had been even larger. In March 1988, the prison population had reached 1,803...
>
> ... Improvements had been made to the living conditions at the prison during the previous three years. However, on April 1, 1990, the physical conditions, in addition to being grossly overcrowded, were still insanitary and degrading."

The Report also stated (at para. 3.432):

> "The object of those who initiated the disturbance was to draw attention to their perceived grievances, which in the case of some inmates were of long standing. They related to the way they were treated by the Prison Service and the conditions in which they were required to live, not only at Manchester but at other prisons as well. These inmates contend that they had no other effective method of ventilating their grievances. It is unlikely that they contemplated taking over the whole of the prison...
>
> A large proportion of the inmates in the prison were sympathetic to the instigators of the disturbance and antagonistic towards the Prison Service because of the conditions in which they were housed at the time at Strangeways ... As the inmates repeatedly told the Inquiry, if they were treated like animals they would behave like animals. The prison was overcrowded, and the inmates were provided with insufficient activities and association. The inmates were spending too

long in their cells without sanitation and without the opportunity, with reasonable frequency, to bathe and to change their clothes. The conditions which contributed to the antagonism of the majority of the inmates towards the prison system in general was not the responsibility of the staff and management of the prison ... the management and staff at the prison were faced with immense problems due to the failure of Governments in the past to provide the resources to the Prison Service which were needed to enable the Service to provide for an increased prison population in a humane manner. The long overdue improvements in the prison which were recognised as being needed at the time of the riot should already have been implemented."

4. Part II of the Woolf Inquiry deals with more general questions relating to the administration of the prison system. This starts with an examination of the proper role of the Prison Service.

Prison Disturbances April 1990: **Report of an Inquiry by Lord Justice Woolf and Judge Stephen Tumim, Cm. 1456 (1991) paras, 10.18–10.24, 10.27–10.29, 10.35, 10.39–10.44, 15.4–15.5.**

10.18 The Courts send prisoners to prison because in their judgement justice requires that the prisoner should receive a sentence of imprisonment. Imprisonment is the gravest punishment which it is open to the Courts to impose. The Courts do not, as they did at one time for some types of sentence, specify what form that punishment should take. They do not sentence someone to hard labour, or corrective training. They leave it to the Prison Service to decide how to provide the conditions of containment which are appropriate for that individual, having regard to all the relevant factors, including the length of sentence which he has to serve.

10.19 If the Prison Service contains that prisoner in conditions which are inhumane or degrading, or which are otherwise wholly inappropriate, then a punishment of imprisonment which was justly imposed, will result in injustice. It is no doubt for this reason, as well as because any other approach would offend the values of our society, that the Statement of Purpose acknowledges that it is the Prison Service's duty to look after prisoners with humanity. If it fulfils this duty, the Prison Service is partly achieving what the Court must be taken to have intended when it passed a sentence of imprisonment. This must be that, while the prisoner should be subjected to the stigma of imprisonment and should be confined in a prison, the prisoner is not to be subjected to inhumane or degrading treatment.

10.20 The condensed language of the [Prison Board's] Statement of Purpose does not (at least to the ordinary reader) draw attention expressly to the importance of treating a prisoner with justice. The definition of the word humanity in the Shorter Oxford Dictionary makes no reference to justice. It does, however, refer to "human attributes ... that appeal to man". It is entirely acceptable to argue that the requirement to treat prisoners with humanity includes an obligation to treat them with justice. However, the two terms are not strictly synonymous. If a prisoner is provided with a dry cell, with integral sanitation and as much exercise, activities, association and food as he likes, many people would regard him as being treated with humanity. They would continue to do so even if the prisoner had a deep sense of grievance because he had been transferred from one prison to another without any reason being given and, the prisoner felt, without any satisfactory means of redress. That would be a failure principally of justice. Only at the extreme could it be properly interpreted as failing the test of humanity.

10.21 Part I of the Inquiry made it abundantly clear that, while some prisoners were angry over the physical conditions or food, there were others who were antagonistic and disruptive because they felt they had been treated unjustly and there was no independent person to whom they could turn for redress. They were aggrieved over a failure of justice.

10.22 The failure of the Statement of Purpose to refer expressly to the requirement to provide justice in prisons, is shared by [Prison] Rules 1 and 2 and the proposed May Amendment. This omission is explicable when it is appreciated that the extent of the entitlement of a prisoner to justice has only been clearly developed by the Courts since 1979 (see *R v. Board of Visitors of Hull Prison* [1979] QB). It is now clear that, contrary to what was previously contended, in spite of his imprisonment a convicted prisoner retains all his civil rights which are not taken away expressly or by necessary implication. If, for example, a governor does not treat a prisoner justly in disciplinary proceedings, the prisoner can obtain judicial review.

10.23 In extending the remedies available to the prisoner, the Courts are only reflecting what are regarded by society as minimum acceptable standards. Where an institution has the sort of power over an individual which the Prison Service has, that institution must at all times be conscious of the importance of justice. This requirement is underlined when the institution is part of the Criminal Justice System. In due course, the Prison Rules should be amended to reflect the requirement that prisoners should be treated with justice.

10.24 There is a third consequence of the Prison Service's position as part of the Criminal Justice System. The objectives of the Criminal Justice System include discouraging crime. A sentence of imprisonment is imposed by the Court partly in order to deter offending. The objective of deterrence implicitly includes the underlying purpose of reducing criminal behaviour. In so far as this is possible, and within the constraints imposed by the fact that imprisonment is inevitably coercive, the Prison Service should therefore, as part of its role, be seeking to minimise the prospect of the prisoner re-offending after serving his sentence. This is fully consistent with the Prison Service's duty "to help them lead law abiding and useful lives in custody and after release"....

10.27 The evidence before the Inquiry suggests that at least part of the explanation for imprisonment not being more successful in preventing reoffending is that the prisoner has so little responsibility for what happens to him during the period of the sentence. It is also clear from the evidence which the Inquiry has received from prisoners, that the conditions which exist at present in our prisons causes a substantial number of prisoners to leave prison more embittered and hostile to society than when they arrived. They leave prison, therefore, in a state of mind where they are more likely to re-offend. Furthermore, the sentence tends to make it more difficult for them to obtain employment. And it tends to weaken their connections with their families and their local communities.

10.28 If it is to further the objectives of the Criminal Justice System, the Prison Service has to address these factors. In particular, if the second half of the Statement of Purpose is not to be subject to ridicule, the Prison Service has to tackle the problems which arise from the conditions and restricted regimes in many prison establishments and in particular in the local prisons.

10.29 In order to do so it must seek to minimise the negative effects of imprisonment which make reoffending more likely. It must require the offender to confront and take responsibility for the wrong doing which resulted in his having to serve a sentence of imprisonment. It must encourage the prisoner to take some responsibility for what happens to him in prison. It must seek to provide the prisoner with an opportunity to obtain skills which will make it easier to obtain and keep employment and enable him to maintain his family and community contacts. It must seek to ensure that life in prison will be as close to life outside as the demands of imprisonment permit. It must, above all, ensure, through these and other means, that the prisoner is properly prepared for his return to society...

10.35 There is a fourth requirement on the Prison Service in its role as part of the Criminal Justice System. It is fundamental to this role that it holds the prisoner securely. The Statement of Purpose does not expressly refer to security. However it is implicit in the words in the first part of the statement that the Service "serves the public by keeping in custody those committed by the Courts". The Criminal Justice System cannot operate effectively if the decisions that are made by one part of the system, in this case the Courts, are not effectively implemented by another part, the Prison Service. The public and the Courts have a right to expect that when a prisoner is sent to prison, he or she stays there until the proper time for his release....

10.39 The achievement of security in this wider sense of including control is important in Prison Service establishments. But the attention paid to security should not be at the expense of the other aspects of the role of the Prison Service. Part of the reason for this is because, as Mr Ian Dunbar, a member of the Prison Service, has made clear in his report, A Sense of Direction, the other aspects of the role will help to provide "Dynamic Security". This is as important to the security of an establishment as physical containment. Prisons are of their nature establishments to which offenders do not wish to go and where they must be held securely; but prisons need not make those who are serving sentences in them feel bitter, hostile or degraded.

10.40 Part of the present difficulties of the Prison Service can be attributed to the fact that, since the Mountbatten Report, the Prison Service has not been in a position to pay sufficient attention to aspects of their role other than security. Overcrowding, and the fact that the prison estate was largely insanitary and run down, has made it necessary for the Prison Service to expend too great a proportion of its energy in crisis management, coping with the consequences of overcrowding and lack of sanitation. It is only in recent years that Governments have been prepared to make the resources available to tackle the inadequacies of the prison estate. As a result, the prospects for the Prison Service are now better than they have been for many years. It should now therefore be possible for the Prison Service to have proper regard for what should be its full role.

10.41 The full role of the Prison Service, as explained in section 9 of the Report, requires the Prison Service to address three aspects. They are: security, control, and justice within prisons. The three aspects complement each other. The Prison Service must give each its due weight. And it must maintain the proper balance between them. If security is breached and a prisoner is allowed to escape, that frustrates the sentence imposed by the Court. There is a failure of both security and justice. If sufficient control is not provided and prisoners riot, security is put at risk and the ability of the Service to provide conditions which accord with justice will be impaired.

10.42 A proper concentration on these three aspects of the Prison Service's role would accord with the intent of the Statement of Purpose. It would involve the prisoner being treated with humanity and being helped to lead a law abiding life while in prison and after release. It would further the objectives of the Criminal Justice System.

10.43 This is a challenging, constructive and worthwhile role. It involves the Prison Service making a recognised and constructive contribution to the Criminal Justice System's task of maintaining public order and justice. If the challenge is met by the Prison Service, it will result in the prison system making a more worthwhile contribution to society than it does at present. While it may not achieve the reform of many prisoners, it will at least give prisoners upon their discharge from prison, a better opportunity than exists at present of their becoming law abiding members of the community, if they choose to do so. It will also result in a more stable prison system, less vulnerable to repeated serious disturbances.

10.44 The achievement of this role, however, depends on there being a proper balance within prisons between security and control on the one hand and humanity and justice on the other.....

15.4 Our 12 recommendations are stated in paragraph 1.167. They are briefly explained in the subsequent paragraphs of that section.

15.5 *We recommend:*

1. Closer co-operation between the different parts of the Criminal Justice System. For this purpose a national forum and local committees should be established (paragraphs 1.169 to 1.172);

2. More visible leadership of the Prison Service by a Director General who is and is seen to be the operational head and in day to day charge of the Service. To achieve this there should be a published "compact" or "contract" given by Ministers to the Director General of the Prison Service, who should be responsible for the performance of that "contract" and publicly answerable for the day to day operations of the Prison Service (paragraphs 1.173 to 1.178);

3. Increased delegation of responsibility to Governors of establishments (paragraph 1.179);

4. An enhanced role for prison officers (paragraphs 1.180 to 1.182);

5. A "compact" or "contract" for each prisoner setting out the prisoner's expectations and responsibilities in the prison in which he or she is held (paragraphs 1.183 to 1.185);

6. A national system of Accredited Standards, with which, in time, each prison establishment would be required to comply (paragraphs 1.186 and 1.187);

7. A new Prison Rule that no establishment should hold more prisoners than is provided for in its certified normal level of accommodation, with provisions for Parliament to be informed if exceptionally there is to be a material departure from that rule (paragraphs 1.188 to 1.191);

8. A public commitment from Ministers setting a timetable to provide access to sanitation for all inmates at the earliest practicable date not later than February 1996 (paragraphs 1.192 and 1.193);

9. Better prospects for prisoners to maintain their links with families and the community through more visits and home leaves and through being located in community prisons as near to their homes as possible (paragraphs 1.194 to 1.196);

10. A division of prison establishments into small and more manageable and secure units (paragraphs 1.197 to 1.203);

11. A separate statement of purpose, separate conditions and generally a lower security categorisation for remand prisoners (paragraphs 1.204 to 1.206);

12. Improved standards of justice within prisons involving the giving of reasons to a prisoner for any decision which materially and adversely affects him; a grievance procedure and disciplinary proceedings which ensure that the Governor deals with most matters under his present powers; relieving Boards of Visitors of their adjudicatory role; and providing for final access to an independent Complaints Adjudicator (paragraphs 1.207 to 1.209).

Notes

1. Many critics of the prison system had called for a major independent inquiry for many years, pointing out that since the Gladstone Report at the end of the last century there had been no such critical review of the function of imprisonment in this country. (The May Committee, it will be remembered, was rather disappointing in this respect). It is sadly ironic that

it took the events of April 1990 to give the necessary impetus for the setting up of what effectively amounted to an unofficial Royal Commission on the prison system.

2.   The terms of reference for the inquiry were liberally construed by Woolf. He went beyond merely documenting the immediate causes and consequences of the most serious riots, by examining the structural reforms which were necessary to create a more just and secure system in the future. The inquiry received a vast amount of evidence, both oral and written. There were numerous meetings with prisoners, staff, individuals and organisations. There was also a series of public seminars. (For details of the methods used by the inquiry, see Rod Morgan, "Woolf in Retrospect and Prospect" (1991) 54 M.L.R. 249).

3.   It reflects much credit on the Woolf Report that it succeeded in winning the support and appreciation of many different groups. The inquiry was conducted in an open and thorough manner and the resulting conclusions were widely acclaimed. Some critics have observed that there was nothing particularly innovative about the Report's recommendations, many of which had been canvassed previously in various official reports and penological articles. However, the timing of the Report was crucial, together with the considerable authority which Woolf himself, and his chosen methodology, bestowed upon the Report.

The Government's response was swift with its White Paper, *Custody, Care and Justice*, Cm. 1647 (1991), in which support for Woolf was also expressed. It states (at para. 13):

> "The Woolf Report has made a considerable contribution to deter-
> mining the Government's policy for the Prison Service. The Govern-
> ment accepts the central propositions in the Report that security and
> control must be kept in balance with justice and humanity and that
> each must be set at the right level. It has examined closely each of the
> 12 central recommendations in the Report and all of its 204 supporting
> proposals. The Woolf Report describes the recommendations as sign-
> posts setting the direction for the Prison Service in the years ahead.
> The Government has accepted the direction set by those rec-
> ommendations. It has accepted the principal proposals which identify
> the route to follow."

4.   To some extent, the appeal of the Woolf Report's conclusions lies in the fact that they deal with general principles rather than operational details. They also attract support from people with quite differing views on the priorities which should determine the task of the Prison Service. This point is developed in the extract which follows.

Prisons After Woolf, **(E. Player and M. Jenkins eds., 1994) Introduction, pp. 11–14.**

The Woolf Report was published virtually twenty-five years after the Mountbatten Report (Home Office 1966). The intervening quarter-century had been a maelstrom for prisoners, prison staff and administrators. The demise of the rehabilitative ethos at the beginning of this period had left the Prison Service without a clearly defined mission. The May Committee (Home Office 1979) argued for "positive custody" but the Service seemed to settle for "humane containment" and often failed to achieve even that. In consequence, the task of prison staff came to be seen, at best, as an exercise in damage-limitation, so little confidence was there in the value of imprisonment. This ideological crisis coincided with a period of considerable organisational strain, brought about by the relentless growth in the numbers of prisoners, the deterioration of prison buildings and an operational preoccupation with issues of security and dangerousness. Against this backdrop industrial relations within the Prison Service deteriorated and industrial action by prison officers came to dominate the agenda for those responsible for running the Prison Service. The old dilemmas about what to do with prisoners were unceremoniously overtaken by a new and compelling urgency to do something about staff. Woolf acknowledged at the outset that: "The Prison Service had already started to tackle some of the worst features of the prison system ... Long term problems were, for the first time being confronted" (para. 1.6). Fresh Start provided a new deal for prison officers and governors. Faith in a new managerialism took hold: governor grades were reincarnated as prison "managers", who worked to achieve "corporate objectives", within a re-designed public service. Such changes brought problems as well as dividends, as Woolf concluded the paragraph above: "However, as often happens at times of change, the improvements that were being introduced brought with them periods of increased instability which made the prison system particularly vulnerable to disturbances. The riots interrupted that process of improvements" (para. 1.6).

A fundamental truth unearthed by Woolf during the course of his Inquiry was that many of those involved in prisons shared a common perspective on what was wrong with the system. Priorities differed, as did the detailed proposals for reform, but, by painting with a broad brush, Woolf succeeded in highlighting the common ground and skirting around the cracks of division. However, agreeing on the signposts and the general route to be followed is considerably less controversial than agreeing on the particular methods of transport and the timing of the journey. In addressing potentially controversial questions about the objectives which prisons should pursue, Woolf does not delve into an examination of the competing theoretical justifications and purposes of imprisonment, but adopts what might be described as a more pragmatic approach. He accepts, as given, the principles set out in the Prison Service's Statement of Purpose:

> The Statement of Purpose recognises that the Prison Service has three tasks: (a) to keep secure those whom the courts put in their custody; (b) to treat those who are in their custody with humanity; and (c) to look after those in its custody in such a way as to help them to "lead law abiding and useful lives" (i) while they are in custody and (ii) after release. (para. 10.11)

Woolf stresses, however, that these tasks must be construed within the context of the criminal justice system as a whole and maintains that there are certain consequences which flow from this for their interpretation and realisation. The first of these is that prisons should operate less introspectively and demonstrate an awareness of a common purpose shared with other members of the criminal justice system. Thus, a primary objective of the Prison Service should be to ensure that prisoners are treated with justice. Woolf argues that the condensed language of the Statement of Purpose does not place sufficient emphasis upon this obligation. The Report notes that although there is a requirement to treat prisoners with "humanity", this is not necessarily synonymous with "justice" and that the Prison Rules should be amended accordingly (para. 10.23). Woolf's definition of justice extends beyond issues of procedure and due process to encompass prison conditions: "If the Prison

Service contains that prisoner in conditions which are inhumane or degrading ...
then a punishment of imprisonment which was justly imposed, will result in injustice"
(para. 10.19). Since the Woolf Report, the Government has agreed to the publication
of the Report of the European Committee for the Prevention of Torture and
Inhuman or Degrading Treatment or Punishment (Council of Europe 1991). This
condemned conditions in three large local prisons in England as both inhuman and
degrading. The Government's response pointed to improvements being made and
rejected the Committee's judgements.

Woolf also insists that, as an integral component of the criminal justice system,
the Prison Service has an obligation to discourage crime and reduce the likelihood
of reoffending, especially by co-operating with the Probation Service in delivering
effective throughcare. The Report, however, draws a distinction between the old
discredited model of rehabilitative *treatment* whereby the offender was sentenced to
imprisonment *for* reformative treatment, and the new rehabilitative approach. This
can be accommodated within the sentencing framework of "just deserts" and is
based not upon a concept of treatment, but on *providing opportunities* for prisoners
to minimise the negative effects of custody and to prepare themselves for release
without recourse to further offending. Hence, it is the promotion of individual
responsibility and the prevention of "a creeping and all pervading dependency by
prisoners on the prison authorities" (para. 14.13), that imbues and characterises
Woolf's conception of the rehabilitative task.

Finally, Woolf acknowledges that, as part of the criminal justice system, prisons
must be seen to uphold law and order, and that a central task for the Prison Service
in this respect is the maintenance of security within establishments. He emphasises,
however, that "attention paid to security should not be at the expense of the other
aspects of the role of the Prison Service" (para. 10.39).

Working from the existing Statement of Purpose Woolf reaches a synthesis,
namely "a proper balance between security and control on the one hand and
humanity and justice on the other" (para. 10.44). This synthesis of ideas, painted
with a broad brush and at this particular juncture in history, is at the heart of
Woolf's successful reception. First the Report gives hope, reinforcement and
direction to those who aspire to the re-establishment of a rehabilitative purpose
in prisons. Doubtless this tradition was never totally abandoned, although the
disillusionment surrounding its unfulfilled expectations arguably drove its expression
underground. Second, despite appeasing this particular sector of consumer interest,
Woolf skilfully avoids alienating the potentially competing faction of the "law and
order" lobby. The task of looking after prisoners with humanity and helping them
to lead law-abiding and useful lives is presented in the Report not as a wishy-washy
act of do-gooding, but as an obligation on the part of the Prison Service to protect
society by helping to reduce reoffending. The Report's proposals on how this should
be accomplished also help to allay anxieties that Woolf is soft on offenders. The
emphasis he and Tumim place upon enabling prisoners to be held responsible and
accountable for what happens to them in prison is wholly consistent with the
neo-libertarian ideology current within the Conservative Party. Indeed the then
Home Secretary, Kenneth Baker, speaking at the publication of *Custody, Care and
Justice*, announced that the White Paper was entirely consistent with the principles and proposals set out in the Citizen's Charter. Finally, the third constituency
with which Woolf establishes a rapport may be described as the "justice" lobby.
By emphasising the need to redress the existing imbalance between security,
control and justice, Woolf deliberately raises the profile of justice in prisons and
enhances its status as a critical objective which the Prison Service must achieve
in order to ameliorate the existing crisis. In so doing he advocates the other side
of the libertarian coin which specifies the duties and obligations which the state
owes to the citizen, or in this case, the prison authorities owe to the individual
prisoner.

Notes
1.   The authors suggest that it is the "synthesis of ideas" which is the key
to the Woolf Report's favourable reception: put simply, there is something
in it for everyone.
2.   What lessons did the Woolf Report think could be learned from the
disturbances of 1990? It was stated (at para. 9.23) that "there is no single
cause of riots and no simple solution or action which will prevent rioting."
Woolf argued (at para. 9.19) that in order to achieve a stable prison system,
there are three essential requirements: security, control and justice. There
needs to be a balance maintained between these three elements, each of
which has to receive sufficient attention. Failure to achieve this balance,
leads to an unstable prison system which then becomes susceptible to riots
and other disturbances, as evidenced by the events of April 1990. The
Report stated (at paras 9.24 *et seq*):

> "A recurring theme in the evidence from prisoners who may have
> instigated, and who were involved in, the riots was that their actions
> were a response to the manner in which they were treated by the prison
> system. Although they did not always use these terms, they felt a lack
> of justice. If what they say is true, the failure of the Prison Service to
> fulfil its responsibilities to act with justice created in 1990 serious
> difficulties in maintaining security and control in prisons ... The
> evidence of prisoners is that they will not join in disturbances in any
> numbers if they feel conditions are reasonable and relationships are
> satisfactory. These are matters which the Prison Service must address
> more closely. They are fundamental to maintaining a stable prison
> system which is able to withstand and reject the depredations of
> disruptive and violent individuals ... There are undoubtedly within the
> prison system of this country a number of prisoners who, given the
> opportunity and whatever the conditions within the prison, would seek
> either to escape or to be disruptive. No improvement in the conditions
> of containment will alter this situation. For this group of prisoners, a
> reasonable and effective degree of security is needed. The prison system
> has to be managed in a way which will enable the required degree of
> security and control to be provided. But even for these prisoners, it is
> important that a proper balance is struck. No more security safeguards
> should be applied than are strictly required. No more control should
> be exercised than is necessary. Excessive security and control can have
> the opposite effect to the ones desired. Prisoners will feel unnecessarily
> oppressed. They will feel a genuine grievance which will attract sym-
> pathy and support from their fellow inmates."

It is clear from this that Woolf thought that security and control had
been over-emphasised in the past, with insufficient attention given to the
requirement of justice.
3.   Amongst the many positive suggestions for improving the prison system
advocated by Woolf, it is worth highlighting his support for community

prisons – prisons which are physically close to, and have close connections with, the community from which their inmates are drawn. (See Woolf Report, para. 11.49 *et seq.* Also see, *Doing Time or Using Time*, Report of a Review by HM Chief Inspector of Prisons, Cm. 2128 (1993)). After listing the obvious practical advantages to prisoners in being in a local prison, the Woolf Report continued (at paras. 11.56–11.66):

"The fact that the prison is within reasonably close proximity to the prisoner's home has further advantages. It assists in preparing a prisoner for release and when he is released from prison. Arrangements can be made more easily to ensure that, as far as practical, he will receive support when he returns to the community. Accommodation or jobs will be more easily found. The probation officer or the prison officer involved in a pre-release scheme will be in a much better position to assist ... The case for a community style prison is further strengthened when it is recognised that the majority of the prison population are in prison for a relatively short period of time.

... There is one further important factor which was identified from the disturbances considered in Part I of this Inquiry [*i.e.*] the disturbing effect which the transfer of prisoners had on prisoners. If the community prisons are provided with small units, that should enable a broader range of regimes to be offered within prisons nearer to the prisoner's home. The Prison Service should then be able to plan a prisoner's sentence in a way which avoids his being moved so far from the community from which he comes. This would avoid the unsettling effect of a transfer away from his locality.

We therefore recommend that the Prison Service should adopt a policy objective of accommodating the majority of prisoners in community prisons. Local prisons already largely conform to this policy. Training and dispersal prisons frequently do not. With time, however, and by careful strategic planning of the prison estate, it should be possible to extend this policy in the long term to the majority of prisons.

In the long term, therefore, we envisage the majority of prisoners being held in prisons near to their homes. There would still need to be some specialist prisons ... but otherwise we would expect the principle of localisation to have precedence...

One way in which we think the Prison Service would be able to achieve the objective of community prisons is through the clustering of establishments within a particular locality or area. Within the cluster, it should be possible to provide the range of services and conditions which prisoners need. This would enable young offenders, remands and women prisoners to be held. Separately, it should also provide for the full range of security categories and for the full range of sentence lengths."

This important recommendation of the Woolf Report would, if followed, involve a significant departure from previous policy based on the "local" and "training" prison dichotomy. In its White Paper, *Custody, Care and Justice*, the Government wanted to retain flexibility in its use of resources and did not accept all of Woolf's ideas about the allocation of prisoners. Although the Government accepted that it was desirable "to hold prisoners in establishments which are near to their homes" (para. 5.4), it pointed out that this is only one of a number of competing aims in deciding on the allocation of prisoners. For example, allocation must also take into account the need to make the best use of available accommodation and to reduce overcrowding within the system.

4.   Although the Woolf Report met with general approval and support, it remains to be seen how much of a catalyst for change it will prove to be. (For recent HM Chief Inspector of Prisons reports, see Part V. of this chapter). Until problems of overcrowding are successfully dealt with by the courts relying less heavily on custodial sentences, and by reducing the length of those sentences where imprisonment is unavoidable, it is difficult to be optimistic about the prospects for the implementation of the Woolf Report's recommendations.

5.   Not all commentators were so impressed with the Woolf Report. The following extract is provided as an example of a more critical approach. The author starts by pointing out that the Woolf Report received "uncritical acclaim" and that his article aims to "deconstruct the hagiography surrounding the report" and provide a critical analysis of a number of Woolf's key recommendations.

Joe Sim, "Reforming the Penal Wasteland?", in *Prisons After Woolf*, (E. Player and M. Jenkins eds., 1994), pp. 35–6, 38–9, 41–5.

[On the subject of Woolf's methodology, and the contention that it was characterised by fairness in relation to the different parties giving evidence]...

    A close examination and rigorous deconstruction of the final Report raises some serious questions about this contention. Despite the apparent openness and fluidity in the Inquiry's methodology, it is clear that the accounts by prisoners were still treated with scepticism. In other words, whose account was to count in the last analysis was based on a hierarchical vision of penal truth in which the definition of reality articulated by the confined was secondary to the reality defined by state servants. There are a number of examples of this in the final draft of the Report which touch on some fundamental areas of prison life. For example, the scathing critique made by prisoners of the regime at Dartmoor – a critique which goes back to the nineteenth century – is significantly qualified by Woolf's remark that "it is important to remember these accounts by prisoners were not given on oath. They have not, unless they were given in oral evidence been subject to cross examination" (Woolf 1991, para. 5.27). Similarly, the Report cites a letter from one prisoner who argued that "if prisoners are treated like animals, sworn at, degraded and psychologically toyed with week after week, they in turn lose their respect for society at large" (para. 14.3). Once again, the Report qualifies the prisoner's testimony: "this letter reflects the prisoner's relationship with the Prison Service. We do not suggest that it accurately reflects the experience of all prisoners in prisons; or that it is an accurate and fair description of life in prison" (para. 14.4). Finally, prisoner's accounts of the Pucklechurch disturbance, in which they maintained that they were beaten and strip-searched, is again heavily qualified. At the same time, the Report points to the limitations of the inquiry in confronting these issues:

> It is possible that some of the screams and yells of pain which were allegedly heard by inmates could be attributed to the use of C and R [Control and Restraint] holds. It is accepted that C and R was used for bringing some prisoners into the cells. Others' screams and yells might have been deliberately misleading – "put on" by inmates who wanted to make out that they were being hurt. For the reasons I explained at the public hearing and set out in Section 2 of this Report, it is not possible for me to make any findings about these allegations. I am conscious, however, that my inability to do so would be unfair to staff who were not in a position to rebut these and other allegations which were made in public. This is, I am afraid, a limitation of an inquiry of this sort – it is not practical to do more than record the fact of the allegations and the fact, which is equally important, that they are denied. (para. 8.142)

In contrast, no such qualifications are made with respect to the evidence given by state servants in general and prison officers in particular. Thus, the Report notes that "the overwhelming impression created by [Prison Service staff] evidence is that the vast majority of the staff have a deep sense of loyalty to the Prison Service. They have a genuine desire to see conditions for prisoners improve" (para. 13.2). This uncritical acceptance of staff benevolence can be contrasted with the evidence contained both in the Report itself and more widely in prisoners' autobiographies as well as in the critical sociology literature on prisons. In the Report, Woolf notes that the largest number of comments in the prisoners' letters were about prison officers. The subject was "mentioned in 294 letters, 245 of these letters (40 per cent of all respondents) were critical and 49 (8 per cent) favourable or neutral" (Annex 2E, Ch. 2, para. II2). Even when a "small minority" of prison officers are criticised for "irresponsible behaviour" as after the Pucklechurch demonstration – the behaviour involved telling surrendering prisoners that their arms and legs would be broken – this is again done with some heavy qualifications....

... The third dimension I wish to highlight is Woolf's argument concerning the responsible prisoner and prison contracts. Both are central to his vision for future penal arrangements.

The following extract provides a clear illustration of how the responsible prisoner is to be conceptualised:

> Prisoners must ... be given the opportunity to make choices. They must be held accountable for those choices. Prisoners must come to recognise that it is for them to make positive use of their sentence. They should have a responsibility for how they serve their sentence and for how they will live after release. It is right that the Prison Service should provide every opportunity for prisoners to exercise that responsibility. (para. 14.14)

The concept of responsibility is underpinned by a second recommendation, the introduction of prison contracts. The report argues that a series of contracts should be established which would specify the obligations of the state to its servants and to the confined. Area managers, for example, would have a contract with prison governors which among other things "would be a statement of what the establishment should be achieving during the year ahead and what it should be seeking to do in the longer-term" (para. 15.35). Prisoners would also receive contracts:

> In that "contract", the establishment would state in as precise terms as possible, what it would provide for the prisoner. In return, the prisoner would agree to comply with the responsibilities which the "contract" placed upon him ... The prisoner would also receive progressively more under the contract as he

> progressed through his sentence. On the other hand, he could lose for a period
> of time some of the features of his "contract" in consequence of a finding of
> ill discipline. (paras. 12.120–12.122)

Woolf's construction of the responsible prisoner and the social contract between
the state and the confined has added another dimension to the current debate
concerning the relationship between the free market and the process of punishment.
The classical liberal notion of free-floating, responsible individuals contracted to the
wider society through the neutral arbitration of state authority has thus worked its
way into the discourse of twentieth-century penal reform. However, as a number of
writers have pointed out, this classical conceptualisation of human behaviour, and
the philosophy of utilitarianism which underpins it, is problematic. These writers
have noted how classical liberalism failed to consider the material impact of wider
structural relationships on individuals living in a grossly unequal society. Choice
for many was (and is) severely restricted because of the divisions which flow from
these structural relationships which are manifested along the fault lines of social
class, gender, race, age and sexuality. Within this model, the state, despite its
inherent contradictions and dislocations, reinforces these divisions. I do not intend to
pursue this argument here as it has been well documented and analysed elsewhere....
   In the final part of this chapter I want briefly to explore the dynamics of the
Woolf Report from another angle, and to position it within the broader context of
the direction of penal policy and the state in the 1990s. There are two problems in
particular that I wish to highlight. The first is concerned with the relationship
between the Report's recommendations and the ongoing issues of discipline and
coercion which lie at the heart of contemporary penality. The second problem
relates to the place of the prison in the wider context of developments within the
state in the last decade, particularly the consolidation of what has been termed the
"strong" or "authoritarian" state and the concomitant subversion of the brittle
structures of democratic accountability and civil liberties within the institutions of
state and civil society. As I shall illustrate, the model of accountability, which is
mainly implied rather than clearly explicated in Woolf, will do little to confront this
broader issue and may ultimately reinforce the drive towards the centralisation of
social authority and power through the ideological dressage of limited penal reform.
   I noted at the beginning of this chapter how the Woolf Report had transcended
the divisions between politicians, penal reformers and media personnel and how it
united the different interests of these groups on the ideological terrain of penal
reform. However, in concentrating on what they understood to be the positive
aspects of the Inquiry these commentators missed an obvious and crucial sociological
point, namely that many politicians and state servants – despite the contradictions
and conflicts between them – are still committed to maintaining the prison's social
order through repression. The coercive strategies discussed above, which have been
utilised in the last twenty-five years and which have often brought further dislocation,
none the less remain central in the repertoire of responses available when the
"exhaustion of consent" leads to the breakdown of institutional authority and
control. The solutions offered by Woolf to deal with the crisis are unlikely to
marginalise the ideological and material support for these strategies. Indeed in his
speech in the House of Commons on the day that Woolf reported, Kenneth Baker,
the then Home Secretary, was quite explicit about the message that prisoners and
those in the wider society should receive. After condemning "utterly the small
minority of the prisoners who joined in [the] orgy of destruction" at Strangeways
and other prisons, he then outlined the reforms which had been introduced following
the disturbances. These included: establishing a new incident control centre; over-
hauling contingency plans; clarifying lines of responsibility; training more staff in
the new and improved techniques of riot control; increasing the stock of riot-control
equipment; and reviewing the physical security of prisons. He went on to point out:

The country will not tolerate the kind of disgraceful behaviour witnessed last April. We must make clear our utter condemnation of it by introducing a new deterrent. We shall therefore, as we have already made clear, bring before the House proposals to create a new offence of prison mutiny, which will carry a maximum penalty of 10 extra years in prison. (Hansard February 25, 1991, col. 659)

Finally, he referred to the prison building programme, the jewel in the government's penal crown, and indicated that another 12 new prisons were to be opened by 1993. It was only after listing these changes that Baker turned to the issues which many prisoners had identified as important in the genesis of the disturbances: overcrowding, slopping out, the lack of rehabilitation and the fracturing of family ties (Hansard February 25, 1991, col. 660).

In September 1991 the Home Secretary reiterated his coercive intentions in his speech to the annual conference of the Boards of Visitors. He announced that the offence of prison mutiny would be included in the Queen's speech to Parliament and the nation the following November. Furthermore, he made it clear that

prisoners must understand that they will have to pay the price for rioting – by spending longer in prison and by waiting longer for improvements in prison conditions ... The repairs required will ... have to be made at the expense of other improvements the prisoners themselves would like to see. (*Guardian*, September 7, 1991)

He repeated this argument at the Conservative Party Conference in October and added some further dimensions to his vision of the prison's future: ten years for aiding and abetting escapes, a privately run prison, "plus the promise that prisoners will quickly learn that rioting was not 'a cost-free option'" (*Guardian*, October 10, 1991).

Baker's emphasis on maintaining order through coercion has been supported most notably by the Prison Officer's Association. At its annual conference in May 1990 the Association called for the establishment of an emergency task force of 1,000 officers to deal with prison disturbances...

The emphasis on paramilitarism can be seen in the Woolf Report itself. Woolf points to the advantages of the "new" Control and Restraint (C and R) techniques which have been developed to replace the infamous MUFTI techniques secretly introduced in the late 1970s. By April 1990, 2,234 members of staff had completed basic C and R training. The target was 4,200 staff who would then have refresher courses. Woolf hoped that "as standards within the prison system improve ... a reduction in the C and R training programme will be possible" (para. 9.92). At the same time, he concealed that the use of C and R techniques was "closely related to a military operation" (para. 12.152).

The marginalisation of coercion and discipline in recent debates about the future of the prisons and their subordination within Woolf's reformist rhetoric can be linked to a set of wider issues which are also marginalised in the Report but which are likely to have a crucial influence on the nature and form of imprisonment in the 1990s. In particular, there is the question of the democratic accountability of state institutions. Although the term tended to be used often uncritically in the late 1980s, it was none the less part of a key political debate which emerged during the decade in the UK and Europe where it was linked to the issues of citizenship and human rights. Within the UK this debate has had a particular reasonance in the context of more general sociological and political discussions about the emergence of the authoritarian or strong state. The consolidation of this state form can be seen not only in the criminal justice system through the centralisation of power, the militarisation of different institutions and the fracturing of already heavily circumscribed civil and political liberties but also within state welfare provision where the erosion of welfare rights has been legitimated through the ideological construction of the "genuine claimant".

The drive towards the centralisation of power and the concomitant marginalisation of democratic accountability in the 1980s, provides a sharp contrast to the evolutionary and highly conventional view of accountability implicit in the Woolf Report. The few references which mention accountability only underline the Report's conventional stance. Thus Woolf notes that "the Home Secretary, assisted by one of his junior Ministers, is directly responsible for all aspects of Prison Service work" (para. 12.35). This pluralistic, organisational model of the prison hierarchy can be contrasted with the critiques which have been made in relation to the problems associated specifically with prison accountability and the nature of power within the institution. More generally, it can also be contrasted with the failure of the parliamentary model of politics, which in its present form, has failed to deliver a sustainable model of accountability built on the regulation and control of state institutions and their servants....

... [I]t could be argued that it has been the failure of the parliamentary model of democracy to deliver a supportive, rights-based regime based on the accountability of those who manage the system that also contributed to the crisis behind the walls. Woolf's model of accountability will do little to challenge the perception held by the confined that there is little control, regulation or fairness within the system notwithstanding the principles of justice and independence which Woolf argues should be introduced into future penal arrangements....

... Taken together, the issues discussed in this chapter raise some serious questions about the viability of the Woolf Report to provide a programme that will tackle the prison crisis and deliver far-reaching and fundamental change. Already the portents for the future are not good. The sharp rise in the prison population in the first nine months of 1991, the continuing debate over the treatment of remand prisoners and the ongoing issues concerning deaths in custody have all been highlighted in one form or another since Woolf reported. In addition there have been further disturbances in Leicester, Moorland, Durham, Lindholme, Frankland, Everthorpe, Shotts and the Crumlin Road. These disturbances indicate that the troubling issues confronting the confined remain unresolved. At the same time their expectations that reforms – however limited – may be introduced in the wake of Woolf (and *Opportunity and Responsibility* (Scottish Office 1990) in Scotland) have been heightened. If the authorities fail to strike an ideological chord with the imprisoned by providing a vision for the future which deals humanely and seriously with these heightened expectations then they might find that the fire next time will burn even more severely in British prisons with catastrophic consequences for all concerned.

Notes

1. Perhaps the Woolf Report could have been more critical in places (for example, in relation to the role of prison staff) but it would have risked alienating various interest groups in the process. It is both a weakness and a strength of the report that it managed to appeal to such a wide cross-section of opinion. To try to avoid his recommendations being left on a shelf to gather dust, Woolf had to ensure that his methodology and findings were realistic from a political point of view.

2. Sim is correct to conclude that many of the grievances felt by inmates still persist. In November 1993, the Home Secretary, Michael Howard, announced stricter disciplinary powers for prison governors, insisting on "decent but austere" regimes in prisons. There also seems to have been

some abandonment on the part of the Government of its commitment to introducing minimum standards for all prisoners (see *The Observer*, April 17, 1994). With prison overcrowding once again threatening to overshadow the need for reform, the penal landscape remains bleak. There are also fears that the Criminal Justice and Public Order Act 1994 might lead to an increase in the number of people being imprisoned for minor offences and fine default. As well as condemning this as an injustice in itself, prison governors and other organisations within the criminal justice system are concerned that the new Act will increase the existing pressures on the prison system.

3.   After the armed attempted escape by a number of prisoners from the maximum-security Whitemoor Prison, in September 1994, considerable alarm was expressed about the lax security arrangements which existed in the prison. Shortly afterwards, the discovery of Semtex explosive and detonators added to this concern about Whitemoor's security. The chairman of the Boards of Prison Visitors criticised the Home Secretary for taking insufficient notice of the warnings that he had received about Whitemoor, both from its Board of Visitors and from an unpublished report by the Chief Inspector of Prisons. (The Tumim Report is thought to be highly critical of arrangements within the secure unit of the prison, and the too "cosy relationship" between prison staff and inmates. See *The Guardian*, September 23, 1994).

4.   Further prison escapes in January 1995, including that of three life sentence prisoners from Parkhurst maximum security jail, have not only embarrassed the government but have also increased the pressure on the Home Secretary to tighten security arrangements.

5.   In a report on Leeds Prison, published in February 1995, the Chief Inspector of Prisons stated that serious overcrowding has led to very unsatisfactory conditions. Judge Tumim could find little evidence of any progress since the earlier inspection of 1989. There appeared to be no immediate prospect of dealing with the overcrowding problem and the conditions inside the prison were found to be well below standard.

VII. Prison Populations

In February 1994, Lord Woolf warned that overcrowding in prisons was jeopardising the process of prison reform, stating that there were now 11 local prisons (mostly in the north west), in which the population was more than double the official capacity. The prison population in mid-February 1994 stood at 47,870, a figure which exceeded the system's official capacity by approximately 600. According to statistics published by the Howard League in February 1994, the Council of Europe placed Britain's use of imprisonment as the highest in western Europe, with 92.1 per 100,000 population subjected to imprisonment. This rate of imprisonment is sustained at considerable financial cost, both in terms of keeping an offender in prison and in terms of building new custodial institutions.

It is often argued that prison overcrowding is simply an inevitable consequence of rising rates of crime and that the prison system must be able to cater for this "demand". This is a seductive argument, as it would seem to be a matter of common sense that the crime rate and the size of the prison population are directly related. Yet such a relationship is not axiomatic. In some countries (including our own prior to 1939) the prison population has fallen at a time of rising levels of recorded crime. There are many ways in which offenders can be diverted or "filtered" out of the criminal justice process, and the success of various strategies for doing so, will be a crucial determinant of prison numbers. In his valuable study, *Prisons and the Process of Justice*, Andrew Rutherford uses three examples of prison systems which followed a reductionist path: England (1908–38), Japan (1950–75), and Holland (1950–75). His conclusions are presented in the following extract.

A. Rutherford, *Prisons and the Process of Justice* (1984), pp. 145–148.

Three examples have been described of prison populations being reduced and sustained at a new low level. Two general conditions have emerged. In each of the three countries, key decision-makers shared a profound scepticism as to what benefits, if any, derive from imprisonment. This viewpoint is exemplified by an official statement of the Japanese government in 1980, which held that although imprisonment ... "may achieve the correctional aims advanced to justify it, the disadvantages suffered by those undergoing imprisonment must not be overlooked. Indeed, the adverse effects are not limited to loss of liberty during confinement; imprisonment affects prisoners' social life after release, an aftermath from which their families are not exempt. Moreover, incarceration, particularly over a long period of time, weakens the ability of offenders to adapt themselves to society following release and destroys the foundation of free community life experience indispensible to reintegration into society. This in turn strongly enhances the likelihood that they will recidivate. It should also be stressed that indiscriminate and widespread use of imprisonment as a sanction against criminal conduct that is not truly serious not only imposes an unneeded financial burden on the community, but also dilutes the deterrent impact of imprisonment generally in potential criminals and thus may promote rather than hinder the commission of heinous or serious offences."

In the Netherlands widespread doubts as to the utility of prisons are expressed by many leading criminal justice practitioners who are well versed as to the negative research findings on imprisonment. One student of the Dutch penal scene has concluded: "... the judiciary in the Netherlands have evolved a distinctive occupational culture, central to which is the strongly negative value placed upon imprisonment, which is viewed as at best a necessary evil, and at least as a process likely to inflict progressive damage on a person's capacity to re-enter the community."

Likewise, in England between 1908 and 1938 there was considerable questioning of the prison system....

The second general conclusion to emerge from the three case examples is that the crucial factor in understanding changes in prison population is less the level of recorded crime or known offenders but, more significant, the responses to crime by officials engaged throughout the criminal justice process. Of particular importance, in the Netherlands and Japan the criminal courts have been insulated from the impact of increasing numbers of offenders as a consequence of action taken by public prosecutors. Prosecutorial decisions to dismiss charges have been one of the most important mechanisms for achieving and sustaining reductions in prison population size. In England, during the inter-war period, total numbers of persons dealt with by the courts remained fairly stable, but this was due to fewer offences cleared up by the police rather than shifts in prosecutorial practice. The critical intervening tactic was the movement away from custody in sentencing practice by the courts. In 1908, of all offences, indictable and non-indictable combined, 16 per cent received prison sentences compared with three per cent in 1938.

A further crucial component of the sustained low level of imprisonment in the Netherlands and Japan is a profound intolerance of overcrowding in prisons. In the Netherlands, since 1950 there has been a statutory prohibition on more than one prisoner being placed in a cell designed for one person. Under these circumstances, capacity acts as a powerful constraint on prison population growth and, in the absence of new construction, places a ceiling on prison population size. In Japan in the late 1940s there was also revulsion at the level of overcrowding which then existed. Total capacity of the prison system in Japan remained constant during the subsequent period of prison population decline, and by the mid-1960s there was much excess capacity.

By contrast, in England during the inter-war years capacity declined alongside a reduction in prison population size. Average daily prison population fell from 22,000 to 11,000 between 1908 and 1938, and capacity declined from 22,600 to 15,700. There was virtually no prison construction during this period, and indeed some 25 prisons were closed. In the English case, however, it is doubtful that capacity would at that time have acted as a brake on population growth. There was overcrowding at various times during the nineteenth century and first decade of the twentieth century, and excess capacity in the period up to the Second World War. Once prison population expansion got underway soon after the Second World War, overcrowding quickly reappeared. The high tolerance for crowding in England played an important part in the expansionist phase which began after 1945. It is crucial to understand why tolerance for prison overcrowding should differ so markedly from one country to another.

The experiences of the three prison systems examined [here] demonstrate that although reductionist policies can be pursued successfully there remain powerful tendencies towards expansion. The thirty-year reductionist phase of the English prison system was followed by a phase of relentless expansion which has persisted for over forty years. As a rate per 100,000 inhabitants the prison population is rapidly approaching what it was at its earlier zenith of the mid-nineteenth century. The contrast of two phases of the English prison system, 1908–38 and the period since 1945, provides a sober reminder of the inherent problem of sustaining reductionist initiatives. Similarly, in the Netherlands and Japan contemporary strains on the prison system in part reflect new criminal justice concerns such as the increased processing of drug-related offences. The availability of the prison system makes it especially vulnerable to new uses and serves to discourage inventive thinking as to alternative resolution.

Notes

1. Rutherford stresses that, in order to achieve reduction and to sustain low levels of imprisonment, central figures in the criminal justice system must entertain profound doubts about the practical utility of imprisoning offenders. As many of those involved in running our penal system have been overtly critical of prison conditions, and the wastefulness of imprisonment in human terms, it is surprising that a successful reductionist programme has not been implemented in this country. Although there was some optimism

in the early 1990s that prison numbers could be reduced, this seems to have been short-lived. As we have seen, it has proved difficult to restrict sentencing discretion in the use of imprisonment and there is still the problem that some politicians equate the use of imprisonment, and "austere" regimes within prisons, with a positive "get tough" approach to dealing with rising crime rates. This has led the current Home Secretary, Michael Howard, to claim that imprisonment does deter and to emphasise the paramount need to protect the public. This could lead one to question whether the lessons of April 1990 have been learnt. Recent events have led to Lord Woolf's timely reminder to the Government that the "corrosive influence" of overcrowding was undermining recent reforms, adding:

> "For the majority of offences prison is an immensely expensive process and should be reserved only for those for whom it is appropriate. As a result of the change in climate the importance of avoiding custody where it is appropriate to do so has been forgotten. The increase in the prison population is an expensive way of making the criminal justice system even less effective" (*The Guardian*, February 3, 1994).

Lord Woolf also warned that overcrowding resulted in many prisoners being incarcerated a long way from their home areas. He stated that "we are building up a significant number of prisoners who have a justifiable grudge against the prison department who have made them move so far from home."
2.   In his final chapter, Rutherford lists nine items on the reductionist agenda (at pp. 175–176), as follows:

> "The physical capacity of the prison system should be substantially reduced. There should be a precise statement of minimum standards as to the physical conditions of imprisonment and these should be legally enforceable. The optimal prison system staff-to-prisoner ratio should be determined and implemented. The prison system should have at its disposal early release mechanisms and use these to avoid overcrowding. Certain categories of persons sentenced to imprisonment should, if space be not immediately available, wait until called up by the prison system. Sentencing discretion should be structured towards use of the least restrictive sanction. Breach or default of non-custodial sanctions should only exceptionally be dealt with by imprisonment. The range of non-imprisonable offences should be widened to include certain categories of theft. The scope of the criminal law should be considerably narrowed."

Some of the above suggestions have been adopted, but with varying degrees of commitment. For example, the White Paper *Custody, Care and Justice* Cm. 1647 (1991), stated that the Government shared the view of the Woolf Report, and of successive Chief Inspectors of Prisons, that priority should be given to providing sanitation for all prisoners. It stated (at para. 6.8) that by the end of 1994 all prisoners within the prison system will have access to sanitation at all times. The White Paper stated:

> "The scale of this work will inevitably involve a temporary loss of places and therefore short-term pressures, but the work will be carried out as speedily as possible. The temporary pressures on prison places will be more than justified by the assurance that no prisoner will have to endure the inhumane and degrading practice of slopping out after the end of 1994" (para. 6.8).

This commitment by the Government was an important one in view of the critical findings of the Council of Europe's Committee for the Prevention of Torture or Degrading Treatment or Punishment which inspected British prisons in 1990. In its report (December, 1991), the Committee expressed its concern about the overcrowding, lack of sanitation and inadequate regime activities in some local prisons. Yet, in February 1994, the Home Secretary announced that the Government would not be able to meet its promise to end slopping out for all prisoners by the end of 1994. It was anticipated that it will now take until February 1996 to honour its commitment. One of the reasons given for this delay, was that resources were being diverted to create a further 2,000 places in prison. The Government, in 1991, also rejected a recommendation of the Council of Europe Committee (see above) that a limit be set on each prison's population to prevent excessive overcrowding.

3.   The English prison system once more appears to be set on an expansionist course. Revised official estimates predict that the prison population will soon exceed 50,000 and perhaps reach 55,000 by the end of the 1990s. (For further details of recent increases in the prison population, see the Prison Reform Trust's *Prison Overcrowding: A Crisis Waiting in the Wings*, (1993)).

4.   It is generally assumed that Britain's rate of imprisonment, which is the highest in Western Europe, reflects an excessively punitive response to crime in this country. For example, the director of the Howard League, Frances Crook, recently stated:

> "For over a decade the Government's criminal justice policies have relied on punishment and retribution, and have placed prison at the centre of the process. The UK has a larger prison population than any other country in Europe. This scandal will only get worse if the Government pursues its current prison-centred policies. The hysterically tough posturing by the current Home Secretary is bringing international opprobrium whilst it is singularly ineffective." (*The Guardian*, February 15, 1994).

However, there are some expert commentators who challenge the conventional assumptions about Britain's use of imprisonment. In a recent article entitled "Changes in the Use of Imprisonment in England and Wales 1950–91", [1994] Crim. L.R. 316, Chris Nuttall and Ken Pease warn of the dangers of over-simplistic analyses of cross-national comparisons. The authors argue that the expression of prison use in terms of the number of prisoners per head of general population, which has led to assumptions about excessive severity in Britain, gives rise to problems of interpretation. National differences, the authors state, could be attributed, *inter alia*, "to country differences in age profile, crime rates, clearance rates, conviction rates, judicial severity, parole differences, or any combination of these and other factors" (p. 316).

Although no method of comparing national differences in the use of imprisonment is free from problems, it should be remembered that there are alternative methodologies to that of concentrating on the number of prisoners per head of general population. In a further article, Ken Pease explored alternative indices, for example the rate of imprisonment as a proportion of the number convicted, and he found that the various indices gave rise to very different impressions of national variations in the use of imprisonment. Interestingly, Britain did not emerge as punitive, in comparative terms, from this piece of research. (See K. Pease, "Punitiveness and Prison Populations: An International Comparison", *Justice of the Peace*, June 27, (1992) 405).

The following extract is taken from another recent article by the same author.

Ken Pease, "Cross-National Imprisonment Rates", B.J. Crim., Vol. 34, Special Issue, 1994, pp. 117–118; 125–129.

... The problem of interpretation becomes acute when differences in prison use are expressed in relation to national population, particularly since the inference of underlying differences in punitiveness is seldom far from the surface.

The measurement of prison use in this way has particular dangers in that there is often common political interest across a wide spectrum to characterise national use of imprisonment as excessive. Imprisonment is expensive and apparently unproductive, and control of its use commends itself to politicians and officials in Justice ministries. Likewise, penal reformers have traditionally espoused the cause of limiting the size of the prison population, alongside that of improving the conditions in which prisoners are held. In such diverse hands, the descriptive "more than elsewhere" tends to slide into the moral "too many". In the last analysis, the questions about the right amount of custody is a moral one, although it could be informed more than it now is by an understanding of the patterning of criminal careers. What should be avoided is the shrill assertion of national punitiveness on the strength of superficial interpretation. "Fewer prisoners than elsewhere" could still be too many. "More prisoners than elsewhere" could still be too few, according to taste. The academic's role is surely to break the issue down as far as possible for analysis, to enable a more informed debate to take place...

[the author then goes on to consider the notion of "punitiveness" in some detail]...

A Summary on "Punitiveness"

The purpose of the discussion of punitiveness above is twofold. First, it seeks to discredit the measurement of international differences in prison use by the conventional means; *i.e.*, by expressing prison population in relation to national population. Such measurement is useless for all practical and intellectual purposes.

Secondly, it seeks to suggest ways of presenting and manipulating data which provide usable, albeit partial, insights into what is happening in different national systems. Within the second, and more constructive, part of the purpose, what is argued for is calculation of a number of indices, and calculation of the likelihood of transitions between adjacent states to yield a more sophisticated understanding of the calibration or responses to crime. While superficial statistical accounts do good service as bullets for politicians to fire, they do a disservice for the reasoned development of criminal justice. Furthermore, they do little in the long term to advance the cause of penal reform in the United Kingdom, despite short-term shame evoked by the spurious conclusion that we are the penal sadists of Europe. At the time of writing, the Home Secretary has just announced legislative changes which will (*inter alia*) allows courts to punish persistent offenders more severely because of their record. A penal reform movement which yokes the cause of improving prison conditions so rigidly to the reduction of prisoner numbers is seriously compromised in *both* these purposes by the public mood which forced the Home Secretary to make his announcement.

If compelled to take a position on the current severity of the English/Welsh system, it would have to be that pronounced sentences *may* be marginally more severe than elsewhere in Europe, but that the severity of sentencing after taking account of the effects of discretionary release is, for all offences save homicide, lower than international practice generally, including those few European comparisons which are possible.

Remands: A Reappraisal
While the liberal consensus has been that English prison use has been too high by Western European standards, this has been less statistically marked for the remand than for the sentenced population. Put crudely, the superficial political interpretation invited by the figures has been that the United Kingdom keeps too many people in prison, but that the problem rests more with sentenced than remand populations. The 1985 Prison Information Bulletin of the Council of Europe, reproduced in Table 7, shows, in column 1, the percentages of the prison population on remand by country, which tends to confirm that impression. However, the figures are not comparable, since mainland European countries count a prisoner as being on remand after sentence until the last possible date for appeal against conviction has passed. In England and Wales, a sentenced prisoner is counted as such from day one of his or her sentence. To make the proper comparison between countries would require a detailed knowledge of the law on appeals against sentencing throughout Europe, knowledge which the author does not have. However, what is clear is that the English method of calculation overstates the proportion of the population under sentence and understates the proportion on remand relative to continental Europe. Column 2 of Table 7 recalculates the Council of Europe figures, reclassifying those serving the first four weeks of sentence in England and Wales (the period during which an appeal is possible) as remand prisoners, in order to facilitate more reasonable comparisons.

It will be seen that this markedly changes the observed composition of the prison population for England and Wales, and makes the remand population a more significant factor in determining the size of UK prison populations in comparison with others. It therefore also has the effect, not observable from Table 7, of reducing the contribution of the sentenced population. This makes the system severity of England and Wales rather less than in the more conventional presentation, and strengthens the tentative conclusions reached earlier in this paper.

International Comparisons: Playing to the Strengths
International comparisons allow many points of contrast or similarity to be identified. Of particular interest are cases where countries that one would take to be

TABLE 7 *Proportion of Prison Population on Remand*
1985*

Country	Uncorrected remand (%)	Corrected remand (%)
Iceland	6	6
Cyprus	6	6
Ireland	6	6
Sweden	18	18
N. Ireland	19	24
Scotland	22	31
England/Wales	23	32
Austria	23	23
Switzerland	23	23
Denmark	23	23
W. Germany	24	24
Greece	24	24
Norway	25	25
Belgium	31	31
Malta	33	33
Luxembourg	35	35
Turkey	35	35
Netherlands	36	36
Portugal	37	37
Spain	50	50
France	51	51
Italy	64	64

* As presented in the original *Council of Europe Bulletin* (col. 2) and as corrected to take account of different status of prisoners eligible to appeal.

similar differ markedly in some penal practice. Such a contrast should never be taken at face value, but should be the starting point for more detailed comparison. The other category of comparison which may be thought especially interesting is where there is a change across most countries in most regimes of the world.

As an instance of the first type of comparison, preference for different sizes of prison can be identified, for which data are presented as Table 8.

From this it will be noted that there is a Northern European preference for small institutions and an apparent mid and Eastern European preference for larger institutions. In this comparison, the United Kingdom seems closer to the mid-European than the Northern European pattern. Apart from this specific identification of an unexpected difference, the comparison as a whole is intrinsically interesting, given Farrington and Nuttall's (1980) identification of prison size as a possible factor leading to criminogenic effects for those housed therein.

Another comparison of interest concerns the composition of prison staff by function, which is presented as Table 9.

While there are obvious ambiguities surrounding staff not included in the table (designated as "other staff" by responding countries), the table damages some possible preconceptions, such as the relationship between penal "treatment" and the reputation for penal liberality. Bulgaria and Poland, for example, have a higher proportion of treatment staff in prisons than countries like Denmark and Finland. The Netherlands is the only country in the table with both a reputation for penal liberality and a high proportion of staff designated as having a treatment function. It does seem that countries with a liberal reputation are characterised more by richness of staffing (a large number of staff per prisoner) than a treatment ethos, at least as reflected in declared staff function. This kind of analysis of system function

TABLE 8 *Percentages of Penal Institutions by Size*

Country	0–99 places	100–499 places	500–999 places	1,000 + places	No. of prisons
Austria	11	78	11	0	32
Bulgaria	24	31	38	7	29
Denmark	83	16	1	0	63
W. Germany	28	50	18	4	153
Finland	19	81	0	0	16
Italy	73	24	2	2	385
Netherlands	62	38	0	0	60
Norway	83	17	0	0	46
Poland	8	60	19	12	213
Portugal	53	39	8	0	38
Switzerland	93	7	0	0	144
UK	10	67	20	3	100

Source: Responses to Third United Nations Crime Survey.

has more potential for informing change than those more commonly encountered. It could be taken further even within the limits of the United Nations Surveys and would hopefully form the basis of a new generation of cross-national comparisons. The development of the United Nations Criminal Justice Information Network is likely to make secondary analysis of international data sets much easier than hitherto and is to be warmly welcomed. The close analysis of disparities in experience between relatively similar countries is also the motif of a forthcoming review of the literature and the addition of new analyses by Warren Young.

An example of the second type of comparison, where a surprising uniformity of change is found across nations, is that concerning the involvement of women in criminal justice as processed offenders. This reveals that over the years from 1975

TABLE 9 *Prison Staff in 1986, Total, by Function and Number of Prisoners per Staff Member*

Country	Manager (%)	Custody (%)	Treat- ment (%)	Prisoners per staff member
Austria	3	90	6	2.5
Bulgaria	6	58	13	6.1
Cyprus	5	90	3	1.2
Denmark	10	65	8	0.9
Finland	18	60	8	1.7
France	9	80	8	2.7
FRG	13	72	7	2.0
Greece	10	85	4	3.3
Italy	6	75	14	1.1
Netherlands	2	61	19	–
Norway	22	65	2	1.3
Poland	2	53	16	4.5
Portugal	1	68	7	2.3
England/Wales	14	72	8	1.8*
N. Ireland	11	66	3	–
Scotland	3	81	3	–

Source: Adapted from Pease and Hukkila 1990.
Note: The percentages do not sum to 100 because of the omission of "other staff".
* U.K. figure.

to 1986, women comprised an increasing proportion of those officially processed but not an increasing proportion of those in prison. This kind of analysis suggests something close to a worldwide movement in criminal justice. Further analyses of the same kind are to be undertaken comparing age distributions over time using United Nations Survey data.

Conclusions

The substantive views reached earlier in this paper are by no means to be regarded as settled conclusions. It does seem that the penal system in England and Wales is not punitive in some of the ways it was claimed to be. It does seem that discretionary release plays a huge part in moderating the extent of its intervention in the lives of convicted offenders so that less serious offenders are treated more leniently here than in many other countries. However, the purpose of the paper is not to express such views as determined fact (although the available evidence does point in the directions suggested) but to argue for more sensitive and imaginative use of comparative statistical data.

Cross-national comparison enlarges the repertoire of the nationally thinkable and is to be encouraged. Open-minded practitioners and applied academics visiting other countries return with notions of how to do things better or (which tends to the same end) motivated to think through the reasons for current national practice. Cross-national statistics of penal practice have proved of more doubtful benefit, not just because their undoubted distortions nullify their value, but also because their usual mode of presentation has (it is argued) been over-simple and misleading. Use of them has primarily been by those with a political or reformist point to make, and assertions made have been ignored or accepted by politicians and scholars, rather than forming the basis of a debate on their meaning and development. The availability of United Nations Survey data (information from the Fourth Survey will be available in 1994) makes possible a much wider and fuller secondary analysis of data allowing national comparison of penal practice. It is ardently hoped that use will be made of the data to inform national debate, and that more refined European or worldwide studies will be mounted to clarify and extend the lessons learned from the United Nations data. Some of the possible growth points in the United Nations data have been identified in this paper.

Notes
1.   The author provides a useful warning of the dangers of over-simple interpretation of cross-national prison statistics, especially where prison numbers are expressed in relation to national population. He observes that use of these statistics is often made by reformist groups to make a political point. However, there is little doubt that Britain's poor performance in European "league tables" of imprisonment, albeit a crude measure of comparison, is a useful political weapon in the hands of penal reformers right across the political spectrum.
2.   A country with a well established liberal reputation for its penal policy is the Netherlands. It is not surprising that our overcrowded prison system is often compared (unfavourably) with the more humane Dutch system. For a valuable discussion of Dutch penal policy since the second world war, see David Downes, "The Origins and Consequences of Dutch Penal Policy Since 1945" (1982) 22 B.J. Crim. 325, and also D. Downes, *Contrasts in Tolerance: Post-War Penal Policies in the Netherlands and England and*

Wales (1988). There has been much academic interest in the use made of imprisonment by various countries and the considerable differences in prison population from one system to another. For a review of the relevant literature, see W. Young, "Influences Upon the Use of Imprisonment: A Review of the Literature" (1986), 25 *Howard Journal*, 125 and, by the same author, "The Use of Imprisonment: Trends and Cross-National Comparisons", in *Crime and Justice* (M. Tonry and N. Morris, eds., 1994). Also of interest is C. Fitzmaurice and K. Pease, "Prison Sentences and Population: a Comparison of some European Countries", (1982) Justice of the Peace, 575; and J. P. Lynch, *Imprisonment in Four Countries* (1987).

3.   Discussion of the prison population tends to focus on the total number of people in prison, as opposed to the composition of that overall figure. Yet it is important to analyse the structure of the prison population in this country and to assess the extent to which it differs from the general population, for example in terms of age, sex, social class and ethnic group. Useful information on this and a number of other subjects can be found in the National Prison Survey of 1991. This survey was undertaken with three main objectives: to obtain systematic information about the background characteristics of prisoners, to study prisoners' perspectives on prison regimes and prison life, and to attempt to provide some insight into the roots of the prisoners' criminality. (See R. Walmsley *et al.*, *The National Prison Survey 1991 – Main Findings* (1992) Home Office Research Study 128).

Chapter Five

NON-CUSTODIAL SENTENCES

I. The Search for Alternatives to Imprisonment

Before looking at specific alternatives to imprisonment and other non-custodial penalties, it is interesting to consider the policies underlying the development of new penal measures. This subject is considered in the following extract which, though rather dated, provides a useful starting point.

R. Hood, "Criminology and Penal Change", in *Crime, Criminology and Public Policy* **(Hood ed., 1974), pp. 376–377.**

A quarter of a century of rising rates of recorded crime, of minimal progress in the provision of penal facilities which might give even the semblance of "treatment institutions" and the lack of evidence that longer incarceration increases the likelihood of reform have caused a retreat from ... penal optimism. Emphasis is no longer on providing measures which increase the opportunities for prisoners to be detained longer in order to achieve their reform ... The growth of serious crime has itself ensured an increasing prison population and an increased tariff of penalties. The problem has been to find means of restricting the use of imprisonment and of releasing those within through the parole system before they "deteriorate". Post-war penal policy has therefore been set upon a task of contriving alternatives to custody in a political climate where the increasing alarm about crime and the growing scepticism about the relevance of welfare measures ... has dispelled some of the earlier enthusiasms for dealing with the more serious offender within the community as a problem solely for social casework and supervision. In analysing recent changes in policy it is less difficult to understand why imprisonment is being seen as a punishment of "last resort" than it is to understand why *particular* alternatives have been devised for it ...

The problem of devising alternatives to imprisonment for those who have no claims for special treatment has been extremely difficulty. It might seem at first sight that the logical step would have been to expand the probation service so as to provide within the community a degree of supervision, control and social aid which apparently had formerly been the aim of their treatment within prison. But there seem to have been a number of reasons why this was not acceptable. First, whatever happened within prison (and it was rarely anything that could be called treatment anyway) the purpose of the sentence – whether short or long – had usually been to deter. Secondly, in the context of what was regarded as widespread public anxiety about crime, alternatives without a "bite" may not have been politically acceptable. Third, the constant repetition of the stereotype of the new affluent criminal created an image to which social casework hardly seemed appropriate. Fourth, and perhaps most important, in these circumstances it would have been hard for governments to justify a vastly increased expenditure on the "treatment" of offenders, on measures which were undoubtedly generally regarded as soft. Expenditure upon control was of course a difficult matter, public anxiety about that ensured there was no difficulty in expending very large sums on tightening security after the Mountbatten Report (1966) on the "scandal" of escapes. It is very unlikely that any government would have been able to spend this amount on the provision of professional or social services for improvements within prisons or outside. Generally speaking, expenditure on controlling crime is not in competition with expenditure on social services where those who have offended, a clientele with no political power, consistently have the lowest priority. In political terms it is not so surprising that the repeated claim that intensive social work is far less expensive than imprisonment still falls largely upon deaf ears...

[Hood then explains that he has made a particular study of the background to the introduction of suspended sentences and the community service order.]

... My argument is that the adoption of both these methods of punishment was due to the appeal of their ideologies and that, particularly in the case of community service, there was no attempt to justify the new penalty in terms of a coherent analysis of crime, criminal behaviour or the effects of penalties. In other words, the part played by criminological analysis, theory and research was minimal. Some would claim that this was inevitable because of the piecemeal way in which policy was formulated and argue instead for an overall analysis of the penal system in the light of knowledge about those who commit crime, in order that a consistent master-strategy could be implemented. Others would argue that there is no criminological knowledge which is of use in formulating legislation and that change can only be on a trial and error basis fully supported by evaluative research.

Notes

1.   Alternatives to imprisonment were therefore considered to be a matter of necessity from the 1960s onwards, in view of the overcrowding in custodial institutions. The theory was that sentencers required more options if they were to assist in keeping offenders out of prison. But what form were these new measures to take? They needed to satisfy various criteria, especially the semblance of being genuine alternatives to prison, whilst also being economically viable. For this reason, as Hood observes, the existing alternative of probation was unfashionable and its use by the courts declined quite sharply between the late 1960s and the end of the 1970s. (See: *Statistics of the Criminal Justice System England and Wales 1969–79*, pp. 67–9). It would seem, then, that the search for credible alternatives to imprisonment was driven more by political and pragmatic considerations than it was by criminological or penological research.

2.   Hood observes that some commentators claim "that change can only be on a trial and error basis" and that penal research is of limited value in formulating legislation. But there were ways in which comparative research might have been utilised to avoid certain pitfalls in the introduction of new measures. For example, the suspended sentence had been in use in some other countries for many years before its introduction here in 1968 (see Marc Ancel, *Suspended Sentence* (1971)), and there were valuable lessons to be learnt from the experience of those countries. There is also a need for a comprehensive understanding of the whole of the sentencing system when penal reform is contemplated. But, in practice, new measures were introduced in this country without such understanding and the resulting

confusion was perhaps inevitable. As Richard Sparks stated in his article, "The Use of the Suspended Sentence" [1971] Crim. L.R. 384 (at pp. 400–401):

> "In any case, a general lesson to be learned from the experience of the suspended sentence is surely that the established sentencing policies and practices of the courts must be understood, and taken into account, when a structural change in the penal system or in sentencing policy is contemplated. The measures which collectively comprise the English penal system do not function in isolation from one another, and allocation of offenders to these measures is in no sense random; the courts' own perceptions of their objectives, and of offenders will in the last resort largely determine the use which they make of any new form of sentence which is introduced. Experience with the suspended sentence to date suggests that these elementary penological facts cannot be ignored, when attempts to change the penal system are made."

3. Attempts to limit the use of imprisonment since the 1960s were also analysed in an essay by Anthony Bottoms in 1987, in which he stated that "England and Wales has now become well known internationally as a jurisdiction which, more than most, has attempted in the last twenty years to develop alternatives to custody." (See A. E. Bottoms, "Limiting Prison Use: Experience in England and Wales", (1987), 26 *Howard Journal*, at 177). Bottoms reviewed the introduction of suspended sentences, community service orders, and probation orders with special conditions. He pointed out that this policy has not been particularly successful in its primary aim of reducing the prison population, and also that there is little evidence to support the view that the gradual adoption of non-custodial measures will, in time, diminish the central importance of imprisonment within the penal system. The author concluded (at p. 198):

> "Some of the [new] measures seem in certain respects to have had some modest success, yet almost all of them can also be shown to have run into severe difficulties of one kind or another. Perhaps most significantly of all, at the end of this twenty-year period the prison population in England stands at a record high level.
> ... Not surprisingly, in such a situation those who wish actively to reduce the prison population in England see little point in pursuing further initiatives of the kind reported in this paper."

4. For an interesting assessment of the "alternatives to custody" policy see Anthony Vass, *Alternatives to Prison* (1990), especially Chapter 3, from which the following extract is taken.

A. Vass, *Alternatives to Prison* (1990), pp. 62–63; 65–66; 68–69; 71–73.

Support for alternatives to custody seems to be guided by a need to be optimistic, and to appear loyal to what, after all, is for most commentators a good cause: a need to offer more humane treatment, and to search for new ways in dealing with offenders which may not be totally effective and foolproof against failures or criticisms but which, nonetheless, are more appropriate and desirable than locking up people in prisons. The practice of resigning to the view that alternatives may not be that much "better" in terms of effectiveness than prisons and that not too much in terms of practical results should be expected from them, other than more humane treatment – and perhaps savings for the public purse – is shared by even some of the original, most fervent supporters of community-based penal programmes ... This apparent failure of alternatives to show in terms of measurement any substantial rehabilitative impact on offenders, and the unlimited urge expressed by politicians to search for new alternatives and methods of sanctioning offenders in the community led to predictions on both sides of the Atlantic that penal policy would experience a throwback to a philosophy of "just deserts" characterised by a more overt emphasis on punitive penal measures and with "punishment" being the new vogue word of the 1980s and beyond. In many respects, such a prophecy, at least in terms of expansion of the means of punishment and control, has come true – depending, of course, on one's perspective. Since the late 1970s, criminal justice policy has not only expanded on an unprecedented scale but has also shifted towards the more traditional conceptions of punishment and deterrence...

... It is apparent from what has been covered so far that a major justification for alternatives to custody is that financial savings are accrued by such methods of dealing with offenders. If they do not rehabilitate, or fail to act as true alternatives, they can at least save money for the public purse. In that respect, governments, as well as advocates of such penal measures, in the past and present, have put forward the proposition that alternatives are cheaper than custody and thus more desirable. Certainly the statistical evidence supports this proposition.

The available statistics which compare the costs of custodial versus non-custodial sentences are quite impressive: they do support the argument that alternatives *are* substantially cheaper than custodial establishments ... [F]rom the known figures and estimates supplied by official sources, the differences in costs between custody and alternatives are quite real. It costs, on average, £14,300 to keep a person in prison for a year at 1987–8 prices. In comparison, it costs about £700 to supervise an offender under the requirements of a community service order at 1986–7 prices!...

... Suggestions then that alternatives to custody are preferable because they are cheaper appear to be well founded. However, there are uncomfortable flaws in such a rigid interpretation. Arguments that alternatives are preferable to custodial institutions because they are more cost-effective must, if they are to bear any real credibility, be accompanied by either a clear *diversion* of resources from custodial institutions or by a formidable increase of expenditure in the field to accommodate the desirable measures. As has already become apparent, when the actual and projected expenditure by both central and local government is considered, the picture is far from satisfactory. Expenditure in the last 20 years (particularly since the early 1980s) on custodial institutions far outstrips the resources made available for the administration and expansion of alternatives to custody...

[The author then points out the difficulties in accurately estimating the relative costs of custodial and non-custodial measures].

... In addition to the reservations voiced that cost-benefits are hard to determine, there is also the less appreciated economic and political need to constantly reinforce the virtues of the cost-effectiveness of such measures by keeping them cheap. Claims which are often unjustified can be taken for granted and used by resource-allocation bodies (voluntary or statutory) as a basis for cutting back expenditure on community alternatives to prove that they are cheaper and to make savings. In effect, such a policy starves administrators and practitioners of the necessary funds and staff resources in dealing successfully with the demands and pressures of supervising offenders in the community. Indeed, as has always been the case, there is a lot of rhetoric about the desirability and cheapness of "community", but little practical illustration that governments are willing to demonstrate that belief through proper financial and other investment in community programmes. For instance, the classic example is that of closing down mental institutions, and thereby forcing the mentally ill to live not only rough in an "uncaring" community but also to find refuge – occasionally through their own choice as a matter of last resort in securing a roof over their heads – in prison establishments ... The panacea of community can thus be exploited by governments to abdicate their moral and financial responsibilities towards really viable alternatives to custodial institutions. It works on the principle of a self-fulfilling prophecy: community programmes are cheaper than custodial institutions. If they are cheaper, it means that a lot is being done and can be done through the community's goodwill and care. So, why spend more than we have to, when that would be a waste, and when the money can be used more profitably elsewhere? ... As the budget for community alternatives is cut, it keeps those alternatives cheap. In turn, that then filters through and appears in statistical form which in turn reinforces the original belief that community programmes are after all cheaper than custodial establishments.

Notes

1. Alternatives to imprisonment are certainly more humane and cheaper than custodial sentences and, in the case of "community" penalties, also more constructive. Whether they are more "effective" in rehabilitative terms is very difficult to assess. It is perhaps advisable to avoid the "nothing works" pessimism of the 1970s. (See A. Bottomley and K. Pease, *Crime and Punishment: Interpreting the Data* (1986), where the authors advocate a more open-minded approach to this issue). Generalisations on this subject should be avoided. Punishment, or treatment, is an interactive process and, as a matter of common sense, different individuals will respond differently to particular penalties. Some penal measures may have a positive effect on a particular type of person, but not on others. The length or severity of the penal measure may also lead to different results.

Measurement of "effectiveness" of penal measures is particularly problematic due to the fact that sentences reflect a variety of aims and functions. (For a useful review of the literature on evaluative research, see S. R. Brody, *The Effectiveness of Sentencing*, Home Office Research Study No. 35 (1976)). Researchers interested in the use of a particular sentence, or the outcome of a particular sentencing policy, first need to distinguish between the *effects* and the *effectiveness* of a particular measure. If any changes occur in an offender's circumstances or his personal relationships as a result of a particular sentence, these may be described as the effects of that sentence – which may be positive or negative. The efficacy or effectiveness of a measure is a narrower concept concerned with the degree of success (if any) achieved by the sentence in relation to what was intended by the sentencer. (For an interesting study of the impact of sentences on motoring offenders, and an attempt to draw a distinction between the effects and the effectiveness of sentences, see T. C. Willett, *Drivers After Sentence* (1973)).

Another major difficulty with the assessment of measures in terms of corrective efficacy is the notion of "correction". Not all sentencing measures are "penal" in a strict sense – contrast a sentence of imprisonment with a probation order – so on what basis can they be compared as "correctives"? How is "correction" to be measured: is it to be based solely on reconviction rates, or should we attempt to investigate more subtle changes in attitude and relationships on the part of the offender? The point was made in 1962, by the Morison Committee on the Probation Service (Cmnd. 1650, para. 22) which claimed that reconviction rates were a poor measure of assessing the rehabilitation of an offender and any positive change of attitudes which may have occurred. The Committee argued that the commission of a further offence might signify nothing more than a temporary setback in the rehabilitative process. Furthermore, if reconviction is to be used as a measure of corrective efficacy, then further questions have to be pursued. For example, how long has the offender gone before reconviction? Was the reconviction for an offence of a similar nature to the original crime – was it more, or less serious? (For a defence of the use of reconviction as a measure of corrective efficacy, see Nigel Walker, *Sentencing in a Rational Society* (1972) pp. 115–9. For a good account of methodological problems inherent in measuring the effectiveness of punishment, see R. Hood and R. Sparks, *Key Issues in Criminology* (1970), especially pp. 175–186).

2. The sentencing of offenders may express a variety of aims and objectives – such as satisfying public notions of justice, humanitarianism, public protection, and economy – apart from the correction of the offender. (See S. Brody, "Research into the Aims and Effectiveness of Sentencing" (1978) 17 *Howard Journal* 133). An obvious alternative to attempting to measure corrective efficacy is to compare sentences on the basis of their costs. However, as Vass observes, this needs to be done with some caution, as there are problems in obtaining reliable figures. The actual cost of any penal measure depends on the type of indirect or hidden expenses that are included.

In 1980, NACRO published the first comprehensive account of the costs of penal measures in this country: see Stephen Shaw, *An Analysis of the Cost of Penal Sanctions*. The author observed that his study was motivated, in part, by the disappointing results of research into reconviction rates and the need for new criteria for assessing sentences. One point which emerged clearly from Shaw's study is that in comparison to the direct costs of non- custodial penalties, custodial measures are very expensive. Moreover, the real cost of imprisonment, which includes "indirect" costs, is considerably greater than the simple direct prison budget would appear to indicate.

The regular publication of relative costs of penal measures, notwithstanding the problematic nature of these figures, plays a useful part in campaigning for less punitive sentencing policies. For example, the following comparative figures were published by NACRO in December 1992.

NACRO Briefing 23 (1992) *The Cost of Penal Measures*

In the financial year 1991/2, the average cost of keeping a person in prison in England and Wales was £442 per week. The costs ranged from £316 per week for open prisons to £807 per week for maximum security dispersal prisons, as follows:

	£
Local prisons and adult remand centres	437
Dispersal prisons	807
Category B training prisons	438
Category C training prisons	363
Open adult prisons	316
Closed youth establishments	452
Open youth establishments	551
Female establishments	629
Overall average	442

Staff costs accounted for 76 per cent of the net operating costs in penal establishments.

In the previous financial year 1990/1, the average cost of keeping a person in prison was £406 per week.

In comparison, the latest available figures for the costs of certain other penal measures are as follows:

Probation orders: In 1990/1, the estimated annual cost of supervising an offender on probation was £1,070.

Community service orders: In 1990/1, the estimated annual cost of supervising an offender on a community service order was some £920.

Attendance centres: The average cost of an attendance centre order in 1990 was estimated to have been £171.

Probation hostels: In 1990/1, the average annual cost to the Home Office of a place in an approved probation/bail hostel was £6,881. This represents 80 per cent of the total running costs of these hostels, the balance provided by payments from local authorities.

After-care hostels: In 1990/1, the average Home Office grant towards the cost of a place in a voluntary after-care hostel for offenders was £1,600.

Fines: Fines raise rather than cost money. The total income from fines, fees and fixed penalties collected by magistrates' courts in England and Wales in 1990/1 was £269,088,000.

Conclusion

Community penalties are significantly less expensive than imprisonment. The figures suggest that keeping an offender in prison for **three weeks** is more expensive than supervising him or her on community service for a year; that the weekly cost of prison is 20 times more than probation and 23 times more than community service; that three young offenders can be given attendance centre orders for about the same cost as keeping one person in a young offender institution for a week; and that even the most expensive community penalties, such as probation hostels, are only half the cost of prison. Fines actually bring in substantial income to the Exchequer.

However, further indirect if hidden costs are often involved in the administration of penalties, both custodial and non-custodial. Research by the Personal Social Services Research Unit at the University of Kent, taking into account these additional costs, has found that in Scotland supervising an offender on community service for a year cost approximately the same as imprisoning him or her for six weeks. (The comparative hidden costs would not necessarily be the same in England and Wales.)

Notes

1.   The above statistics were obtained from the *Report on the Work of the Prison Service 1991/2*, Cmnd. 2087 (1992) and from a number of answers to questions in Parliament.

2.   The introduction of alternatives to prison since the 1960s has not been particularly successful as a means of reducing the prison population. There has been a tendency for sentencers to use new measures, such as the suspended sentence or community service, not just as alternatives to imprisonment, but also as alternatives to other non-custodial penalties, such as fines or probation. This failure to persuade sentencers to use these new measures as intended has had counter-productive consequences, with many offenders ending up in prison (*e.g.* after the activation of their suspended sentence) for offences which, in the past, would not have led to their incarceration. (This is considered in more detail under the specific penal measures, below).

Despite these problems, the search for viable alternatives to imprisonment has continued. There has been a special enthusiasm for "community" based penalties. In the White Paper (1990), *Crime, Justice and Protecting the Public*, the government announced its plans for a re-structuring of the sentencing system. It stated that although those who committed very serious crimes should receive long prison sentences, "many other crimes can be punished in the community, with greater emphasis on bringing home to the criminal the consequences of his actions, compensation to the victim and reparation to the community" (para. 2.2). It was also stated that although imprisonment was justifiable in terms of public protection, denunciation and retribution, "it can be an expensive way of making bad people worse. The prospects of reforming offenders are usually much better if they stay in the community, provided the public is properly protected." (para. 2.7).

II. The Suspended Sentence

Technically, the suspended sentence is classified as a custodial sentence (*e.g.* see Powers of Criminal Courts Act 1973, s. 22(6)(a)), albeit one which will not be implemented if the offender stays out of trouble in the future. It is, therefore, a difficult sentence to categorise. Strictly speaking, it could be dealt with under the heading "custodial sentences". However, it was actually introduced as an *alternative* to imprisonment and, of course, it is non-custodial (in its effect) at the time the sentence is imposed upon the offender. The rationale of this measure is that it will have a deterrent effect on the offender, who will refrain from future law-breaking for fear of his suspended sentence being activated. As the dominant philosophy under the Criminal Justice Act 1991 is now that of "just deserts" (or proportionality), the present role of the suspended sentence in the sentencing repertoire is less assured than at the time of its introduction. The partly suspended sentence, introduced as recently as 1982, was abolished by the CJA 1991 (section 5(2)(b)). It remains to be seen how prominent a position the suspended sentence will occupy, in future, in the sentencing system (see below).

The suspended sentence of imprisonment was introduced under the Criminal Justice Act 1967, and the main provisions relating to its use are now contained in PCCA 1973, sections 22–5 (as amended, notably by CJA 1991, s. 5(1)). Briefly, a court may suspend a prison sentence of not more than two years for a period (the "operational period") of between one and two years. The "operational period" represents the length of time that the offender is at risk of having his sentence activated should he commit a further imprisonable offence (see PCCA 1973, s. 22(1)). The prison sentence will not be activated unless the offender commits another imprisonable offence within this period. But if a further imprisonable offence is committed, within the operational period, the offender is at risk of having the suspended prison sentence activated. The powers of a court in dealing with an offender who commits such a breach of a suspended sentence are set out in PCCA 1973 section 23(1), as amended by CJA 1982, s. 31:

> "Where an offender is convicted of an offence punishable with imprisonment committed during the operational period of a suspended sentence ... [the] court shall consider his case and deal with him by one of the following methods: –
>
> > (a) the court may order that the suspended sentence shall take effect with the original term unaltered;
> > (b) it may order that the sentence shall take effect with the substitution of a lesser term for the original term;
> > (c) it may by order vary the original order under section 22(1) of this Act by substituting for the period specified therein a period expiring not later than two years from the date of the variation; or
> > (d) it may make no order with respect to the suspended sentence;
>
> and a court shall make an order under paragraph (a) of this subsection unless the court is of the opinion that it would be unjust to do so in view of all the circumstances, including the facts of the subsequent offence, and where it is of that opinion the court shall state its reasons."

After the introduction of the suspended sentence in the late 1960s, it was stressed that a court should not pass a suspended sentence unless it was first satisfied that imprisonment was the appropriate way of dealing with the offender before going on to consider the question of suspension. (See *O'Keefe* [1969] 1 All E.R. 426 at pp. 427–8 and PCCA 1973, s. 22(2)). Important restrictions on the use of the suspended sentence are now contained in PCCA 1973, s. 22(2), as amended by the Criminal Justice Act 1991, s. 5. This states:

"(2) A court shall not deal with an offender by means of a suspended sentence unless it is of the opinion –

(a) that the case is one in which a sentence of imprisonment would have been appropriate even without the power to suspend the sentence; and
(b) that the exercise of that power can be justified by the exceptional circumstances of the case."

The imposition of a suspended sentence by a court is subject to the statutory restrictions on imposing custodial sentences contained in the Criminal Justice Act 1991, ss. 1–3 (see Chapter 4). For example, the court must be satisfied that the offence, or the combination of the offence and one or more offences associated with it, is so serious that only a custodial sentence can be justified. But if a court wishes to suspend that sentence, it may do so only if such a course of action "can be justified by the exceptional circumstances of the case". This provision now severely restricts the availability of suspended sentences to the courts (as we shall see later). Another restriction on the practical utility of this measure, is that a sentence of detention in a young offender institution cannot be suspended. (The Criminal Justice Act 1982 first removed from the courts the power to impose a suspended sentence on a person under 21 years of age).

Before returning to the current use of the suspended sentence, it is interesting to reflect on the rise and fall of this measure. The background to its introduction is a fine example of the frequently confused objectives of those responsible for formulating penal policy. Initially, the Advisory Council on the Treatment of Offenders (1952), after a superficial discussion on the matter, stated that "the suspended sentence is wrong in principle and to a large extent impracticable. It should not be adopted, either in conjunction with probation or otherwise" (para. 23). This dismissal of the suspended sentence was followed, unhesitatingly, in the 1957 report by the same body. Yet within a decade of this second rejection, it was introduced into our penal system.

A. E. Bottoms, "The Suspended Sentence in England 1967–78" (1981) 21 B.J. Crim. 1, pp. 2–3.

Two Theories of the Suspended Sentence

Prior to the introduction of the suspended sentence, its two most celebrated individual advocates in England were Sir Leo Page in the 1950s and Mr Brian Leighton in the 1960s, both magistrates.

Page's views were summarised by the Advisory Council in 1952. First, he compared the suspended sentence favourably with probation. It was, he thought, likely to be better understood by the recipient, because the consequence of re-offending was known and certain; for the same reason, he thought it would be a *more effective deterrent to the individual offender*. Many others have since used this argument, and not a few have specifically compared the suspended sentence, in this sense, with the efficacious classical image of the "Sword of Damocles".

Secondly, Page argued that in certain cases the suspended sentence should be used in place of imprisonment. Its use "would allow courts to avoid sending an offender to prison, and at the same time to show their sense of the gravity of his offence." (Advisory Council 1957, Appendix D, para. 2).

I shall call these two approaches to the suspended sentence the "special deterrent theory" and the "avoiding imprisonment theory". The first compares the sentence favourably with *non-custodial sentences*: one would expect courts influenced by it to use the suspended sentence in some cases where they had previously used non-custodial measures. The second theory, on the other hand, necessarily supposes that, in the absence of any power to suspend, a sentence of imprisonment would be passed. There is nothing illogical or inconsistent in holding both theories together, as Page did; one can argue that both are appropriate, but for different types of offender.

In the 1960s, Brian Leighton, a prominent member of the Magistrates' Association, was apparently particularly influential in securing the acceptance of the suspended sentence despite its rejection by A.C.T.O. It is clear from his memorandum to the Royal Commission on the Penal System that he fully supported both the special deterrent theory ("probation alone has its limitations") and the avoiding prison theory ("as some 80 per cent of first offenders never return to prison the suspended sentence might be equally effective as a deterrent with little cost to the state in the majority of cases"). Like Page, therefore, Leighton clearly foresaw the use of the suspended sentence in place of both existing custodial and non-custodial measures.

But, although the two most prominent advocates of the suspended sentence thus supported both theories behind the measure, in its official life only the second theory of the suspended sentence, the "avoiding prison theory", has ever been accepted.

Notes

1. The introduction of the suspended sentence (in the Criminal Justice Act 1967) as an alternative to short terms of imprisonment – not as an alternative to non-custodial measures – caused some confusion amongst sentencers. In the 1960s, much had been made of the possibility of the suspended sentence being introduced to "add teeth" to existing non- custodial measures, like probation and the conditional discharge. Moreover, in the House of Commons debates the then Home Secretary, Roy Jenkins, referred to the suspended sentence as a deterrent measure on more than one occasion. As it is difficult to comprehend how the suspended sentence could be regarded as a greater deterrent than immediate imprisonment, it is not surprising that some sentencers inferred (erroneously) that the new measure was intended, at least for some offenders, as an alternative to non-custodial penalties.

2. It is evident that the purpose behind the introduction of the suspended sentence was not conveyed to sentencers with sufficient clarity. It was introduced largely out of political expediency, due to fears about the rising prison population, and defended by vague, and potentially misleading, references to its supposed deterrent value. Initially, little was done to help sentencers cope with the difficulties which were inherent in this new measure. Despite being introduced as a sentence of imprisonment (albeit suspended), the sentencer was aware that he was passing a sentence which was non-custodial in its operation. So where did this new measure fit in to the range of existing sentences available to the courts? Confusion as to the appropriate

use of the suspended sentence, and its exact location on the "penal ladder", was perhaps inevitable. (See R. Sparks, "The Use of the Suspended Sentence" [1971] Crim. L.R. 384, pp. 396–7).

3. Guidance was eventually given to sentencers by the Court of Appeal. In *O'Keefe* [1969] 1 All E.R. 426, it was observed that lower courts were frequently using suspended sentences incorrectly, "as what one might call a soft option, when the court is not quite certain what to do, and in particular ... [there were] many cases when suspended sentences have been given when the proper order was a probation order" (at p. 427). The Court emphasised that before arriving at a suspended sentence: "the court must go through the process of eliminating other possible courses such as absolute discharge, conditional discharge, probation order, fines and then say to itself: this is a case for imprisonment, and the final question, it being a case for imprisonment, is immediate imprisonment required, or can I give a suspended sentence?" (at p. 428). It is unfortunate that this process was not laid down by Parliament when the suspended sentence was first introduced. Eventually, the *O'Keefe* guidance was put into statutory form in the Criminal Justice Act 1972 and is now to be found in the PCCA 1973, s. 22(2) as amended by the CJA 1991, s. 5. (For further illustrations of this principle, see *Watts* (1984) 6 Cr. App. R.(S) 61, *Jeffrey* (1985) 7 Cr. App. R.(S) 11, and *Smith* (1990) 12 Cr. App. R.(S) 85).

4. There is evidence that sentencers had difficulty complying with the decision-making process laid down in *O'Keefe*. Suspended sentences were given frequently to offenders who would *not* have been sent to prison prior to the CJA 1967. In an article in 1972, two researchers from the Home Office Research and Statistics Department stated:

> "It is only reasonable to conclude that courts have used the suspended sentence both to replace immediate imprisonment, and as a sentence in its own right ... It has been estimated that of all persons awarded a suspended sentence, only somewhere between 40 per cent, and 50 per cent would, but for the new provisions, have been sentenced to imprisonment for the original offence" (E. Oatham and F. Simon, "Are Suspended Sentences Working?" (1972) *New Society*, 233).

In an influential article, Sparks (*op cit.* (1971)) argued that magistrates' courts in particular did not follow the *O'Keefe* guidance. How accurate is this claim?

A. E. Bottoms, "The Suspended Sentence in England 1967–78" (1981) 21 B.J. Crim. pp. 8 and 15.

Sparks described the early experience under the 1967 Act as a "malfunction", and there can be no doubt that this is a correct description, given the intentions of the then Government in passing the legislation. The widespread use of suspended sentences in places of fines and probation, and the magistrates' tendency to impose longer sentences when suspending, were not legislatively intended. Nor was the failure of the measure to have a marked impact in reducing the prison population –

it did this for a short time, but not surprisingly this fall was checked as people originally given suspended sentences instead of non- custodial penalties began to re-offend and have their sentences activated; and the effect on the prison population was exacerbated both by the Court of Appeal's ruling (apparently largely followed) that the new and activated sentences should run consecutively and not concurrently [*Ithell* (1969) 53 Cr. App. R. 210], and by the tendency for magistrates' courts to give longer sentences when originally suspending. The exact effects of the suspended sentence on the prison population in 1968–72 have been a matter of some controversy ... [and] for technical reasons the true effect cannot be precisely calculated, but even if we take the most optimistic view, it is still clear that the Act had not had the reductive effect on the prison population which had been intended....

A final statistical issue is to reconsider, in the light of the latest available evidence, the current situation as regards the main 1967 malfunction, namely the tendency to use suspended sentences in places of fines and probation rather than where imprisonment would otherwise have been imposed ... We can obtain a simple guide to this malfunction by testing the level of imprisonment plus suspended sentence *combined*, as against the pre-1967 level for imprisonment alone. These data are summarised in Table 5. As may be seen, in the Crown Court there is every evidence

Table 5

The 1967 malfunction reconsidered

(Proportion of convicted defendants over 21 awarded imprisonment, immediate *and* suspended, 1966–78).

	Magistrates' Courts*		Higher Courts	
	Males	Females	Males	Females
1966–7	16.2	3.0	61.4	31.1
1968–9	24.9	6.4	74.8	44.8
1970–2	21.4	5.7	71.8	42.5
1973–4	14.9	4.4	68.1	42.7
1975–6	16.0	4.9	69.7	44.3
1977	16.6	5.8	69.8	46.7
1978	17.2	5.3	68.7	46.8

*Indictable offence only

of the continuation of this malfunction: since 1970 about 70 per cent of males have been awarded immediate or suspended imprisonment, as against only 61 per cent given immediate imprisonment in 1966–7. In the magistrates' courts, however, a rather different picture obtains at least for males, because from 1973–7 the level of immediate and suspended imprisonment combined was at or below the immediate imprisonment level for 1966–7 (the rate rose somewhat in 1978). This apparent tendency for the lower courts to be more strictly following the legislative intent was, it will be recalled, also apparent in the extent of the displacement of fines and probation in the years before 1972. However, as in that earlier period, when one comes to consider the question of lengths of sentence, it is still the case on the latest figures (1978) that magistrates' courts impose consistently longer sentences when suspending sentence than when imposing immediate imprisonment, whereas the Crown Court judges and recorders do not. Thus there is still evidence of the continuation of the 1967 malfunction, in both lower and higher courts.

Notes

1.   The confusion surrounding the introduction of the suspended sentence, in its early years, can best be summed up by the fact that although it was introduced in the hope of reducing the prison population, it was soon being blamed for a rise in prison numbers. (See *Report of the Prison Department*, Cmnd. 4486, (1969), para. 5).

2.   The obligation of a court to activate a suspended sentence where an offender is reconvicted of an imprisonable offence within the operational period, was a major reason for the adverse effect that the new measure had on the prison population. (For the relevant provisions dealing with breach of a suspended sentence, see the Powers of Criminal Courts Act 1973, s. 23(1), as amended by the Criminal Justice Act 1982, s. 31). As some offenders received suspended sentences for crimes that (prior to 1967) would have led only to a fine or probation order, their chances of being sent to prison, on reconviction, were substantially increased.

3.   Unless it is unjust to do so, a court should order that the suspended sentence be activated with the term unaltered, in the event of breach of the original sentence. This rule has been quite strictly applied, over many years, by the Court of Appeal in numerous decisions. For example, in *Saunders* (1970) 54 Cr. App. R. 247, it was stated (at p. 250):

> "[I]t has been suggested [on behalf of the appellant] ... that since the current offences here were of a completely different character from the offence in respect of which the suspended sentence was imposed, it may be that there would be a reason for not bringing the suspended sentence into force. It is an argument which is becoming rather prevalent these days, and this Court would like to say firmly that the mere fact that the current offence is of a different character from the offence for which the suspended sentence was given is no ground whatever for not bringing that suspended sentence into force. If the current offence is a trivial offence, the position may be different. An example of this is to be found in *Moylan* (1969) 53 Cr. App. R. 590, where Widgery L.J., in giving the judgment of the Court, said at p. 593: 'We think it quite clear that a court may properly consider as unjust the activation of a suspended sentence where the new offence is a comparatively trivial offence and, particularly, where it is in a different category from that of the offence for which the suspended sentence is imposed'...."

Also, in *Craine* (1981) 3 Cr. App. R.(S) 198 at (p. 200), Russell J. stated:

> "Complaint is made before us that the suspended sentence should not have been activated but ... it cannot be made too plain that when suspended sentences of imprisonment are imposed they mean what they say. Only in exceptional circumstances, if further offences involving imprisonment are committed, will those suspended sentences not be activated."

This principle was also affirmed in *Clitheroe* [1987] Crim. L.R. 583, where decisions to the contrary were held to have been reached *per incuriam*. In his commentary on *Clitheroe* in [1987] Crim. L.R. 584, David Thomas observes that the decision "is a clear and unambiguous reaffirmation of the principle stated in *Saunders*, that the fact that the later offence is of a different type from the original offence is not in itself a ground for not activating a suspended sentence." (Also see *Wells* [1987] Crim. L.R. 429).

Of course, this does not affect the principle stated in *Moylan* (above) that it may well be unjust to activate a suspended sentence where the subsequent offence is a comparatively trivial one. This is further illustrated by the case of *Brooks* (1991) 12 Cr. App. R.(S) 756, in which the appellant had previously been given a suspended prison sentence of nine months for possession of cannabis with intent to supply. During the operational period (of two years), he was convicted of possessing a small quantity of cannabis. On conviction of this subsequent offence, the magistrates committed him to the Crown Court for sentence. Brooks was sentenced to one month's imprisonment for the latest offence, with the suspended sentence activated in full. The Court of Appeal stated (at pp. 756–757):

> "In our view, it would have been sufficient for the judge to have dealt with the breach offence by way of a fine. That being so, the next question is whether if the judge had imposed a fine, he would have been justified in activating the suspended sentence of nine months' imprisonment. This Court has now held on several occasions ... that the fact that a subsequent offence does not warrant a custodial sentence is a strong argument for not activating the suspended sentence. That is apparent from, among other, the following authorities *Cline* (1979) 1 Cr. App. R.(S) 40, *McElhorne* (1983) 5 Cr. App. R.(S) 53, and *Jagodzinski* (1986) 8 Cr. App. R.(S) 151.
>
> As those authorities indicate, this is not a matter of principle but a matter of strong argument for counsel when mitigating in such a case, either at first instance or by way of appeal. Whilst the argument is particularly strong when a later offence is of a different character from the earlier one as well as being comparatively trivial ... it is not confined to such a case."

The Court of Appeal held, in *Brooks*, that the judge should have imposed a fine for the subsequent offence and made no order for activation of the original sentence. (Also see *Bee* [1993] Crim. L.R. 464).

4. Another reason for the adverse effect of suspended sentences upon the prison population was the ruling of the Court of Appeal in *Ithell* (1969) 53 Cr. App. R. 210. Here, it was held that where a further offence is committed during the operational period of a suspended sentence, the new and the activated sentences should run consecutively and not concurrently, "unless there are some quite exceptional circumstances" (at p. 212). (This approved the decision in *Brown* [1969] Crim. L. R. 20). There is some evidence that these decisions contributed to an increase in the average length of prison

sentences which occurred at this time. In his influential article, Sparks (*op. cit.*, 1971) observed (at p. 393):

"There has been a drastic shift in the lengths of sentences of men received into prison since 1968: about half of those sentences have been for over six months, compared with less than a third in 1967. It would not be surprising if implemented suspended sentences had doubled the effective lengths (allowing for remission, etc.) of offenders imprisoned after having been given a suspended sentence. The effect of this, in turn, could well be to increase the prison population by as much as 25–30 per cent...."

5. In view of the confusion about the rationale of the suspended sentence, its inappropriate use by many sentencers, and its lack of success in halting the rise of the prison population, it is perhaps surprising that it took until 1991 for its future to be seriously threatened. Why was it, until recently, such an important and established part of the sentencing system?

A. Bottoms, "The Suspended Sentence in England, 1967–78" (1981) 21 B.J. Crim. 22

The Practical Utility of the Suspended Sentence

We have seen that the suspended sentence, as applied in England, is open to attack on the theoretical level both from the neo-classical position and because of the existence of related measures; it also faces criticism from those who see it as an insufficient penalty.

It might be thought that such a critique would leave the suspended sentence in a relatively weak and vulnerable position within the English penal system, but actually nothing could be further from the truth. It is indeed now so firmly established as one of our major penal measures that the Advisory Council on the Penal System (1978), in a recent review, concluded that "no major changes" in its operation should be made, even though the Council explicitly recognised that "the accumulated evidence (of the operation of the suspended sentence since 1967) is not very encouraging" (paras. 265–7).

What accounts for this apparent impregnability of the suspended sentence? The answer is relatively straightforward – it derives its curious strength from its supposed practical utility in the present state of the English penal system.

Since the Second World War, the English prison population has risen from 11,000 (in 1938) to over 44,000 (in 1980) ... But during this same period the proportion of persons sentenced to immediate custodial sentences has dropped – in the case of adult indictable offenders, from 33 to 15 per cent. What principally lies behind these apparently contradictory trends is the vast rise in the annual total of convictions, corresponding with the rise in recorded crime during the period. The situation now confronting the penal system, as evidenced in various recent official reviews, is a need to hold steady or actually reduce the prison population at a time when public money is short but the rate of convictions continues to increase. Hence the recent calls for a further switch to non-custodial sentences if possible, coupled with an urgent appeal to sentencers to reduce the terms of imprisonment being awarded to most offenders.

In such a climate, it seems impossible to contemplate the abolition of the suspended sentence, whatever its theoretical vulnerability and however much the courts apparently continue to misuse it. For, undeniably, the suspended sentence has been a major contributor to the switch away from the use of sentences of immediate imprisonment since 1967. Thus the suspended sentence seems urgently necessary as a practical measure for penal administrators, however much it may be open to academic criticism.

Notes

1. For further thoughts on the suspended sentence by the same writer, see A. Bottoms, "Limiting Prison Use: Experience in England and Wales" (1987), *Howard Journal*, 177.

2. As a result of the Criminal Justice Act 1991, s. 5 encouragement is given to sentencers to consider when suspending a sentence, "whether the circumstances of the case are such as to warrant in addition the imposition of a fine or the making of a compensation order." (Powers of Criminal Courts Act 1973, s. 22(2A)). But the other amendments contained in the same section of the Criminal Justice Act 1991 suggest that the use of the suspended sentence is now to be severely circumscribed. A court is not to impose a suspended sentence unless the case is one in which a sentence of imprisonment would have been appropriate in the absence of the power to suspend, *and* "that the exercise of that power can be justified by the exceptional circumstances of the case." This new and important restriction has led to doubts about the future of the suspended sentence. While this measure no longer enjoys the "apparent impregnability" referred to by Bottoms, predictions of its virtual disappearance from the penal system are possibly premature. (For an interesting discussion see J. Q. Campbell, "A Sentencer's Lament on the Imminent Death of the Suspended Sentence" [1995] Crim. L.R. 293).

The Use of Suspended Sentences Since the Criminal Justice Act 1991

Nigel Stone, "The Suspended Sentence Since the Criminal Justice Act 1991" [1994] Crim. L.R. 399, pp. 399–400, 407–408.

Speculation about the fate of the suspended sentence of imprisonment since the implementation of the Criminal Justice Act 1991 has so far centred on the handful of Court of Appeal decisions which have illuminated the presence or absence of "exceptional circumstances" justifying such a sentence under section 22(2)(*b*) of Powers of Criminal Courts Act 1973. In his commentary on one of the most recently reported cases, *Ullah Khan* (in which a fraudulent solicitor's serious health problems were considered sufficiently exceptional), David Thomas considers it "unlikely that a consistent approach will be found to the meaning of the new restriction" and suggests that "inconsistency in the use of suspended sentences will be inevitable." He concludes that "either this restriction ... should be repealed or the suspended sentence itself should be abolished." Writing from his perspective as liaison probation officer at the Court of Appeal, David Foot is less troubled by this diversity and individuality of approach and feels that it can be left "to the good sense of magistrates and judges to determine whether, on the facts before them in a particular case, such (exceptional) circumstances exist."

To gain a better understanding of how that "good sense" is actually being exercised in the daily world of sentencing practice, I examined the residual use of the suspended sentence during the first operational year of the 1991 Act, October 1992–September 1993, in one shire county. It has not been possible to obtain the statistical returns of the courts (including two Crown Court centres) which sit in that county but I was able to use the data held by the local probation service on sentences passed following the preparation of pre-sentence reports by its staff. The figures thus available do not constitute the total number of suspended sentences imposed by the county's courts, because such sentences may be made upon defendants residing outside the county whose reports were prepared by other probation areas. Similarly, a few reports prepared locally resulting in suspended sentences were submitted to out-of-county courts. Nevertheless, this trawl may be considered to provide a reasonably good indication of courts' present preparedness to use this measure. I was able to read all the pre-sentence reports resulting in suspended terms of imprisonment to seek clues to the exceptionality of each case. I also sought any indication from the probation service record of sentencers' reasons for finding exceptionality. It was also possible to examine all reports in which suspension of sentence was proposed but not adopted.

A total of 33 suspended sentences (none of which included a supervision order) were imposed, 28 by courts within the county and five by out-of-county courts. The 12 suspended sentences made by magistrates within the county were imposed by three of the county's six petty sessions areas. The 33 sentences were not spread evenly over the year. Sixteen of the 19 Crown Court sentences and nine of the 14 magistrates' courts sentences were imposed in the first six months after the 1991 Act came into force.

This trend probably reflects the gradual trickle-down impact of early Court of Appeal decisions giving a firm indication that exceptionality should not be found in relatively commonplace features such as youth, previous good character, early plea of guilt, the adverse consequences of conviction, etc. The most prevalent principal offences resulting in suspended terms were: theft and deception (nine), violence and public disorder (five), burglary (five), drug crime (four) and driving offences (four).

Basis for suspension

A reasoned basis for finding exceptionality was recorded in 11 instances, all at Crown Court level, and I am unaware whether any justification was articulated or any reference made to the statutory restriction in the other cases. David Thomas has commented that even the Court of Appeal sometimes makes no reference to the statute or simply mentions the "exceptional" nature of the case without further elaboration. I have thus had to rely primarily on the mitigating circumstances or unusual features revealed by the pre-sentence reports.

There is no neat pattern or rational logic to explain exceptionality in this sample of cases, merely some trends or clusterings which throw light on the continuing serviceability of the suspended term in the sentencing armoury....

... Few and far between?

In the view of the Lord Chief Justice in *Robinson*, "the instances in which a suspended sentence will be appropriate will be few and far between." On the strength of this, commentators have concluded that "for all practical purposes, the suspended sentence has been abolished except for a tiny number of extraordinary cases." The evidence of this admittedly small study is to the contrary, suggesting that the measure retains an enduring pragmatic appeal and has not been completely marginalised by the 1991 Act.

The courts in this sample clearly wished to mark the offence with a custodial sentence without requiring the offender to incur the pains of imprisonment. This sentencing tactic was sometimes observable even in the absence of any of the exceptional factors identified above, for example in dealing with breach of a regulatory court order (such as keeping a dog whilst disqualified or being involved in the management of a company while an undischarged bankrupt). Here the court perhaps hoped to leave the offender in no doubt of the unacceptability of such behaviour while holding back from the ultimate sanction. In other instances the court seemed simply very reluctant to send the offender to prison and thus seized upon the suspended sentence as a convenient route of retreat with dignity. For example, in sentencing a woman (28) convicted of cruelty to a child, described in the pre-sentence report as reluctant to take responsibility for her behaviour and very preoccupied with her own emotional needs and drug dependence, the judge justified suspension of sentence by referring to her guilty plea, the fact that the case had been pending for over a year, the unlikelihood that she would resume care of the child in the immediate future and the "lamentable lack of support and advice" from her mother during the critical period.

This evidence of the suspended sentence's resilience is supported by Home Office data comparing the proportionate use of particular types of sentence between July and August 1992 with the first two months of 1993. Overall, use of the fully suspended sentence at 10 Crown Court centres for offenders convicted of indictable offences fell from 18 per cent to a far from negligible 5 per cent. Centres varied in their pattern of adaptation. While Kingston dropped from an unusually high rate of 30 per cent in 1992 to only 3 per cent in 1993, the impact of the Act was far smaller at Newcastle where the 1992 rate of 10 per cent dropped to 7 per cent in January 1993 and 8 per cent in February.

Few if any of the cases resulting in a suspended sentence in this study would have satisfied the stringent approach of the Court of Appeal demonstrated in *Lowery* and *Robinson*. However, only 2 per cent of offenders sentenced to suspended sentences at Crown Court in 1992 appealed against sentence and that appeal rate is now likely to be even smaller. As a consequence, although "exceptional circumstances" may seem a somewhat questionable or even spurious concept, it is likely that courts will continue to opt for an exceptional course of sentence for a variety of familiar reasons. Furthermore, the more recent Court of Appeal decisions finding exceptionality may signal greater flexibility and bolster the courts' reluctance to "kill off" the suspended sentence.

Notes

1. In another part of the article, Stone observes that the pre-sentence reports in his sample had limited influence, as their writers suggested suspension of sentence in only four of the 33 cases which resulted in a suspended sentence.

2. Before turning our attention to the Court of Appeal guidance on the use of suspended sentences since 1991, it is worth asking whether the Court should even try to define what is meant by "exceptional circumstances" under the Powers of Criminal Courts Act 1973, s. 22(2)(b). In the article referred to (above) by Stone, David Foot argues that the term is not susceptible to precise definition and that its interpretation ought to be left to the common-sense of sentencers. (See D. Foot, "The Use of Suspended Sentences", (1993) 157 *Justice of the Peace*, 565). He states (at p. 567):

> "To attempt an exhaustive list of exceptional features would have been a Sisyphean task. Scarcely more possible would have been the attempt, by some process of semantic analysis, to arrive at an operationally useful definition of the word 'exceptional'. Questions as to how exceptional is

exceptional would always remain. Opinions will differ. To the believer, all human actions are unique; an action appears common place only because our inquiry has been superficial or unimaginative or the actor is uncommunicative. To the sceptic, any appearance of exceptionality is an illusion created by the superior ability of some defendants or their representatives to weave a good story."

As Nigel Stone suggests, it seems that in many cases where a sentence is suspended, the court simply wishes to avoid imposing the ultimate sanction, rather than there being any "exceptional circumstances" which would satisfy the strict approach of the Court of Appeal (see below).

Appellate Guidance on the Criminal Justice Act 1991, section 5(1)

In *Okinikan* [1993] 1 W.L.R. 173, Lord Taylor C.J. considered the meaning of section 5(1) of the Criminal Justice Act 1991, in the Court of Appeal. He stated (at p. 176):

"The significant amendment is the new emphasis on the exceptional nature of a suspended sentence. Parliament has given statutory force to the principle that a suspended sentence should not be regarded as a soft option, but should only be imposed in exceptional circumstances.

This court cannot lay down a definition of 'exceptional circumstances'. They will inevitably depend on the facts of each individual case. However, taken on their own, or in combination, good character, youth and an early plea are not exceptional circumstances justifying a suspended sentence. They are common features of many cases. They may amount to mitigation sufficient to persuade the court that a custodial sentence should not be passed or to reduce its length. The statutory language is clear and unequivocal."

A good illustration of the strict approach of the Court of Appeal can be found in the case of *Lowery* [1993] Crim. L.R. 225, where the appellant pleaded guilty to 11 counts of false accounting. He was a police officer of almost twenty years' standing, whose wife became seriously disabled. Due to adapting their house for his wife, the appellant ran into financial trouble. He collected fines paid at police stations in discharge of warrants issued by magistrates' courts (which was one of his duties), but on 11 occasions he failed to hand over the money to the court office. The total amount involved was £1,500. As a result of these offences, he was dismissed from his job and lost his police house. Furthermore, he had made two suicide attempts and had been receiving psychiatric care for depressions. The Court of Appeal stated that these mitigating circumstances did not alter the fact that the appellant's offences were an extremely serious breach of trust, committed by a police officer in the course of his responsibility for the administration of justice. In considering whether the custodial sentence could have been suspended, the Court held that the appellant's circumstances did not amount to "exceptional circumstances" such as would justify the application of section 5 of the 1991 Act. (In fact, the Court extended the privilege of mercy and the original sentence of three months' imprisonment was varied to one of 42 days, so as to permit the appellant's immediate release).

In his commentary on this decision and that of *Sanderson* [1993] Crim. L.R. 224, David Thomas summarised the effect of the new statutory provision as follows ([1993] Crim. L.R. 226):

> "These two decisions, taken together with *Okinikan* indicate that the Court is taking a strict view of the meaning of 'exceptional circumstances' ... The combined effect of the three decisions appears to be that previous good character, youth, a long period of public services, provocation, a plea of guilty, the commission of the offence as a result of significant domestic difficulties, extra-legal consequences in the form of loss of career, home, and substantial diminution of pension rights, and the needs of dependent relatives, cannot constitute 'exceptional circumstances' for this purpose, either alone or in combination with each other. It seems clear that in future suspended sentences will be permissible only in extremely unusual cases, where the mitigating factors are both rare and compelling. The practical importance of the effective disappearance of the suspended sentence is enormous ... It seems likely that at least some of those who would have received suspended sentences under the old law will now be sentenced to immediate imprisonment..."

For further illustrations of the Court of Appeal's strict interpretation of section 5 of the Criminal Justice Act 1991, see *Robinson* (1993) 14 Cr. App. R.(S) 559, and *Attorney-General's Reference (No. 5 of 1993) (R v. Hartland)* [1993] Crim. L.R. 794. However, there have been recent Court of Appeal decisions which suggest a more flexible approach might be taken in the future. In *Cameron* (1993) 14 Cr. App. R.(S) 801, an immediate custodial sentence was suspended by the Court of Appeal, despite the serious nature of the offence (assault on a young child by his father), as there were very exceptional circumstances. These circumstances were the desirability of reuniting and rehabilitating the appellant's family under supervision. In *Huntley* (1993) 14 Cr. App. R.(S) 795, the Court of Appeal reduced a sentence of imprisonment and suspended it, having been persuaded that there were very special circumstances. Although the offence was for unlawful wounding – the appellant had struck her tormentor on the head with a bottle – there was a history of provocation by the victim.

The confusion that now surrounds the interpretation of section 5 of the Criminal Justice Act 1991, and the availability of the suspended sentence, can be well illustrated by two recent appellate decisions. In *French* (1994) 15 Cr. App. R.(S) 194, the appellant pleaded guilty to conspiracy to obtain property by deception, having participated in a fraudulent insurance claim for £5,500 and was sentenced to six months' imprisonment. The Court of Appeal decided that there were exceptional circumstances which justified suspension of the prison sentence; before the offence, the appellant had experienced severe financial and emotional difficulties and she was under psychiatric care for depression. Her prospects of recovery would have been hampered by a custodial sentence.

In *Bradley* [1994] Crim. L.R. 381, the appellant, who was head of a department in a college, pleaded guilty to four offences of forgery, two of obtaining by deception and one of theft. (She diverted about £7,000 of the college's money into her own account). Although the appellant had a history of mental health problems and had been in hospital for treatment for severe reactive depression, the Court held that the facts of the case were not so exceptional as to justify suspension of the custodial sentence. The Court merely reduced the sentence of immediate imprisonment from nine to four months.

It is clearly difficult to reconcile these recent, inconsistent decisions of the Court of Appeal. But it would seem from recent research (Nigel Stone (1994), discussed above) that lower courts are not unduly concerned by the apparent restrictions of the new section 22(2) PCCA 1973. The "enduring pragmatic appeal" of the suspended sentence, to which Stone refers, may well ensure its survival.

Suspended Sentence Supervision Orders

The Advisory Council on the Penal System, in its report *Non-Custodial and Semi-Custodial Penalties* (1970, para. 191) advocated giving sentencers the power to combine a suspended sentence with compulsory supervision. Some commentators argued that, without such a power, offenders could not receive supervision during the operational period of their sentence. (Because a suspended sentence and a probation order cannot be combined by a court in dealing with an offender; section 22(3) of the Powers of Criminal Courts Act 1973). To remedy this problem, section 26 of the 1973 Act provides that when a court passes a suspended sentence of more than six months for a single offence, the court may make a suspended sentence supervision order placing the offender under the supervision of a probation officer for a period not exceeding the operational period of the suspended sentence.

The limitation of suspended sentence supervision orders (SSSOs) to sentences of over six months effectively makes this measure irrelevant to magistrates' courts. Also, the SSSO differs from a probation order, notably because the court cannot include any special requirements in an SSSO, which it can in a probation order. Under a suspended sentence supervision order, the offender must simply keep in touch with the probation officer, as directed, and in particular, notify the officer of any change of address (section 26(4) of the Powers of Criminal Courts Act 1973). An offender who fails to comply with this requirement (under section 26(4)) may be brought before a magistrates' court and fined up to £1000. However, such a breach of the order does not make the offender liable to have his suspended sentence activated. This can only happen if a further imprisonable offence is committed during the operational period. (The relevant principles in relation to activation of suspended sentences are discussed earlier in this section).

The suspended sentence supervision order is not used very frequently by the courts. In view of the tortuous process of reasoning that is required of a sentencer before arriving at a decision to impose this measure, its unpopularity is hardly surprising. A sentencer has first to decide that a custodial sentence of between six months and two years is required, complying with all the requirements of the Criminal Justice Act 1991. Secondly, he must be able to justify suspending that sentence in accordance with the strict requirements of section 5(1) of the Criminal Justice Act 1991. (According to the Court of Appeal in *Robinson* (1993) 14 Cr. App. R.(S) 559 at 561: "Since the commencement of the CJA 1991, the instances in which a suspended sentence will be appropriate will be few and far between"). Finally, if supervision is appropriate, the sentencer must decide whether to impose a supervision order as well. Conforming to this decision-making process is an unenviable task for sentencers. They must, of course, resist the temptation to use a suspended sentence supervision order in circumstances where a probation order would have been appropriate.

III. Community Sentences

Community Sentences (General)

White Paper, *Crime, Justice and Protecting the Public*, Cm. 965 (1990), paragraphs 4.3–4.7.

4.3 The Government believes a new approach is needed if the use of custody is to be reduced. Punishment in the community should be an effective way of dealing with many offenders, particularly those convicted of property crimes and less serious offences of violence, when financial penalties are insufficient. The punishment should be in the restrictions on liberty and in the enforcement of the orders. All community service orders place some restrictions on an offender's liberty and so may probation orders when, for example, they require an offender to attend a day centre for a lengthy period. The discipline exerted by these orders on offenders may extend over many months. These orders intrude on normal freedom, and the court should be satisfied that this is justified.

4.4 It is the loss of liberty involved in carrying out the terms of the order rather than the activities carried out during the order which is the punishment. The purpose of the activities will differ. Community service work provides reparation to the community. A probation order, on the other hand, should help offenders not to re-offend. It is not the intention that the activities carried out during a community service order should deliberately be made unpleasant in the expectation that this will deter either the offender or other potential offenders, but rather that they should be demanding in a number of ways. There is nothing demeaning in hard manual labour or working with disabled or elderly people. Many people do similar work as volunteers to improve the local environment or to help people in their communities. What is needed is useful work of benefit to the community. Both community service orders and probation should try to strengthen offenders' links with the community and not weaken them.

4.5 Restrictions on liberty would become the connecting thread in a range of community penalties as well as custody. By matching the severity of the restrictions on liberty to the seriousness of the offence, the courts should find it easier to achieve consistency of approach in sentencing. The more serious the offence is, the greater the restrictions on liberty which would be justified as a punishment.

New legislative provisions

4.6 The legislation will provide that, before making an order which places restrictions on liberty, a court would have to be satisfied that the offence for which the offender had been convicted by the court was so serious that restrictions on liberty were justified but not serious enough to deserve a custodial sentence. It would also have to be satisfied that the seriousness of the offence justified the severity of the restrictions on liberty which would be imposed by the order which was being made. The court would therefore have to be satisfied both that any restrictions on liberty were justified and that the scale or degree of restrictions which the order imposed were justified by the seriousness of the offence. This would be the equivalent of a decision to use custody and the decision on the length of the sentence. The aim is to ensure that the more restrictive, and usually more expensive, community sentences are used for more serious offenders, such as persistent thieves and non-domestic burglars, and not for those who have committed minor offences.

4.7 The Government proposes to restructure community sentences for adult and young adult offenders to reflect the concept of graduated restrictions on liberty, which are related to the seriousness of the offending. This is consistent with the just desserts principle. There would be a wide range of options for the court, which could be used with greater flexibility and linked with financial penalties, particularly compensation to the victim. The main options for adults would be a probation order; a probation order with additional requirements such as attendance at a day centre or other activities; community service of between 40 and 240 hours; and a new combined order which would link community service and probation with or without additional requirements. There will be a new curfew order, which could be used by itself or with other orders. Sentencers would be able to select the precise form of punishment in the community best suited to each offender, relating the severity of the punishment to the seriousness of the offence...

Notes

1. The White Paper expressed the Government's enthusiasm for punishment in the community. The value of community penalties, it was claimed, is their suitability for dealing with offences in the medium range of seriousness: for example, property crimes and less serious offences of violence. In cases which are not so serious as to require imprisonment, yet which warrant some restriction on liberty, it was argued that punishment in the community would be an effective sentence. The sentences which the government had in mind were a stricter form of probation order, the community service order, a new combined order linking community service and probation, and also a newly proposed curfew order. Restrictions on liberty were to be the "thread" which connected this range of penalties, and sentences would be in proportion to the seriousness of the offence committed. It was stated that "sentencers would be able to select the precise form of punishment in the community best suited to each offender, relating

the severity of the punishment to the seriousness of the offence." (at paragraph 4.7).

2.   Despite the confident assertions made in the White Paper, there were some problems with its line of reasoning. It is easy to see how the use of custodial sentences can be subjected to a guiding principle of just deserts. But can community penalties be imposed on the same basis, but for less serious offences? To attempt to do so presupposes that they are punitive, rather than rehabilitative measures, and that different community penalties can be ranked in terms of their supposed severity. For this reason, the White Paper stressed the need to strengthen probation orders and it also referred to the established use of community service orders according to "desert" principles. But is it possible to create a meaningful scale of community penalties which can be consistently applied by sentencers? Are there not dangers in trying to adapt an essentially rehabilitative measure, like probation, to a new punitive ethos, where sentences are imposed on a just deserts basis?

3.   Some interesting comments on an earlier version of the government's proposals – contained in the Green Paper, *Punishment, Custody and the Community* (1988) – can be found in Antony Vass' book, entitled *Alternatives to Prison* (1990). He argues (at p. 170):

> "In short, part of the problem with government 'policy', the rising prison population, and the punitiveness of the system as a whole, has to do with low levels of 'tolerance' ... tolerance *should* be a necessary precondition and an integral part of any attempts to destructure the prison establishment. In that respect, alternatives to custody can only function as real alternatives if they can demonstrate more flexibility and tolerance than is currently practised by the criminal justice process in general. By being expected to compromise that tolerance with harsher methods of supervision and a tough approach to offenders, the government is not heading for reductions in the prison population but for an escalation of the prison crisis."

4.   It is clear that the government's intention was to create tougher community penalties, with stricter enforcement procedures, so as to persuade sentencers to use them instead of imprisonment for medium range offenders. To ensure that they were not to be used for relatively minor offences, it was stated that, before imposing such a sentence, the court must be "satisfied both that any restrictions on liberty were justified and that the scale or degree of restrictions which the order imposed were justified by the seriousness of the offence" (para. 4.6). Although one can detect a certain logic behind the government's intentions, it is equally clear sentencers might well experience some difficulty in translating these intentions into practice with any degree of consistency.

The government's proposals relating to community sentences were brought into effect by the Criminal Justice Act 1991. The provisions of general application are reproduced below, and those relating to particular community orders will be dealt with in turn.

Criminal Justice Act 1991, sections 6–7 (as amended by the Criminal Justice Act 1993, section 66(4) and (5)).

Restrictions on imposing community sentences.
6. – (1) A court shall not pass on an offender a community sentence, that is to say, a sentence which consists of or includes one or more community orders, unless it is of the opinion that the offence, or the combination of the offence and one or more offences associated with it, was serious enough to warrant such a sentence.

(2) Subject to subsection (3) below, where a court passes a community sentence –

(a) the particular order or orders comprising or forming part of the sentence shall be such as in the opinion of the court is, or taken together are, the most suitable for the offender; and

(b) the restrictions on liberty imposed by the order or orders shall be such as in the opinion of the court are commensurate with the seriousness of the offence, or the combination of the offence and one or more offences associated with it.

(3) In consequence of the provision made by section 11 below with respect to combination orders, a community sentence shall not consist of or include both a probation order and a community service order.

(4) In this Part "community order" means any of the following orders, namely –

(a) a probation order;
(b) a community service order;
(c) a combination order;
(d) a curfew order;
(e) a supervision order; and
(f) an attendance centre order.

Procedural requirements for community sentences.
7. – (1) In forming any such opinion as is mentioned in subsection (1) or (2)(b) of section 6 above, a court shall take into account all such information about the circumstances of the offence or (as the case may be) of the offence and the offence or offences associated with it (including any aggravating or mitigating factors) as is available to it.

(2) In forming any such opinion as is mentioned in subsection (2)(a) of that section, a court may take into account any information about the offender which is before it.

(3) A court shall obtain and consider a pre-sentence report before forming an opinion as to the suitability for the offender of one or more of the following orders, namely –

(a) a probation order which includes additional requirements authorised by Schedule 1A to the 1973 Act;
(b) a community service order;
(c) a combination order; and
(d) a supervision order which includes requirements imposed under section 12, 12A, 12AA, 12B or 12C of the Children and Young Persons Act 1969 ("the 1969 Act").

(4) No community sentence which consists of or includes such an order as is

mentioned in subsection (3) above shall be invalidated by the failure of a court to comply with that subsection, but any court on an appeal against such a sentence –

> (a) shall obtain a pre-sentence report if none was obtained by the court below; and
> (b) shall consider any such report obtained by it or by that court.

Notes

1.   The community orders available to the courts are listed in section 6(4) of the 1991 Act as follows: a probation order, a community service order, a combination order, a curfew order, a supervision order and an attendance centre order. (The power to impose a curfew order has not yet been brought into force). A community sentence consists of one or more of these orders. Although some of these community orders originally started life as rehabilitative measures (*e.g.* probation orders used to be imposed instead of sentencing an offender), it is clear that they are now to be regarded as punitive sentences under the new framework. Community orders involve restrictions on liberty and such a sentence should reflect the guiding principle of just deserts (see section 6(2)(b)).

It is intended that community sentences will be imposed where a custodial sentence cannot be justified, but where a fine or discharge would not be sufficiently punitive. In an attempt to ensure that community sentences do not slide too far down the sentencing scale, and be used inappropriately for relatively minor offences, section 6(1) states that a court shall not pass a community sentence:

> "unless it is of the opinion that the offence, or the combination of the offence and one or more offences associated with it, was serious enough to warrant such a sentence."

Of course, an offence may be "serious enough" to justify a community sentence without the court deciding to impose one. So presumably there will be cases where a sentencer could choose, with equal justification, between a less severe community sentence and a fine.

2.   Having decided that a community sentence is justified and appropriate, the court must then have regard to two further principles. The sentencer must select the particular order or orders which are the most suitable for the offender (section 6(2)(a)), *and* he must ensure that the restrictions on liberty which the sentence will impose are proportional to the seriousness of the offence(s) committed (section 6(2)(b)). As observed earlier, courts may well experience some difficulty, in practice, in balancing the "just deserts" and the rehabilitative elements of section 6(2). (But see M. Wasik and A. von Hirsch, "Non-Custodial Penalties and the Principles of Desert" [1988] Crim. L.R. 555. Also see M. Wasik, "Rethinking Information and Advise for Sentencers", in *Sentencing, Judicial Discretion and Training*, (Munro and Wasik eds., 1992)).

Before imposing certain orders, a court must consider a pre-sentence report (section 7(3)): these orders are a probation order which includes additional requirements under Schedule 1(A), a community service order, a combination order, and a supervision order which includes specified requirements. Where a court selects an order for which a pre-sentence report is not mandatory, it may still be good practice to obtain such a report. (For a recent amendment to section 7(3), see the Criminal Justice and Public Order Act 1994, schedule 9, paragraph 40).

3.   Although section 6(3) states that a community sentence shall not consist of or include both a probation order and a community service order, it should be noted that section 11 permits a combination of these measures (with restrictions) in the new "combination order". Apart from the prohibition under section 6(3), two or more orders may be lawfully combined by sentencers and, additionally, a fine or compensation order may be imposed.

4.   There are six orders which come within the community sentence category. Of these, the supervision order and attendance centre order apply to young offenders and will be looked at in Chapter 6. The other orders are considered in the sections which follow.

A. Probation Orders

Introduction

Probation was first introduced into the penal system by the Probation of Offenders Act 1907. Prior to this official recognition, there had been a number of unofficial schemes involving supervision in the community during the nineteenth century. For instance, in 1876, police court missions were established by the Church of England Temperance Society out of concern for the growing social problem of drunkenness. The missionaries made enquiries about the offender's background and sometimes helped to supervise offenders that were released by the courts. What characterised the various schemes, these embryonic forms of probation, was a growing dissatisfaction with prison conditions and administration, together with changing ideas about the causes of crime and the purpose of punishment. There was a growing interest in the individual criminal and the need for positive steps to assist his and her reform. (For an interesting historical account of these developments, see D. Bochel, *Probation and After-Care*, (1976)).

   In an otherwise hostile penal system, the probation service was the sole agency devoted to assisting and advising offenders. Traditionally, the probation service has been a civilising and constructive influence on the courts and the administration of justice. As the range of supervisory measures and after-care work increased, so too did the duties of the probation service. In addition to supervising offenders placed on probation, the service became involved, *inter alia*, in the preparation of social enquiry (now pre-sentence) reports, the supervision of juvenile offenders, social work within penal institutions, after-care, liaison work with the courts and rehabilitation schemes.

This far from exhaustive list amply demonstrates the valuable contribution made by the probation service to the administration of criminal justice and the humane treatment of offenders. However, in a penal climate that has come increasingly to talk in terms of just deserts, rather than reform and rehabilitation, the role of the probation service, and the philosophy underlying its work, have become a matter for debate. (For a very useful series of four articles by W. McWilliams on the changing philosophy of the probation system since its introduction, see "The Mission to the English Police Courts 1876–1936" (1983), 22 *Howard Journal* 129; "The Mission Transformed: Professionalisation of Probation Between the Wars" (1985), 24 *Howard Journal* 241; "The English Probation System and the Diagnostic Ideal" (1986) 25 *Howard Journal* 257; and "Probation, Pragmatism and Policy" (1987) 26 *Howard Journal* 97). The following brief extract is taken from the final article in this series.

W. McWilliams, "Probation, Pragmatism and Policy", (1987), 26 *Howard Journal*, 97, pp. 114–115.

To summarise succinctly the conceptual history of the probation endeavour as I have portrayed it in these four essays, we may say that the service began as a straightforward enterprise intended to save offenders from harsh punishments with a view to their salvation through divine grace. The missionaries' work in the courts began as one expression of their wider mission of saving souls and, it is important to remark, their underlying purpose provided sufficient *justification* for their court work. The changes which followed the rise of "scientific" understandings of offenders radically altered the *nature* of the original mission, but it is quite clear from the writings of the more dedicated social diagnosticians that the *sense* of mission continued unabated; its ontology had changed, its overarching objective had changed, and its justifying purpose had changed, but it remained missionary in its zeal and sense of the righteousness of its cause, the "cure" of offenders through scientific treatment.

The decline of confidence in the treatment ethic had profound effects upon the probation service in general, but especially on its court work. The social enquiry report could no longer be a simple plea for mercy for the accused in the face of harsh punishment, the scientific ideal had put paid to that; but no longer could the report of the probation officer purport to be a vehicle of accurate diagnosis either. The answer to these fundamental problems in the phase of pragmatism was to begin to see the report to court as an instrument of the policy of diverting offenders from custody ... Unfortunately, it is at this point that a gap between the theory of policy formulation and the reality of practice becomes apparent.

In the post-diagnostic era the probation service has not actually lost its sense of mission (although it must be noted that the conception of that mission now varies as between the different schools of thought); rather it is that the loss which the service has suffered is that of any satisfying transcendent *justification* for its present concerns with providing realistic alternatives to imprisonment. It is true (at least in most instances) that there are cost advantages in dealing with offenders outside penal institutions, and it is equally true that many non-custodial disposals can be held to be more humane than their custodial counterparts, but justifications such as these, no matter how ardently they are reiterated for public consumption, do not actually provide the sort of inspirational justifications which both the phases of special pleading and diagnosis could command. The contemporary claim that one can deal with offenders somewhat more cheaply and more humanely than might otherwise be the case may appeal to economists with a soft spot for their fellow men, but it hardly has the cachet, or indeed the rectitude, of a claim to save men's souls or change their psyches.

For those in the higher ranks of the service the collapse of confidence in the diagnostic-treatment model was a severe blow ... but at least for them there was the growth in the management ideal into which they could retreat, and the fast-developing notions of policy towards which they could divert their energies and idealism. For those at the basic level of the service, however, those continuing to be involved in the daily business of practice, no such escape was possible; and, if anything, the new managerialism in the upper reaches of the organisation was felt to be more of a burden than a helpfully liberating force ... The practitioners, despite the collapse of confidence, remained obliged to continue to perform in that most public of arenas, the criminal courts, and to produce social enquiry reports even though the currency of those reports had been debased and their *raison d'être* undermined.

Small wonder that the practitioners retreated somewhat and that practice failed to meet the ideals of policy even on points of consensus.

Notes

1.   For the case in favour of restoring the rehabilitation of offenders as the central philosophical ideal of the probation service, see W. McWilliams and K. Pease, "Probation Practice and an End to Punishment" (1990) 29 *Howard Journal* 14.

2.   For a criticism of the direction in which the probation service was being forced to move in the late 1980s, see Judith Rumgay, "Probation – the Next Five Years: A Comment" (1988) 27 *Howard Journal* 198. She states that "the pressures on the probation service to establish credibility as a provider of alternatives to custody have encouraged the development of 'tough' approaches about which the service is deeply divided internally" (at p. 199). She also refers to the growing concern amongst many probation officers that certain developments in supervision have unacceptable implications for the freedom of choice of those subject to extra conditions in probation orders. Moreover, whilst tougher supervision has not been markedly successful in reducing the use of imprisonment, it has resulted in "more intrusive intervention in the lives of those who could be dealt with by the traditional non-custodial measures" (p. 200). (Also of interest, but raising slightly different issues, see A. Vass and A. Weston, "Probation Day Centres as an Alternative to Custody", (1990) 30 B.J. Crim. 189).

3.   It is easy to appreciate why probation officers, attracted and recruited to a service which has traditionally represented rehabilitative and humane ideals, should have balked at the official adoption of the language of punishment. But how effective has the probation service been in asserting the value of rehabilitation? Has the service's lack of confidence in its traditional ideals made it vulnerable to being incorporated into a more punitive ethos? For an interesting discussion of these issues, see Judith Rumgay, "Talking Tough: Empty Threats in Probation Practice" (1989) 28

Howard Journal 177. She points out the irony that, by promoting community-based programmes which were sufficiently punishment-oriented to appeal to sentencers as credible alternatives to prison, the probation service was undermining its own traditional foundations built on rehabilitative ideals. She concludes that the "credibility of probation ... has much to do with the positive, active and public embrace of the rehabilitative goal and the methods by which it is to be achieved. It is perhaps unlikely that anyone else will assert confidence in the rehabilitative work of the probation service if probation officers themselves display uncertainty about its worth in the language invoked to describe policy and practice" (p. 185).

4.   The government put forward its proposals for reforming the probation service in the Green Paper, *Supervision and Punishment in the Community: A Framework for Action*, Cm. 966 (1990). In addition to the sweeping changes proposed for the management and administration of the service, it was clear that the government wanted to see less emphasis on social work and more on punishment. It also wished to bring about the closer co-operation of the service with other criminal justice agencies. These proposals were directly related to the White Paper, Cm. 965 (1990) – discussed at the start of this chapter – with its emphasis on tougher community penalties as alternatives to custody. The Green Paper emphasised the responsibilities of probation officers to the criminal justice system as a whole as well as to individual offenders. Running through the Green Paper was a concentration on value for money and management effectiveness. (The Green Paper was followed, in May 1991, by the Home Office's publication of *Organising Supervision and Punishment in the Community: A Decision Document*, which announced its plans for the restructuring and financing of the probation service. For a discussion, see "Plans For the Probation Service" (1991) 30 *Howard Journal* 337).

5.   National Standards for the Supervision of Offenders in the Community were published in 1992. These provide guidance on pre-sentence reports, probation and other community orders, and the supervision of offenders before and after release from custody. The official "Statement of Purpose for the Probation Service" (1992) states that "the probation service serves the courts and the public by supervising offenders in the community; helping them lead law-abiding lives; safeguarding the welfare of children in family proceedings". The shift in emphasis in relation to the rationale and philosophy of probation work, was accompanied (under the Criminal Justice Act 1991) by the introduction of tougher community sentences and important changes to the social enquiry (now pre-sentence) work of the service.

6.   For an insight into how probation staff divided their time between different tasks prior to the Criminal Justice Act 1991, see the *National Probation Survey* (1990), Home Office Research and Planning Unit Paper No. 72. This Survey is discussed in an article by M. Hough and C. May, *Surveying the Work of Probation Officers*, (1993), Home Office Research Bulletin, 15.

Probation Orders

Criminal Justice Act 1991, section 8.

Probation and community service orders

8. – (1) For section 2 of the 1973 Act there shall be substituted the following section –

"Probation"

2. – (1) Where a court by or before which a person of or over the age of sixteen years is convicted of an offence (not being an offence for which the sentence is fixed by law) is of the opinion that the supervision of the offender by a probation officer is desirable in the interests of –

    (a) securing the rehabilitation of the offender; or
    (b) protecting the public from harm from him or preventing the commission by him of further offences,

the court may make a probation order, that is to say, an order requiring him to be under the supervision of a probation officer for a period specified in the order of not less than six months nor more than three years.

For the purposes of this subsection the age of a person shall be deemed to be that which it appears to the court to be after considering any available evidence...

... (3) Before making a probation order, the court shall explain to the offender in ordinary language –

    (a) the effect of the order (including any additional requirements proposed to be included in the order in accordance with section 3 below);
    (b) the consequences which may follow under Schedule 2 to the Criminal Justice Act 1991 if he fails to comply with any of the requirements of the order; and
    (c) that the court has under the Schedule power to review the order on the application either of the offender or of the supervising officer,

and the court shall not make the order unless he expresses his willingness to comply with its requirements.

(4) The court by which a probation order is made shall forthwith give copies of the order to a probation officer assigned to the court, and he shall give a copy –

    (a) to the offender;
    (b) to the probation officer responsible for the offender's supervision; and
    (c) to the person in charge of any institution in which the offender is required by the order to reside...

... (6) An offender in respect of whom a probation order is made shall keep in touch with the probation officer responsible for his supervision in accordance with such instructions as he may from time to time be given by that officer and shall notify him of any change of address.

(7) The Secretary of State may by order direct that subsection (1) above shall be amended by substituting, for the minimum or maximum period specified in that subsection as originally enacted or as previously amended under this subsection, such period as may be specified in the order...

Notes

1. These new provisions have brought about considerable changes to the probation order. However, as with the old law, the consent of an offender is required before a probation order can be made by the court. But, under section 1(3) of the Act, a court can pass a custodial sentence if the offender refuses to give his consent to a community sentence, in which case the restrictions on imposing prison sentences under section 1(2) will not apply.
2. A court may make a probation order on an offender over 16 years old, requiring him to be under the supervision of a probation officer for a period of between six months and three years. As a result of section 8 of the Criminal Justice Act 1991, the probation order is now to be regarded as a sentence of the court, whereas formerly such an order was imposed "instead of sentencing" an offender. In keeping with the policy expressed in the White Paper, *Crime, Justice and Protecting the Public* Cm. 965 (1990) pp. 20–1), the new provisions have incorporated the probation order within the punishment framework of the Act. Although a probation order cannot be combined with a sentence of imprisonment, it may be combined with a fine or with a compensation order.

It will be remembered that the probation order is now one of six community orders which comprise the community sentence. Section 6(1) states that a court is not to pass a community sentence, which consists of one or more of the community orders, unless the offence committed was serious enough to justify such a sentence. With the exception of murder, a probation order can be made in respect of any offence; but the offence (or the combination of the offence and one or more offences associated with it) must satisfy the threshold referred to in section 6(1). A probation order should not be imposed for a trivial offence.

Section 2(1) of the Powers of Criminal Courts Act 1973 now states that, in order to impose a probation order on an offender, the court must be of the opinion that supervision of that offender by a probation officer is desirable in the interests of:

> "(a) securing the rehabilitation of the offender; or
> (b) protecting the public from harm from him, or preventing the commission by him of further offences."

3. Before making a probation order, the court must explain to the offender in ordinary language the effect of the order, including any additional requirements which are to be included in the order. The court must also explain the consequences for the offender of any failure to comply with the requirements of the order, and that the court has the power to review the order on the application either of the offender or of the supervising officer. (See section 2(3) of the Powers of Criminal Courts Act 1973). A copy of the probation order must also be given to the offender, via the court probation officer.
4. The offender on whom an order is imposed will be under the supervision

of a probation officer for a specified period of between six months and three years. Section 2(6) states that, during this time, the offender must keep in touch with his probation officer, as directed by that officer, and he must notify the officer of any change of address. To ensure that these basic requirements are not to be regarded as too lenient, both the White Paper (1990) and the National Standards for the Supervision of Offenders in the Community (1992) stress the more demanding qualities of a probation order. As well as securing the offender's compliance with the order and enforcing its terms, supervision by an officer should involve "challenging" the offender to accept responsibility for his crime and its consequences. The National Standards also require that supervision is established promptly (within 5 days) of a probation order being made, and that a "supervision plan" is drawn up. Meetings between officer and offender are to be "frequent": where practical, there should be 12 (and a minimum of six) in the initial three months of the order. During the next three months there should be six meetings, with at least one meeting each month thereafter until the completion of the order.

5. A court may include additional requirements in a probation order. Section 3(1) of the Powers of Criminal Courts Act 1973 (as substituted by section 9 of the Criminal Justice Act 1991) states:

"... a probation order may in addition require the offender to comply during the whole or any part of the probation period with such requirements as the court, having regard to the circumstances of the case, considers desirable in the interest of –

    (a) securing the rehabilitation of the offender; or
    (b) protecting the public from harm from him or preventing the commission by him of further offences."

This sub-section does not specify particular requirements which may be imposed. But note that s. 3(2) states that the payment of compensation to a victim cannot be made a *requirement* of a probation order – although a compensation order and a probation order may be imposed at the same time.

In addition to this general power to include requirements in an order, Schedule 1A to the Powers of Criminal Courts Act 1973 (inserted by Schedule 1, Part II, Criminal Justice Act 1991) provides for the inclusion of specific requirements. Before forming an opinion as to the suitability of an offender for a probation order with requirements authorised by schedule 1A, a court must obtain and consider a pre-sentence report (section 7(3) of the Criminal Justice Act 1991). But the effect of section 7(3) of the 1991 Act has been weakened by paragraph 40 of Schedule 9 to the Criminal Justice and Public Order Act 1994.

The Criminal Justice Act 1991, Schedule 1, Part II, Schedule 1A: Additional Requirements in Probation Orders

Requirements as to residence

1. – (1) Subject to sub-paragraphs (2) and (3) below, a probation order may include requirements as to the residence of the offender.

(2) Before making a probation order containing any such requirement, the court shall consider the home surroundings of the offender.

(3) Where a probation order requires the offender to reside in an approved hostel or any other institution, the period for which he is so required to reside shall be specified in the order.

Requirements as to activities etc.

2. – (1) Subject to the provisions of this paragraph, a probation order may require the offender –

  (a) to present himself to a person or persons specified in the order at a place or places so specified;
  (b) to participate or refrain from participating in activities specified in the order –

    (i) on a day or days so specified; or
    (ii) during the probation period or such portion of it as may be so specified.

(2) A court shall not include in a probation order a requirement such as is mentioned in sub-paragraph (1) above unless –

  (a) it has consulted a probation officer; and
  (b) it is satisfied that it is feasible to secure compliance with the requirement....

Requirements as to attendance at probation centre

3. – (1) Subject to the provisions of this paragraph, a probation order may require the offender during the probation period to attend at a probation centre specified in the order.

(2) A court shall not include such a requirement in a probation order unless –

  (a) it has consulted a probation officer; and
  (b) it is satisfied –
    (i) that arrangements can be made for the offender's attendance at a centre; and
    (ii) that the person in charge of the centre consents to the inclusion of the requirement.

(3) A requirement under sub-paragraph (1) above shall operate to require the offender –

  (a) in accordance with instructions given by the probation officer responsible for his supervision, to attend on not more than 60 days at the centre specified in the order; and
  (b) while attending there to comply with instructions given by, or under the authority of, the person in charge of the centre.

(4) Instructions given by a probation officer under sub-paragraph (3) above shall,

so far as is practicable, be such as to avoid any interference with the times, if any, at which the offender normally works or attends a school or other educational establishment . . . .

Requirements as to treatment for mental conditions, etc.

5. – (1) This paragraph applies where a court proposing to make a probation order is satisfied, on the evidence of a duly qualified medical practitioner approved for the purpose of section 12 of the Mental Health Act 1983, that the mental condition of the offender –

(a) is such as requires and may be susceptible to treatment; but
(b) is not such as to warrant the making of a hospital order or guardianship order within the meaning of that Act.

(2) The probation order may include a requirement that the offender shall submit, during the whole of the probation period or during such part of that period as may be specified in the order, to treatment by or under the direction of a duly qualified medical practitioner with a view to the improvement of the offender's mental condition . . .

Requirements as to treatment for drug or alcohol dependency

6. – (1) This paragraph applies where a court proposing to make a probation order is satisfied –

(a) that the offender is dependent on drugs or alcohol;
(b) that his dependency caused or contributed to the offence in respect of which the order is proposed to be made; and
(c) that his dependency is such as requires and may be susceptible to treatment.

(2) The probation order may include a requirement that the offender shall submit, during the whole of the probation period or during such part of that period as may be specified in the order, to treatment by or under the direction of a person having the necessary qualifications or experience with a view to the reduction or elimination of the offender's dependency on drugs or alcohol . . .

. . . (9) In this paragraph the reference to the offender being dependent on drugs or alcohol includes a reference to his having a propensity towards the misuse of drugs or alcohol, and references to his dependency on drugs or alcohol shall be construed accordingly.

Notes

1. Schedule 1A contains new provisions on requirements in probation orders relating to residence, specified activities, attendance at a probation centre, treatment for a mental condition, and treatment for drug or alcohol dependency. If a court wishes to impose such a condition, it must ensure (under section 6(2)) that the restrictions on liberty imposed by the order are commensurate with the seriousness of the offence, or the combination of the offence and one or more offences associated with it.

2. The probation order may require an offender to live at a particular address, or at an approved probation hostel, or at another approved institution, for a period specified in the order. Before imposing such a condition, the court must consider the home environment of the offender.

A requirement that the offender resides in a probation hostel may well be made if the offender's home background is particularly unsupportive. Probation hostels enable a period of closer supervision for the offender, and the running of these institutions is now regulated by the Home Office National Standards. The specified period of a residence requirement will not usually be as long as the probation order itself, in order to permit some period of normal supervision once the offender has left the hostel.

3.   A probation order may require an offender to participate in specified activities, as directed by his supervising probation officer, for up to 60 days. Thus, an offender may be required to take part in schemes or activities organised by the probation service or other bodies, such as NACRO. Alternatively, the order may stipulate that the offender should not take part in specified activities (for example, going to football matches).

4.   A probation order may now include a requirement that, during the whole or a specified part of the order, the offender shall submit to treatment by a suitably qualified person "with a view to the reduction or elimination of [his] dependency on drugs or alcohol." (paragraph 6.2). The specified place where such treatment is to take place may require the offender's attendance as either a resident or a non-resident (paragraph 6.3). Before including such a requirement in an order, the court must be satisfied that the offender suffers from alcohol or drug dependency, that this dependency contributed to the offence for which he is being sentenced, and that it is susceptible to, and in need of, treatment (paragraph 6(1)). It should be noted that "dependency" is defined widely, so as to include instances where the offender has a "propensity towards the misuse of drugs or alcohol" (paragraph 6(9)).

5.   The power of a court to include a requirement in a probation order that the offender undergo treatment for a mental condition is looked at in Chapter 7, which discusses mentally disordered offenders.

6.   A court may include in a probation order a requirement that the offender attends a probation centre (formerly known as a "day centre") for up to 60 days (paragraphs 3(1) and 3(3)). A probation centre means premises "at which non-residential facilities are provided for use in connection with the rehabilitation of offenders", and which are approved by the Secretary of State as providing suitable facilities (paragraph 3(7)). (For further discussions, see G. Mair, *Probation Day Centres*, Home Office Research Study No. 100 (1988); A. Vass, *Alternatives to Prison* (1990), Chap. 6; and A. Vass and A. Weston, Probation Centres as an Alternative to Custody" (1990) 30 B.J. Crim. 189). One significant change brought about by the 1991 Act, is that probation centres are now subject to approval by the Home Secretary. Formerly, the organisation and activities of these centres varied considerably from one to another and presumably there will now be greater standardisation.

The rationale of a day centre requirement in a probation order, when first introduced in 1972, was that it could offer help to probationers, where appropriate, with their employment prospects, their literacy, and with the provision of "life skills". It was hoped that attendance at these centres would also help to divert offenders, especially younger ones, from getting into trouble. But some probation officers expressed concern that the introduction of such conditions into a probation order was evidence of a movement towards exerting greater control over probationers and towards tougher community penalties (see Vass, *Alternatives to Prison* (1990), pp. 132 *et seq*).

B. Community Service Orders

Introduction

Community service orders were first introduced into the penal system, in 1973, on an experimental basis in six probation areas. After a cursory but favourable review by the Home Office, of the early workings of this new measure in these "pilot" areas, the government decided in 1975 that the scheme should be introduced nationally. The law relating to community service orders is set out in the Powers of Criminal Court Act 1973, s. 14, as amended by the Criminal Justice Act 1991, s. 10. A community service order can be imposed on offenders aged 16 or over, convicted of an offence for which an adult can be punished with imprisonment. (As one of the "community orders" since 1991, it is subject to the restrictions placed on imposing community sentences – discussed at the start of this chapter). Before making a community service order, a court must have considered a pre-sentence report (Criminal Justice Act, 1991, s. 7(3)), and the offender must consent to the making of the order. A court may impose anything from 40 to 240 hours of community service, and the number of hours specified should, as a guiding principle, be in proportion to the seriousness of the offence committed. The work is to be completed within a twelve month period, in the offender's leisure time. Under the Criminal Justice Act, 1991, s. 10(1), a community service order may now be combined with a fine.

Community service work consists of unpaid work for the community under the supervision of either people employed by the probation service, or by members of the public or voluntary organisations. The administration of community service orders is the responsibility of the probation service. The tasks undertaken by offenders performing community service vary considerably; they may be of a practical nature (e.g. decorating and gardening for the elderly, assisting with conservation projects and constructing adventure play areas), or they may involve more direct contact with the elderly, or with handicapped children. These tasks may involve working together with volunteers. Since 1989, there have been National Standards for community service orders, to promote consistency and to ensure that such an order operates as a genuine restriction on liberty, which is neither regarded as a "let-off" by offenders, nor distrusted by sentencers.

Although community service orders are now used wisely and are an integral part of the penal system, (see *Statistics on CSOs*, Bulletin, 13/92, Home Office Research and Statistics Department), it is interesting to reflect on the origins of this measure. In the early 1970s there was much discussion about the need for new, non-custodial options for sentencers. But why was the community service order, in particular, introduced and what was its underlying philosophy? As the following extracts reveal, this is a subject for debate. First, the view of the Wootton Committee (1970) which led to the introduction of the community service order.

The Advisory Council on the Penal System, *Non-Custodial and Semi-Custodial Penalties* **(1970), paras. 33–34.**

But in general the proposition that some offenders should be required to undertake community service should appeal to adherents of different varieties of penal philosophy. To some it would be simply a more constructive and cheaper alternative to short sentences of imprisonment; by others it would be seen as introducing into the penal system a new dimension with an emphasis on reparation to the community; others again would regard it as a means of giving effect to the old adage that the punishment should fit the crime; while still others would stress the value of bringing offenders into close touch with those members of the community who are most in need of help and support.

These different approaches are by no means incompatible. A court order which deprived an offender of his leisure and required him to undertake tasks for the community would necessarily be felt to have a punitive element. What attracts us, however, is the opportunity which it could give for constructive activity in the form of personal service to the community, and the possibility of a changed outlook on the part of the offender. We would hope that offenders required to perform community service would come to see it in this light, and not as wholly negative and punitive.

In contrast to the Wootton Committee's uncritical enthusiasm for the community service order, Roger Hood concentrated on its lack of a coherent rationale.

R. Hood, "Criminology and Penal Change", in *Crime, Criminology and Public Policy* **(R. Hood ed., 1974) pp. 410–412.**

Did [the Wootton Committee] believe, for example, that such offenders are any different from the majority of the population in the value they place on mutual support and in the sympathy they feel for the sick, disabled and incapacitated aged? After all, relatively few of the law-abiding majority are active in organised voluntary movements. Was the offender viewed as basically lacking empathy, and that this could be remedied by revealing the true state of the sick? Or was he seen as labouring under a feeling of inferiority ... which would be dispelled by revelation of the true underprivileged? Or was he simply hedonistic and selfish; a fact to be brought home to him by the selflessness of volunteers? Where was the consideration of the problem in the light of criminological ideas and knowledge? Most sociological research and theory, emphasising as it does the importance of the delinquent's sense of identity, the broader problems of attaining status in school and work and the "dissociation" from conventional leisure activities, indicate a picture of the delinquent, let alone the adult criminal, who may have moved far beyond the point of being influenced simply by the "wholesome influence of those who choose voluntarily to help in the community". But then in trying to understand the report, one is also faced by the fact that it does not try to define the types of offender concerned. Presumably, if community service were to be a genuine alternative to imprisonment, they were already well on their career, having experienced the majority of other nominal alternative penalties, or were first offenders who had committed an offence of the type the courts wished especially to deter. In either case it is not self-evident why the remedy of community service is appropriate. To the extent that many repetitive minor offenders are among the most deprived members of the community – those lacking parental support, affection, educational or work-skills, stability and friendships – they are hardly in need of "bringing ... into close touch with those members of the community who are most in need of help and support." ...

... I am not here trying to argue a case for one view of the offender over another or even to claim *a priori* that the concept of Community Service is wrong or likely to prove particularly ineffective as a suitable alternative to imprisonment for a least some offenders. The important point is that the Committee failed to provide any analysis of the case for its proposals in terms of criminological and penological knowledge ... In another sphere, also, the Committee conspicuously failed to ... provide a convincing analysis of why the methods already available had failed or need "re-inforcing". It could of course, be said that the Committee's only problem was to suggest alternatives that would be acceptable to courts and to parliament in order to decrease the overcrowding within the prisons. But the issue should have been conceived in broader terms than this. Firstly, it was essential to know why the existing alternatives (especially probation) were not being used more frequently or could not be extended in use, why were they regarded as unsatisfactory or unsuccessful or both? ... Lastly, the Committee should have satisfied itself these available penalties were themselves working satisfactorily and at their maximum effectiveness – for if they were not, the solution might lie in first improving them before embarking on anything new.

Notes

1. The Wootton Report emphasised the appeal which the community service order would have to sentencers possessing a variety of attitudes to punishment. (For a critique, see Warren Young, *Community Service Orders*, 1979, at p. 33). This pragmatic appeal of the measure may well account for the steady increase in its use since its introduction, and also for the ease with which it was incorporated within the new sentencing framework in 1991.

2. As one of the orders which now comprise the category of "community sentences" the use of community service orders is subject to the statutory restrictions discussed earlier in this chapter. Under the Criminal Justice Act 1991, s. 6(1), a court cannot pass a community sentence unless it thinks that the offence, or the combination of the offence and one or more offences associated with it, "was serious enough to warrant such a sentence". It is clear that community sentences are intended to be used for dealing with offences in the middle range of seriousness; that is, those which are not so serious as to require imprisonment, yet which merit some restriction on the offender's liberty.

But when the community service order was first introduced, its exact location within the existing sentencing framework was far from clear. From the outset, in the six "pilot" areas where the new measure was introduced, opinions were fairly evenly divided on the question whether the community service order was simply an alternative to a custodial sentence, or whether it was an alternative to both custodial and non-custodial measures. Early studies suggested that only 45–50 per cent of offenders who received a community service order got them as an alternative to custody (see Home Office Research Study No. 39, (1977)). There was some uncertainty as to where the community service order fitted into the range of measures available to sentencers. The reasons for this uncertainty are explored in the following extracts.

Andrew Willis, "Community Service as an Alternative to Imprisonment" (1977) 24 *Probation Journal* 120–122.

The Wootton Report, without doubt, sets the stage for the future uncertainties and ambiguities: remember, for example, the lengthy catalogue of possible justifications for Community Service ... potentially difficult problems never materialise as such because the authors simply refuse to consider the issues. Small wonder, then, that early commentators were uncertain as to the true nature of this penal "chameleon" they are required to operate.

However, in the midst of this uncertainty, there appeared to be one incontrovertible element, namely, that Community Service should comprise, to some extent, a viable alternative to imprisonment. The evidence appears on first analysis, unequivocal. The Report states clearly that it considers Community Service to be both "inappropriate for trivial offences" and hopes that it "would be felt by the courts to constitute an adequate alternative to a short custodial sentence". It might well have been the case that Community Service was a vaguely determined project in that it could appeal to varieties of penal philosophies but, in practice, the initial aim seemed clear enough: it should be made available for offenders who might otherwise be dealt with by imprisonment.

But, just as the authors wanted *Everyman* to subscribe to the ideology of Community Service, so too they strove to ensure that *Anyman* (and not just the candidate for a custodial disposition) could be awarded this new sentence. Specifically, there are four occasions in the Report where it is possible to interpret Community Service as being another alternative to the existing range of non-custodial dispositions, rather than as an alternative to imprisonment....

... My first point, then, is this: Community Service, as enunciated in the Wootton Report, is totally confused, for the authors posit it both as an alternative to imprisonment and, at the same time, view it as being reserved for minor, non-imprisonable offences. More disturbing, however, is the further point that this contradiction is evidenced elsewhere. On the one hand, consider the view of the Parliamentary Under-Secretary of State who envisaged the sentence becoming "a type of order which the courts may come to use freely ... as an alternative to short custodial sentences", which clearly implies subscription to the alternative-to-imprisonment model. And, on the other hand, consider the recent Report of the Advisory Council on the Penal System (1977) which argues: "We remain convinced that Community Service could be of particular value as a disposal in the less serious, non-imprisonable cases" which represents endorsement of the model which would reserve Community Service for non-serious offenders. Paradoxically, both parties would, and, as we have seen, could, refer to the Wootton Report to support their views....

... Clearly, then, the literature offers a number of not wholly compatible conceptions – as an alternative to imprisonment; as being restricted to a range of non-serious, non-imprisonable offences; or, for all types of offence. These ambiguities have not been without repercussions. For, apart from inhibiting any theoretical development of the notion of Community Service as a penal disposition, it has also caused unavoidable ambiguities in its practice. Given the philosophical uncertainty that surrounds the concept, what, in practice, has actually happened?

[Willis goes on to suggest that there is empirical evidence to support the view that the CSO was being used instead of other non-custodial measures, rather than in place of imprisonment – "in short, that Community Service and imprisonment do not exist as penal alternatives."]

Ken Pease, *Community Service Orders – A First Decade of Promise* (1981), pp. 23–25.

Now, there can be any combination of views, among the various individuals involved, about the position of community service relative to custody. A probation officer can, for example, recommend a community service order, believing it to be an alternative to custody, the court can accept or reject that recommendation, believing it not to be an alternative to custody, and the offender's perception could be either. If the offender has his order revoked, the revoking court can have a view of community service relative to custody which is different from that of the sentencing court and/or the probation officer who originally recommended it. The particularly poignant kinds of misunderstanding can arise when the probation officer, believing the sentence not to be primarily an alternative to custody, does not recommend community service, and the court thereupon locks up the offender believing that the probation officer would have recommended community service if he had thought that it was an appropriate alternative to custody in the case. Another example is when the revoking court locks up someone who has failed on his community service order although the court making the order did not think that the original offence should be punished by imprisonment. Knowing community service practice reasonably well, I would also argue that probation officers recommending community service tend to stress the alternative-to-imprisonment aspect to the offender to obtain his consent even when a custodial sentence is not in fact likely. This is very understandable. It is surely worse for someone to be given a prison sentence when he is not expecting it than to be given a non-custodial sentence when he is expecting to be sent to prison.

On a more mundane level, there is the ludicrous position at present that the use of community service relative to custody depends upon the view of the most influential of court personnel, the justices' clerk. The day before writing this paragraph, I was talking about community service in a small area where, I was told, two justices' clerks operated. One of them regarded community service as exclusively an alternative to a custodial sentence, the other regarded it as a sentence in its own right, with no presumption about the sentence which might be passed if a community service order were not to be made. Thus offenders living on opposite sides of the road which formed the boundary between the two areas faced fundamentally different sentencing policies in relation to community service.

The important thing which I would argue should be guaranteed in any sentence is that the offender should know the sentence to which community service is an alternative, and this should be a matter of public record. In England and Wales, I see two possible resolutions of the problem. The first would be a two-tier community service order scheme in which it was generally understood that orders in excess of 100 hours in length were alternatives to custody and those of less were not. In this way, when invited to consent to an order of a particular length, the offender would grant or withhold his consent knowing what the alternative was likely to be. If he withheld his consent to a short order but the court proceeded to lock him up, this could and should be dealt with by the appellate courts.

An alternative and simpler scheme which may find more favour involves simply telling each individual offender what the alternative sentence would be and recording that for the possible use of a revoking court. The offender can then make an informed consent, or withhold such consent. This kind of scheme would have the additional advantage of avoiding the uncertainty which a probation officer at present feels in making a recommendation of community service.

Notes

1.   For a further discussion of the suggestions made by Pease, see K. Pease, "Community Service and the Tariff" [1978] Crim. L.R. 269 and A. Willis, "Community Service and the Tariff" [1978] Crim. L.R. 540. For a more recent study of the extent to which community service succeeded in diverting offenders from custody, see G. McIvor, "Community Service and Custody in Scotland" (1990) 29 *Howard Journal* 101.

2.   In view of the early uncertainty about the appropriate use of community service orders, the Court of Appeal provided some guidance to sentencers. The Court encouraged the use of this measure in cases which might otherwise have been dealt with by imprisonment. For example, in a series of judgments, it quashed custodial sentences on young burglars and substituted community service. In *Lawrence* [1982] Crim. L.R. 377 the appellant's 18 month prison sentence for burglary was reduced to 150 hours of community service. The burglary was from commercial premises, where the appellant took television and video equipment. He had some previous convictions, but had not been in trouble for some time. The appellant was 23 years old and the Court thought that he showed signs of settling down and remaining a useful member of society. The Court of Appeal stated:

> "Generally speaking it was wrong to order a small number of community service hours where the alternative order would have been, as in the present case, a sentence of imprisonment. A short period of community service would usually be reserved for cases in which the court was not minded otherwise to impose a custodial sentence. In the present case, the court would probably have ordered about 190 hours service if the appellant had not spent a little time in prison before being released on bail; as it was, 150 hours would suffice" (at p. 377).

This decision went even further than in *Brown* [1982] Crim. L.R. 126, where the appellant, also a burglar, was younger and had no previous convictions and the Court described the case as "tailor-made" for a community service order. (For a similar case to *Lawrence*, see *Canfield* [1982] Crim. L.R. 460). In a case which was very close to the custody threshold, *Seymour* [1983] Crim L.R. 635, the Court reduced an eighteen month prison sentence to 80 hours' community service (the appellant had already spent some time in prison). Here, an eighteen year old with a number of previous convictions pleaded guilty to burglary of a dwelling. The Court, in varying the sentence to one of community service, placed much reliance on the favourable social enquiry report which stated that the appellant was showing signs of greater maturity.

Although all of the above decisions relate to burglars, community service may also be imposed for other property offences, such as theft, fraud and criminal damage. Less commonly, but in appropriate cases, community service may be imposed for less serious, isolated crimes of violence for example, see *McDermot* [1985] Crim. L.R. 245) and for quite serious instances of reckless driving (see *Eynon* (1988) 10 Cr. App. R.(S) 437).

3. The debate as to whether community service is an "alternative to custody" is not so relevant, perhaps, since 1991. The government expressed its dislike of the term "alternatives to custody" (see White Paper (1990), para. 4.1) and pointed out that custody is not the only "real" punishment. The new category of "community sentences" is intended to provide a credible form of punishment for offences of moderate seriousness. As community service is quite a demanding form of community sentence, it may well be appropriate to use other community orders for less serious offences. In this way, community service might be reserved for the higher end of the scale of community penalties.

It should be remembered that the Criminal Justice Act 1991, s. 6(2), states that where a court passes a community sentence, the particular order or orders should be the most suitable for the offender, and the restrictions on liberty should be commensurate with the seriousness of the offence. In short, if a community service order is appropriate (*e.g.* the offender does not need close supervision by a probation officer), then the number of hours imposed by the court should reflect the seriousness of the offence(s) committed.

4. For further discussion of the use and practice of community service before 1991, see A. Bottoms, "Limiting Prison Use: Experience in England and Wales" (1987) 26 *Howard Journal* 177, pp. 191–5, and A. Vass, *Alternatives to Prison*, (1990, Chap. 7). The following extract is taken from the latter.

A. Vass, *Alternatives to Prison* (1990), pp. 128–131.

In an attempt to regulate the way in which the community service is enforced and to limit discretion, the Home Office has drawn up national standards for the operation of community service orders. The statutory rules, which took effect from April 1989, focus on the following main areas of concern:

1. *Making the order appear harsh punishment.* Thus, every offender serving an order of 60 hours or more should spend at least 21 hours in a group placement. People who are physically or mentally unsuited to work in a group, who might disrupt work or be a bad influence, those who need to travel at least two hours in each direction in order to attend a group placement, and those who have special domestic responsibilities (for upbringing of children for example) and need to travel at least one hour in each direction in order to attend a group placement, are exempted.

2. *Exercising more control over offenders' choices and structuring working arrangements.* Community service should not be performed at the convenience of offenders.

Offenders must be given clear instructions and a leaflet which sets out the requirements of the order. They must attend for the first work session within 10 days of notification of the order being received by the probation service unless there are legitimate delays or because of offenders' health or other exceptional circumstances. Community service schemes should aim to ensure a work rate of a minimum of five hours per week throughout the order. Generally no offenders should be allowed to work more than 21 hours in a week, unless previous absences make this necessary to complete the order within 12 months. Only work done at the time and place specified counts towards the community service order. Offenders who report for work without an appointment should not be allowed to work. Travelling time does not count towards the completion of an order, except when offenders are travelling under the supervision of community service staff. In addition to other requirements, lunch breaks which count towards the completion of an order must not last longer than half an hour. If other breaks are allowed, these must not last longer than ten minutes and any excess should not be counted towards completion of an order. Offenders should not be allowed to leave the site unless authorised to do so by the supervising officer. In bad weather, which may necessitate cancellation of work, no more than one hour can be credited to the work record of offenders for any one session, for time lost.

3. *Enforcing discipline and required standards of work.* If offenders fail to meet the stated required standards of performance and behaviour, the reasons for that should be identified, and those offenders should be warned of the possible consequences. If unsatisfactory work or behaviour continues, offenders should be reported and be liable to be sent home, and treated as if they had failed to attend (including forfeiture of any hours worked on that day). If offenders are late in arriving for work without a reasonable excuse, they are liable to be sent home and a failure to attend should be recorded. Those who are more than half an hour late, without a reasonable excuse, should not be allowed to work on that day. When offenders fail to attend work appointments or behave or work unsatisfactorily, action by supervising officers should be taken within two days. First, an explanation must be sought for each failure to comply with the requirements of the order. Secondly, action taken must be recorded. Thirdly, the offenders' explanation for those failures to comply with the requirements of the order must be recorded as either acceptable or unacceptable. Fourthly, if explanations are accepted, that choice must be clarified. Acceptable reasons for failure to attend are medical grounds, family or religious responsibilities, requirements of usual paid employment and educational training commitments, and circumstances beyond the control of offenders. Where medical reasons are accepted, these must be supported by a certificate signed by a doctor. If frequent absences are recorded on grounds of ill-health, further evidence should be obtained about offenders' state of health, and if necessary by requiring offenders to undergo an independent medical examination at the expense of the probation service.

After the first instance of a failure to attend or unsatisfactory performance without an acceptable explanation, offenders should either be taken to court or be warned in writing that further breaches of the order will make them liable to court proceedings. After the second such instance, the case should be referred to the senior probation officer who must decide the next appropriate action. Breach proceedings should normally be started following no more than three instances of unacceptable absence, work or behaviour.... Whether the national standards will work or their requirements will be followed and enforced by supervising officers is an open question....

However, as the effect of those statutory rules will not be known for some time and until there is more empirical work on the subject, the preceding discussion should be regarded as a factual representation of current activity....

In sum, in this brief account of the interactions between supervisors and offenders in the context of community service, I have attempted to show that in organising and enforcing this alternative to custody, supervisors play a crucial role in the process of defining and determining, among other issues, the outcomes of their supervision of offenders. In advocating alternative means of control to either supplement or supersede the authoritative sanctions installed by law, officers evolve a screening process which is characterised by a degree of *tolerance* for technical infractions of the law. This principle of tolerance remains operative, for the majority of offenders, at the *cautioning* level without advancing against such offenders any special or severe penalties. By expanding the sanctions and scaling them against a background of pressures, officers manage to determine the rate of successful completions of orders. This process indirectly promotes in public the value of community service as an effective penal measure, and in private protects many offenders from re-entering the criminal justice system as defaulters of their order. In essence, the tolerance expressed by those officers and their elastic responses to infractions of the order, may be *instrumental in expanding the opportunities open to offenders to remain in the community and outside the walls of prison establishments.* In other words, by using formal sanctions as a last resort and focusing instead on methods which allow a protracted process of negotiation, those officers may in fact, without realising it, be promoting the basic and fundamental justification for providing and running *alternatives* to custody. In some circles (for instance over-zealous politicians or managers of the probation service who are divorced from practice) this tolerance, informal exchanges, and means of enforcing an order may appear to represent an abdication of professional responsibility and an attempt to downgrade or indeed violate the spirit of the court order. They are quite wrong. What is happening in community service, in an unofficial capacity, is not so different to the officially promoted and condoned policy of "police cautioning" of juveniles in an attempt to divert them from courts. Hard as it may seem, tolerance of some rule-breaking, and, overall, some discretion and elasticity in the way offenders are treated, are necessary and integral parts of the administration, organisation and enforcement of laws; for the preservation of stability in social relationships; and for keeping prison populations down. The statutory rules discussed earlier are in contradiction to that principle of tolerance and if successful in their aims, they may well structure community service but they will not destructure the prison.

Notes

1. Vass described community service as a "process of tolerance", but it was the perceived leniency in the enforcement of orders which led some people to suggest that the courts were losing confidence in this penal measure. (Research suggested variations in use between courts, and a decline in the number of orders in the mid-1980s). In a study of the use of community service orders after the introduction of national standards, Lloyd argued that there was evidence of a revival of confidence in the measure. (See C. Lloyd, *National Standards for Community Service Orders: The First Two Years of Operation*, Home Office Research Bulletin, No. 31 (1991), 16). He stated (at p. 21):

"... [I]t could be that the stricter breach policy and other more rigid codes of practice introduced by the Standards have affected sentencers' attitudes in a positive way. The Probation Statistics show that the decline in the use of community service orders up until 1989 was reversed in 1990, and the monitoring data shows an increased use of community service orders through to the first quarter of 1991. More-

over, this increase has occurred without any diminution in the proportion of offenders given community service orders who have previous
custodial experience. These developments could be due to greater
confidence in the community service order on the part of sentencers."

2.   In another study of community service practice in the late 1980s, Skinns
did not find the same pattern of informality suggested by Vass' earlier
research (A. Vass, *Sentenced to Labour* (1984)). Skinns' study suggested
that there had been "a shift not only in the working ideology, from
rehabilitation to a more juridical model, but that this shift [was] connected
with the shift in personnel concerned with the day-to-day management of
community service, away from probation staff qualified in social work and
towards ancillaries". (See C. Skinns, "Community Service Practice" (1990),
30 B.J. Crim. 65 at 76). The introduction of national standards, he suggested,
was likely to further the shift from a rehabilitative approach to one of
formality and uniformity.

3.   The "chameleon"-like qualities of community service which so appealed
to the Wootton Committee, have enabled the measure to be adapted to
successive shifts in penal policy. It now fits comfortably within the "just
deserts" framework and it is a measure well suited to the idea of punishment
in the community. There was never any clear evidence of its reformative
qualities (see Home Office Research Study No. 39 (1977), and Home Office
Statistical Bulletin 18/83), but this is something which is notoriously difficult
to quantify with any accuracy. In any case, its rehabilitative credentials are
no longer (officially) of any great concern. It is a constructive penalty and
one which is consistent with the notion of an offender paying back something
to society, although not to any particular victim. The other frequent claim
for community service is that it represents a relatively cheap means of
dealing with offenders. How valid is this claim?

**M. Knapp, E. Robertson, and G. McIvor, "The Comparative Costs of Community
Service and Custody in Scotland" (1992) 31 *Howard Journal 8*, pp. 8–10; 26–30.**

   In this paper we examine the costs of community service orders in Scotland in
comparison to the costs of custody and fines. Although a small amount of evidence
exists on the costs of different penal sanctions in Britain, the costings presented here
bring more comprehensive and purposive evidence to illuminate the implications of
alternative decisions for adult offenders. The cost results reported in this paper are
part of a larger evaluative study of community service. The results presented are of
more than academic interest. Funding of community service orders in Scotland is
ultimately the responsibility of central government, which reimburses regional social
work departments (there are no probation departments) for the appropriate costs
incurred. The diversity of policy and practice which has developed during the short
history of community service orders makes it imperative to examine how the costs
of this service vary from region to region, scheme to scheme and perhaps even
activity to activity. There is, for example, much to learn from observed differences
in costs between community service schemes organised along different lines, pursuing
marginally different objectives, and undertaking different services within local
communities.

Although offenders are sentenced to community service orders under different legislation in Scotland than elsewhere in the UK, and although the orders are supervised from within social work departments rather than probation departments as in England and Wales, there are many similarities between the Scottish arrangements and those operating elsewhere, and there are conclusions to draw from this research for the UK as a whole.

Appropriate Costings: The Research Methodology

There are four comparatively simple rules to obey when conducting cost studies for public or other services. First, costs should be comprehensively measured across the full range of agencies and individuals affected by policy or practice decisions. Second, variations in cost from one part of the country to another, or between different individuals served, should be noted, examined and "explained". Third, comparisons between services, areas of the country, agencies, or individuals should only be made on a like-with-like basis. Finally, costs results should preferably be integrated with findings on outcomes or effectiveness. Whilst simple to state, these rules can present formidable conceptual and practical problems. Compromises will be necessary. Nevertheless, one does not have to search long to find prize examples of erroneous conclusions, sometimes dangerous in their implications, drawn from mis-specified costings. In this study of community service orders and their alternatives we do not have outcome data, so not all of the rules apply.

The cost study was focussed on twelve community service schemes, but because of the way in which accounting information is compiled in two of the regions, we are working here with ten "costed" community service schemes. The schemes were selected so that they would differ from each other procedurally in various respects but would, as a whole, be representative of Scottish practice nationally. Data were collected directly from community service organisers and their colleagues, from individual case files, from offenders with community service sentences, from regional headquarters, and from appropriate central government departments. To preserve anonymity, the schemes have been assigned an alphabetic code...

Conclusion

Although we have been able to measure some of the costs of community service and its alternatives only with some informed guesswork, this paper offers what we believe to be the most comprehensive costing of this penal measure to date. The direct costs of community service have been disaggregated to the four principal component activities – assessment, matching, ongoing supervision and processing breaches – on the basis of focussed work in a dozen schemes (conflated to ten because of accounting procedures in one region). To these direct costs we have added estimates of the indirect or hidden costs. Equivalent procedures have been employed in the costing of custody, giving us a comprehensive base for the comparison of these two penal alternatives. We commented earlier that reliance on the published costings of central government departments suggests that community service is a good deal less expensive than custody. The direct costs of the two options, as more accurately and consistently computed in this paper, led us to reach the same conclusion. What, then, is the impact of the addition of the indirect costs?

From ... [our findings] it is clear that a successfully completed community service order is noticeably cheaper than the likely costs of custody, having adjusted the latter to take account of the typical characteristics of offenders given orders. However, the full cost of a breach order, building in the court and sentence costs, is high. Breaches represented only 11% of completions in the study sample, so that the probabilistic cost estimate averages approximately £1,044 per community service order, which compares favourably with the equivalent costing of a custodial sentence (£2,268).

We would draw four general conclusions from this comparative costing exercise. First, whilst cheaper than custody, community service is not *as* cheap as central government figures suggest. The various additions and adjustments necessary to place the costings on a comparable footing, and to build in their full service ramifications, leave community service looking rather more expensive than previously published figures suggest, and custody is left looking less expensive than before. It would be foolish to plan a penal policy solely on the basis of comparative costs, but the efficiency streak running through public policy discussions and initiatives is putting greater reliance on financial indicators. These indicators should therefore be *accurate*. We earlier quoted the NACRO conclusion drawn from published Home Office data that a three week prison sentence costs more than community service. This statement needs amendment in the light of our more accurate costings: community service costs the same as about *six* weeks of imprisonment. NACRO have already taken these cost adjustments on board.

A second conclusion is that the costs of these two penal sanctions fall to a variety of sectors within society. The indirect costs are not huge, but any major shift in the pattern of sentencing could quickly push up the burden falling to social work departments (other than the community service schemes within them) and the health service.

Third, an important factor in the narrowing of the cost difference between community service and custody was the probability of breach because of non-compliance with the order. Currently in Scotland about 10% of orders breach (about the same proportion as in England), with costly ramifications in terms of court time and the likelihood of a custodial sentence...

... To what extent does community service function as an alternative to custody? It has been shown that only 45% of offenders on community service are likely to have been diverted from custody. For these offenders, the cost savings of being placed on community service will be substantial. For many offenders, however, community service is likely to be a comparatively costly disposal, given the minimal costs of other disposals such as a fine. On the basis of the costs presented here, the cost of 100 offenders sentenced to community service would be £102,000. If 45 of these offenders have been diverted from custody, the total cost of the custodial sentences that have been replaced would be £102,060. The cost implications are clear. If community service is used *less* than at present as a direct alternative to custody, then it will cease overall to be a relatively cheap penal option. An *increase* in the use of community service orders in lieu of custody will, on the other hand, result in savings to other parts of the penal system and justify the increased resourcing of community service schemes.

Finally, it must not be forgotten that community service is intended to generate positive benefits for communities and, although the order is in itself a punishment, it hopefully also produces positive "rehabilitative" benefits for offenders. In a subsequent study of recipients' attitudes towards the work carried out by offenders on community service orders, McIvor found that the vast majority of individuals and agencies who responded believed the work to have been of a high standard and of considerable benefit to them...

... This economic study of community service and its two main alternatives – custody and fines – has suggested that routinely published costs data are very inaccurate, even though the inaccuracies do not reverse the ordering of these alternatives in terms of their drain on society's services and other resources.

Note

1. As we saw at the start of this chapter, much of the research into the corrective efficacy of penal measures is inconclusive. This has led to a growing interest in studying other aspects of sentences, such as their

respective costs. Care must be taken, of course, to allow for the "hidden" costs of penal measures when research of this type is undertaken. The study of community service costs by Knapp *et al.* is of considerable interest both in relation to its methodology and to its conclusions.

C. Combination Orders

Section 11, Criminal Justice Act 1991

11. – (1) Where a court by or before which a person of or over the age of sixteen years is convicted of an offence punishable with imprisonment (not being an offence for which the sentence is fixed by law) is of the opinion mentioned in subsection (2) below, the court may make a combination order, that is to say, an order requiring him both –

    (a) to be under the supervision of a probation officer for a period specified in the order, being not less than twelve months nor more than three years; and

    (b) to perform unpaid work for a number of hours so specified, being in the aggregate not less than 40 nor more than 100.

(2) The opinion referred to in subsection (1) above is that the making of a combination order is desirable in the interests of –

    (a) securing the rehabilitation of the offender; or

    (b) protecting the public from harm from him or preventing the commission by him of further offences.

(3) Subject to subsection (1) above, Part I of the 1973 Act shall apply in relation to combination orders –

    (a) in so far as they impose such a requirement as is mentioned in paragraph (a) of that subsection, as if they were probation orders; and

    (b) in so far as they impose such a requirement as is mentioned in paragraph (b) of that subsection, as if they were community service orders.

The combination order is a new penalty introduced under the Criminal Justice Act 1991, s. 11, and it can be made in respect of offenders aged 16 or over, convicted of an imprisonable offence. As one of the orders which comprise the category of community sentences, the combination order is subject to the restrictions set out in the Criminal Justice Act 1991, s. 6(1), (discussed earlier). This new measure enables a court to combine a probation order of 12 months to three years with community service of between 40 and 100 hours. (For the relevant law in relation to the making of probation orders and community service orders, see the preceding sections of this chapter). Before making a combination order, a court must consider a pre-sentence report (the Criminal Justice Act 1991, s. 7(3)) and the offender's consent to the making of such an order is also required.

Why was the new combination order introduced? The White Paper *Crime, Justice and Protecting the Public* (1990), para. 4.16 stated:

"The Government proposes to introduce a new power to enable the courts to combine a probation order and community service. The power to combine probation and community service is already available to the courts in Scotland. Under this new order, an offender could be required to carry out a period of community service work while under the supervision of a probation officer and subject to any of the requirements which could be attached to a probation order. It would enable the courts to introduce an element of reparation but, at the same time, to provide the probation service with an opportunity to work with offenders, to reduce the likelihood of future offending. It will be possible to combine community service either with basic probation supervision or with probation with specified activities. This new order should be particularly suitable for some persistent property offenders. About 10,000 of those in custody sentenced for burglary, theft, handling, fraud and forgery, have three or more previous convictions."

The combination order was devised, therefore, as a demanding form of community sentence, particularly suitable for moderately serious offenders with a poor record. Prior to 1991, this type of offender frequently ended up in prison more as a result of persistent law-breaking, than as a consequence of the offence itself. This new order, situated at the more punitive end of the scale of community sentences, combines elements of both reparation and supervision. Although additional requirements may be added to the probation part of the sentence, a sentencer must ensure that the overall sentence is not too demanding for the offender. A combination order may be further combined with a fine or compensation order.

D. Curfew Orders

Section 12, Criminal Justice Act 1991

Curfew orders

12. – (1) Where a person of or over the age of sixteen years is convicted of an offence (not being an offence for which the sentence is fixed by law), the court by or before which he is convicted may make a curfew order, that is to say, an order requiring him to remain, for periods specified in the order, at a place so specified.

(2) A curfew order may specify different places or different periods for different days, but shall not specify –

(a) periods which fall outside the period of six months beginning with the day on which it is made; or
(b) periods which amount to less than 2 hours or more than 12 hours in any one day.

(3) The requirements in a curfew order shall, as far as practicable, be such as to avoid –

(a) any conflict with the offender's religious beliefs or with the requirements of any other community order to which he may be subject; and
(b) any interference with the times, if any, at which he normally works or attends school or other educational establishment.

(4) A curfew order shall include provision for making a person responsible for monitoring the offender's whereabouts during the curfew periods specified in the order; and a person who is made so responsible shall be of a description specified in an order made by the Secretary of State...

This section of the Act provides for the making of curfew orders by a court but, as yet, section 12 has not been brought into force. A curfew order is a new measure which (when implemented) will give courts the power to require an offender, of 16 years old or over, to remain at a specified location for between two and twelve hours per day for not more than six months. (It should be noted that a curfew order may "specify different places or different periods for different days"). A curfew order may be made in respect of any offence except murder but, as a community order, it is subject to the statutory restrictions on imposing this type of sentence. Before making a curfew order, a court must explain the effect of such an order to the offender, and the consequence of any failure to comply with it. The offender must agree to the making of the order. Although the obtaining of a pre-sentence report is not a statutory prerequisite for making a curfew order, a court may well see fit to obtain and consider a report before making such an order.

What was the rationale behind this new measure? The White Paper ((1990), paras. 4.20 and 4.23) stated:

"The Green Paper, *Punishment, Custody and the Community* raised the question of whether it would be useful for the courts to have powers to make curfew orders, confining people to their homes at certain times. It is not the intention to keep people at home for most of the day. The aim is to enable them to go to work, to attend training courses or probation centres, to carry out community service or to receive treatment for drug abuse. Curfews could be helpful in reducing some forms of crime, thefts of and from cars, pub brawls and other types of disorder. A curfew order could be used to keep offenders away from particular places, such as shopping centres or pubs, or to keep them at home in the evenings or at weekends.

... The court would have to consider whether making the order would be likely to reduce further offending while it is in force, and the likely effect on the offender's family and those living at the same address. If the order is made as a penalty, the court would have to be satisfied that the seriousness of the offence justified imposing the order."

Although the White Paper stated that a curfew order might be used as "an order in its own right" (para. 4.24), it was clearly intended that it could be combined usefully with other community orders, such as probation or community service. A curfew order may also be imposed together with a financial penalty.

Electronic Monitoring

The White Paper also expressed enthusiasm for electronic monitoring as a method of enforcing curfew orders (see paragraph 4.21). It announced that the government had set up "pilot" schemes to test the feasibility of this idea and which were to be carried out by the private sector, under the control of the courts and with the co-operation of the police. The White Paper stated (at paragraph 4.22):

> "There are those who criticise electronic monitoring as an infringement of civil liberty. Of course, any restriction on liberty must be justified. But, if restrictions are justified, most people would prefer electronic monitoring to a remand in custody or a term of imprisonment. The criminal justice system should take advantage of modern technology when it is sensible and practical to do so ... The Home Office experimental projects will test the effectiveness of electronic monitoring and the results should be available in 1990."

Despite the far from reassuring experience of electronic monitoring in the three trial areas (see G. Mair and C. Nee, *Electronic Monitoring: The Trials and Their Results*, Home Office Research Study, No. 120, (1990)), the government pressed on with its support for this idea. Section 13 of the Criminal Justice Act 1991 states:

> 13(1) Subject to subsection (2) below, a curfew order may in addition include requirements for securing the electronic monitoring of the offender's whereabouts during the curfew period in the order.
>
> (2) A court shall not make a curfew order which includes such requirements unless the court –
>
> (a) has been notified by the Secretary of State that electronic monitoring arrangements are available in the area in which the place proposed to be specified in the order is situated; and
> (b) is satisfied that the necessary provision can be made under those arrangements.
>
> (3) Electronic monitoring arrangements made by the Secretary of State under this section may include entering into contracts with other persons for the electronic monitoring by them of offenders' whereabouts.

(Note: As with the provision relating to curfew orders, section 13 has not yet been implemented).

A court cannot include an electronic monitoring requirement as part of a curfew order unless the offender agrees to it (see s. 12(5)). But in spite of this, and the assurances in the White Paper (at para. 4.22) that electronic monitoring is a justifiable restriction on liberty, the proposed scheme has encountered much hostility (not least from the probation service). The arguments for and against electronic monitoring are clearly presented in the following extract.

NACRO Briefing Paper, *The Electronic Monitoring of Offenders* **(May 1989), pp. 10–12.**

Arguments for and against

Those in favour of electronic monitoring of offenders say that it is less costly than imprisonment and can:

- reduce the use of custody without putting the public at risk;
- avoid the contamination effect of imprisonment through which first offenders mix with more experienced offenders and learn new "tricks of the trade";
- avoid the stigma attached to having served a prison sentence;
- assist rehabilitation by allowing the offender to support his or her family and maintain social ties.

Those opposed to electronic monitoring of offenders argue:

For an offender to be eligible for electronic monitoring as part of home confinement, he or she must have a home and a telephone. Offenders who have committed minor offences and have a stable homelife with a regular income are already likely to be considered suitable for supervision in the community without the additional penalty of electronic surveillance.

There is a danger of "widening the net" of social control and an unwarranted escalation of penalties. Courts are likely to use electronic monitoring for offenders who would otherwise receive a less restrictive non-custodial penalty. According to early research following the introduction of community service orders, 55% were used instead of other non-custodial penalties and the evidence suggests that this is also true of many suspended sentences. It is even more likely to be true of electronic monitoring, which has so far been used in the USA for socially stable offenders who in this country would be good prospects for other non-custodial penalties.

If electronic monitoring were applied to offenders who would not otherwise have been sent to prison, this would defeat the argument that monitoring is less intrusive and less costly than prison.

Little as yet is known about the types of offenders best suited for these programmes, the effect on re-offending and the psychological impact of monitoring. Reports suggest that the failure rate goes up if the sentence is imposed over too long a period.

Little, too, is known about the impact of electronic monitoring on the offender's family. However, it is reported that enforced home confinement has led to family tensions and, in some cases, to domestic violence.

If electronic monitoring is seen as an adjunct to a probation order or parole licence, it is worth noting that the vast majority of probationers and parolees in this country complete their period of supervision successfully without electronic monitoring. 80% of probation orders and community service orders are satisfactorily completed. Moreover, they are applied to a much wider variety of offenders than the highly selected group considered suitable for electronic monitoring in the USA and last for much longer than periods of electronic home confinement. It is therefore difficult to see what additional benefit electronic monitoring would offer in the supervision of offenders.

Electronic monitoring only allows the authorities to know where an offender is, not what he or she is doing. If he or she is committing an offence from home the authorities are none the wiser.

Requiring someone to walk around with a transmitter permanently strapped to his or her neck, wrist or ankle is degrading and stigmatising in a way which other high tariff non-custodial measures, such as community service orders, residence at a probation hostel, or attendance at a day centre, are not. (The European Convention on Human Rights forbids "degrading punishment".) It is also purely restrictive, whereas the other options are not. It is therefore preferable to promote the use of more positive and less stigmatising non-custodial measures.

Notes

1. The study by G. Mair and C. Nee for the Home Office (*Electronic Monitoring: The Trials and their Results* (1990), Home Office Research Study No. 120) found little evidence of the "net-widening" referred to in the NACRO paper. But, if electronic monitoring were to be available nationally, rather than in a few carefully prepared and scrutinised "trial" areas, it is likely that the scheme would widen the net of social control and be used in inappropriate cases.

2. The experimental schemes, which were targeted at remand prisoners, also suggested a reluctance on the part of the courts to use electronic monitoring, as there was a surprisingly low take-up rate. Other problems included technical difficulties with monitoring equipment, frequent violation of restrictions by remandees, and very high costs of implementation.

3. For an interesting attempt at predicting the effect on sentencing (and remand) decisions when "tagging" is an available option, see the empirical study of Sally Frost and Geoffrey Stephenson, "A Simulation Study of Electronic Tagging as a Sentencing Option" (1989) 28 *Howard Journal* 91.

4. For a useful overview of the "tagging" debate, see M. Nellis, "The Electronic Monitoring of Offenders in England and Wales", (1991) 32 B.J. Crim. 165. The following extract is taken from Nellis' article.

M. Nellis, "The Electronic Monitoring of Offenders in England and Wales" (1991) 31 B.J. Crim. 165, pp. 178–181.

To a number of commentators the central moral/political issue with tagging, as with all so-called "alternatives to custody", is that of targeting. So long as it is targeted properly, that is, actually used on people who would otherwise have gone into custody, it is acceptable. As we have seen, this is how the Home Office would see tagging used. Both liberal newspapers such as the *Guardian* (February 23, 1988) and probation commentators such as Wade have given qualified support to this position, simply on the grounds that electronic monitoring is "obviously" not as bad as imprisonment. Now, although there is deep concern in Britain that when allegedly tough "alternatives to custody" are introduced (community service, day centres, suspended sentences), they tend to replace other, more lenient alternative sentences (ordinary probation, fines, conditional discharges), rather than prison itself, there is also growing evidence, especially in the juvenile justice field, that successful targeting can be achieved. That is not to say that perpetual vigilance to avoid "slippage" or net-widening is not needed, merely that total pessimism is unwarranted.

However, not all parties agree that tagging *should* be restricted to those specifically at risk of custody. The Offender Tag Association takes the view that net-widening is unimportant: tagging can and should be used on any offender, minor or serious, at risk of custody or not, because it is not *per se* as intrusive as other measures. In his evidence to the All-Party Penal Affairs Group on January 26, 1988, Tom Stacey resisted the restriction of tagging to serious offenders who were specifically at risk of custody as "an unnecessary proviso", adding that "it could apply to a lot of people ... as a second serious warning"...

... But even if electronic monitoring were targeted "properly", and used as a genuine alternative to custody, it is still not clear that no new moral or political issues arise. To accept that tagging is not as bad as prison (the stock comment of all its supporters) is not *per se* to endorse it: each non-custodial measure needs to be judged on its own merits, and some raise issues that others do not. The OTA is right to say that tagging "is fundamentally different in kind to any other kind of correction", although the Association itself is rather naïve about the ethical principles involved. In principle tagging does enable offenders to remain "in the community" in contact with family and friends, available for work; and, as with other non-custodial measures – this is indisputably more humane than imprisonment in many cases. But that is in fact quite a limited way of conceptualizing what tagging – unlike other non-custodial measures – *also* does. With "tracking tagging" (if it develops), and already with "curfew tagging", some of the public and private spaces in which an adult citizen's whereabouts has hitherto been regarded as a matter of unscrutinised free choice come to be redefined as penal space, an area in which movement can be monitored and constrained by *unseen* state (or state-mandated) personnel. This does indeed represent a fundamental alteration in the type and degree of control which a state can exert over its offending citizens, and one which might significantly diminish the amount of personal, professional contact – whether for support or control – that up to now has been an integral feature of community-based social work with offenders.

Can – indeed, should – this new form of control be resisted? Most of its supporters doubt that it can be ... Tom Stacey sees much of the resistance to it as simply the opinions of "vested interests" in the civil libertarian, penal reform, and social work lobbies. In a quite literal sense this is true, but a commitment to existing approaches, to a reasoned defence of tradition, does not in itself invalidate criticism of electronic tagging. To Stacey, it merely "brings to mind the fact that most of those operating the transport system in 1900 opposed the motor car"; the opponents of tagging "are making fools of themselves in the sight of history"...

... Tagging also has behind it (potentially at least) the power of vested interests in the range of new businesses concerned with "personal communication networks", part of the so-called "sunrise industries", for whom the electronic policing of urban space could become a lucrative sideline in the 1990s or in the next century. Given that the market for tagging will always be relatively small (compared to those for videos, personal computers, portable telephones, and night security systems for shopping malls) it may never be more than marginally profitable (although as we noted earlier it may not need to be any more than this to be commercially viable). But the electronic/telecommunications/security industries of which it is already a part dwarf into insignificance the vested interests of the civil libertarians and penal reform groups who so preoccupy Stacey, and for all his visionary, rugged-individualist-against-the-welfare-bureaucracies pose, he acts, consciously or not, as an advertising man for them.

There remains an image problem with tagging – "Orwellian" connotations on the one hand, gimmickry on the other – which some of the OTA's own pronouncements have done little to ameliorate. It is therefore of interest that in its recent White Paper the Home Office made a straightforward appeal to the image of "benign technology", linking tagging (by association) with developments such as high-tech heart surgery, pacemakers, and alarm systems for old people that only the most shameless of Luddites could oppose...

322 NON-CUSTODIAL SENTENCES

... In so far as this kind of imagery characterises tagging as a "supportive" rather than a "punitive" technology, it remains to be seen what appeal it will have in neutralising opposition and securing support. But now that the Home Office has given the green light to electronic monitoring, as part of its general encouragement to "independent sector" involvement in the criminal justice system, Stacey could be right about the inevitability of its expansion during the next century (whatever its image is then), even if development is still slow in the last decade of this one. That does not absolve us from the responsibility of developing a critical response to it, but it does demonstrate the difficulty of deciding precisely what kind of penal measure electronic monitoring is, and it does remind us of the scale of the forces on whose crest it has arrived, and is still riding.

Notes

1. In an earlier part of this article, which traces the development of the debate on tagging, Nellis explains (at p. 168) that the "Offender Tag Association was formed in 1982 as an alternative to custody and as a means of reducing crime. It was founded by an ex-*Sunday Times* journalist, novelist, and prison visitor called Tom Stacey, and has since attracted support from a variety of politicians, ex-offenders, church ministers, academics, electronics industry representatives, and, perhaps most notably, the Chief Inspector of Prisons, Stephen Tumim." (The writings of Stacey, to which Nellis refers, are "Why Tagging Should be Used to Reduce Incarceration" (1989) *Social Work Today*, April 20, 18–19; a letter in (1989) *Social Work Today*, June 29, and "Tracking Tagging – The British Contribution" in *The Electronic Monitoring of Offenders* (K. Russell and R. Lilley eds., 1989), a Leicester Polytechnic Law School Monograph).

2. There has been strong opposition to "tagging", as we have noted, from civil libertarians and penal reform groups. The probation service has been particularly hostile to the concept. In another overview of the subject, J. R. Lilley castigates critics of electronic monitoring for their "*a priori* reasoning, professional self-interest, misinformation [and] fear." (See J. R. Lilley, "Tagging Reviewed" (1990) 29 *Howard Journal* 229 at 241). He argues that the subject has yet to be "debated in terms of its intrusiveness or in terms informed by the broader cultural context from which it sprung", and concludes that "the new age of surveillance technology is part of post-modernism and is not likely to go away" (at p. 242).

3. In view of the practical difficulties and the ethical objections associated with electronic monitoring, it is perhaps surprising that the government has persisted with its plans to implement the scheme in the near future. Such persistence is even more remarkable in the face of an internal Home Office briefing paper which was pessimistic about the effectiveness of "tagging" (reported in *The Guardian*, May 31, 1994). The briefing paper revealed that private security companies were being asked to bid for contracts to fit the tagging devices and to monitor violations. In the *Guardian* article (*ibid.*), Harry Fletcher of the National Association of Probation Officers is quoted as follows:

"The [tagging] trials are only being reintroduced because ministers have ordered the officials to introduce them. It is about sounding good for the right wing of the Tory party and increasing the involvement of the private sector in the criminal justice system. Despite all the technical problems of preventing reoffending ministers continue to be obsessed with this technological wizardry."

Enforcement of Community Orders

The following discussion is concerned with the arrangements for breach and revocation of probation, community service, combination and curfew orders. As a result of section 14 and Schedule 2 of the Criminal Justice Act 1991, these arrangements have been substantially altered. Dissatisfaction with the previous procedures was expressed in the White Paper (1990, para. 4.18):

"The Government intends to simplify the arrangements for enforcing probation orders, community service orders and the new combined order and curfew order. The present powers are complex and inconsistent. The courts need powers to deal effectively with both failure to comply with the requirements of an order and reconviction for another offence while the order is in force. There is a careful balance to be drawn here. If the procedures are too lax, confidence in the effectiveness of these community penalties will be undermined. On the other hand, if the procedures are too strict, for example, if they allow minor disciplinary infractions to be punished with custody, there is a danger that offenders who are otherwise not at risk of custody will find themselves in prison. There should be three stages in enforcing the requirements of an order: warnings and possibly administrative sanctions by the supervisor; a decision, if necessary, to take the offender back to court; and the court's decision. The Government intends to introduce more order and consistency in the arrangements."

The government's intentions were implemented in the Criminal Justice Act 1991 and parts of the relevant section and Schedule are reproduced here.

Section 14 and Schedule 2, Criminal Justice Act 1991.

14. – (1) Schedule 2 to this Act (which makes provision for dealing with failures to comply with the requirements of certain community orders, for amending such orders and for revoking them with or without the substitution of other sentences) shall have effect.

(2) Sections 5, 6, 16 and 17 of, and Schedule 1 to, the 1973 Act (which are superseded by Schedule 2 to this Act) shall cease to have effect.

SCHEDULE 2

ENFORCEMENT, ETC., OF COMMUNITY ORDERS. . . .

. . . PART II

BREACH OF REQUIREMENT OF ORDER

Issue of summons or warrant

2. – (1) If at any time while a relevant order is in force in respect of an offender it appears on information to a justice of the peace acting for the petty sessions area concerned that the offender has failed to comply with any of the requirements of the order, the justice may –

    (a) issue a summons requiring the offender to appear at the place and time specified in it; or

    (b) if the information is in writing and on oath, issue a warrant for his arrest.

(2) Any summons or warrant issued under this paragraph shall direct the offender to appear or be brought before a magistrates' court acting for the petty sessions area concerned.

Powers of magistrates' court

3. – (1) If it is proved to the satisfaction of the magistrates' court before which an offender appears or is brought under paragraph 2 above that he has failed without reasonable excuse to comply with any of the requirements of the relevant order, the court may deal with him in respect of the failure in any one of the following ways, namely –

    (a) it may impose on him a fine not exceeding £1,000;

    (b) subject to paragraph 6(3) to (5) below, it may make a community service order in respect of him;

    (c) where the relevant order is a probation order and the case is one to which section 17 of the 1982 Act applies, it may make an order under that section requiring him to attend at an attendance centre; or

    (d) where the relevant order was made by a magistrates' court, it may revoke the order and deal with him, for the offence in respect of which the order was made, in any manner in which it could deal with him if he had just been convicted by the court of the offence . . . .

(3) Where a relevant order was made by the Crown Court and a magistrates' court has power to deal with the offender under sub-paragraph (1)(a), (b) or (c) above, it may instead commit him to custody or release him on bail until he can be brought or appear before the Crown Court. . . .

Powers of Crown Court

4. – (1) Where by virtue of paragraph 3(3) above an offender is brought or appears before the Crown Court and it is proved to the satisfaction of the court that he has failed to comply with any of the requirements of the relevant order, that court may deal with him in respect of the failure in any one of the following ways, namely –

(a) it may impose on him a fine not exceeding £1,000;

(b) subject to paragraph 6(3) to (5) below, it may make a community service order in respect of him;

(c) where the relevant order is a probation order and the case is one to which section 17 of the 1982 Act applies, it may make an order under that section requiring him to attend at an attendance centre; or

(d) it may revoke the order and deal with him, for the offence in respect of which the order was made, in any manner in which it could deal with him if he had just been convicted by or before the court of the offence....

Exclusions

5. – (1) Without prejudice to paragraphs 7 and 8 below, an offender who is convicted of a further offence while a relevant order is in force in respect of him shall not on that account be liable to be dealt with under paragraph 3 or 4 above in respect of a failure to comply with any requirement of the order.

(2) An offender who is required by a probation order to submit to treatment for his mental condition, or his dependency on drugs or alcohol, shall not be treated for the purposes of paragraph 3 or 4 above as having failed to comply with that requirement on the ground only that he has refused to undergo any surgical, electrical or other treatment if, in the opinion of the court, his refusal was reasonable having regard to all the circumstances.

Supplemental

6. – (1) Any exercise by a court of its powers under paragraph 3(1)(a), (b) or (c) or 4(1)(a) or (b) above shall be without prejudice to the continuance of the relevant order....

PART III

REVOCATION OF ORDER

Revocation of order with or without re-sentencing

7. – (1) This paragraph applies where a relevant order is in force in respect of any offender and, on the application of the offender or the responsible officer, it appears to a magistrates' court acting for the petty sessions area concerned that, having regard to circumstances which have arisen since the order was made, it would be in the interests of justice –

(a) that the order should be revoked; or

(b) that the offender should be dealt with in some other manner for the offence in respect of which the order was made.

(2) The court may –

(a) if the order was made by a magistrates' court—

(i) revoke the order; or

(ii) revoke the order and deal with the offender, for the offence in respect of which the order was made, in any manner in which it could deal with him if he had just been convicted by the court of the offence; or

   (b) if the order was made by the Crown Court, commit him to custody or release him on bail until he can be brought or appear before the Crown Court.

(3) The circumstances in which a probation order may be revoked under sub-paragraph (2)(a)(i) above shall include the offender's making good progress or his responding satisfactorily to supervision.

(4) In dealing with an offender under sub-paragraph (2)(a)(ii) above, a magistrates' court shall take into account the extent to which the offender has complied with the requirements of the relevant order.

(5) An offender sentenced under sub-paragraph (2)(a)(ii) above may appeal to the Crown Court against the sentence...

   8. – (1) This paragraph applies where an offender in respect of whom a relevant order is in force –

   (a) is convicted of an offence before the Crown Court; or

   (b) is committed by a magistrates' court to the Crown Court for sentence and is brought or appears before the Crown Court; or

   (c) by virtue of paragraph 7(2)(b) above is brought or appears before the Crown Court.

(2) If it appears to the Crown Court to be in the interests of justice to do so, having regard to circumstances which have arisen since the order was made, the Crown Court may –

   (a) revoke the order; or

   (b) revoke the order and deal with the offender, for the offence in respect of which the order was made, in any manner in which it could deal with him if he had just been convicted by or before the court of the offence.

(3) The circumstances in which a probation order may be revoked under sub-paragraph (2)(a) above shall include the offender's making good progress or his responding satisfactorily to supervision.

(4) In dealing with an offender under sub-paragraph (2)(b) above, the Crown Court shall take into account the extent to which the offender has complied with the requirements of the relevant order.

Revocation of order following custodial sentence

   9. – (1) This paragraph applies where –

   (a) an offender in respect of whom a relevant order is in force is convicted of an offence before a magistrates' court other than a magistrates' court acting for the petty sessions area concerned; and

   (b) the court imposes a custodial sentence on the offender.

(2) If it appears to the court, on the application of the offender or the responsible officer, that it would be in the interests of justice to do so having regard to circumstances which have arisen since the order was made, the court may –

   (a) if the order was made by a magistrates' court, revoke it; and

   (b) if the order was made by the Crown Court, commit the offender in custody or release him on bail until he can be brought or appear before the Crown Court.

Notes

1. For the powers of the courts in relation to amending community orders, see Schedule 2, Part IV of the Criminal Justice Act 1991.

2. In making the important decision whether to commence breach proceedings against an offender, reference should be made to the national standards for community service and for probation orders.

3. The rather complex provisions of Schedule 2 are explained lucidly in the following extract.

A. Ashworth, *Sentencing and Criminal Justice* (1992), pp. 272–273.

A large part of the success of the new community orders in reducing the numbers sent to prison will depend on the courts' treatment of breach cases. On breach of a conditional discharge, the court may pass any sentence which could have been passed for the original offence. But for breach of one or more of the four community orders examined above (probation, curfew, community service or combination order), the 1991 Act introduces new procedures.

The court's powers, reformulated in Schedule 2 to the Act, depend on the nature of the breach. For an ordinary breach of the order, *i.e.* a failure without reasonable excuse to comply with its conditions, the court has three main alternatives. It may impose a fine of up to £1,000, and leave the original order in force; it may make a community service order of up to 60 hours, and leave the original order in force; or it may revoke the order and deal with the offender afresh for the original offence. The court may call upon stronger powers in cases where it finds that the offender has "wilfully and persistently failed to comply" with the order. In such circumstances, the court may revoke the order and may assume that the offender has refused to consent to a community sentence. In other words, custody becomes a possibility. But before the court reaches this conclusion, it is required to take account of any part performance of the original order. The White Paper warned that if "minor infractions [are] to be punished with custody, there is a danger that offenders who are otherwise not at risk of custody will find themselves in prison". However, the Act itself contains no specific requirements designed to avoid this.

What is needed is guidance, at least by means of general principle, on the assessment of breaches. Of course the Act requires the breaches to have been wilful and persistent before these stronger powers become available. But if the original offence was considerably below the level of seriousness necessary for custody – as should often be the case, if the Act's provisions are properly applied – how should failure to comply with the original order be viewed? In their influential article, Wasik and von Hirsch argued that the defaulter certainly deserves something more, but that it should only be a modest increase in the severity of the sanction, so as to preserve some proportionality with the original offence. They therefore proposed that cases of default might be dealt with by applying the next most severe sanction. The difficulty in applying this to the new English scheme is that there is no agreed scale of sanction severity. Yet their approach does at least suggest some principles which might be applied. The problem with the Act is that it does not.

The commission of a further offence during the currency of a community order does not constitute a breach, but may lead to revocation of the order by the court in the subsequent case. Schedule 2 of the 1991 Act gives the Crown Court wide powers of re-sentencing in this situation, but the powers of magistrates' courts are limited.

Notes

1. The influential article referred to by Ashworth is that of M. Wasik and A. von Hirsch, "Non-Custodial Penalties and the Principles of Desert" [1988] Crim. L.R. 555.

2. For more detailed discussion of the enforcement of community orders under the 1991 legislation, see M. Wasik and R. Taylor, *Criminal Justice Act 1991* (2nd ed., 1994), pp. 72–76; and R. Leng and C. Manchester, *A Guide to the Criminal Justice Act 1991* (1991), pp. 81–90.

3. The national standards for probation orders state that breach action under schedule 2 may be appropriate immediately where the offender's failure to comply is a serious one (*e.g.* failure to notify of a change of address so as to avoid carrying out the order); but, in other cases, "the supervising officer may consider that the purpose of the order is best served by giving a warning in the first and second instances ... but breach action should normally be taken after no more than three instances of failure to comply with the order."

Although some flexibility is desirable, national standards on enforcement procedures are to be welcomed. The considerable discretion exercised by supervising officers, in the past, led to much inconsistency and criticism. (For an interesting, but rather dated, empirical study of breach of probation orders in Essex, 1973–5, see Colin Lawson, *The Probation Officer as Prosecutor* (1978)). Formerly, a probation officer's discretion whether to institute breach proceedings involved a conflict going to the root of the service itself. On the one hand, officers were social workers with a duty to advise and help offenders whilst, on the other, they were agents of the courts and of social control. In view of the movement away from the rehabilitation model, towards probation officers as agents of punishment in the community, the role of supervising officers in enforcement procedures is now less ambiguous.

4. How effective are these enforcement procedures? A recent survey by probation officers suggests that many offenders in breach of community sentences are not being brought back before the courts. The National Association of Probation Officers claims that there are around 2,200 outstanding summonses against such offenders in London alone, with a further 400 in the Bristol area. (This survey is reported in *The Guardian*, September 30, 1994).

IV. FINES

Fines can be imposed by the higher and lower courts for any offence for which the sentence is not fixed by law. In practice, it is the sentence most frequently used by the courts. This is hardly surprising in view of the vast number of summary offences, road traffic, strict liability and regulatory offences dealt with each year by the courts. The usefulness of a fine as a means of dealing with serious crimes is obviously more limited. In any case, its use is subject to the new sentencing framework laid down by the Criminal

Justice Act 1991 (discussed in earlier sections of this book) which creates distinct "thresholds" for the use of certain penalties. If an offence is so serious that only a custodial sentence can be justified (section 1(2)(a)), then a fine will clearly not suffice. Under section 6(1), a court must not impose a community sentence unless the offence was "serious enough to warrant such a sentence". This is a more equivocal restriction, and clearly a court may decline the opportunity of passing a community sentence even though the offence is serious enough to justify imposing one. In such a case, it may well choose to impose a fine on the offender instead. Thus, although the fine occupies a place towards the base of the sentencing "pyramid", there is some overlap between fines and community penalties in their suitability for dealing with offences of moderate seriousness. There can be little doubt, however, that – in view of its restriction on liberty – a community sentence is generally to be regarded as more punitive than a fine. (A fine may well be *combined* with a community order).

Generally, there is no statutory limit to the amount that an offender may be fined in the Crown Court after conviction on indictment. For example, in *Ronson and Parnes* [1991] Crim. L.R. 794, the first appellant was convicted of conspiracy, theft, and false accounting. In addition to receiving a 12 month prison sentence, he was fined a total of £5 million. This fine was held not to be excessive by the Court of Appeal in view of the appellant's means. It should be noted, however, that the Criminal Justice Act 1991, s. 18(2) (as amended) states that the amount of any fine fixed by a court should reflect the seriousness of the offence.

The use of fines is particularly common in the magistrates' court. The maximum fine on summary conviction for an offence triable either way is now £5,000 (CJA 1991, s. 17(2)(c)). To overcome problems of inconsistent maxima and inflation, CJA 1982, s. 37 introduced a new standard scale of maximum fines for summary offences. Under this system, existing fines were adapted to the standard scale, which permitted amounts specified in "the scale" to be more easily amended and updated. The standard scale was amended by section 17(2) of the 1991 Act as follows:

Level on the scale	Amount of fine
1	£200
2	£500
3	£1,000
4	£2,500
5	£5,000

The Utility of Fines

The fine is the most frequently used measure by the courts and it is easy to appreciate its practical value. Fines provide a considerable source of revenue, they can be fixed so as to reflect the seriousness of the offence (taking account of the offender's means), they do not involve incarceration, supervision or other such resources. They are easy for both public and offender to understand and they are not based on any ephemeral penological trend or theory. The Howe Report (*Fine Default*, NACRO, 1981) stressed the considerable merits of the fine, as follows:

> "The fine is attractive to sentencers because it is flexible and is seen to combine elements of both reparation and deterrence. In terms of reconviction rates it compares well with other sentences and is also economical, even when the costs of enforcement and imprisonment for default are taken in to account. It is this general satisfaction with the fine which is its greatest strength." (para. 1.12).

The White Paper *Crime, Justice and Protecting the Public*, Cm. 965 (1990) stated:

> "The great majority of criminal offences are dealt with by fines. In 1988, the courts convicted 1.6 million people, of whom 1.25 million received fines. The fine has great advantages for the public as well as the offender. It involves the offender actually paying back to the community something in return for the damage he has done, rather than requiring society to spend even more money upon him so that he can repay that debt. A fine, if properly assessed, can punish the offender without damaging his opportunities for employment or his responsibilities towards his family. The limitations of the fine are threefold: it is not regarded as suitable for very serious offences; it depends upon the offender having some financial resources which can be taken away; and the level of fine normally awarded can seem derisory if applied to the, admittedly small, number of 'well-off' offenders. The advantages and limitations of financial penalties have until very recently received much less attention than other forms of punishment. The fine has been taken for granted. The Government believes that there are substantial benefits to be gained from maximising the effectiveness of fines." (para. 5.1).

Before returning to the problem of setting the amount of fines so as to reflect a just approach to sentencing, it is interesting to consider the Howe report's conclusion that, in terms of reconviction rates, the fine compares favourably with other sentences. In early editions of the handbook for sentencers, *The Sentence of the Court* (*e.g.* 2nd ed. at p. 67), the Home Office stated that fines "were followed by fewer reconvictions than any other method of treatment for almost every age group." Such a claim should, perhaps, be treated with caution.

A. E. Bottoms, "The Efficacy of the Fine: The Case for Agnosticism" [1973] Crim. L.R. 543, pp. 544–549.

[The author explains that the *Sentence of the Court* statement was based on a comparison of the actual as opposed to the expected reconviction rates of various samples of offenders, with the results then tabulated].

... It is common ground among penologists that the comparison of the reconviction rates of offenders given different treatments in itself tells us nothing about effectiveness: we would expect those sent to prison to be worse risks for reconviction than those given discharges, and hence the better success rate for the latter may simply reflect a better "intake" into the treatment. It is also usually agreed that if we can "control" or "match" the intake into different treatments on enough variables (so that, as far as possible, we are comparing like with like) then significant differences in the reconviction rates will probably reflect real differences in the effectiveness of treatment. Hence the dispute about *The Sentence of the Court* figures is a dispute about the adequacy of the control or matching technique used.

In computing the "expected" rate for comparison purposes, W. H. Hammond, the author of the relevant section of *The Sentence of the Court*, controlled on three factors only, namely (i) age, (ii) the type of the current offence, and (iii) the number of previous convictions (or, for first offenders, the number of offences currently charged and taken into consideration)....

... Control on only three factors is a less full matching of intake than most penologists would want in an ideal research situation, particularly when the three factors have not been selected as the result of a full prediction-technique study. Nevertheless, there is some control here, and that is a great deal better than none. But there remains the choice of interpretation: "face-value" interpreters have to assert the degree of control is sufficient to make meaningful assertions from the table as it stands; while those who take the "sceptical" interpretation argue that the degree of control is insufficient since courts consistently take account of other variables when selecting offenders for various treatments.

The best general argument for the face-value interpretation has been put by Nigel Walker in the following terms:

> "Sentencers ... are influenced by age, type of offence, and criminal record; these are strongly associated with the probability of reconviction; and Hammond's table takes them into account ... If we believe that the table reflects sentencers' skill rather than efficacy, we must be prepared to maintain that sentencers were able to weigh in their minds not only Hammond's three factors but also a number of subtler ones. Moreover, we must also maintain that the sentencers' main aim was to allot offenders to different measures according to their estimated probability of reconviction. It is highly improbable that sentencers are either so skilful in their calculation or so utilitarian in their aims."

But this argument is not fully convincing, for two reasons:

(i) It is certain that courts do not always sentence with primary regard to the future conduct of the offender. But it is not correct to assert, as Walker appears to, that this automatically rules out the "sceptical" interpretation. Provided that the courts have in mind the future conduct of the offender as one of the main considerations in a substantial proportion of cases, the sceptical interpretation is still logically possible.

(ii) To believe that courts are incapable of making consistent judgments over and above the three very basic factors of age, previous convictions, and type of current offence, is to require a very considerable scepticism about the consistency of magistrates' reactions to, *e.g.* home background, employment record, and gravity of the offence within the legal category. It is true that magistrates are not noted for their consistency in sentencing; and it is also true that "human subjective assessment is not as reliable an estimator of probabilities of reconviction as are methods of rigorous analysis by means of models." But it appears very unconvincing to assert that magistrates taken as a whole react in effect in a random way in their appreciation of (say) the degree of stability in a work record, a factor known to be associated with the probability of reconviction from many research studies . . .

[Bottoms then discusses how courts tend to use probation, more frequently than fines, when sentencing "problem" or "poor risk" offenders; he then returns to the question of the efficacy of fines].

. . . I began with the effectiveness of the fine, and may seem to have wandered far from it. However, the above discussion is relevant since for a position of thoroughgoing agnosticism one must be able to argue both that courts may select good risks for fines and discharges over and above the three controlled factors, and that they can similarly select poor risks for probation (and hence, *a fortiori*, for custodial sentences). And such a case is, I have tried to show, entirely plausible.

The conclusion of this argument seems to be that we can salvage very little indeed by way of face-value interpretation of Hammond's data. Indeed, the only possibility of such interpretation which seems to me to be in any way legitimately open is to argue that the fine is more effective than the discharge. In relation to all but one of the groups of offenders in *The Sentence of the Court* table, the fine scores better than the discharge; yet *prima facie* it seems difficult to argue that discharge will consistently be imposed for cases with greater social problems. However, in view of our almost total lack of knowledge to date on the kinds of offenders given discharges and in view also of the very limited degree of matching control in Hammond's table, I would not wish to press even this conclusion as being anything other than highly tentative.

Some additional support for my general position comes from a Home Office research study of fines imposed on probationers. Using a fairly stringent method of matching control, eight "risk groups" for reconviction were isolated and, within each, probationers fined and not fined were distinguished. It was found, contrary to what might have been expected from *The Sentence of the Court*, that there was "a consistent tendency for probationers who have been 'fined' to have a relatively high failure rate." Although (as the author notes) this result is not without its technical problems, and although of course we cannot generalise from it to those fined without also being placed on probation, nevertheless there is, to put it at its lowest, no strong suggestion here of the deterrent effect of fining.

I recognise that my sceptical approach is a far cry from some of the bold conclusions that have been drawn from *The Sentence of the Court*. But the time for a frank recognition of the difficulties of interpretation of the data seems overdue, and one hopes that claims about the fine being "an especially effective measure" will cease – at least until some better evidence is produced. This is not to say, of course, that one cannot advocate the use of the fine on other grounds. Sceptical as I am of the apparent reductivist efficacy of the fine, I would on humanitarian grounds like to see it used more often in place of short sentences of imprisonment. But that is another story, and another argument.

Notes

1.   In later editions of *The Sentence of the Court* it was admitted that the research, on which earlier claims were made about the effectiveness of fines,

was rather unsophisticated. Nigel Walker, in a later book (*Sentencing: Theory, Law and Practice* (1985)), also referred to:

> "The possibility that when courts content themselves with financial penalties they are selecting offenders who are less likely to be reconvicted than those, for example, whom they put on probation, or in prison. Even an analysis which allows for age, previous convictions and type of offence cannot rule out the possibility that courts are influenced in their choice of financial or other measures by some factor which is also associated with a higher or lower reconviction rate." (p. 249).

Indeed, Home Office Research Study No. 46 (Softley, 1978) found that unemployed offenders were significantly less likely to be fined and that unemployed offenders had a higher rate of reconviction than those who were employed. It concluded that, whilst its findings were consistent with earlier research that fines were followed by fewer convictions than other forms of disposal, "it is by no means certain whether the apparent slight superiority of the fine in terms of reconviction is an effect of the fine itself or of unknown factors." (see pp. 5–9).

2. Despite the well supported "case for agnosticism" there is an enduring impression, which is not contradicted by the empirical evidence available, that fines are reasonably effective when judged in terms of reconviction rates. Although the evidence in support of this efficacy is equivocal, it does lend weight to those who favour the use of fines on other grounds.

Sentencing Principles

As a guiding principle, the decision of a court to impose a fine should reflect the seriousness of the offence. If an offence is very trivial and could be dealt with more appropriately by (for example) a conditional discharge, a fine should not be imposed. Equally, a court should not impose a fine if the seriousness of the offence merits a custodial sentence. Furthermore, a wealthy person must not be allowed to avoid imprisonment merely because he has the means to pay a large fine instead (see *Markwick* (1953) 37 Cr. App. R. 125).

These principles, and the problem of achieving a fair approach to setting the *amount* of a fine, are considered in the following extract.

G. Dingwall, "Making Fines Work – or Learning from our Mistakes" (1994) 47 *Criminal Lawyer* 3, pp. 3–5.

There is, however, one immense difficulty with the fine – setting the amount. If one adopts a fixed statutory amount this creates uniformity, but at the expense of justice. An affluent offender may hardly feel the punitive effect whereas for a poor offender it may be so onerous that its effect on his lifestyle, and that of any dependants, may be out of all proportion to the gravity of the offence. In extreme cases the poor offender may become involved in additional criminal activity to pay off the fine or may end up in prison for fine default. The aim of this article is to look at how the courts traditionally set the level of the fine and at the attempts to gain proportionality via "Unit Fines". It will argue that the return to discretion following the abolition of the Unit Fine will not remedy this underlying problem and that a statutory system is not only desirable but necessary to ensure that fines have their desired effect.

Ignoring fines where the penalty was set by statute, the major consideration for the court in calculating the amount of the fine used to be the severity of the offence. The offender was only to be fined where his conduct merited this and if the "punishment did not fit the crime", other methods were to be employed. This could happen both where the offence was considered too trivial or too serious. Therefore the Court of Appeal substituted a fine with a conditional discharge in *Jamieson* (1975) 60 Cr. App. R. 318 where it was held that a fine was too severe where the defendant – of previously good character, and with strong mitigating factors – stole a half-bottle of whisky. On the other hand the Court of Appeal was equally critical of a decision to combine a fine with a suspended sentence in *Sisodia* (1979) 1 Cr. App. R. (S) 291. Here the defendant had been involved in a VAT fraud worth £500,000 and hence the use of a fine was judged to be "astonishingly lenient". Imprisonment was held to have been more appropriate.

It was however recognised that certain offenders would have difficulty in paying a fine and the courts were aware that this could have the undesirable effect of the offender being imprisoned for fine default. This was somewhat mitigated by allowing the fine to be paid over a period of time. Usually this was a year, but the Court in *Olliver* (1989) 11 Cr. App. R. (S) 10 stated that, provided the total amount of the fine was not disproportionate to the actual offence, a longer repayment period could be justified.

Having established that the fine was the correct penalty given the severity of the offence, the court would then have regard to the offender's means in calculating the final amount. This principle was embodied in s. 35 of the Magistrates' Court Act 1980. Although it was stated in broad terms the courts appeared to have construed it narrowly to mean that the amount would only be altered if the offender was unable to pay the original amount. With those living on the poverty line that could mean a very small fine paid over a long period of time.

In *Ball* [1982] CLR 131 for example the defendant was a single parent of eighteen who was dependent on social security to provide for her young son and herself. She pleaded guilty to stealing some children's clothing, a jumper and six cassettes. The magistrate however had great difficulty in finding an appropriate way of dealing with her. She could not be given a conditional discharge as she had been given one previously for handling stolen goods. Similarly, as she had a "very narrow margin on which to live", it was felt that a fine would be unrealistic. Probation was deemed inappropriate as she was felt to be a basically honest person who was coping fairly well in a difficult situation and had the support of family and friends. The magistrate gave her a suspended prison sentence of two months. Whilst the Court of Appeal recognised the difficulty in finding a just way of dealing with Ball, they held that imprisonment was too severe a punishment in relation to the offence. In its place they substituted a fine of £25 to be paid over six months. This case certainly offered guidance to magistrates over the correct treatment of poor defendants; the combination of small fines spread over a period of time was the correct approach to crimes of the requisite severity. To use another method solely because of the defendant's lack of means would be unjust.

The problem did not however disappear completely. Even a small fine could well place such a defendant in a position where they would not be able to meet the payments and, as a result, could end up being imprisoned for default. Social security payments are designed, at least theoretically, to be the minimum amount needed to provide for essential needs. Any fine would therefore place the offender below what the State regards as the minimum acceptable standard of living.

If the courts were willing on occasion to reduce fines for poor offenders there appeared to be a reluctance to increase fines for wealthy offenders. Clearly a fine's punitive aspect depends upon the economic status of the offender. A fine of £100 would have drastically different effects upon someone in receipt of social security and a millionaire.

The authorities on this issue are not particularly clear. The courts appeared to justify their decisions objectively on the severity of the offence without accepting that the desired effect of the fine then involved a subjective element in linking it to the offenders ability to pay. In *Fairbairn* (1980) 2 Cr. App. R. (S) 315 the defendant was fined £7,500 and sentenced to nine months' imprisonment for stealing a variety of parcels in the course of his job with British Rail. It transpired that he was of considerable personal means. On appeal the fine was reduced to £1,000. The Court of Appeal did not state categorically that it was wrong to increase a fine in the case of a rich defendant; however, it was said that: "In principle, the amount of the fine should be determined in relation to the gravity of the offence, and then – and only then – *should the offender's means be considered to decide whether he has the capacity to pay such an amount*" (emphasis added).

In other words, the court should only consider the offender's financial situation to see if he can pay the fine. If he could it would appear that the courts should not have increased it if he could pay it with ease. It should be remembered that the fine was imposed with imprisonment so the punishment remained severe. Five months later the Court of Appeal had to consider a case where the only punishment was a substantial fine. *Messana* (1981) 3 Cr. App. R. (S) 88 had been fined £20,000 for handling stolen goods worth £11,500. He had been fined this amount as it was felt this would reflect the seriousness of the offence on a wealthy defendant. Again the Court of Appeal reduced the fine, claiming it was disproportionate to the severity of the offence. The court claimed the first priority on the part of the sentencer is to decide upon the most appropriate punishment having regard to the gravity of the offence. It was argued that if the trial judge believed a fine of £20,000 was the correct punishment he must have regarded the crime as very serious and therefore imprisonment should have been employed. The fine was reduced to £5,000.

It is respectfully submitted that the Court of Appeal's logic is flawed. The trial judge's first concern was to find the most appropriate punishment based on the severity of the case. He opted for a fine in preference to imprisonment. This, it is submitted, was based on his assessment of the gravity of the offence, having regard to any aggravating and mitigating circumstances. Having decided upon the correct method of punishment the trial judge then had to decide upon the amount that would have the desired punitive effect on the offender. As the defendant was of considerable wealth a fine of £20,000 was imposed. It could be argued that the figure was adopted so that it had a punitive effect on Messana, proportional to that which a lower fine would have on a defendant of more modest means.

This lack of clarity combined with the problems of poor defendants being imprisoned for fine default and rich defendants being fined amounts which had little punitive effect resulted in the move towards Unit Fines in the United Kingdom.

Notes

1. Dingwall goes on to discuss the introduction of the unit fine to magistrates' courts under the CJA 1991 and the abolition of this scheme in the CJA 1993. Section 18(2) of the Criminal Justice Act 1991 formerly stated that the amount of the fine was to be the product of a number of units which was to reflect the seriousness of the offence, and the value of the unit calculated in relation to the offender's disposable income. The purpose of the scheme was to achieve a greater equality of impact in fining

offenders. (See White Paper, *Crime, Justice and Protecting the Public* (1990), paras. 5.2–5.5). For details of the unit fine system see B. Gibson, "Criminal Justice Act 1991 – Unit Fines" (1992) 156 J.P. 371, and B. Gibson, *Unit Fines* (1990). For a discussion of the experimental use of unit fines in four magistrates' courts in 1989, see Home Office Research and Planning Unit Paper No. 59, *Unit Fines: Experiments in Four Courts* (1990).

After less than a year, during which time the unit fine was heavily (and often unfairly) criticised in some quarters, the government decided to abolish it. A useful account of the brief history of unit fines in magistrates' courts is contained in C. Emmins and M. Wasik's *Emmins on Sentencing* (1993), pp. 381–384. There can be no doubt that the unit fine system, as introduced by the 1991 Act, had certain shortcomings and anomalies, but some commentators have argued that the government acted too hastily in deciding to abolish, rather than "fine-tune", the scheme. For a forceful criticism of the government's policy in relation to the CJA 1993, see A. Ashworth and B. Gibson, "Altering the Sentencing Framework" [1994] Crim. L.R. 101, where the authors state:

> "Section 65 of the 1993 Act sweeps away sections 18 and 19 of the 1991 Act, and with them the whole of the unit fine system. It substitutes a new section 18, and risks returning the system of fining to its former diversity and indiscipline. This is a change which will, in retrospect, be seen as particularly short-sighted – a prime example of throwing the baby out with the bath water. However, there are indications that many magistrates' courts are continuing with a form of unit fines on a voluntary basis, or at least a 'unit approach' in which seriousness and means are kept separate in a structured fashion. There is nothing in law to prevent this. The scheme in the 1993 Act *is* means-related but leaves courts with complete flexibility as to how means are taken into account. Had this been the approach from the outset, unit fines may well have survived in statutory form."

2.   Section 18 of the Criminal Justice Act 1991 (as substituted by section 65(1) of the CJA 1993) states:

> "**18** – (1) Before fixing the amount of any fine, a court shall inquire into the financial circumstances of the offender.
>
> (2) The amount of any fine fixed by a court shall be such as, in the opinion of the court, reflects the seriousness of the offence.
>
> (3) In fixing the amount of any fine, a court shall take in to account the circumstances of the case including, among other things, the financial circumstances of the offender so far as they are known, or appear to the court ...
>
> ... (5) Subsection 3 (above) applies whether taking into account the financial circumstances of the offender has the effect of increasing or reducing the amount of the fine.
>
> (2) Section 19 of the Act of 1991 (fixing the fines in cases to which

the unit fines system did not apply) shall cease to have effect..."

[Note: Minor amendments to section 18 of the CJA 1991 (as substituted by the CJA 1993) are provided by paragraph 42 of Schedule 9 to the Criminal Justice and Public Order Act 1994].

If a court decides that a fine is the appropriate way of dealing with a case, s. 18 (as amended) states that its first task is to fix the amount which reflects the seriousness of the offence. However, the section also enables the courts, in fixing the fine, to take into account the impact that the fine will have on the offender in view of his financial circumstances; and this principle applies equally to where it results in the fine being increased, as it does to it being decreased. In other words, there are two (possibly conflicting) principles for the sentencer to bear in mind. On the one hand, the fine should reflect the seriousness of the offence, but on the other, it should also take account of the offender's financial circumstances. Obviously there must be limits to how far a fine should be lowered or raised to take account of the offender's ability to pay, otherwise it might end up being disproportionate to the crime committed.

It is difficult to predict, with any confidence, the way in which the Criminal Justice Act 1991, s. 18 (as amended by section 65(1) of the Criminal Justice Act 1993) will be interpreted by the courts. Some commentators have been pessimistic, with Ashworth and Gibson (1994), *op cit*, pp. 107–108) stating:

> "The new provisions could be viewed as coming close to the law before the 1991 Act, which was criticised on the ground that courts were reluctant to fine poor offenders, often giving them more severe measures because they could not bear to impose a fine that would appear derisory; that many of those poor offenders who were fined were fined more than they could afford; and that imprisonment for fine default was higher than it need be, if fines had been properly calculated in the first place ... ... [T]o return to a system that promises ... less fairness, fewer fines and greater difficulty in enforcing them, is eloquent testimony to the power of short-term political gain over sound penal policy."

This assessment of the new provisions is not shared by all commentators on the Criminal Justice Act 1993. The following extract contains a more favourable response to the new section 18.

J. N. Spencer, "Current Thinking on the Imposition of a Fine as a Sentence – or the Re-Introduction of the Unit Fine System by the Back Door?" (1994) 158 *Justice of the Peace*, pp. 115–117.

... There is another side to the matter. Many magistrates' courts have been trying to decide what method to adopt in place of the unit fine system, when assessing the amount appropriate to the offender. It is not possible to revert to the position as it was before the 1991 Act. This is because the substituted s. 18 is somewhat differently worded from the situation which existed before the unit fine system was introduced.

The substituted s. 18 provides that "before fixing the amount of any fine, a court *shall inquire* into the financial circumstances of the offender" (s. 18(1)) (our italics). The amount of any fine fixed by a court must be such as, in the opinion of the court, reflects the seriousness of the offence (s. 18(2)). In fixing the amount, the "court *shall* take into account the circumstances of the case, including, among other things, the financial circumstances of the offender so far as they are known, or appear, to the court" (s. 18(3)) (again, our italics)...

... More importantly, s. 18(5) states:

> "Subsection 3 above applies whether taking into account the financial circumstances of the offender has the effect of increasing or reducing the amount of the fine."

Poverty and wealth

Section 19 of the 1991 Act was repealed by the 1993 Act, but the substituted s. 18(5), quoted above, as inserted by the 1993 Act, picks up and re-instates one of the more important provisions of s. 19. Moreover, it was a provision which did not exist prior to the 1991 Act and over which there had been previously considerable doubt as to the legal position.

It was well recognised that a fine could be reduced to take account of poverty. This conclusion was derived from s. 35 of the Magistrates' Courts Act 1980 ("in fixing the amount of a fine, the court shall take into consideration among other things the means of the person on whom the fine is imposed so far as they are known to the court").

Before the passing of the 1991 Act, there was considerable doubt as to whether a fine could be increased to take account of wealth...

... This doubt over poverty and wealth, and whether wealth, as well as poverty, could be taken into account, was resolved by s. 19 and now by s. 18(5).

The crucial point is that courts must remember that, in this respect, the law is different from what it was prior to the 1991 Act and that it is essential for the courts to continue to take this aspect into account when imposing a fine on an offender; this is an aspect which was introduced originally in conjunction with the unit fine system, but which has survived the abolition of that system.

The original s. 19(1) provided for the exceptional offences which were outside the unit fine system. It also made it clear that when any court was imposing one of these fines, an offender's means should be taken into account so far as they appear or are known to the court. This was merely a restatement in statutory form of a long recognised principle of general application. Section 19(2), however, gave express effect to the proposal in the White Paper, "Crime, Justice and Protecting the Public", and went on to state: "subs. (1) above applies whether taking into account the means of the offender has the effect of increasing or reducing the amount of the fine". Section 19 was not limited by its terms in the courts to which it applied and, therefore, also had to be applied in the Crown Court. So far as unit fines in magistrates' courts were concerned, the variation in accordance with the comparative wealth or poverty of the offender was achieved automatically by the unit fine system itself. This principle of adjustment for wealth as well as poverty, is re-stated, for all fines, and for all courts, in s. 18(5).

Assessing the consequences of poverty and wealth

The question arises, therefore, as to how courts are properly to carry out this statutory function when imposing a fine and how they are properly to assess the liability of the offender in accordance with his financial circumstances and, in particular, after having due regard to his relevant affluence or poverty. This is a statutory responsibility which was, in effect, introduced in clear fashion by the 1991 Act and expressly retained by the 1993 Act.

Some of the courts have given considerable thought to the matter and have stumbled across the ideal solution. Their answer is to re-introduce the unit fine system! At first sight, they are under no statutory obligation to do so, but, equally, there is no reason why they should not make use of it on a voluntary basis. Indeed, it is the easiest way of fixing the fine correctly in the light of the respective wealth or poverty of the offender.

The great advantage the courts have is that they are not stuck with an inappropriate result. The new s. 18(2) introduced by the 1993 Act makes it clear that the fine imposed must reflect the seriousness of the offence. If the result obtained by applying a voluntary version of the unit fine system produces an absurd result which does not reflect the seriousness of the offence, the courts are clearly entitled to ignore it...

Conclusion

It is clear from the provisions of the replaced version of s. 18, that a court is under a statutory obligation to take into account the means of each offender whenever the imposition of a fine is under consideration. This requirement includes an obligatory statutory need to adjust the result in line with the offender. This need to take wealth into account is a new statutory requirement specifically imposed since the 1991 Act, in place of the doubts which previously existed as to the correct legal position.

Any court which does not fulfil these obligatory requirements would be in breach of its statutory duty. Advocates and representatives will no doubt keep this aspect in mind when reviewing what happened in court for the purpose of any appeal.

A "fine" is widely defined in s. 150(1) of the Magistrates' Courts Act 1980, as including any pecuniary penalty, forfeiture or compensation. The new s. 18, like the old ss. 18 and 19, does not define what is meant by a "fine" but the meaning seems to be narrower and to be limited to a fine alone (*cf.* the special meaning in s. 24). It would be inappropriate to apply any version of the unit fine system to an order for costs or compensation. Different criteria clearly apply to these.

There seems to be no reason why it should not be adopted for monetary penalties, including fines and penalties which were outside the system originally. There seems to be no reason even why the Crown Court should not make use of the system. It might well be of assistance in reaching the best solution, especially when the Crown Court is faced with a wealthy offender.

The great irony, therefore, is that by abolishing the unit fine system, Parliament may have considerably extended its scope. At the same time, there is the double advantage in that Parliament has removed the difficulties and anomalies.

Notes

1.   For a rather different assessment of the new provisions see G. Dingwall, "The Dangers of Discretion in Determining a Just Fine after the Abolition of the Unit Fine in the Criminal Justice Act 1993" (1994) 158 *Justice of the Peace*, 545. Dingwall argues in favour of a return to a statutory unit scheme, and criticises the wide discretion which has now been given to sentencers in making decisions as to the amount of fines. He does not share Spencer's enthusiasm for the new section 18 of the 1991 Act. He states (at p. 546):

"The amount of the fine, therefore, has to be relative both to the seriousness of the offence and the offender's ability to pay. It is advocated by Mr Spencer that the discretion afforded by the 1993 Act will allow the courts to achieve this on an equitable basis, but it is respectfully submitted that what will follow will be inconsistent decisions centring on the extent to which a wealthy offender, and, for that matter, a poor offender, will have their fine adjusted to reflect their economic position. The ambiguity of the position prior to unit fines was well documented ... This uncertainty will not magically vanish now that the general presumption that rich offenders should pay more has gained statutory force. The problem of how much a fine should be altered remains unanswered."

2.   A return to sentencing practices which result in fines being imposed in an unjust way would be most regrettable. In its pre-1991 report, the Prison Reform Trust (*Tackling Fine Default*, (1990)) estimated that several thousand prison receptions each year could be avoided if fines were fixed at more realistic levels and enforcement procedures were improved. In another research paper, published before the Criminal Justice Act 1991, it was reported that fine defaulters are likely to be either unemployed or near the poverty line (see NACRO Briefing, *Fines and Fine Default*, (January 1990)). Earlier NACRO research also suggested that unemployed offenders were less likely to receive a fine. In view of these findings, and the lingering doubts whether sentencers will achieve equality of impact when sentencing wealthier offenders, the premature end of the unit fine scheme is a cause for concern.

3.   For useful further reading, see *Paying for Crime* (P. Carlen and D. Cook eds., 1989); A. Morris and L. Gelsthorpe, "Not Paying for Crime: Issues in Fine Enforcement" [1990] Crim. L.R. 839; P. Softley, *Fines in Magistrates' Courts*, Home Office Research Study No. 46 (1978); W. Sabol, "Imprisonment, Fines and Diverting Offenders From Custody: Implications of Sentencing Discretion" (1990) 29 *Howard Journal* 25; and D. Moxon, M. Sutton and C. Hedderman, *Deductions from Benefits for Fine Default* (1990) Home Office Research and Planning Unit Paper No. 60.

V. COMPENSATION ORDERS

It is important that the issue of punishing offenders should not obscure the need, in appropriate cases, for compensating victims of crime. In the past, it was often argued that our criminal justice system paid insufficient attention to the needs of victims. In more recent times, however, greater concern for the treatment of victims has been shown at various stages in the criminal justice process, and one example of this is the development of powers given to courts to award compensation to victims. The first step in this direction was taken by the introduction of the compensation order, in the Criminal Justice Act 1972, enabling a court to order an offender to pay compensation for any personal injury, loss or damage resulting from the offence. The purpose of such an order, as stated in *Inwood* (1974) 60 Cr.

App. R. 70, is to allow the victim a simple and effective means of obtaining compensation from an offender who can afford to pay, without the need to resort to expensive and time-consuming civil litigation. (For the relevant legislation, see the PCCA 1973, ss. 35–8; for amendments see below).

At first the Powers of the Criminal Court Act 1973, s. 35 gave courts the power to make a compensation order only in addition to dealing with the offender in any other way. But, as amended in 1982, this provision now enables a court to make such an order "instead of or in addition to" any other way of dealing with him. An order may be made without any application by the victim to the court. (But see T. Newburn, *The Use and Enforcement of Compensation Orders in Magistrates' Courts*, (1988), Home Office Research Study No. 102, in which he reported that the courts often overlooked the possibility of compensation). In order to encourage the use of compensation orders by the courts, CJA 1988, section 104 (amending section 35 of the PCCA, 1973) states that "a court shall give reasons, on passing sentence, if it does not make [a compensation] order where [section 35] empowers it to do so." The White Paper, *Crime, Justice and Protecting the Public* (1990) stated at para. 4.25 that "there was considerable support for compensation orders and the priority which the courts are now required to give them in considering the possibility of making compensation orders in all suitable cases."

The impact of the 1988 legislation on the use of compensation orders was investigated by the Home Office Research and Planning Unit. The following extract is taken from a summary of this research (which was published as Home Office Research Study No. 126).

D. Moxon, *Use of Compensation Orders in Magistrates' Courts* (1993) Home Office Research Bulletin, pp. 25–29

Home Office statistics provided an overview of changes, in terms of developments in the use of compensation orders for different types of offence. For a more detailed examination of the factors which influenced decisions in individual cases information was collected from nine magistrates' courts for a period 12 months before and 12 months after the new provisions came into force. Less common offences were excluded, as they would not have yielded sufficient numbers for comparison. The offences covered were common assault, assault occasioning actual bodily harm, criminal damage, fraud and forgery, non-domestic burglary and "other theft". Shoplifting was excluded because compensation is rarely an issue (because the goods are usually recovered). Finally, case studies were used in sentencing exercises at seven of the courts, to see how different benches approached compensation in cases which raised particular problems.

The impact of the Act
By far the most important change in the year after the 1988 Act came into force was that the proportion of assault cases in which compensation was awarded doubled, at both magistrates' courts and the Crown Court – to 46 per cent of such cases dealt with at magistrates' courts, and 28 per cent at the Crown Court. As an adjunct to the legislative changes, courts were given guidance as to the sums that were considered appropriate for different types of offences, based on the figures

drawn up by the Criminal Injuries Compensation Board. In general, the amounts awarded for minor injuries such as cuts and bruises were within the range suggested by the guidelines. But for more serious injuries the sums awarded were usually far below the recommended levels. Thus the average sum awarded in 1988–9 for a broken nose was £187 compared with guideline figures of £550 to £850 depending on the type of fracture.

For property offences the increases in the use of compensation were much more modest. To take some examples, the proportion of victims of theft from a vehicle who were awarded compensation increased from 33 to 37 per cent, for burglary from a dwelling the number increased from 31 to 34 per cent and for summary criminal damage, too, there was a three per cent rise, to 78 per cent. Similar increases were recorded at the Crown Court although offenders sentenced at the higher court were less than half as likely as those dealt with by magistrates to be ordered to pay compensation.

The overall figures conceal very large differences in the use of compensation orders by individual magistrates' courts. Among the nine courts in the study, the number of thieves ordered to pay compensation ranged from 18 per cent to 48 per cent; for fraud and forgery the range was 27 to 73 per cent and for assault occasioning actual bodily harm the range was 51 to 89 per cent. Clearly, at all courts and for all types of offence, there were many cases in which the court did not feel it was appropriate to award compensation. Often, reasons for not awarding compensation, or for awarding less than the full amount of any loss, were noted in court records.

Courts may order compensation to be paid whether or not there is a specific claim. However, where there is no claim there is often little information on which to base any award. So it is perhaps not surprising that the most common reason for not awarding compensation noted in court records was that it had not been sought. The second main reason for either making no order or for reducing the amount, related to the means of the offender. It was not surprising, therefore, that in 1988–9 only 59 per cent of unemployed offenders in the sample were ordered to pay compensation compared with 74 per cent of employed offenders.

The power courts have to make a compensation order on its own has never been used very often, and this remains the case although the proportion of compensation orders used on their own did rise from four per cent to six per cent in the year after the new provisions came into force. And in a further 19 per cent of cases in 1988–9 (a slight increase on the previous year) the accompanying sentence was a conditional discharge. However, in more than half the cases in which a compensation order was made, the offender was fined as well. Compensation was rarely ordered where an immediate custodial sentence was imposed, in line with guidance that offenders should not be faced with a burden of debt on release from prison . . .

[The author then goes on to discuss the sentencing exercises, given to 44 benches, which were designed to examine how magistrates approached some of the more difficult issues relating to compensation].

One point which emerged both from the sentencing exercises and from the court data was that in many instances magistrates imposed a fine and/or costs in cases where the amount of compensation was reduced due to lack of means. This breaches the statutory requirement to give priority to compensation where the means of the offender are insufficient to pay a fine and costs as well. Another key finding was that cases in which there is no clear cash value involved gave rise to a very wide range of views as to whether compensation was appropriate, and if so how much. In the absence of formal advice courts have only their own views to guide them, and so there is no "right" answer. But the differences in the way both victims and offenders are treated according to where they are dealt with gives obvious cause for concern.

Enforcement

Payment details were extracted from court records, so that the terms of payment set by the court and the time taken to pay could be examined. Courts generally drew a distinction between the maximum time they would normally expect a compensation order to be payable and the absolute maximum that they would consider. Of the nine courts, three said they would, exceptionally, impose orders which would be payable over three years (in line with *Olliver and Olliver* where the Court of Appeal said that three years might be appropriate on occasions). At the other courts the maximum was usually two years, but again this was seen as exceptional. In the general run of cases, however, courts preferred to impose orders that could be collected much more quickly in recognition of the problems that very long orders create for individual offenders and, in consequence, for enforcement. Almost three-quarters of the offenders in the sample were allowed to pay by instalments. (Most of the rest were required to pay within two or four weeks.)

In practice, even when orders were recorded as having been reduced due to lack of means, 86 per cent were due to have been paid within 12 months and 40 per cent within six months. Overall, 77 per cent of offenders were due to have paid within 6 months, and 60 per cent had done so. At 12 months, 93 per cent were due to have paid in full and 80 per cent had done so. Payment was strongly related to the sums involved: 14 per cent of awards of less than £25 and 58 per cent of awards of more than £500 were still outstanding after 12 months. There were also large differences in the success of individual courts in collecting sums imposed. The differences in the proportion of orders due to have been paid within a year ranged from 87 to 98 per cent, but the sums actually collected ranged from 56 to 86 per cent. The problems were most acute where the offender was unemployed, and it is hoped that the power to attach income support, will make it easier to secure payment in such cases.

Discussion

It was encouraging to find that the 1988 Criminal Justice Act had stimulated courts to use compensation orders in significantly more cases, particularly for violent offences. However, the study showed that awards were often for much less than the extent of material loss or the guideline figures for personal injury suggested was appropriate, and the wide variation in courts' use of compensation suggested there was substantial scope for greater use of compensation orders.

It is inevitable that some orders will fall short of full compensation because the offender lacks the means to pay the full amount. But it was clear that to some extent victims were losing out because of courts' continuing reluctance to impose compensation on its own, with the result that part of whatever limited sums were available were going to pay fines or costs rather than compensation. In training relating to the Criminal Justice Act 1991 the opportunity has been taken to remind magistrates of the need to give precedence to compensation where additional financial impositions would reduce the sum available to the victim.

As in previous studies, the fact that compensation was not sought was a major reason for it not being awarded. This underlies the need for the police and CPS to ensure that relevant details are provided to the court. This is a point made in *The Victim's Charter*, (Home Office 1990) which stresses the need for effective mechanisms for communicating information about the loss or injury sustained by the victim to the court.

The substantial variation in approach revealed by the sentencing exercises shows a need for additional guidance, to cover the kinds of circumstances which may occur infrequently, but which give rise to very different responses by different benches when they do. The Home Office plans to issue further guidance to courts on the use of compensation orders, which will take account of some of the problems identified by the research.

Notes

1. Although a compensation order can be made without any application being made by the victim, it seems that it is not advisable for victims to rely on the courts in this matter. In any case, without a specific claim by the victim, the court may lack information on which to base an award for compensation.

2. The reluctance of sentencers to make wide use of the power to impose a compensation order on its own, and not in addition to another sentence, is not entirely surprising. (Even prior to the statutory amendment to the Powers of Criminal Courts Act 1973, section 35, in 1982, it was always possible to combine a compensation order with a conditional or an absolute discharge). The present law tends to confuse the separate notions of punishment and compensation. Where a compensation order is made as the sole method of dealing with an offender, it gives the misleading impression of being the "penalty" for the offence. It is understandable that the government wanted to demonstrate its commitment to the idea of compensation for victims, but it is obviously rather difficult for sentencers to accept the compensation order as a measure in its own right (rather than as an adjunct to other sentences). The debate on this issue is well summed up by Andrew Ashworth (1992, p. 250) as follows:

> "... [S]ome have found the task of justification harder when the compensation order is the principal or sole order in the case. How can this be regarded as sentencing when, in effect, the court is merely making a relatively swift and rough award of damages to the victim? The offender would have been civilly liable to the victim in almost all cases and therefore, the argument goes, the court's order amounts to nothing – certainly no punishment, but rather a kind of civil award made by a criminal court. One counter-argument to this is that, in practice, very few victims sue their offenders; therefore, in practice, the compensation order does transfer from the offender to the victim money which the offender would not otherwise have been made to pay. It is thus realistic to regard the compensation order as punitive in its effect on the offender, as well as reparative in relation to the victim."

Sentencing and Compensation Orders

As we have seen, a compensation order may be imposed in addition to some other sentence, or it may be made on its own. If a court considers that it would be appropriate to impose a fine together with a compensation order, yet it thinks that the offender lacks the means to pay both, it should give priority to compensation (see section 35(4A) of the Powers of Criminal Courts Act 1973). From the Home Office research (discussed above), it seems that the courts do not always comply with this statutory obligation to give precedence to compensation where a fine is also imposed.

A compensation order can be made in respect of personal injury, loss or damage, and this includes where the offence causes distress and anxiety to the victim (see *Bond v. Chief Constable of Kent* (1982) 4 Cr. App. R(S) 314). Section 104(1) of the Criminal Justice Act 1988 introduced amendments to section 35 of the Powers of Criminal Courts Act 1973 so as to enable compensation (subject to restrictions) for "funeral expenses or bereavement in respect of a death resulting from any such offence, other than a death due to an accident arising out of the presence of a motor vehicle on a road."

Magistrates' courts cannot order compensation of amounts in excess of £5000 for any offence, but the Crown Court is not restricted in this way. In deciding whether to make a compensation order, or in assessing the amount of any order, the court must take account of the offender's means (Powers of Criminal Courts Act 1973, s. 35(4)). An order must not be made where "there is real doubt as to whether the convicted man can find compensation" (*per* Lord Scarman in *Inwood* (1974) 60 Cr. App. R. 70 at 73). In *Bagga and Others* [1990] Crim. L. R. 128, the three appellants were convicted of assault occasioning actual bodily harm after kicking and punching the proprietor of a restaurant. In addition to the four months' imprisonment imposed in each case, the trial court also ordered each of them to pay £200 compensation and £200 prosecution costs. Their appeal concerned the compensation orders, as one of them (Bagga) was unemployed and living on benefit and the other two were in quite low-paid employment. The Court of Appeal did not interfere with the orders against the two employed appellants, but in Bagga's case the order was quashed. The Court stated that it was wrong to make a compensation order where the offender lacked the means to pay, and that this principle was clearly set out in the Powers of Criminal Courts Act 1973, s. 35(4). The Court also upheld the principle that a compensation order should not be made for such an amount that the offender would have little prospect of paying within the foreseeable future. In his comment on the case (*ibid.* p. 129), David Thomas stated:

"The case is interesting for a number of reasons. It demonstrates in particular that the legislative encouragement to make compensation orders contained in recent legislation ... does not derogate from the principle that the court must have regard to the means of the offender, so far as they appear or are known to the court ... The decision also implies that where several offenders are convicted jointly, and some have means while others do not, there is no unjust disparity in making compensation orders only against those who have the means ... A third point is that the Court indicates that four years is too long a period over which to allow a compensation order to stretch. It was recognised in *Olliver and Olliver* (1989) 11 Cr. App. R(S) 10 that twelve months was not the limit for such orders, that orders payable over two years were appropriate, and three years would not necessarily be too long. It may be that this decision indicates that four years is outside the limit, although it should be remembered that [Bagga] had virtually no means at all."

Compensation orders are not to be used so as "to enable the convicted to buy themselves out of the penalties for crime" (*per* Lord Scarman, *Inwood* (1974) 60 Cr. App. R. 70 or 73). For example, the ability to pay compensation should not allow an offender to avoid imprisonment if that is the appropriate way of dealing with him. This point was emphasised in *Copley* (1979) 1 Cr. App. R.(S) 55 at p. 57, and it has been reiterated in many subsequent decisions. For example, in *Barney* [1990] Crim. L.R. 209, the offender was convicted of obtaining over £2000 from an elderly victim, having deceived a householder about work which B purported to have carried out on his property. The trial judge imposed a sentence of five years' imprisonment on B, and indicated that if B had been able to pay compensation to his victim, the sentence would have been reduced. But as B lacked the means for such an order, the court would impose the maximum that it had in mind for the offence. The Court of Appeal criticised this approach and reduced the sentence to three and a half years' imprisonment. The Court restated the principle that it must not be thought that an offender can buy himself out of imprisonment, or any part if it, because he has the means to pay compensation.

As we have seen, compensation orders may be imposed on their own, or in addition to other measures. Where an order is made at the same time as a custodial sentence, the court must be careful to ensure that the demands made on the offender are not too severe. In the words of Lord Scarman (in *Inwood* (1974) 60 Cr. App. R. 70 at 73): "Compensation orders, which may appear at the trial to the convicted man to be a life line, can, however, become a millstone round his neck, when he is released from prison. They can be counter-productive, and force him back into crime to find the money."

In the recent case of *Tyce* [1994] Crim. L.R. 71, the Court of Appeal suggested that, as the sentence of six months' detention in a young offender institution was sufficient to mark the seriousness of the offender's conduct, it was wrong to combine a compensation order with that sentence. This surprising statement appears to confuse the ideas of punishment and compensation, and is hard to reconcile with other pronouncements of the Court in relation to compensation orders.

VI. ABSOLUTE AND CONDITIONAL DISCHARGES

In this section, we are looking at the least severe of the non-custodial sentences available to the courts. (It should be noted that a discharge is not a community order within the meaning of section 6(4) of the Criminal Justice Act 1991). The relevant provisions are now contained in the Powers of Criminal Courts Act 1973, s. 1A, which states:

(1) Where a court by or before which a person is convicted of an

offence (not being an offence the sentence for which is fixed by law) is of opinion, having regard to the circumstances including the nature of the offence and the character of the offender, that it is inexpedient to inflict punishment, the court may make an order either –

(a) discharging him absolutely; or
(b) if the court thinks fit, discharging him subject to the condition that he commits no offence during such period, not exceeding three years from the date of the order, as may be specified in the order.

(2) An order discharging a person subject to such a condition is in this Act referred to as "an order for conditional discharge", and the period specified in any such order as "the period of conditional discharge".

(3) Before making an order for conditional discharge the court shall explain to the offender in ordinary language that if he commits another offence during the period of conditional discharge he will be liable to be sentenced for the original offence.

(4) Where, under the following provisions of this Part of this Act, a person conditionally discharged under this section is sentenced for the offence in respect of which the order for conditional discharge was made, that order shall cease to have effect.

Absolute discharges are not used in many cases. It is not a punitive measure and it does not even impose any restrictions on the offender's future behaviour. (For a discussion, see M. Wasik, "The Grant of an Absolute Discharge", (1985) 5 Oxford J.L.S. 211). An absolute discharge will be appropriate in cases where little or no blame attaches to the offender (*e.g.* see *Lundt-Smith* [1964] 2 Q.B. 167), or where the offence is of a trivial nature, or where there is considerable mitigation. Where a case can be dealt with appropriately by means of an absolute discharge, it might be questioned whether a prosecution should have been brought in the first place. In such cases, a caution by the police, or a decision not to proceed by the Crown Prosecution Service, might have been expected. But not all cases resulting in an absolute discharge can be dismissed as prosecution errors (see M. Wasik, *op cit*).

The conditional discharge carries more of a threat to an offender about his future conduct, and it can be useful as a way of dealing with less serious instances of certain indictable offences, such as theft. (See D. Moxon, *Sentencing Practice in the Crown Court* (1988), Home Office Research Study No. 103). A conditional discharge should not be confused with a suspended sentence (see section II of this chapter). The latter is a custodial sentence and the consequences of breach lead (in most cases) to the activation of the original sentence. *The Sentence of the Court* ((1986), para. 4.4) states:

"[The conditional discharge] differs from a suspended sentence in that if the offender commits a further offence during the period of discharge there is no statutory obligation on the court to deal with him for his original offence, and if it does so the sentence is not pre-determined ... but is considered afresh by the court."

CHAPTER SIX

YOUNG OFFENDERS

I. UNDERLYING PRINCIPLES AND PHILOSOPHY

There has been a gradual and clearly enunciated movement during the last 100 years towards a separate system of dealing with younger offenders (for purposes of the British penal system, this category must be understood to include offenders under the age of 21; those over the age of 18 are now usually termed "young adult offenders"). This approach is based on the assumption that (a) the reasons for juvenile law-breaking and (b) the optimum response to the problem in terms of both procedures and penal and corrective measures require a differentiation between "adult" and "juvenile" offenders. This is now an article of legal as much as penological faith. For instance, Article 10 of the International Covenant on Civil and Political Rights (a treaty to which the United Kingdom is party) requires that "accused juvenile persons should be separated from adults ..." and that "juvenile offenders should be segregated from adults and be accorded treatment appropriate to their age and legal status" (an approach further consolidated by the General Assembly's adoption of the United Nations Minimum Standard Rules for the Administration of Juvenile Justice (Beijing Rules) in 1985). Despite the generality of such an obligation and the number of questions begged by that kind of provision, the underlying policy is clear enough and would be unsurprising to most contemporary people.

Yet it should be remembered that this distinction between "adult" and "child" is of relatively modern origin. Before the last century, children were treated in a more functional manner. Allison Morris and Mary McIsaac (1978) note: "until the nineteenth century children were treated as adults as soon as they were considered capable of doing without their mothers. They did not have distinctive clothing or books, but rather shared in the work and play of adults" (p. 1). No doubt a number of factors combined to change this view of children. Most obviously, on the surface, there was a reaction against the exploitation of child labour in the aftermath of the industrial revolution. Also, as the nineteenth century advanced, there was a growing awareness of the significance and complexity of child psychology and its contribution to adult development, which served to focus attention on the position and role of younger members of society, for purposes of both care and control. Indeed, the view is now increasingly put forward, with justification, that the philanphropic and humanitarian intervention in the lives of young people from the nineteenth century onwards was partly, if not largely, a cloak for motives of societal control. Thus Phyllida Parsloe ((1978), p. 3) has commented:

> "The juvenile justice system is one of a number of institutions which society has developed for the purpose of socialising and controlling children, and particularly lower class city children. All societies have developed some such institutions, since the future of society and the culture it develops depend upon socialisation processes. Most have placed a primary responsibility for socialisation upon the family unit but, where the family has proved inadequate, other institutions have been developed to supplement, support or supplant the parents."

It is important to bear in mind, therefore, that the whole legal framework which has been constructed to provide institutions, measures and procedures for dealing with young people "in trouble" or breaking the law may be interpreted in different ways. In an earlier period, there was a greater tendency to see the whole as a benign development, concerning itself with the welfare of children. More recently, the "welfare" justification has been handled with more scepticism (see, for example, Stephen Humphries (1981); David Garland (1985)), resulting in a critical identification of a class-inspired manipulation of developing personalities.

Such conflicting interpretations of legal and social policy developments are clearly controversial. But, at the very least, it is useful to probe the coherence of the adult-young person dichotomy on which the existing legal structure is based. It cannot be seriously doubted that young children require a large measure of direction, supervision and control; but, beyond a certain age of childhood, the necessity for this is, upon even the most superficial comparative analysis of different societies, open to question. As already noted, present concepts relating to childhood and youth derive in a large part from a nineteenth century revolution in thinking; and the present movement in favour of children's rights (see M. D. A. Freeman (1981)) questions the wisdom of and need for such extensive adult intervention. Certainly, the legislation in this area, as regards both civil and criminal law, nowhere spells out the justification for measures of supervision and control, such justification being easily assumed in the now pervasive and ambiguous concepts of the "welfare" and "best interests" of the child.

At a more practical level, these assumptions are productive of difficulty and anomaly. The apparatus of control and supervision must also reflect the progression from childhood to adult capacity and this has entailed the introduction of age categories to govern questions of criminal liability and the application of different measures. Such categories are necessarily arbitrary and are vulnerable to changing moral and social conceptions. For instance, it is now the legal position that a person is adult and of full legal capacity at the age of 18, but is not treated as a fully adult offender until the age of 21.

It is fair to say, therefore, that the legal structure for dealing with young offenders now to be considered is based upon questionable assumptions.

This fact has produced, particularly in the last 30 years, a vigorous debate concerning underlying principle, a tension within the system itself as between welfare concerns and considerations of legality and justice, and a pendulum effect as between discretionary and more structured methods and procedures. For a useful account of the development of policy regarding young offenders during the second part of the twentieth century, see Loraine Gelsthorpe and Allison Morris (1994).

Stewart Asquith, "Justice, Retribution and Children," in *Providing Criminal Justice for Children* **(Allison Morris and Henri Giller eds., 1983), pp. 7–11.**

The current attack on what might be termed a welfare philosophy as the basis for systems of juvenile justice is composed of two main elements, both conceptually linked.

The first is that children's rights receive insufficient protection in systems based on welfarism for a number of reasons. Theoretically, the critics argue ... that welfarism is based on philosophically unsound principles insomuch as it is not possible to identify criteria which can either be employed to explain delinquent behaviour or to inform the measures to which children are subjected in their "best interests". In short, if we do not really know what we are doing with children we should not pretend to by employing the rhetoric of therapy when what is being exercised is a very subtle form of social control. Semantic and linguistic devices too readily conceal the ambiguity and confusion which is seen to be at the very root of welfarism. Practically, the justice movement deplores the absence of sufficient legal and judicial safeguards in a system of control based on welfare principles and in that respect their claims are reminiscent of the arguments made in relation to the infamous Gault and Kent cases which fostered a policy of constitutional revisionism in the United States in the 1960s ... The "return to justice" movement as currently conceived then includes arguments in favour of a court hearing, judicial review of decisions and legal representation. Only in this way, it is said, can children avail themselves of the safeguards commonly available to adults caught up in the criminal justice system. It is no surprise to find that the Scottish system of juvenile justice in which hearings take the form of administrative tribunals comes in for particular comment and criticism along these lines. Indeed, there has more recently been empirical evidence to the effect that even the minimal statutory requirements which should govern children's hearings in Scotland are in practice often being ignored.

The second argument is that measures imposed on children should be offence (rather than child) oriented and that children can, therefore, be legitimately punished for what they have done. Advocacy of children's rights and of punishing is, within the terms of a justice approach, conceptually linked: only in a system in which children are punished for what they have done can their rights best be protected. Within a welfare philosophy children can be subjected to measures which are indeterminate and which may appear inconsistent with the measures inflicted on children who have committed prima facie similar offences. Accordingly, the main proponents of the justice movement include amongst their main principles the proposal that measures should be determinate, proportional (to the offence) and consistent (with other offences). Needless to say these in themselves provide for a decision-making process that is, in theory at least, more structured and restrictive than that manifested in a welfare system in which wide discretionary powers are available to decision-making personnel. A retributively oriented philosophy underpinning a legally and judicially constituted form of decision-making is seen as the most appropriate and most just basis for a system of juvenile justice.

What is particularly interesting about such arguments is the extent to which they are currently being voiced in a number of countries. Very similar arguments are contained in proposals made by the ABA/IJA Standards Project (1977) in the USA, the Black Committee (1979) for Northern Ireland, Morris *et al.* for England and Wales and Joutsen in the Republic of Ireland. There are a number of differences in the recommendations made by these different bodies and individuals but what they have in common is the commitment to punishment (as opposed to welfarism) as the means of dealing with children who offend and to judicial proceedings (as opposed to what are seen to be wide discretionary powers available within administrative forms of decision making)...

... the concept of justice employed by many of the proponents of a justice approach reflects concern with the procedural injustices which may arise within systems of delinquency control espousing a commitment to welfare. As such, proposals for change, even in the advocacy of retributive sanctions, are primarily directed at promoting greater procedural justice within systems of control and there is often little discussion of how these are, or ought to be, related to the material conditions of social life.

Second, in the pursuit of greater protection for children within systems of control, further consideration has to be given to the distinction between dealing with children and dealing with adults and, consequently, between children's rights and adults' rights. The perception of the offender in retributive thinking is rational and responsible and this poses particular problems for any social institution dealing with those whose status as morally autonomous agents needs careful consideration. The extent to which children can be considered criminally or morally responsible or both is a crucial question. The mental capacity of the individual has always been singled out as a prime factor to be taken into account in determining the character of retributive sanctions. Walker, for example, argues that "the amount and therefore the severity of the penalty should be governed by the offender's intentions and not by the actual result". In this respect, the issues involved in dealing with juveniles parallel very closely the debates about the punishment of the mentally ill since both involve questions of moral agency and moral competency.

Notes

1.   The above extract summarises some of the arguments used to limit a "welfare" approach in dealing with young offenders. However, Asquith distinguishes between a crude swing of the pendulum, simply allowing a return to more penal methods, and a response which separates the need for "due process" or procedural guarantees from the resort to penal measures. Implicit in his argument is the notion that proponents of a penal approach have not yet demonstrated that in itself it is either more just or more appropriate for younger offenders. He points out that the question of the extent to which children can be considered to be criminally or morally responsible is still unresolved. He concludes, towards the end of his paper, that

> "policies which ignore the social and economic realities in which children find themselves, while promoting greater equality and justice within formal systems of control, may not only ignore but may compound the structural and material inequalities which have been historically associated with criminal behaviour. The provision of justice for children will require a fundamental reappraisal of the social distribution of life opportunities offered to children" (at p. 17).

2.   Concern for the "social and economic realities in which children find themselves," as a factor in the explanation of juvenile rule-breaking, has been to the forefront of some more recent discussion in this area. For instance, Stephen Humphries (1981) has investigated the enforcement of criminal law in relation to certain aspects of juvenile behaviour in the period 1880–1930 and interprets much "delinquent" behaviour as a (justifiable?) reaction against the attempted imposition of particular values. In a paper advocating discussions in terms of children's rights, M. D. A. Freeman (1981) asserts: "All underprivileged groups, but children particularly, are a soft touch. They can be blamed for society's ills and hitherto have been slow to mobilise protest ..." (p. 211). Generally, there has been a re-assessment of the central concept of juvenile delinquency. Doreen Elliott (Chapter 2 in *Society Against Crime* (Howard Jones ed., 1981)) concludes: "There is ample evidence from research studies to support the conclusion of Morris and Hawkins (*The Honest Politician's Guide to Crime Control* (1970)) that

> "delinquent behaviour of some kind among young people, if not universal, is at least far too widespread to be regarded as abnormal. The knowledge that most juvenile delinquents do not become adult criminals adds strength to the argument that much juvenile delinquency is widespread, normal behaviour at a certain stage of development. Systems of juvenile justice which have set up a sophisticated 'treatment' approach, thus implying abnormality in the offender, may therefore be in danger of missing the point completely" (at pp. 45–46).

The reaction in both policy and practice against the "welfare" approach in dealing with young offenders, especially as embodied in the 1969 Children and Young Persons Act, is analysed in the following terms by Gelsthorpe and Morris (1994):

> "More broadly speaking, two opposing trends – first an increase in punitive dispositions generally and in custodial dispositions in par-ticular, and second an increase in the use of diversion – occurred in the 1970s. Neither is overtly linked with welfare; quite the contrary, in fact. But both were undoubtedly created by the consequences of perceptions of welfare – or more accurately perhaps, by perceptions of those promoting welfare practices. A third and paradoxical trend also occurred: a decline in the use of welfare-orientated dispositions despite the intentions underlying the Act."

3.   The Gault and Kent cases in the United States, referred to by Asquith, were Supreme Court decisions fostering an emphasis on due process in relation to juvenile court proceedings, a development pre-dating British concern by a decade. (*Re the Application of Paul L. Gault*, 387 U.S. 1 (1967); and *Morris A. Kent v. U.S.*, 383 U.S. 541 (1966)). The Gault case contained a dissenting opinion by Mr Justice Stewart, part of which may be quoted:

"Juvenile proceedings are not criminal trials. They are not civil trials. They are simply not adversary proceedings. Whether treating with a delinquent child, a neglected child, a defective child or a dependent child, a juvenile proceeding's whole purpose and mission is the very opposite of the mission and purpose of a prosecution in a criminal court. The object of one is correction of a condition. The object of the other is conviction and punishment for a criminal act."

Does such a view subscribe to what Nigel Walker ((1972), p. 130), would refer to as the "diagnostic fallacy"?

M. D. A. Freeman, "The rights of children when they do 'wrong'" (1981) 21 B.J. Crim. 210, pp. 217–220.

Status offences are a   particularly troublesome feature of juvenile justice. They are a matter of concern because they legitimise state intervention in the lives of children, rather than the population as a whole, and are thus discriminatory. However, they also exemplify certain procedures and practices which are endemic in the juvenile justice system whether it is dealing with criminal offences or such matters as promiscuity or truancy. For in all cases what is in issue is not the act itself, whether this be theft or vandalism or staying out late or running away, but the fact that the act is deemed to be symptomatic of an underlying psychological condition which is believed to be its cause. It is difficult to justify status offences. Although other justifications may be posited, in general there are two grounds commonly asserted to support the retention of such offences. First, the behaviour in question is supposed to typify more serious problems in the child and thus to allow intervention to solve those problems. Secondly, it is assumed that children who are promiscuous or smoke or truant or whatever are more likely than other children to commit serious delinquent behaviour in the future. As prevention is better than cure, early intervention is seen as desirable if these children are to be "saved". An underlying assumption is that intervention will deter the child from subsequently engaging in "harmful" or delinquent activities.

These arguments make a number of claims and there is no empirical evidence to support any of them. Furthermore, intervention causes any number of evils, notably stigmatisation with the attendant problems for employment prospects and self-image and the fact that it is likely to lead to increased police surveillance. It is difficult to see what is being treated and how: "being an unruly child is not, any more than being an obnoxious adult, a treatable condition". The goal is said to be rehabilitation but this is to suggest that intervention is justified not for what the child has done but for what it is feared he might do in the future. There is no evidence at all that there is any connection between suffering from some kind of psychological disorder and committing a status offence. But then no one has established any causal link between any personality disorder the delinquency and it is not likely that anyone ever will. We are simply asked by those who support status offences to take too much on trust. After all, the arguments used in support could be used to make similar behaviour illegal in the case of adults...

The American Bar Association Juvenile Justice Standards Project has proposed the elimination of the general juvenile court jurisdiction over status offences in non-criminal juvenile misbehaviour. Instead, the standards place primary reliance on "a system of voluntary referral to service provided outside the juvenile justice system". They envisage the need for "some carefully limited official intervention" in emergency situations where there is "immediate jeopardy" and the standards provide for this. In general the standards reject judicialisation and coercion. "Removal of the status offense jurisdiction will", the Project submits, "encourage more people to get more effective help; stimulate the creation and extension of a wider range of voluntary services than is presently available, and the corrosive effects of treating non-criminal youth as though they had committed crimes; and free up a substantial part of the resources of the juvenile justice system to deal with the cases of delinquency and of abused and neglected children that belong to it" (American Bar Association, 1977). Whilst endorsing in general this proposal, I believe its implications should be considered carefully. The substitution of "help", however "voluntary", looks like a familiar invocation of welfare philosophy. Some adolescents may need advice, befriending or assistance but many will not. Help assumes the existence of a problem: this may amount to nothing more than the interpretation of fairly normal adolescent behaviour by welfare officials for whom the norm is different. The removal of both the education condition and the moral danger condition as grounds for a care order should be undertaken forthwith. Coercive intervention in the lives of young people should be limited to those who commit a criminal offence or who are abused or neglected. Children should only be punished for offences for which adults are punished and, however we conceptualise them, children see care orders, particularly where they involve removal from home, as punishment.

Notes

1. Here Freeman is pointing out the dangers of a policy of "decriminalisation," as recommended by the American Bar Association Juvenile Justice Standards Project. A virtue of criminal proceedings is its (usual) assumption of the need for "due process." The risk to an individual under a "welfare" approach is, not only that it may be too easy to assume the existence of "problems" requiring attention, but that there is also a tendency to remove the matter from public scrutiny into a more closed, discretionary decision-making environment.

2. A jurist would probably object to the categorisation of a care order (when it was available to deal with convicted young offenders) as a kind of punishment (see the discussion in Chapter 1), since it was not intended to blame or hold responsible the young person in such a case for any unacceptable behaviour. On the other hand, is it right to disregard the subjective experience of the measure or its actual content, which may have penal features? (*cf.* The discussion in relation to remand in custody, in Chapter 2). The care order ceased to be available as a measure to deal with convicted juvenile offenders under section 90 of the Children Act 1989.

II. THE LEGAL FRAMEWORK

Children and Young Persons Act 1969, s. 70(1) (as amended).
  70. – (1) ... "child", except in Part II (including Schedule 3) and sections 27, 63, 64 and 65 of this Act, means a person under the age of fourteen, and in that Part (including that Schedule) and those sections means a person under the age of eighteen and a person who has attained the age of eighteen and is the subject of care order; ...

  [Editor's note: Part II of the Act and the other sections referred to concern the courts' power to make a care order.]

  ... "Young person" means a person who has attained the age of fourteen and is under the age of eighteen years; ...

Children and Young Persons Act 1933, s. 44(1).

44. – (1) Every court in dealing with a child or young person who is brought before it, either as an offender or otherwise, shall have regard to the welfare of the child or young person and shall in a proper case take steps for removing him from undesirable surroundings, and for securing that proper provision is made for his education and training.

Children and Young Persons Act 1933, s. 50 (as amended).

50. – It shall be conclusively presumed that no child under the age of ten years can be guilty of any offence.

Criminal Justice Act 1982, s. 1.

1. – (1) Subject to subsection (2) below, no court shall pass a sentence of imprisonment on a person under 21 years of age or commit such a person to prison for any reason.

(2) Nothing in subsection (1) above shall prevent the committal to prison of a person under 21 years of age who is remanded in custody or committed in custody for trial or sentence.

Notes

1.   The application of penal and other measures to children and young persons depends upon two sets of criteria in relation to age. First, the matter is partly determined by the rules as to criminal liability: legally no person under the age of ten years can commit a criminal offence, or therefore be convicted or sentenced (Children and Young Persons Act 1933, s. 50). Until recently, a child (for these purposes, a person under the age of 14 years, although see section 70(1) of the 1969 Act) between the age of 10 and 13 was presumed to be incapable of committing a criminal offence, although this was rebuttable upon proof of what was sometimes called a "mischievous discretion" – broadly, an awareness of the wrongful nature of the act in question. The present position is that children over the age of ten, and then those who are termed "young persons" (aged between 14 and 17) and those described as "young adult offenders" (a non-statutory term for those aged 18 to 20) may commit offences and fall within the sentencing powers of the courts. But, at the same time, children and other young persons under the age of seventeen who have not committed any criminal offence may still be compulsorily dealt with under family proceedings on grounds other than the commission of an offence (Part IV of the Children Act 1989).

2.   Secondly, the use of a particular measure depends upon the age of the young person, in that certain measures cannot be used in relation to persons below a stated age. The table below summarises the availability of the

CHILDREN	1–9 years	family proceedings: care or supervision orders (non- criminal)
	10–13 years	care (family proceedings); supervision (family or criminal proceedings); fine; discharge; hospital order; attendance centre order; secure training order (12 years-old and above); detention under section 53(1) and (2)(b) CYPA 1933
YOUNG PERSONS	14–17 years	care (family proceedings); supervision (family or criminal proceedings); fine; discharge; hospital order; attendance centre order; compensation order; secure training order (14 years-old); detention in a young offender institution (15 years-old and above); detention under section 53(1) and (2)(a) CYPA 1933
YOUNG ADULT OFFENDERS	18–20 years	all measures available to deal with adult offenders, plus attendance centre orders, but imprisonment is replaced by detention in a young offender institution (and this may not be suspended), and custody for life under section 8 of the CJA 1982

various penal and other measures according to age group.

3. The Children and Young Persons Act 1969 had envisaged the use of care proceedings as a primary response to juvenile delinquency. There were (until 1992) provisions in that legislation for the reduction of criminal proceedings and the removal of certain types of penal measure in relation to children and young persons. Section 4 provided that a child (*i.e.* a person below the age of 14) shall not be convicted of any offence except homicide; section 5 laid down restrictions on criminal proceedings for offences committed by young persons; section 7(1) provided for the minimum age for

borstal training to be raised to 17 years; and section 7(3) contemplated the phasing out of attendance and detention centres. These provisions were never brought into force; as Gelsthorpe and Morris (1994) comment:

> "Like many Acts of Parliament certain sections in the Children and Young Persons Act 1969 were to be implemented at some future date. However, a Conservative Government replaced the Labour one in 1970 and the Conservatives made it clear that they would not fully implement the Act. So, from its beginnings, the Act in practice reflected compromise. And when the Labour party were re-elected in 1974, it was no longer politically or popularly viable to implement the Act in full. Thus new welfare measures were added on to, but did not replace, the old punitive ones."

4.   The term "young adult offender" is commonly but informally used; it was given vogue by the Advisory Council on the Penal System following their Report, "Young Adult Offenders" (1974). It mainly serves to indicate the scope for custodial measures in relation to this age group. Since 1982 (see section 1 of the Criminal Justice Act of that year), a sentence of imprisonment may not be used, but detention in a young offender institution is available. Under the 1991 Criminal Justice Act, 17 year-old offenders were removed from this category to that of young persons, so falling to be dealt with in criminal proceedings by the youth court. In the Government's White Paper, *Crime, Justice and Protecting the Public* (1990), the view was put forward that there was little to distinguish between 16 and 17 year-olds in this context and they should all therefore be dealt with in a way that separates them from adult offenders.

5.   The rebuttable presumption against criminal liability for children below the age of 14 years was removed by the Divisional Court in the case of *C (a Minor) v. DPP* (1994) 3 W.L.R. 888; the presumption was regarded as no longer corresponding with the view of society. In any case the number of criminal proceedings within this age group had declined significantly during the last 20 years, as an increasing number of offenders were cautioned. In 1982, 16,668 persons aged over 10 and under 14 were the subject of criminal proceedings in England and Wales; in 1989, the total was 5,459; in 1990, it was 2,800.

6.   It is important to bear in mind that an increasing number of young offenders are being diverted from court proceedings through the use of cautioning (see Chapter Two, above, and section IV, below, for a wider discussion of cautioning). Thus during the 1980s the proportion of juvenile offenders cautioned for indictable offences increased from 66 per cent (1979) to 88 per cent (1989) in the ten to thirteen years age group; from 35 per cent (1979) to 64 per cent (1989) in the 14 to 16 years age group; and from three per cent of male offenders (1980) to 17 per cent (1989) in the 17 to 20 years age group. This trend clearly had a significant impact on the number of young offenders being dealt with in criminal court proceedings.

III. The Forum for Proceedings: the Youth Court

Phyllida Parsloe, *Juvenile Justice in Britain and the United States* (1978), pp. 140–145.

Juvenile courts were established in 1908. At that time they constituted a special sitting of the magistrates court to hear cases relating to those under sixteen. The juvenile court remains the court in which most troubled and troublesome juveniles appear, but over the years the courts have become rather more specialised and more easily distinguished from magistrates courts dealing with adults. It is part of the lowest level of courts with the most localised jurisdiction in the English judicial structure, and, like any other magistrates court, it has both criminal and civil jurisdiction.

The Children and Young Persons Acts of 1933 and 1937 made it a requirement that a juvenile court should "sit either in a different building or room from that in which sittings of courts other than juvenile courts are held, or on different days from those on which sittings of such courts are held". The separation of adults from juveniles was thus carried a step further, although in 1963 the law was changed in response to the pressure on court buildings, and now a juvenile court may not sit in a room in which sittings of another court have been or will be held within an hour of the juvenile court's sitting. The reasons for this change are administrative and economic, but the effect is to weaken the welfare approach. Juveniles are now more likely to mix with adult offenders, not in the court room itself, but in the corridors and waiting rooms. Such mixing is unlikely to lead to any direct corruption of juveniles by adults, although this is possible; much more damaging may be the effect upon the self image of the juvenile. If they meet and wait with adult offenders, they are more likely to begin to see themselves as criminals, and, according to the labelling theorists, such a change in self image is a vital step on the road to a delinquent career. . . .

. . . Although it was important to establish the principle that children and young people should appear before specially selected magistrates, it has proved difficult to ensure that these magistrates are in fact particularly well suited to their job. The method by which the juvenile court rota is chosen is by an election amongst the magistrates of each administrative area known as a petty sessional division. Their choice is limited to existing magistrates, and the guide lines on which they operate are necessarily broad. Home Office circulars suggest that those selected should have particular interest or experience with young people, and since 1966 training has been required. Even imposing an age limit on the service of juvenile court magistrates took a long time. Mr Lunn, MP, had interrupted the opening speech on the Second Reading of the 1933 Act to exclaim: "There ought to be more modern magistrates. A lot of them are old maids". Mr Stanley replied: "Well, the Hon. Member is no doubt a better judge of old maids than I am"; and an age limit was not introduced until 1936. Elkin states that, before the new panels were elected in 1936, of approximately 10,000 justices in England and Wales on juvenile court panels, 1,284 were aged between seventy and eighty, and 130 were over ninety years. Even the present requirement that they be not over 65 years of age results in many being the age of the grandparents, rather than of the parents, of the young people with whom they are concerned.

The great difference in age between magistrates and the juveniles who appear before them is important. Ideas about what is tolerable behaviour in young people change over the generations, and juveniles tend to feel they have a greater chance of being understood by people near their own age. Briggs, in his account of his experiences before a juvenile court, shows how impossible it was for him to convey how he felt to the court, and anything that increases that difficulty, such as the distance and perhaps the deafness of old age, lessens the chance of individualising justice.

Apart from attempts to regulate age, the law also refers to the sex of magistrates. The 1933 Act required that, where possible, each juvenile court bench should include a man and a woman magistrate, and the 1926 Juvenile Courts (Scotland) Act made provision for a woman magistrate to sit as an assessor in juvenile courts in Scottish burghs where the presiding magistrate was a man.

Alongside the development of special panels of juvenile court justices has gone the development of restrictions upon the numbers of people involved in a juvenile court hearing. The present size of a juvenile court bench is three, but although this was the most common number when the Children's Branch of the Home Office issued one of its periodic reports in 1925 it was not the number in a majority of courts.

When a large number of magistrates sit, it is clearly even harder to achieve an atmosphere in which the child and his parents can understand what is happening and explain their own views to the bench. This is the aim of a court concerned with the welfare of children, and restricting the numbers to three helps to make it nearer a reality.

The same applies to the presence of other people in the court. The 1908 Act had intended to allow access only to those involved in the particular case. Juvenile courts never were, as are adult courts, open to the public. However, in 1927 a departmental committee discovered that as many as fifty people were present in some juvenile courts and that twenty was not an unusual number. They recommended that the number of people present be kept as low as possible.

Although juvenile courts have never been open to the public, the press have been allowed to attend. The departmental committee report in 1927 stated that most courts had made informal arrangements with the press that they would not disclose details which would allow a child or young person to be identified. They considered excluding the press entirely, but decided to recommend a statutory ban on the publication of identifying details, to be lifted in individual instances only by order of the Secretary of State. This was enacted in the 1933 and 1937 Acts, and remained unchanged until 1969 when, for England and Wales, publication was forbidden unless the court considered it to be in the interests of a child or young person for the press to give identifying details. The thinking behind this new clause is that in cases where one child or group of children are suspected of acts which in fact were carried out by others, publication may be necessary to serve the welfare of the innocent children or young people. In general, however, those appearing before juvenile courts do not suffer the exposure to the public inflicted on adult offenders, because a concern for their welfare overrides the need to stigmatise and expose them.

Besides the magistrates, the child and his parents, and the press, the other people usually present throughout an English juvenile court hearing are the clerk to the justices, members of the local police, when they are prosecuting in a criminal case, and social workers from the probation service and/or the local authority social service department.

Although some justices may have had a legal training, this is not required, and the juvenile court is served by a clerk to the justices. He must have legal training, and is usually a solicitor with at least five years' practice. The function of the clerk is twofold: he serves as the administrator of the court and he advises the justices upon legal questions.

Criminal Justice Act 1991, s. 70

70. – (1) Juvenile courts shall be renamed youth courts and juvenile court panels shall be renamed youth court panels.

(2) Any reference to juvenile courts or juvenile court panels in any enactment

passed or instrument made before the commencement of this section shall be construed in accordance with subsection (1) above.

Notes

1.   During the 1960s, with the "welfare" approach clearly in the ascendant, there were proposals for the replacement of the juvenile courts, most notably in the Government White Paper *The Child, the Family and the Young Offender*, Cmnd. 2742 (1965). This was particularly critical of the fact that the procedure in the juvenile courts was still broadly based upon that of the criminal courts. It was therefore proposed (para. 11) "to remove young people so far as possible from the jurisdiction of the court, and to empower each local authority, through its children's committee, to appoint local family councils to deal with each case as far as possible in consultation and agreement with the parents." This proposed system included the possibility of a further reference to "family courts" (also to be set up under these proposals) and procedural safeguards for the children and young persons being dealt with. There was a critical reaction to the White Paper: see, *e.g.*, P. J. Fitzgerald, "The Child, the White Paper and the Criminal Law: Some Reflections" 1966 Crim. L.R. 607; "The Child, the Family and the Young Offender," Memorandum by the Council of the Law Society, June 1966; the Magistrates' Association, "The Association's Views on the White Paper on the Child, the Family and the Young Offender," November 1965. The proposals proved to be too radical to be politically acceptable and when the law was changed in 1969, on the basis of the White Paper *Children in Trouble*, Cmnd. 3601 (1968), it was achieved by preserving the juvenile court system, but at the same time introducing new measures and shifting responsibility for their implementation in the direction of the social services agencies (see below in relation to care and supervision). See the discussion by Ball (1992) and Gelsthorpe and Morris (1994).

2.   Radical change proved easier to achieve in Scotland where, under the Social Work (Scotland) Act 1968, children's hearings were established in 1971, using panels drawn from members of the public: these were intended to be both socially representative and staffed by non-professionals with the necessary experience and understanding of children's problems. This has been the most significant move within the British system away from the restricted "professional" background of most judges and magistrates. The question remains, however, whether such a shift in social background has actually been achieved in the Scottish system. Another doubt raised by some earlier research into the working of the system of children's hearings concerned the degree of influence on the panels' decisions exercised by the recommendations of professional social workers. For instance, Allison Morris and Mary McIsaac (1978) argued that the "panel is a professionally orientated group; even if it was at the outset representative of the community it served, training made it less so" and that "... panel members ... readily accept, possibly because of their training in the values and ethics of social work, the recommendations of social workers" (pp. 117–118). See in general

Chapter 7 of their work, "The Children's hearings: a study in ambiguity." The authors' conclusion was that the factors of community representation and social work training may combine to produce in the panels an ambiguity between criminal justice and social welfare values inherent in the juvenile courts which had been superseded. There has been less research recently into the working of the Scottish system, but Murray and Hill (1991) present a less dated view.

Criminal Justice Act 1982, s. 3 (as amended).

3. Restriction on imposing custodial sentences on persons under 21 not legally represented
(1) A magistrates' court on summary conviction or the Crown Court on committal for sentence or on conviction on indictment shall not –

(a) pass a sentence of detention in a young offender institution under section 1A above;
(c) pass a sentence of custody for life under section 8(2) below; or
(d) make an order for detention under section 53(2) of the Children and Young Persons Act 1933,

in respect of or on a person who is not legally represented in that court, unless either—

(i) he applied for legal aid and the application was refused on the ground that it did not appear his means were such that he required assistance; or
(ii) having been informed of his right to apply for legal aid and had the opportunity to do so, he refused or failed to apply.

(2) For the purposes of this section a person is to be treated as legally represented in a court if, but only if, he has the assistance of counsel or a solicitor to represent him in the proceedings in that court at some time after he is found guilty and before he is sentenced, and in subsection (1)(i) and (ii) above "legal aid" means legal aid for the purposes of proceedings in that court, whether the whole proceedings or the proceedings on or in relation to sentence: but in the case of a person committed to the Crown Court for sentence or trial, it is immaterial whether he applied for legal aid in the Crown Court to, or was informed of his right to apply by, that court or the court which committed him.

Notes
1.   A similar provision in section 24 of the 1982 Act relating to care orders was repealed by the Children Act 1989
2.   This provision clearly reflects a shift towards "legalism" and a suspicion of "welfare totalitarianism" in juvenile court proceedings. But, if it is felt that children and young persons require such legal protection, does legal representation in itself guarantee this? The following extract raises doubts as to the effectiveness of the kind of change introduced by the 1982 legislation.

Allison Morris: "Legal representation and justice," in *Providing Criminal Justice for Children* **(Allison Morris and Henri Giller eds., 1983), pp. 134–135.**

Research in both England and the United States suggests that more legal representation does not necessarily mean better legal representation: the mere provision of legal services may have little impact on the quality of the decisions made about children or the quality of the care offered to them. Procedural formality by itself does not promote children's interests. Take, for example, the findings of Morris and Giller (1977): that children and parents find the juvenile court a bewildering experience; that they have communication problems; that they are afraid to participate actively in the proceedings; that they feel that matters are pre-determined and that nothing they say will influence the outcome. In fact, over half of the respondents in their pilot survey could not correctly identify the magistrates and did not know who made the decision in court. One might expect the presence of a lawyer to improve this, but this would not necessarily be so. In a Canadian project (Catton and Erickson 1975), 22 children who were legally represented were asked "who was on your side in court?" Only seven mentioned their lawyer; four referred to the judge. Only six children thought their lawyer helped them in court and only four thought that the lawyer was the best person to whom to tell their story. Some children did not even realise they had a lawyer and, where they did realise it, some did not think that he had been there to assist them. These findings are perhaps not surprising in view of the fact that in just under half of the cases the lawyer said nothing at all in court! Further, Joanna Shapland's study of barristers in English courts (1979) found that a considerable proportion did not discuss with their client the recommendation they would present to the judge. One can assume that this disregard for clients' wishes is even more extensive in the juvenile court.

The author poses a number of important questions at the beginning of her discussion (p. 125):

The extent of legal representation in England and Wales has greatly increased in recent years. In 1969, three per cent of children appearing in the juvenile court were represented; by 1980 the figure had reached at least 27 per cent. There has, however, been very little discussion of the role which a lawyer in the juvenile court should play. Does the inexperience and immaturity of the juvenile inevitably (and appropriately) require the lawyer to have a different role from that of representing an adult accused of crime? Does the lawyer represent the child or his parents? Does he independently assess the child's interests or follow the wishes of the child or his parents? Does he independently assess the child's interests or follow the wishes of the child or his parent? Does he act as an advocate for the child or as an officer of the court? These are difficult questions in themselves but they beg a more important question: what do we want a juvenile justice system to achieve, for the nature of the lawyer's role must ultimately depend on that? Should he protect the child's legal rights or try to promote his welfare? Should he try to get the child off or get appropriate treatment for him? Should he sacrifice the child's legal rights if the child's general welfare seems to require it? Should he look to the child's legal rights and his welfare?

See also: Allison Morris and Henri Giller, "The juvenile court – the clients' perspective" 1977 Crim. L.R. 198; T. Catton and P. Erikson, "The juvenile's perception of the role of defence counsel in the juvenile court," Working Paper of the Centre of Criminology, University of Toronto (1975); Joanna Shapland, "The construction of a mitigation," in Psychology, Law and Legal Processes (D. Farrington *et al.* eds., 1979); Elizabeth Burney, *Sentencing Young People* (1985a).

IV. DIVERSION OF YOUNG OFFENDERS

See also the more general discussion of diversion and cautioning in Chapter Two, above.

Loraine Gelsthorpe and Henri Giller, "More Justice for Juveniles: Does More Mean Better?" (1990) Crim. L.R. 153, pp. 153–154, 161–164.

The Crown Prosecution Service was created to take over from the police the primary responsibility for the prosecution of crimes in England and Wales. But with juveniles prosecution is clearly meant to be a last resort. The *Code for Crown Prosecutors* makes special reference to juvenile offenders and suggests that:

> "There may be positive advantages for the individual and for society, in using prosecution as a last resort and in general there is in the case of juvenile offenders a much stronger presumption in favour of methods of disposal which fall short of prosecution unless the seriousness of the offence or other exceptional circumstances dictate otherwise. The objective should be to divert juveniles from court wherever possible. Prosecution should always be regarded as a severe step" (para.16).

The Code continues this theme by stressing that prosecutors must satisfy themselves that the spirit of cautioning guidelines[1] have been applied by the police in reaching the decision to prosecute and alerts them to the need for consultation between different agencies where appropriate.[2] How then do Crown Prosecutors deal with those juvenile cases which the police reject as unsuitable for diversion? How do they make sense of their Code and translate its formal directives into operation?

As part of an evaluation of the work of the CPS with respect to juvenile offenders we examined how this policy statement was put into everyday practice.[3] In this analysis we are not concerned with the question of whether the CPS "succeeds" or "fails" in implementing its stated goals, but how these "mission statements" are translated into the reality of decision-making and how such decisions are created and sustained.

In answering this question we sought to establish the "operational philosophy" of the Crown Prosecutors with juvenile offenders. By this term, we mean the system of ideas and procedures for constructing and implementing decision-making under the specific organisational conditions of the Prosecution Service. One immediate difficulty in doing this was that despite the official emphasis on diversion with juveniles, the CPS (as its name suggests) was primarily concerned with prosecution. Overall 95.8 per cent, of cases recommended for prosecution by the police in the sample were prosecuted (458 out of 478 cases).

Given the "routine" nature of prosecution decision-making and the organisational

---

[1] Home Office circular 14/1985. "The Cautioning of Offenders."

[2] *Code for Crown Prosecutions*, para. 17.

[3] The evaluation was part of a two year project sponsored by the ESRC into police and prosecutor decision-making in Cheshire and South Yorkshire (ESRC Ref. No.: 11250002). Nearly 1,000 files were followed through the prosecution process. Interviews were undertaken with personnel in both the Police forces and Crown Prosecution Service. Details of the full evaluation are available in Gelsthorpe, L., Giller, H. & Tutt, N., *The Impact of the Crown Prosecution Service on Juvenile Justice* (1990).

context in which decisions were taken, we initially hypothesised that those everyday "operational philosophies" were best exposed by examining the features of cases in which the presumption in favour of prosecution had been undermined or deconstructed.[4] In this way we aimed to establish those features which made cases "non-routine" and "potentially problematic" and from them examine similarities and differences with the characteristics of their counterparts (*i.e.* those cases which were routine and non-problematic)...

Dissent and independence

The Crown Prosecution Service was set up as an "independent" service to "promote consistency and fairness" and to "reduce the proportion of cases pursued despite lack of sufficient evidence" amongst other things. Indeed, one of the underlying themes in the setting up of the Service was that it should be an important counterbalance to the increased police powers provided by the Police and Criminal Evidence Act 1984.[5]

Despite this, the Crown Prosecution Service remains dependent upon the police for information. Since the raison d'etre of the police is to detect and prevent crime we might reasonably expect a presumption in favour of prosecution with respect to those cases they refer to the Crown Prosecution Service. Andrew Sanders has shown how information from the police is constructed in such a way as to suggest that prosecution is both expedient and desirable.[6] He refers to the potential for discounting evidence, to the fact that the police do not actively seek information that could establish innocence and to the fact that the police do not see their role extending to checking the defence story if doing so would be difficult, even when, for example, following up the story is beyond the resources of the defence. Sanders establishes that cases are not simply about sets of objective facts which can be ascertained once and for all. The police try to construct strong cases by eliminating ambiguity and removing features which undermine cases.[7] Those cases which they present to the Crown Prosecution Service are generally only those cases which they want to prosecute.[8] The Crown Prosecution Service has inquisitorial power to vet cases, to screen them and to halt those which are evidentially insufficient, but is has no resources to explore the cases in depth. The Crown Prosecution Service remains *dependent* upon the police for the carefully constructed accounts it receives. Indeed, many Crown Prosecutors we interviewed resisted the idea of receiving information from any source other than the police, or at least, resisted the idea of unlimited information.

What is of interest here in the context of juvenile cases, is that we found the police used the same set of conceptual categories as Crown Prosecutors in their decisions to divert or refer cases to court.[9] For those recommended for prosecution the police "construction" of the cases provides the basis for Crown Prosecution

---

[4] Given the limited number of "disagreement" cases this group was supplemented with a further sub-sample of 14 cases derived from 133 police recommendations for prosecution from Division C (Rotherham) in South Yorkshire during June to August 1988.

[5] K. de Gama, "Police Powers and Public Prosecutions: Winning by Appearing to Lose," (1988) 16 *Int. J. of Sociology of Law* 339.

[6] A. Sanders, "Constructing the Case for the Prosecution," (1987) 14 *Jo. Law & Society* 229.

[7] This does not mean that the police try to make a strong case out of every incident. The police are often reluctant to choose a "domestic violence" case where an incident indicates that an alternative case may be made: see T. Faragher, "The Police Response to Violence against Women in the Home" in *Private Violence and Public Policy* (J. Pahl ed., 1985); F., Wasoff, "Legal Protection from Wifebeating" (1982) 10 *Int. J. of Sociology of Law* 187.

[8] This is not to undermine the importance of the system whereby the police initially seek advice from the Crown Prosecution Service before issuing summons.

[9] Those interested in the findings with respect to the police should see Gelsthorpe *et al.* (above, n. 3).

Service assessment and review. The Crown Prosecutors depend on the police for a core of information which could be quickly and routinely checked. Information on offenders and their offences is transmitted to the Crown Prosecution Service with the tacit understanding that these are all cases which deserve to go to court. There was a commonality in their approach and use of their conceptual categories. But the question remains, if the police and Crown Prosecutors use similar conceptual categories in their approach to decision-making, why is it that disagreements occur? A superficial analysis here might be to suggest that the police and Crown Prosecutors have different tolerance levels of "trouble," different standards or different policies. This is not the case. Rather, it is that perceptions of "trouble" need to be redefined by the Crown Prosecution Service in the context of its own organisational goals. Thus despite Crown Prosecutors' reliance on police constructions of cases, they do assess cases in the light of the exigencies of everyday organisational practice and it is these which shape their "operational philosophy."[10]

At its simplest an organisational priority of the Crown Prosecution Service is to effect a smooth-functioning of the prosecution process. The chief "problem relevance" in pursuing this is the limitation on available time and human resources. The "operational philosophy" adopted is one which tests out whether the case as presented by the police is "routine" or "potentially problematic." This is done by assessing the case for the factors we have identified. This assessment is a two-fold process: first the case is assessed by reference to technical considerations – evidential sufficiency, previous referrals, procedural soundness, seriousness of the offence. Where potential problems arise in this assessment reference is made to secondary considerations – agency intervention, personal circumstances, tariff-guessing and the ability to bide one's time.

In the majority of cases the police provide sufficient technical information and there is little (if any) reference to secondary materials. In routine cases there is little in the way of "character assessment." The more problematic the information to substantiate the first-order technical considerations, however, the more pressure there is to rebut the presumption in favour of prosecution. The presence of problematic technical considerations in a case potentially threatens the smooth-functioning of the prosecution process. In these circumstances Prosecutors examine the information around the secondary considerations to determine whether a potentially problematic prosecution should be given an organisational priority. "Independence," therefore, emerges not from some Olympian platform of values nor from some discrete professional ideology but from the organisational context – from what we have termed the "operational philosophy."

From operational philosophy to professional ideology

Interestingly, the recent Crown Prosecution Service Report on Juvenile Proceedings (1989) envisages change in the organisational context of prosecution decisions. One of the main recommendations states that:

"The Crown Prosecution Service should be seen to be promoting multi-agency panels. If properly constituted they offer the best method of achieving the *correct* decision in individual cases (para. 6.4, our emphasis)."

The Report notes the following points in their favour:

(i)   they provide a structured forum where all agencies can make their views known;

(ii) a *better* decision should be reached if all interested parties are involved;

[10] It is also important to note that this information is also interpreted in the light of the "public interest", whatever that means – see A. Sanders (below, n. 14), and A. Ashworth, "The Public Interest Element in Prosecutions" [1987] Crim. L.R. 595.

(iii) the Crown Prosecution Service should only receive cases where a prosecution is deemed to be necessary;

(iv) the Crown Prosecution Service would not be open to the accusation that
it was simply rubber stamping a police decision to prosecute. (para. 6.1,
our emphasis).

The recommendation begs a number of questions: why does the Crown Prosecution
Service want information from other agencies? What information is required? Would
this information be filtered through to the Crown Prosecution Service independently
of the police? How would the information be used? Does more information
necessarily mean better decisions?[11]

Clearly, more information from agencies is expected to lead to "better" decision-
making and to the enhancement of the independent status of the Crown Prosecution
Service. But this does not address the fact that organisational priorities and
constraints currently "drive" practice considerations. On the one hand the Crown
Prosecution Service appears to function on the basis of an "operational philosophy" – the smooth functioning of the prosecution process – on the other, it
appears resistant to the development of a "professional ideology" which would,
above all other things, mark it independent status.

The development of a "professional ideology" would involve an explicit declaration of beliefs, principles and objectives. Secondly, strategies would have to be
adopted to achieve the objectives. Thirdly, the objectives would have to be translated
into measurable criteria and targets set. Fourthly, monitoring would have to be
carried out to assess whether or not targets had been met. Lastly, policies and
practices would have to be evaluated in the light of data derived from monitoring
processes.

Such a development would bring both advantages and difficulties. Positively, such
an approach would reinforce the central position of the Crown Prosecution Service
in the criminal justice system. But areas of difficulty include the issue of accountability
and the problem of the lack of coherency and consistency. To whom would the
Crown Prosecution Service be accountable, central government or local government?
What if the Crown Prosecution Service were to develop objectives based on a
percentage usage of custodial sentences per court and local government declared
itself a "custody-free zone"? With regard to the issue of coherency and consistency
it is not at all clear how objectives would be set. Given that there is presently wide
variation in views amongst juvenile specialists in the Crown Prosecution Service,
who would determine the values and principles to be used? While the current *Code
for Crown Prosecutors* does provide a general statement of intent with respect to
the diversion of juveniles from court, it does not provide specific objectives. Sanders
makes much the same point in his discussion of the "public interest".[12]

"[There is an] absence of any clearly stated view of the 'public interest' ... Even
the existence, let alone the content, of one universal 'public interest' is far from
self-evident. If any concept of public interest is to have legitimacy, it must be
based on specific, clearly articulated and publicly debated values."

The analogy is clear: an articulated set of objectives which can be measured and
monitored would enable the Crown Prosecution Service to develop a professional

[11] The role of the Crown Prosecutor in relation to the multi-agency panels is not clearly
defined. At a conference of Juvenile Specialists in February 1989 it emerged that there were
widely differing perceptions of the role of Crown Prosecutors *vis-à-vis* panels. Whilst some
Crown prosecutors envisaged an observer role, others envisaged no contact at all with the
panels. One thing that was clear, however, was an unequivocal resistance to actual
participation in the decision- making processes of the panels.

[12] A. Sanders "Incorporating the 'Public Interest' in the Decision to Prosecute," in *The Role
of the Crown Prosecutor* (J. E. Hall Williams ed., 1988), at p. 40.

ideology and with it a privotal position in the criminal justice system. The current practice of an "operational philosophy" does not achieve this.

Notes

1. The statistical background to this discussion is one of increased resort to the cautioning of juveniles during the 1980s (see p. 358 above). But at the same time some researchers warned that there were geographical variations in cautioning practice in relation to young offenders. Wilkinson and Evans (1990) commented that:

> "Cautioning rates have increased, particularly for 14–16-year-olds, and variations in rates between forces have narrowed slightly. The variations that remain, however, are attributable more to differences in cautioning practice than differences in crime pattern or cautioning policy. Also force cautioning rates hide considerable variation in practice within forces." (at p. 175)

2. Gelsthorpe and Giller's conclusion stresses the pragmatic quality of CPS decisions on juvenile diversion and the apparent difficulty in evolving a detailed policy, based on an agreed ideology, this difficulty being compounded by a "wide variation in views among juvenile specialists in the Crown Prosecution Service".

3. Cautioning and net-widening: some commentators have warned that a move towards a non-judicial disposal of juvenile offenders could have a net-widening effect. For instance, Tutt and Giller (1987), stated that:

> "Between 1980 and 1985 a 30 per cent decrease in the number of juveniles entering the court and receiving a finding of guilt has been matched by a concomitant increase in the use of cautions. Nevertheless over the same period the actual juvenile population has declined by some 10 per cent, indicating, at least circumstantially, that a degree of 'net-widening' has taken place." (at p. 374)

Arguments about net-widening in this context have been contradicted, however, by other writers: see, for instance, Bottoms *et al.* (1990), below; and Gelsthorpe and Morris (1994), who assert that, in the mid-1990s, net-widening is not occurring on account of a declining youth population during the 1980s (although this is predicted to increase again during the 1990s) and changes in police practice.

V. SUPERVISION

The supervision order was introduced in tandem with the care order in the 1969 Children and Young Persons Act as a central element in the welfare-oriented strategy of that legislation. The demise of the care order in criminal proceedings – it was removed by the Children Act of 1989 – and its possible consequences are considered in the following extract.

Caroline Ball, "Young Offenders and the Youth Court", (1992) Crim. L.R. 277, pp. 285–286

The effectively indeterminate sentence of a care order made under the Children and Young Persons Act 1969, s. 7(7) is no longer available in criminal proceedings, having been replaced (Children Act 1989, s. 90 and Sched. 12) by the power, in certain circumstances when specified criteria are met, to add a requirement to an existing supervision order that a child or young person shall live in local authority accommodation for up to six months (Children and Young Persons Act 1969, s. 12AA). Use of care orders as a disposal in criminal proceedings had already substantially declined even prior to statutory restrictions being imposed on their use by the Criminal Justice Act 1982. This was largely as a result of research findings which revealed that the effectively severe sentence of remaining in the care of the local authority until the age of 18 failed to prevent further offending and often led to a swift entry to penal custody.[13] This was compounded by evidence that the care order was often imposed for very minor offences, or as a result of educational rather than child care factors.[14] By 1990 the incidence of care orders made in criminal proceedings had declined to such an extent that it was possible that they were only being used in the few cases in which long term local authority care was an appropriate response to serious offending by very disturbed children, who might otherwise, if old enough, have received a custodial sentence.

There is some concern that, with only the much less draconian section 12AA requirement under the 1969 Act available for offenders of 14 years committing serious offences when on a supervision order, some courts may feel that they have insufficient powers to deal with 14-year-olds charged with grave crimes and may commit more of them to the Crown Court under section 53(2) of the 1933 Act. This concern is linked, as is that considered in relation to 16-year-olds, with a possible change in the ethos of the juvenile court resulting from implementation of the Children Act. A recent NACRO publication refers to the "more welfare-minded sentencing ethos of the juvenile court"[15] as being one of the advantages to 17-year-olds of their transfer to a different jurisdiction. It may be questioned whether the youth court will in fact inherit that ethos. Ever since a special magistrates' court for juveniles was introduced by the Children Act 1908 that court has had a dual criminal jurisdiction over young offenders and a concurrent jurisdiction, in care and related proceedings, over children in need of protection or control. In terms of a suitable forum for child care cases the quasi-criminal nature of care proceedings and the hearing of related civil proceedings in what is essentially a criminal court has been recognised as a profoundly unsatisfactory arrangement. The bonus was, however, that the work of the juvenile court was varied, interesting and demanding, with the result that many high quality magistrates with considerable commitment to both young offenders and care cases were attracted to the juvenile panel and made substantial personal investment in its work.

The 1989 Act moved all care and related proceedings from the juvenile court to the magistrates' new family proceedings court, leaving the former with, for the time being, a criminal jurisdiction over all except the most seriously offending 10–16-year-olds, soon to be joined by large numbers of 17-year-olds. An unpublished survey of membership of the shadow family panels, which were set up before implementation of the Children Act, shows that in 92 out of 207 new panels (45 per cent) more than half of shadow family panel justices were previously on the

[13] S. Millham *et al.*, *Locking up Children: Secure Provision within the Child Care System* (1978).
[14] See for example P. Cawson, *Young Offenders in Care* (1981) and C. Ball, "The Use and Significance of School Reports in Juvenile Court Criminal Proceedings: a Research Note" (1981) 11 *British Journal of Social Work* 479–83.
[15] NACRO (1991) Briefing Paper, *Criminal Justice Bill 1990*.

juvenile panel.[16] Since serving on both panels is discouraged it seems likely that a substantial proportion of very experienced justices, many of whom may have been actively involved in strategies to reduce the use of custody in their juvenile courts, will not be involved in the work of the youth court.

Children and Young Persons Act 1969, s. 12AA

12AA Requirement for young offender to live in local authority accommodation
(1) Where the conditions mentioned in subsection (6) of this section are satisfied, a supervision order may impose a requirement ("a residence requirement") that a child or young person shall live for a specified period in local authority accommodation.

(2) A residence requirement shall designate the local authority who are to receive the child or young person and that authority shall be the authority in whose area the child or young person resides.

(3) The court shall not impose a residence requirement without first consulting the designated authority.

(4) A residence requirement may stipulate that the child or young person shall not live with a named person.

(5) The maximum period which may be specified in a residence requirement is six months.

(6) The conditions are that –

    (*a*) a supervision order has previously been made in respect of the child or young person;

    (*b*) that order imposed –
        (i)   a requirement under section 12A(3) or this Act; or
        (ii) a residence requirement;

    (*c*) he is found guilty of an offence which –
        (i)   was committed while that order was in force;
        (ii) if it had been committed by a person over the age of twenty-one, would have been punishable with imprisonment; and
        (iii) in the opinion of the court is serious; and

    (*d*) the court is satisfied that the behaviour which constituted the offence was due, to a significant extent, to the circumstances in which he was living.

except that the condition in paragraph (d) of this subsection does not apply where the condition in paragraph (b)(ii) is satisfied.

(9) A court shall not include a residence requirement in respect of a child or young person who is not legally represented at the relevant time in that court unless –

    (*a*) he has applied for legal aid for the purposes of the proceedings and the application was refused on the ground that it did not appear that his resources were such that he required assistance; or

    (*b*) he has been informed of his right to apply for legal aid for the purposes of the proceedings and has had the opportunity to do so, but nevertheless refused or failed to apply.

(10) In subsection (9) of this section –

    (*a*) "the relevant time" means the time when the court is considering whether or not to impose the requirement; and

    (*b*) "the proceedings" means –
        (i)   the whole proceedings; or

---

[16] C. Ball (1991) Unpublished survey, University of East Anglia, Norwich.

(ii) the part of the proceedings relating to the imposition of the requirement.

(11) A supervision order imposing a residence requirement may also impose any of the requirements mentioned in sections 12, 12A, 12B or 12C of this Act.

Since 1989, therefore, supervision has become the principal welfare-based strategy for dealing with convicted young offenders (although this is not to deny the existence of some welfare elements in the attendance centre order and in some custodial measures; see below). Like the attendance centre order, the supervision order is now classified as a "community sentence" under section 6 of the 1991 Criminal Justice Act (see Chapter 5, above) and is thus subject to the threshold criteria of seriousness contained in section 6, and to the procedural requirements laid down in sections 6 and 7 of that Act. The upper age limit for supervision was raised by the 1991 Act (section 68 and schedule 8) to include 17-year-olds, in line with the revised jurisdiction of the Youth Court.

Children and Young Persons Act 1969, ss. 12(1), (2), (3), 14 and 17 (as amended).

12. – (1) A supervision order may require the supervised person to reside with an individual named in the order who agrees to the requirement, but a requirement imposed by a supervision order in pursuance of this subsection shall be subject to any such requirement of the order as is authorised by the following provisions of this section or by section 12A, 12B or 12C below...

(2) Subject to section 19(12) of this Act, a supervision order may require the supervised person to comply with such directions given from time to time by the supervisor and requiring him to do all or any of the following things –

(a) to live at a place or places specified in the directions for a period or periods so specified,
(b) to present himself to a person or persons specified in the directions at a place or places and on a day or days so specified,
(c) to participate in activities specified in the directions on a day or days so specified;

but it shall be for the supervisor to decide whether and to what extent he exercises any power to give directions conferred on him by virtue of the preceding provisions of this subsection and to decide the form of any directions; and a requirement imposed by a supervision order in pursuance of this subsection shall be subject to any such requirement of the order as is authorised by section 12B(1) of this Act.

(3) The total number of days in respect of which a supervised person may be required to comply with directions given by virtue of paragraphs (a), (b) or (c) of subsection (2) above in pursuance of a supervision order shall not exceed 90 or such lesser number, if any, as the order may specify for the purposes of this subsection; and for the purpose of calculating the total number of days in respect of which such directions were previously given in pursuance of the order and on which the directions were not complied with.

14. – While a supervision order is in force it shall be the duty of the supervisor to advise, assist and befriend the supervised person.

17. – A supervision order shall, unless it has previously been discharged, cease to have effect –

> (a) in any case, on the expiration of the period of three years, or such shorter period as may be specified in the order, beginning with the date on which the order was originally made...

Notes

1. On the variation and discharge of supervision orders, see section 15 of the Children and Young Persons Act 1969, as amended by section 66 and schedule 7 of the Criminal Justice Act 1991.

2. The supervision order can be made under both family and criminal proceedings. In essence, it is a form of probation for younger offenders although it is administered for the most part by local authority social workers and only exceptionally by the probation service (see section 13(2) and (3) or the 1969 Act). Unlike probation, supervision – except for particular aspects – does not require the consent of the person subject to the order.

3. The content of the supervision is provided for in section 12 of the 1969 Act, as amended in particular by the Criminal Justice Acts of 1982 and 1988. Requirements as to residence (section 12(1) – this would allow for short-term residential treatment) or mental treatment (section 12B) may be inserted, and there is also provision for "intermediate treatment" (section 12(2) and (3)). Intermediate treatment (often referred to as "I.T.") is not a statutory term; it originated in the White Paper, *Children in Trouble*, Cmnd. 3601 (1968), which stated that "some form or forms of intermediate treatment should be available to the courts, allowing the child to remain in his own home but bringing him also into contact with a different environment" (para. 25). Intermediate treatment has developed around a number of community-based programmes, varying from one local authority to another but including, typically, remedial education, work training, community service, group activities, expeditions and the development of skills or interests.

4. Section 12A of the 1969 Act (as introduced by section 20 of the Criminal Justice Act 1982) enables the court to determine in advance some aspects of the supervision, so limiting the discretion of the social workers: particular forms of intermediate treatment may be directed; restrictions may be placed on the juvenile's night-time movements (a "night restriction" or "curfew" order); or certain types of activity may be prohibited. However, very little use has been made by courts of "night restriction orders" in practice (a fact that imports a sense of unreality into the prospects for the curfew order for adults introduced by the 1991 Criminal Justice Act, but as yet unimplemented).

Anthony Bottoms *et al.*, *Intermediate Treatment and Juvenile Justice: Key Findings and Implications from a National Survey of Intermediate Treatment Policy and Practice* (1990), pp. 2–4.

The term "intermediate treatment" was created in the 1968 White Paper which preceded the enactment of the Children and Young Persons Act 1969, a welfare-oriented statute on juvenile justice. As originally conceived, I.T. was to be available as a requirement of a supervision order under s. 12(2) of the 1969 Act, but it was additionally intended as a form of community-based treatment or activity to be available also, at a social worker's or probation officer's discretion and if the client agreed, to other offenders and to non-offenders. (For a definition of intermediate treatment provided by the D.H.S.S. in the early 1980s, see Appendix A).

The 1970s were a time of confusion and of inter-agency conflict in English juvenile justice, following the partial implementation of the Children and Young Persons Act 1969. Rates of custodial sentencing rose (though the use of care orders in criminal proceedings did not), and the eventual replacement of detention centres by I.T. schemes, which the 1969 Act had envisaged, seemed impossibly remote. Intermediate treatment made little effective headway in the first half of the decade, and thereafter was developed mainly for offenders low on the tariff scale, or for non-offenders, within a predominantly "preventive" policy framework.

Vigorous initiatives followed to relocate intermediate treatment at a higher point in the tariff, first by the Personal Social Services Council, and secondly and more influentially by a group of academics from Lancaster University.

It turned out that these initiatives were given powerful additional impetus by two pieces of Government action in the early 1980s. First, the Criminal Justice Act 1982 contained certain restrictions on the custodial sentencing of persons aged under 21 (s. 1(4)), together with a remodelling of the provisions relating to requirements in supervision orders to create, among other things, a new "supervised activities requirement" (s. 12(3C)(a) of the Children and Young Persons Act 1969) which, unlike the original I.T. requirement under s. 12(2) (which remained on the statute book) bound both supervisor and supervisee. While the restrictions on custodial sentencing apparently had little direct impact on sentencers, at least initially, the Act as a whole provided a very real impetus to social services departments and probation services to consider their social inquiry report practice, and the credibility to courts of their intermediate treatment provision as an alternative to custody and residential care. Secondly, the D.H.S.S. and the Welsh Office in 1983 issued circulars (Circulars LAC 83/3, WOC 48/83) offering bridging finance (to a total of over £15 million) to local authorities and voluntary agencies in partnership, specifically in order to develop I.T. projects as alternatives to custody and care; and, in due course, over a hundred local projects were funded under the umbrella of these circulars.

In parallel with these governmental developments, many intermediate treatment practitioners were evolving a new style of working. This involved a move away from the traditional "welfare" approach based primarily upon meeting the social and emotional needs of individuals, towards an approach which was both more offence and tariff-oriented and, at the same time, took greater cognisance of the role of intermediate treatment within local juvenile justice systems, with a particular stress upon the importance of developing so-called "heavy end" or "high-tariff" I.T. specifically as an alternative to custody or residential care for offenders. This practitioner movement of the 1980s has been called, with some justice, "the new orthodoxy". Pitts (1988, pp. 90–3) has produced an interesting, but somewhat overstated and controversial list of the main characteristics of "the new orthodoxy". Considerably modifying his words, but keeping some of the key ideas, the central tenets of the new orthodoxy can perhaps be described as follows:

(i)   the helping professions are sometimes a major source of hindrance to young offenders, because they pathologise them, intervene in their lives too readily and too intensively, and may therefore unwittingly encourage courts to use institutional disposals if and when welfare-based community treatments eventually fail;

(ii) placing young offenders in residential or custodial institutions is to be avoided whenever possible, because such institutions have an adverse effect on the criminality and social development of these offenders;

(iii) placing young offenders in community-based alternatives is clearly to be preferred to institutional sentencing;

(iv) minimum intervention is the best approach, if practicable given magistrates' sentencing philosophies and other constraints of the system; hence, among other things, cautioning young offenders is clearly to be preferred to taking them to court;

(v) welfare considerations should not be predominant in the juvenile court, or in decisions whether to caution or prosecute;

(vi) I.T. should concern itself only with adjudicated offenders, especially those at risk of receiving custodial or residential sentences;

(vii) in developing I.T. programmes, credibility with the courts (in order to reduce rates of sentencing to custody or residential care) is at least as important as what one subsequently does with the clients;

(viii) research and monitoring of local juvenile justice systems is vital in order to discover, for example, what kinds of cases have recently been sent to custody, what recommendations were made in the social inquiry reports in those cases, etc. However, the job of research and monitoring may be confined to analysis of the workings of the system; it is not usually thought necessary, for example, to explain crime, devise cures for it, or analyse re-offending rates after various disposals.

It will be apparent from this brief description that "the new orthodoxy" draws its inspiration from a mixture of theoretical sources. These include (i) labelling theory (the view that professional intervention can often escalate and inflate individual criminality); (ii) aspects of a "justice" approach to sentencing; (iii) systems theory (perception of the local juvenile justice organisation as a system, with an advocacy of careful monitoring of information about the system, and creative intervention at key points in order to attempt to achieve desired ends, especially the reduction of custody and care and diversion from prosecution; and, finally, (iv) a view of adolescent offending as essentially transient, and dependent upon the situational context at least as much as any more deep-seated personality difficulty.

The philosophical turn-around, in the dominant discourse about I.T., from "preventive" concepts in the late 1970s to "the new orthodoxy" in the mid-1980s, was a remarkably rapid one.

Notes

1. The above extract places intermediate treatment (I.T.) programmes within the context of evolving juvenile justice policy during the 1970s and 1980s. The research, based at the University of Cambridge Institute of Criminology, comprised an examination of I.T. programmes during 1984–5 and the key findings emphasise the major shift in the philosophy of I.T. during the early 1980s. The authors of the research recommend a clearer delineation between the welfare (voluntary) and disciplinary (compulsory) programmes within the whole field of I.T. and their conclusions to some extent anticipate the transformation of supervision into a "community sentence" under the 1991 Criminal Justice Act and its more definite location on a tariff of offence seriousness.

2. The research by Bottoms *et al* considers also the issue of inter-agency co-operation and liaison in the context of I.T. As noted in the extract, inter-agency collaboration had played an important role in the reduction of custody and care for juvenile offenders during the 1980s. A notable example of such collaboration is presented by Bowden and Stevens (1986) in relation to Northampton. But Bottoms *et al.* argue that inter-agency collaboration (for instance, police/social services departments (SSDs)/probation services) requires more carefully thought-out definitions and objectives and that "one has to begin by asking (as, we suggest, one should ask in all inter-agency issues) whether there is any strong policy or structural reason why the work should continue to be divided between two agencies" (1990, p. 90). In the context of I.T. the authors urge that social services departments should take over the entire responsibility for social work services for juveniles (1990, p. 91).

VI. ATTENDANCE CENTRES

Criminal Justice Act 1982, s. 16(1), (2) and s. 17(1)–(5) (as amended).

16. – (1) The Secretary of State may continue to provide attendance centres.

(2) In this Act "attendance centre" means a place at which offenders under 21 years of age may be required to attend and be given under supervision appropriate occupation or instruction, in pursuance of orders made –
(a) by the Crown Court of magistrates' courts under section 17 below;
(b) by youth courts or other magistrates' courts under section 15(2A) or (4) of the Children and Young Persons Act 1969 (attendance centre orders made on breach of requirements in supervision orders); or
(c) by magistrates' courts under section 6(3)(c) of the Powers of Criminal Courts Act 1973 (attendance centre orders made on breach of requirements in probation orders).

17. – (1) Subject to subsection (3) and (4) below, where a court –
(a) would have power, but for section 1 above, to pass a sentence of imprisonment on a person who is under 21 years of age or to commit such a person to prison in default of payment of any sum of money or for failing to do or abstain from doing anything required to be done or left undone; or
(b) has power to deal with any such person under Schedule 2, Part II of the Criminal Justice Act 1991 for failure to comply with any of the requirements of a probation order,

the court may, if it has been notified by the Secretary of State that an attendance centre is available for the reception of persons of his description, order him to attend at such a centre, to be specified in the order, for such number of hours as may be so specified.

(2) An order under this section is referred to in this Act as an "attendance centre order". . . .

(4) The aggregate number of hours for which an attendance centre order may require an offender to attend at an attendance centre shall not be less than 12 except where he is under 14 years of age and the court is of opinion that 12 hours would be excessive, having regard to his age or any other circumstances.

(5) The aggregate number of hours shall not exceed 12 except where the court is

of opinion, having regard to all the circumstances, that 12 hours would be inadequate, and in that case shall not exceed 24 where the offender is under 16 years of age, or 36 hours where the offender is under 21 but not less than 16 years of age.

Notes
1. On the discharge and variation of these orders, see section 18 of the Criminal Justice Act 1982; on breaches of attendance centre orders or rules, see section 19.
2. Attendance centre orders were first introduced in the Criminal Justice Act 1948; section 7(3) of the 1969 Children and Young persons Act envisaged their eventual phasing out (along with detention centres), but they gradually recovered official support and section 16(1) of the 1982 legislation confirms their survival. In 1992 there were 66 "junior attendance centres" (males under 17 years), 18 "junior mixed attendance centres" (males and females under 17 years) and 26 "senior" centres (males 17–20 years). However, the number of attendance centre orders made by the courts declined during the 1980s: from over 14,000 in respect of indictable offences in 1981, to just over 5,300 in 1989. Under the Criminal Justice Act of 1991, the attendance centre order, like the supervision order, became a community sentence, subject to the general provisions for such sentences under that legislation (see Chapter Five, above, and notes on the supervision order).
3. The earlier conventional perception of the attendance centre is presented by Cross and Ashworth (1981), where it is said (at p. 77): "Attendance centres are for the most part run by police officers in their spare time in schools, youth clubs or police premises; the emphasis is upon discipline, and the regime normally includes physical training and instruction on matters relating to good citizenship." However, research into the operation of the centres suggested a more complex and variegated sentencing and penal phenomenon.

Loraine Gelsthorpe and Norman Tutt, "The Attendance Centre Order" (1986) Crim. L.R. 146, pp. 146, 151–3.

Recent Home Office pronouncements in the wake of episodes of football hooliganism that the Attendance Centre Order is "tailor-made for football tearaways" may well encourage new interest in this alternative weekend activity. Indeed, the former Home Secretary claimed that whilst a short Detention Centre Order would be appropriate for some offenders and youth custody appropriate for those who revealed their "addiction" to violence "in less serious cases, where a custodial sentence was not necessary, magistrates should bear in mind the basic preventive aim of keeping the offender away from future matches."

In spite of their current popularity, Attendance Centres have received surprisingly little attention since they were conceived in the Criminal Justice Bill of 1938. They came into being through the Criminal Justice Act 1948, but since then have rarely been the subject of research. The reason for this is partly attributable to the fact that by the middle of the 1960s Attendance Centres were considered to be otiose. Indeed, in the White Papers and plans of the day they were to be replaced by intermediate treatment (Home Office, 1968). Nevertheless, despite the passing of the

1969 Children and Young Persons Act, they survived, and by 1972 the then government (Conservative) decided to retain them and in 1981 parties of all political persuasion agreed that they should be expanded. Ten new centres opened in 1978, 11 in 1979, 13 in 1980 and there are now over 100 centres in England and Wales (87 for boys, 7 for girls and 13 mixed centres). In 1971 the proportionate use of Attendance Centres was 12 per cent (10–14 years) and 7 per cent (14–17 years). By 1981 proportionate use was 19 per cent and 16 per cent respectively. The Criminal Statistics for 1983 reveal that 21 per cent of juveniles (10–14 years) sentenced for indictable offences received an Attendance Centre Order and that 17 per cent of those aged 14–17 years received the Order.

These figures, however, mask important differences which occur in sentencing patterns across the country. Moreover, official statistics leave unexplored a wide range of questions regarding the age and types of offenders who receive this sentence and for what offences...

... In this paper we have described how the Attendance Centre Order is used in six specific areas of England. That there is variation in its use is unsurprising given the rather chequered history of the Attendance Centre Order. Nevertheless, these findings give rise to a number of issues.

First, in spite of exhortations to use Attendance Centre Orders for "football hooligans," Attendance Centres are not used for any specific group of offenders but match the range of offending generally. Moreover, Attendance Centre Orders are passed on the full age spread of juvenile offenders, not just the older group eligible for custody. They are not normally an alternative to custody, although for a minority of cases (10 per cent) they appear to be used in this way. In some areas the Attendance Centre Order is apparently an alternative to fines or supervision orders. In this respect, Attendance Centre Orders in the juvenile court appear to occupy the same role, and suffer the same problems, as Community Service Orders in the adult court. Pease argued that lack of clear objectives for Community Service Orders meant that they were more likely to be used down tariff, *i.e.* replacing fines and probation orders, than be used as alternatives to custody. Similarly, attendance Centre Orders are more likely to replace fines and supervision orders, than detention centre orders. This is particularly true because the "public image" of the Attendance Centre is that it is run (indirectly) by the police; structured (hours and attendance), and carefully programmed (physical training and constructive hobbies); all these factors have greater appeal to magistrates than the unstructured and less specific arrangements of a supervision order to a social worker.

This movement down tariff is in fact aided by the advisers to the bench, since as we have shown, most Attendance Centre Orders follow the recommendation put to the bench by a social worker or probation officer.

Previous commentators have suggested that the tariff system is relatively clear and agreed upon by all parties at its upper and lower extremes, but in the middle range is highly confused. This is borne out in the findings where the use of Supervision Orders, with or without intermediate treatment, and Attendance Centres all appear in an undifferentiated and interchangeable middle range. Findings presented in this paper, which show that the Attendance Centre Order is used for both relatively inexperienced and experienced offenders, confirm this. Despite these points, however, and a general confusion surrounding the use of the Attendance Centre Order, it is interesting to note that in popular (though informed) conception, the Attendance Centre Order still appears as a "heavy end" disposal. Indeed, a paper on the Attendance Centre Order was included at a recent conference at Cambridge University alongside papers relating to the use of custody. The theme of the conference was "the use of intermittent custody."

This view may persist since the Attendance Centre Order appears to demand some deprivation of liberty. In this respect it appears to have greater credibility than the Supervision Order, with or without intermediate treatment, which may incur greater loss of free time (if not the deprivation of liberty). However, it is clear that Attendance Centres, like intermediate treatment, vary across the country, some are "welfare orientated," others have a more "punitive orientation." Whilst some centres concentrate on remedial reading skills, social skills, practical skills and even individual counselling, other emphasise immediate obedience, vigorous exercise, cleanliness, and punishment, and yet this variation is obscured when compared with the comments about variations in social services provision.

The "key factor" in magistrates' and others' (positive) perception of Attendance Centres is the fact that they are in the main run by the police. In fact two are run by Social Services Departments and one by an Education Department.

What is forgotten in this (positive) perception is the possibility of adverse consequences. Whilst not wishing to criticise staff for their efforts, it is perhaps important to question the possibility of juveniles' behaviour in this post-court facility being recorded and remembered by the police in such a way as to influence future decisions by the police if the juvenile reoffends. Indeed, in a recent paper to the Cambridge conference, Norman Tutt emphasised that it is essential that both policy makers and practitioners be alert to the dangers of the police becoming not only "'judge and jury' but also 'jailers for juveniles.'"

The danger is that exploitation of the Attendance Centre Order for both relatively inexperienced and experienced offenders may lead to escalation. That is, offenders may not be given the opportunity of experiencing a wide range of penalties prior to custody if it is perceived that this penalty has failed to curtail the offending behaviour of those who appear in court on a first or second occasion. From the evidence, we know that there is no set perspective on the Attendance Centre Order, that it is, in fact, used for a wide range of offenders and offences. But this possibility of escalation, this risk, serves to emphasise the importance of the continuous monitoring of local juvenile criminal justice systems. Another risk is that the use of the Attendance Centre Order for a wide range of offenders and offences may lead to the eclipse of certain other penalties. Here too there is a need for monitoring. There needs to be a careful watch on the possibility of Attendance Centre staff and social workers *competing* for the same clients, when all may make useful contributions to the range of disposals available.

Notes

1. As the authors of this extract point out, despite their extensive use by the early 1980s, there had been surprisingly little research into attendance centres. For other research findings, see Dunlop (1980), and Gelsthorpe and Morris (1983). Overall, such research stressed that in practice the centres received a wide range of juvenile offenders and carried out a spectrum of functions, welfare as well as penal, so belying their popular image as places of Saturday afternoon detention for "football hooligans".

2. There had been some concern that the detention centre order had been operating "down tariff", that is, used as an alternative to non-custodial measures and, by virtue of its welfare orientation, poaching clients from the sphere of supervision. Gelsthorpe and Morris (1983), for example, urged that the order be used unambiguously as a "tough" measure: "There is a need for an 'ace' in the pack of juvenile court dispositions which would act as an unequivocal warning about the implications of future offending. We believe that attendance centres should be used in this way."

VII. Custody

The development of custodial measures for younger offenders over the last hundred years has reflected the gradual abandonment of imprisonment for all offenders under the age of 21 (see section 1 of the Criminal Justice Act 1982, above) and the emergence of specialised institutions: industrial and reformatory schools, later reorganised as approved schools and then as community homes as a component of the care order; borstals, replaced in the 1982 Criminal Justice Act by youth custody centres; and detention centres (both youth custody and detention centres being replaced in turn by young offender institutions under the 1988 Criminal Justice Act). For a general account of the development of these institutions, see Harding *et al.* (1985), pp. 240–9. In more recent years, policy has been characterised by attempts (judged to be largely successful in the 1980s and early 1990s) to move away from the use of custody towards community-based measures for young offenders. The criteria for the use of custody are now those general criteria laid down in section 1 of the Criminal Justice Act 1991. The relevant successive provisions of the 1982, 1988 and 1991 Criminal Justice Acts are now consolidated in section 1A and 1B of the 1982 Act.

Rob Allen, "Out of Jail: The Reduction in the Use of Penal Custody for Male Juveniles, 1981–8" (1991) 30 Howard Journal 30, pp. 30–31, 49–51

The number of male juvenile offenders receiving custodial orders in England and Wales since 1981 has declined dramatically. 3,200 males aged 14–16 were given custodial disposals in 1988, less then half the number of those in 1984 and under 42 per cent of those in 1981. There were about a third of [male juveniles in custody] on June 30, 1988 as had been there on the same date in 1981 ... the marked fall in the eighties is noteworthy for a number of reasons.

First, the government in power during the entire period of the decline has been an unlikely one to preside over a process of decarceration. Although, there has been a marked ambivalence in their policy towards juvenile and young adult offenders, the Conservative Party had prior to 1979 expressed strong views on law and order and the decline of moral standards which found rapid translation into measures such as the "short sharp shock". Many observers were not convinced by the apparent commitment to community based penalties shown in the White Paper *Young Offenders* and feared that custodial institutions would play a yet more central role in the government's plans for dealing with juvenile crime.

Secondly, the years 1981–8 have not seen a similar trend towards decarceration amongst other age groups of offender. Although the latter part of the period has seen a decline in the custodial sentencing of 17–20 year olds, the prison population under sentence has remained fairly stable.

Thirdly, the years 1981–8 have not seen a similar fall in the numbers of juveniles remanded in care or custody prior to sentence; although the abolition of borstal training and its replacement by youth custody orders which could be passed by magistrates as well as Crown Court judges reduced the number who were held between trial and sentence after 1983, there has been no substantial change in the numbers of *untried* juveniles held in custody.

With prison overcrowding a continuing problem and the official government policy that prison should be used as a last resort, the reasons for the reduction in the population of sentenced juveniles would clearly repay careful study. By untangling and evaluating the different changes and developments that have taken place, it may be possible to apply lessons elsewhere in the system.

Conclusions

This brief review of factors associated with the declining use of custody is of necessity partial: there is still enormous regional and local variation in the extent to which it is used. This can only partly be explained by the varying level of non-custodial provision. There must also be concern about the fact that there are a disproportionate number of black young people amongst the residual custodial population, suggesting that the factors that have served to keep juveniles in the community have not acted equally throughout the population.

It seems clear however that a number of important changes have contributed to the reduction in the use of sentences nationally. A declining population of juveniles and a declining population of sentenced juveniles do much to account for the fall in custody. Changes in law, policy and practice have also played an important role. In as much as the juvenile justice system is a collection of local systems, the relative significance of different factors will have varied between police force area, psd, local authority and probation areas and even within them.

It appears however that the various changes, many of which were not related in origin have worked together or at least not against each other. To repeat one example, the way in which the increased use of police cautioning did not erode the lower tariff sentences but acted "across the board" has been an important and unexpected "interactive" effect. This may have been in large part due to the tariff management strategies of welfare professionals. Without these, the effect of increased cautioning could have been very different. Any attempts to transfer measures which have produced change to older age groups will need to attend to these interactive effects as well as identifying individual steps to be taken by agencies and organisations.

Criminal Justice Act 1982, s. 1A and s. 1B (as amended).

1A Detention in a young offender institution

(1) Subject to section 8 below and to section 53 of the Children and Young Persons Act 1933, where –

(a) an offender under 21 but not less than 15 years of age is convicted of an offence which is punishable with imprisonment in the case of a person aged 21 or over; and

(b) the court is of the opinion that either or both of paragraphs (a) and (b) of subsection (2) of section 1 of the Criminal Justice Act 1991 apply or the case falls within subsection (3) of that section

the sentence that the court is to pass is a sentence of detention in a young offender institution.

(2) Subject to section 1B(2) below, the maximum term of detention in a young offender institution that a court may impose for an offence is the same as the maximum term of imprisonment that it may impose for that offence.

(3) Subject to subsection (4) below ... a court shall not pass a sentence for an offender's detention in a young offender institution for less than the minimum period applicable to the offender under subsection (4A) below.

(4) A court may pass a sentence of detention in a young offender institution for less than the minimum period applicable for an offence under section 65(6) of the Criminal Justice Act 1991.

(4A) For the purposes of subsections (3) and (4) above, the minimum period of detention applicable to an offender is –

(a) in the case of an offender under 21 but not less than 18 years of age, the period of 21 days; and

(b) in the case of an offender under 18 years of age, the period of two months.

(5) Subject to section 1B(4) below, where

(a) an offender is convicted of more than one offence for which he is liable to a sentence of detention in a young offender institution; or

(b) an offender who is serving a sentence of detention in a young offender institution is convicted of one or more further offences for which he is liable to such a sentence.

the court shall have the same power to pass consecutive sentences of detention in a young offender institution as if they were sentences of imprisonment.

(6) Where an offender who –

(a) is serving a sentence of detention in a young offender institution; and

(b) is aged over 21 years.

is convicted of one or more further offences for which he is liable to imprisonment, the court shall have the power to pass one or more sentences of imprisonment to run consecutively upon the sentence of detention in a young offender institution.

1B Special provision for offenders under 17

(1)...

(2) In the case of an offender aged 15, 16 or 17 the maximum term of detention in a young offender institution that a court may impose is whichever is the lesser of –

    (a) the maximum term of imprisonment the court may impose for the offence; and

    (b) 12 months.

(3)...

(4) A court shall not pass on an offender aged 15, 16 or 17 a sentence of detention in a young offender institution whose effect would be that the offender would be sentenced to a total term which exceeds 12 months.

(5) Where the total term of detention in a young offender institution to which an offender aged 15, 16 or 17 is sentenced exceeds 12 months, so much of the term as exceeds 12 months shall be treated as remitted.

(6) In this section "total term" means - -

    (a) in the case of an offender sentenced (whether or not on the same occasion) to two or more terms of detention in a young offender institution which are consecutive or wholly or partly concurrent, the aggregate of those terms;

    (b) in the case of any other offender, the term of the sentence of detention in a young offender institution in question.

Notes

1. As may be seen from Allen's discussion there was during the 1980s a substantial although gradual decline in the number of young offenders subject to custody (youth custody and detention centres prior to 1988, subsequently young offender institutions). Although this trend has to be seen against a demographic background of a declining juvenile population, policy considerations clearly also played a major part in the outcome. The juvenile courts' approach in relation to custodial dispositions was slow to change: 12 per cent of juvenile court dispositions in 1979, 11 per cent in 1986 and seven per cent in 1990. However, the use of custody as a proportion of the whole of the known juvenile offender population declined

dramatically, from eight per cent in 1981 to one per cent in 1990. This prompts Gelsthorpe and Morris (1994) to conclude:

> "This indicates that it was the impact of diversion (cautioning) practices rather than deinstitutionalisation (I.T.) practices, the increased use of fines, compensation or community service, the introduction of criteria to restrict the use of custody or legal representation, which reduced custody" (1994, pp. 976–7).

Their analysis relates to Allen's emphasis on the fact that police cautioning acted across the board, with important "interactive" effects.

2. There would therefore appear to be grounds for asserting that a declining use of custody is not so much the result of legislative exhortation to sentencers (as in the Criminal Justice Acts of 1982 and 1991) as of the perceptions and decisions of enforcement agencies. Graham (1990) reaches a similar conclusion as regards the notable decline in the use of custody in the Federal Republic of Germany in recent years:

> "Neither has the decline been brought about by legislative changes. The most persuasive explanation appears to be that the decline stems from a radical change in the practice of public prosecutors and judges, which in turn has been brought about by a shift in their perceptions of the efficacy and legitimacy of incarceration.
>
> The shift in thinking appears to have been initiated through a fundamental questioning of the legitimacy of pre-trial detention, especially for young offenders, and the rehabilitative efficacy of short-term imprisonment." (1990, p. 167)

3. The legal framework of custody for young offenders has in effect been simplified under the 1991 Criminal Justice Act. The single sentence of detention in a young offender institution is available for male and female offenders aged between 15 and 20 years (no longer for 14-year-old males: section 63(1) of the 1991 Act), for a minimum term of two months for offenders aged 15 to 17 years, or 21 days for those aged 18 to 21 years. The maximum term for 15 to 17-year-old offenders is 24 months, (section 17 of the 1994 Criminal Justice and Public Order Act) or the maximum term of imprisonment for the offence in question, whichever is the shorter. The total term for that age group (that is to say, taking into account consecutive terms) cannot exceed 12 months. For those aged 18 to 20 years, the maximum is that which could be imposed in relation to adult offenders. The longer minimum period for 15 to 17-year-olds is to ensure that custody is only used in relation to offences which are serious enough to justify at least two months detention. Following the 1991 legislation, there is no longer any differential provision for male and female offenders as regards detention in a young offender institution. Abolition of the sentence for the small number of 15 to 17-year-old female offenders who receive it in practice was considered but not eventually included in the 1991 Act.

4. Detention under section 53 of the Children and Young Persons Act

1933. This has now evolved into a special form of custody for homicidal and other "dangerous" juvenile offenders: detention "during Her Majesty's pleasure" if convicted of murder (subsection 1); "section 53(2) detention" if convicted of other serious offences. A person aged 18 to 20 years, convicted of murder or any other offence the sentence for which is fixed as life imprisonment, would be sentenced to "custody for life" under section 8 of the Criminal Justice Act 1982. But a child under the age of ten involved in comparable behaviour would have to be dealt with in family proceedings. Originally there was little appropriate provision for severely disturbed children, whether taken into care or dealt with under section 53. There is provision under section 64 of the Children and Young Persons Act 1969 for youth treatment centres, on which see Parker (1985), and Millham, Bullock and Hosic (1978). More recently, section 60 of the Criminal Justice Act of 1991 has provided for remand and committal to local authority secure accommodation for children aged 15 years and above.

Criminal Justice and Public Order Act 1994, section 1(1)–(11)

Secure training orders
1. – (1) Subject to section 8(1) of the Criminal Justice Act 1982 and section 53(1) of the Children and Young Persons Act 1933 (sentences of custody for life and long term detention), where –
(a) a person of not less than 12 but under 15 years of age is convicted of an imprisonable offence; and
(b) the court is satisfied of the matters specified in subject (5) below,
the court may make a secure training order.
(2) A secure training order is an order that the offender in respect of whom it is made shall be subject to a period of detention in a secure training centre followed by a period of supervision.
(3) The period of detention and supervision shall be such as the court determines and specifies in the order, being not less than six months nor more than two years.
(4) The period of detention which the offender is liable to serve under a secure training order shall be one half of the total period specified by the court in making the order.
(5) The court shall not make a secure training order unless it is satisfied –
(a) that the offender was not less than 12 years of age when the offence for which he is to be dealt with by the court was committed;
(b) that the offender has been convicted of three or more imprisonable offences; and
(c) that the offender, either on this or a previous occasion –
    (i) has been found by a court to be in breach of a supervision order under the Children and Young Persons Act 1969, or
    (ii) has been convicted of an imprisonable offence committed whilst he was subject to such a supervision order.
(6) A secure training order is a custodial sentence for the purposes of sections 1 to 4 of the Criminal Justice Act 1991 (restrictions etc. as to custodial sentences).
(7) Where a court makes a secure training order, it shall be its duty to state in open court that it is of the opinion that the conditions specified in subsection (5) above are satisfied.
(8) In this section "imprisonable offence" means an offence (not being one for which the sentence is fixed by law) which is punishable with imprisonment in the case of a person aged 21 or over.

Notes
1. Section 1 of the 1994 Criminal Justice and Public Order Act provides for a new kind of order, to be known as a "secure training order", to deal with recalcitrant, "out of control" 12 to 14-year-old male offenders. The order is a combination of secure detention and supervision, for a total period of between six months and two years, one half of which is to be spent in detention. The detention will be in either a secure training centre (within the management of the Prison Service) or local authority secure accommodation. The conditions for such an order to be made are listed in section 1(8): primarily, conviction for a minimum of three imprisonable offences, lack of response to non-custodial penalties, and breach of supervision requirements or conviction for imprisonable offences while previously under supervision. This new measure has been criticised as a panic response to media hysteria related to a perceived increase in juvenile offending (see, for instance, (1993) 32 *Howard Journal*, p. 252).
2. Secure institutions for juvenile offenders straddle uneasily the dividing line between welfare-oriented and punitive approaches; the provision for alternative secure accommodation within the organisational framework of the Prison Service and social services departments under the Criminal Justice and Public Order Act reinforces this obfuscation of purpose. For a study of secure custody for younger juvenile offenders in Scotland, see Kelly (1992), who describes (in contrast) an institution in which the "prison aspects ... are denied; the deprivation of liberty is seen as part of an overall caring process and is justified in terms of a child's need for treatment" (p. 199).

VIII. PARENTAL RESPONSIBILITY

The 1990 White Paper, *Crime, Justice and Protecting the Public*, emphasised the importance of parents and guardians being involved in court proceedings against their children. Section 56 of the 1991 Criminal Justice Act reinforces the requirement of attendance at court of a parent or guardian where a child or young person is charged with an offence or otherwise brought before a court; in the case of juveniles under the age of 16, a court must require the attendance of the parents or guardian unless in all the circumstances it would be unreasonable to do so (section 34 of the Children and Young Persons Act 1933, replaced by section 34A of the 1991 Act).

However, as regards responsibility for financial penalties, section 57 of the 1991 Act amends the provision under section 55 of the 1933 Children and Young Persons Act that a parent or guardian should pay any fine, order for costs or compensation imposed on an offender who has reached the age of 16; there is now a power on the court's part to order such payment by the parent, rather than a duty, reflecting the view that juveniles of 16 or 17 years of age should be regarded, when appropriate, as independent of their parents and responsible for their own actions.

Parental responsibility has also been emphasised under section 58 of the

1991 Criminal Justice Act, which places courts under a duty to bind over parents of offenders under the age of 16 years, if satisfied that to do so would be in the interests of preventing the commission of further offences by such young offenders. Any court which is not of a mind to make such an order must give its reasons for not doing so. The intention here is to encourage courts to make more use of a power which was hitherto used only in a small number of cases. On the other hand, an earlier controversial proposal of 1989 to enact a criminal offence for parents who failed to make reasonable efforts to prevent their children from committing offences was not pursued in the face of strong opposition.

The concept and rationale of parental responsibility has origins in the late nineteenth and earlier twentieth centuries, as demonstrated in the following extract.

Leon Radzinowicz and Roger Hood, *A History of English Criminal Law, Volume 5: The Emergence of Penal Policy* (1986), pp. 655–657

One possible way of reducing dependence upon incarceration as a method of controlling or punishing juvenile offenders was to throw back the responsibility for these functions upon parents. Until the middle of the nineteenth century the idea of making parents in some ways responsible for the offences committed by their children was hardly ever considered. The Criminal Law Commissioners, although appointed to review the treatment of young offenders, made no reference to it.[17] In 1847 a Select Committee of the House of Lords endorsed the principle when they recommended that, wherever possible, part of the cost of convicting and punishing juvenile offenders should be legally chargeable to their parents.[18] This idea was later to be embodied in the law and practice regulating reformatory and industrial schools.

The idea re-emerged in 1880 in a variety of forms and found its way into several Bills before finally reaching the Statute Book in 1901 and 1908. The most radical formula was punishment of parents as well as of their children. This concept of double punishment found many supporters among the do-gooders and, most significantly, among a large portion of the magistracy.[19] It was believed it could be justified by proving gross parental negligence, or more precisely, drunkenness, cruelty or wilful neglect. An even more extreme version of this was a proposal to make general negligence in the care and control of a child a statutory offence, for which parents were to be punished by a small fine, ordered to pay compensation,

[17] The Commissioners ignored the only suggestion made by a witness that parents should be liable for the misconduct as well as the maintenance of their children while undergoing punishment. "Third Report from the Commissioners on Criminal Law (Juvenile Offenders)" 1837, *Parl. Papers* (1837), vol. 31, p. 1, at p. 24.
[18] "Second Report from the Select Committee of the House of Lords on the Execution of the Criminal Law," *op. cit.* (1847), vol. 7, p. 10.
[19] See, for example, Letter from Sir James Ingham, the Chief Metropolitan Magistrate, to the Home Office, November 8, 1880, in H.O. 45/9593/93897/72; Lord Norton, Letter to the *The Times*, October 25, 1880, p. 10. Many suggestions were made along these lines in "Reports on the State of the Law relating to the Treatment and Punishment of Juvenile Offenders," *op. cit.* (1881), vol. 35, for example, the Report of the City of Manchester Juvenile Offenders Executive Committee, at p. 829; also H.O. 45/10158/B23010C/52, 54, 65, Howard Association, *Report*, 1900, pp. 10–1, and "Report from the Departmental Committee on Prisons" (C. 7702), 1895, *Parl. Papers* (1895), vol. 56, p. 1, at p. 33.

and be subject to imprisonment in default.[20] This, however, was rejected, on the grounds that it would "not be practicable ... to make the offence of the child directly the offence of the parent," and that it would "throw upon the prosecutor the obligation to prove neglect in the parent, which will often prove impossible."[21] These were convincing reasons.

A less extreme, but still arbitrary, formula was the binding over of the parents to ensure the good conduct of their children. To make sure that they could not get away with an empty promise, failure was to be punished by a fine. It was hoped that this would be sufficient to encourage parents to discipline their children, preferably by administering a whipping.[22] Subsequently it was suggested that they should give a formal undertaking to punish their children in return for the court agreeing to refrain from passing sentence.[23]

Ultimately the legislation followed a middle course. Parents or guardians were to be summoned to attend court where there was reason to believe that they had "conduced" to the commission of an alleged offence by failing to exercise due care and control over children in their care. If such failure were proved, they could be ordered to pay the fine, costs or damages imposed on the children or young persons. In case of default they would become liable to imprisonment like other defaulters. This formula was adopted by the Youthful Offenders Act of 1901 and sharpened in the Children Act of 1908.[24] Henceforth parental responsibility was to be assumed: a parent could not escape liability for fines imposed on his child unless the court was "satisfied that the parent or guardian cannot be found or that he has not conduced to the commission of the offence by neglecting to exercise due care of the child or young person."

This search for ways to bring home to parents their responsibility for the delinquencies of their children, reflected the growing influence of the ameliorative and moral creed, which assumed that crime was largely a product of disorganised family life. It also reflected the new perception of the responsibilities of the State, extending gradually but substantially its frontiers of intervention and control. Although in practice it did not have a great deal of impact, socially and politically it was a significant development.

---

[20] See the "Youthful Offenders Bill (H.L.)" (349), 1890, *Parl. Papers* (1890), vol. 9, pp. 523–4; "Summary Jurisdiction (Youthful Offenders) Bill [H.L.]" (194), 1891, *Parl. Papers* (1890–1), vol. 10, pp. 269–70; "Youthful Offenders Bill" (189), 1900, *Parl. Papers* (1900), vol. 5, pp. 695–703. The maximum fine in the 1900 Bill was to be £5, the whole or any part of which could be ordered to be paid as compensation to the victim. See also Thomas Holmes, "Youthful Offenders and Parental Responsibility" *The Contemporary Review* (1900), vol. 77, pp. 845–54, at pp. 851–2.

[21] Memoranda of Sir Godfrey Lushington, dated October 5, 1880, in H.O. 45/9594/93897H/18 and March 19, 1887, *ibid.* /20.

[22] For example, Sir Rupert Kettle, "How can the System of Police be Improved in regard to the Repression and Detection of Crime?" *Transactions* N.A.P.S.S. 1880 (1881), pp. 317–26, at pp. 325–6. On Kettle (1817–94), see *D.N.B. Supplement*, vol. 22, p. 934.

[23] This solution was embodied in the first draft of a Bill prepared in the Home Office in 1887, but was never resurrected. See H.O. 45/9594/93897H.

[24] See 1 Edw. 7, c. 20, s. 2. See Home Office circular A 62,846 in H.O. 45/10050/A62846/18. 8 Edw. 7, c. 67, s. 99.

CHAPTER SEVEN

MENTALLY DISORDERED OFFENDERS

I. INTRODUCTION

It has only been relatively recently that a distinct system for dealing with mentally disordered offenders has evolved in this country. The theoretical basis of the legal system's response to the problem of crime resulting from or associated with mental disorder remains unsatisfactory, largely on account of the limited availability of legal defences based upon such disorders. Theoretically, there exists a general defence to criminal liability: the plea of insanity, defined in the "M'Naghten Rules," formulated in 1843. However, this defence is not often used. Technically and properly speaking, it applies to a narrow range of disorders, and before 1992 was unattractive to defendants since its successful employment led to compulsory and indeterminate confinement in a mental health institution. The only other defences are that of diminished responsibility, under section 2 of the Homicide Act 1957, which has been interpreted to cover a wider spectrum of disorders, but can only be used in a limited number of cases where the charge is murder (and, if successful, will result in conviction for manslaughter and consequent sentencing flexibility); and non-insane automatism, which would, if successfully pleaded, lead to acquittal in rather rare and difficult-to-prove cases of involuntary physical action (such as sleepwalking or concussive acts). In practice, therefore, there is little that a mentally disordered defendant can of would wish to do in order to avoid criminal liability.

It must be admitted that English substantive criminal law has been slow to take on board the impact of mental disorder on questions of responsibility. At one time this may have been largely explicable in terms of a general lack of awareness or ignorance in relation to psychological questions. In 1925 Lord Chief Justice Hewart rejected an attempt to widen the defence of insanity by accommodating the idea of an act being performed under an "irresistible impulse": "It is the fantastic theory of uncontrollable impulse which, if it were to become part of our criminal law, would be merely subversive. it is not yet part of the criminal law, and it is to be hoped that the time is far distant when it will be made so." (Judgment in *Kopsch* (1925–6) 19 Crim. App. R. 51–2). Judges and lawyers are now much more conversant with and receptive to psychiatric discussion, but are still reluctant to extend the scope of defences without the lead of a statute. In more recent years, for example, while the effects of pre-menstrual tension have been taken into account for purposes of the defence of diminished responsibility, attempts to generalise a defence based on such mental disturbance have been rejected.

(On the substantive criminal law in relation to issues of mental disorder, see: Smith and Hogan, *Criminal Law* (7th ed., 1992), pp. 192–215; C. M. Clarkson and H. M. Keating, *Criminal Law: Text and Materials* (2nd ed., 1990), pp. 345–75; Smith and Hogan, *Criminal Law: Cases and Materials* (5th ed., 1993), Chapter 10.)

Moreover, despite policy statements and legislative initiatives intended to encourage diversion of mentally disordered offenders from the formal criminal justice process in recent years (see below), a significant proportion of seriously disturbed offenders still find their way into the court and penal systems. The outcome, that an offender, who is in some way mentally disordered and therefore may not be, in moral terms, fully responsible for the behaviour in question is nonetheless likely to be convicted, is clearly open to criticism. However, this state of affairs is less objectionable in practice since the sentencer's decision as to what measures should be applied can take into account the existence of mental disorder to a large extent, so that the outcome may be some (hopefully appropriate) treatment and in some cases no penal measure as such being used. Nonetheless, with the exception of a limited number of situations (discussed below), a mentally disordered offender may well be convicted, *i.e.* publicly condemned, before the court proceeds to say, in effect, that he or she is not wholly responsible for their act and may need treatment rather than punishment. The proposals of the Butler Committee on Mentally Abnormal Offenders (1975) included the correction of this illogical situation by providing for a wider general defence based on mental disorder but also powers for compulsory treatment or measures of public protection if the defence was successful. This approach was also adopted by the Law Commission in Clause 38 of its Draft Criminal Code (1985). The Butler Committee considered that a "mental disorder verdict" should allow a court to order hospital in-patient treatment, with the possibility of a restriction order; hospital out-patient treatment; forfeiture of any fire-arm, motor vehicle, etc., used in any crime; guardianship; disqualification; or discharge. What was envisaged, therefore, was a sensible re-ordering, on a non-penal basis, of many of the measures presently available to deal with convicted mentally disturbed offenders. Legislation of 1991 went some way towards achieving this objective by providing for such a range of dispositions for those defendants found to be unfit to plead or who successfully pleaded the (still narrowly drafted) insanity defence.

It should be borne in mind that, at present, disordered persons involved in minor offences may not be prosecuted and may be left to receive help or treatment informally. But for present purposes any discussion must proceed on the assumption that a number of disordered offenders dealt with by the criminal courts will be processed as convicted criminals. The main task, therefore, is to consider what measures, penal or otherwise, are available to deal with such cases; and when, in terms of the underlying disorder and other considerations of penality and public protection, each of these measures is appropriate. First, however, it would be helpful to outline the principal generally recognised and accepted categories of mental disorder.

II. CRIMINALITY AND MENTAL DISORDER

Report of the (Butler) Committee on Mentally Abnormal Offenders, Cmnd. 6244 (1975), para. 1.12.

(1) "Mental Disorder" and "Mental Abnormality"

1.12 We have considered what significance if any should be attached to the distinction apparently drawn between "mental disorder" and "mental abnormality". We assume that together these terms were intended to be comprehensive. The inconvenience of not having available a single expression covering all forms of mental ill health (and, one might add, mental disability) was pointed out by the Royal Commission on the Law Relating to Mental Illness and Mental Deficiency 1954–7 in their Report. The term "abnormality of mind" had been used in the provision for diminished responsibility in section 2(1) of the Homicide Act 1957. The Royal Commission thought that "abnormality" implied a permanent condition; they preferred "mental disorder" as a comprehensive term and this was the term used in the Mental Health Act 1959. The use of the phrase "mental abnormality" as more or less a synonym for "mental disorder" is in our view unfortunate, since there are people who can be said to be mentally abnormal, in the sense of diverging from the statistical norm of mental functioning, although not necessarily disordered. Examples are religious fanatics, occasional drunks and people with unusual mental capacities such as "photographic memories". The use of the term "abnormality" as synonymous with "disorder", implying that the condition in question should if possible be remedied, is liable to lead to misunderstanding. Throughout our Report, therefore, we shall avoid the term "mental abnormality". Nevertheless, the use of both phrases in our terms of reference has been an advantage, since it has enabled us to discuss the problems raised by offences committed under the influence of alcohol and other drugs without begging the question whether such offences involve mental disorder.

Herschel Prins, Offenders, Deviants or Patients? (1980), pp. 42–50.

An important problem arises in trying to establish any causal connections or relationship between mental disorder and criminality, namely that of attempting to make connections between very divergent behaviours. The substance and definition of mental illness has been open to much challenge and dispute in recent years; there are commentators such as Szasz and Laing and Esterson, who see current definitions of mental illness largely as ploys by which the state and its agents seek to control those whose behaviour is seen by them as merely different and socially unacceptable. This summary statement may seem to be somewhat unfairly dismissive of some very useful points that have been made by proponents of the so-called "anti-psychiatry" school. Even if we tend to dismiss some of the more polemical writing on mental disorder, it is only fair to state that there is considerable divergence of opinion amongst contemporary psychiatric practitioners as to the precise nature of mental illness and its causes. Gunn states the problem succinctly from the psychiatrist's point of view: "Yet most of us believe that somewhere in the confusion there is a biological reality of mental disorder, and that this reality is a complex mixture of diverse conditions, some organic, some functional, some inherited, some learned, some acquired, some curable, others unremitting." The question of causation and classification is dealt with in more detail later in this chapter.

Similar problems arise when we consider the nature of criminality. For, at its simplest, crime is merely that form of behaviour defined as illegal by the criminal law. We know that at various times in our history, acts judged as criminal have been redefined, or even removed from the statute books. In a sense, crimes "come and go" according to changes in public opinion. The fact that the crimes of attempted suicide, and homosexual acts in private between adult consenting males have been removed from the statute book are two illustrations of this phenomenon. New offences are also created, particularly in times of war or of serious crisis; moreover, our increasingly complex society has necessitated the introduction of all manner of laws and regulations to govern aspects of our conduct. Croft has summarised the position very well.

"Not only has crime been defined variously at different periods in history but the opprobrium which crime attracts, and the degree of gravity with which particular crimes are regarded, has also changed. Not doubt this has something to do with the prevalence of certain sorts of crimes and the reaction of society (more precisely, the reaction of those responsible for the enforcement of the law) to them but an assessment of the frequency of some particular form of behaviour is not of course synonymous with the definition of that behaviour as criminal. Indeed, it is safer to assume that we are all criminals, or at least have the potential to be criminals given the right conditions, and to take courage from the fact that some people at least are not apparently regular offenders. If such a view seems unduly cynical, it is because the breaking of the rules and conventions which regulate human behaviour is widespread and it becomes an issue of policy, even of political philosophy, to determine whether the criminal law, as distinct from the many other formal and informal methods of controlling conduct, should be invoked to regulate certain sorts of activities." (Croft, 1978)

Since much "criminal behaviour" is thus somewhat arbitrarily defined and there is serious disagreement as to the existence and definition of mental disorder, it is hardly surprising that we find difficulties in trying to establish connections between these two somewhat ill-defined and complex forms of behaviour. Nevertheless, it would seem worthwhile to attempt some examination of their possible relationships, acknowledging that any conclusions must be tentative and seen against the background of the inherent difficulties referred to above.

Studies of Penal and Other Populatons

Over the years, various efforts have been made to estimate the prevalence of mental disorder in criminal and penal populations. I have already made reference to two of the difficulties involved in such attempts, namely the problem in defining both crime and mental disorder and the difficulties in drawing satisfactory links between the two conditions. Moreover, nearly all the studies that have been carried out have been of inmates of penal or correctional establishments or specialist court clinics. Thus, one is bound to be drawing conclusions from highly selected populations. This fact has important implications. For example, it is quite likely the imprisonment itself may well exacerbate certain underlying psychiatric conditions, or the impact and effects of such imprisonment may be so severe as to precipitate mental disorder in certain individuals. Feldman speculates that it may also be the case that those who are in fact in some way mentally disordered may be less skilful in crime and thus caught more easily. He also suggests that the police may tend to charge some of these offenders more readily and that in addition pleas of "guilty" may be more frequent. It is difficult to substantiate any of these speculations, but certainly one must be very careful in drawing firm conclusions as to the relationships between mental disorder and crime from studies of such highly selected groups.

Scott has suggested that even if we allow for the high degree of selectivity in penal populations the proportion of clearly identifiable psychiatric diagnoses is something in the region of 15 to 20 per cent. More recently, Gunn *et al.* have estimated that about one third of the sample of 629 prisoners they studied could have been regarded as requiring psychiatric attention at the time of interview. This does not mean that all would have been diagnosed as suffering necessarily from a formal psychiatric illness . . . .

Prevalence of Criminality in Psychiatric Populations

Reference has already been made in the preceding discussion to the numerous difficulties that occur in attempting to draw specific conclusions from studies of mental disorder in penal and similar populations. In order to offer conclusive evidence of association or lack of it we would need to show the prevalence of criminality in psychiatric hospitals and similar samples. To date, very little work has been done on this, largely, as Gunn points out, because of the ethical difficulties involved in investigating the criminal backgrounds (if any) of hospitalised psychiatric patients. However, a few studies have attempted to investigate this area, and these are now reported upon. Walker has estimated on the basis of various epidemiological studies, that about 12 in every 1,000 of the population will suffer from some kind of identifiable psychiatric disorder. Gunn on the basis of calculations made by McClintock and Avison suggests that approximately 1 in 3 of the male population and 1 in 12 of the female population would be convicted of a "standard list" (fairly serious) offence in their lifetime. In the light of these combinations of figures, it would be surprising (as Gunn suggests) if psychiatric hospitals did not contain an appreciable number of persons with criminal records. Guze examined a population of some 500 patients attending a psychiatric clinic in the United States. He found that 4 per cent had a history of the commission of a serious offence. (The offences included robbery, burglary and sex offending.) Guze also quotes another American study by Brill and Malzberg (undated report) in which the arrest records of 5,354 male ex-patients from New York State Mental Hospitals were examined for the period 1946–8. The authors concluded that "patients with no record of crime or arrest have a strikingly low rate of arrest after release", and that "patients who have a prior record of arrest have a rearrest rate which compares favourably with figures available for persons in the general population who have an arrest record. . ." Guze also quotes studies by Ashley, Pollock, and Cohen and Freeman which indicate a lower arrest rate for former psychiatric in-patients than is found in the general population. However, he also reports contrary finding by Rappeport and Lassen indicating that "women with a history of psychiatric hospitalisation are more likely to be arrested for aggressive assault than are women in the general population . . ." and that males have "a significantly higher arrest rate . . ." for robbery than did the general population. Unfortunately diagnostic criteria are not described altogether adequately so that it is difficult to draw too many firm conclusions from these apparently conflicting results. Gunn reports a study made by Tidmarsh and Wood (unpublished) of persons using London's largest Reception Centre. (Such centres being the successors to the old "casual wards" and providing accommodation for persons without a settled way of life.) Of 4,000 persons who had been at the centre at some time in the past, they estimated that 79 per cent had previous convictions and 58 per cent had been in prison. Tidmarsh made psychiatric assessments and found about 1,200 men had been diagnosed as mentally ill or sub-normal. Only just over one quarter were said to have no psychiatric disorder. Gunn reports three other findings by Tidmarsh and Wood which are of particular interest from our point of view. First, men with no psychiatric abnormalities were least likely to have had convictions. Second, most of those without prison sentences had not been in psychiatric hospital. Third, most of those who had not been in psychiatric hospital had not been in prison either, while "conversely those who had been in either type of institution had usually been in both". This study seems to support the view of psychiatrists such as Rollin that there is a "stage army" of persons who drift in and out of each type of institution. He came to this conclusion as a result of an almost unique study of patients admitted to one of our large psychiatric hospitals in the Home Counties (Horton Hospital). The catchment area included part of the Metropolitan District of London. Rollin found that some 83 per cent of his sample were diagnosed as suffering from schizophrenia. He examined the records of those admitted without recourse to a court (that is, under Part IV of the Mental Health Act, 1959 – and sometimes through the use of Section 136) ... Of seventy-eight such cases, he found the following distribution of offences: sex offences, 10 per cent; violence, 13 per cent; stealing, 9 per cent; public order offences, 57 per cent. When he enquired into the records of such non-prosecuted patients he found that 40 per cent had a criminal record, 36 per cent of them being persistent offenders. He also examined the prosecuted group; that is, those admitted for psychiatric treatment under the relevant sections of Part V of the Act ... finding that 63 per cent had previous convictions and that 44 per cent had previously been subject to a custodial sentence. Thus, it is not hard to see that there is a considerable degree of overlap between the two groupings. However, to be able to offer more precise data as to possible causal or associative factors one would need not only to examine substantial samples of psychiatric hospital patients, but also cohorts of offenders appearing before the courts. As far as I am aware this has never been carried out and the ethical objections referred to by Gunn are of course considerable. Some authorities, such as Penrose, have stated that the populations of prisons and psychiatric hospitals are inversely related. Penrose attempted to demonstrate that before the Second World War, those European countries with a large psychiatric hospital population had a small penal institution population and vice versa. Penrose's so called "law" might well be cited today since our prison staffs are complaining that they are having to cope with too many mentally disordered offenders and our psychiatric hospitals seem for their part very reluctant to take them – not infrequently in the face of the express wishes of High Court judges and other sentencers.

Notes

1.   It may be seen that this is a subject fraught with both definitional and aetiological problems. Convenient shorthand terms are necessary. Yet expressions such as "abnormality" and "disordered" beg many questions. "Mental disorder," as the Butler Committee argues, is probably now accepted as the most satisfactory term to denote in a broad collective sense the range of problems under discussion. But, as will be seen below, most of the terms used to describe more specific conditions are often open to objection of both psychiatric and linguistic ground.

2.   Tracing the relationship between mental disorder and criminality is highly problematical. In the first place, these basic concepts – and even the existence of conditions of disorder and criminality – are subject of interpretation and manipulation. Secondly, even if a theoretical framework for discussion may be agreed upon, the summary provided by Prins indicates that research so far into the character of both penal and psychiatric populations does not allow us to draw very specific conclusions about the role of mental disorder in the emergence of criminal behaviour. Nonetheless, there do appear to be some grounds for asserting that there exists a "stage army" of problematical personalities which is dealt with alternatively or

even interchangeably by penal and psychiatric methods. This phenomenon could not lead to any assertion of a clear relation between mental disorder and criminality, but does at least suggest that some forms of disorder may well manifest themselves in outwardly criminal behaviour. It is then the concern of the criminal justice system to identify such cases and decide upon an appropriate moral and practical response. For recent surveys and analyses of the incidence and character of mental disorder, both in its broader and more specific senses, in penal populations, see: Gunn *et al.* (1978); Home Office/DHSS (1987); Prins (1990); Gunn *et al.* (1991). Such research prompts the conclusion by Peay (1994) that "offenders with mental disorder are not a minority group of only marginal concern to the criminal justice system" (1994, p. 1128).

Mental Health Act 1983, s. 1(2) and (3).

1. – ... (2) in this Act –

"mental disorder" means mental illness, arrested or incomplete development of mind, psychopathic disorder and any other disorder or disability of mind and "mentally disordered" shall be construed accordingly;

"severe mental impairment" means a state of arrested or incomplete development of mind which includes severe impairment of intelligence and social functioning and is associated with abnormally aggressive or seriously irresponsible conduct on the part of the person concerned and "severely mentally impaired" shall be construed accordingly;

"mental impairment" means a state of arrested or incomplete development of mind (not amounting to severe mental impairment) which includes significant impairment of intelligence and social functioning and is associated with abnormally aggressive or seriously irresponsible conduct on the part of the person concerned and "mentally impaired" shall be construed accordingly;

"psychopathic disorder" means a persistent disorder or disability of mind (whether or not including significant impairment of intelligence) which results in abnormally aggressive or seriously irresponsible conduct on the part of the person concerned ...

(3) Nothing in subsection (2) above shall be construed as implying that a person may be dealt with under this Act as suffering from mental disorder, or from any form of mental disorder described in this section, by reason only of promiscuity or other immoral conduct, sexual deviancy or dependence on alcohol or drugs.

Law Commission, Draft Criminal Code, Clause 38.

38. Mental Disorder Verdict
  (1) A mental disorder verdict shall be returned where:

  (a) the defendant is proved to have committed an offence but it is proved on the balance of probabilities (whether by the prosecution or by the defendant) that he was at the time suffering from severe mental illness or severe subnormality; or

  (b) (i) the defendant is found not to have committed an offence on the ground only that, by reason of mental disorder or a combination of mental disorder and intoxication, he acted or may have acted in a state of automatism, or without the fault required for the offence, or believing that an exempting circumstance existed; and

(ii) it is proved on the balance of probabilities (whether by the prosecution or by the defendant) that he was suffering from mental disorder at the time of the act.

(2) (a) "Mental disorder" means mental illness, arrested or incomplete development of mind, psychopathic disorder, and (subject to paragraph (b)) any other disorder or disability of mind.

(b) "Mental disorder" does not include:
(i) intoxication, whether voluntary or involuntary; or
(ii) any disorder caused by illness, injury, shock or hypnosis, or occurring during sleep, unless it is a feature of a condition (whether continuing or recurring) that may cause a similar disorder on another occasion.

(c) "Psychopathic disorder" means a persistent disorder or disability of mind (whether or not including significant impairment of intelligence) which results in abnormally aggressive or seriously irresponsible conduct.

(d) "Return a mental disorder verdict" means:
(i) in relation to trial in indictment, return a verdict that the defendant is not guilty on evidence of mental disorder; and
(ii) in relation to summary trial, dismiss the information on evidence of mental disorder.

Herschel Prins, *Offenders, Deviant or Patients?* (1980), pp. 51–90.

... we are particularly concerned with the question of "socially considerate behaviour" and the extent to which a lack of it should bring penal or quasi-penal sanctions into play. Although it is difficult to define mental ill-health (mental disorder) I think it is important to make my own position clear. I take it to be a term to be applied to those people who, for psychological and other reasons, are frequently unable to fulfil their lives to their own satisfaction or (frequently) to the satisfaction of others. In addition they may, from time to time, become so disturbed as to require some form of psychiatric or other intervention. I am aware that the term "disturbed" is contentious and that some people can be contained within, and supported by, their social environments, while others require specialist help outside it. It follows, therefore, that the terms I am using suffer from a certain degree of imprecision and a wide range of interpretation. Wing has alerted us to the fact that some of the confusion seems to arise because the term "illness" is used in two quite different ways. "In one usage, people are regarded as sick or regard themselves as sick, because of some experience or behaviour that departs from a standard of health generally accepted in the community." Wing agrees with Mechanic that this is rightly called "illness behaviour", and that standards for the designation of this kind of illness vary very widely not only from community to community but also over time. In respect of the second use of the term, Wing reserves this for notions of "disease" proper; "a limited and relatively specific theory about some aspect of psychological or biological functioning (that) is put forward because it is thought to be relevant to the reduction of some recognisable impairment which causes disability or distress." Wing suggests that these "two usages represent different types of theory. Over the centuries, the second usage has become more and more precisely differentiated from the first, but has also become more restricted." Wing further suggests that this has meant that much "illness behaviour" cannot helpfully be explained in terms of disease theories. Although Wing is making these statements in a paper primarily about schizophrenia – a condition, he says, which can be explained medically, socially, and psychologically – they have a more general applicability. They also support my earlier contention that the understanding of mental disorders is facilitated by a multi-causal (explanatory) and multi-disciplinary perspective in which boundaries will inevitably be blurred. For those who have devoted themselves to the study of the phenomena of mental disorders, this multi-causal and multi-disciplinary approach presents at one and the same time a dilemma and a stimulating challenge....

... Mental disorders have been classified in a variety of ways and there is no universal acceptance of any one classification, although from time to time the World Health Organisation has endeavoured to introduce uniformly accepted classifications and definitions. The following is a simplified classification accompanied by some explanatory comment (see *Table 3(2)*).

Table 3(2)   Outline Classification

The functional psychoses	the affective disorders schizophrenic illnesses
The neuroses (psychoneuroses)	mild depression anxiety states hysteria obsessional states
Mental disorder as a result of infection, disease, metabolic disturbances, and trauma	(including epilepsy)
Mental disorder due to the ageing process	(for example, the pre-senile and senile dementias)
Abnormalities of personality and psycho-sexual disorders	
Alcohol and other drug addictions	
Mental subnormality (deficiency, handicap, retardation)	(including chromosomal abnormalities)

... The term functional psychoses is used for that group of "severe mental disorders in which no evidence of underlying organic brain dysfunction has been proved to exist" (Munro and McCulloch). It would probably be more true to assert that the phrase "not *yet* been proved to exist" would be preferable since there is a substantial body of opinion indicating that for these particular mental disorders there is the possibility of a clear biochemical cause. The two illnesses subsumed under the heading functional psychoses are (1) the affective disorders (manic-depressive illness) and (2) schizophrenia (or the schizophrenias as some would prefer to describe them)....

... The underlying characteristic of an affective disorder is a basic disturbance of mood; in cases of *mild* depressive disorder the disturbance of mood (or affects as it is sometimes called) may be quite slight and may often be almost unnoticeable to those quite close to the person. In *severe* affective disorder, the mood disturbance is much more pronounced; a useful "aide memoire" is that the main characteristics are those of "loss" – of energy, of libido (sexual drive and energy), weight, appetite, interest in oneself and one's surroundings...

... At the other end of the spectrum of the affective illnesses with should note that periods of depressive disorder may be interspersed with occasional attacks of mania – a condition in which the patient develops grandiose ideas, may become uncontrollably excitable, overactive, and socially disinhibited. In addition, insight may be entirely lacking and any attempt to interfere with the patient's activities may be strongly resisted – sometimes to the extent that severe physical violence will be used. Mania in its extreme form is a comparatively rare illness, but just occasionally the behaviour of severely manic individual may bring them into conflict with the law – sometimes in bizarre circumstances....

... From time to time, we find cases in which it has been alleged that a person charged with a serious offence (murder for example) was suffering from a severe depressive disorder at the time of the commission of the offence. West made a study of cases of *Murder Followed by Suicide*. He was able to show from his very careful case histories that a substantial number of these particular murderers were suffering from serious mental illness – in particular depression. He says that sufferers from psychotic depression may,

> "become so convinced of the helplessness of their misery that death becomes a happy escape. Sometimes before committing suicide, they first kill their children and other members of the family ... Under the delusion of a future without hope and the inevitability of catastrophe overtaking their nearest and dearest as well as themselves, they desire to kill in order to spare their loved ones suffering...."

... It is customary to use the term schizophrenia in the singular when describing what seem to be a wide range of illnesses. Moreover, it has become clear in recent years that although the illness has certain basic characteristics there are in fact many variants of it, so that it is probably more accurate to use the descriptive term schizophrenic *illness* or the *schizophrenias*....

... The most important single characteristic feature of schizophrenic illnesses is the disintegration and (in some cases) apparent destruction of the personality. It should be noted here that the term schizophrenia is frequently used incorrectly in two ways. First of all, lay people tend to use the term to denote the state of being in "two minds", no doubt a derivation from the old descriptive term – "split mind". Second, people sometimes use it to describe *Jekyll and Hyde* characteristics – being sane one minute and mad the next. Both interpretations are quite erroneous; in the schizophrenic illnesses we are dealing with what can best be regarded as a splintering of the mind – "the personality shatters and disintegrates into a mass of poorly co-operating components rather than into a neat division into two parts. In particular, there is incongruity between thoughts and emotions"....

... Despite their numerically small representation, it is worth looking briefly at some of the situations in which schizophrenic illness may play a causal or explanatory part in criminal acts. I would wish the stress here that from time to time, the onset and course of such an illness and its possible relationship to a crime may have been overlooked – sometimes with tragic consequences....

... (1) *Schizophrenic illness and violent crime*. As has already been observed, the patient suffering from catatonic schizophrenia may occasionally erupt into violence and "lash out" at those around him, but the circumstances in which such behaviour will bring about a confrontation with the law are comparatively rare....

... The seriously *paranoid* individual is quite likely to appear to be sane and intelligent in all other respects. To the unwary and inexperienced interviewer, the delusional system may be so well encapsulated that it may not emerge unless the matters upon which the system has fastened are broached in the examination. The severely paranoid and the morbidly jealous individual can be a very dangerous person indeed – probably one of the most potentially dangerous that the penal and hospital systems have to cope with. The ideas and preoccupations of such persons are so fixed and long-lasting that they may persist in pursuing their alleged unfaithful spouse or other subject of their delusions from one part of the country to the next despite all attempts at intervention. No form of rational persuasion to get them to alter their beliefs seems to be effective in such cases.

(2) *Other offence behaviour.* In schizophrenic illness of insidious onset there is often, as we have seen, an accompanying decline of social functioning and competence. In such cases, the individual may well succumb to temptations (sometimes prompted by others) that he would have well resisted had he been in normal mental health. We sometimes find cases of shoplifting or other thefts being committed in these circumstances.

(3) *Schizophrenic illness, vagrancy, and kindred offences.* In cases of persons suffering from so-called simple schizophrenia we have seen that the deterioration may take the form of a steady diminution of social functioning accompanied by a withdrawal from society. Such persons may come to the attention of the courts for offences such as begging, breach of the peace (insulting words and behaviour), or vandalism (wilful damage). Rollin found a very high proportion of such cases in his Horton Hospital "stage-army" sample. Such an offender/patient who is shunted between hospital, prison, and community, can best be described as a society nuisance rather than as a society menace. Just occasionally, however, such a person may commit a serious crime as a result of "hearing the voices"; arson being one such example....

(4) *Schizophrenic illness and the bizarre crime.* Occasionally a crime is committed which shocks the community because of its ferocity or depravity. Such offences may be committed by persons who seem to have behaved with senseless and quite appalling cruelty. They show a lack of feeling for their victims which seems quite incomprehensible to most of us. In such cases, it is sometimes found that a schizophrenic illness of insidious onset has occurred, but its presence has been overlooked. It seems probably that some cases of sadistic sexual murder may be committed by such a schizophrenic though it is sometimes very difficult to differentiate the diagnosis in such a case from a similar offence committed by the cold and callous psychopath....

... The terms neuroses or psychoneuroses (which are for the most part synonymous), when used correctly, describe a wide range of conditions which are characterised by certain fairly specific mental and physical symptoms and signs; they usually have as their origin the existence of some mental conflict of which the sufferer may frequently be quite unaware. The neuroses are usually regarded as being less severe in nature than the psychoses mainly because the sufferer is not likely to be out of touch with reality, is less floridly ill and behaves quite rationally in most respects. However, many neurotic conditions (particularly the obsessive states) are severely disabling and some psychiatrists prefer not to make too sharp a distinction between some forms of neuroses and the functional psychoses – depressive disorder being a good case in point. (See earlier discussion.)

Although there is no absolute consensus of opinion concerning classification, the following seems to be acceptable to most people:

> mild depression;
> anxiety states;
> hysteria;
> obsessional states....

... A special problem arises in any discussion of the neuroses. Many of us show – albeit in varying degrees – a number of "neurotic" traits. For example, how many of us do not show a high level of anxiety in certain unfamiliar or threatening situations, become mildly depressed when things go badly, or have certain obsessional traits which enable us to carry out some tasks more effectively?...

... Few people would disagree with the view that the specific label of neurotic illness should be reserved for those instances where the patient/sufferer is seriously disabled and where although he may have a degree of insight into his condition he is powerless to do anything about it. Neurotic illnesses in their classical presentation do not feature significantly amongst the ranks of criminals. Woddis found only three cases of psychoneurosis and two dissociated states in his sample of ninety-one offender/patients; Faulk only found one. Despite this small proportion, the relevance of these conditions (in common with those described earlier) may be of considerable importance in specific cases....

Mental Subnormality (Deficiency, Handicap, Retardation)

These terms are frequently used synonymously; however, in recent years the term mental *retardation* seems to be preferred to others. The layman often, but understandably, confuses mental illness with mental retardation; the two conditions are entirely separate though they may coexist in some patients. In general and oversimplified terms, it can be said that the mentally ill individual starts life with normal intellectual endowments, but for some of the reasons described earlier in this chapter, he may become ill and thus deviate from normality, whereas the subnormal person never had the endowment of intellectual normality, or lost it in infancy or in early life. This point is demonstrated very clearly in the use of the older descriptive term for subnormality – *amentia* – which means literally "lack of mind"....

... It is highly unlikely that the profoundly subnormal will come to the attention of the courts for their condition is sadly almost inevitably accompanied by severe physical disability so that they spend most of their lives in hospital care. We are more likely to be concerned with those showing mild or moderate degrees of mental subnormality. In this context we need to remember that in any event most criminological studies show a lack of direct association between intelligence and crime *per se*. Woodward in what is still probably the most comprehensive study of the subject, concluded that offenders were not more than eight points below the general average; but even this slight depression may be explained in part by the fact that these could well be the offenders who are caught and therefore subjected to study....

... In whatever manner we interpret the disparities in the statistics relating to mental subnormality and crime, we are faced with the inevitable fact that the penal and allied services will have to deal from time to time with a number of offenders who suffer from subnormality in varying degrees. Indeed, one of our "special" hospitals – Rampton in Nottinghamshire – caters specifically for such subnormal offender/patients...

Report of the (Butler) Committee on Mentally Abnormal Offenders, Cmnd. 6244 (1975), Chapter 5 *et seq.*

5.2 Since its introduction more than 90 years ago the term "psychopathic disorder" has been subject to a variety of different practical usages: it has been taken to cover either a narrow or a broad group of mental disorders, and to indicate differences either of causation or of clinical manifestation from other mental disorders. In consequence there is now a multiplicity of opinions as to the aetiology, symptoms and treatment of "psychopathy", which is only to be understood by reference to the particular sense in which the term is being employed by the psychiatrist in question....

... 5.4 It is probably that philosophers and physicians had recognised the group of so-called "psychopathic disorders" as early as the seventeenth century. Certainly 150 years ago French and German psychiatrists had done so. In 1801 Phillippe Pinel described "manie sans délire", of which the specific features were on the one hand absence of any appreciable alteration in the intellectual functions, perception, judgement, imagination, memory, but on the other hand pronounced disorder of the affective (emotional) functions and blind impulse to acts of violence, even murderous fury. In 1818 in Germany "moral diseases of the mind" were described, including "moral dullness", "congenital brutality" and "moral imbecility". In England the notion of a defect or disease of the moral faculty (ie the emotional faculty) was popularised by J. C. Prichard (1835) who saw it as a "morbid perversion of the natural feelings, affections, inclinations, temper, habits, moral dispositions and natural impulses, without any remarkable disorder of defect of the intellect knowing or reasoning faculties and particularly without any insane illusion or hallucination" . . . .

. . . 5.10 An important impetus to the development in this country of the idea of psychopathy as a clinical entity was provided during the middle decades of the present century by the work and teaching of Sir David Henderson. He drew attention to what he regarded as the essential elements of psychopathic disorder, particularly its anti-social aspects, using the definition in a restricted and rather specific sense:

"The term psychopathic state is the name we apply to those individuals who conform to a certain intellectual standard, sometimes high, sometimes approaching the realm of defect but not amounting to it, who throughout their lives or from a comparatively early age, have exhibited disorders of conduct of an anti-social or asocial nature, usually of a recurrent or episodic type which in many instances have proved difficult to influence by methods of social, penal and medical care and treatment or for whom we have no adequate provision of a preventive or curative nature. The inadequacy or deviation or failure to adjust to ordinary social life is not mere wilfulness or badness which can be threatened or thrashed out of the individual so involved but constitutes a true illness for which we have no specific explanation".

5.11 Henderson's psychological concepts have not been adopted in any official medical classification but his work has encouraged the popular belief that the psychopathic personality may be categorised as either aggressive or inadequate. Such terms refer to overt observable behaviour rather than behaviour interpreted by inference from psychological theory, and their use is therefore largely at variance with Henderson's own formulation. Nevertheless Henderson's ideas have done much to influence clinical practice and research and have made their mark on legislation . . . .

. . . 5.16 It is evident that it was necessary to divorce as far as possible from any definition or classification any reference to alleged causes, to psychological theories and to hypothetical psychological mechanisms. This task has been undertaken by the World Health Organisation which started its work in this area in 1947. Since then there have been eight revisions of the International Statistical Classification of Disease (ICD), Section V of which refers to Mental Disorders. The latest revision appreared in 1968. A number of countries, including the United Kingdom, have accepted it for official administrative purposes, and national and personal classifications are being abandoned.

5.17 The ICD (1968 Revision) recognises three major groups of mental disorders: the psychoses (the major mental illnesses); mental retardation (severe subnormality and subnormality); and the neuroses (personality disorders and other non-psychotic mental disorders) of which there are nine sub-categories. Among these are personality disorders, sexual deviation, alcoholism and drug dependence. Each category has a number of recognised sub-categories, which are to some extent arbitrary, since they do not rest upon any objective clinical, psychological or other differences. The terms "psychopath", "psychopathic disorder" and "psychopathic personality" are not used. However, in the British Glossary to the classification prepared by a sub-committee of the Registrar-General's Advisory Committee on Medical Nomenclature and Statistics, under the main category of Personality Disorders (301) it is stated that this category "includes what is sometimes called 'psychopathic personality'." More specifically the Glossary states that the sub-category "Anti-social" (301.7) includes those individuals who are classified in the Mental Health Act 1959 as suffering from "psychopathic disorder". The British Committee refer to those suffering from personality disorder of the anti-social type as follows:

> "This term should be confined to those individuals who offend against society, who show a lack of sympathetic feeling, and whose behaviour is not readily modifiable by experience including punishment. They are affectively cold and callous. They may tend to abnormally aggressive and seriously irresponsible conduct".

It is evident however that some other sub-categories of personality disorder describe patients who for reasons connected with their particular disability may well come within the definition of psychopathic disorder in the Mental Health Act. The "explosive" (301.3) for example shows "marked instability of mood with particular liability to outbursts of irritability, anger, aggression and impulsive behaviour", but "are not otherwise prone to anti-social behaviour"...

Notes

1. The classification of mental disorders, let alone an examination of their causes and effects, is in itself a large and complex subject which is constantly subject to revision. It is not possible to be exact in any description of these conditions, the identification of which may be made more difficult by the overlapping of categories. However, in introducing the subject, a broad exposition is inevitable and the Mental Health legislation is also based upon a wide and simplified categorisation. For immediate purposes it must suffice to distinguish between psychoses, neuroses, retardation (or impairment or subnormality) and psychopathic (or personality) disorder. Generally, and so far as the criminal justice system is concerned, the most significant problems tend to arise in relation to certain types of psychosis and in connection with the difficult condition of psychopathy.

2. The terminology employed in both the Mental Health legislation and the Law Commission's Draft Code tends not only to be based on broad concepts but also to avoid detailed definition. In so far as any definition is attempted, it is in terms of outward behaviour and anti-social consequences and in particular relies on the idea of abnormally aggressive and seriously irresponsible conduct. Certain conditions are excluded from the ambit of "mental disorder": promiscuity, immoral conduct, sexual deviancy and drug or alcohol dependence, under section 1(3) of the 1983 Act; intoxication or occasional disorder brought about by illness, injury, shock, hypnosis or occurring during sleep, in Clause 38 of the Draft Code. "Mental illness" is not defined, but may be taken to include the range of psychoses and neuroses; whether such illness is "severe" for purposes of clause 38 will inevitably depend to a large extent on medical opinion. As far as mental impairment and psychopathic disorder are concerned, these are defined according to their result and this follows from the legal concern underlying these provisions, which is the search for a justification for committal to hospital or the use of other compulsory measures. The mentally retarded person or "mild" psychopath, whose behaviour is not unusually aggressive or socially irresponsible, is not a subject for these procedures but should be

dealt with "in the community." It is not surprising that specific definition is eschewed; as already noted, many of these conditions do not easily lend themselves to precise description, and expert opinion may shift rapidly on certain questions. Terminology itself is a matter of fashion: the term "subnormality" used in the Mental Health Act 1959 has been replaced by "impairment"; but despite a wide preference for "personality disorder," the term "psychopathic disorder" has been retained. A residual problem is that medical and legal concepts are used for different purposes and translation from one discipline to another is notoriously difficult, a problem which has bedevilled the search for a satisfactory "insanity defence" (see on this Herbert Fingarette (1972), especially Chapter 1). Peay (1994) at p. 1123 comments:

"There is no pure form of mentally disordered offender. To assume that there is would be both to mislead and to negate the transparent and frequently reiterated need for flexibility within the mental health and criminal justice agencies."

3.   Persons suffering from a psychosis, especially a schizophrenia, will usually qualify in the layman's view for what is "mad" or "insane." Many of the well-known criminal insanity cases, including that of Daniel M'Naghten, involved personalities diagnosed as psychotic. For an earlier judicial rejection of the relevance of such diagnosis, see the dismissive comments of Lord Chief Justice Goddard in *Rivett* (1950) 34 Crim. App. R. 87.

4.   Prins points out that, in the category of mental impairment, it is the moderately retarded or impaired person who is likely to come within the ambit of the criminal law. The Mental Deficiency Act 1913 diverted a large number of more seriously impaired persons away from the criminal justice system to more appropriate institutions. Prins goes on (pp. 90–92) to explain how this kind of person may become involved in criminal activities, through such avenues as manipulation by others, other people's misunderstanding of motives or actions, or vulnerability to society pressures.

5.   The psychopathic personality has presented particular problems for the criminal justice system. This is a condition which is rarely "treatable" in the same way as much mental illness and whose anti-social manifestations may well attract general opprobium. The Butler Committee's Report gave particular attention to the problems of dealing with psychopathic offenders and, reacting to the fact that many such "untreatable" cases find their way into the prison system, recommended the setting up of a new type of institution to cater for the dangerous psychopathic offender. This problem is further considered below.

III. DIVERSION OF MENTALLY DISORDERED OFFENDERS

Mental Health Act 1983, ss. 136, 135(6), 35(1)–(3) and 36(1)–(2).

135. – (6) In this section "place of safety" means residential accommodation

provided by a local social services authority under Part III of the National Assistance Act 1948 or under paragraph 2 of Schedule 8 to the National Health Service Act 1977, a hospital as defined by this Act, a police station, a mental nursing home or residential home for mentally disordered persons or any other suitable place the occupier of which is willing temporarily to receive the patient.

136. – (1) If a constable finds in a place to which the public have access a person who appears to him to be suffering from mental disorder and to be in immediate need of care or control, the constable may, if he thinks it necessary to do so in the interests of that person or for the protection of other persons, remove that person to a place of safety within the meaning of section 135 above.

(2) A person removed to a place of safety under this section may be detained there for a period not exceeding 72 hours for the purpose of enabling him to be examined by a registered medical practitioner and to be interviewed by an approved social worker and of making any necessary arrangements for his treatment or care.

35. – (1) Subject to the provisions of this section, the Crown Court or a magistrate's court may remand an accused person to a hospital specified by the court for a report on his mental condition.

(2) For the purposes of this section an accused person is –

(a) in relation to the Crown Court, any person who is awaiting trial before the court for an offence punishable with imprisonment or who has been arraigned before the court for such an offence and has not yet been sentenced or otherwise dealt with for the offence on which he has been arraigned;

(b) in relation to a magistrates' court, any person who has been convicted by the court of an offence punishable on summary conviction with imprisonment and any person charged with such an offence if the court is satisfied that he did the act or made the omission charged or he has consented to the exercise by the court of the powers conferred by this section.

(3) Subject to subsection (4) below, the powers conferred by this section may be exercised if –

(a) the court is satisfied, on the written or oral evidence of a registered medical practitioner, that there is reason to suspect that the accused person is suffering from mental illness, psychopathic disorder, severe mental impairment or mental impairment; and

(b) the court is of the opinion that it would be impracticable for a report on his mental condition to be made if he were remanded on bail;

but those powers shall not be exercised by the Crown Court in respect of a person who has been convicted before the court if the sentence for the offence of which he has been convicted is fixed by law.

36. – (1) Subject to the provisions of this section, the Crown Court may, instead of remanding an accused person in custody, remand him to a hospital specified by the court if satisfied, on the written or oral evidence of two registered medical practitioners, that he is suffering from mental illness or severe mental impairment of a nature or degree which makes it appropriate for him to be detained in a hospital for medical treatment.

(2) For the purposes of this section an accused person is any person who is in custody awaiting trial before the Crown Court for an offence punishable with imprisonment (other than an offence the sentence for which is fixed by law) or who at any time before sentence is in custody in the course of a trial before that court for such an offence.

Jill Peay "Mentally Disordered Offenders", Chapter 23 in M. Maguire, R. Morgan and R. Reiner, *The Oxford Handbook of Criminology* (1994), pp. 1131–1135.

One of the more telling anomalies emerges from the disparity between the Government's stated policy of treating and caring for the mentally disordered offender outwith custodial care and the numbers of mentally disordered offenders still to be found in custody who could benefit from care and treatment under alternative regimes. The intention of Home Office Circular No 66/90, "Provision for Mentally Disordered Offenders", was twofold: first, to draw to the attention of criminal justice agencies those legal powers relevant to the mentally disordered; second, to reinforce the desirability of ensuring the best use of resources and to ensure that the mentally disordered were not prosecuted where this was not required by the public interest. Where prosecution was necessary, Circular 66/90 stressed the importance of finding non-penal disposals wherever appropriate. Clearly, however effective diversion schemes become, there will always be mentally disordered offenders in the penal system, either because of late onset of the disorder or because the nature of the offending/disorder makes a penal disposal inevitable...

The Mental Health Act 1983 attempted to rectify the partial failure of the 1959 Act to realise a treatment-based approach by introducing measures to divert offenders into the hospital system at an earlier stage. Hence, s. 35 permitted remand to hospital for reports (but not compulsory treatment); s. 36 provided for remand to hospital for treatment; and s. 38 initiated interim hospital orders. All these provisions were designed to ensure early identification of those with mental disorders in need of treatment and appropriate disposal of them, with interim hospital orders designed to avoid the difficulty that could arise out of the "once-and-for-all" disposal to hospital under s. 37. The interim hospital order lasts, with renewals, up to a maximum of six months, at which point the court may make a full hospital order or any other available disposal. In effect, it permits hedging of bets. Although a punitive order should not follow where "instant cure" at hospital occurs, a punitive approach may be adopted where it becomes apparent that no cure is possible.

However, none of these orders has been frequently used by the courts. Fennell (1991: 337–9) notes that there were only thirty-four s. 36 orders in 1988/9, and although there were 328 s. 35 orders in the same period, this compares very unfavourably with the 5,569 psychiatric reports carried out by prison medical officers following remand in 1989. Indeed, recent research on mentally disordered remanded prisoners by Dell *et al.* (1991) noted that courts remand in custody essentially for psychiatric and social reasons, rather than for reasons of public safety or the seriousness of offence – as the denial of bail implies. The Reed Report (1991: Prison Advisory Group para. 3.3) recommends that "the appropriate powers in the Bail Act 1976 and Magistrate's Court Act 1980 should be reviewed with a view to amendment or repeal" to prevent magistrates sending the accused to prison solely for medical reports – a practice regarded as wrong in principle and an unjustifiable use of the prison system. Such limitations on magistrates' powers might result in an increase in their limited use of s. 35, although clearly not all offenders would fit the necessary Mental Health Act classifications, nor would sufficiently secure provisions necessarily be available. Equally, as Fennell notes (1991: 338) if all those offenders currently remanded to prison were remanded to hospital, it would result in a 30–35 per cent increase in the numbers of compulsory admissions to hospitals.

By the end of the 1980s, and partly in recognition of the under-use, non-use, and delay these provisions entailed, a movement developed towards even earlier assessment and diversion. Court-based psychiatric assessments (not dissimilar to the duty solicitor schemes) enabled the courts to receive speedy medical advice and to ensure that, where appropriate arrangements could be made, mentally disordered offenders would be admitted to hospital (1) as a condition of bail; (2) under s. 35(2)(b) of the Mental Health Act 1983 by magistrates following conviction, or where the magistrates were satisfied before conviction that the accused did the act or made the omission charged and was suffering from one of the four narrow classifications; (3) under s. 35 if the accused consents; (4) using civil powers of admission under s. 2 or s. 3; (5) by a hospital order under s. 37; (6) by a psychiatric probation order; or (7) under s. 36 (remanding to hospital for treatment).

Although these schemes all take different forms, they share the innovative and proactive approach of getting psychiatrist, Crown Prosecution Service (CPS), mentally disordered alleged offender, and sentencer together at court. They aim to prevent offenders having to be remanded in custody for reports merely because they do not enjoy stable community ties or because of the absence of bail hostels; ultimately, disposal into a custodial setting should be avoided where a therapeutic one would be more appropriate. The Reed Report (1991: Community Advisory Group para. 2.37(x)) recommends that "there should be nationwide provision of court psychiatrist or similar schemes for assessment and diversion of mentally disordered offenders". This recommendation notably comes on top of a series of recommendations to ensure earlier and earlier diversion, including diversion from police stations as a place of safety under s. 136, specialised bail hostels, and extension of the "public interest" case assessment. As para. 2.25 notes, "comprehensive and reliable information about the suspect's mental condition" should be available so that the CPS may consider the desirability of proceeding against a person who is mentally disordered.

Such an overall approach, which implies exemption from prosecution, is not without its problems. Some commentators believe that those with mental handicap should be prosecuted and held responsible where responsibility exists (Carson 1989). Although the Code for Crown Prosecutors already requires the CPS to consider a defendant's mental condition, disorder *per se* is not regarded as a sufficient basis for not proceeding. Indeed, the Home Office Circular no. 66/90, paralleling the Code, distinguishes in para. 6 those forms of mental disorder made worse by the institution of proceedings and those which come about by reason of instituting proceedings. It has also been suggested (Robertson 1988) that the presence of disorder may make prosecution more likely where a guilty plea is anticipated. Hence it is important to distinguish the additional safeguards all mentally disordered people should enjoy under the Codes of Practice and the Police and Criminal Evidence Act (PACE), while in police custody, from the decision to prosecute. In the latter instance, the presence of mental disorder may act as a mitigating factor and pre-empt prosecution, or it may act as an incentive to proceedings being taken.

Curiously, under PACE, the presence or suspicion of mental disorder as defined in the Mental Health Act 1983 (i.e. including psychopathic disorder) should trigger all of the protections and additional rights to which the mentally vulnerable are entitled in police custody, including the right to have an appropriate adult present during questioning (Code C, paras 1.4, 3.9, 3.12, 11.14). It would be interesting to know how frequently the police's definition of a "psychopath" impels them to adhere to these special protections for the mentally disordered under PACE...

Thus, the public interest in ensuring that the offence will not be repeated needs to be weighed against that of the welfare of the person in question. Equally, there are difficulties concerning potential net-widening, such schemes work best for trivial offences which might, in the absence of an assured diversion scheme, have never even come before the courts. And there are problems of due process (*e.g.* the question of being unfit to plead) where the earlier ... involvement of psychiatrists will inevitably favour welfarism over legalism; are alleged offenders being made offers they cannot refuse? Finally, as Fennell notes (1991: 336–7); assuming that an offender is prepared to be diverted, "hospital authorities and local authorities have considerable discretion as to whether to accept responsibility for that person. If he is a persistent petty offender, or is potentially disruptive, he is unlikely to be afforded priority status in the queue for scarce resources." With the drop at district level in in-patient beds for the adult mentally ill from around 150,000 in the 1950s to approximately 63,000 in the early 1990s, and a reluctance by some to see offender-patients integrated with "non-offenders", diversion and community care may have real limits to their ability to absorb all those whom the courts might wish so to allocate.

References

Phil Fennell, "Diversion of Mentally Disordered Offenders from Custody", (1991) Crim. L.R. 333

S. Dell, A. Grounds, K. James and G. Robertson, "Mentally Disordered Remanded Prisoners: Report to the Home Office", (unpublished, 1991)

Reed Report, "Review of Health and Social Services for Mentally Disordered Offenders and Others Requiring Similar Services" (Department of Health/Home Office, 1991)

D. Carson, "Prosecuting People with Mental Handicaps", (1989) Crim. L.R. 87

D. James and L. Hamilton, "Setting Up Psychiatric Liaison Schemes to Magistrates' Courts: Problems and Practicalities", (1992) 32 *Medicine, Science and the Law* 167.

G. Robertson, "Arrest Patterns Among Mentally Disordered Offenders", (1988) 153 *British Journal of Psychiatry* 313.

Notes

1.   Official policy, as expressed in particular in Home Office Circular 66/90, is to encourage diversion of mentally disordered offenders from the formal process of prosecution, trial and sentence. The powers laid down in sections 35, 36 and 136 of the Mental Health Act 1983 may be exercised to divert such offenders from prosecution but, as shown in Fennell's research, the powers contained in sections 35 and 36 are not used to a large extent. However, a more pro-active inter-agency approach to diversion, from the end of the 1980s, is reported in the extract from Peay.

2.   It is difficult to state accurately the extent of "police diversion" under section 136 of the Mental Health Act since there are no centrally recorded statistics: only for those cases resulting in hospital admission.

   Police involvement in psychiatric referrals is probably much greater than would be suggested by hospital admission figures alone; see Hoggett (1990), pp. 145–9; Rogers and Faulkner (1987) and *Carter v. Metropolitan Police Commissioner* [1975] 1 W.L.R. 507.

Criminal Procedure (Insanity and Unfitness to Plead) Act 1991, ss. 2,3 (amending ss. 4 and 5 of the Criminal Procedure (Insanity) Act 1964)

   2. For section 4 of the Criminal Procedure (Insanity) Act 1964 ("the 1964 Act") there shall be substituted the following sections –
   4. – (1) This section applies where on the trial of a person the question arises (at

the instance of the defence or otherwise) whether the accused is under a disability, that is to say, under any disability such that apart from this Act it would constitute a bar to his being tried.

(2) If, having regard to the nature of the supposed disability, the court are of opinion that it is expedient to do so and in the interests of the accused, they may postpone consideration of the question of fitness to be tried until any time up to the opening of the case for the defence.

(3) If, before the question of fitness to be tried falls to be determined, the jury return a verdict of acquittal on the count of each of the counts on which the accused is being tried, that question shall not be determined.

(4) Subject to subsections (2) and (3) above, the question of fitness to be tried shall be determined as soon as it arises.

(5) The question of fitness to be tried shall be determined by a jury and –
    (a) where it falls to be determined on the arraignment of the accused and the trial proceeds, the accused shall be tried by a jury other than that which determined that question;
    (b) where it falls to be determined at any later time, it shall be determined by a separate jury or by the jury by whom the accused is being tried, as the court may direct.

(6) A jury shall not make a determination under subsection (5) above except on the written or oral evidence of two or more registered medical practitioners at least one of whom is duly approved.

4A. – (1) This section applies where in accordance with section 4(5) above it is determined by a jury that the accused is under a disability.

(2) The trial shall not proceed or further proceed but it shall be determined by a jury –
    (a) on the evidence (if any) already given in the trial; and
    (b) on such evidence as may be adduced or further adduced by the prosecution, or adduced by a person appointed by the court under this section to put the case for the defence.

whether they are satisfied, as respects the count or each of the counts on which the accused was to be or was being tried, that he did the act or made the omission charged against him as the offence.

(3) If as respects that count or any of those counts the jury are satisfied as mentioned in subsection (2) above, they shall make a finding that the accused did the act or made the omission charged against him.

(4) If as respects that count or any of those counts the jury are not so satisfied , they shall return a verdict of acquittal as if on the count in question the trial had proceeded to a conclusion.

(5) A determination under subsection (2) above shall be made –
    (a) where the question of disability was determined on the arraignment of the accused, by a jury other than that which determined that question; and
    (b) where that question was determined at any later time, by the jury by whom the accused was being tried."

3. For section 5 of the 1964 Act there shall be substituted the following section –
5. – (1) This section applies where –
    (a) a special verdict is returned that the accused is not guilty by reason of insanity; or
    (b) findings are recorded that the accused is under a disability and that he did the act or made the omission charged against him.

(2) Subject to subsection (3) below, the court shall either –
    (a) make an order that the accused be admitted, in accordance with the provisions of Schedule 1 to the Criminal Procedure (Insanity and Unfitness

to Plead) Act 1991, to such hospital as may be specified by the Secretary of State; or

(b) where they have the power to do so by virtue of section 5 of that Act, make in respect of the accused such one of the following orders as they think most suitable in all the circumstances of the case, namely –

(i) a guardianship order within the meaning of the Mental Health Act 1983;

(ii) a supervision and treatment order within the meaning of Schedule 2 to the said Act of 1991; and

(iii) an order for his absolute discharge.

(3) Paragraph (b) of subsection (2) above shall not apply where the offence to which the special verdict or findings relate is an offence the sentence for which is fixed by law."

Mental Health Act 1983, s. 37(3).

37. – (3) Where a person is charged before a magistrates' court with any act or omission as an offence and the court would have power, on convicting him of that offence, to make an order under subsection (1) above in his case as being a person suffering from mental illness or severe mental impairment, then, if the court is satisfied that the accused did the act or made the omission charged, the court may, if it thinks fit, make such an order without convicting him.

Notes

1. Greater flexibility has been introduced by the 1991 legislation as regards the disposal of both defendants found unfit to plead at the trial and those who at trial successfully rely on the insanity defence. Previously, both categories of defendant were liable to be detained in a hospital for treatment as though subject to a hospital order with restrictions and without time limits (on hospital orders, see below). A jury finding of unfitness to plead is now accompanied by a trial on the facts. If the latter results in a finding that the defendant did the act or made the omission charged, such a finding (though it is not a conviction) opens the way to one of the disposal options listed in section 3. A negative finding of fact results in an acquittal in the usual sense. The range of options for the court in the case of both unfit to plead and "insane" defendants now comprises: a hospital order, with or without restrictions; a guardianship order; a supervision and treatment order; absolute discharge.

2. Research into the first year of operation of the new Act (1992) revealed a continuing reluctance on the part of lawyers to put forward arguments of either unfitness to plead or insanity (a total of 13 unfitness findings and five insanity verdicts during that year). The court disposal of these cases, however, demonstrated a willingness to make use of the full range of options: see Mackay and Kearns (1994), and also the earlier research by Mackay (1990).

3. Magistrates also have a power under section 37(3) of the Mental Health Act 1983 to commit to hospital for treatment defendants diagnosed as suffering from mental illness or severe mental impairment on a finding that

the act of the criminal offence has been committed (as in the case of jury findings of unfitness to plead).

Mental Health Act 1983, s. 48(1), (2)

48. – (1) If in the case of a person to whom this section applies the Secretary of State is satisfied by the same reports as are required for the purposes of section 47 above that that person is suffering from mental illness or severe mental impairment of a nature or degree which makes it appropriate for him to be detained in a hospital for medical treatment and that he is in urgent need of such treatment, the Secretary of State shall have the same power of giving a transfer direction in respect of him under that section as if he were serving a sentence of imprisonment.

(2) This section applies to the following persons, that is to say –

> (a) persons detained in a prison or remand centre, not being persons serving a sentence of imprisonment or persons falling within the following paragraphs of this subsection;
>
> (b) persons remanded in custody by a magistrates' court;
>
> (c) civil prisoners, that is to say, persons committed by a court to prison for a limited term (including persons committed to prison in pursuance of a writ of attachment), who are not persons falling to be dealt with under section 47 above;
>
> (d) persons detained under the Immigration Act 1971.

Mental Health Act 1983, s. 51(5), (6).

51. – (5) If ... it appears to the court having jurisdiction to try or otherwise deal with the detainee –

> (a) that it is impracticable or inappropriate to bring the detainee before the court; and
>
> (b) that the conditions set out in subsection (6) below are satisfied, the court may make a hospital order (with or without a restriction order) in his case in his absence and, in the case of a person awaiting trial, without convicting him.

(6) A hospital order may be made in respect of a person under subsection (5) above if the court –

> (a) is satisfied, on the written or oral evidence of at least two registered medical practitioners, that the detainee is suffering from mental illness or severe mental impairment of a nature or degree which makes it appropriate for the patient to be detained in a hospital for medical treatment; and
>
> (b) is of the opinion, after considering any depositions or other documents required to be sent to the proper officer of the court, that it is proper to make such an order.

Notes

1.   While a mentally disordered person is awaiting trial, a court can only grant bail or remand in custody; it has no power to commit to hospital for treatment. But the Home Secretary can order the transfer to hospital of any persons awaiting trial in custody, if there is urgent need for treatment. The transfer thus carried out under section 48 takes effect as a hospital

order, except that remanded prisoners, if transferred, are subject to restriction (section 49(1)). The transfer to hospital will normally last for the period of remand, but if treatment is no longer necessary or effective, then a magistrates' court, the Home Secretary or a Crown Court may transfer the defendant back to prison, but the Crown Court also has power to release on bail in such a case (see sections 51 and 52 of the Act). On transfers from remand in prison to hospital under section 48, see Fennell (1991), at pp. 339–40.

2. The procedure laid down in section 51 supplies another method of committing a defendant for hospital treatment, without the need for trial, provided that he or she is already in hospital (having been remanded and then transferred under section 48). The court must be satisfied that the defendant is suffering from mental illness or severe impairment and that this would be the "proper" course to take, and that appearance before court would be impracticable or inappropriate. Such an order may be made with or without restrictions.

IV. Psychiatric Orders Following Conviction

Criminal Justice Act 1991, Schedule 1, Part II, section 5.
Requirements as to treatment for mental condition, etc.

5. – (1) This paragraph applies where a court proposing to make a probation order is satisfied, on the evidence of a duly qualified medical practitioner approved for the purposes of section 12 of the Mental Health Act 1983, that the mental condition of the offender –
  (a) is such as requires and may be susceptible to treatment; but
  (b) is not such as to warrant the making of a hospital order or guardianship order within the meaning of that Act.

(2) The probation order may include a requirement that the offender shall submit, during the whole of the probation period or during such part of that period as may be specified in the order, to treatment by or under the direction of a duly qualified medical practitioner with a view to the improvement of the offender's mental condition.

(3) The treatment required by any such order shall be such one of the following kinds of treatment as may be specified in the order, that is to say –
  (a) treatment as a resident patient in a mental hospital;
  (b) treatment as a non-resident patient at such institution or place as may be specified in the order; and
  (c) treatment by or under the direction of such duly qualified medical practitioner as may be so specified;
but the nature of the treatment shall not be specified in the order except as mentioned in paragraph (a), (b) or (c) above.

(4) A court shall not by virtue of this paragraph include in a probation order a requirement that the offender shall submit to treatment for his mental condition unless it is satisfied that arrangements have been made for the treatment intended to be specified in the order (including arrangements for the reception of the offender where he is to be required to submit to treatment as a resident).

(5) While the offender is under treatment as a resident patient in pursuance of a requirement of the probation order, the probation officer responsible for his

supervision shall carry out the supervision to such extent only as may be necessary for the purpose of the revocation or amendment of the order.

(6) Where the medical practitioner by whom or under whose direction an offender is being treated for his mental condition in pursuance of a probation order is of the opinion that part of the treatment can be better or more conveniently given in or at an institution or place which –

    (a) is not specified in the order; and

    (b) is one in or at which the treatment of the offender will be given by or under the direction of a duly qualified medical practitioner, he may, with the consent of the offender, make arrangements for him to be treated accordingly.

(7) Such arrangements as are mentioned in sub-paragraph (6) above may provide for the offender to receive part of his treatment as a resident patient in an institution or place notwithstanding that the institution or place is not one which could have been specified for that purpose in the probation order.

(8) Where any such arrangements as are mentioned in sub-paragraph (6) above are made for the treatment of an offender –

    (a) the medical practitioner by whom the arrangements are made shall give notice in writing to the probation officer responsible for the supervision of the offender, specifying the institution or place in or at which the treatment is to be carried out; and

    (b) the treatment provided for by the arrangements shall be deemed to be treatment to which he is required to submit in pursuance of the probation order.

See also section 12B of the Children and Young Persons Act 1969, which contains a comparable provisions in relation to supervision for young offenders.

Note

This form of probation developed unofficially in the 1930s and was specifically provided for in section 4 of the Criminal Justice Act 1948 and remains today a popular means of providing psychiatric treatment in criminal cases, allowing for in-patient treatment (though not in a special hospital), out-patient treatment or treatment by a named doctor. The measure inevitably depends upon a successful liaison between supervisor and doctor:

"... opinions differ as to the efficacy of the order. Therapeutically, it may be preferable to a hospital order because there is less and less need for even the most seriously disordered to be detained in hospital and the order allows a flexible combination of medical care and supervision. On the other hand, evasion is relatively easy, and there have been failures of communication between the medical and supervising authorities." (Brenda Hoggett (1990), p. 177; see also, Lewis (1980); Jones (1989)).

Mental Health Act 1983, s. 37 (excluding subs. 3)).

37. – (1) Where a person is convicted before the Crown Court of an offence punishable with imprisonment other than an offence the sentence for which is fixed by law, or is convicted by a magistrates' court of an offence punishable on summary conviction with imprisonment, and the conditions mentioned in subsection (2) below are satisfied, the court may by order authorise his admission to and detention in such hospital as may be specified in the order or, as the case may be, place him under the guardianship of a local social services authority or of such other person approved by a local social services authority as may be so specified.

(2) The conditions referred to in subsection (1) above are that –

(a) the court is satisfied, on the written or oral evidence of two registered medical practitioners, that the offender is suffering from mental illness, psychopathic disorder, severe mental impairment or mental impairment and that either –

    (i) the mental disorder from which the offender is suffering is of a nature or degree which makes it appropriate for him to be detained in a hospital for medical treatment and, in the case of psychopathic disorder of mental impairment, that such treatment is likely to alleviate or prevent a deterioration of his condition; or

    (ii) in the case of an offender who has attained the age of 16 years, the mental disorder is of a nature or degree which warrants his reception into guardianship under this Act; and

(b) the court is of the opinion, having regard to all the circumstances including the nature of the offence and the character and antecedents of the offender, and to the other available methods of dealing with him, that the most suitable method of disposing of the case is by means of an order under this section . . .

. . . (4) An order for the admission of an offender to a hospital (in this Act referred to as "a hospital order") shall not be made under this section unless the court is satisfied on the written or oral evidence of the registered medical practitioner who would be in charge of his treatment or of some other person representing the managers of the hospital that arrangements have been made for his admission to that hospital in the event of such an order being made by the court, and for his admission to it within the period of 28 days beginning with the date of the making of such an order; and the court may, pending his admission within that period, give such directions as it thinks fit for his conveyance to and detention in a place of safety.

(5) If within the said period of 28 days it appears to the Secretary of State that by reasons of an emergency or other special circumstances it is not practicable for the patient to be received into the hospital specified in the order, he may give directions for the admission of the patient to such other hospital as appears to be appropriate instead of the hospital so specified; and where such directions are given –

(a) the Secretary of State shall cause the person having the custody of the patient to be informed, and

(b) the hospital order shall have effect as if the hospital specified in the directions were substituted for the hospital specified in the order.

(6) An order placing an offender under the guardianship of a local social services authority or of any other person (in this Act referred to as "a guardianship order") shall not be made under this section unless the court is satisfied that that authority or person is willing to receive the offender into guardianship.

(7) A hospital order or guardianship order shall specify the form or forms of mental disorder referred to in subsection (2)(a) above from which, upon the evidence taken into account under that subsection, the offender is found by the court to be suffering; and no such order shall be made unless the offender is described by each of the practitioners whose evidence is taken into account under that subsection as suffering from the some one of those forms of mental disorder, whether or not he is also described by either of them as suffering from another of them.

(8) Where an order is made under this section, the court shall not pass sentence of imprisonment or impose a fine or make a probation order in respect of the

offence or make any such order as is mentioned in paragraph (b) or (c) of section 7(7) of the Children and Young Persons Act 1969 in respect of the offender, but may make any other order which the court has power to make apart from this section; and for the purposes of this subsection "sentence of imprisonment" includes any sentence or order for detention.

Criminal Justice Act 1991, s. 4(1)–(4)

4. – (1) Subject to subsection (2) below, in any case where section 3(1) above applies and the offender is or appears to be mentally disordered, the court shall obtain and consider a medical report before passing a custodial sentence other than one fixed by law.

(2) Subsection (1) above does not apply if, in the circumstances of the case, the court is of the opinion that it is unnecessary to obtain a medical report.

(3) Before passing a custodial sentence other than one fixed by law on an offender who is or appears to be mentally disordered, a court shall consider –
  (a) any information before it which relates to his mental condition (whether given in a medical report, a pre-sentence report or otherwise); and
  (b) the likely effect of such a sentence on that condition and on any treatment which may be available for it.

(4) No custodial sentence which is passed in a case to which subsection (1) above applies shall be invalidated by the failure of a court to comply with that subsection, but any court on an appeal against such a sentence –
  (a) shall obtain a medical report if none was obtained by the court below; and
  (b) shall consider any such report obtained by it or by that court.

(5) In this section –
"duly approved", in relation to a registered medical practitioner, means approved for the purposes of section 12 of the Mental Health Act 1983 ("the 1983 Act") by the Secretary of State as having special experience in the diagnosis or treatment of mental disorder;
"medical report" means a report as to an offender's mental condition made or submitted orally or in writing by a registered medical practitioner who is duly approved.

(6) Nothing in this section shall be taken as prejudicing the generality of section 3 above.

Notes

1. Hospital orders were first introduced in the Mental Health Act 1959. They are broadly designed to provide necessary treatment for more serious disorders (*i.e.* mental illness, impairment and psychopathic disorder, the last two conditions entailing, by definition under section 1 of the 1983 Act, abnormally aggressive or seriously irresponsible conduct) following conviction for more serious, *i.e.* imprisonable, offences. The underlying philosophy of this measure is to allow for treatment in place of punishment, so that any penal approach is categorically excluded (section 37(8)). However, although penal considerations are alien to the making of such orders, it is difficult to resist some notions of proportionality and justice for the patient and these may be logically admitted even in the absence of penal objectives. Moreover, section 37(2)(b) refers to the nature of the offence as one of the factors to be taken into account in deciding upon the suitability of a hospital order. Considerations of proportionality have arisen

in particular in relation to the use of restriction orders and whether orders should be indeterminate or not (see further discussion below).

2.   The pivotal consideration in deciding upon a hospital order is that of the patient's treatability. This is referred to in section 37(2)(a) and, in relation to psychopathic offenders, it must now be shown that the case is one where treatment is likely to alleviate or prevent a deterioration of the condition (this was not a requirement of the 1959 legislation). Under the 1983 Act, it is much less easy to justify the admission of impaired or psychopathic offenders to hospital. This accommodates the current medical view that there is very little that can usually be done for such persons in hospital. The decision as to treatability is clearly a medical one, and the hospital's control over such admissions is increased by the requirement under section 37(4) that a court must have evidence that a hospital bed will be available within 28 days in order to make a hospital order. In practice, this entails the willingness of both psychiatric and nursing staff to receive certain types of patient.

3.   On the way in which medical reports are prepared and evidence of this kind given to courts, see Chapter 11 of the Butler Committee's Report, and Hoggett (1990), pp. 155–160. The Butler Committee expressed concern about reports being prepared inside prisons, if defendants had been remanded in custody, and section 35 of the 1983 Act now provides for remand to hospital for a report to be made in some cases. Note that section 4 of the 1991 Criminal Justice Act now requires as a matter of principle that a court considers a medical report before passing a custodial sentence on an offender who is or appears to be mentally disordered.

4.   The effect of an order under section 37 is virtually the same as that of an admission under civil procedures as regards such matters as the duration and renewal of detention and discharge from hospital (for a detailed discussion of these questions, see Hoggett (1990), generally). The only significant differences are that a patient cannot be discharged upon application of his or her nearest relative and cannot appeal to a tribunal within the first six months of his or her admission to hospital.

5.   The number of hospital orders has declined over the period of this legislation, reflecting the shift in professional opinion away from hospital treatment for certain types of patient. During the 1960s the annual number of orders was well over a thousand; by the end of the 1970s it had dropped to between seven and eight hundred and in 1988–89 it was 501: an annual average decline of 13 per cent during the second part of the 1980s. Although there has also been a decline in the number of psychiatric probation orders since the early 1970s, there were still around a thousand of these orders made annually at the end of the 1980s, making it the most popular form of psychiatric disposal (not surprisingly, in view of its flexibility and its accommodation of the movement towards community-based treatment).

6.   Guardianship orders have been provided for alongside hospital orders in both the 1959 and 1983 legislation. In practice, minimal use is made of guardianship by the courts, despite repeated expressions of regret at its

under-utilisation, for instance, by the Butler Committee. This situation may be a result, as the Committee suggested, of the reluctance on the part of social services departments of local authorities to add to their heavy workload, and the greater familiarity of the courts with the probation system, which would seem in this respect to have competed successfully with the guardianship order. In fact, guardianship has more bite than probation (see section 8(1) of the 1983 Act). It is perhaps unfortunate that those under the age of 16 and also impaired persons who are neither abnormally aggressive or seriously irresponsible are excluded from the scope of the order (section 37(2)(a)).

7.   A profile of offenders detained in hospital can be gained from the Home Office Research and Statistics Department's *Statistics of Mentally Disordered Offenders* (England and Wales, 1989 and 1990, issue 29/31). For 1990 the largest proportion of this group were diagnosed as having mental illness (67 per cent), while 22 per cent were diagnosed as psychopathic and ten per cent as having some form of impairment. Of those admitted in 1990, 50 per cent had committed acts of violence against the person.

Report of the (Butler) Committee on Mentally Abnormal Offenders, Cmnd. 6244 (1975), para. 12.5.

... In our discussions with medical witnesses we gained the impression that many doctors found it difficult to decide whether to recommend that a hospital order should be made where they have been able to examine the patient only briefly in a prison hospital under the pressure of impending court proceedings, since it was often impossible to know how he would react subsequently to the psychiatric hospital regime. At present a hospital order may be made on medical recommendation but it may subsequently become clear that no treatment is possible; the patient may be unresponsive or disruptive, or he may even be found through continuous observation in hospital to have been feigning mental disorder to the time he was first examined. As the order cannot subsequently be replaced by a punitive sentence the hospital has no alternative in such a case but to discharge the patient, and he is then beyond the reach of the court. This difficulty could in part be solved if the courts had power to make what might be termed a "interim hospital order", committing the defendant to a specified hospital for a limited period of compulsory detention for diagnosis and assessment. at the latest at the expiry of the interim period, the court would again consider the case and would have discretion to confirm the order in the medical report so recommended, or, if the report indicated that a hospital order was inappropriate, to reconsider the matter and impose any other available disposal, including where appropriate a custodial sentence...

Mental Health Act 1983, s. 38(1), (5).

38. – (1) Where a person is convicted before the Crown Court of a offence punishable with imprisonment (other than an offence the sentence for which is fixed by law) or is convicted by a magistrates' court of an offence punishable on summary conviction with imprisonment a the court before or by which he is convicted if satisfied, on the written or oral evidence of two registered medical practitioners –

(a) that the offender is suffering from mental illness, psychopathic disorder, severe mental impairment or mental impairment; and

(b) that there is reason to suppose that the mental disorder from which the offender is suffering is such that it may be appropriate for a hospital order to be made in his case,

the court may, before making a hospital order or dealing with him in some other way, make an order (in this Act referred to as "an interim hospital order") authorising his admission to such hospital as may be specified in the order and his detention there in accordance with this section...

... (5) An interim hospital order –

(a) shall be in force for such period, not exceeding 12 weeks, as the court may specify when making the order; but

(b) may be renewed for further periods of not more than 28 days at a time if it appears to the court, on the written or oral evidence or the responsible medical officer, that the continuation of the order is warranted;

but no such order shall continue in force for more than six months in all and the court shall terminate the order if it makes a hospital order in respect of the offender or decides after considering the written or oral evidence of the responsible medical officer to deal with the offender in some other way.

Notes

1. It should be noted that, in the case of a interim hospital order, no application may be made to a tribunal and the patient cannot be discharged or granted leave of absence.

2. If, at the end of the period of an interim order, it is clear the no further treatment would be necessary or beneficial, (a) would a further short custodial sentence be justifiable? (b) would a penalty be justifiable if the interim order has effected a cure?

Mental Health 1983, s. 41(1), (2), (3), s. 42(1), (2), (3) and s. 43(1).

41. – (1) Where a hospital order is made in respect of a offender by the Crown Court, and it appears to the court, having regard to the nature of the offence, the antecedents of the offender and the risk of his committing further offences if set at large, that it is necessary for the protection of the public from serious harm so to do, the court may, subject to the provisions of this section, further order that the offender shall be subjected to the special restrictions set out in this section, either without limit of time or during such period as may be specified in the order; and an order under this section shall be known as "a restriction order".

(2) A restriction order shall not be made in the case of any person unless at least one of the registered medical practitioners whose evidence is taken into account by the court under section 37(2)(a) above has given evidence orally before the court.

(3) The special restrictions applicable to a patient in respect of whom a restriction order is in force are as follows –

(a) none of the provisions of Part II of this Act relating to the duration, renewal and expiration of authority for the detention of patients shall apply, and the patient shall continue to be liable to be detained by virtue of the relevant hospital order until he is duly discharged under the said Part II or absolutely discharged under section 42, 73, 74 or 75 below;

(b) no application shall be made to a Mental Health Review Tribunal in respect of a patient under section 66 or 69(1) below;

    (c) the following powers shall be exercisable only with the consent of the Secretary of State, namely –

        (i) power to grant leave of absence to the patient under section 17 above;

        (ii) power to transfer the patient in pursuance of regulations under section 19 above; and

        (iii) power to order the discharge of the patient under section 23 above;

and if leave of absence is granted under the said section 17 power to recall the patient under that section shall vest in the Secretary of State as well as the responsible medical officer; and

    (d) the power of the Secretary of State to recall the patient under the said section 17 and power to take the patient into custody and return him under section 18 above may be exercised at any time;

and in relation to any such patient section 40(4) above shall have effect as if it referred to Part II of Schedule 1 to this Act instead of Part I of that Schedule.

42.. – (1) If the Secretary of State is satisfied that in the case of any patient a restriction order is no longer required for the protection of the public from serious harm, he may direct that the patient shall cease to be subject to the special restrictions set out in section 41(3) above...

    ... (2) At any time while a restriction order is in force in respect of a patient, the Secretary of State may, if he thinks fit, by warrant discharge the patient from hospital, either absolutely or subject to conditions; and where a person is absolutely discharged under this subsection, he shall thereupon cease to be liable to be detained by virtue of the relevant hospital order, and the restriction order shall cease to have effect accordingly.

    (3) The Secretary of State may at any time during the continuance in force of a restriction order in respect of a patient who has been conditionally discharged under subsection (2) above by warrant recall the patient to such hospital as may be specified in the warrant.

43. – (1) If in the case of a person of or over the age of 14 years who is convicted by a magistrates' court of an offence punishable on summary conviction with imprisonment –

    (a) the conditions which under section 37(1) above are required to be satisfied for the making of a hospital order are satisfied in respect of the offender; but

    (b) it appears to the court, having regard to the nature of the offence, the antecedents of the offender and the risk of his committing further offences if set at large, that if a hospital order is made a restriction order should also be made,

the court may, instead of making a hospital order or dealing with him in any other manner, commit him in custody to the Crown Court to be dealt with in respect of the offence.

Sections 66, 69, 73, 74 and 75 relate to the powers of Mental Health Review Tribunals (see below). Part II of Schedule 1 deals with the position of patients subject to special restrictions.

Statement by Lord Chief Justice Parker in *Gardiner* (1967) 51 Crim. App. R. 187, pp. 192–193.

This is not meant to suggest that restriction orders should be made in every case, but it is very advisable that they should be made in all cases where it is thought that the protection of the public is required. Thus in, for example, the case of crimes of violence, and of the more serious sexual offences, particularly if the prisoner has a record of such offences, or if there is a history of mental disorder involving violent behaviour, it is suggested that there must be compelling reasons to explain why a restriction order should not be made.

Nevertheless, experience has shown that there are an alarming number of cases in which in such circumstances no restriction order has been made...

... since in most cases the prognosis cannot be certain the safer course is to make any restriction order unlimited in point of time. The only exception is where the doctors are able to assert confidently that recovery will take place within a fixed period when the restriction order can properly be limited to that period.

Report of the (Butler) Committee on Mentally Abnormal Offenders, Cmnd. 6244 (1975), para. 14 *et seq*.

14.24 The making of a restriction order has potentially serious consequences for the defendant because of the special procedural steps, involving the Home Secretary, taken to establish that he is fit to be discharged, and that adequate after-care arrangements have been made, and because of his liability to remain subject to supervisory conditions. (Figures supplied by the Home Office based on a count of the restricted patients discharged from all hospitals in 1974 give the average period of detention under a section 65 order as about $4\frac{1}{2}$ years – see paragraph 7.23. Detention could continue for life.) For this reason and, less importantly, because of the administrative difficulties they involve, restriction orders should not be made unless they are fully justified. Evidence given to us by the Home Office has indicated the probability that these orders are imposed in numbers of cases where their severity is not appropriate. In the words of the section the court may impose restrictions where "... it appears to the court, having regard to the nature of the offence, the antecedents of the offender, and the risk of his committing further offences if set at large, that it is necessary for the protection of the public so to do ...". There is no indication of the seriousness of the offences from which the public is intended to be protected by the restriction order provisions and some courts have evidently imposed restrictions on, for example, the petty recidivist because of the virtual certainty that he will persist in similar offences in the future. In our view this is not the sort of case in which a section 65 order should be imposed. The restriction order provisions drive from recommendations made by the Royal Commission on the Law Relating to Mental Illness and Mental Deficiency and paragraph 519 of their Report recommends these arrangements where "there is a real danger of the commission of further *serious* offences ..." (our italics). Figures supplied by the Home Office indicate that there has been a decline over recent years in the number of cases in which restriction orders have been imposed for the "less serious offences" (that is to say, offences other than homicide, attempted homicide, sexual offences, other offences against the person, and criminal damage). This is a welcome trend, but nevertheless we think that the wording of section 65(1) should be more tightly drawn to indicate its true intention, namely to protect the public from serious harm. A more restrictive wording of the section would help the courts in making the difficult decision whether it is appropriate to impose this severe form of control. Contributory factors to the inappropriate use of restriction orders by the courts are shortage of time and scarcity of resources which often mean that they lack complete information when assessing a defendant's suitability for restriction: we hope that our proposals for remands to hospital (paragraphs 12.2–12.3) and interim hospital orders (paragraphs 12.5–12.6) will help overcome these other difficulties.

Notes

1.   The restriction order, basically a measure of public protection which is coupled with a hospital order, has extreme effects. The detention does not have to be renewed and will continue indefinitely (unless the order has been made for a fixed period – something considered to be illogical by the Butler Committee). Even if detention is no longer medically justified, it may be very difficult to convince the Home Office that the patient should be released (see *Kynaston v. Secretary of State for Home Affairs* (1981) 73 Crim. App. R. 281). However, following the decision of the European Court of Human Rights in *X v. U.K.* ((1981), see below), the continued restriction may now be appealed to a Mental Health Review Tribunal.

2.   The Butler Committee considered that restriction orders were being used too readily, in that cases which entailed a nuisance rather than a danger to the public were being dealt with in this manner. For instance, in *Toland* (1974) 58 Crim. App. R. 453, Roskill L.J. said: "... the case is not in the same category as a case of a violent sexual offender ... But this boy is certainly an anti-social person. He is a pest ... somebody from whom the public is entitled to be protected." The case of Nigel Smith, referred to by Scarman L.J. in *McFarlane* (1975) 60 Crim. App. Rep. 320, provides another example of inappropriate use of restrictions. Section 41 now requires the court to find it necessary to protect the public from serious harm, before making a restriction order. However, even before the 1983 Act, the number of orders coupled with restriction had begun to decline and the number of property offenders entering hospital as restricted patients fell during the 1970s. The daily average population of restricted patients fell to 1,692 in 1985, since when it has increased once again (by 16 per cent to 1,964 at the end of 1990). Moreover, more restricted patients are now being detained outside the special hospitals (on which see the note below). See Home Office Research and Statistics Department, *Statistics of Mentally Disordered Offenders*, England and Wales, 1989 and 1990, issue 29/31. (*Cf.* p. 414).

3.   For a restriction order to be effective, a patient needs to be kept in secure conditions, which in practice may well mean one of the "special" hospitals (Broadmoor, Rampton and Ashworth). Section 4 of the National Health Service Act 1977 governs the position of such special hospitals for Mental Health Act detainees who, in the opinion of the Secretary of State, require treatment under conditions of special security. These hospitals are managed directly by the Department of Health. There had been very critical reports on Broadmoor (the Butler Committee's Interim Report, 1974) and Rampton, Cmnd. 8073 (1980) and eventually in 1989 a Special Hospitals Service Authority was established to "develop policies relating to the

provision and management" of the special hospitals. For a more detailed and critical account of the special hospitals, see Hoggett (1990), pp. 31–33. 4.   The limited number of places in the special hospitals (about 1800 beds in total) has led to pressure for further secure hospital provision. The Butler Committee in 1974 recommended the provision of secure units in each NHS region as a matter of urgency. Funds were provided in the late 1970s and several permanent secure units have now been established; however, the units tend to be selective as to the patients they are prepared to accept, being careful to ensure that they can be transferred out, either up or down the scale of security, as necessary. See further, Blugrass (1985) and Snowden (1986).

European Convention on Human Rights, Article 5(1)(a), (e); 5(4).

Article 5
1. Everyone has the right to liberty and security of person.
No one shall be deprived of his liberty save in the following cases and in accordance with a procedure prescribed by law;

> (a) the lawful detention of a person after conviction by a competent court...
> ... (e) the lawful detention of persons for the prevention of the spreading of infectious diseases, of persons of unsound mind, alcoholics or drug addicts, or vagrants...

... 4. Everyone who is deprived of his liberty by arrest or detention shall be entitled to take proceedings by which the lawfulness of his detention shall be decided speedily by a court and his release ordered if the detention is not lawful.

Judgement of the European Court of Human Rights in *X v. U.K. (Re Detention of a Mental Patient)* (October 24, 1981) (1982) 4 European Human Rights Reports 188.

In November 1968, X was convicted of an offence of wounding another with intent to cause grievous bodily harm. He was sent to a secure mental hospital. In May 1971, the Home Secretary authorised his conditional discharge. As a result of information received, the Home Secretary issued a warrant for his recall to the mental hospital in April 1974 in accordance with section 66 of the Mental Health act 1959. An application for a writ of habeas corpus made on X's behalf was refused in June 1974. Following an application to a Mental Health Review Tribunal and a favourable recommendation by the responsible medical officer, X was allowed out on leave in February 1976; in July of the same year, he was again conditionally discharged. X complained, inter alia, that his recall in April 1974 constituted an unlawful deprivation of liberty contrary to Article 5(1) of the European Convention on Human Rights and that he has not had an opportunity the have the lawfulness of his detention after recall speedily decided by a court guaranteed by Article 5(4)...

Judgment
... 40. In its WINTERWERP judgment[1] the Court stated three minimum conditions which have to be satisfied in order for there the be "the lawful detention of a person

---

[1] See *Winterwerp v. The Netherlands* (1979) 2 E.H.R.R. 387, 402, para. 39.

of unsound mind" within the meaning of Article 5(1) (e): except in emergency cases, the individual concerned must be reliably shown to be of unsound mind, that is to say, a true mental disorder must be established before a competent authority on the basis of objective medical expertise; the mental disorder must be of kind or degree warranting compulsory confinement; and the validity of continued confinement depends upon the persistence of such a disorder.

41. The applicant's counsel argued that the recall procedures established under section 66 of the 1959 Act, since they do not lay down any minimum conditions comparable to those stated in the WINTERWERP judgment, and in particular the need for objective medical evidence, were incompatible with Article 5 (1) (e). The unfettered discretion vested in the Home Secretary meant, so it was submitted, that any recall decision, even one taken in good faith, must by its very nature be arbitrary.

Section 66 (3) is, it is true, framed in very wide terms; the Home Secretary may at any time recall to hospital a "restricted patient" who has been conditionally discharged. Nevertheless, it is apparent from other sections in the Act that the Home Secretary's discretionary power under section 66 (3) is not unlimited. Section 147 (1) defines a "patient" as a person suffering or appearing to be suffering for mental disorder" and section 4 (1) defines "mental disorder" as "mental illness, arrested or incomplete development of mind, psychopathic disorder, and any other disorder or disability of mind". According to the Government, it is implicit in section 66 (3) that unless the Home Secretary on the medical evidence available to him decides that the candidate for recall falls within this statutory definition, no power of recall can arise.

Certainly, the domestic law itself must be in conformity with the Convention, including the general principles expressed or implied therein. However, section 66 (3), it should not be forgotten, is concerned with the recall, perhaps in circumstances when some danger is apprehended, of patients whose discharge from hospital has been restricted for the protection of the public. The WINTERWERP judgment expressly identified "emergency cases" as constituting an exception to the principle that the individual concerned should not be deprived of his liberty "unless he has been reliably shown to be of 'unsound mind' "; neither can it be inferred from the WINTERWERP judgment that the "objective medical expertise" must in all conceivable cases be obtained before rather than after confinement of a person on the ground of unsoundness of mind. Clearly, where a provision of domestic law is designed, amongst other things, to authorise emergency confinement of persons capable of presenting a danger to others, it would be impracticable to require thorough medical examination prior to any arrest or detention. A wide discretion must in the nature of things be enjoyed by the national authority empowered to order such emergency confinements. In the Court's view, the terms of section 66(3), read in their context, do not grant an arbitrary power to the Home Secretary; nor are they such that they exclude observance in individual cases of the principles stated in the WINTERWERP judgment.

Having regard to the foregoing considerations, the conditions under the 1959 Act governing the recall to hospital of restricted patients do not appear to be incompatible with the meaning under the Convention of the expression "the lawful detention ... of persons of unsound mind". What remains to be determined is whether the manner in which section 66(3) was in fact applied in relation to X gave rise to a breach of Article 5(1)(e)...

... In such circumstances, the interests of the protection of the public prevail over the individual's right to liberty to the extend of justifying an emergency confinement in the absence of the usual guarantees implied in Article 5(1)(e) (see para. 41, third sub-para., above). On the facts of the present case, there was sufficient reason for the Home Secretary to have considered that the applicant's continued liberty constituted a danger to the public, and in particular to his wife...

... On the other hand, in the Court's opinion, a judicial review as limited as that available in the habeas corpus procedure in the present case is not sufficient for a continuing confinement such as the one undergone by X. Article 5 (4), the Government are quite correct to affirm, does not embody a right to judicial control of such scope as to empower the court, on all aspects of the case, to substitute its own discretion for that of the decision-making authority. The review should, however, be wide enough to bear on those conditions which, according to the Convention, are essential for the "lawful" detention of a person on the ground of unsoundness of mind, especially as the reasons capable of initially justifying such a detention may cease to exist (see paras. 40 and 52, above). This means that in the instant case Article 5 (4) required an appropriate procedure allowing a court to examine whether the patient's disorder still persisted and whether the Home Secretary was entitled to think that a continuation of the compulsory confinement was necessary in the interests of public safety.

59. The habeas corpus proceedings brought by X in 1974 did not therefore secure him the enjoyment of the right guaranteed by Article 5(4); this would also have been the case had he made any fresh application at a later date...

... 61. The Government drew the Court's attention to four ways by which the continued need for detention may come to be reviewed by the Home Office, namely a recommendation from the responsible medical officer that the patient be discharged, the intervention of a Member of Parliament with the Home Secretary a direct request by the patient to the Home Secretary asking for release or for his case to be referred to a Mental Health Review Tribunal...

The first three do not, however, bring into play any independent review procedure, whether judicial or administrative.

The fourth calls for closer examination since, in relation to the confinement of restricted patients, the 1959 Act provides the opportunity for a periodic review on a comprehensive factual basis by Mental Health Review Tribunals. There is nothing to preclude a specialised body of this kind being considered as a "court" within the meaning of Article 5 (4), provided it enjoys the necessary independence and offers sufficient procedural safeguards appropriate to the category of deprivation of liberty being dealt with. Nonetheless even supposing Mental Health Review Tribunals fulfilled these conditions, they lack the competence to decide "the lawfulness of the detention" and to order release if the detention is unlawful, as they have advisory functions only...

... Therefore, without underestimating the undoubted value of the safeguards thereby provided, the Court does not find that the other machinery adverted to by the Government serves to remedy the inadequacy, for the purposes of Article 5 (4), of the remedy of habeas corpus.

Mental Health Act 1983, s. 72(1) and s. 73(1)–(4).

72. – (1) Where application is made to a Mental Health Review Tribunal by or in respect of a patient who is liable to be detained under this Act, the tribunal may in any case direct that the patient be discharged, and –

(a) the tribunal shall direct the discharge of a patient liable to be detained under section 2 above if they are satisfied –
  (i) that he is not then suffering from mental disorder or from mental disorder of a nature or degree which warrants his detention in a hospital for assessment (or for assessment followed by medical treatment) for at least a limited period; or
  (ii) that his detention as aforesaid is not justified in the interests of his own health or safety or with a view to the protection of other persons;

(b) the tribunal shall direct the discharge of a patient liable to be detained otherwise than under section 2 above if they are satisfied –
   (i) that he is not then suffering from mental illness, psychopathic disorder, severe mental impairment or mental impairment or from any of those forms of disorder of a nature or degree which makes it appropriate for him to be liable to be detained in a hospital for medical treatment; or
   (ii) that it is not necessary for the health or safety of the patient or for the protection of other persons that he should receive such treatment; or
   (iii) in the case of an application by virtue of paragraph (g) of section 66(1) above, that the patient, if released, would not be likely to act in a manner dangerous to other persons or to himself...

... **73.** – (1) Where an application to a Mental Health Review Tribunal is made by a restricted patient who is subject to a restriction order, or where the case of such a patient is referred to such a tribunal, the tribunal shall direct the absolute discharge of the patient if satisfied –

(a) as to the matters mentioned in paragraph (b)(i) or (ii) of section 72(1) above; and
(b) that it is not appropriate for the patient to remain liable to be recalled to hospital for further treatment.

(2) Where in the case of any such patient as is mentioned in subsection (1) above the tribunal are satisified as to the matters referred to in paragraph (a) of that subsection but not as to the matter referred to in paragraph (b) of that subsection the tribunal shall direct the conditional discharge of the patient.
(3) Where a patient is absolutely discharged under this section he shall thereupon cease to be liable to be detained by virtue of the relevant hospital order, and the restriction order shall cease to have effect accordingly.
(4) Where a patient is conditionally discharged under this section –

(a) he may be recalled by the Secretary of State under subsection (3) of section 42 above as if he had been conditionally discharged under subsection (2) of that section; and
(b) the patient shall comply with such conditions (if any) as may be imposed at the time of discharge by the tribunal or at any subsequent time by the Secretary of State...

See L. Gostin, "Human Rights, Judicial Review and the Mentally Disordered Offender" 1982 Crim. L.R. 779.

Note
The opportunity was taken, with the revision of the Mental Health legislation, to bring the law into conformity with the European Convention, as required by the European Court's judgement. The net result is that detention is no longer lawful if based upon a perceived danger to the public rather than need for treatment. Section 41(6) of the Act requires the Home Secretary to consider reports on a restricted patient's condition at intervals of at most a year. If the Home Secretary refuses to agree to the discharge of a patient who no longer fulfils the criteria for detention, his decision can be taken to a Mental Health Review Tribunal, which has a power of discharge under section 73. This may reduce the effectiveness of the restriction order as a measure of public protection, but it was made clear by Lane, L.C.J. in *Howell* (1985) 7 Cr. App. R. (S) 360 that, if an offender is

suitable for and can be placed in a secure hospital, a court should not resort to life imprisonment to avoid the risk of release by a Mental Health Review Tribunal.

V. THE USE OF IMPRISONMENT

At the present time the prison system deals with a significant proportion of mentality disordered offenders as well as a number with non-psychiatric problems such as alcohol or drug addiction. From a sentencing point of view, these are cases that naturally fall outside the scope of the psychiatric orders to referred to above. For the most part such cases comprise offenders suffering from a disorder or problems which are outside the categories listed in the Mental Health Act, or are not considered to be treatable. Significant examples would include many instances of psychopathic (personality) disorder and also addicted persons convicted of more serious offences. In addition, there may be a number of offenders who could be dealt with in hospital but who are seen as requiring secure accommodation which is not presently available. These may be sentenced to imprisonment in the hope that they can later be transferred to hospital under section 47 of the Mental Health Act 1983. There is now a substantial case-law on the appropriate use of imprisonment for mentally disordered offenders, summarised in the extract below.

Brenda Hoggett, *Mental Health Law* (3rd ed., 1990). pp. 195–197.

When he is not suitable for or cannot be found a place in a special hospital, however, a mentally disturbed offender who commits very serious offences is undoubtedly at greater risk of a sentence of life imprisonment than are other offenders. The criteria are, first, that the offences themselves are serious enough to justify very long sentences; secondly, that there is evidence, usually but not invariably medical evidence, of "mental instability" indicating that the offender is likely to go on committing such offences; and thirdly, that the consequences to others will be "specially injurious" (see *R. v. Hodgson* (1967) 52 Cr. App. R. 113; examples include *R. v. Herpels* (1979) 1 Cr. App. R.(S.) 209; *R. v. Dempster* (1987) 9 Cr. App. R.(S.) 176; *R. v. Birch* (1987) 9 Cr. App. R.(S.) 509). However, in *R. v. Pither* (1979) 1 Cr. App. R.(S.) 209, this was confined to exceptional cases where the offender is subject to a "marked degree of mental instability." Persistent delinquent behaviour is not enough. In *R. v. Spencer* (1979) 1 Cr. App. R.(S.) 75 (see also *R. v. Laycock* (1981) 3 Cr. App. R.(S.) 104), the court emphasised that a life sentence should not be imposed unless the offender was also a serious and consistent danger to the public. The defendant was a former mental patient who set fire to a car while labouring under a misguided sense of grievance, but he had taken pains to avoid endangering life, and the court substituted a sentence of five years.

Lower down the scale, there have been cases such as *R. v. Arrowsmith* [1976] Crim. L.R. 636, in which a woman with a long history of disturbed and aggressive behaviour was given three years' imprisonment on breach of probation for a minor offence because the medical and social services could not cope with her any longer. But in *R. v. Clarke* (1975) 61 Cr. App. R. 320, Lawton L.J. observed that "Her Majesty's courts are not dustbins into which the social services can sweep difficult members of the public. ... If the courts became disposers of those who are socially inconvenient the road ahead would lead to the destruction of liberty. It should be clearly understood that Her Majesty's judges stand on that road barring the way. The courts exist to punish according to law those convicted of offences. Sentences should fit crimes." A £2.00 fine was substituted for a sentence of 18 months' imprisonment upon a former Rampton patient who was admittedly very difficult to handle but had only been convicted of breaking a flower pot.

In *R. v. Tolley* (1978) 68 Cr. App. R. 323, the Court of Appeal preferred the approach in *Clarke* to that in *Arrowsmith*. They ordered the immediate release of a man who had been diagnosed schizophrenic and sentenced to two years imprisonment for possessing a small amount of cannabis, even though he was obviously doing very well in the prison hospital. A fixed term of imprisonment should not exceed a length commensurate with the gravity of the offence. The fact that his mental condition made it likely that if set at large he would be a danger to himself or others did not justify using the penal system to supplement the shortcomings of the social services and mental health system.

These cases may be seen as part of a judicial campaign to keep mentally disordered people out of prison. To the extent that they emphasise that punishments should fit crimes, they are welcome. But they are also part of a campaign to persuade the medical authorities to accept responsibility. A good example is *R. v. Porter (Wendy)*, *The Times*, January 22, 1985, where the Court of Appeal substituted an indefinite restriction order in Moss Side for a sentence of life imprisonment, while commenting forcibly on the lack of suitable intermediate facilities. While the *Tolley* approach is still good law, especially for offences of dishonesty (see, for example, *R. v. Judge* July 31, 1980; *R. v. Fisher* (1981) 3 Cr. App. R. (S.) 112), mental instability is certainly taken into account in justifying sentences at the top end of the "tariff" for violent offenders who for one reason or another cannot be sent to hospital (see, for example, *R. v. Scanlon* (1979) 1 Cr. App. R.(S.) 60; *R. v. Walsh* (1981) 3 Cr. App. R.(S.) 359). No matter how many secure units are built, they will not solve the problem of people like Dawn Clarke, who was repeatedly discharged from Rampton by a tribunal. There are many people who are not dangerous in any sensible meaning of the term, but who are difficult and a nuisance to all and sundry, and for whom there is precious little that hospitals as such can do. Hospitals are not dustbins any more than prisons are. The alternative of good facilities in the community simply does not exist in many places. The courts, and the rest of us, may have to accept that there are some troublesome people whom we must try to tolerate as best we can.

Research in the 1970s based upon a one per cent, census sample of prisoners in the South-East Prison Region suggested that about one-third of the prisoners there would be designated as psychiatric cases on the basis of I.C.D. (International Classification of Diseases) criteria: 21 per cent suffered from personality disorder, 12 per cent were alcoholic, nine per cent were neurotic, three per cent sexually deviant, three per cent drug dependant, and two per cent psychotic (see J. Gunn, G. Robertson, S. Dell, and C. Way (1978)). A 1986 census of male prisoners serving sentences of six months or more indicated a total of 1,497 who were mentally disordered or disturbed in some way, although only 115 of these could have been committed to hospital under the Mental Health Act (Home Office/DHSS, Report of the Interdepartmental Working Group on Mentally Disturbed Offenders in the Prison System in England and Wales). Such a situation naturally prompts questions concerning the kind of facility available in the prison system to deal with such problems and the prospect of alternative and more appropriate custody, if custody is necessary.

John Gunn, "Psychiatry and the Prison Medical Service," in *Secure Provision* (Larry Gostin ed., 1985), pp. 131–134, 144–146.

[See also the discussion by Gunn *et al.*, referred to above.]

Psychotherapy in Prison

Wormwood scrubs is one of the largest prisons in Britain and has a strong medical tradition. In 1971 it was investigate as part of a series of enquiries into some of the psychiatric aspects of imprisonment (Gunn *et al.*). When the research started there were 1,300 prisoners. As in many other English prisons, much of the basic medical work was done by visiting GPs, who conducted a sick parade. The GPs and senior prison staff sometimes referred men to a full-time medical officer for a psychiatric assessment. Some prisoners were kept in the prison hospital as in-patients. At the time of our study there were twenty-eight psychiatric beds available and an average bed occupancy of twenty-one. A few of the hospitalised men were transferred to mental hospitals under the Mental Health Act but the majority were treated and returned to ordinary locations. The average length of stay in the prison hospital was twenty-five days. Less severe cases were dealt with by conventional out-patient care (*i.e.* support plus medication) within the prison or by referral to a visiting psychotherapist. A few were transferred to Grendon Prison. In 1971 there were seven visiting psychotherapists. Most were consultant psychiatrists in the NHS and they normally worked two half-day sessions each week. Five practised psychotherapy on an individual basis, one specialised in the group treatment of substance-abusers, and the seventh ran a clinic for men with sexual problems, the treatment consisting mainly of hormone implants given shortly before discharge.

During a twelve-month period four of the five individual psychotherapists took on forty-four new patients at Wormwood Scrubs (the fifth doctor took on no new patients as his books were full!). We studied twenty-nine cases treated individually and thirteen men treated in groups. The individual treatments lasted from four months (sixteen men) to nine months or longer. The group-treated men tended to improve their self-esteem whilst the individually treated men reduced their; this is a finding of some important for it suggests that the support afforded by group treatment may help to counteract the ordinary demeaning experience of imprisonment. Both group- and individually treated men improved in terms of psychiatric symptomatology. However, there was little evidence in the sample of changes in motivation towards either crime or treatment or of changes in attitude towards authority figures. The only hint of improvement came from the group-treated men. They had initially expressed exceptionally low opinions of police and magistrates, but they later rated those figures in the same way as the rest of the sample. The group-treated men showed some increase in positive motivation towards treatment.

Indeed, for the recovering or recovered depressive who has killed a loved family member, and does not present a danger to the public, a probation order with a condition of treatment is a disposal that has many advantages: it provides in- or out-patient treatment as necessary, and it has an excellent built-in system of after-care through the probation service. Moreover, there are provisions for bringing the offender back to court if the arrangements made do not work satisfactorily. Yet, as we have seen, doctors in their reports seldom referred to the possibility of making these orders, and judges made little use of them. In a few cases where the option was put to them, the judges preferred to impose imprisonment: the case was cited earlier of the elderly man who developed a depressive psychosis in the course of looking after his mentally ill wife, and killed her before attempting to kill himself. The court reports said that he presented no danger to others, that he no longer required hospitialisation that psychiatric surveillance was desirable, and that this could be exercised either in prison or in the community through a probation order. He was sentenced to two years' imprisonment. Such judicial preference for retributive sentencing account for at least some of the increased use of imprisonment which followed the decline in the proportion of cases where doctors recommended hospital disposals.

We also studied Grendon Prison, where treatment was different. The prison evolved from the East-Hubert report of 1939 but became a psychotherapeutic institution taking personality-disordered, neurotic prisoners of average intelligence or above (see Gunn *et al.*, and Gunn and Robertson for full details). The prison in 1971/2 housed 150–200 men and boys in five separate wings. Unlike all other prisons it was governed by a doctor who was a trained psychiatrist. Our research was concerned only with the three wings containing adults. Each wing consisted of thirty to forty inmates, some ten prison officers and two therapists (doctors or psychologists usually). No individual treatments were given, drugs were eschewed, and the whole system was run as democratically as is possible in a maximum-security institution. This meant that all decisions were discussed, there was open and free communication between the staff and the men, and formal group meetings of all kinds were held regularly. The courts have no powers to send offenders to Grendon. The prisoners who went there were chosen from the general prison population by the prison medical staff. Nobody was forced to go to or stay at Grendon and a period at Grendon did not have much influence on the eventual date of release from prison. Men with psychoses or with mental handicap were excluded.

We studied a consecutive sample of admissions comprising 107 men, 27 of whom left prematurely (often at their own request). To summarise a great deal of data we found that the men showed a significant reduction in neurotic pathology, an increase in social self-confidence, and an improvement in attitude towards authority figures. Embittered neurotic men damaged by institutionalisation were improved in mental health and social attitudes. Sex offenders and violent men who had proved difficult to manage in other prisons became manageable in Grendon. What we could *not* show was a lowered reconviction rate compared with similar prisoners after leaving prison, but it seems unreasonable to expect one prison to differ from another in criminological terms. As our data showed, criminality and neuroticism are independent variables. Offending in the community is much more likely to be influenced by community factors such as support, opportunity, peer-group pressure, police activities, and the like than by what happens during a period of imprisonment (see Gunn *et al.* for a discussion).

Although Wormwood Scrubs and Grendon Prisons were catering for dissimilar groups (*e.g.* Grendon dealt with recidivists – old hands – and Scrubs with first-time prisoners – "stars"), there seemed some evidence from the research to suggest that individual psychotherapy in prison is of limited value, group psychotherapy within an ordinary prison brings some benefits, but the best prison results (in terms of psychiatric improvement and attitude change) come from a total therapeutic community.

It has to be remembered of course that these studies were conducted twelve years ago. Since that time a number of changes have taken place, particularly at Grendon. In 1975 the governor/medical director changed, but this did not alter the basic medical philosophy. A new development has been the introduction of a ten-day induction period. Now candidates are assessed within the hospital area of the prison before they are allowed on the wings and quite a lot are rejected at this stage. The assessment service is also used to provide the PMS with information about prisoners who are not going into the therapeutic community at Grendon. Grendon is also taking more prisoners than it did in 1971 because a sixth wing (making four adult wings in all) has been opened. Our research findings have been used to consolidate the work the prison is doing with violent offenders and sexual offenders. More men in each of these categories are now being taken. At the time of writing the future of Grendon is in some doubt and there has been some slippage of medical control. When the medical director died in 1983, his temporary replacement was a non-medical governor and the advertisement for his successor asked for both doctors and non-medical governors to apply . . .

The Role of Psychiatry in Prison

There seem to be four basic jobs for the psychiatrist inn a prison: (1) to provide psychiatric reports in a number of different circumstances; (2) to provided general psychiatric treatment; (3) to provide psychotherapy and psychotherapeutic regimes; and (4) to influence the general milieu of prisons.

The provision of psychiatric reports seems straightforward. The bulk of such reports are requested by courts, which ask in effect, does this man have a psychiatric disorder, if so should he be punished, have you advice about his management? There is no obvious reason why the questions should be addressed to prison doctors. The fact that most psychiatric reports to court are provided by prison doctors seems an historical accident. Justice, the strain on prisoners, and the quality of reports would all be improved by a shift away from prisons to the NHS for this service. HM Government has weakly acknowledged this by the inclusion in the new Mental Health Act of possible provisions for remand to hospitals. If the NHS is to undertake a lot of court work, it will need a substantial increase in funds and staff.

Other psychiatric reports are required within prisons which cannot legitimately be provided by the NHS, although the work can be carried out by visiting psychiatrists as well as by prison doctors. These reports include those sent to the Parole Board, those given to governors who are dealing with breaches of discipline, and recommendations for courses of treatment (e.g. at Grendon Prison).

The second role for the psychiatrists in prison is the provision of treatment. In England the prison doctor will struggle, often unsuccessfully, to get the sick psychiatric patients into the NHS; where he fails (often because of a complicating personality problem, drug-abuse or alcoholism), or where the disorder is of a lesser degree and the patient consents, it seems reasonable for the psychiatrist to provide treatment in prison. This might be anything from ECT to psychotropic drugs, from anticonvulsants to supportive counselling. Compulsory treatment is, however, not permitted within the prisons.

It seems likely that for the foreseeable future prisons are to be the main repositories for individuals with personality disorder who break the law. It is also clear that prison psychiatry has developed to respond to this group. Individual psychotherapy is provided in many prisons and group psychotherapy has developed in some establishments. Most importantly Grendon prison has shown the advantages in developing therapeutic communities within secure conditions.

The first three roles for prison psychiatry seem then to be fairly largely within the mainstream of medicine. The fourth role is more debatable and esoteric. Grendon Prison, as our research has shown, improves neurotic disorder and changes attitudes, but it does more than that. It provides a humane system of management for some otherwise unmanageable prisoners. It is debateable whether all unmanageable prisoners are "sick" or in any way medically disordered; some are simply reacting to authority in a quasi-political fashion. The more that unmanageability is political the less likely it is to respond to a therapeutic community (the IRA prisoners creating their dirty protest) but in some cases it is difficult to determine how much is political and how much is neurotic; therapeutic communities may be helpful in cases where there is a suspicion of a politicall element. Let us take an example. The Scottish prison service had a group of long-term (mostly lifer) prisoners who were proving unmanageable because of persistent violence. The Grendon model was copied and a special wing in Barlinnie prison, Glasgow, was set up. Some highly dangerous, severely violent men were managed there and showed a good deal of personal growth. One prisoner, Jimmy Boyle, made himself famous by his sculpture and his writings. Was Jimmy Boyle mentally disordered or was he simply reacting to stress? Perhaps he was reacting against a life sentence he regarded as unjust, perhaps the conditions he found himself in (including the cages at Peterhead) were too much for him, perhaps he has an impulsive and volatile personality (see his book to make an assessment). Whatever the explanation, the special unit transformed him.

Psychiatry should not be hesitant about going beyond a concern with the mentally ill provided (and note the italics) it has something scientific to say which is testable and refutable. Psychiatry has been rightly ridiculed in the past for dabbling in politics, warfare, the arts, and all sorts of human activities with no basis at all. However, medicine does have things to say about non-pathological matters in some biosocial circumstances. Who would doubt the value and pertinence of medicine in the phenomena of pregnancy and childbirth? The science of physical hygiene is partly medical, partly social, but it is largely responsible for our high standard of health today. In prisons doctors can use their knowledge of group psychotherapy, therapeutic communities, and the consequences of stress to give advice about better management. This surely is as much a role for the prison doctor as is giving advice about correct feeding, hygiene, ventilation, and the like. Indeed ultimately such a preventive role could be developed into the most important psychiatric role of all within the prisons.

Notes

1.   The Report by Norwood East, Prison Medical Commissioner, and W. H. de B. Hubert, of St. Thomas' Hospital, *Psychological Treatment of Crime* (1939), was influential in promoting the idea of a psychotherapeutic institution. Grendon psychiatric prison in Buckinghamshire was opened in 1962 initially under the direction of a psychiatrist as medical superintendent. In 1985 it was decided that Grendon Prison should specialise in "sociopaths", short-term acute management, lifer career plans and sex offenders, and a unit catering for the needs of the latter group was subsequently opened. The prison has a good reputation in dealing successfully with the behavioural problems of its inmates during their time there. See Gunn and Robertson (1987); Genders and Player (1989).

2.   The research carried out by Gunn and others suggests that the achievement of prison psychotherapy has been not so much in the area of reducing criminality as in relation to the problem of managing difficult disturbed personalities in an institutional setting. In so far as institutions such as Grendon are necessary, for reasons of public protection, then at least some progress has been made towards the evolution of a tolerable and humane regime. See as well, in this connection, Jimmy Boyle's autobiographical work, *A Sense of Freedom* (1977), and its discussion of the Barlinnie special unit.

Report of the (Butler) Committee on Mentally Abnormal Offenders, Cmnd. 6244 (1975), Chapter 5 et seq.

5.34 This lack of material progress in provision for the diagnosis and treatment of psychopathic conditions, with associated research, within the National Health Service is apparently matched by continuing uncertainty as to the treatability of the various conditions. The great weight of evidence presented to us tends to support the conclusion that psychopaths are not, in general, treatable, at least in medical terms. The Home Office and the Department of Health and Social Security stated in a joint memorandum that understanding of causes and of response to treatment is still very slight. The views expressed to us by individual consultant psychiatrists and senior medical officers of the Prison Medical Service have been almost uniformly pessimistic: "There are no agreed criteria for assessing treatability in psychopaths and indeed no agreed combination or sequence of therapeutic procedures for their treatment"; "There is no known treatment for the great majority of psychopaths and control is all that medicine has to offer"; "The possibility of treatment of aggressive psychopaths is extremely debatable – the aim has to be day to day management and support, concentrating on helping the individual through his crises with the minimum damage to himself and others"; "The belief that the psychopath is responsive to medical treatment has not been substantiated in the period since the Mental Health Act came into force"; "Court orders directing the admission of psychopathic personalities to hospital for treatment are in the most part unsuitable, since there is no recognised effective treatment at present for such personality defects"; and the British Psychological Society have pointed out that there is "No solid evidence of the effectiveness of treatment for psychopaths in this country"...

... 5.37 In this country there are at present broadly two main methods of treatment for psychopaths. On the one hand there are the various types of therapeutic community treatment, practised, for example, at Grendon Prison and Garth Angharad Hospital; on the other hand there are the various methods of behaviour modification (e.g. social skills training and aversion or operant conditioning) practised by clinical psychologists in certain hospitals. Although successful results are claimed by some hospitals and by Grendon Prison in the treatment of selected patients, these methods are not suitable for many of the more aggressive offenders who are often not willing or not able to co-operate in the treatment offered. Their behaviour is often disruptive, liable to extreme variations and unpredictable. They require secure containment. In prison or hospital they are a source of anxiety to their fellow prisoners or patients, as well as to staff. If they are located with the rest of the prison or hospital population they represent an unsettling element and the risk of unexpected violence has to be accepted and lived with. If on the other hand they are located separately, they make a further demand on scarce accommodation and staff, and may present special problems of control. On any of these counts, they are not usually suitably placed in local psychiatric hospitals. Apart from the reluctance of the hospitals to accommodate people who will not co-operate, or for whom no treatment is available, the local psychiatric hospitals do not contain facilities to cope over long periods of time with dangerous patients in whom the dangerousness may be the outstanding clinical problem, and it would be unreasonable to expect them to do so. These dangerous psychopaths have therefore usually been sent to prison.

5.38 We think that the penal system should continue to receive them and that, if certain attitudes and policies, which we describe later, were adopted it could become capable of offering the prospect of important advances in the understanding and treatment, in the broadest sense, of the dangerous psychopath...

... 5.49 For offenders suffering from personality disorders who may not display any strong or continuing motivation for treatment, and who may on occasions prove violent and disruptive, we see a need for a treatment institution founded on principles different from those of Grendon and employing different methods, based essentially on the idea of training. The Grendon approach towards resocialisation is based in considerable part on promoting insight through self-analysis and self-questioning on the part of the offender in the hope of enabling him to come to terms with the problems which lie behind his law-breaking. But not all offenders suffering from personality disorders which manifest themselves in seriously anti-social behaviour are amenable to such an approach. In many cases the need appears to be developed in the offender patterns of social behaviour which are normally acquired during childhood and adolescence but have never been satisfactorily learned by the psychopath. In the present state of knowledge it is believed that this may come about either in a psychotherapeutic setting or in a behaviour therapy setting and for this type of offender such treatments could be developed only in a structured environment providing a degree of control and security. In our view it would be appropriate for the new units to set out to establish a realistic regime on these lines, based on roughly equal periods of work and social activity but adjusted to the particular needs of individual inmates. We accept that some would argue that it is inappropriate in a treatment situation to impose a particular regime based on certain arbitrary assumptions about normality, and we agree that the training programme must be matched to the individual. But we are not impressed by the results which have been achieved by the approach which some of us saw adopted in certain Continental institutions, whereby patients were allowed to do nothing. Work and activity have always been the cornerstones of education and rehabilitation and it is difficult to see what effective alternative regime could be offered to an offender suffering from a psychopathic disorder to enable him to find his place in the community on release.

5.50 We should make it clear that we do not intend that the proposed units should cater for those cases in which psychopathic behaviour is a function of some underlying mental or organic illness where medical treatment might be helpful. Nor do we think that the regime will, in general, be suitable for the younger inadequate prisoner, who requires intensive long-term support but presents little physical risk to the community, although he is likely to be an annoyance and a nuisance. It is our intention that training units should cater for psychopaths with dangerous anti-social tendencies aged between 17 or 18 and 35, for whom special psychiatric treatment is not available, who are willing to undertake the training offered and are likely to be able to benefit from it and will have a chance of employment on release, but who in the meantime require secure containment. The offender's consent should be obtained before admission to a unit. We would emphasise that the age limits we have mentioned are to be regarded as illustrative rather than precise. The lower age limits we have proposed are linked with the minimum ages at which an offender is normally dealt with in an adult court and a sentence of imprisonment imposed, as well as representing the lowest ages at which most doctors would be willing to attach any diagnostic label to an offender. The upper limit is intended to exclude the older inadequate personality.

Note

There is little prospect of this proposal being implemented so that the more serious psychopathic offender is likely to remain the responsibility of the prison system.

Mental Health Act 1983, s. 47(1), (3), s. 49(1), (2), and s. 50(1), (2).

47. – (1) If in the case of a person serving a sentence of imprisonment the Secretary of State is satisfied, by reports from at least two registered medical practitioners –

(a) that the said person is suffering from mental illness, psychopathic disorder, severe mental impairment or mental impairment; and
(b) that the mental disorder from which that person is suffering is of a nature or degree which makes it appropriate for him to be detained in a hospital for medical treatment and, in the case of psychopathic disorder or mental impairment, that such treatment is likely to alleviate or prevent a deterioration of his condition;

the Secretary of State may, if he is of the opinion having regard to the public interest and all the circumstances that it is expedient so to do, by warrant direct that that person be removed to and detained in such hospital (not being a mental nursing home) as may be specified in the direction; and a direction under this section shall be known as "a transfer direction".

(3) A transfer direction with respect to any person shall have the same effect as a hospital order made in his case.

49. – (1) Where a transfer direction is given in respect of any person, the Secretary of State, if he thinks fit, may by warrant further direct that that person shall be subject to the special restrictions set out in section 41 above...

(2) A direction under this section shall have the same effect as a restriction order made under section 41 above and shall be known as "a restriction direction".

50. – (1) Where a transfer direction and a restriction direction have been given in respect of a person serving a sentence of imprisonment and before the expiration of that person's sentence the Secretary of State is notified by the responsible medical officer, any other registered medical practitioner or a Mental Health Review Tribunal that that person no longer requires treatment in hospital for mental disorder or that no effective treatment for his disorder can be given in the hospital to which he has been removed, the Secretary of State may –

(a) by warrant direct that he be remitted to any prison or other institution in which he might have been detained if he had not been removed to hospital, there to be dealt with as if he had not been so removed; or
(b) exercise any power of releasing him on licence or discharging him under supervision which would have been exercisable if he had been remitted to such a prison or institution as aforesaid,

and on his arrival in the prison or other institution or, as the case may be, his release or discharge as aforesaid, the transfer direction and the restriction direction shall cease to have effect.

(2) A restriction direction in the case of a person serving a sentence of imprisonment shall cease to have effect on the expiration of the sentence.

Note
It had become customary to warn sentencers about being too ready to commit offenders to prison in the expectation that there could be a subsequent transfer to hospital. In 1961 there were 179 such transfers; in 1976 only 30. This was largely a reflection of the hospitals' "open-door" policy (*i.e.* the use of community-based rather than custodial care and

treatment) and the reduced availability of hospital places. However, the Prison Medical Service campaigned for a greater receptivity on the part of the Health Service and during the 1980s the number of prisoners transferred to hospital was usually between 200 and 250 each year. In the early 1990s the number increased further (445 with restrictions in 1991, for example). Certainly the Home Office has expressed its concern to secure the transfer of such prisoners (a notorious example of which was Peter Sutcliffe, the "Yorkshire Ripper.") See further on this issue, Grounds (1991).

VI. APPLICATIONS TO MENTAL HEALTH REVIEW TRIBUNALS

[See also the discussion above concerning the review of restriction orders and the impact of applications under the European Convention on Human Rights.]

The tribunals were set up under the Mental Health Act 1959 as a means of safeguarding the rights of individuals dealt with compulsorily under the Act. Each tribunal is composed of a lawyer, a psychiatrist and a lay member. Under section 66 of the 1983 Act, ordinary hospital order patients can apply to a tribunal once during each period for which their detention is renewed, *i.e.* once during their second six months of detention and in every year after that. The same applies to patients who have been transferred from prison without restriction. The detention of restricted patients is not renewed, but under sections 70 and 79 they have the right to apply to the tribunal within equivalent periods. The tribunal's role is not to consider the legality of the patient's admission to hospital or the mode of treatment there, but whether the detention may legally continue. In the case of unrestricted patients it may, as well as discharge, recommend leave of absence, transfer to another hospital or to guardianship, or reclassify the mental disorder on which the detention is based. For the tribunal's powers in relation to restricted patients, see section 73 of the Act, above.

Jill Peay, *Tribunals on Trial: A Study of Decision-Making Under the Mental Health Act 1983* (1989), pp. 202–203, 206, 209–210, 227–228, 231–232.

... even if legalism had largely been embraced, this alone would have been insufficient to protect and enshrine patients' rights. It will be asserted, on the basis of the research findings, that it is wholly unrealistic to conceive of an effective legal safeguard in an inherently therapeutic environment. ... tribunals do not necessarily fulfil the function of remedying abuse. Rather I would argue that the operation of the law is context-specific. Thirdly, in the quasi-legal setting in which the tribunals function, applying the law so as to protect fully the rights of individual patients is peculiarly reliant upon the willingness and inclinations of those with the statutory authority so to do. Since there is evidence that the philosophy behind the Act has not been absorbed and that some of those influential within the system have chosen to ignore or even reject it, the Act's fundamental principles are clearly endangered. The fourth theme evolves from the third. If those who operate the system start with the paternalistic assumptions that public safety and therapeutic considerations should take precedence over individual rights, then they will not only conceive of the Act as an obstacle, but also deem other determinants more critical. In respect of tribunal decision- making, these concern the assessment of risk . . .

. . . The research findings suggest that many of those who operate the system believe that its bedrock in individual rights is not necessarily the most appropriate. Professionals working in the field were found to be either unfamiliar with the provisions of the Act, resistant to them, or, in some instances, unwilling to enforce them. Similarly, although patients' legal representatives may help to prevent sloppy thinking by tribunals, they cannot guarantee that members will necessarily give sufficient credence to the fine detail of the law. In some instances, representatives were found to collude in a negation of the appropriate legal criteria; in others, this occurred in arenas to which they had no access, for example during the tribunals' deliberations. Arguments raised by representatives based on the statutory criteria frequently failed to impress the tribunal; those based on the principles of equity received even shorter shrift. There may, therefore, be limits both to what the appeal process can achieve and, indeed, to what any changes in the statute might achieve. Without winning the "hearts and minds" of these fulcral individuals, the Act is impotent. Arguably, changes in the system personnel, particularly by appointing those who are prepared to tolerate a certain level of discomfort to facilitate enforcement of the provisions of the Act, may be more effective than progressively hardening the letter of the law.

In the light of this, the decision to appoint judges to the tribunal appears particularly astute. By balancing changes in the law, forced upon the government as a result of the European Court's ruling in *X. v. the United Kingdom* (1981), with changes in the membership of the tribunal, the government may have favoured the impact the latter may induce. Thus, with one or two notable exceptions, the reasoning adopted in practice by the judges has not substantially departed from the traditional view of successive Home Secretaries, namely, that the discretion to release restricted patients is to be exercised cautiously, if at all. Previous research had, of course, suggested that more "judicious" decision-making went hand in hand with greater responsibility for the decisions taken. The appointment of the judges may therefore have been only a form of double insurance; none the less, it was clearly regarded as a price well worth paying. . . .

. . . Although the absolute number of cases in the study is small, the research findings suggest that, rather than making decisions in the sense of exercising choice between real options, the tribunals invariably endorsed the recommendations made to them. While the findings do not support the assertion that tribunals were wholly constrained in these "choices", they do reveal that the evidence as presented to them inevitably tended to support one decision or another, and that tribunals routinely acquiesced, almost irrespective of the content of the recommendation. This assessment may appear harsh, but the following may be taken as support.

1. The different rates of discharge by the tribunals serving the two different Special Hospital regions were sustained even where comparable samples were examined. Hence, similar cases were seemingly treated differently.
2. In 86 per cent of the sample cases the tribunals' decisions paralleled the recommendations made by the RMOs.[2] In those rare instances where the tribunals went against the advice of the RMOs, it was usually in order to ensure outcomes of a more cautious nature than the RMOs were advocating (69 per cent of cases).

[2] Since the tribunals' decisions correlated with those of the RMOs it might be maintained that both groups arrived at similar decisions, but independently, because of the nature of the cases. However, given that the tribunals agreed with the decisions of the RMOs and these were, in turn, quite flexible depending on, for example, the hospital at which the RMO worked, it seems more credible that the tribunals adopted a passive role. Hence, the RMOs opinions more than merely correlated with the tribunals' decisions; they had an arguable causative impact.

Moreover, in five of these cases, the tribunal had to go against the concurring advice of both the RMO and an IP. Since such decisions would prevent any radical change taking place in a patient's circumstances, they may primarily be regarded as "non-decisions".

3. The nature of the advice given by RMOs in Acheland and Bendene differed; the impact of the prevailing ethos at each location cannot be ignored.

4. The advice the RMOs offered to the tribunals did not derive irrevocably from the facts of patients' circumstances, but was, in turn, constructed according to both their views of the case and their professional experience. Hence, different RMOs reached different conclusions given predominantly similar evidence (as, for example, when a patient changed RMO). Also, the conclusions of two or more doctors reviewing the same case at about the same time would differ (see, for example, discordant conclusions drawn by RMOs, their colleagues, IPs, and medical members of the tribunal). Finally, the conclusion drawn by a single RMO could be changed independently of any changes in the facts of the case (where, for example, pressure was exerted by the Responsible Authority).

5. There was similarly no irrevocable connection between the evidence presented and the tribunals' outcomes. In some cases, evidence was available which, had the tribunal been so minded, could have supported an alternative decision. Indeed, on occasions the same case reviewed sequentially by two different tribunals would result in two contradictory decisions, even when the patient's condition remained stable. Hence, evidence was open to interpretation and to selection.

There is, therefore, a process of construction which occurs in any given case which starts at a point considerably prior to the tribunal hearing. The case, as presented to the tribunal, has been refined for their consideration, principally by the RMO and the patient or his or her legal representative. The tribunal's decision, like that of many other decision-making bodies hearing evidence, amounts largely to a ratification of a decision which has been structured by earlier choices.

... the tribunal system does not exist in a vacuum. It represents only one aspect of a system of checks and balances for dealing with mentally disordered individuals. Since the research has identified the RMOs as the key figures in the sequence of decision-making, perhaps it is their decision-making skills which should properly form the focus for reform. Or, as Webster and Menzies (1987: 202) have asserted, "the activities of forensic practitioners deserve to be a focus of systematic evaluation quite as much as the characteristics of offenders". Improving the decision-making abilities of RMOs might, in the long run, be a more effective route to better decisions than any action that could be taken in respect of the tribunals...

... It is inevitable that the process of weighing the laudable yet competing objectives of patients' rights, therapeutic goals, and wide-ranging social considerations will be fraught with difficulties. Too rigid an approach – the substantive justice route – is unlikely to produce a satisfactory solution, and therefore one that will be readily employed; routine abrogation of the law is anyway undesirable. But too lax an approach cannot protect patients from unjustifiable deprivation of their liberty. Greater procedural regulation, particularly if inappropriate attributions of "dangerousness" are to be made, is a necessary first step. But in the light of the research findings, this would be insufficient. Decisions to discharge are resource and reality-oriented, not rule and law- oriented; scope must be provided for tribunals to deal in these realities. Hence, if the tribunal setting is not conducive to a strict application of the law it may be that an improvement will be achieved not so much in reform of the law but in the context within which the safeguard operates and the consequences that stem from its effective use.

[RMO: responsible medical officer

 IP: independent psychiatrist]

Note

The findings of Peay's research into the operation of the Mental Health Review Tribunals, carried out in the mid 1980s, echo the rather pessimistic conclusions of her earlier study of the tribunals (1982) as regards the effectiveness of legal safeguards of patients' interests. At that earlier point in time she argued that legal change in the form of greater opportunity to apply for review and wider terms of reference for review had a limited impact in the face of problems such as informational bias and an uneven familiarity with the legal and medical aspects of the applications. Structural problems are also identified in Peay's later research: the tribunals are presented as operating in "an inherently therapeutic environment" and the tribunals' decisions as a "ratification of a decision which has been structured by earlier choices."

VII. THE CONCEPT OF DANGEROUSNESS

Many decisions in relation to mentally disordered offenders are based upon a prediction of dangerousness or risk to the public, most obviously decisions in connection with restriction orders or secure custody. The concept of dangerousness has of course a wider relevance, in relation to other forms of custodial disposal and decisions concerning imprisonment, early release and even bail. The concept was considered by the Butler Committee in the context of the problems of disordered fixed term prisoners who may be a risk to the public upon release and in respect of whom the Committee proposed a new indeterminate, reviewable sentence, release depending upon the issue of dangerousness (see paras. 4.34 to 4.45). However, the whole question of predicting future dangerous behaviour has been controversial in the last fifteen years, with a growing recognition of the fallibility of such predictions. There is now a substantial body of official and academic literature on these questions, the discussion and report by the Floud Committee (Floud and Young (1981)), set up by the Howard League for Penal Reform, having both identified the lines of discussion and generated further debate.

Although some aspects of the Floud Committee's discussion and proposals stimulated a critical response (see for example the articles by Radzinowicz and Hood, and Bottoms and Brownsword, referred to below), the "Report" did clear the ground for the debate by frankly confronting the nature of the harm to be guarded against, by stressing the need for legal protection of individuals subjected to such procedures and by rejecting any optimistic acceptance of a predictive formula for assessing the likelihood of future dangerous behaviour. It is the assertion that, in the end, this is something which can only be determined by the exercise of a broad discretion, which remains controversial.

Significant contributions to this debate, both preceding and after the Floud proposals, include the following: Report of the Butler Committee (1975), Chapter 4; Scottish Council on Crime, *Crime and the Prevention of*

Crime (1975), Chapter 4; A. E. Bottoms, "Reflections on the Renaissance of Dangerousness," (1977) 16 *Howard Journal* 70; Jean Floud and Warren Young, "Dangerousness and Criminal Justice" (Cambridge Studies in Criminology 47 (1981)); L. Radzinowicz and R. Hood, "Dangerousness and Crim Justice: A Few Reflections" 1981 Crim. L.R. 756; A. E. Bottoms and R. Brownsword, "The Dangerousness Debate after the Floud Report" (1982) 22 B.J. Crim. 229; Floud, "Dangerousness and Criminal Justice" (1982) 22 B.J. Crim. 213; N. Walker, "Unscientific, Unwise, Unprofitable or Unjust?" (1982) 22 B. J.Crim. 276; *Dangerousness: Problems of Assessment and Prediction* (J. W. Hinton ed., 1982); *Dangerousness: Probability and Prediction, Psychiatry and Public Policy* (Christopher Webster, Mark Ben-Aron, Stephen Hucker eds., 1985); Herschell Prins, *Dangerous Behaviour, The Law and Mental Disorder* (1986).

BIBLIOGRAPHY

Advisory Council on the Treatment of Offenders (1952), *Report* (HMSO, London).

Advisory Council on the Treatment of Offenders (1957), *Alternatives to Short Terms of Imprisonment* (HMSO, London).

Advisory Council on the Penal System (1970), *Non-Custodial and Semi-Custodial Penalties* (HMSO, London).

Allen, R. (1991), "Out of Jail: The Reduction in the Use of Penal Custody for Male Juveniles, 1981–1988", 30 *Howard Journal* 30.

Alschuler, A. (1991), "The Failure of Sentencing Commissions", *New Law Journal* 829.

Ancel, M. (1971), *Suspended Sentence* (Heinemann).

Antilla, I. (1966), "Sentencing and the Changing Role of the Court", 15 *Howard Journal* 1.

Ashworth, Andrew (1982a), "Reducing the Prison Population in the 1980s: the Need for Sentencing Reform", in *A Prison System for the '80s and Beyond* (NACRO).

Ashworth, Andrew (1982b), "Judicial Independence and Sentencing Reform" in *The Future of Sentencing* (Thomas, D. A. ed., University of Cambridge).

Ashworth, Andrew *et al.* (1984a), *Sentencing in the Crown Court* (Oxford University Centre for Criminological Research).

Ashworth, Andrew (1984b), "Prosecution, Police and the Public—A Guide to Good Gatekeeping?", (1984) 23 *Howard Journal* 65.

Ashworth, Andrew (1986), "Punishment and Compensation: Victims, Offenders and the State", (1986) 6 Oxford J.L.St. 86

Ashworth, Andrew (1992a), *Sentencing and Criminal Justice* (Weidenfeld and Nicolson).

Ashworth, Andrew (1992b), "The Criminal Justice Act 1991", in *Sentencing, Judicial Discretion and Training* (Munro, C. and Wasik, M. eds., Sweet & Maxwell).

Ashworth, Andrew (1992c), "Non-Custodial Sentences", Crim.L.R. 242.

Ashworth, Andrew and Gibson, Bryan (1994), "Altering the Sentencing Framework", Crim.L.R. 101.

Atiyah's Accidents, Compensation and the Law (1987) (4th ed. by P. Cane, Weidenfeld and Nicolson).

Baldwin, J. R. (1975), "The Compulsory Training of the Magistracy" [1975] Crim.L.R. 634.

Baldwin, J. R. and McConville, M. (1977), *Negotiated Justice* (Martin Robertson).

Baldwin, J. R. (1985a), "Pre-Trial Settlement in Magistrates' Courts" 24 *Howard Journal* 108.

Baldwin, J. R. (1985b), *Pre-Trial Justice* (Blackwell).

Baldwin, J. R. and Mulvancy, A. (1987), "Advance Disclosure in the Magistrates Courts" Crim.L.R. 315.

Ball, Caroline (1992), "Young Offenders and the Youth Court", Crim.L.R. 277.

Banks, C. and Fairhead, S. (1976), *The Petty Short-Term Prisoner* (Barry Rose).

Barak-Glantz, I. (1981), "Towards a Conceptual Scheme of Prison Management Styles", 61 *Prison Journal*, issue 2.

Barnatt, G. N. (1983), "Section 48—A Viable Alternative?" 147 *Justice of the Peace* 117.

Blom-Cooper, Louis (1974), *Progress in Penal Reform* (O.U.P).

Blugrass, R. (1985), "The Development of Regional Secure Units". in *Secure Provision* (Gostin, L. ed., Tavistock).

Bochel, Dorothy (1976), *Probation and After-Care* (Edinburgh University Press).

Bottomley, A. K. and Pease, K. (1986), *Crime and Punishment: Interpreting the Data* (O.U.P.). .

Bottoms, A. E. (1973), "The Efficacy of the Fine: The Case for Agnosticism" Crim.L.R. 543.

Bottoms, A. E. (1977), "Reflections on the Renaissance of Dangerousness" 16 *Howard Journal* 70.

Bottoms, A. E. (1981), "The Suspended Sentence in England 1967–1978" 21 B.J.Crim. 1.

Bottoms, A. E. (1987), "Limiting Prison Use: Experience in England and Wales", 26 *Howard Journal* 177.

Bottoms, A. E. and Brownsword, R. (1982), "The Dangerousness Debate after the Floud Report" 22 B.J.Crim. 229.

Bottoms, A. E. (1983), "Neglected Features of Contemporary Penal Systems", in *The Power to Punish: Contemporary Penality and Social Analysis* (Garland, David and Young, Peter eds, Heinemann).

Bottoms, A. E. and McWilliams, W. (1979), "A Non-Treatment Paradigm for Probation Practice" 9 *British Journal of Social Work* 159.

Bottoms, A. E. and Light, R, (eds) (1987), *Problems of Long-Term Imprisonment* (Institute of Criminology, Cambridge).

Bottoms, A. E. *et al.* (1990), *Intermediate Treatment and Juvenile Justice: Key Findings and Implications from a National Survey of Intermediate Treatment Policy and Practice* (HMSO, London).

Bowden, J. and Stevens, M. (1986), "Justice for Juveniles: A Corporate Strategy in Northampton", 150 *Justice of the Peace* 326, 345.

Box, Steven (1983), *Power, Crime and Mystification* (Tavistock).

Boyle, Jimmy (1977), *A Sense of Freedom* (Pan Books).

Braithwaite, John (1988), *Crime, Shame and Reintegration* (Cambridge University Press).

Brants, Chrisje (1994), "The System's Rigged—Or Is It? The Prosecution of White Collar and Corporate Crime in the Netherlands", 21 *Crime, Law and Social Change* 103.

Brants, Chrisje and Field, Stewart (1995), "Discretion and Accountability in Prosecution: a Comparative Perspective on Keeping Crime out of Court", in *Criminal Justice in Europe* (Fennell *et al.* eds., Clarendon Press).

Bredar, J. K. (1992), *Justice Informed: The Pre-Sentence Report Pilot Trials in the Crown Court*, Vol. 1 (HMSO, London).

Bridge, Lord (1978), *Report of the Working Party on Judicial Studies and Information* (HMSO, London).

Brody, S. (1976), *The Effectiveness of Sentencing*, H.O.R.S. No. 35 (HMSO, London).

Brody, S. (1978), "Research into the Aims and Effectiveness of Sentencing" 17 *Howard Journal* 133.

Brown, I. and Hullin, R. (1992), "A Study of Sentencing in the Leeds Magistrates' Courts: The Treatment of Ethnic Minority and White Offenders", 32 B.J.Crim. 41.

Burney, Elizabeth (1985), *Sentencing Young People* (Gower).

Butler Committee (1975), *Report of the Committee on Mentally Abnormal Offenders*, Cmnd. 6244.

Carlen, P. and Cook, D. (eds.) (1989), *Paying for Crime* (O.U.P.).

Carlen, P. (1990), *Alternatives to Women's Imprisonment* (O.U.P.).

Carlisle Committee (1988), Report, *The Parole System in England and Wales*, Cm. 532 (HMSO, London).

Carson, D. (1989), "Prosecuting People with Mental Handicaps", Crim.L.R. 87.

Casale, S. (1989), *Women Inside* (Civil Liberties Trust).

Catton, T. and Erikson, P. (1975), "The Juvenile's Perception of the Role of Defence Counsel in the Juvenile Court" (University of Toronto Centre of Criminology Working Paper).

Cavadino, Paul (1990), "The White Paper—Will it Achieve its Objectives?", 80 *Prison Service Journal* 5.

Champion, D. J. (1991), *The U.S. Sentencing Guidelines: Implications for Criminal Justice* (Praeger).

Clarkson, C. M. and Keating, H. M. (1990), *Criminal Law: Text and Materials* (2nd ed., Sweet & Maxwell).

Chief Inspector of Prisons (1981), *Annual Report*, Cmnd. 8532.

Chief Inspector of Prisons (1993), *Doing Time or Using Time (Report of a Review)*, Cm. 2128 (HMSO, London).

Cohen, Stanley and Taylor, Laurie (1972), *Psychological Survival* (Penguin).

Cohen, Stanley and Taylor, Laurie (1978), *Prison Secrets* (NCCL/RAP).

Cohen, Stanley (1979), "The Punitive City: Notes on the Dispersal of Social Control", 3 *Contemporary Crises* 339.

Cohen, Stanley (1985), *Visions of Social Control: Crime, Punishment and Classification* (Polity Press).

Control Review Committee (1984), *Managing the Long-Term Prison System* (HMSO, London).

Council of the Law Society (1966), *Memorandum: The Child, the Family and the Young Offender*.

Criminal Law Revision Committee (1980), *Report on Offences against the Person*, Cmnd. 7844.

Croall, Hazel (1992), *White Collar Crime* (O.U.P.).

Cross, Rupert and Ashworth, Andrew (1981), *The English Sentencing System* (3rd ed., Butterworth).

Crow, I. (1987), "Black People and Criminal Justice in the U.K.", 26 *Howard Journal* 303.

Crow, I. and Cove, J. (1984), "Ethnic Minorities and the Courts", Crim.L.R. 413.

Davies, M. (1974), "Social Inquiry for the Courts" 14 B.J.Crim. 18.

Davies, M. and Knopf, A. (1973), *Social Inquiry Reports and the Probation Service*, H.O.R.S. No. 18 (HMSO, London).

Davies, C. (1970), "The Innocent Who Plead Guilty" *Law Guardian*, March 9, 1970.

De Haan, Willem (1990), *The Politics of Redress: Crime, Punishment and Penal Abolition* (Unwin Hyman).

De la Motta, K. (1984), *Blacks in the Criminal Justice System*, Unpublished thesis, Aston University.

Devlin, Sir Patrick (1979), *The Judge* (O.U.P.).

Dingwall, G. (1994a), "Making Fines Work—or Learning from our Mistakes", 47 *Criminal Lawyer* 3.

Dingwall, G. (1994b), "The Dangers of Discretion in Determining a Just Fine after the Abolition of the Unit Fine in the Criminal Justice Act 1993", 158 *Justice of the Peace* 545.

Ditchfield, John (1990), *Control in Prisons: Review of the Literature*, H.O.R.S. No. 118 (HMSO, London).

Doherty, M. and East, R. (1985), "Bail Decisions in Magistrates' Courts", 25 B.J.Crim. 251.

Downes, D. (1982), "The Origins and Consequences of Dutch Penal Policy Since 1945", 22 B.J.Crim. 325.

Downes, D. (1988), *Contrasts in Tolerance: Post-war Penal Policy in the Netherlands and England and Wales* (Clarendon Press).

Dunlop, A. B. (1980), *Junior Attendance Centres*, H.O.R.S. No. 60 (HMSO, London).

Dyer, C. (1990), "Making a Snap Decision", *The Guardian*, February 14, 1990.

East, Norwood and Hubert, W. H. de B. (1939), *Psychological Treatment of Crime* (HMSO, London).
Emmins, C. and Wasik, M. (1993), *Emmins on Sentencing* (2nd ed., Blackstone).

Farrington, D. *et al.* (1979), (eds.) *Psychology, Law and Legal Processes* (Macmillan).
Fennell, P. (1991), "Diversion of Mentally Disordered Offenders from Custody", Crim.L.R. 333.
Fennell, P. *et al* (1995) (eds.) *Criminal Justice in Europe* (Clarendon Press).
Field, Stewart and Jorg, Nico (1991), "Corporate Liability and Manslaughter: should we be going Dutch?", Crim.L.R. 156.
Fingarette, Herbert (1974), *The Meaning of Criminal Insanity* (University of California Press).
Fisse, Brent and Braithwaite, John (1988), "The Allocation of Responsibility for Corporate Crime", 11 *Sydney Law Review*, 468.
Fitzgerald, Mike and Sim, Joe (1982), *British Prisons*, (2nd ed., Blackwell).
Fitzgerald, P. J. (1966), "The Child, the White Paper and the Criminal Law: Some Reflections" [1966] Crim.L.R. 607.
Fitzmaurice, C. and Pease, K. (1982), "Prison Sentences and Population: a Comparison of some European Countries" [1982] *Justice of the Peace* 575.
Fitzmaurice, C. and Pease, K. (1986), *The Psychology of Judicial Sentencing* (Manchester University Press).
Floud, J. and Young, W. (1981), *Dangerousness and Criminal Justice* (Cambridge Studies in Criminology 47).
Floud, J. (1982), "Dangerousness and Criminal Justice" 22 B.J.Crim. 213.
Foot, D. (1993), "The Use of Suspended Sentences", 157 *Justice of the Peace* 565.
Ford, P. (1972), *Advising Sentencers* (Oxford University Penal Research Unit Occasional Paper No. 5).
Foucault, Michel (1977, 1979), *Discipline and Punish: The Birth of the Prison* (Penguin).
Freeman, M. D. A. (1981), "The Rights of Children When They Do 'Wrong'", 21 B.J.Crim. 210.
French, P. (1984), *Collective and Corporate Responsibility* (Columbia University Press).
Frost, S. and Stephenson, G. (1989), "A Simulation Study of Electronic Tagging as a Sentencing Option", 28 *Howard Journal* 91.
Fry, M. (1944), "The Future Treatment of the Adult Offender" (*Howard League*).

Garland, David (1985), *Punishment and Welfare* (Gower).
Garland, David and Young, Peter (1983) (eds), *The Power to Punish: Contemporary Penality and Social Analysis* (Heinemann).

Gelsthorpe, L. and Giller, H. (1990), "More Justice for Juveniles: Does More Mean Better?" Crim.L.R. 153.

Gelsthorpe, L. and Morris, A. (1983), "Attendance Centres: Policy and Practice", 22 *Howard Journal* 101.

Gelsthorpe, L. and Morris, A. (1994), "Juvenile Justice 1945–1992", in *The Oxford Handbook of Criminology* (Maguire, M., Morgan, R. and Reiner, R. eds., Clarendon Press).

Gelsthorpe, L. and Tutt, N. (1986), "The Attendance Centre Order" Crim.L.R. 146.

Genders, E. and Player, E. (1989), "Grendon: A Study of a Therapeutic Community within the Prison System", (Report to the Home Office).

Gerber, R. J. and McAnany, P. D. (1972), *Contemporary Punishment* (Notre Dame Press).

Gibson, B. (1987), "Why Bournemouth?", *Justice of the Peace* 520.

Gibson, B. (1990), *Unit Fines* (Waterside Press).

Gibson, B. (1992a), "Information and Pre-Sentence Reports", 89 *Law Society Gazette* 28.

Gibson, B. (1992b), "Criminal Justice Act 1991—Unit Fines", 156 *Justice of the Peace* 371.

Gladstone Committee (1895), *Report of the Departmental Committee on Prisons*, C. 7702.

Glidewell, Lord Justice (1992), "The Judicial Studies Board", in *Sentencing, Judicial Discretion and Training* (Munro, C. and Wasik, M. eds., Sweet & Maxwell).

Gostin, Larry (1982), "Human Rights, Judicial Review and the Mentally Disordered Offender" Crim.L.R. 779.

Gostin, Larry (1985), *Secure Provision* (Tavistock).

Gostin, Larry and Staunton, Marie (1985), "The Case for Prison Standards: Conditions of Confinement, Segregation and Medical Treatment", in *Accountability and Prisons*, (Maguire, M., Vagg, J. and Morgan, R. eds., Tavistock).

Graham, J. (1990), "Decarceration in the Federal Republic of Germany", 30 B.J.Crim. 150.

Grounds, A. (1991), "Transfers of Sentenced Prisoners to Hospitals", Crim.L.R. 544.

Gunn, J. (1985), "Psychiatry and the Prison Medical Service", in *Secure Provision* (Gostin, L., ed., Tavistock).

Gunn, J., Robertson, G., Dell, S. and Way, C. (1978), *Psychiatric Aspects of Imprisonment* (Academic Press).

Gunn, J. and Robertson, G. (1987), "A Ten-Year Follow-Up of Men Discharged from Grendon Prison", 151 *B. Journal of Psychiatry* 674.

Gunn, J., Maden, A. and Swinton, M. (1991), "Treatment Needs of Patients with Psychiatric Disorders", *B. Medical Journal* 338.

Halliday, J. (1992), "Providing a Legislative Framework for Sentencing", in *Sentencing, Judicial Discretion and Training* (Munro, C. and Wasik, M. eds., Sweet & Maxwell).

Harding, C., Hines, B., Ireland, R. and Rawlings, P. (1985), *Imprisonment in England and Wales, a Concise History* (Croom Helm).

Harding, C. and Ireland, R. W. (1989), *Punishment: Rhetoric, Rule and Practice* (Routledge).

Harding, C. (1993), *European Community Investigations and Sanctions* (Leicester University Press).

Harris, B. (1979), "Recommendations in Social Enquiry Reports" [1979] Crim.L.R. 73.

Hart, H. L. A. (1968), *Punishment and Responsibility* (O.U.P.).

Henham, Ralph (1990), *Sentencing Principles and Magistrates' Sentencing Behaviour* (Avebury).

Henham, Ralph (1994), "Attorney-General's References and Sentencing Policy", Crim.L.R. 499.

Hine, J., McWilliams, W. and Pease, K. (1978), "Recommendations, Social Information and Sentencing", 17 *Howard Journal* 91.

Hinton, J. W. (1982) (ed.), *Dangerousness: problems of assessment and prediction* (Allen & Unwin).

Hogarth, J. (1971), *Sentencing as a Human Process* (University of Toronto Press).

Hoggett, Brenda (1990), *Mental Health Law* (4th ed., Sweet & Maxwell).

Home Office, *The Sentence of the Court, a Handbook for Courts on the Treatment of Offenders* (1st ed., 1964; 2nd ed., 1969; 3rd ed., 2nd Impression, 1979; 4th ed., 1986; 5th ed., 1990).

Home Office/DHSS (1987), "Report of the Interdepartmental Working Group on Mentally Disturbed Offenders in the Prison System in England and Wales".

Home Office (1990), *Unit Fines: Experiments in Four Courts*, Research and Planning Unit Paper No. 59 (HMSO, London).

Hood, Roger (1962), *Sentencing in Magistrates' Courts* (Stevens).

Hood, Roger (1972), *Sentencing the Motoring Offender* (Heinemann).

Hood, Roger (1974), "Criminology and Penal Change" in *Crime, Criminology and Public Policy* (Hood, Roger ed., Heinemann).

Hood, Roger (1992), *Race and Sentencing: A Study in the Crown Court* (Clarendon Press).

Hood, Roger and Sparks, Richard (1970), *Key Issues in Criminology* (Weidenfeld).

Hough, M. and Mayhew, P. (1983), *The British Crime Survey*, H.O.R.S. No. 76 (HMSO, London).

Hough, M. and Mayhew, P. (1984), *The British Crime Survey*, H.O.R.S. No. 85 (HMSO, London).

Hough, M. and May, C. (1993), *Surveying the Work of Probation Officers*, H.O. Research Bulletin 15.

House of Lords Select Committee (1992), *Murder and Life Imprisonment* (HMSO, London).

House of Lords Select Committee on the European Communities (1993), *Enforcement of Community Competition Rules* (HMSO, London).

Howe Report (1981), *Fine Default* (NACRO).

Hudson, B. (1990), *Justice through Punishment: A Critique of the Justice Model of Corrections* (Macmillan).

Humphries, Stephen (1981), *Rebels or Hooligans?* (Blackwell).

James, D. and Hamilton, L. (1992), "Setting Up Psychiatric Liaison Schemes to Magistrates' Courts: Problems and Practicalities", 32 *Medicine Science and the Law* 167.

Jones, Gail (1989), "The Use and Effectiveness of the Probation Order with a Condition for Psychiatric Treatment in North Wales", 20 Cambrian L.Rev. 63

Jones, Howard (1981) (ed.) *Society Against Crime* (Penguin).

Jones, M. (1980), *Crime, Punishment and the Press* (NACRO).

Justice (1983), *Justice in Prison* (Justice).

Justice (1993), *Negotiated Justice: A Closer Look at the Implications of Plea Bargains* (Justice).

Keith Committee (1983), *Report on the Enforcement of Revenue Legislation*, Cmnd. 8222 (HMSO, London).

Kelly, Barbara (1992), *Children Inside: Rhetoric and Practice in a Locked Institution for Children* (Routledge).

Kelk, C., Koffman, L. and Silvis, J. (1995), "Sentencing Practice, Policy and Discretion", in *Criminal Justice in Europe* (Fennell, P. *et al.* eds., Clarendon Press).

King, J. (1979) (ed.), *Pressures and Change in the Probation Service*, Report of the 11th Cropwood Conference (Institute of Criminology, Cambridge).

King, Michael (1971), *Bail or Custody* (Cobden Trust).

King, Michael (1981), *The Framework of Criminal Justice* (Croom Helm).

King, Roy and Morgan, Rod (1980), *The Future of the Prison System* (Gower).

King, Roy and Maguire, Mike (1994), *Prisons in Context* (Clarendon Press).

Knapp, M., Robertson, E. and McIvor, G. (1992), "The Comparative Costs of Community Service and Custody in Scotland", 31 *Howard Journal* 8.

Lacey, Nicola (1988), *State Punishment: Political Principles and Community Values* (Routledge).

Langbein, John H. (1973), "Controlling Prosecutorial Discretion in Germany", 41 *University of Chicago L.R.* 439.

Law Commission (1985), *Draft Criminal Code*, Law Commission No. 143, (HMSO, London).

Leigh, L. and Brown, S. (1980), "Crimes in Bankruptcy" in *Economic Crime in Europe* (Leigh, L. ed., Macmillan).

Leng, R. and Manchester, C. (1991), *A Guide to the Criminal Justice Act 1991* (Fourmat).

Levi, M. (1987), *Regulating Fraud: White-Collar Crime and the Criminal Process* (Tavistock).

Levi, M. (1991), "Sentencing White-Collar Crime in the Dark? Reflections on the Guinness Four", 30 *Howard Journal* 257.

Lewis, H. and Mair, G. (1989), *The Use of London Probation Bail Hostels for Bailees*, Home Office Research and Planning Unit Paper, No. 50 (HMSO, London).

Lewis, P. (1980), *Psychiatric Probation Orders: Roles and Expectations of Probation Officers and Psychiatrists* (Institute of Criminology, Cambridge).

Liberty (1992), *Unequal Before the Law: Sentencing in Magistrates' Courts in England and Wales 1981–1991* (Liberty).

Lidstone, K. W., Hogg, R. and Sutcliffe, F. (1980), *Prosecution by Private Individuals and Non-Police Agencies*, Royal Commission on Criminal Procedure Research Study No. 10.

Liebling, Alison (1992), *Suicides in Prison* (Routledge).

Lilley, J. R. (1990), "Tagging Reviewed", 29 *Howard Journal* 229.

Livingstone, Stephen and Owen, Tim (1993), *Prison Law: Text and Materials* (Clarendon Press).

Lloyd, C. (1991), *National Standards for Community Service Orders: The First Two Years of Operation*, H.O. Research Bulletin 31.

Lovegrove, A. (1992), "Sentencing Guidance and Judicial Training in Australia", in *Sentencing, Judicial Discretion and Training* (Munro, C. and Wasik, M. eds., Sweet & Maxwell).

Lynch, J. P. (1987), *Imprisonment in Four Countries* (U.S. Department of Justice).

Mackay, R. D. (1990), "Fact and Fiction about the Insanity Defence", Crim.L.R. 247.

Mackay, R. D. and Kearns, G. (1994), "The Continued Underuse of Unfitness to Plead and the Insanity Defence", Crim.L.R. 576.

Magistrates' Association (1965), "The Association's Views on the White Paper on the Child, the Family and the Young Offender" (November 1965).

Maguire, M., Vagg, J. and Morgan, R. (1985) (eds.) *Accountability and Prisons* (Tavistock).

Maguire, M. and Pointing, J. (1988), *Victims of Crime: A New Deal?* (O.U.P.).

Maguire, M., Morgan, R. and Reiner, R. (1994), *The Oxford Handbook of Criminology* (Clarendon Press).

Mair, G. (1986), "Ethnic Minorities, Probation and the Magistrates' Courts", 26 B.J.Crim. 147.

Mair, G. (1988), *Probation Day Centres* H.O.R.S. No. 100 (HMSO, London).

Mair, G. and Nee, C. (1990), *Electronic Monitoring: The Trials and Their Results* H.O.R.S. No. 120 (HMSO, London).

Martin, J. P. and Webster, D. (1971), *The Social Consequences of Conviction* (Heinemann).

Mathieson, T. (1983), "The Future of Control Systems—The Case of Norway", in *The Power to Punish* (Garland, David and Young, Peter eds., Heinemann).

May Committee (1979), *Report of the Committee of Inquiry into the United Kingdom Prison Services*, Cmnd. 7673.

McConville, M. and Baldwin, J. (1982), "The Influence of Race on Sentencing in England", Crim.L.R. 652.

McConville, S. (1975) (ed.), *The Use of Imprisonment* (R.K.P.).

McIvor, G. (1990), "Community Service and Custody in Scotland", 29 *Howard Journal* 101.

McMahon, Maeve W. (1990), "Net-Widening: Vagaries in the Use of the Concept", 30 B.J.Crim. 121.

McMahon, Maeve W. (1992), *The Persistent Prison? Rethinking Decarceration and Penal Reform* (University of Toronto Press).

McWilliams, W. (1981), "The Probation Officer at Court: from Friend to Acquaintance" 20 *Howard Journal* 97.

McWilliams, W. (1983), "The Mission to the English Police Courts, 1876–1936", 22 *Howard Journal* 129.

McWilliams, W. (1985), "The Mission Transformed: Professionalisation of Probation Between the Wars", 24 *Howard Journal* 257.

McWilliams, W. (1986), "The English Probation System and the Diagnostic Ideal", 25 *Howard Journal* 241.

McWilliams, W. (1987), "Probation, Pragmatism and Policy", 26 *Howard Journal* 97.

McWilliams, W. and Pease, K. (1990), "Probation Practice and an End to Punishment", 29 *Howard Journal* 14.

Miers, D. A. (1978), *Responses to Victimisation* (Professional Books).

Miers, D. A. (1990), *Compensation for Criminal Injuries* (Butterworth).

Miers, D. A. (1992), "The Responsibilities and Rights of Victims of Crime", 55 M.L.R. 483.

Millham, S., Bullock, R. and Hosic, K. (1978), *Locking up Children* (Saxon House).

Moody, S. R. and Tombs, J. (1982), *Prosecution in the Public Interest* (Scottish Academic Press).

Morgan, Rod and King, Roy (1976), *A Taste of Prison* (R.K.P.).

Morgan, Rod and King, Roy (1977), "A Trying Time for the Untried" 15 *Howard Journal* 32.

Morgan, Rod (1989), "Remands in Custody: Problems and Prospects", Crim.L.R. 481.

Morgan, Rod (1991), "Woolf in Retrospect and Prospect", 54 M.L.R. 249.

Morison Committee (1962), *Report of the Departmental Committee on the Probation Service*, Cmnd. 1650.

Morris, A. and Giller, H. (1977), "The Juvenile Court—The Client's Perspective" Crim.L.R. 198.

Morris, A. and Giller, H. (1983) (eds.), *Providing Criminal Justice for Children* (Edward Arnold).

Morris, A. and McIsaac, M. (1978), *Juvenile Justice* (Heinemann).

Morris, A. and Gelsthorpe, L. (1990), "Not Paying for Crime: Issues in Fine Enforcement", Crim.L.R. 839.

Morris, J. (1986), "The Structure of Criminal Law and Deterrence" [1986] Crim.L.R. 524.

Morris, N. and Hawkins, G. (1970), *The Honest Politician's Guide to Crime Control* (University of Chicago Press).

Mountbatten Report (1966), *Report of the Inquiry into Prison Escapes and Security*, Cmnd. 3175.

Moxon, D. (1988), *Sentencing Practice in the Crown Court* H.O.R.S. No. 103 (HMSO, London).

Moxon, D., Sutton, M. and Hedderman, C. (1990), *Deductions from Benefits for Fine Default*, H.O. Research and Planning Unit Paper No. 60 (HMSO, London).

Moxon, D. (1990), *The Use of Compensation Orders in Magistrates' Courts*, H.O. Research Bulletin (HMSO, London).

Mulcahy, A., Brownlee, I. and Walker, C. (1993), *An Evaluation of Pre-Trial Review in Leeds and Bradford Magistrates' Courts*, 33 Home Office Research Bulletin 10 (HMSO, London).

Munro, C. and Wasik, M. (1992), (eds.) *Sentencing, Judicial Discretion and Training* (Sweet & Maxwell).

Murray, K. and Hill, M. (1991), The Recent History of Scottish Child Welfare", Children and Society 5/3, 266.

NACRO Race Issues Advisory Committee (1986), *Black People and the Criminal Justice System* (NACRO).

NACRO (1989), *The Electronic Monitoring of Offenders* (NACRO (briefing paper)).

NACRO (1990), *Fines and Fine Default* (NACRO).

NACRO (1991), *Race and Criminal Justice* (NACRO).

NACRO (1992), *Statistics on Black People Working in the Criminal Justice System* (NACRO).

Nelken, David (1989), "Discipline and Punish: Some Notes on the Margin", 28 *Howard Journal* 245.

Nellis, M. (1991), "The Electronic Monitoring of Offenders in England and Wales", 31 B.J.Crim. 165.

Newburn, T. (1988), *The Use and Enforcement of Compensation Orders in Magistrates' Courts*, H.O.R.S. No. 102 (HMSO, London).

Nunn, S. (1992), "Pre-Sentence Reports—A Defence Perspective", *Justice of the Peace* 755.

Nuttall, C. P. *et al.* (1977), *Parole in England and Wales*, H.O.R.S. No. 38 (HMSO, London).

Nuttall, C. P. and Pease, K. (1994), "Changes in the Use of Imprisonment in England and Wales 1950–1991", Crim.L.R. 316.

Oatham E. and Simon F. (1972), "Are Suspended Sentences Working?", (August 3, 1972) *New Society* 233.

Packer, Herbert L. (1969), *Limits of the Criminal Sanction* (Stanford University Press).

Padfield, Nicola (1993), "Parole and the Life Sentence Prisoner", 32 *Howard Journal* 187.

Paterson, Alexander (1951), "Why Prisons?" in *Paterson on Prisons*, Chapter 1 (Ruck, S. K. ed., Muller).

Parker, Elizabeth (1985), "The Development of Secure Provision", in *Secure Provision* (Gostin, L. ed., Tavistock).

Parker, H., Sumner, M. and Jarvis, G. (1989), *Unmasking the Magistrates* (O.U.P.).

Parliamentary All-Party Penal Affairs Group (1980), *Too Many Prisoners* (Barry Rose).

Parsloe, Phyllida (1978), *Juvenile Justice in Britain and the United States* (R.K.P.).

Paterson, A. A. and Bates, T. St. J. N. (1993), *The Legal System of Scotland* (3rd ed., W. Green/Sweet & Maxwell).

Pease, K. (1978), "Community Service and the Tariff" [1978] Crim.L.R. 269.

Pease, K. (1981a), *Community Service Orders—A First Decade of Promise* (Howard League).

Pease, K. (1981b), "The Size of the Prison Population", 21 B.J.Crim. 71.

Pease, K. and Wasik, M. (eds.) (1987), *Sentencing Reform: Guidance or Guidelines?* (Manchester University Press).

Pease, K. (1992), "Punitiveness and Prison Populations: An International Comparison", *Justice of the Peace* 405.

Pease, K. (1994), "Cross-National Imprisonment Rates", 34 B.J.Crim. 117.

Peay, Jill (1982), "Mental Health Review Tribunals and the Mental Health (Amendment) Act" Crim.L.R. 794.

Peay, Jill (1989), *Tribunals on Trial: A Study of Decision-Making under the Mental Health Act 1983* (Clarendon Press).

Peay, Jill (1994), "Mentally Disordered Offenders", in Maguire, M., Morgan, R. and Reiner, R., *Oxford Handbook of Criminology* (Clarendon Press).

Pointing, J. (1986), (ed.) *Alternatives to Custody* (Blackwell).

Player, E. and Jenkins, M. (1994) (eds.), *Prisons After Woolf* (Routledge).

Porter, R. (1990), "The Privatization of Prisons in the United States: A Policy that Britain Should Not Emulate", 29 *Howard Journal* 65.

Pratt, J. and Bray, K. (1985), "Bail Hostels—Alternatives to Custody?", 25 B.J.Crim. 160.

Priestly, Philip (1985), *Victorian Prison Lives* (Methuen).

Prins, Herschel (1980), *Offenders, Deviants or Patients?* (Tavistock).

Prins, Herschel (1986), *Dangerous Behaviour, The Law and Mental Disorder* (Tavistock).

Prins, Herschel (1990), "Mental Abnormality and Criminality: An Uncertain Relationship", *B. Medical Journal* 338.

Prison Reform Trust (1990), *Tackling Fine Default* (Prison Reform Trust).

Prison Reform Trust (1993a), *Prison Overcrowding: A Crisis Waiting in the Wings* (Prison Reform Trust).

Prison Reform Trust (1993b), *Working Guide to Prison Rules* (Prison Reform Trust).

Prison Reform Trust (1994), *Wolds Remand Prison Contracting-Out: A First Year Report* (Prison Reform Trust).

Purves, R. (1971), "That Plea-Bargaining Business: Some Conclusions from Research" Crim.L.R. 470.

Radzinowicz, L. and Hood, R. (1981), "Dangerousness and Criminal Justice: A Few Reflections" Crim.L.R. 756.

Radzinowicz, L. and Hood, R. (1986), *A History of English Criminal Law, Vol. 5: The Emergence of Penal Policy* (Stevens).

Radzinowicz, L. and King, J. (1977), *The Growth of Crime* (Hamilton).

Reed Report (1991), *Review of Health and Social Services for Mentally Disordered Offenders and Others Requiring Similar Services* (Department of Health/H.O.).

Research and Advisory Group on the Long-Term Prison System (1987), *Special Units for Long-term Prisoners: Regimes, Management and Research* (HMSO, London).

Richardson, Genevra (1993), *Law, Process and Custody: Prisoners and Patients* (Weidenfeld and Nicolson).

Robens Committee (1972), *Report of the Committee on Safety and Health at Work*, Cmnd. 5034.

Roberts, J. and Roberts, C. (1982), "Social Enquiry Reports and Sentencing" 21 *Howard Journal* 76.

Robertson, G. (1988), "Arrest Patterns Among Mentally Disordered Offenders", 153 *B. Journal of Psychiatry* 313.

Rock, Paul (1990), *Helping Victims of Crime* (Clarendon Press).

Rogers, A. and Faulkner, A. (1987), "A Place of Safety: MIND's Research into Police Referrals to the Psychiatric Services" (MIND).

Ross, Alf (1975), *On Guilt, Responsibility and Punishment* (Stevens).

Ross, H. *et al.* (1970), "Detecting the Social Effects of a Legal Reform: the British 'Breathalyser' Crackdown of 1967" 13 *American Behavioural Scientist* 493.

Royal Commission on Criminal Procedure (1981), *Report* Cmnd. 8092 (HMSO, London).

Royal Commission on Criminal Justice (Runciman Commission) (1993), *Report*, Cm. 2263 (HMSO, London).

Rumgay, J. (1988), "Probation—The Next Five Years: A Comment", 27 *Howard Journal* 198.

Rumgay, J. (1989), "Talking Tough: Empty Threats in Probation Practice", 28 *Howard Journal* 177.

Rutherford, Andrew (1984), *Prisons and the Process of Justice* (Heinemann).

Rutherford, Andrew (1984a), "Deeper into the Quagmire: Observations on the Latest Prison Building Programme" 23 *Howard Journal* 129.

Ryan, M. and Ward, T. (1989), *Privatization and the Penal System: The American Experience and the Debate in Britain* (O.U.P.).

Sabol, W. (1990), "Imprisonment, Fines and Diverting Offenders from Custody: Implications for Sentencing Discretion", 29 *Howard Journal* 25.

Sanders, A. (1986), "An Independent Crown Prosecution Service?" Crim.L.R. 16.

Sanders, A. and Young, R. (1994), *Criminal Justice* (Butterworths).

Scottish Council on Crime (1975), *Crime and the Prevention of Crime.*

Scull, A. T. (1977), *Decarceration: Community Treatment and the Deviant— A Radical View* (Prentice Hall); (2nd ed., 1984, Polity Press).

Seabrook Committee (1992), *The Efficient Disposal of Business in the Crown Court* (General Council of the Bar).

Shapland, J. (1979), "The Construction of a Mitigation", in *Psychology, Law and Legal Processes* (Farrington, D. *et al.* eds., Macmillan).

Shapland, J. (1981), *Between Conviction and Sentence* (R.K.P.).

Shapland, J., Willmore, J. and Duff, P. (1985), *Victims in the Criminal Justice System* (Gower).

Shapland, J. and Cohen, O. (1987), "Facilities for Victims: The Role of the Police and the Courts", Crim.L.R. 28.

Shaw, S. (1980), *An Analysis of the Cost of Penal Sanctions* (NACRO).

Sim, Joe (1994), "Reforming the Penal Wasteland", in *Prisons After Woolf* (Player, E. and Jenkins, M. eds., Routledge).

Simon, F. and Wilson, S. (1975), *Field Wing Bail Hostel: The First Nine Months*, H.O.R.S. No. 40 (HMSO, London).

Skinns, C. (1990), "Community Service Practice", 30 B.J.Crim. 65.

Skyme, Sir T. (1979), *The Changing Image of the Magistracy* (Macmillan).

Smellie, E. and Crow, I. (1991), *Black People's Experience of Criminal Justice* (NACRO).

Smith, J. C. and Hogan, B. (1992), *Criminal Law* (7th ed., Butterworths).

Smith, J. C. and Hogan, B. (1993), *Criminal Law: Cases and Materials* (5th ed., Butterworths).

Snowden, P. (1986), "Forensic Psychiatry Services and Regional Secure Units in England and Wales: An Overview" Crim.L.R. 790.

Softley, P. (1978), *Fines in Magistrates' Courts*, H.O.R.S. No. 46 (HMSO, London).

Sparks, R. (1971), "The Use of the Suspended Sentence" Crim.L.R. 384.

Spencer, J. N. (1994), "Current Thinking on the Imposition of a Fine as a Sentence—or the Re-Introduction of the Unit Fine System by the Back Door?" 158 *Justice of the Peace* 115.

Spencer, J. R. (1985), "No Prosecution Appeal Against Sentence?" 149 *Justice of the Peace* 262.

Spencer, J. R. (1987), "Do We Need a Prosecution Appeal Against Sentence?" Crim.L.R. 724.

Stacey, Tom (1989a), "Why Tagging Should Be Used to Reduce Incarceration", *Social Work Today*, April 20, 1989, 18–19.

Stacey, Tom (1989b), "Tracking Tagging—The British Contribution", in *The Electronic Monitoring of Offenders* (Russell, K. and Lilly, R. eds., Leicester Polytechnic).

Stern, V. (1993), *Bricks of Shame* (2nd ed., Penguin).

Stone, N. (1992), "Pre-Sentence Reports, Culpability and the 1991 Act", Crim.L.R. 558.

Stone, N. (1994), "The Suspended Sentence since the Criminal Justice Act 1991", Crim.L.R. 399.

Streatfeild Committee (1961), *Report of the Interdepartmental Committee on the Business of the Criminal Courts*, Cmnd. 1289 (HMSO, London).

Stuart-White, C. (Judge) (1989), "The Exercise of Judicial Discretion in Sentencing Decisions", 45 *The Magistrate* 194.

Sutherland, Edwin H. (1949), *White Collar Crime* (Dryden).

Taylor, Laurie (1985), *In the Underworld* (Guild Publishing).

Taylor, M. and Pease, K. (1989), "Private Prisons and Penal Purpose", in *Privatizing Criminal Justice* (Matthews, R. ed., Sage).

Thomas, D. A. (1965), "Sentencing the Mentally Disturbed Offender" Crim.L.R. 685.

Thomas, D. A. (1979), *Principles of Sentencing* (2nd ed., Heinemann).

Thomas, D. A. (1982), "The Justice Model of Sentencing—Its Implications for the English Sentencing System" in *The Future of Sentencing* (Institute of Criminology, Cambridge).

Thomas, D. A. (1990) "Penalties Without a Plan", *The Times*, February 13, 1990.

Thomas, D. A. (1992), "The Criminal Justice Act 1991: (1) Custodial Sentences", Crim.L.R. 232.

Thomas, D. A. (1993), "Law That's Hard to Judge", *The Guardian*, March 30, 1993.

Thomas, D. A. (1994), "Why the Sentence Fits the Crime", *The Guardian*, March 22, 1994.

Thomas, J. E. (1972), *The English Prison Officer since 1850* (R.K.P.).

Thomas, J. E. (1974), "Policy and Administration in Penal Establishments" in *Progress in Penal Reform* (Blom-Cooper, L. ed., O.U.P.).

Thorpe, J. and Pease, K. (1976), "The Relationship between

Recommendations made to the Court and the Sentences Passed" 16 B.J.Crim. 393.

Thorpe, J. (1979), *Social Inquiry Reports: A Survey*, H.O.R.S. No. 48 (HMSO, London).

Tonry, M. (1991), "The Politics and Processes of Sentencing Commissions", 37 *Crime and Delinquency* 307.

Tonry, M. and Morris, N. (1978), "Sentencing Reforms in America" in *Reshaping the Criminal Law* (Glasbrook, P. ed., Sweet & Maxwell).

Tonry, M. (1987), "Sentencing Guidelines and Sentencing Commissions— The Second Generation", in *Sentencing Reform* (Pease, K. and Wasik, M. eds., Manchester University Press).

Treverton-Jones, G. (1989), *Imprisonment: The Legal Status and Rights of Prisoners* (Sweet & Maxwell).

Tumim, S. (Judge) (1990), *Report of a Review by H.M. Chief Inspector of Prisons of Suicide and Self-Harm in Prison Service Establishments in England and Wales*, Cm. 1383 (HMSO, London).

Turner, A. J. (1992), "Sentencing in the Magistrates' Court", in *Sentencing, Judicial Discretion and Training* (Munro, C. and Wasik, M. eds., Sweet & Maxwell).

Tutt, N. and Giller, H. (1987), "Police Cautioning of Juveniles: The Continuing Practice of Diversity", Crim.L.R. 367.

Uglow, S. (1984), "Defrauding the Public Purse", Crim.L.R. 128.

Vass, A. A. (1984), *Sentenced to Labour* (Venus Academica).

Vass, A. A. (1990), *Alternatives to Prison* (Sage).

Vass, A. A. and Weston, A. (1990), "Probation Day Centres as an Alternative to Custody", 30 B.J.Crim. 189.

Voakes, R. and Fowler, Q. (1989), *Sentencing, Race and Social Enquiry Reports* (West Yorkshire Probation Service).

von Hirsch, A. (1987), "Guidance by Numbers or Words? Numerical Versus Narrative Guidelines for Sentencing", in *Sentencing Reform* (Pease, K. and Wasik, M. eds., Manchester University Press).

von Hirsch, A., Knapp, K. and Tonry, M. (1987), *The Sentencing Commission and its Guidelines* (Northeastern University Press).

von Hirsch, A. and Sareborg, N. (1989), "Swedish Sentencing Statute Enacted", Crim.L.R. 275.

Waddington, P. (1983), *The Training of Prison Governors—Role Ambiguity and Socialisation* (Croom Helm).

Walker, Nigel (1972), *Sentencing in a Rational Society* (Penguin).

Walker, Nigel (1982), "Unscientific, Unwise, Unprofitable or Unjust?" 22 B.J.Crim. 276.

Walker, Nigel (1985), *Sentencing: Theory, Law and Practice* (Butterworths).

Walker, Nigel and McCabe, Sarah (1973), *Crime and Insanity in England (Vol. 2)* (Edinburgh University Press).

Walmsley, R. (1989), *Special Security Units*, H.O.R.S. No. 109 (HMSO, London).

Walmsley, R. (ed.) (1991), *Managing Difficult Prisons: The Parkhurst Special Unit*, H.O.R.S. No. 122 (HMSO, London).

Walmsley, R., Howard, L. and White, S. (1991), *National Prison Survey 1991: Main Findings*, H.O.R.S. No. 128 (HMSO, London).

Walmsley, R. *et al.* (1992), *The National Prison Survey 1991—Main Findings*, H.O.R.S. No. 128 (HMSO, London).

Wasik, M. (1985), "The Grant of an Absolute Discharge", 5 Oxford J.L.St. 211.

Wasik, M. (1992a), "Rethinking Information and Advice for Sentencers", in *Sentencing, Judicial Discretion and Training* (Munro, C. and Wasik, M. eds., Sweet & Maxwell).

Wasik, M. (1992b), "The Criminal Justice Act 1991: (3) Arrangements for Early Release", Crim.L.R. 252.

Wasik, M. and von Hirsch, A. (1988), "Non-Custodial Penalties and the Principles of Desert", Crim.L.R. 555.

Wasik, M. and von Hirsch, A. (1990), "Statutory Sentencing Principles: The 1990 White Paper", 53 M.L.R. 508.

Wasik, M. and von Hirsch, A. (1994), "Section 29 Revisited: Previous Convictions in Sentencing", Crim.L.R. 409.

Wasik, M. and Turner, A. (1993), "Sentencing Guidelines for the Magistrates' Courts", Crim.L.R. 345.

Wasik, M. and Taylor, R. (1994), *The Criminal Justice Act 1991* (2nd ed., Blackstone).

Webster, Christopher, Ben-Aron, Mark and Hucker, Stephen (1985) (eds.), *Dangerousness: probability and prediction, psychiatry and public policy* (Cambridge University Press).

Wells, Celia (1993), *Corporations and Criminal Responsibility* (Clarendon Press).

West Midlands Probation Service (1987), "Birmingham Social Enquiry Report Monitoring Exercise".

White, Karen and Brody, Stephen (1980), "The Use of Bail Hostels" Crim.L.R. 420.

Wilkinson, C. and Evans, R. (1990), "Police Cautioning of Juveniles: The Impact of Home Office Circular 14/1985", Crim.L.R. 165.

Willcock, H. D. and Stokes, J. (1968), *Deterrents to Crime Among Youths Aged 15–21*, Government Social Survey Report No. 55, 356 Pt. II (HMSO, London).

Willett, T. (1973), *Drivers after Sentence* (Heinemann).

Williamson, Derek (1990), "Questions of Punishment", 80 *Prison Service Journal*, 18.

Willis, A. (1977), "Community Service as an Alternative to Imprisonment" 24 *Probation Journal* 120.

Willis, A. (1978), "Community Service and the Tariff" Crim.L.R. 540.

Willis, A. (1986), "Alternatives to Imprisonment: An Elusive Paradise?" in *Alternatives to Custody* (Pointing, J. ed., Blackwell).

Windlesham, Lord (1993), "Life Sentences: Law, Practice and Release Decisions, 1989–1993", Crim.L.R. 644.

Woolf Report (1990), *Prison Disturbances, April 1990: Report of an Inquiry by Lord Justice Woolf and Judge Stephen Tumim*, Cm. 1456 (HMSO, London).

Wootton Report (1970). *See* Advisory Council on the Penal System.

Wootton, Barbara (1963), *Crime and the Criminal Law* (2nd ed., 1981, Stevens).

Young, P. (1986), "Review of S. Cohen, Visions of Social Control", 34 *Sociological Review* 222.

Young, W. (1986), "Influences upon the Use of Imprisonment: A Review of the Literature" 25 *Howard Journal* 125.

Young, W. (1994), "The Use of Imprisonment: Trends and Cross-National Comparisons", in *Crime and Justice* (Tonry, M. and Morris, N. eds., University of Chicago Press).

Zander, Michael (1979), "What is the Evidence on Law and Order?" *New Society* 591.

Zander, Michael and Henderson, Paul (1992), *The Crown Court Study*, Royal Commission Research Study, No. 19.

Zedner, Lucia (1994), "Victims" Chap. 25 in *The Oxford Handbook of Criminology* (Maguire, M., Morgan, R. and Reiner, R. eds., Clarendon Press).

INDEX